to Painting

A   B I L I N G U A L   E D I T I O N

Northwestern University Press
Evanston, Illinois

to Painting

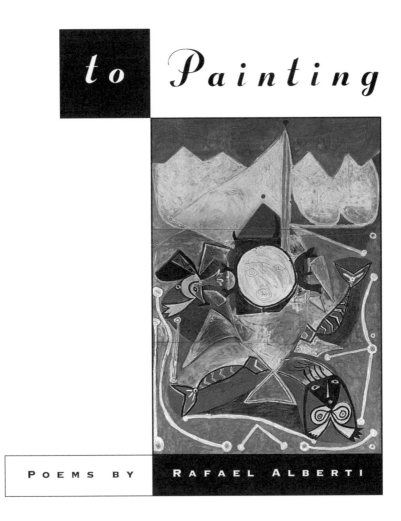

POEMS BY RAFAEL ALBERTI

Translated and with an

Introduction and Notes by

Carolyn L. Tipton

Hydra Books
Northwestern University Press
Evanston, Illinois 60208-4210

First paperback printing 1999

The preparation of this work was made possible in part by a grant from the National Endowment for the Humanities, an independent federal agency.

Printed in the United States of America

ISBN 0-8101-1725-1

Library of Congress Cataloging-in-Publication Data

Alberti, Rafael, 1902–
    [A la pintura. English and Spanish]
    To painting : poems / by Rafael Alberti ; translated and with an
introduction and notes by Carolyn L. Tipton.
        p. cm.
    ISBN 0-8101-1351-1 (alk. paper). —ISBN 0-8101-1725-1 (pbk.: alk. paper)
    1. Artists—Poetry. 2. Painting—Poetry. I. Tipton, Carolyn L. II. Title.
PQ6601.L2A6213 1997
861'.62—dc21   97-35657
                                                            CIP

To Picasso

This translation is dedicated to the memory of

Peter Whigham and John K. Walsh,

inspired masters of the art of translation

and much beloved teachers.

contents

Acknowledgments xi

Introduction xiii

A la pintura

A la pintura 2

Giotto 4

A la retina 8

A la mano 10

Botticelli 12

A la paleta 14

Azul 16

Rafael 24

Tiziano 28

Rojo 32

Tintoretto 40

Al pincel 44

Veronés 46

A la línea 50

El Bosco 52

A la perspectiva 58

Durero 60

To Painting

To Painting 3

Giotto 5

To the Retina 9

To the Hand 11

Botticelli 13

To the Palette 15

Blue 17

Raphael 25

Titian 29

Red 33

Tintoretto 41

To the Paintbrush 45

Veronese 47

To Line 51

Bosch 53

To Perspective 59

Dürer 61

Amarillo 62

Rubens 70

A la composición 74

Verde 76

Pedro Berruguete 86

Al ropaje 90

Zurbarán 92

A la luz 96

Velázquez 98

Valdés Leal 108

Negro 112

Goya 120

Delacroix 126

Al desnudo 128

Cézanne 130

A la gracia 134

Renoir 136

Blanco 140

Van Gogh 148

A la acuarela 152

A la divina proporción 154

Picasso 156

Yellow 63

Rubens 71

To Composition 75

Green 77

Pedro Berruguete 87

To Clothing 91

Zurbarán 93

To Light 97

Velázquez 99

Valdés Leal 109

Black 113

Goya 121

Delacroix 127

To the Nude 129

Cézanne 131

To Grace 135

Renoir 137

White 141

Van Gogh 149

To Watercolor 153

To Divine Proportion 155

Picasso 157

Notes on the Translations 165

acknowledgments

It is a pleasure to be able to thank the many people who have helped me with this book. First, I owe a deep debt of gratitude to the National Endowment for the Humanities, whose generous grant enabled me to finish this translation. I would particularly like to thank Christina Miner, formerly of the NEH, for her competent, efficient handling of various matters pertaining to my grant, her generous willingness to answer all my questions, and the enthusiasm and goodwill with which she met every query and problem addressed to her. For help given early on, I would also like to thank the U.C. Berkeley Phi Beta Kappa Executive Council for a graduate fellowship that enabled me to attend the U.C. Santa Cruz Translation Institute, where I was able to work with Gabriel Berns and Paul Mann. Finally, I would like to thank U.C. Berkeley's Graduate Division, whose Humanities Graduate Research Grant provided me with the funds to travel to Spain for the first time in order to meet Rafael Alberti.

To Rafael Alberti himself I am deeply grateful, and I thank him for having created—after all of his suffering—this work of beauty, for having generously given me his permission to translate it, and for having extended his friendship to me. For putting me together with Rafael Alberti for the first time, I would like to thank Tom Entwistle and Marcos Ana, and for facilitating later meetings, Dick Winslow, Teresa Sánchez Alberti, and María Asunción Mateo. For their hospitality to me in Spain, and their help with the interpretation of certain poems, I am grateful to Robert Harvey and Juan Carlos Blanca.

I would particularly like to thank Professor Luis Monguió, who corresponded with me, answering numerous questions about the Spanish text, and who invited me to stay at his home, where he and his wife, Alicia de Columbí, offered both help and encouragement. Professor Monguió has contributed immeasurably to my understanding of Alberti's poetry. I would also like to thank Professor Howard Young, whose generous support, encouragement, and continued interest have buoyed me.

I would like to thank, too, the American Literary Translators Association, whose talented members have given me so much advice about all aspects of translation. I am grateful to all who have shared their knowledge and experience with me. For their particular help and practical suggestions, I would especially like to thank John DuVal, Cola Franzen, Dorothy Gilbert, Stephen Kessler, Will Kirkland, David Kornacker, Elizabeth Miller, Christopher Sawyer-Lauçanno, and Rainer Schulte. For his continued counsel and inspiring example, I would like to thank Roger Greenwald.

I am very grateful to Susan Harris, editor-in-chief of Northwestern University Press, whose enthusiasm, dedication, and vision have been a great gift to me. I would also like to thank Ellen Feldman, managing editor of Northwestern University Press, for her meticulous editing.

A bouquet of thanks to Amy Einsohn and Marta Maretich, who have helped me with everything from Spanish prosody to English phrasing, from poem selection to disk preparation. I am deeply grateful for their kind and active friendship. Thanks, too, to Leslie Daniels and Holly Schmidt, whose belief in my work has sustained me.

Finally, I would like to thank my family, particularly my parents, James and Elizabeth Tipton, for all their moral and material support; my brother Jamie Tipton, for his suggestions about specific lines of poetry; my dog, Moonnight, spiritual cousin of Alberti's Niebla, for his quiet companionship; and my husband, Frank Kucera, who celebrated with me as this work took shape, and who aided every stage of its emergence.

Grateful acknowledgment is made to the following periodicals in which these translations first appeared: *The Atavist*: "Velázquez"; *The Berkeley Poetry Review*: "Cézanne," "To Light," "Green," "Van Gogh," "Picasso"; *Blue Unicorn*: "Giotto," "Renoir"; *First Leaves*: "To the Palette," "Tintoretto"; *Hawai'i Review*: "Blue," "Yellow"; *Modern Poetry in Translation*: "Valdés Leal"; *Muse*: "Bosch"; *O.ARS*: "Goya"; *Partisan Review*: "To the Hand"; *Poetry Miscellany*: "Delacroix," "To Perspective," "To Clothing"; *Sequoia*: "Botticelli"; *Translation*: "White," "Zurbarán". "Renoir" was named in *The Pushcart Prize IV: Best of the Small Presses*. To Divine Proportion" was hand set and printed as a broadside by Jack Stauffacher of The Greenwood Press.

C.L.T.
Berkeley, 1997

introduction

Rafael Alberti: A Biographical Sketch

Over the course of Rafael Alberti's long and varied artistic career, he has not only practiced painting and poetry singly, but he has also found a number of inventive ways to bring the two arts together. Among these combinations—intersections of the verbal and visual realms—doubtless the most richly imagined is *A la pintura* (*To Painting*), written at the heart of his artistic career, when he and the twentieth century were each near their midpoints.

Rafael Alberti and the twentieth century have progressed together: born in its infancy, he experienced the excitement and novelty of all the artistic movements of the 1920s in his youth—Cubism, Cinematic Imagism, Surrealism; participated as an adult in the political upheaval of the 1930s, working ardently for a more equitable society; and then, having suffered war and exile, finally reached a place of quiet at the end of the 1940s, a place of maturity out of which he created—and would continue to create for years to come—with insight and a profound nostalgia for the world of his youth.

Rafael Alberti was born in 1902 in the south of Spain, in the village of Puerto de Santa María on the Bay of Cádiz, along whose shores he spent most of the hours of what he calls his "saltwork childhood." Almost from the time he first became aware of his world, he wanted to be a painter. His first drawings are of the waters of the bay, its boats, its waves patterning the beach. He had no aspirations at that time to be a poet and he wrote no poems as a boy, but the images he soaked up then fill the poetry of his adulthood.

During the year he turned fifteen, his family moved to Madrid. Alberti experienced a profound sense of dislocation and imagined he could never be happy again, as far inland from the sea as he now found himself. It was the Prado Museum, which he was later to call "the house of my adolescence," that rescued him. Dazzled by his first view of paintings he had hitherto seen only in poor reproductions, he spent hours every day there, often setting up his easel to copy some of the Masters, including Zurbarán and Goya. He also painted outside, wandering the outskirts of Madrid to find suitable Impressionist subjects—like ruins in the moonlight—with which to experiment. He soon began to experiment, too, with the new Cubism. Along with Robert Delaunay and other avant-garde painters, he showed his work in a controversial exhibition at the Salón Nacional de Otoño. Later, in 1922, he held a one-man show at Madrid's prestigious Ateneo.

With this show, he believed he was saying farewell to the vocation of his youth, for during this period his health had begun to deteriorate. Forced ultimately to endure long periods of bedrest, he was also forced to give up painting, which had always been for him an active and peripatetic pursuit. Lying on his back, he began to read extensively. What he found himself most attracted to was the traditional lyric poetry of the fifteenth, sixteenth, and seventeenth centuries; he was drawn both to the folksongs collected from the oral tradition and to the Golden Age poets' sophisticated variations upon them. He began to write poems himself, and soon he began composing his own formal songs. Writing in this ancient Spanish tradition, he created poems imbued with his nostalgia for the sea. He came to call this collection *Marinero en tierra* (*Sailor on Land*). These thematically linked poems are remarkable not only for their lightness, grace, and musicality, but also because of their imagistic evocation of the indigos, aquamarines, and whitewash, the kelp and shells of the seaside world of his childhood: Alberti was still painting, in effect, but now he was using words. In 1925, not yet twenty-three years old, at the suggestion of a friend he sent this first book of poetry to the National Literary Competition, one of whose judges was Antonio Machado. To his surprise and delight, he won the National Prize for Literature.

Over the next few years, Alberti was drawn into the circle of poets who came to be known as the Generation of '27. This group, which included Federico García Lorca, Pedro Salinas, Jorge Guillén, and Vicente Aleixandre, among others, and who often gathered together in the cafés of Madrid, brought about a literary renaissance there in the late 1920s. These writers enjoyed practicing a variety of poetic forms;

they revived classical forms, experimented with creating new ones, and combined the old and the new in unusual ways. Without knowing Ezra Pound, these Madrid poets were nevertheless practicing the maxim he was articulating elsewhere at that same time: Make It New. Alberti's work at this time, for example, includes a "continuation" of a work by the sixteenth-century poet Góngora, whose hermeticism, cult of the metaphor, and technique of piling image upon image was joyously seized upon by Alberti's generation, who found in the old poet a voice surprisingly consonant with that of the poetic vanguard of the 1920s. Alberti also composed an "open letter" poem deliberately "missing" its first and last pages; a group of poems that employ cinematic techniques and offer an imitative tribute to the silent film comedians; and a madrigal to a tram ticket, in which the poet excitedly praises in an impeccably classical style not his lover but "tú, billete, flor nueva" ("you, ticket, new flower").

These were ebullient times. Toward the end of the decade, however, Alberti's vision of the world began to darken. In 1929, the same year in which Lorca published *Poeta en Nueva York* (*Poet in New York*), and in which Pablo Neruda, far away in Java, was working on *Residencia en la tierra* (*Residence on Earth*), Alberti wrote *Sobre los ángeles* (*Concerning the Angels*); all three works are informed by a dark Surrealism. *Sobre los ángeles* was written during a time of despair and turmoil for Alberti, who had come to feel that the world, whose myriad voices he had formerly interpreted, no longer spoke to him. Suffering the sense of a paradise lost, depressed and confused, Alberti nevertheless, as was his way, created a brilliantly unified and organized work. *Sobre los ángeles* is populated by a tribe of angels, each of whom symbolizes something in Alberti's inner or outer world, and to each of whom he has given a voice. The angels, Alberti would later say, gave shape to the tangle in which he struggled; through them, he was able to articulate all of the elements of the nightmare in which he found himself, and to grope forward toward light.

He eventually reached day again, not only through the struggles of his art but also through a confluence of events both political and romantic. On the first day of the new decade, January 1, 1930, Alberti wrote his first "civic" poem. This was to be the decade that saw him become politically involved and begin to write "poetry of engagement." Alberti's despair had gradually hardened into an anger that he realized was felt not only on his own behalf, but also on behalf of others. Politically awakened by the student demonstrations in Madrid against the abuses of the dictator Primo de Rivera, he began to be concerned with the problems of Spain. Soon he joined in these demonstrations himself. It was also at this time that he met the writer María Teresa León, the woman who was to become his lifelong companion. He immediately fell in love with her, and soon afterward married her. No longer alone and adrift, but now doubly committed, Alberti worked together with his wife to help topple the dictator and bring the Republic into being. In these years, he became a "poet in the street," reciting poems at demonstrations and tacking them up on walls.

In 1931 a republic was created, and soon afterward the new government gave Alberti and his wife a grant to travel abroad and study the new theater movement in Europe. They had rich and fascinating discussions with many artists on this trip: they met Pablo Picasso, César Vallejo, Henri Michaux, Alejo Carpentier, Boris Pasternak, Maxim Gorky, Sergei Eisenstein, and Louis Aragon; this was the beginning of Alberti's lifelong friendship with Picasso (it was to Alberti, at this time, that Picasso first read his poems). Yet they also witnessed firsthand the rising menace of Fascism in Europe. They were present at the burning of the Reichstag. Radicalized by what he had seen, Alberti returned to Spain and put his poetry at the "service of the people." He rejoiced when the Popular Front—a coalition advocating land, educational, military, and economic reform—was voted into power in 1936.

Franco's Fascists rose up against the government that July. During the Civil War that followed, Alberti was very active in the Republic's defense. He served as secretary of the Alliance of Antifascist Intellectuals; he organized the Second International Congress of Writers to help publicize Spain's predicament, traveling to Paris and Moscow to invite the delegates, who included Stephen Spender, André Malraux, Langston Hughes, Nicolás Guillén, and Octavio Paz; he presented short theatrical pieces ("theater of urgency") at the front; he served as director of the Museo Romántico, an annex of the Prado, and was responsible for securing it against attack; he put out a magazine in which most of the important writing of the time reached the front; he even joined the air force. The single activity to which he was most dedicated, however, was reading at the front; whenever there were pauses in the fighting, Alberti read aloud, to assemblies of troops, poems that he had composed specifically for them. He achieved in the best of these poems a synthesis of the public and the private hitherto unknown in his poetry; the poems were both personal and inspiriting to all who heard them. One such poem is addressed to the orphaned dog who was the wartime companion of Alberti and his friend Pablo Neruda, who had moved to Spain and who lived and worked with the Albertis during the war. In this poem, "A Niebla, mi perro" ("To Niebla, My Dog"), Alberti speaks of all the horror they have seen together, but then ends on a note of great exaltation as he tells Niebla what enables them to go on: "Niebla, mi camarada" ("Niebla, my comrade"), he concludes, "aunque tú no lo sabes, nos queda todavía, / en medio de esta heroica pena bombardeada, / la fe, que es alegría, alegría, alegría" ("though you don't know it, there remains for us still / in the midst of this heroic, bombarded, painful time / a faith, which is joy, which is joy, which is joy").

Alberti struggled hard in the months that followed to keep this faith, for with the aid of Mussolini and Hitler, the Spanish Fascist forces were crushing the Republicans. By March of 1939, Spain had fallen to Franco. Lorca had been murdered by Fascists in Granada, Antonio Machado had died in a refugee camp in France, and Miguel Hernández had been imprisoned; most of the survivors of Alberti's generation had already left Spain, and now Alberti fled for his life. He and his wife made a miraculous escape by plane to Orán, and finally reached Paris, where they lived with Neruda and worked as translators. By September, however, World War II had begun, and the Pétain government withdrew the work and residence permits of Alberti and his wife. Out of work and facing the threat of German troops, they decided to follow Neruda's advice and go to Latin America. In February of 1940, they escaped Europe on a boat bound from Marseilles to Buenos Aires. Warmly welcomed in Buenos Aires, they decided to settle there.

It had been in Paris, at the beginning of an exile that was to last nearly forty years, that Alberti had begun the first volume of his nostalgic memoirs, *La arboleda perdida* (*The Lost Grove*). In Argentina he continued to write in this nostalgic mode for many years, mourning his lost country and his lost comrades. As late as 1952, when he published *Retornos de lo vivo lejano* (*Returns of the Vital, Distant Past*), hauntingly beautiful poems that evoke the people, places, and emotions of his youth, and even as late as 1954, when he published *Baladas y canciones del Paraná* (*Ballads and Songs of the Paraná*), which includes poignant lyrics like "Ballad of the Lost Andalusian," he was still looking backward to Spain. By this time, however, the anger, bitterness, and sorrow that characterized much of the early work of his "high maturity" had become tempered.

The title of his first work of this period, *Entre el clavel y la espada*

(*Between the Carnation and the Sword*), describes Alberti's existential state. For years he wrote elegies to the Spanish dead, as well as pamphlets about the Spanish refugees and petitions to free the prisoners in Franco's jails; his poetry was informed by his exile, and he never ceased to think of himself first as a citizen of La España Peregrina (Wandering Spain). Almost from the beginning, however, a part of him wrote not just under the sign of the sword and the shadow of war, but also under the sign of the carnation, taking pleasure in the beauty of the natural world and feeling hope that renewal might be possible.

Very gradually, he began to write more and more under the sign of the carnation. A daughter was born to him. He found himself once again, after so many years, able to compose at his leisure, to pick words with great care, to explore new forms. He had longed for this in Madrid, during the war, when he had written, in a wish poem entitled "De ayer para hoy" ("From Yesterday for Today"): "Después de este desorden impuesto, de esta prisa, / de esta urgente gramática necesaria en que vivo / vuelva a mí toda virgen la palabra precisa / virgen el verbo exacto con el justo adjetivo" ("After this imposed disorder, this haste, / this urgent grammar of necessity in which I live / let there return to me all virginal the precise word / virginal, the exactly right verb with the perfect adjective"). Alberti had hoped, of course, to experience the serenity of slow and deliberate composition in a Spain that had returned to tranquillity, having vanquished its enemy. This did not come to pass, and yet the wish itself came true.

In Alberti's work, we see him gradually coming back to life again after all the horror and bloodshed. He entered into a period of creative expansion. He wrote plays that were produced in Buenos Aires. He collaborated in compositions and performances with musicians: one of his works of this time is named, with a bow to Baudelaire, *Invitación a un viaje sonoro* (*Invitation to a Sonorous Voyage*); it is a group of lyrics that Alberti set to musical pieces by Lully, Rameau, Purcell, Scarlatti, Bach, Mozart, Borodin, Albéniz, and Falla. Most importantly, however, he began to collaborate with visual artists; thus was a love for his first vocation reawakened.

Alberti had never ceased looking at the world through the eyes of a painter. Even when he ceased to paint actively, he retained an essentially visual orientation toward the world. Critics have often pointed out the painterly quality of Alberti's work, the predominance of imagery in all his poetry, beginning with his earliest book.[1] "Without doubt,"

Alberti has said, "I am a poet whose eyes are the hands of his poetry." Yet, as I have said, from the time he began to write seriously, he ceased to paint. There are a few exceptions—his illustrations for his second book of poems, for example, as well as a "poem-design" or two for his war magazine—but for the better part of the 1920s and 1930s, Alberti's paintings were purely verbal. Nor did he even take painting as the subject of his writing. Though he had been moved, during the troubled 1930s, by the work of his friend Picasso and by that of Diego Rivera and David Alfaro Siqueiros, it was only now, suddenly at leisure in the mid-1940s, in the midst of forging a new life, that he let the paintings of his friend and fellow Spanish exile Manolo Ángeles Ortiz move him to write accompanying poems.

What began, however, as an interest in Ortiz's work and a desire to participate with him soon grew into an overwhelming nostalgia for the days of his youth when he himself was a painter and spent so much time in the Prado amid the classics of European art. The Prado, Alberti thought, was now forever lost to him. Ultimately, he decided to re-create its beauty and impact in words so that he and others in his position might be able to re-experience it.

This was the inception of *A la pintura*. It is, then, written in the same spirit in which Alberti had written the first volume of his autobiography, *La arboleda perdida*, and was later to write *Retornos de lo vivo lejano:* it grew out of his desire to make of the past a living presence. But there is more to *A la pintura* than nostalgia, for it is not just a re-creation, but also a creation, a deft and lovely shaping of reality. Alberti has said that he hoped *A la pintura* might contribute, in some small way, to the reemergence of beauty, harmony, and order in his ravaged world. These are the values that emerge both from the poems and from the structure of *A la pintura*, which is not a sprawling heterogeneous collection but a unified presentation on a single theme, as were his great prewar books *Marinero en tierra* and *Sobre los ángeles*. *A la pintura*, published in 1948, was fashioned, Alberti has said, "after all the chaos" and set up in opposition to it; this is why he first offered it as an "homage to peace."

Besides being an important work for his readers, *A la pintura* was also a watershed work for Alberti. In addition to being the first major postwar volume in which he manifested no bitterness and anger—Alberti had at last emerged from the shadow of the sword—it was also the first work in which he brought together his two vocations. After *A la pintura*, Alberti's poetry was to be increasingly informed by his love of painting.

One critic has even suggested that all of Alberti's late work has simply been an "interrupted continuation of *A la pintura*."[2] Since its composition, Alberti has sought to intermingle the two arts. With *A la pintura*, Alberti says, "I began to enlace poetry with painting."

This enlacing has been effected in an astonishing variety of ways. This is because, inspired by *A la pintura*, he took up his brushes again after more than twenty years, thus dramatically increasing the number of ways in which he could combine the verbal and the visual. Since *A la pintura*, Alberti has not only continued to write poems about paintings and painters, including four separate works all dedicated to the art of Picasso, but he has also illustrated his own poems (as well as those of Lorca), painted in the margins of his poems, composed colorful *calligrammes*, and even invented a new form, the "liricografía," or "painted poem." In 1953 he named the homage he had composed for the three-thousandth-year anniversary of the founding of Cádiz—a combination of poems and drawings—an "homenaje lirico-plastico," and in 1969, still seeking new ways to bring together language and visual art, he created for an exhibition in Milan a collection of drawings based on the alphabet, entitled *Lirismo del alfabeto*.

A new chapter in Alberti's life began in 1963: the worsening political situation in Argentina compelled him to find a new home-in-exile for his family, and he chose Italy, home of his paternal grandparents. During his years in Italy, and during the final years of his stay in Argentina, Alberti's life began to fill with exhibitions. Now that he had begun to paint again, he had also begun to exhibit again. (This is a practice he was to continue; indeed, since the late 1940s he has held hundreds of exhibitions of his artwork throughout Europe and Latin America.) These years were also filled with poetic recitals, with conferences (both literary and political), and especially with travel. As early as the mid-1950s, he began to travel extensively, making trips to China, Russia, and Eastern Europe. Much of his literary work of these years would take the form of poetic travelogues. He also began to write more dramatic poems, which he used as performance pieces in his frequent recitals. For the recitals, too, he began to compose more and more humorous poems; many of the poems in *Roma, peligro para caminantes* (*Rome, Dangerous for Pedestrians*) (1964) were written in this vein. Many of his later poems are occasional, and others might be described as "diaristic," consisting of brief observations about where he is and what he is doing at the moment.

On the whole, his poems have gradually become shorter, and his verse less rigorous and more free.

Perhaps the most successful and striking of his late works is *Los 8 nombres de Picasso* (*The 8 Names of Picasso*), a delightful collection of poems which Alberti wrote to honor his friend on the occasion of his eighty-ninth birthday in 1970. Despite the fact that Spain was still in the grip of Franco and subject to his strict censorship policies, Alberti managed to have *Los 8 nombres* brought out in Barcelona and in an inexpensive paperback edition available to all. It is a work very reminiscent of *A la pintura*, both in its formal diversity and in its combination of ekphrastic poems that speak of specific paintings and more psychological poems that speak about the painter; it even recapitulates *A la pintura*'s closing poem.

In April of 1977, after the death of Franco and following an invitation by King Juan Carlos himself, Rafael Alberti and his wife María Teresa, who was not to live many years longer, finally returned to Spain after an exile of almost four decades; hundreds were in the jubilant crowd that greeted them at the airport in Madrid. In the years following the Spanish diaspora, Alberti, more than many others of his generation, had become a symbol of survival, of resistance, of the unquenchable flame of the artistic spirit. Finding himself a much revered public figure upon his arrival home, Alberti actively entered into Spanish political and cultural life: he served briefly in the Spanish Cortes (Parliament) as the Communist Party candidate from Cádiz; he appeared constantly at Madrid functions, giving talks and readings; he held local exhibitions of his paintings and "painted poems"; for many years, he even wrote a weekly column in the Madrid newspaper *El País*.

In the last few decades, Alberti has also been awarded many prizes and honors; in 1965 alone he won both the Rome Figurative Arts Prize for his engravings and the Lenin Peace Prize. Most of his more recent awards, however, including the Premio Cervantes, Spain's most prestigious literary prize, awarded to Alberti in 1983, have been literary, and seek to honor a lifetime of literary achievement: he has published, to date, some twenty-four volumes of poetry, produced over seven decades, as well as several plays, some nonfiction prose, and a five-volume autobiography.

Recently, the Fundación Rafael Alberti has been created, and in Alberti's old childhood home of Puerto de Santa María it has established an archive of his books and paintings. The town government has also given Alberti a house, which he has named Ora Marítima (Seacoast), after the title of one of his volumes of poetry. Of late, he has begun to spend most of his time in Puerto de Santa María, realizing, he says, by this return to his native village, "all the dreams of my exile." Delighted that he has finally closed a circle first opened by his departure from the Puerto as a child nearly eighty years ago, he dwells contentedly at Ora Marítima with his second wife, the scholar María Asunción Mateo. Here, he continues, as ever, to paint and write poetry. He has also hinted that he may even begin yet another volume of his autobiography, a work he says, in a manner both wistful and joking, that will surely include events of the new century.

A Brief Explication of *A la pintura / To Painting*

A la pintura is a celebration of painting. With his title, Alberti both defines the nature of his book as an homage, or salute, to painting and wittily echoes the name of another work on painting by another Alberti: *Della Pittura (On Painting)*, the first modern analytical study of painting, written in 1436 by Leon Battista Alberti. This playful identification of his own book with the famous work of his illustrious predecessor has not been unjustified, however, for readers have found themselves dazzled by this book. *A la pintura* is, indeed, a stunning work, not only because of the quality of its individual poems, but also because of the humanistic vision and elaborate design that underlie the whole.

Examining this design, we notice first that there are three different types of poems in the book: poems to colors, poems to the instruments of painting, and poems to painters. Moreover, each type of poem has its own form. First, the poems dedicated to colors are configured in an unusual way: they take the form of numbered lists, each item of which names either a use to which a certain painter has put the particular color, or a specific shade taken by the color in painting or in nature, or an association the poet has with the color. Sometimes the poet speaks, but just as often it is the color itself who addresses us, sketching its own self-portrait. Ángel Crespo has called these novel poems "greguerías" (a Spanish word denoting "impressionistic imagery in epigram style"),[3] an apt term for Alberti's lists, which take the form of a series of aphorisms but whose content is subjective, impressionistic, and visual.

In striking contrast, the poems dedicated to the various instruments and components of painting are all traditional sonnets. Each sonnet except the first, "To Painting," which introduces the subjects of future sonnets, possesses the same classical scheme of rhythm and rhyme. Moreover, again excepting the first sonnet, each of these poems shows the same pattern. The first three stanzas of each sonnet always begin with the words "To you," which are followed by the poet's various names for, and descriptions of, the sonnet's subject; these lines often read like extended toasts to the subject, as if the poet has just lifted a glass of champagne. Similarly, the final line of each sonnet begins with the words "To you" and ends with the word "Painting";[4] here, in a last evocation of the subject, the poet always tries to define its relation to Painting.

Finally, the third group of poems—those dedicated to painters—not only varies from the other two but is itself dramatically varied, for almost every poem in it has a different form. This is because each of the poems to painters strives to imitate, in some way, the style of the painter whom it is addressing, or is given a form particularly appropriate to him. "Giotto," for example, takes the form of a medieval lauda, while "Picasso" is a free-form poem whose words are spaced over the page in an unconventional manner.

Alberti has ordered these three different types of poems with particular care. In the tradition of works like Baudelaire's *Les Fleurs du mal*, *A la pintura* is no mere gathering of an odd assortment of poems, but a deliberately structured, carefully put together whole, part of whose effect is attained by the placement of the poems. We notice first that each group of poems possesses its own order. The poems to the painters appear in a roughly chronological order and are also arranged by nationality. The series begins with Giotto and a group of Italian painters of the thirteenth through sixteenth centuries, then moves to Northern painters of the fifteenth through seventeenth centuries, then to Spanish painters of the fifteenth through eighteenth centuries, then to painters of nineteenth-century France, and ends with Alberti's contemporary, Picasso. Next, the poems dedicated to the colors are ordered so that the three primary colors—blue, red, and yellow—come first, followed by green, black, and white, which although not technically primary colors are defined, along with blue, red, and yellow, as "psychological primaries"; black and white follow green because, unlike it, they are "noncolors." Finally, the sonnets begin with the introductory "To Painting" and then progress from poems dedicated to basics—the retina, the hand, the palette—through poems that celebrate new conceptions and new materials in the order in which artists began to make use of them—perspective, watercolor—to a final poem dedicated to a quality whose presence marks a culmination of centuries of trial and experimentation: divine proportion.

Alberti did not stop here though, for he then took the three carefully arranged strands of this book and wove them together, intercalating the sonnets and color poems with the poems to painters. Thus another whole dimension was added to the collection: we can read the poems either singly or in combination, appreciating the delightful and didactic juxtapositions that Alberti has created with his careful intercalation. If we choose to read them in combination, we can read them in groups or in pairs. In the 1948 edition of *A la pintura*, considered by most scholars to be the authoritative edition, Alberti pairs in succession each of his poems with another, beginning with "To Painting" and "Giotto" and ending with "To Divine Proportion" and "Picasso." Although the 1948 edition is the source of my translation, I have left out certain poems, and as a result, some of Alberti's pairings no longer exist. I will speak a little later about my excisions, but for now I would like to examine the remaining original pairs.

There exist many different types of pairs. Some seem merely fitting and appropriate: that Alberti should pair "Black," with "Goya," creator of the Black Paintings, seems exactly right, as does his placing of "Red" next to "Tintoretto," whose paintings are replete with scarlet robes, curtains, and silks. Similarly, once we think about it, "To Clothing" may be seen to fit well with its partner, "Zurbarán": many viewers of his paintings are struck first by the solidity of the robes of his monks, which seem to have a presence of their own. And certainly it seems appropriate that the introductory poem be placed next to "Giotto," the artist credited, first by Boccaccio and since then by countless others, with introducing modern painting. Finally, the pairing of "Renoir" and "To Grace" seems perfect and inevitable.

Other pairings we come across, however, seem more idiosyncratic and tell us more perhaps about the poet than about his subject; they open an interesting window onto Alberti's tastes, prejudices, and personal associations. That he should choose to pair "Green" with "Pedro Berruguete," for example, tells us how affected he was by the latter's portrayal of scenes of the Inquisition, in which the color green played such a prominent part. Berruguete's work can be found in the Prado, as can that of most of the painters in *A la pintura*, including Rubens, who is one of Alberti's great favorites. It was undoubtedly the lovely long tresses, coils, curls, braids, and falls of blond hair lighting the Rubens canvases in the Prado that Alberti was thinking of when he made the rather personal pairing of "Rubens" and "Yellow."

Alberti seems to have linked other poems in order to point out certain connections to his readers. Thus, "Dürer" is placed next to "To Perspective" to remind us of Dürer's contributions to the study of perspective, while "Bosch" is juxtaposed to "To Line" so that we will particularly remark his use of it. Similarly, "Veronese" was probably put together with "To the Paintbrush" in order to underline his unusual technique by means of which individual brushstrokes seem to stand out. And Alberti seems to have linked "Botticelli" with "To the Hand" in order that we might focus for a moment on Botticelli's hand, which, unstopping, often created shapes using a single line, and whose designs Alberti calls attention to by subtitling his Botticellian poem "Arabesque."

Some of his didactic pairings are not immediately comprehensible, however. Alberti created these juxtapositions, I believe, hoping we would puzzle over them and eventually discover the lesson each contains. One such pairing is that of "Velázquez" with "To Light." Rather than make an obvious pairing of "To Light" with a poem celebrating an Impressionist painter, Alberti positions it with "Velázquez," thereby emphasizing the latter's groundbreaking use of light; indeed, the Spanish master is said to have been the first to paint light itself rather than merely depict its effect. Similarly, we may conclude that Alberti probably pairs "Cézanne" and "To the Nude" in order to highlight Cézanne's little-known but historically important nudes, whose angular and geometric forms, repeated in the landscape around them and in their groupings together on the canvas, were precursors of Picasso's later and more famous Cubist nudes. Alberti's linking of "Van Gogh" with "White" is probably even more unexpected. Why link this supreme colorist with white instead of with what the painter himself called the "devilish yellow" that so obsessed him, or at least with some intense color? We may conjecture that Alberti knew we would associate Van Gogh with color; thus, his pairing of this painter with "White" is a way of reminding us of the paradox that white reflects to the eye all the rays of the spectrum combined, that it is, in fact, "The builder of the colors." Lastly, by putting "Picasso" next to "To Divine Proportion," Alberti hoped that we would consider how they might belong together. I believe that this pairing of "Picasso" and "To Divine "Proportion" is an homage to his friend Picasso, to whom *A la pintura* is dedicated; it is the poet's way of imparting to us his belief that his friend's deliberate distortion, his dislocation of classical forms, and his destruction of traditional measure ultimately led to the creation of a more profound symmetry, a deeper harmony, an arrangement—as in *Guernica*—of disproportionate parts whose whole, nevertheless, reflects a "divine proportion."

At this point, I would like to speak briefly about my excisions. I have cut out of my translation six sonnets and seven poems to painters. I've left these poems out because I think that most of them tend not to be as strong as the other poems, and I felt that their inclusion would weaken the whole.[5] In doing so, however, I have left certain poems without their partners. "To the Retina" originally went with "Piero della Francesca," "To the Palette" with "Leonardo," "Raphael" with "To the Mural," "Titian" with "To the Canvas," "Blue" with "Michelangelo," "To Composition" with "Poussin," "Valdés Leal" with "To Shadow," "Delacroix" with "To Movement," and "To Watercolor" with "Gutiérrez Solana."[6] Although the excision of these poems at first may seem a travesty, I would like to mention two facts that may mitigate this view. First, there have been many editions of *A la pintura*, and almost every one of these editions has contained a different group of poems. The authoritative 1948 edition was preceded by a very early edition that contained only six poems; it has been followed by a host of successive editions to and from which Alberti himself has both added and subtracted poems, disarranging his original structure and thus creating a precedent for his translator to do likewise.

The second fact is that, while the poems in *A la pintura* may be read in pairs, they may also be read in larger groups, as I said above. For example, a reader can find many triplets in the collection: just as a poem written in careful couplets sometimes contains a line that may be read both with the line that precedes it and the line that follows it, so here there are certain poems each of which may be read both with its partner and with the poem on its other side. Thus, the poem dedicated to Dürer, the melancholy painter, may be read with both "To Perspective" and with "Yellow," and one may read "Renoir" with "White" as well as with "To Grace." Because the poems possess this combinatory flexibility, then, even if a poem is missing its partner, it may still be possible to read it with other poems. So, for example, "Titian" may be read together with "Red" and "Tintoretto," and "Valdés Leal" with "Black" and "Goya."

If the placement of the poems, delicately managed to ensure an optimum of juxtapositional richness, yields us a variety of lessons in art history, the content of the poems gives us something even more worthwhile: a vision of beauty, harmony, and order. While Alberti, as a socially committed artist, has written many poems that lament injustice, and while he has frequently, like Picasso in *Guernica*, delineated and decried evil, he has more often sought to describe and praise what is good. He has articulated an ideal of harmony that is simultaneously social and aesthetic. In *A la pintura* particularly, both the subjects he has chosen and the words he has written manifest this ideal.

Let us look first at his subjects. Speaking of the painters Alberti has chosen to write about, Ángel Crespo points out that, with a very few exceptions, they are all interested in figurative art—in the human form—and express themselves concretely. He notes that there are only two landscape artists, and that there is a complete absence of "primitives," abstract Impressionists, modern Expressionists, and Surrealists.[7] If, with Crespo, we conclude that, judging from his selection of painters, Alberti seems to cherish order, proportion, and form, this conclusion is only strengthened by a study of those instruments of painting to which Alberti dedicates poems, for the subjects of these poems include, as we have seen, not only such obvious components of painting as the hand, the retina, the palette, and the brush, but also line, perspective, composition, grace, and divine proportion.

If we now look at the language of the poems themselves, we find that Alberti again and again celebrates the same things: form and structure, mathematical order and discipline, harmony and symmetry, love, beauty, and grace. He has Giotto say, "O Lord, praise be to the human form, / ardent analogue of her vaster / Sister Architecture . . . Praise be . . . to . . . symmetry." In "Zurbarán" he speaks of the painter's "fight for form," in "Cézanne" of the latter's "glorying in form," and he praises the "Nude" as the "palpable dream of a Form expressed." He sings in "To Composition" of "sweet order." He begins his sonnet to divine proportion, "To you, amazing discipline," and then he continues, "source of beauty without flaw . . . mysterious wellspring of moderation / that gives rise to harmonious Creation." He praises "Line" as "geometry that dances" and as the "contour of human grace".

Geometry and grace are also celebrated in "Botticelli," love and grace in "Veronese," beauty and grace in "Raphael," and beauty, love, and grace together in both "Titian" and "Rubens." Alberti, in fact, dedicates a whole sonnet to Grace, whom he praises as "lovely" and "divine," and even though Beauty has no sonnet of its own, in his celebration of the retina, Alberti praises this organ of sight because, he says, it is "where beauty . . . lies."

Luis Monguió summarizes Alberti's enthusiasms:

> In Alberti's poems on painters we perceive his love of an art truer than life, reflecting an ideal of order and discipline, a world of enjoyment of the senses, of elegance, happiness, love, and beauty. In his sonnets on the instrumentalities of painting we discovered the same enthusiasm for harmony, truly loved order, measure, restraint, civility, form, beauty within the willingly accepted law of golden proportion.
>
> More than specific social perspective on the world's problems which one can extract here and there from his verse, it is this worldview, this humane perspective, this vision of life and art in Rafael Alberti's poetry that I find entrancing, compelling, elevating. It is civilized and civilizing. It is in the great tradition of humanism. The poet preserves what is humane in mankind and dreams the reality of a more beautiful life, a more humane world.[8]

Finally, there is one more important aspect of this work. Let us not forget, while we are praising his humanistic vision and lauding his complex design, that Rafael Alberti has been hailed as one of the great poets of the twentieth century, and that this judgment is based mainly on his stunning ability with language. Readers have always been enchanted by the verbal music he makes, and in *A la pintura* in particular they have been delighted by the circular song of "Botticelli," the nursery-rhyme repetitions of "Bosch," the eerie refrain of "Valdés Leal," the smooth, lilting flow of "Renoir," the staccato rhythm of "Van Gogh," the Cante Jondo flamenco sound of parts of "Picasso." Even more than as a verbal musician, however, Rafael Alberti is known as a consummate imagist; it is for his images that he is most cherished as a poet. And *A la pintura*, because of its ekphrastic nature, is particularly rich with a full range of Albertian images. Some of these images, in trying to get us to imagine something in a new way, are gently thought-provoking; here, for example, are his quiet closing apostrophes to the hand, "For the paintbrush, you are not an open rose: / you make your living happily half-closed," and to the palette, "For vision's bread, you provide the leaven. / The placid rainbow grazes on your heaven." Some give us exquisite pictures, as when he says we may find blue "Winding within mother-of-pearl flesh / as a blissful vein in Rubens," or as when he describes a woman's nipple, in "Red," as "The carnation that springs / from the squeezed ivory / of a cupped breast." Some startle with the beauty of the unexpected, as when he says of Velázquez, "He dipt his quiet / brush in the bright air" and made "The children ring out like blond / bells: peals of color." Some of his images even expand like opening flowers: he writes in "Rubens," for example, of "a stream / like the rosy back of a woman who has smiled, / widening the woods, dogs barking, deer."

In conclusion, *A la pintura* is one of those rare books that satisfies on both the macrocosmic and the microcosmic level, a book of grand design and noble vision whose most compelling draw is, nevertheless, the beauty of its music and, especially, of its myriad images. I wish the reader joy in the discovery of these poems, appearing here for the first time in English.

Notes

1. See, for example, Ana María Winkelmann's "Pintura y poesía en Rafael Alberti," *Papeles de Son Armadans* 88 (1963): 151, or Carlos Areán's "La imagen pictórica en la poesía de Alberti," *Cuadernos Hispanoamericanos* 289–90 (1974): 198–209.

2. Manuel Bayo, *Sobre Alberti* (Madrid: C.V.S. Ediciones, 1974), 93.

3. Ángel Crespo, "Realismo y pitagorismo en el libro de Alberti *A la pintura*," *Papeles de Son Armadans* 88 (1963): 102.

4. There is a single exception to this generalization: the final word of the final sonnet, "To Divine Proportion," is not "Painting" but "gold."

5. A few poems were also left out because of their excessive length, including the lovely poem that introduces the collection, "1917," in which Alberti recounts the thrill of his initial discovery of the Prado.

6. My excision also includes the complete pairs "Rembrandt" and "Chiaroscuro," and "El Greco" and "To Color."

7. Crespo, "Realismo y pitagorismo," 106.

8. Luis Monguió, "Rafael Alberti: Poetry and Painting," *Crítica Hispánica* 1 (1979): 83–84.

1. Botticelli, *The Birth of Venus* (ca. 1480), Uffizi Gallery, Florence (Credit: Scala/Art Resource, NY)

2. Fra Angelico, *The Annunciation* (1430–45), Museo del Prado, Madrid
(*Credit: Scala/Art Resource, NY*)

3. Titian, *Bacchanal* (1525), Museo del Prado, Madrid (*Credit: Scala/Art Resource, NY*)

4. Monet, *Red Poppies, near Argenteuil* (1873), Musée d'Orsay, Paris
(*Credit: Lessing/Art Resource, NY*)

5. Tintoretto, *Battle between the Christians and the Moors* (1588–89), Museo del Prado, Madrid (*Credit: Scala/Art Resource, NY*)

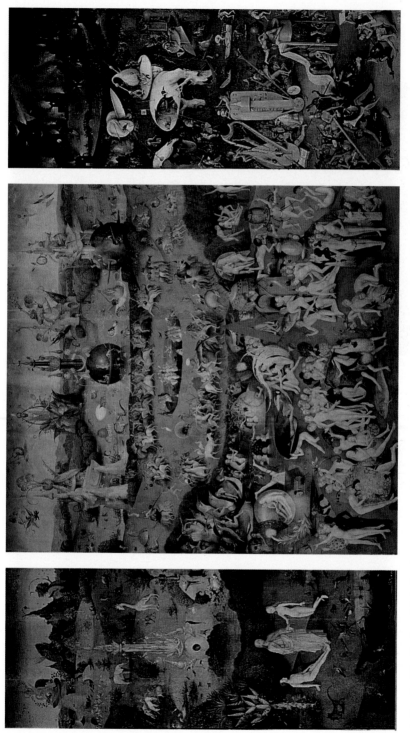

6. Bosch, *The Garden of Delights* (1500–1510), Museo del Prado, Madrid (Credit: *Lessing/Art Resource, NY*)

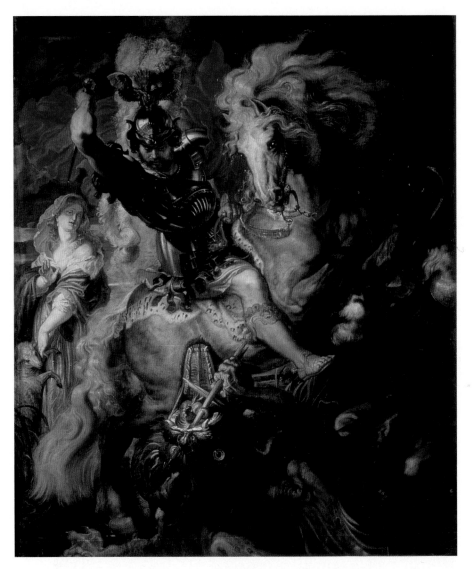

7. Rubens, *St. George and the Dragon* (1606), Museo del Prado, Madrid
(Credit: *Bridgeman/Art Resource, NY*)

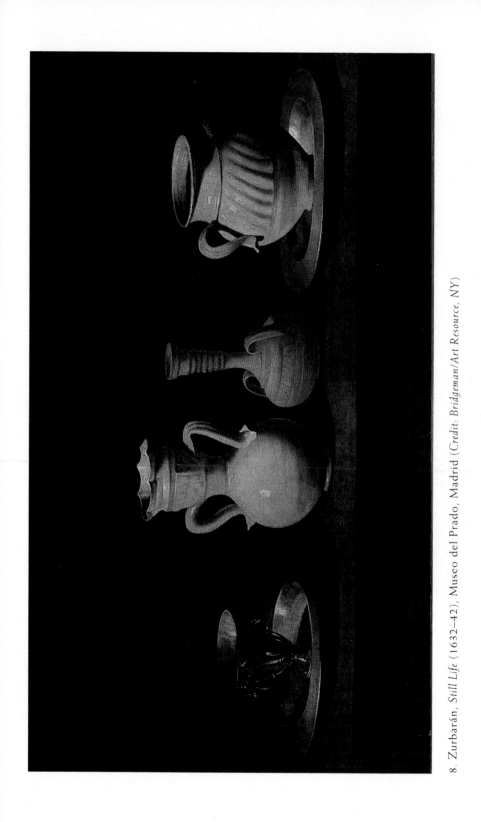

8. Zurbarán, *Still Life* (1632–42), Museo del Prado, Madrid (*Credit: Bridgeman/Art Resource, NY*)

9. Velázquez, *Prince Balthasar Carlos in Hunting Dress, with Two Dogs* (1635–36), Museo del Prado, Madrid (*Credit: Scala/Art Resource, NY*)

10. Picasso, *Design in India Ink*, Aguilar Archive, Madrid (*Copyright © 1997 Estate of Pablo Picasso/Artists Rights Society [ARS], NY*)

11. Goya, *The Witches' Sabbath* (1821–23), Museo del Prado, Madrid (*Credit: Scala/Art Resource, NY*)

12. Cézanne, *The Bridge of Maincy* (1879), Musée d'Orsay, Paris
(*Credit: Lessing/Art Resource, NY*)

13. Renoir, *Bathing Women* (1910), National Museum, Stockholm
(*Credit: Bodil Karlsson, 1993*)

14. Manet, *Branch of White Peonies and Shears* (1864), Musée d'Orsay, Paris
(*Credit: Lessing/Art Resource, NY*)

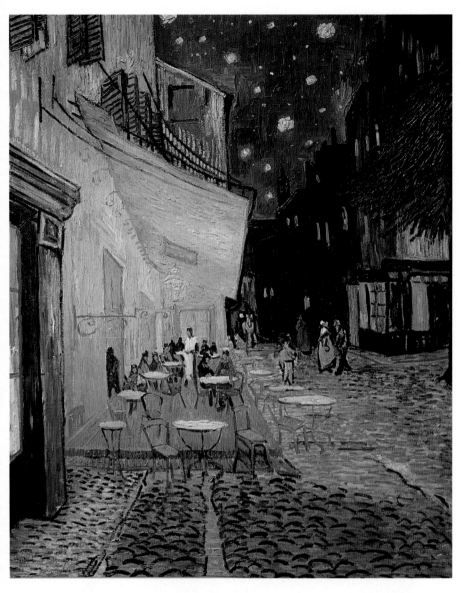

15. Van Gogh, *Outdoor Café at Night* (1888), Kröller-Müller Museum, Otterlo
(*Credit: Lessing/Art Resource, NY*)

16. Picasso, *Guernica* (1937), Centro d'Arte Reina Sofía, Madrid (Credit: *Giraudon/Art Resource, NY. Copyright © 1997 Estate of Pablo Picasso/Artist Rights Society [ARS], NY*).

a la Pintura

to Painting

A la pintura

A ti, lino en el campo. A ti, extendida
superficie, a los ojos, en espera.
A ti, imaginación, helor u hoguera,
diseño fiel o llama desceñida.

A ti, línea impensada o concebida.
A ti, pincel heroico, roca o cera,
obediente al estilo o la manera,
dócil a la medida o desmedida.

A ti, forma; color, sonoro empeño
por que la vida ya volumen hable,
sombra entre luz, luz entre sol, oscura.

A ti, fingida realidad del sueño.
A ti, materia plástica palpable.
A ti, mano, pintor de la Pintura.

To Painting

To you, flax in the field. To you, expanse
of surface for the eyes: expectant glance.
To you, imagination, ice or coal,
exact design or fire out of control.

To you, line unforeseen or always known.
To you, heroic paintbrush, wax or stone,
compliant to whatever style's envisioned,
to measure or the lack of all precision.

To you, form; color, resonating scheme
by which life shows the volume of its space,
dark next to light, light next to sun, now fainter.

To you, fictive reality of dream.
To you, real object, palpable, in place.
To you at last, the hand, all Painting's painter.

Giotto

Laude, Señor Dios mío,
al hermano pincel. Él se ha mojado
de tu divino rostro de rocío
y al fundirle la sangre, iluminado.

Laude, Señor Dios mío,
al sometido, abierto hermano muro,
a la cal fresca, hirviente, resistida
del aire, del calor, el agua, el frío;
la hermana cal, su puro
blanco y perenne sueño de la vida.

Laude, Señor Dios mío,
al lápiz, a la pluma
que al hermano diseño delinea.
Laude al esbozo erguido de la bruma,
laude a la hermana luz que lo recrea.

Laude, Señor Dios mío,
a la humana figura,
ardiente paralela, recta hermana
de la infinita hermana arquitectura.

Laude, Señor Dios mío,
al hermano color, a los colores:
al fraternal violeta,
al verde, al blanco, al rojo, al amarillo,
al negro, al oro, al rosa
y al que es lengua pintando tus loores
cuando se eleva airosa
a humilde, a pobrecillo
pájaro fiel mi mano:
el claro azul, el buen añil hermano.

Giotto

O Lord, praise be
    to Brother Paintbrush. In Thy divine
    face of dew he has moistened himself, & dipped
    into Thy blood has come to shine.

O Lord, praise be
    to Brother Wall, open to me,
    to fresh lime, able to beat
    cold, water, air, heat—
    Sister Lime, with her pure white
    everlasting dream of life.

O Lord, praise be
    to the pencil, to the pen who drafts Brother Design.
    Praise be to the outline
    manifesting itself out of mist;
    praise be to Sister Light who clarifies it.

O Lord, praise be
    to the human form,
    ardent analogue of her vaster
    Sister Architecture.

O Lord, praise be
    to Brother Color, to his rainbow:
    to green, to white, to red & yellow,
    to black & gold & rose,
    to fraternal violet, and
    to the one whose bright language paints Thy praise
    when, looking up, I raise
    my hand to gather in the humble birds,
    and see/hear the lauding words
    of blue, of good Brother Indigo.

Laude, Señor Dios mío,
al pausado, solemne movimiento,
al hierático mar y rígido paisaje.
Laude al ángel que boga sin el hermano viento,
al simétrico orden sin hastío
y al salmo rectilíneo del ropaje.

Laude, Señor Dios mío,
porque me armaste dulce, cariñoso,
y en una edad oscura
me concediste el hábito glorioso
del hermano mayor de la Pintura.

O Lord, praise be
    to solemn & deliberate movement,
    to the rigid landscape & hieratic sea. Praise be
    to the angel: a sail who has no need of Brother Wind,
    to a symmetry not tiresome to behold,
    to the rectilinear psalm of the robe.

O Lord, praisèd be
    what Thou hast done for me.
    In this dark age Thou hast made me sweet & gentle,
    and clothed me in a garment like no other:
    the bright habit of Painting's eldest brother.

A la retina

A ti, jardín redondo, donde mora
de par en par pintada la belleza;
flor circular que irisa en su cabeza
del rayo negro al rubio de la aurora.

A ti, profundo espejo que atesora
todo el sinfín de la naturaleza;
si sol cerrado, noche de grandeza;
si abierta luna, hora de sol sin hora.

A ti, siempre vivaz, aunque dormida,
torre del homenaje de la vida,
ajimez a la mar de la ventura.

¿Qué sería sin ti de los colores,
niña de luz, pintor de los pintores?
A ti, fuente inmortal de la Pintura.

To the Retina

To you, rounded garden, where beauty, like
an open window's view, lies clearly drawn;
curved flower iridescing in the eye
from band's-end blackness to the blond of dawn.

To you, mirror in whom the infinity
of Nature's images is held like treasure:
occluded sun, night of sublimity;
open moon, sunlit hour without measure.

To you, animated even during sleep,
chivalric in the oath to life you keep,
mullioned window on the sea of fortune.

Without you, what would be the colors' plight,
painter of the painters, child of light?
To you, always Painting's source & origin.

A la mano

A ti, firmeza y tiemblo, conductiva
de ese enhebrado, misterioso hilo
que de los ojos fluye y prende al filo
del pincel una luz germinativa.

A ti, flor en acción, copulativa
cómplice permanente del estilo;
tacto, obediencia, lentitud, sigilo,
cuando no disparada disyuntiva.

A ti, siempre solícita viajera,
llevadora del tallo que genera
la más maravillosa criatura.

No eres para el pincel la abierta rosa.
Semicerrarte es tu vivir dichosa.
A ti, alma del jardín de la Pintura.

To the Hand

To you, tremor & steadiness, guide
of the eyes' thread, mysterious line of sight
which flows thence to the brush's underside,
and sets to it a germinative light.

To you, flower in action, copula,
permanent accomplice of the pen,
tactful, slow, obedient, discreet
unless flung out— disjunctive only then.

To you, cross-canvas traveler, helpmate,
bearer of the stalk that generates
blossoming creatures, marvelous & ardent.

For the paintbrush, you are not an open rose:
you make your living happily half-closed.
To you, the tutelar god of Painting's garden.

Botticelli

(Arabesco)

La Gracia que se vuela,
que se escapa en sonrisa,
pincelada a la vela,
brisa en curva deprisa,
aire claro de tela
alisada,
concisa,
céfiros blandos en camisa,
por el mar, sobre el mar,
todo rizo huidizo,
torneado ondear,
rizado hechizo;
geometría
que el viento que no enfría
promueve
a contorno que llueve
pájaro y flor en geometría;
contorno, línea en danza,
primavera bailable
en el espacio estable
para la bienaventuranza
del querubín en coro,
del serafín en ronda, de la mano
del arcángel canoro,
gregoriano,
que se escapa en sonrisa
tras la gracia que vuela,
brisa en curva deprisa,
aire claro de tela
alisada,
concisa,
pálida Venus sin camisa.

Botticelli

(Arabesque)

Grace escapes,
leaves a smile, and flees,
painted undersail,
the curve of a breeze,
air like a drape
with a lustrous sheen,
quick, coming into shape,
the winds in their cape,
and over the sea, upon the sea,
all is curling witchery,
twirling curl
& rippling wave;
a geometric order
carried to the border
by uncooling winds that shower
bird & flower
in a geometric order;
a border, a dancing line,
the ballet of Spring
in the space designed
for the angels to sing,
blissful cherubim in chorus,
seraphs in the round,
and for the hand of the archangel
of melodious sound,
who leaves a smile, and flees,
behind the grace that escapes,
the curve of a breeze,
air like a drape
with a lustrous sheen,
quick, coming into shape,
Venus, pale, with no cape.

A la paleta

A ti, infinita haz, campo sembrado
donde siega el pincel, gavilla, amasa
y entre color, luces y sombras, pasa
de mar radiante a tiempo anubarrado.

A ti, pozo y brocal, donde asomado
medita, viene y va, mide, acompasa;
frente asida a la mano que traspasa
tu ojo de Polifemo enamorado.

A ti, abanico, ala redonda, escudo,
espejo que al vestir queda desnudo
y nuevamente superficie pura.

En ti se cuece la visión que nace.
Tu firmamento el arcoiris pace.
A ti, lecho y crisol de la Pintura.

To the Palette

To you, infinite sheaf, field rich with seeds:
here the brush harvests, gathers, blends together,
and mid color, lights & shade proceeds
from ocean-radiance to cloudy weather.

To you, well at whose edge we linger,
peering down, then looking up at how things lie;
brow, linked to a hand whose mythic finger
pokes through your single Polypheman eye.

To you, opened fan, round wing, a shield;
the more you dress, the more you are revealed;
when bare: a mirror, once more usable.

For vision's bread, you provide the leaven.
The placid rainbow grazes on your heaven.
To you, Painting's bed & crucible.

Azul

1

Llegó el azul. Y se pintó su tiempo.

2

¿Cuántos azules dio el Mediterráneo?

3

Venus, madre del mar de los azules.

4

El azul de los griegos
descansa, como un dios, sobre columnas.

5

El azul Edad Media delicado.

6

Trajo su virginal azul la Virgen:
azul María, azul Nuestra Señora.

7

A su paleta descendió. Traía
el azul más oculto de los cielos.
De rodillas pintaba sus azules.
Lo bautizaron con azul los ángeles.
Le pusieron: Beato Azul Angélico.

8

Hay paletas celestes como alas
descendidas del blanco de las nubes.

Blue

Blue arrived in time
to paint its coming.

How many blues has the Mediterranean conjured?

Venus, mother of the sea of blues.

Blue of Greece,
leaning like a god against the columns.

Delicate, medieval blue.

The Virgin's contribution:
Mary-blue, the pale blue of Our Lady.

It descended to his palette from above.
Heaven's secret blue: when he used
this blue, he painted on his knees.
Angels came to baptize him with blue: Blessèd
Blue Angelico they called him.

Palette of celestial blue: swoop
of a wing white with the clouds.

9

Los azules de Italia,
los azules de España,
los azules de Francia . . .

10

Rafael tenía alas.
Tambíen el Perugino tenía alas
que al pintar derramaban sus azules.

11

Pinceles que son plumas,
azul añil, cuando de ti se tiñen.

12

Venecia del azul Tiziano en oro.

13

Roma de los azules Poussin entre los pinos.

14

Me enveneno de azules Tintoretto.

15

Azul azufre alcohol fósforo Greco.
Greco azul ponzoñoso cardenillo.

16

En la paleta de Velázquez tengo
otro nombre: me llamo Guadarrama.

17

Cuando serpeo entre las carnes nácar,
me llamo alegre azul vena de Rubens.

9

Blues of France,
blues of Spain,
blues of Italy . . .

10

Raphael had wings.
Perugino, too, had wings,
scattering blue like feathers as he painted.

11

Blue indigo, your dye
turns brushes into pens.

12

Venice of Titian blue in gold.

13

Rome, blues of Poussin between the pines.

14

Tainted by Tintoretto blues.

15

Sulfur blue phosphor galena El Greco.
Greco blue poisonous verdigris.

16

On the palette of Velázquez I've
another name: Sierra Guadarrama.

17

Winding within mother-of-pearl flesh
as a blissful vein in Rubens.

18

Y por la madrugada de los lagos,
con un azul clareo, que repiten
los ecos de la umbría: Patinir.

19

Hay un azul Murillo Inmaculada,
precursor del brillante de los cromos.

20

También dio azules Tiépolo a su siglo.

21

Soy una banda, una ligera cinta
azul de Goya tenue, diluido.

22

Te diría:
                    —Eres bella, eres tan bella
como el azul glorioso de los techos.

23

Explosiones de azul en las alegorías.

24

En el azul Manet cantan los ecos
de un azul español en lejanía.

25

También me llamo Renoir. Me gritan.
Pero respondo a veces
con voz azul transparentada en lila.

18

And across the early morning of the lakes:
a light created out of blue, repeated
by the echoes of the grove—Patinir.

19

Immaculate Murillo blue:
gaudy on the glossy holy-cards.

20

Tiepolo, too, donated a blue to his epoch.

21

I am a sash in Goya, a ribbon of
light blue, diluted, pale.

22

A compliment for you:
                            —You're as beautiful
as the blue of the frescoed ceilings.

23

In the allegories: bursts of blue.

24

Manet's blue, where the echoes sing
of a Spanish blue in the distance.

25

I'm also called Renoir. They shout at me.
But mainly I respond with a blue voice—
stream-clear and running into lilac.

26

Soy la sombra azulada,
la clara silueta de tu cuerpo.
Para los viejos ojos, el escándalo.

27

Dieron las Baleares su azul a la Pintura.

28

El mar invade a veces la paleta
del pintor y le pone
un cielo azul que sólo da en secreto.

29

La sombra es más azul cuando ya el cuerpo
que la proyecta se ha desvanecido.

30

Tiene el azul estático nostalgia
de haber sido azul puro en movimiento.

31

Aunque el azul no esté dentro del cuadro,
como un fanal lo envuelve.

32

Dijo el azul un día:
—Hoy tengo un nuevo nombre. Se me llama:
Azul Pablo Ruiz Azul Picasso.

26

Blue shadow, plainly
outlining your body:
for old eyes, a scandal in itself!

27

A gift to Painting from the Islands: Balearic blue.

28

Sometimes, the sea invades
the palette, setting there
the blue sky it can only bring in secret.

29

A shadow: bluest when the body
casting it has already vanished.

30

Static blue feels nostalgia for a time
when it was pure blue in motion.

31

A given painting may contain no blue,
and yet blue hovers round it like a bell glass.

32

Blue said one day,
—I have a new name now:
my name is Pablo Blue Ruiz Picasso.

Rafael

He aquí el festín, el gran banquete,
la esperada comida.
Es la celebración del nacimiento
de una fuente desconocida.

Corre la adolescencia,
perpetuo encantamiento,
oreada de transparencia.

Tendidos los manteles,
de buril en pincel, de los pinceles,
viene y va la armonía.

Es el día.
        ¡Oh, es el día,
el señalado día del espacio,
su vibración sonora,
la música real de las esferas!

Es nada, o menos, todo muro,
poco todo palacio
para tan alta hora,
tan altas horas venideras.

Al fin va a descorrerse,
a levantarse
el bosque de la maravilla,
y el agua antigua a refrescarse,
desnuda, en su nueva orilla.

De rumor de Amorcillos,
sus plumas enlazadas
a las de las palomas en grecas de frutales,

Raphael

The banquet's spread: a feast!
It is the food so long awaited,
the celebration of an unknown
fountain, just created.

      Flowing adolescence,
           the constant plash of magic,
                refreshment as transparent as the rain.

The table's all set
        with burin & paintbrush;
harmony's glint comes & goes.

      This is the day,
           the appointed day
      when space's dream coheres,
      when its sonorous vibrations
      are the music of the spheres.

All this wall is nothing at all,
the palace, little room
for what is to transpire here
in the hours soon to come.

      The enchanted forest
        will open up again
          —two curtains parting—
      its ancient stream, a young nude
          lying cool on a new shore.

Away from the murmuring Cupids,
      whose wings echo those of each dove
        in the border above,

se ladean los arbolillos,
las cabelleras encintadas
y el aliento de los cendales.

Gracioso manadero
tranquilo, de dulzura,
masculina inocencia femenina.
El aire es un venero
de fina arquitectura
y áurea sección divina.

Ungido, preferido
de la delicadeza.
Muda muchacha, la Belleza
te da su único vestido.

De rodillas las Gracias te llevan, te llevaron.
Tu alma no yace. Ondea
serenamente y pura
en la sonrisa que dejaron
Venus, Apolo y Galatea
por el cielo de tu pintura.

lean the little willow trees,
                    long hair adorned with ribbons
                              & the gauze of breeze.

Two wellsprings: you, a source
of sweetness, grace,
androgynous innocence;
the air is charged
with architecture, vibrant
with invisible golden sections.

Anointed one, touched
                    by tenderness.
Beauty is the silent girl
                    who wraps you in her dress.

                    It is the Graces who support you. They,
                    who carried you away.
                              But your spirit didn't follow:
                                        it floats free, apart,
                    fluttering in the smile
                              left by Venus, Galatea, & Apollo
                                        in the heavens of your art.

Tiziano

Fue Dánae, fue Calixto, fue Diana,
fue Adonis y fue Baco, fue Cupido;
la cortesana azul mar veneciana,
el ceñidor de Venus desceñido,
la bucólica plástica suprema.
Fue a toda luz, a toda voz el tema.

¡Oh juventud! Tu numbre es el Tiziano.
Tu música, su fuente calurosa.
Tu belleza, el concierto de su mano.
Tu gracia, su sonrisa numerosa.
Lúdica edad, preámbulo sonoro,
divina y fiel desproporción de oro.

El alto vientre esférico, el agudo
pezón saltante, errático en la orgía,
las más secretas sombras al desnudo.
Bacanal del color: su mediodía.
Colorean los ríos los Amores,
surtiendo en arco de sus ingles flores.

No ignoran las alcobas ni el brocado
del cortinón que irisa el escarlata
cuánto acrecienta un cuerpo enamorado
sobre movidas sábanas de plata.
Nunca doró pincel en primavera
mejor cintura ni mayor cadera.

Titian

He was Bacchus, and Diana, Danaë,
Callisto, and Adonis, he was Cupid;
the courtly blue of the Venetian sea,
the gird'ling sash of Venus just removèd,
of pastorals in paint, the one supreme.
He was the full expression of the theme.

Oh youthfulness! Thy happy name is Titian.
Thy music was the wellspring of his art.
Thy beauty, his hand's power to position.
Thy grace, his smile that harmonized all parts.
Playful age, preface to time grown old,
divinely disproportionate with gold.

A spheric belly, nipples that protrude,
upturned in an orgiastic swoon,
the secret, hidden shadows all laid nude.
This Bacchanal of color is their noon.
The Love God aims, and tints the stream with showers,
spurting from his groin an arc of flowers.

The scarlet bedroom curtain's not deceived
about the light that's rainbowing its pleats;
her flesh, in love, grows ready to receive,
still, upon the stirring silver sheets.
Never in Springtime was a paintbrush graced
to gild a greater hip or better waist.

Todo se dora. El siena, que en lo umbrío
cuece la selva en una luz tostada,
dora el ardor del sátiro cabrío
tras de la esquiva sáfica dorada;
y un rubio viento, umbrales y dinteles,
basamentos, columnas, capiteles.

La vid que el alma de Dionisos dora,
del albo rostro de Jesús exuda,
y la Madre de Dios, Nuestra Señora,
de Afrodita de oro se desnuda.
Vuelca el Amor profano su áureo vino
en los manteles del Amor divino.

¡Amor! Eros infante que dispara
la más taladradora calentura;
venablo luminoso, flecha clara,
directa al corazón de la Pintura.
¿Cuándo otra edad vio plenitud más bella,
altor de luna, miramar de estrella?

Pintor del Piave di Cadore, eterno,
dichoso juvenil, vergel florido,
resplandeciente río sin invierno,
en el monte de Venus escondido.
Sean allí a tus prósperos verdores
Príapo el pincel, Adonis los colores.

Everything is golden. In the grove,
ocher bastes the leaves with toasted light,
and gilds the satyr's eagerness, which drove
the shy and sapphic golden girl to flight.
Even the wind is blond, and all it bathes:
sylvan ruins, columns, architraves.

The grape that gilds the soul of Dionysus
from Jesus' pale forehead is transpired,
and Mary, virgin pearl, pure and priceless,
turns Aphrodite, golden and desired.
Profane Love overturns her aureate wine,
drenching Divine Love's altarcloths and shrine.

Eros! Child whose arbalestic art
brings penetrating fever, wakeful fainting;
resplendent arrow, luminescent dart
fired directly at the heart of Painting.
When else was such full beauty held in fee,
so high a moon, a star's view of the sea?

Piave di Cadore's painter, timeless,
blissful youth, fully flowering field,
river without winter, flashing, rimeless,
in the mound of Venus happily concealed.
May Adonis always lend thy art his blush,
and Priapus provide thee with a brush.

Rojo

1

Soy el primer color de la mañana
y el último del día.

2

Lucho en el verde de la fruta y venzo.

3

Lo mismo que mis otros hermanos, sometido
—Giotto—al rigor del éxtasis geométrico.

4

Pleno rubor redondo en la manzana.

5

Me llamo excitación, cólera, rabia,
estallido del día de la ira.

6

Me violento y subo
hasta de pronto reventar en sangre.

7

Coágulo cuando ya
casi mi ser solidifico en negro.

8

Rojo en el labio y menos
en las pequeñas cumbres
donde gustosamente
Venus ganando pierde las batallas.

Red

1

I am morning's first color,
day's last.

2

I wrestle with the green in fruit; I win.

3

With my brothers, I submitted to the rigors
—Giotto—of geometric rapture.

4

The apple's full round blush.

5

My name's excitement, anger, fury
ruptured on the day of wrath.

6

I gather myself & rise till suddenly
I burst forth as blood.

7

I congeal when my being
solidifies in black.

8

Red in the lips, and less
at the small summits
where Venus, winning,
happily loses the battle.

9

Soy el infierno—Brueghel,
Bosch—y el nocturno espanto
en los ojos insomnes de los niños.

10

Pluma en las alas de Luzbel, ardiendo.

11

El rojo recortado
—Flandes—hasta llegar
—Rubens—al derramado de la orgía.

12

Vago en ciertos desnudos,
en ciertas formas diluido en nieve.

13

Rojo para el descanso de los hombros
y la espalda de Venus
—Giorgione—dormida.

14

Me levanto hasta el solio de la púrpura
y desciendo esparcido—¡oh Greco!—en pliegues.

15

El púrpura a través de los cristales
—copa, vaso, botella—
calientes de los vinos.

16

Ven, amarillo. Quiero ser naranja,
cadmio lustroso esférico entre el verde.

9

I am Hell—Brueghel,
Bosch—& nighttime fright
in the sleepless eyes of children.

10

Feather in the wings of Satan, flaming.

11

Red diminished—Flanders—
until Rubens:
all the lavishness of orgy.

12

Indistinct in certain nudes,
diluted by the snow.

13

Red for the repose
in the shoulders & the back
of Venus—Giorgione—fast asleep.

14

High up in the purple canopied throne
then down—Greco—dispersed among the pleats.

15

Purple through glass:
goblets, bottles, tumblers
warm with wine.

16

Come to me cadmium yellow: I want to be orange,
a lustrous sphere amidst the green.

17

¿En la rosa? Diverso, pero único.

18

Pierdo el sentido en rosa,
hasta desvanecerme en casi blanco.

19

Canto en la lengua, tiño
con un húmedo rosa las palabras.

20

Un rosa con escarcha, de Velázquez.

21

Otro—Goya—con aire diluido.

22

Me vertí en rosa—Renoir—y puse
un nuevo nombre—Renoir—al mío.

23

La niña rosa—¡oh sueno!—de Rosales.

24

Bajé hasta el rosa rosa de Picasso.

25

Rojo, contra el azul, de una bandera.

26

A veces desafino hasta la sima
del más profundo rojo insoportable.

17

In roses? Multiple, but always singular.

18

I lose my sense of self
in pink, then disappear
as it approaches white.

19

I sing in the tongue,
I leave a moist rose
trace on words.

20

The frost-pink of Velázquez.

21

In Goya, I'm diluted by the air.

22

I cascaded out in rose—Renoir—& added
a new name—Renoir—to mine.

23

The girl in pink—a vision—by Rosales.

24

All the way down to the rose rose of Picasso.

25

In a flag, against blue.

26

At times, I am so dissonant I reach the edge:
beyond, a red past all endurance.

27

Mas me calman las tierras, el sentirme
de sus hondas umbrías penetrado.

28

Rojo de la bravura en las arenas
rojo español redondo de las plazas.

29

Rojo como el relámpago
espiral de una alegre revolera.

30

Como el clavel que estalla en los ceñidos
marfiles de unos senos apretados.

31

Como el grana fugaz de una amapola.

32

Bañado por el mar y trabajado
por su garganta azul, florezco y subo
fino ramo encendido de corales.

33

Pensad que ando perdido en la más mínima,
humilde violeta.

27

But the lands soothe me, suffuse me
with the shade of their deep groves.

28

The round Spanish bullring;
bravura.

29

Red as the spiral lightning
of the matador's flipped cape.

30

. . . As the carnation that springs
from the squeezed ivory
of a cupped breast.

31

The fleeting scarlet of a poppy.

32

Bathed by the sea and worked
by her blue throat, I grow into
a sharp bouquet: bright coral.

33

Think how I'm lost
in the tiniest violet.

Tintoretto

Rotos los cielos, rotos.
Sombras despedazadas,
acechadoras luces,
desgarradas.

En la noche, estampidos
solemnes, redoblados,
de los aparecidos
fatigados.

Todo se cae, rueda.
Todo se precipita,
se violenta, se excita.
Y todo queda.

Batalla que reaviva,
reinventa el movimiento
allá en la turbulenta,
turbada, trastornada,
perspectiva del viento.

Pintura alta en esguince,
en quebradura.
Turbión que no parara
jamás y que rodara
ciego hacia la Pintura.

Tintoretto

Skies broken to pieces.
Shadows shattered;
light, a tattered
ambush.

Night: solemn
explosions, redoubled
by the troubled
apparitions.

Everyone is falling, rolling,
hurtling through space,
forcing, violent, excited.
Fixed in place.

This battle revivifies,
reinvents motion—
here turbulence, all's
turned around, askew: it's
the wind's point of view.

Painting rich with twisting,
forms breaking apart.
Squall that might not ever
stop, might roll blind
over Art.

No te miro, me anego
en ti, mar agitado,
pincel arrebatado
en un carro de fuego.

Hubiera yo querido
sentirme por tu cólera
hendido, sacudido,
y en medio del paisaje
fluvial, por la hermosura
de la virgen sin traje
que prolonga en el agua su blancura.

I don't view you, I
drown in you: rough ocean,
paintbrush in commotion,
swept off by a chariot of fire.

Always, desire
to feel myself split open
by your fury, by the beauty
—there, in the liquid landscape
where you've caught her—
of the virgin with no dress on
who prolongs her whiteness in the water.

Al pincel

A ti, vara de música rectora,
concertante del mar que te abre el lino,
silencioso, empapado peregrino
de la noche, el crepúsculo y la aurora.

A ti, caricia que el color colora,
fino estilete en el operar fino,
escoba barredera del camino
que te ensancha, te oprime y te aminora.

A ti, espiga en invierno y en verano,
cabeceante al soplo de la mano,
brasa de sombra o yerta quemadura.

La obstinación en ti se resplandece.
Tu vida es tallo que sin tierra crece.
A ti, esbelto albañil de la Pintura.

To the Paintbrush

To you, music-conjuring wand,
conductor of the seas which set
the canvas, as you wander, silent, wet,
across the night, half-light, & dawn.

To you, caress that deepens color,
fine-edged as a needle at a stitch,
or broomlike: on a road on which
you're flattened, pressed down, smothered.

To you, spike of grain above the land,
nodding in the light gusts of the hand,
supple flame, or blight-burnt stalk, erect.

Resistance shines from you: a torch.
Without soil, you put blossoms forth.
To you, Painting's slender architect.

Veronés

(Alegoría de Primavera)

Si los ríos, Amor, Gracia, fuerte, anchurosa,
de dilatadas ansias y caderas;
si los ríos, los jóvenes, más anhelados ríos
se alzaran, se doblaran,
un amanecer largo, y sólo fueran hombros,
pechos altos, abiertos y muslos extendidos . . .
Si pudiera tocarlos,
Amor, Gracia opulenta,
resbalarlos, dormidas las manos por su espalda . . .
¡Oh, navegar, nadar, perderse ahora,
Amor, redonda Gracia, por esa piel que ondea,
trasluciendo el impulso de la sangre,
por su torso en declive,
por sus brazos sin fin
en la ardiente mañana poderosa!
Los aires y las flores, como Amores desnudos,
encendidos, veloces por la orilla;
los ropajes, rizados, temblorosos,
colgados de las ramas,
y las sobredoradas palomas de los arcos,
hacia las balaustradas donde el cielo
vuelca palmas de luz entre murmullos
de ángeles anidados en las nubes.

Veronese

(Allegory of Spring)

What if the rivers, Love,
                    Grace, deep & wide
                                —broadened desires, broadened hips;
what if the rivers most
                    yearned for & young
should rise one dawn
and lay back down as shoulders,
                    high open-budded breasts,
                                        and spreading thighs . . .
What if I could touch them,
                    Love, opulent Grace,
slide up them, let my hands
                    sleep on their back . . .
Oh to sail, to swim, to lose my way,
                    Love, rounded Grace,
across that skin that undulates
                    —the impulse of the blood now glowing through—
down the slope of the torso,
                    up arms without end,
some potent & radiant morning!

Wind-stirrings, blossoms
                    —nude Cupids in air—
fire-touched, flit over the bank;
our clothing, in tremulous ruffles,
hangs from the boughs,
and through the arches: gold-lit doves
toward balustrades
                    beyond whose frame the sky
turns over palms of light, and sets
the angels nested there to murmuring.

¡Ven tú, Amor, ancho Amor, ansioso río!
¡Ven tú, dura, infinita,
clara columna, Gracia corpulenta,
ven a jugar conmigo,
ven ya a gritar, luchar, morir conmigo,
en la despeinadora,
naciente y plena luna saludable!

Come to me, wide Love,

                    passionate river!
Hard, infinite, clear column,

                    come,
come soft-fleshed Grace,
come play with me,

          come struggle, cry out, die
beneath the moon

          —she's taking out her combs,
          spilling her hair—

                    the full & rising,
                    vitalizing moon!

A la línea

A ti, contorno de la gracia humana,
recta, curva, bailable geometría,
delirante en la luz, caligrafía
que diluye la niebla más liviana.

A ti, sumisa cuanto más tirana,
misteriosa de flor y astronomía,
imprescindible al sueño y la poesía,
urgente al curso que tu ley dimana.

A ti, bella expresión de lo distinto,
complejidad, araña, laberinto
donde se mueve presa la figura.

El infinito azul es tu palacio.
Te canta el punto ardiendo en el espacio.
A ti, andamio y sostén de la Pintura.

To Line

To you, contour of human grace,
geometry that dances, straightens, twists,
delirious in light's embrace,
calligraphy that thins the finest mist.

To you, submissive when most arbitrary,
mysterious in astronomy, in roses,
vital to poets and to visionaries,
unwavering from the course your law imposes.

To you, expressing aptly the distinct,
complexity, a spider's, labyrinth
in which the caught form moves about, held short.

Your mansion's the infinity of blue.
The point blazing in space is singing you.
To you, Painting's scaffold and support.

El Bosco

El diablo hocicudo
ojipelambrudo,
cornicapricudo,
perniculimbrudo
y rabudo,
zorrea,
pajarea,
mosquiconejea,.
humea,
ventea,
peditrompetea
por un embudo.
Amar y danzar,
beber y saltar,
cantar y reír,
oler y tocar,
comer, fornicar,
dormir y dormir,
llorar y llorar.

Mandroque, mandroque,
diablo palitroque.

¡Pío, pío, pío!
Cabalgo y me río,
me monto en un gallo
y en un puercoespín,
en burro, en caballo,
en camello, en oso,
en rana, en raposo
en un cornetín.

Bosch

The devil—

blubber-lipped,
asshole-hipped,
anus-eyed,
tail-wide,
& caprihorny,
Beelzebuggering,
cummingbirding,
sniffing,
whiff-emitting,
strumpeting,
fart-trumpeting
through a funnel.
Loving & dancing,
drinking & prancing,
singing & laughing,
smelling & touching,
eating, fucking,
sleeping & sleeping,
weeping & weeping.

Mandrake, mandrake,
The devil has a crooked stake.

Cock-a-doodle-do!
I ride and I crow,
go mounted on a doe
& on a porcupine,
on a camel, on a lion,
on a burro, on a bear,
on a horse, on a hare,
and on a bugler.

Verijo, verijo,
diablo garavijo.

¡Amor hortelano,
desnudo, oh verano!
Jardín del Amor.
En un pie el manzano
y en cuatro la flor.
(Y sus amadores,
céfiros y flores
y aves por el ano.)

Virojo, pirojo,
diablo trampantojo.

El diablo liebre,
tiebre,
notiebre,
sipilipitiebre,
y su comitiva
chiva,
estiva,
sipilipitriva,
cala,
empala,
desala,
traspala,
apuñala
con su lavativa.

Barrigas, narices,
lagartos, lombrices,
delfines volantes,
orejas rodantes,
ojos boquiabiertos,
escobas perdidas,

Cork, cork,
The devil has a small pitchfork.

> Love in a garden,
> nude . . . ah, summer!
> Garden of Delights.
> On one foot the appletree
> & on all fours the flower.
> (And your lovers,
> asses bare to the wind,
> to perching birds, small bouquets.)

> > Prickster, dickster,
> > The devil is a trickster.

The devil jackrabbit
        jackoffrabbit
        packoffrabbit
        fackoffrabbit,
with his satyry,
        summery,
        cuntery
        company,
jabs,
grabs,
dabs,
nabs,
stabs
with an enema.

> Bellies, nostrils,
> lizards' tails,
> dophins flying,
> ears impaled,
> eyes gape-mouthed,
> lost brooms,

barcas aturdidas,
vómitos, heridas,
muertos.

Predica, predica,
diablo pilindrica.

Saltan escaleras,
corren tapaderas,
revientan calderas.
En los orinales
letales, mortales,
los más infernales
pingajos, zancajos,
tristes espantajos
finales.

Guadaña, guadaña,
diablo telaraña.

El beleño,
el sueño,
el impuro,
oscuro,
seguro
botín,
el llanto,
el espanto
y el diente
crujiente
sin
fin.

Pintor en desvelo:
tu paleta vuela al cielo,
y en un cuerno,
tu pincel baja al infierno.

                              boats in dread,
                              vomitings & wounds,
                              the dead.

He preaches, he preaches,
The devil puts on leeches.

                              Ladders sliding,
                              potlids flowing,
                              cauldrons blowing.
                              In the lethal
                              chamberpots,
                              the most infernal
                              rags, shoe-toes—
                              sad, ultimate
                              scarecrows.

He scythes, he scythes,
Devil cobweb harvests lives.

                              Nightshade
                              nightmare,
                              dark,
                              polluted,
                              untransmuted
                              fruits,
                              tears,
                              fear,
                              & gnashing
                              teeth
                              without
                              cease.

Uneasy painter:
your palette ascends to the skies,
but on a horn your paintbrush flies

                              to Hell.

A la perspectiva

A ti, engaño ideal, por quien la vista
anhela hundirse, prolongada en mano,
yendo de lo cercano a lo lejano,
del hondo azul al pálido amatista.

A ti, sinfín, profundidad, conquista
de la espaciada atmósfera en lo plano,
por quien al fondo del balcón cercano
decides que la mar lejana exista.

A ti, aumento, valor de los valores,
vaga disminución de los colores,
música celestial, arquitectura.

Los ámbitos en ti fundan su planta.
La línea con el número te canta.
A ti, brida y timón de la Pintura.

To Perspective

To you, the perfect hoax, through whom the eye,
like a reaching hand, extends its view,
moving to what is far from what's close by,
to paler amethyst from deepest blue.

To you, feigner of depth & endless space,
giving to flat planes profundity,
through whom, beyond the balcony's iron lace,
we think that we can just make out the sea.

To you, value prized above all others,
hazy diminution of the colors,
architecture, music of the spheres.

On you, pictorial space lays its foundation.
Line & number sing your celebration.
To you, the tiller by which Painting steers.

Durero

Nocturno lancinado
por la luz, que domeña
la mano que desgreña
en orden el grabado.

Misteriosa escritura
que irrumpe en agua fuerte
a caballo la Muerte
por una selva oscura.

Drama que se perfila
persistente, hilo a hilo.
Tristeza del estilo
sin pausa que burila.

Lenguaje lanzadera.
Rúbricas que se pierden
por las sombras que muerden
el cobre y la madera.

Pitagórica trama,
calmo desasosiego.
Todo es prueba de fuego,
métrica tinta en llama.

Pintor en cirugía,
paciente inquisitivo.
Tú, el ángel pensativo
de la Melancolía.

Dürer

Nocturne lanc'd by light:
carefully, on the plate,
a hand undoes the night,
dishev'ling to create.

Mysterious writing
erupts into design:
past Death a knight goes riding,
past Satan in a swine.

Drama come to life
through persistence, hatch by hatch.
Sorrow of the knife
continuing to scratch.

Shuttle-language: 'cross the loom.
Initials lost for good
among shadows that consume
the copper & the wood.

Pythagorean woof,
compos'd/unravel'd skein.
A trial by fire, each proof—
measure touch'd by flame.

Investigative surgeon,
patient, above folly.
Your portrait's other version:
angel of Melancholy.

Amarillo

1

Acciono con la luz, soy un activo
cómplice de la luz contra la sombra.

2

Ella me dice: —Hermano.
Pero luego al más mínimo
sobresalto me borra, emblanqueciéndome.

3

. . . Mas tengo el privilegio de ser verde
y desnudarme—otoño—en amarillo.

4

Feliz, risueño, alegre, delicado
—Goethe—, en estado puro.

5

Gualda de sol—pinturas—de Pompeya.

6

Oro en el nimbo de los viejos santos.
Oro ingenuo labrado de Edad Media.

7

Canto en la espiga y canto
cuando, pálido pan,
me recorta la albura
tersa de los manteles.

8

A ti, elevado a pura trasparencia,
tenue, amarillo aéreo de la rosa.

Yellow

1

I am Light's partner, active
accomplice of Light against Shadow.

2

She calls me "Brother,"
but at the slightest alarm
blots me out, whitening me.

3

. . . But it's my privilege to be green
and undress—Autumn—in yellow.

4

In my purest state: cheerful, smiling
—Goethe—tender, gay.

5

The sun's dye—paintings—at Pompeii.

6

Gold in the old saints' halos.
Gold of the Middle Ages: naive, figured.

7

I sing in the spikes of grain
and when, as bread,
I'm set off by the smooth
egg-whiteness of the tablecloth.

8

To you, attained to pure transparency,
faint, ethereal yellow of the rose.

9

Senos áureos, espaldas
—Tiziano—como finas
rodelas de oro puro.

10

Lo vi dorarse, hacerse
vino viejo en los trajes
—Veronés—que colgaban de los hombros.

11

Derivo a bucle, a larga cabellera
sobre el desnudo combo de la espalda.

12

Me amaso con la luz, y con el rosa
de la carne me fundo y permanezco.

13

Seca piel de arrugado pergamino.

14

Me llamo lividez, entumecido
exangüe cadavérico estirado.

15

El pálido amarillo de la muerte.

16

Marfil oculto dentro de la carne.

17

Sonámbulo, espectral, aparecido,
cálido, turbio—Greco—, pantanoso,
gélido, indigestado, vomitado,
diluido, llovido, evaporado,

9

Golden shoulders, breasts
—Titian—fine-bossed
bucklers of pure gold.

10

I saw gold gild itself, become
old wine in cloaks
—Veronese—spilling from the shoulders.

11

I cleave to curl, to long hair
down the bare curve of the back.

12

I knead myself with light, and with the flesh's
pink am lastingly united.

13

A wrinkled parchment's dried-up skin.

14

Lividness: numbed, laid out,
cadaveric, lifeless.

15

Death's pallor.

16

Ivory, hid within the flesh.

17

Somnambulant, phantasmal, eerie,
turbid—El Greco—swampy, warm,
bilious, vomited, pit-cold,
rained down, diluted, disappeared,

difunto, corrompido, disecado,
vivo, resucitado . . .

18
Aparezco de pronto en la tormenta.

19
Hueso amarillo en polvo, desvelado
resplandor de la muerte en movimiento.

20
Esqueleto, y sonora dentadura
luciente de los claves y los pianos.

21
Soy la cera, la lágrima
caliente por el cuello de los cirios.

22
El amarillo Rembrandt revelado.

23
Sin mí, ¿qué hubiera sido
de la estameña en éxtasis
—Zurbarán—de tus monjes?

24
Temo al azul porque me pone verde.

25
Me gritan las naranjas:
—Amarillo limón,
¡ay, quién pudiera,
amarillo limón, ser tu amarillo!

deceased, corrupted, dried,
resurrected, alive . . .

18
Suddenly in the storm.

19
Yellow bone whirled to dust, sleepless
glimmer of death in motion.

20
Skeleton, or shining sonorous
teeth, those piano keys?

21
Wax, I am a hot tear
down the candle's neck.

22
As revealed by Rembrandt.

23
Your monks, Zurbarán—
without me, what would have become
of their "serge in ecstacy"?

24
I'm afraid of Blue because it makes me Green.

25
The oranges on the corner call out as I pass:
"Lemon yellow!
Ah! If only everyone could be
as yellow as you!"

26

Amarillo descarga, amarillento
estampido, lujoso y claro, en Goya.

27

Cuando rompo a volar y mi garganta
suelta un oro de flautas repetidas,
le dan a mi alegría un amarillo:
Amarillo canario.

28

El amarillo del temblor, el tenso
amarillo febril de la demencia.

29

Sueno, resueno, grito
hasta hincarme en el centro
—Van Gogh—de la retina y desgarrarla.

30

Me tuesta el ocre. El rojo
me excita y me suspende hasta la altura
naranja de la llama.

31

El amarillo cromo, satinado.

32

Un ordenado esférico amarillo
naturaleza muerta.

33

Volví a extenderme puro,
a vibrar en mi son del arcoiris,
mas sometido a leyes geométricas.

26

Volleyed fire, a lavish bright
explosion in Goya.

27

When I break into flight, and my throat
lets go the gold of flutes repeating,
they give to my happiness a particular hue:
canary yellow.

28

Trembling-yellow, the tense
fever-yellow of dementia.

29

I sound, I resound, I scream
until I thrust myself into the core
—Van Gogh—of the retina, ripping it.

30

Ocher toasts me. Red
excites me, hangs me at the orange
tip of the flame.

31

Chrome-yellow: satin's luster.

32

Arranged & spherical
—still life.

33

I've come back, an arc of simple yellow,
vibrating in position in the rainbow,
bent to geometric law.

Rubens

Era del año la estación florida . . .

Góngora

Era del hombre la pasión, la vida.
Era el caballo que se eleva a hombre,
relámpago las crines, y los ojos,
rayos de lluvia enamorada.

Era . . .

La edad que no conoce la edad, una corriente
como una espalda rosa de mujer sonreída,
ensanchando los bosques la ladridos y ciervos.
Era, tirante, un músculo en la fija ignorancia
de la hora y el filo que pudieran cortarlo.
Un alcohol siempre alto, una espuma ebria siempre,
rota en nácares blancas y venillas azules.
Era también, preciso y girando en su aguja,
un compás siempre en punto al dibujo de un seno,
tembloroso en las yemas ansiosas de asumirlo
y escapar en la noche un levante de estrellas.
Era además . . .

¡Oh nubes!

Que los ríos no olviden esta lección de agua
que puede dislocarse trasmutando los cielos,
que recuerde la mar y apunte en su memoria
las posibilidades de amanecer sin playas,
que la tormenta piense en el riesgo que corre
de abrirse al firmamento de las alegorías,
y la Belleza bella, en un despertar súbito,
verterse en los cabellos de Diana cazadora.

¡Oh dioses,

dioses,

dioses!

Rubens

It was the flowering season of the year . . .

Góngora

It was man's passion and his life, all here.
It was the horse that rises into man,
mane of lightning bolts, eyes
with the gleam of rain in love.

It was . . .

An age that knows no age, a stream
like the rosy back of a woman who has smiled,
widening the woods, dogs barking, deer.
It was a muscle, taut, in ignorance
of any blade or moment that could cut it.
A liquor always high, intoxicated spume
smashed in pearls and delicate blue veins.
And pivoting around its point,
a compass always fashioning a breast,
fingers trembling to alight, to release
in the night a levanter of stars.
And it was also . . .

clouds!

Let the rivers remember this lesson on water:
it can decamp, transmuting the skies;
let the sea fix in its memory
the thought that it could wake and find no beach;
let the storm fear to open up
the old skies of the allegories, pouring,
soft Beauty spilling all over
the hair of chaste Diana as she hunts.

O gods,

& gods,

& goddesses!

Delirio de la mano por sorprender que Venus
mide igual, de hombro a hombro, que Adonis poseído,
que la cadera pálida de una ninfa en huida
tiembla el mismo color que los ojos del sátiro.
¡Dionisos! ¡Cómo estallan los enjambres de mosto
bajo tu vagabunda risa voluminosa,
cómo ufanas tu vientre circunscrito al escándalo
de las contorneadas y repletas bacantes!
Jardines. Amplias Gracias de la luz que no oculta
más pasión que extenderse desnuda por los cuerpos,
de la línea que sabe en su concreto impulso
ceder anchos espacios al color que los llene.
¡Oh pintor de mayúsculas desmedidas no escritas,
de las exclamaciones que no encontraron signo,
de la boca y los ojos que al intentar decirte
tu hermosura no pueden expresarse y se espantan!
Tú, el Amor, tú los cielos en orgía, tú el árbol
que ha cubierto el mordido pezón flotante en fuga,
la solidificada música más redonda,
tú, el tumulto del sueño en volutas de carne,
tú, en fin, ese caballo que se desborda en hombre,
hinchándole las venas el verde soplo extraño
de erigirse en los tuétanos de la mar como tromba
que lo mueve, lo empuja, lo exalta y lo eterniza.

Delight of the hand, surprised that Venus
has the same breadth as Adonis, that the pale
hip of that fleeing nymph, trembling,
repeats the color of the satyr's eyes.
Dionysus! Swarms of must exploded
by your laugh—vagrant, voluminous—,
your vaunted belly circumscribed by din,
replete Bacchantes all wound round.
Gardens. Ample Graces. Here, the light
hides nothing, lying nude across their bodies;
here, line knows instinctively to cede
broad spaces to the color that will fill them.
                                    O painter
of magnificent, unwritten Capitals,
of exclamations with no matching signs,
of mouths and eyes that never will be able
to describe to you how beautiful you are.
                                    You are
Love; the skies in orgy; leaves that drape
the bitten nipple of that floating breast
—music solidified, a perfect round—;
the tumult of a dream, volutes of flesh;
and last, that white horse flowing into man,
veins filled by a rare green wind, whirled, rising
from the marrow of the sea, a waterspout,
exalting you, pushing, immortalizing.

A la composición

A ti, cimiento azul de la armonía,
sólida trama que una ley sanciona,
suma de acordes que entre sí aprisiona
en su red ideal la geometría.

A ti, premeditada fantasía,
diosa avara de cálculo, ladrona
del pleno espacio puro que corona
la inspiración de la sabiduría.

A ti, intocable flor, orden dilecto,
cabal conjunto, rítmico arquitecto,
inconmovible, mágica armadura.

Tu mejor monumento arde en tu frente.
Te alzas total imperativamente.
A ti, soplo y razón de la Pintura.

To Composition

To you, blue ground of harmony, design
whose solid silken threads a law has set,
a tune: chord-dances blending to confine
geometry within their ideal net.

To you, premeditated fantasy,
goddess hot for calculus, a thief
of pure unplotted space, of vacancy
that wisdom's inspiration will complete.

To you, sweet order, full elusive bloom,
ensemble, architect of rhythmic room,
magic-educing, moveless skeleton.

Your best arrangement burns behind your brow.
It's that one you aspire to even now.
To you, Painting's plans, sail-shaping wind.

Verde

1

Yo soy el verdemar,
subido a azul cuando el azul del cielo
tiende su pecho azul sobre mi espalda.

2

Tengo otro nombre siempre: Primavera.

3

Y alta forma de copa, que los árboles
se encargan presurosos de llenar,
hasta el borde, de verde.

4

Mi forma repetida más constante,
desde que vi la luz, es la de hoja.

5

Soy tallo, esbelto pie
sostenador de todos los colores.

6

Claro, soy la Esperanza.
Pero me descompongo y tengo entonces
cierto horrible matiz: el verde Envidia.

7

Un verde sumergido en las aguas del tiempo.

8

Verde ojival que el sol
oblicuo—catedrales—
penetra sin romperlo ni mancharlo.

Green

1
I am sea-green, lifted
to blue where the sky lays across me,
blue chest over my back.

2
Always, my other name: Springtime.

3
And tall branch-cups,
which the quick trees
brim with green.

4
Since first seeing light,
my most common form: the leaf's.

5
I am the stem, slender stand,
supporter of all the colors.

6
Yes, I'm Hope, but,
out of sorts, I assume
a horrible hue: Envy's green.

7
A green submerged in the waters of time.

8
Ogival green which the sun
slanting—cathedrals—
suffuses without breaking up or mottling.

9

Dio el olivo su verde de Minerva,
y su verde, "el laurel del verde Apolo."

10

Verde de exhalación,
verde relámpago,
en un abrir y en un cerrarse verde.

11

Y tierra verde antiguo en los pinceles
de las manos maestras ya remotas.

12

El alegre, bailable, florecido
verde—Brueghel—flamenco.

13

Aunque soy verde, tengo
muchas veces el alma de amarillo.

14

Cuando sueño ser gris le quito un poco
al negro y al azul de su hermosura.

15

Para Tiziano, un jubiloso, eterno
verde ondear de tréboles floridos.

16

A veces me acelesto y me confundo
con el azul que anhela erguirse verde.

17

Me han dado un nombre—Veronés—que tiene
blasón de principado.

9

The olive gave Athena's green,
the laurel, green Apollo's.

10

Green of a shooting star,
green lightning-flash: sudden
green opening & closing.

11

And an ancient green land
at the tips of brushes
held by masters now gone.

12

Jolly, dancing, blossoming
Flemish—Breughel—green.

13

Though green, I often have
the soul of yellow.

14

Dreaming of gray, I steal
from blue, from black, some of their beauty.

15

For Titian, the joyful, eternal
green waving of flowering clover.

16

At times I turn turquoise and am confounded
with blue yearning to grow green.

17

They have given me a name—Veronese:
emblem of preeminence.

18

El verde solitario de la muerte.

19

El mar vomita un verde umbroso alga
que al expandirse inunda,
tomándola por playa,
la tenebrosa luz que empuja al Tintoretto.

20

Un agónico verde helado Greco,
un verde musgo legamoso Greco,
un disecado verde vidrio Greco,
un verde roto Greco.

21

Verde jubón en un arcabucero
—Velázquez—de "Las lanzas."

22

Voz de verde misterio
—Rembrandt—que se abre paso
desde el fondo de tierra de la sombra.

23

Muchos días me engarza al paisaje
la luz como a un anillo una esmeralda.

24

Para Rubens, un rubio verde viña,
líquido por las plantas oscilantes de Baco.

25

Sigo a veces teniendo
claras sonoridades de cristales
cuando ya para el tacto
soy nada más que tela.

18

The solitary green of death.

19

A shadowy, algae-like green,
thrown up by the sea, floods
the dark light that haunts Tintoretto,
taking it for a beach.

20

Dying chill El Greco green,
dark river-bottom El Greco green,
stuffed underglass El Greco green,
broken El Greco green.

21

Green of the harquebusier's doublet
—Velázquez, "Las Lanzas."

22

Voice of green mystery
—Rembrandt—opening a way
from earth's depths for the shadow.

23

On many days I am the emerald
light sets upon the landscape's ring.

24

For Rubens, the green of golden vineyards,
liquid of the swaying plants of Bacchus.

25

Sometimes, I continue to give off
resonances of crystal,
though to the touch,
I am nothing more than canvas.

26

Un verde popular de romería
y un lazo en fino verde para Goya.

27

Delacroix me exalta hasta dar voces.
Courbet—verde intrincado de selva—me ensombrece.

28

Me lavaron también, me evaporaron
pinceles que a la luz pidieron todo.

29

Cézanne me corta, Renoir me envuelve.

30

A ti, verde lavado,
líquido verde Francia
(Manet, Sisley, Monet,
Pissarro, Renoir . . .)

31

En la sombra persisto.
En la luz arrebato y borro todo.

32

¡Si un día se pudiera
en ciertos momentáneos
verdes que alumbra el mar
hundir por la manaña los pinceles!

33

Desagradables verdes que dan gritos
en pinceles que nadie ve ni escucha.

26

For Goya, the popular green of a rural saint's-day
& a sash of fine green.

27

Delacroix intensifies me till I cry out.
Courbet—entangled forest's green—enshades me.

28

I evaporated, was washed out
by brushes who asked everything of light.

29

Cézanne pares me down, Renoir wraps me round.

30

To you, aquarelle-green,
liquid green France
(Manet, Sisley, Monet,
Pissarro, Renoir . . .)

31

In the shade, I persist.
In the light, I enchant, I eclipse everything.

32

If, into sudden momentary
greens brought to light by the sea,
one could, some day,
plunge all the paintbrushes . . .

33

Vile greens shouting through brush-tips—
no one sees, no one hears you.

34

Y un verde, el más hermoso
de los verdes, que olvido o no recuerdo.

34

And one green, the most beautiful
of all, which I forget, or can't recall.

Pedro Berruguete

Aquí los oros ungidos,
los platas divinamente
      laminados;
las santas facies perdidas,
la piel absorta y sin agua,
      muerto el sueño.

Los espartos y los duros,
secos raigones terrestres,
      amarillos;
los yermos trajes quebrados,
las desveladas aristas
      silenciosas.

La pálida arquitectura
los musitados ladrillos
      y las piedras;
el incansable, en ayuno
ciprés desde las ojivas
      solitario.

Aquí los rojos enjutos,
los blancos óseos crujientes
      y los negros;
la lenta tierra abstraída
que un pensamiento en las nubes
      desmejora.

Barro que el sol come, heladas
arcillas que el sol ahorna,
      mudas gredas;
sangre cocida, cocidos
cuerpos cerrados que un fuego
      petrifica.

Pedro Berruguete

Here, the anointed golds,
divine silver
        laminae;
the holy facades: flesh lost
in thought, dried up, lacking
        dreams.

The esparto grass, and the hard
dry roots, earthbound &
        yellow;
barren robes of broken ground,
the bristles of the weeds sleepless,
        silent.

A pallid architecture,
the mumbling of bricks
        & stone;
through the arch: a fasting
cypress, tireless,
        alone.

Here, the dried-out reds,
bone-cracking whites,
        and blacks;
the slow, daydreaming earth
that a cloud's thought
        could corrupt.

Mud eaten by the sun,
the frozen clay now scorched, a
        muted marl;
boiling blood, baked
bodies, closed by fire, and
        petrified.

Pintor de atril y colores
en la plática y la misa
        consagrados;
pincel de la fe, martillos
y escoplos, sagrada forma
        del tormento:

tu melancólica llama
con la sombra que concierta
        se agavilla.
Aquí la muerte viviente,
aquí la vida muriente,
        de Castilla.

Painter: in the Mass,
your easel & your paints are
        sanctified;
paintbrush of the Faith, hammer,
chisel, shaping sacred
        torture.

Your flame is sheaf-bound
to shadow: the spokes & the space
        in a wheel.
Here, the living death,
here, the dying life
        of Castile.

Al ropaje

A ti, fino, ligero, desatado,
rizada delgadez trémula al viento;
si habitado del cuerpo, ceñimiento,
desceñimiento si deshabitado.

A ti, métrico, rígido, pausado,
llovida solidez sin movimiento;
si estática en acción, ordenamiento,
si acción movida, mar desordenado.

A ti, ágil seda, gasa, encaje, velo,
solemne lana, lino, terciopelo,
piel de la forma, hechizo de su hechura.

Cantan su ley los campos de tu escudo:
vestir de los vestidos el desnudo.
A ti, fiel tejedor de la Pintura.

To Clothing

To you, loosened open, light & thin,
ruffled transparence trembling in the wind;
if dwelt in by a body, belted round,
unbelted if no body can be found.

To you, metrical, rigid, slow, restrained,
a solid fall of stationary rain;
a conduct-ordinance if stiff in motion,
if flexible when worn, chaotic ocean.

To you, vivacious silk, lace, muslin, tulle,
solemn velvet, cambric-linen, wool,
skin that can be peeled and make no martyr.

The verses on your coat of arms conclude:
"to costume with apparel every nude."
To you, Painting's persevering sartor.

Zurbarán

Ni el humo, ni el vapor, ni la neblina.
Lejos de aquí ese aliento que destruye.
Una luz en los huesos determina
y con la sombra cómplice construye.
Pensativa sustancia la pintura,
paraliza de luz la arquitectura.

Meditación del sueño, memorable
visión real que en éxtasis domeña;
severo cielo, tierra razonable
de pan cortado, vino y estameña.
El pincel, la paleta, todo es frente,
medula todo, pensativamente.

Piensa el tabique, piensa el pergamino
del volumen que alumbra la madera;
el pan se abstrae y se ensimisma el vino
sobre el mantel que enclaustra la arpillera.
Y es el membrillo un pensamiento puro
que concentra el frutero en claroscuro.

Ora el plato, y la jarra, de sencilla,
humildemente persevera muda,
y el orden que descansa en la vajilla
se reposa en la luz que la desnuda.
Todo el callado refectorio reza
una oración que exalta la certeza.

La nube es un soporte, es una baja
plataforma celeste suspendida,
donde un arcángel albañil trabaja,
roto el muro, en mostrar que hay otra vida.
Mas lo que muestra es siempre un andamiaje
para enganchar en pliegues el ropaje.

Zurbarán

Neither smoke, vapor, nor mist.
Far from here that killing breath.
A light within the bones delimits,
fashions with the shadow's edge.
Thought makes the painting bright,
paralyzes forms with light.

Meditation during sleep: birth
of a vision, bliss masters the mind;
stern heaven & a reasonable earth
of monk's-cloth serge, cut bread, & wine.
The brush & palette are all brain,
this is intellect's domain.

The thin wall thinks, the vellum thinks
of the lighted volume which it props;
the bread becomes abstracted, the wine sinks
to musing on the cloist'ring tablecloth.
And the quince is a thought, an attention paid
which concentrates the fruit in light & shade.

The platter prays, the pitchers stand
humbly in their muteness, and
the order that rests in the tableware
reposes in the light that lays it bare.
All the still refectory
breathes a prayer exalting certainty.

The cloud's a platform in our view,
hung from a celestial height,
work of an artisan angel who
broke our wall to show heaven's life.
Yet this great stage is but a shape
on which the painter hangs his drape.

Rudo amante del lienzo, recia llama
que blanquecinamente tabletea,
telar del hilo de la flor en rama,
pincel que teje, aguja que tornea.
Nunca la línea revistió más peso
ni el alma paño vivo en carne y hueso.

Fe que da el barro, mística terrena
que el color de la arcilla sube al cielo,
mano real que al ser humano ordena
mirarse ante el divino, paralelo.
La gloria abierta, el monje se extasía
al ver volar la misma alfarería.

Pintor de Extremadura, en ti se extrema,
dura y fatal, la lidia por la forma.
El pan que cuece tu obrador se quema
en el frío troquel que lo conforma.
Gire en tu eternidad la disciplina
de una circunferencia cristalina.

Rough lover of the canvas, flame
that claps white castanets and dances,
thread that flow'rs the pattern on the frame:
brush that weaves, shuttle that advances.
Never has line had greater weight,
nor soul been fleshed in cloth more animate.

Earthenware gives faith: mystic clay
whose color lifts it to the sky,
bestowing hand that gave a shape
to men that mirrors the divine.
Christ's Rise fills the monk with ecstasy:
apotheosis of human pottery!

In you, Extremaduran,
the fight for form goes to extremes.
The bread your workshop bakes is burned
in the cold matrix of the die-machine.
May held shape turn round you perpetually:
a crystalline periphery.

A la luz

(*Impresionismo*)

A ti, temblor y halo del paisaje,
recortadora del perfil y ciega
para el pincel abierto que disgrega
la mancha de la mar y del celaje.

A ti, lavado, líquido lenguaje;
dura al color que su color restriega
contra el árbol preciso que doblega
a imprecisión la copa del ramaje.

A ti, mano de sol, cono perfecto,
denunciadora, igualadora, efecto
desvanecente de la línea pura.

El ala de la sombra en ti se afila.
Te quema el ser que tu cristal destila.
A ti, espejo y fanal de la Pintura.

To Light

(*Impressionism*)

To you, tremulous halo of the fields,
cutter of silhouettes, and turned to dark
by the dusk-creating brush: the sea yields
its color to the clouds, its shine & spark.

To you, gold aquarelle, liquid language,
hard on the forms 'gainst which your softness scrapes:
tree branches reaching out to you in homage
give up to imprecision their clear shapes.

To you, hand of sun, tracing a cone's design,
diffuser of the thinness of a line,
flatt'ner at noon, discloser, causing fear.

In you, the shadow's wing tapers away.
A lens can create fire from your ray.
To you, Painting's lamp, and Painting's mirror.

Velázquez

Se apareció la vida una mañana
y le suplicó:
        —Píntame, retrátame
como soy realmente o como tú
quisieras realmente que yo fuese.
Mírame, aquí, modelo sometido,
sobre un punto, esperando que me fijes.
Soy un espejo en busca de otro espejo.

       *

Mediodía sereno,
descansado
de la Pintura. Pleno
presente Mediodía, sin pasado.

       *

Te veo en mis mañanas madrileñas,
cuando decía: Voy al Pardo, voy
a la Casa del Campo, al Manzanares . . .
Y entraba en el Museo.

       *

. . . Y entraba por la puerta de tus cuadros
al encinar, al monte, al cielo, al río,
con ecos de ladridos, de disparos
y fugitivas ciervas diluidas
en el pintado azul de Guadarrama.

       *

Conocía los troncos y las hojas,
la herradura en la tierra,
la huella del lebrel
y hasta esas briznas

Velázquez

Life came to him one day
appealing,
            "Paint me
as I really am or as
you'd like me to be seen.
Look at me: a willing model,
hovering, waiting to be pinned.
A mirror searching for another mirror."

                    *

Noontime. Painting's
arrest.
Pleninoon, serene,
without past.

                    *

I see you—those Madrid mornings
when I used to say, "I'm going to the Pardo, I'm going
to the Casa de Campo, to the Manzanares River . . . ,"
and I'd enter the Museum.

                    *

. . . And I'd enter through the door of your paintings
the oakgrove, come to the mountain, sky & river:
echoes of gunfire & barking,
fleeting deer fading
into the painted blue of the Guadarrama.

                    *

I came to know the trunks & leaves,
the horseshoe's trace,
the whippet's mark, even
those blades of grass—no more

que en las sombras no son más que el alivio
del pincel que al pasar las acaricia.

*

La majestad del cielo
sobre la melancólica
majestad de la encina que guarece
la tristeza cansada de un retrato.

*

Y también conocía
aquel azul a quien le preguntaba:
—¿Qué es ese azul que apenas
si es montaña, si es nieve, si es azul?

*

Y su respuesta:
        —Soy, pero teniendo
por pincelada y por color el aire.

*

La pintura en tu mano se serena
y el color y la línea se revisten
de hermosura, de aire y "luz no usada."

*

Yo me entré—soy el aire—en el cuadrado
abierto de las telas, en los regios
salones, en las cámaras umbrías,
y allí envolví los muebles, las figuras,
revistiéndolo todo, rodeándolo
de ese vívido hálito que hoy
hace decir:
        —Mojaba su tranquilo
pincel en una atmósfera oreada.

than the slight unburdening
of the brush, grazing the shadows.

*

The majesty of the sky
above the melancholy
majesty of the oak, shelter
of the wistfulness in the portrait.

*

And I also knew
that blue whom I asked,
"Are you mountain or snow . . .
or even blue?"

*

And it replied,
              "The air of Blue is mine,
but by means of tint & brushstroke."

*

Painting, in your hands: a cleared sky;
line & color clothe themselves
in beauty, air, "uncommon light."

*

"I entered"—I'm the air—"through the open
squares of canvas, into royal
reception rooms & shadowed chambers,
enveloping the furniture, the figures,
clothing & suffusing
all, with that vivid breath
that makes one say,
              'He dipt his quiet
brush in the bright air.'"

*

Dice el pincel:
            —Como también soy río,
lo envuelvo todo a veces
en un vaho de plata.

*

La tenue rosa y gris argentería.

*

En tu mano un cincel,
pincel se hubiera vuelto,
pincel, sólo pincel,
pájaro suelto.

*

De las profundidades vaporosas
surjo denso vapor,
humana forma aérea condensada.

*

Dice el borracho:
            —Tengo
noble cara de príncipe y borracho,
de príncipe borracho o de beodo
que fuera rey y borracho a un mismo tiempo.

*

Y el tonto:
            —Me retratan
como a S.M. o al Conde Duque.
Soy D. Bobo Felipe de Coria y Olivares.

*

¿Quién el más noble príncipe? ¿El que alza
el arma cazadora entre sus guantes
o el perro que a sus pies mira tranquilo?

*

His brush says,
                "I am both brush and river,
and can disperse
an atmosphere of silver."

*

Silverspun embroidery; pale rose.

*

A chisel, at your touch,
would've turned into a brush,
in your hands, always
a brush/the rush of wings.

*

"From vaporous depths
I rise and mass, take
floating human form."

*

The drunk says,
                "I have the noble face
of prince & drunk—
of a drunken prince, or of a sot
who could've been a king."

*

And the fool,
                "I am portrayed
as if I were the King or the Count-Duke:
Don Felipe Buffoon de Olivares!"

*

Who's the nobler hunter? The prince who shifts
his gun between gloved fingers, or the dog
who looks out, quiet, at his feet?

*

Sangre azul en los perros de Velázquez.

*

Habla un alano:
                    —Hubiera yo—¿no veis?—,
tan bien pintado, dirigido el reino.

*

Y un lebrel:
                    —Sí, llamadme
S.M. Felipe Lebrel IV.

*

Mas también los caballos le podrían
disputar a los perros la corona.

*

Hago sonar los niños como rubias
campanas repicadas de colores.

*

La Gracia se vistió, la austera Gracia,
pero de pronto se miró desnuda
Venus tranquila al fondo de un espejo.

*

Serio color fluido sin ofensa.
Severidad, mar calma, sin ataque.

*

Los negros como túmulos,
los trajes negros como monumentos.

*

The blue-blooded dogs of Velázquez.

*

A wolfhound says,
               "My portrait is so fine
I am convinced I could've run the realm."

*

And a whippet,
               "Hound prince you may call me . . .
His Majesty Felipe Whippet IV."

*

But the horses, too,
ought to be crowned!

*

"I make the children ring out like blond
bells: peals of color."

*

Grace had dressed austerely,
but found herself a naked, tranquil
Venus in the mirror.

*

Unbrash color: liquid solemnity.
The sea's authority without its crash.

*

Tomblike blacks;
black robes like standing monuments.

*

La distinción le dijo ante la lámina
rigurosa y exacta de un espejo:
—Tengo un nombre. Me llamo . . .
Y el pintor retrató su propia imagen.

*

Nunca la línea se sintió más ágil
y menos responsable del contorno.

*

Soy el volumen que me da la mano
que modela el color y no la arcilla.

*

Soy en la tela un soplo,
el paso detenido de un momento.

*

Y en la historia del tiempo, el ligerísimo
roce fugaz de un ala perdurable.

*

Más vida, sí, más vida,
y tu pintura,
pintor, de haber vivido,
más que real pintura hubiera sido
pintura sugerida,
leve mancha, almo cuerpo diluido.

*

Accuracy spoke to him
before the mirror's exacting space,
"I have a name. My name is . . . "
The painter painted his own face.

*

Never was line more agile,
less bent on contour.

*

"I am volume, issue
of a hand that models color and not clay."

*

"I am breath in the canvas,
a moment's step detained."

*

And in the course of time, the grazing
touch of an eternal wing.

*

"More life! More!"
But painter,
if your work had come to life
it would be fainter—
art's source, but not its solution;
vitality, but dilution.

Valdés Leal

Silencio. ¿Quién sonríe?
Un temblor que se apaga.
Un humo que enmudece.
Ni más ni menos. Nada.

¡Oh virulencia clara,
profunda llama oscura!
Ni más ni menos. Nada.
Viento de la amargura.

Luz de postrimería.
Un ataúd, la caja
de colores, vacía.
Ni más ni menos. Nada.

Duro pincel espada,
pincel mojado en sangre
de garganta cortada.
Ni más ni menos. Nada.

¿Vais a llorar? ¡Grandeza
de agonía enterrada!
Rodando, una cabeza,
otra cabeza. Nada.
Ni más ni menos. Nada.

Vértigos, viejas ramas,
broncas barbas de olivo,
de encendidas retamas.
Color muriendo vivo.
Ni más ni menos. Nada.

Valdés Leal

Silence. Who's there, smiling?
A trembling, stopt; a snuffing.
Wick-smoke, muted, dying.
No more; no less. Nothing.

O darken'd flame, light-sloughing,
o bright malignancy!
No more; no less. Nothing.
A bitter wind; debris.

Eschatological light.
A coffin, paintbox shutting
up lost color, holding night.
No more; no less. Nothing.

Paintbrush sword, firm knife,
brush wet with the gushing
of throats disgorging life.
No more; no less. Nothing.

Will you weep? Be consol'd:
agony is smoth'ring.
First, one head is roll'd,
then another. Nothing.
No more; no less. Nothing.

A dizzy, deadwood maze,
rough olive-twigs, the broom's
flush'd & febrile blaze.
Color dies in bloom.
No more; no less. Nothing.

Línea en ciclón, anchura
de sombra lacerada.
Alma en pena: pintura.
Ni más ni menos. Nada.

¡Oh pintor de la nada!
La paleta en tu mano:
tierra para el gusano,
una guadaña helada.
Ni más ni menos. Nada.

Lines like twists of rain;
shadows, torn & jutting.
This art: a soul in pain.
No more; no less. Nothing.

O painter limning Nothing!
The products of your brushing:
an earth where maggots writhe;
a skeleton-held scythe.
No more; no less. Nothing.

Negro

1

Dio su revés la luz. Y nació el negro.

2

Y abrió un hoyo en lo claro, un agujero
desde el que dijo:

        —Soy también hermoso.

3

Tuve forma de vaso, negro ánfora,
cielo para los dioses del Olimpo.

4

Negro como la tinta, negro como
la que linea el cuerpo del dibujo,
la que muerde la sombra del grabado.

5

Tengo otro grave nombre, un pensativo,
un concentrado nombre—que Durero
me hubiera dado—: el de Melancolía.

6

Negro Rembrandt, punzado
negro en la frente limpia del acero.

7

Negro como la boca de la noche,
como boca de lobo, como abismo
sin fin, como agujero
que recortan los cuerpos en algunas
determinadas claras superficies.

Black

1

Light reversed itself. And black was born.

2

Black opened up a hole in all the brightness,
spoke from inside:
                    I, too, am beautiful.

3

I took a vase's shape, a black
amphora: sky for Greece's gods.

4

Black as ink, black as the line
that shapes the design, black
as the bitten shadow of the etching.

5

I have another name—grave,
concentrated, pensive—Dürer
might have given it to me:
Melancholy.

6

Black Rembrandt, pricked black
into the clean brow of the sword.

7

Black as the mouth of night,
as a wolf's maw, an endless
abyss, as the hole
cut into a light background
by the body's silhouette.

8

Negros de Italia, negros
con un rumor de pinos soleados.

9

Un negro como flor de la alegría.

10

Hosannas en los negros de Tiziano.

11

Negros húmedos, negros
verdinosos, capaces
—Tintoretto—de erguirse
y desplomar de pronto una tormenta.

12

Negro de España, negro
de los cinco sentidos:
negro ver,
negro oír,
negro oler,
negro gustar y negro
—¡oh Pintura!—tocar.

13

Un túmulo de negras sombras, un imponente
manto en caído mar negro del Greco.

14

Me sentí grande, impar, tuve mi trono,
levanté mi imponente monarquía
en la mano tranquila de Velázquez.

15

Fui en el retrato majestad y orgullo.

8

Blacks of Italy:
murmur of sunlit pines.

9

The flower of happiness.

10

Hosannas in the blacks of Titian.

11

Blacks wet & green
—Tintoretto—rising,
toppling suddenly
in storm.

12

The black of Spain, all
five senses black:
black sight,
black sound,
black smell,
black taste,
the Spanish painter's touch.

13

Tomb of black shadows, sweeping
cloak falling black sea of El Greco.

14

I became great, unique—I held
a throne, set up an imposing monarchy—
transformed by the calm hand of Velázquez.

15

In portraits: majesty & pride.

16

Gloria y honor severos del ropaje.

17

Monumento callado de la muerte.

18

Rumor de rezos, voces funerales
de réquiem, largo oficio
de tinieblas y llantos en Carreño.

19

Soy un negro mortaja sepultado.
Mi entretejida eternidad yacente
finará mucho antes
que la amarilla y dura de los huesos.

20

El negro olor a cirios apagados.

21

Negro negro Ribera negro negro.

22

Negro misa solemne Zurbarán.

23

El negro misterioso, secreto, de las minas.

24

El alma negra junto al rojo, en llamas.

25

¿Qué sería del fuego sin ti, qué de la lumbre
sin el negro carbón que la sustenta?

16

Robes of stern glory & honor.

17

The silent monument of death.

18

Murmur of prayers, a requiem's
voice, the long lament
of tenebrae & tears: Carreño.

19

I am a sepulchred shroud.
My weave will last
far shorter
than those hard & yellowed bones.

20

The scent of snuffed candles.

21

Black black Ribera black.

22

The solemn mass of Zurbarán.

23

The mysterious & secret black of mines.

24

Black spirit of a red flame.

25

What would become of fire without you? Of its light
without the black coal that sustains it?

26

Tú eres la luz con antifaz. Lo quitas.
Pero sus ojos siguen siendo negro.

27

Me llamo rasgo, rayo,
rúbrica, erizo, huella y otros nombres
que me suben a más resplandeciente.

28

Soy el hermano del papel, reluzco
en él como caminos paralelos.

29

Horror en Goya, espanto
que eriza hasta el cabello de la sombra.

30

Quisieron rehuirme,
pensando que la luz me rechazaba.
Pero soy tan hermoso,
que llamado por ella a mí volvieron.

31

Negro de pesadilla en los románticos.

32

Tuve siempre un temblor, una caricia
vaporosa en la mano de Manet.

33

Y alguien al fin me vio otra vez la luz
que nadie por ser tanta me veía.

34

Cuando soy puro, cuando
soy tan total como una pared blanca,
respondo por Juan Gris, Braque o Picasso . . .

26

You are light wearing a mask. You take it off.
But still its eyes are black.

27

My name is stroke, spoke, spike, a signer's
flourish, footprint; by other names,
I'm raised to more resplendence.

28

I am the brother of paper;
I shimmer upon him like parallel roads.

29

In Goya: horror, a terror that bristles
even the shadow's hair.

30

They avoided me, thinking
that light herself had shunned me.
But I am so lovely that,
called to by her, they returned.

31

Nightmare in the Romantics.

32

In Manet's hand: touched by trembling
& a vaporous caress.

33

And finally someone saw in me again
the light that no one had been noticing.

34

When I am pure
& whole as a blank wall,
I answer as Picasso, Braque, Juan Gris . . .

Goya

La dulzura, el estupro,
la risa, la violencia,
la sonrisa, la sangre,
el cadalso, la feria.
Hay un diablo demente persiguiendo
a cuchillo la luz y las tinieblas

    De ti me guardo un ojo en el incendio.
    A ti te dentelleo la cabeza.
    Te hago crujir los húmeros. Te sorbo
    el caracol que te hurga en una oreja.
    A ti te entierro solamente
    en el barro las piernas.
        Una pierna.
        Otra pierna.
            Golpea.

    ¡Huir!
    Pero quedarse para ver,
    para morirse sin morir.

¡Oh luz de enfermería!
Ruedo tuerto de la alegría.
Aspavientos de la agonía.
Cuando todo se cae
y en adefesio España se desvae
y una escoba se aleja.

        Volar.

Goya

Sweetness, rape,
laughter, violence,
smiling, blood,
gallows, the fair.
A tortured demon with a knife
chases the light & the darkness.

> Your eye: I keep it in the fire.
> Your head: I nibble on it.
> Your humerus: I crackle it. Your harrying
> inner ear: I suck its snail.
> Your legs: I bury you up to them
> in mud.
>> One leg.
>> Another.
>>> Flailing.

> Run away! But stay
> to witness, to die
> without dying.

O light of the infirmary!
The blind circle of gaiety.
Histrionic agony.
When everything falls down, slips back,
and ridiculous Spain swerves off the track,
and a broom flaps away.

>> Flying.

El demonio, senos de vieja.
Y el torero,
Pedro Romero.
Y el desangrado en amarillo,
Pepe-Hillo.
Y el anverso
de la duquesa con reverso.
Y la Borbón esperpenticia
con su Borbón esperpenticio.
Y la pericia
de la mano del Santo Oficio.
Y el escarmiento
del más espantajado
fusilamiento.
Y el repolludo
cardenal narigado,
narigudo.
Y la puesta de sol en la Pradera.
Y el embozado
con su chistera.
Y la gracia de la desgracia.
Y la desgracia de la gracia.
Y la poesía
de la pintura clara
y la sombría.
Y el mascarón
que se dispara
para
bailar en la procesión.

El mascarón, la muerte,
la Corte, la carencia,
el vómito, la ronda,
la hartura, el hambre negra,
el cornalón, el sueño,
la paz, la guerra.

The devil, breasts of an old woman.
And the torero,
Pedro Romero.
In bloodied yellow,
Pepe-Hillo.
And the reverse
of the Duchess' obverse.
Her Majesty the Grotesque
with His Majesty the Grotesque.
And the prowess
of the hand of the Holy Office.
And the persecution
of that scare-crowed
execution.
The stout
& big-nosed Cardinal:
Snout.
And the Meadow below the rose skies.
And the man in the top hat,
darkly wrapped up to his eyes.
The disgrace of grace,
& the grace of disgrace.
And the poetry
of a painting of light
& a work of the night.
And the great mask
in flight,
gone off
to dance in the procession.

The great mask, death,
the Royal Court, need,
vomiting, the nightly round,
satiety, black hunger,
the long-horned Goat, the dream,
peace, war.

¿De dónde vienes tú, gayumbo extraño, animal fino,
corniveleto,
rojo y zaíno?
¿De dónde vienes, funeral,
feto,
irreal
disparate real,
boceto,
alto
cobalto,
nube rosa,
arboleda,
seda umbrosa,
jubilosa
seda?

      Duendecitos. Soplones.
      Despacha, que despiertan.
      El sí pronuncian y la mano alargan
      al primero que llega.
      Ya es hora.
           ¡Gaudeamus!
              Buen viaje.
      Sueño de la mentira.
                  Y un entierro
      que verdaderamente amedrenta al paisaje.

Pintor.
En tu inmortalidad llore la Gracia
y sonría el Horror.

Where do you come from, strange creature, percipient goat
with upward-snaking horns
& chestnut coat?
Where do you come from, funeral,
fetus,
unreal nonsense
nonetheless true,
sketchings, etchings,
deepest
cobalt blue,
clouds of rose milk,
thicket of trees,
sun-shading
silk, silk
blithe as breeze?

       Little hobgoblins. Informers.
       Get going, they're waking up.
       They say "yes" & give their hand
       to the first man who comes by.
       Now is the hour.
                  Let us rejoice!
                        Bon voyage.
       Dream of the lie.
                             And a burial
       that truly terrifies the countryside.

Painter: throughout your endless years,
may Grace remain in tears
and Horror smile.

Delacroix

El color como drama.
Como luz, la vehemencia.
Como línea, la urgencia
del rapto y de la llama.

Torres de sangre, abiertos
cielos convulsionados,
horizontes quemados
en ciudades de muertos.

Todo es furia y bandera,
estandarte aturdido.
Todo, mar y expandido
caballo a la carrera.

Sin rienda ni atalaje,
luna desguarnecida,
la Libertad, crecida,
cabalga el oleaje.

Pasión en movimiento,
pintor en arrebato.
Tu paleta, un retrato:
la elocuencia del viento.

Delacroix

Color as drama.
Vehemence as light.
As line, the urgency
of kidnap, flames, flight.

Towers of blood, skies
convulsed overhead,
horizons scorched out
beyond cities of dead.

It's all fury & banners,
flags battle-stunned.
All, sea & stretched limbs:
flying horse on the run.

Without harness or reins,
moon all undressed,
Liberty, risen,
rides on the crest.

Passion in movement,
painter in a spin.
Your palette, a portrait:
the eloquence of wind.

Al desnudo

A ti, esqueleto ornamentado, llena
rosa mural en él enguirnaldada;
vestido de los huesos, revocada
luz en relieve y sólida azucena.

A ti, veloz, centella la melena,
rayo en escorzo, mar precipitada;
tranquilo ensalmo, diosa reposada,
sueño palpable de la forma plena.

A ti, contemplación, gusto, recreo,
plástica enamorada del deseo,
trama interior, hermosa cobertura.

La gloria del pincel es modelarte,
vestirte, y al vestirte desnudarte.
A ti, Venus en flor de la Pintura.

To the Nude

To you, skeleton embellished,
full rose garlanding its trellis;
bone-clothes: set in relief, newly
whitewashed light, a solid lily.

To you, swift, loose hair a flash,
lightning foreshorten'd, sea-dash;
tranquil enchantment, goddess at rest,
palpable dream of a Form expressed.

To you, contemplation, play, and pleasure,
delight's malleable treasure,
beautifully covered, tram-wound loom.

The brush's glory is to mold you,
and in clothing, to unclothe you.
To you, Painting's Venus in full bloom.

Cézanne

Tenaz, penoso, lento
aprendiz de pintor. Aprendizaje
en toda la extensión del sufrimiento.
Plantado humilde enfrente de un paisaje.

La plástica, diaria, muda vida
es una interminable, trabajosa mañana,
una cosa cualquiera, definida:
la manzana, el reloj, la damajuana.

¡Oh combatiente,
dulce cruel, oh solitario,
agresivo prudente,
dios primario!
¡Oh pobre, oh preso,
para quien la pintura es una pura
cárcel de un solo nombre: la Pintura,
la solidez, el peso!

Modulado, medido, que acompasa
la nube, el árbol masa,
la dispuesta
tonalidad graduada, yuxtapuesta;
el son, el denso exacto
del mar, bloque compacto;
la perseguida
pincelada
cortada,
dirigida.

Cézanne

Tenacious, slow-to-yield
apprentice in the field
of suffering. Humble man-shape
opposite the landscape.

Still life: the artist's silent days,
the long & quiet labor of a gaze
through which anything might come to be defined:
an apple, a clock, a jug of wine.

O combatant—
                    solitary,
harsh & mild, circumspect
& wild—o primary
god of coloring!
O poor, o captive one,
for whom painting is a prison
pure and simple with a single sense:
Painting, heavy, dense.

Measured modulation
informs the creation
of tree-mass & cloud,
a tonal gradation;
the dense, compact
block of the sea;
brushstrokes
                    that flee,
yet are cut short,
controlled.

Te conoce el azul, te reconoce
el nuevo tema:
la forma, el pleno goce
de la forma, color pleno en esquema.

Muriente encadenado
del cenital pincel, clavada espina;
San Sebastián herido de los ojos, doblado
mártir de la retina.

Pintor: en tu verdad más verdadera
todo se determina
por el cubo, el cilindro y por la esfera.

Blue knows you, and you're
hailed by the new theme:
form—a glorying in form—pure
color the constructor of the scheme.

Like one shackled 'til he dies
to a zenith-bound brush, tearing thorn,
you are St. Sebastian wounded in the eyes,
martyr to a retina, gaze-worn.

Painter, for you, one truth is clear:
everything resolves into
cone, cylinder, & sphere.

A la gracia

A ti, divina, corporal, preciosa,
por quien el aura imperceptible orea
el suspendido seno que recrea
la perfección tranquila de la rosa.

A ti, huidiza, resbalada, airosa,
caricia virginal, sal que aletea
y ante la mano en vuelo delinea
tu fugitiva, rubia espalda, diosa.

A ti, fino relámpago, destello,
sonrisa más delgada que el cabello,
burladora, inefable travesura.

La gracia de tu gracia es resistirte,
correr, volar, asirte, desasirte.
A ti, yo no sé qué de la Pintura.

To Grace

To you, lovely, divine, embodied
                                    grace,
imperceptibly, for you, the mild wind blows,
cools the lifted breast that recreates
the motionless perfection of the rose.

To you, evanescent, light, slipping away
—a virgin's touch—allure become a bird
which, taking wing, flies before our face:
a glimpse, goddess, of your fair back, just turned.

To you, lightning, flash fine-etched on the air,
sparkle, smile more delicate than hair,
Puckishness which raises pranks to art.

You resist yourself—the essence of your grace—
you run, fly, seize yourself, quit your embrace.
To you, hardest to define of Painting's parts.

Renoir

Los colores soñaban. ¡Cuánto tiempo,
oh, cuánto tiempo hacía!
El rosa era quien quería
resbalar por el seno y ser cadera.
El amarillo, caballera.
La cabellera, rosas amarillas.
El añil, diluirse entre los muslos
`y ceñir hecho agua las rodillas.
El plata, ser olivo
y vino de clavel el rojo vivo.
¿Se murió el color negro?
El azul es quien canta
y se destila
en una sombra verde o lila.
Pero es el rosa el de mejor garganta.
El rosa canta junto al mar,
el ancho rosa nalga por el río,
el rosa espalda puesto a espejear
al sol y a resonar
rosa talón por el rocío.

Renoir

Your colors
had long been dreaming—
rose wished to slip
          down the breast
               to the hip,
yellow, to be falling curls
          (while the curls dreamed of falling
                    like roses),
indigo imaged itself
between thighs:
       diluted, it flowed,
             and encircled the knees like dark water.
Silver dreamt
       of olive groves,
deep red,
     of wine
         the shade of bougainvillea.
And black?
      Did it die
         in its sleep?

Blue sings,
      its pure tones
           distilled from green and lilac shadows.

But rose has the better voice
for your songs.
Rose sings by the sea—

           glimpse of a wide rose buttock by the river,
           of a rose back: sun-gleam, color echo
           of a rose heel, elsewhere, in the dew.

Vibra, zumba la vida,
y es un abejorreo de cigarras
en tu agreste pupila estremecida.
El céfiro cobalto clarinea,
el cabello azulea,
nacarea la piel y se platea
de un polvo nítido el paisaje.
Se amorata el follaje
y en la sombra verdea fresco el lila.
Pero es el rosa quien mejor titila
al desnudarse evaporado en rosa.

Pintor: en tu paleta rumorosa,
cuando vierten sus jarras los colores,
ya todos son ramos de flores.
Y rosa.

Life hums
like cicadas
in the countryside
of your eye's pupil.

There the lustrous breeze
is a trumpet of light.
There hair grows blue,
and flesh is mother-of-pearl.

      Your eyes
      throw a fine, shining dust
      over the landscape.

            Deep purple now the foliage,
            the lilac in the shade now coolly green.

But rose, more than the others,
moves slightly
even as you look

      —a rose opening its petals—

            and is slowly diffused into the air around it.

O painter,
when the colors
spill out of their jars
onto your rustling palette,
they are already boughs of blossom
                   and rose.

Blanco

1

Dijo el blanco: —Yo puedo,
feliz, estar en todo, porque soy
la imprescindible sangre para el justo
clarear de la luz en los colores.

2

Mi vieja historia es la pared. Si buscas
deslumbrarte conmigo,
recréate los ojos en su tirante frente.

3

Blanco de las atónitas columnas asombradas.

4

Blanco de Creta, tibio,
caliente, casi azul, reverberante.

5

Blanco como la nieve, blanco como
el papel, blanco blanco
como la cal al sol
de los tranquilos muros andaluces.

6

Yo vi—Rafael Alberti—
la luz entre los blancos populares.

7

Mi infancia fue un rectángulo
de cal fresca, de viva
cal con mi alegre solitaria sombra.

White

1

White said,

      I am happy
because I am the lifeblood
of the colors, lightening
to bring them into being.

2

My oldest tale: the wall. Dazzle
your eyes with me—
let them trace its face.

3

White of the astonished columns, thunderstruck.

4

White of Crete: tepid,
hot, almost blue, shimmering.

5

White as snow, white
as paper, white,
white as lime in the light:
still, Andalusian walls.

6

I, Rafael Alberti, first
saw light amid these common whites.

7

My childhood: a rectangle
of fresh lime, quick
with my lone, playful shadow.

8

Blanco Cádiz de plata en el recuerdo.

9

Yo soy el hijo de la cal más pura.

10

Temo al negro. Me teme
el negro a mí. La noche
tiene miedo del día.
El día, de la noche.

11

Cuando el pincel me toma, me estremezco
como el cristal del ojo que tocara
un cabello invisible extraviado.

12

Soy el más albañil de los colores.

13

Una línea, una letra
sobre mí. ¡Inolvidable maravilla!

14

Una línea, una letra,
un rayón solamente en blanco tiza
sobre el terso nocturno mudo de las pizarras.

15

Canto más en el verde
inicial claro de la primavera.

16

Plegaria matinal:
     —Dame la gracia

8

White Cádiz, silver in memory.

9

Child of the purest lime.

10

I am afraid of black. Black
is afraid of me. The night
fears the day.
The day, the night.

11

When the brush gathers me, I shiver
like the eye's crystal, touched
by an invisible stray hair.

12

Mason among colors.

13

O wonder that the hand above me, moving
on, should leave a line, a letter!

14

A line, a letter,
the crash & flash of chalk
against the mute nocturne of the blackboard.

15

I sing most in the first
light green of Springtime.

16

Morning prayer:

        Grant me the grace

de a Fray Añil volverlo más angélico
y de empalidecer aún más el rosa.

17
De pronto caigo como traje o nube.

18
Soy a veces el arco ágil de un potro
contra el azul sin límites.

19
Aquel—Uccello—viejo pajarillo,
muerto en la araña de la perspectiva,
me hizo saltar en forma de caballo.

20
Y aún más hermoso y más que arquitectura,
Piero della Francesca.

21
Espuma de la mar, galopadora.

22
Soy mantel, alba, níveo
encaje en el cristal de las heladas.

23
Y sobre algunos lienzos, fugaz blanco paloma.

24
Hilo del fácil ceñidor de Venus.
Sábana para el molde de su forma.

25
Blanco toca tirante recortado.
Blanco nieve de Brueghel, campesino.

to make Brother Indigo heavenly,
turn rose paler still.

17

I fall suddenly—as cloak, as cloud.

18

Sometimes, the agile arc
of a colt against boundless blue.

19

That bird snared in
perspective's net—Uccello—made me
leap in the form of a horse.

20

More beautiful, and more
than his architechtonics:
Piero della Francesca.

21

Sea spume, galloping.

22

I am an altarcloth, dawn's light, the snow-
like lace of the frost's crystal.

23

I'm fleeing on some canvases: a dove.

24

Tie-string on the easy belt of Venus.
Bedsheet molded by her form.

25

White outlines the hunters' staves:
Brueghel's village-snow.

26

Blanco de aparición, blanco del éxtasis.

27

Blanco gorguera llama blanca Greco.

28

Aparezco en el sueño como hábito,
como sombra marfil
de plato—Zurbarán—, mantel o monje.

29

Siempre dispuesto a dar
en el blanco escondido de la sombra.

30

Voy a invadir al fin el largo oro,
la desbordada endrina de aquella cabellera.

31

Soleo, aclaro, enturbio,
diluyo, trasparento,
lavo, esfumo, evaporo
(Manet, Sisley, Monet,
Pissarro, Renoir . . .)

32

Blanco puro, total, más prisionero
en un cuadrado, un círculo, un triángulo.

33

Recordad que también yo soy la rosa.

26

Apparitions.   Ecstasy.

27

Neckruff white flame white Greco.

28

I am a habit in his dreams,
the ivory shadow of a hooded monk,
—Zurbarán—a table's cloth, a plate.

29

Drawn to the target's
bull's-eye, past shadow.

30

I will finally invade the long gold,
the spilling sloe-plum of her hair.

31

I lighten, brighten, make
opaque, make clear, dilute,
wash out, tone down, evaporate . . .
(Manet, Sisley, Monet,
Pissarro, Renoir . . .)

32

Pure bit of white, prisoner
inside a circle's line, a triangle, a square.

33

Remember: I, too, flourish as a rose.

Van Gogh

Pincelada
quemada.
Fuente
de aparente
corriente
desordenada.
Matutina,
golondrina
fuente.

Se arremolina,
campesina,
ondula.
Noche en círculo rueda,
azula
la arboleda.

Crepita,
carrasca infinita,
tizo,
el paisaje:
rescoldo movedizo,
mar,
oleaje.

Nuclear
demencia en amarillo,
pincel cuchillo,
girasol,
cruento
amarillo sol,
violento
anillo.

Van Gogh

Sunstruck
brushstroke:
source
of a seeming-
ly orderless
streaming,
morning-
like source
of the swallows.

Whirls,
the countryside
swirls.
Night's wheel twirls,
blues
the grove.

Crackling,
the mazed holly-oak,
a blaze of coals,
the scene:
embers shifting,
an uplifting
of the sea.

Yellow dementia
at its core,
knife-applied
sunflower:
yellow sun-
gore,
violent-eyed
round.

Gualda trigal,
verde alucinación,
naranja, bermellón,
metal,
chilla,
pesadilla
mortal,
humilde silla.
Flor,
candela
amarilla.

Se corta,
se recorta
tu color,
se exalta,
vuela,
pintor.

Mas permanece lo que importa:
alta,
la estela.

Wheat-field of weld,
hallucination in green,
orange, vermilion,
brass
scream—
nightmare,
mortal dream:
humble, in a room,
chair,
yellow candle,
bloom.

Your colors
then cut short,
cut off,
painter,
you rise,
apotheosized.

Yet what you worked
to make
remains:
a starry wake.

A la acuarela

A ti, límpida, inmácula, expandida,
jubilosa, mojada, trasparente.
Para el papel, su abrevadora frente,
agua primaveral, lluvia florida.

A ti, instantánea rosa sumergida,
líquido espejo de mirar corriente.
Para el pincel, su cabellera ardiente,
fresca y mitigadora luz bebida.

A ti, ninfa de acequias y atanores,
alivio de la sed de los colores,
alma ligera, cuerpo de premura.

Llorada de tus ojos, corres, creces,
feliz te agotas, cantas, amaneces.
A ti, río hacia el mar de la Pintura.

To Watercolor

To you, pristine, pellucid, sheer,
jubilant, expansive, clear.
For the paper's wetted brow, a shower
of Springtime's water, raining flower.

To you, a sudden, streaming rose;
mirror of a glance which flows.
For the brush's burning hair, close-tied,
cool & easing light imbibed.

Nymph of irrigated tracts,
through you the colors' thirst is slack'd—
sprite's heart, body of urgency.

Wept from your own eyes, you run,
become diffused & sing: dawn's sun.
To you, river to Painting's sea.

A la divina proporción

A ti, maravillosa disciplina,
media, extrema razón de la hermosura,
que claramente acata la clausura
viva en la malla de tu ley divina.

A ti, cárcel feliz de la retina,
áurea sección, celeste cuadratura,
misteriosa fontana de mesura
que el Universo armónico origina.

A ti, mar de los sueños, angulares,
flor de las cinco formas regulares,
dodecaedro azul, arco sonoro.

Luces por alas un compás ardiente.
Tu canto es una esfera transparente.
A ti, divina proporción de oro.

To Divine Proportion

To you, amazing discipline,
ratio: source of beauty without flaw,
revering the rich life cloistered within
the armored confines of your sacred law.

To you, the retina's beatific jail,
golden section, squaring up to scale,
mysterious wellspring of moderation
that gives rise to harmonious Creation.

To you, ocean of angulated dreams,
flower of the five regular forms,
blue dodecahedron, sonorous arc.

You spark a kindled compass with your wings.
A clear sphere is the song your theorem sings.
To you, divine proportion, gold from dark.

Picasso

Málaga.
      Azul, blanco y añil
      postal y marinero.

De azul se arrancó el toro del toril,
de azul el toro del chiquero.
De azul se arrancó el toro.
             ¡Oh guitarra de oro,
             oh toro por el mar, toro y torero!

España:
fina tela de araña,
guadaña y musaraña,
braña, entraña, cucaña,
saña, pipirigaña,
y todo lo que suena y que consuena
contigo: España, España.

El toro que se estrena y que se llena
de ti y en ti se baña,
se laña y se deslaña,
se estaña y desestaña,
como toro que es toro y azul toro de España.

Picasso

Málaga.
>Blue, white & indigo
>postcard & sailor.

Out of the blue charg'd the bull from its pen,
out of blue charg'd the bull.
Blue charg'd the bull.
>>And gold—sea-strand, guitar-sound;
>>bull & fighter in the round.

Spain:
deep-song's domain,
a spider's hand, web-strumming,
the thin design set humming
a refrain—Spain,
skein, plain & pain,
all you contain, and all that rhymes
& chimes with you: Spain, Spain.

The bull that springs from you, rings with you,
is sustain'd but constrain'd,
chain'd, then unchain'd,
the quintessential bull: the blue bull of Spain.

Picasso:

maternidad azul, arlequín rosa.
Es la alegría pura una niña preñada;
la gracia, el ángel, una cabra dichosa,
rosadamente rosa,
tras otra niña sonrosada.
Y la tristeza más tristeza,
una mujer que plancha, doblada la cabeza,
azulada.

¿Quién sabrá de la suerte de la línea,
de la aventura del color?
                              Una manaña,
vaciados los ojos de receta,
se arrojan a la mar: una paleta.
Y se descubre esa ventana
que se entreabre al mediodía
de otro nuevo planeta
desnudo y con rigor de geometría.

La Fábrica de Horta de Ebro.
La Arlesiana.
              El modelo.
                         Clovis Sagot.
                                   El violinista.
(¿Qué queda de la mano real, del instrumento,
del sonido?
Un invento,
un nuevo dios sin parecido.)

Entre el ayer y el hoy se desgaja
lo que más se asemeja a un cataclismo.
Trae rigideces de mortaja,
separación de abismo.

P i c a s s o :

blue "maternités" & rose harlequins.
A pregnant girl in gaiety's flush—
an angel, a grace, rose petaling rose—
a delighted goat in a different pose,
and a child beside with a blush for clothes.
So much sadder are you:
woman ironing, bent with sorrow,
blue.

How could line know of its luck,
or color, its adventure?
                    One morning,
eyes emptied of prescript
are cast to sea: a palette.
And a window is found
set open to noon
on a naked, new planet,
Geometry's moon.

The Factory at Horta de Ebro.
The Arlésienne.
                The model.
                            Clovis Sagot.
                                        The violinist.
(What's left of the sounding instrument,
of the hand that touch'd the string?
Invention, and a new
god, unlike anything.)

Between yesterday & today, an up-
heaval, earthquakes:
the rise of stiff shrouds,
abysses like lakes.

Le journal.
                    Una pipa.
                              Una guitarra.
                                        Una botella.

               El cubismo.

Pero todo pasado—¡ah, ah!—por otra estrella.

¿Cuál será la arrancada
del toro—¿acorralado?—
en un duro, aparente
callejón sin salida?
                    Miedo.
¡Fuera, fuera la gente!
Para mí es poco ancho todo el ruedo.
Por sobre los tejados
se divisan la raya
de la mar y mujeres charlando en una fuente
y desnudos corriendo por la playa.

          Vida, vida, vida.
          Sangre, pura pasión de toro bravo.
          Aquí el toro torea a veces al torero.
          Es el toro quien teme la cogida.
          Con las astas dibuja.
          ¿Quién vio punta de aguja
          torear más ceñida?

          El taller.
          Una mujer
es apenas un cuarto de sombrero,
mujer casi almohadón,
caderas de butaca,
los senos en la alfombra, y el trasero,
asomado al balcón.

The *newspaper.*

A pipe.

A bottle.

Guitar.

C u b i s m .

Turn'd from, to spark a new star.

What will be the sally
of the bull from his blind alley?
Apparently,
he's corner'd.

Fear.

Get these people out of here!
For me, there's little room in this wide ring.
For beyond I can see
the stripe of the sea, ocean-strand,
and women chatting at a spring,
and nudes running on the sand.

Life at its most full.
The blood & passion of a fighting bull
who sometimes flourishes the cape
and feels, himself, the fear of being gor'd.
It is with his hornpoints that he paints.
Who ever saw a pair of horns make
tighter passes or more graceful feints?

The studio.

Women—beware!

Women can turn into portions of hats over there.
One became a striped cushion,
her hips are a chair,
her breast's in the rug and her butt's on the balcony,
sticking out into the air.

Monstruos.
　　　¡Oh monstruos, razón de la pintura,
　　　sueño de la poesía!
Precipicios extraños,
secretas expediciones
hasta los fosos de la luz oscura.
　　　Arabescos. Revelaciones.
Canta el color con otra ortografía
y la mano dispara una nueva escritura.

　　　La guerra: la española.
　　　¿Cual será la arrancada
　　　del toro que le parten en la cruz una pica?
　　　Banderillas de fuego.
Una ola, otra ola desollada.
　　　　　　　Guernica.
　　　　　　　Dolor al rojo vivo.

. . . Y aquí el juego del arte comienza a ser un juego
explosivo.

Monsters.
        Arising out of painting's logic,
        out of poetry's dreams.
Strange heights,
secret expeditions
to the caves of the dark light.
        Arabesques. Revelations.
Color sings through words that make it bright:
the hand fires automatically, and writes.

        Spanish Civil War.
    What will be the sally
    of the bull stabb'd with the pica?
        Banderillas of fire.
    Every rally broken.
            Guernica.
            White-hot pain, corrosive.

. . . And what had been before a game of art became
explosive.

notes on the translations

List of Abbreviations

Alberti, *Antología* = Rafael Alberti, *Antología comentada*, ed. María Asunción Mateo (Madrid: Ediciones de la Torre, 1990).

Alberti, *Lo que canté* = Rafael Alberti, *Lo que canté y dije de Picasso* (Barcelona: Editorial Bruguera, 1981).

Barskaya = Anna Barskaya, *Paul Cézanne*, trans. Natalia Johnstone (Leningrad: Aurora Art Publishers, 1975).

Bicchi = Ugo Bicchi, *Spanish Painting* (New York: Golden Press, 1963).

Berti = Luciano Berti, *Raphael*, trans. Sylvia Sprigge (New York: Norton, 1961).

DeWald = Ernest T. DeWald, *Italian Painting: 1200–1600* (New York: Holt, Rinehart, and Winston, 1961).

Freedberg = S. J. Freedberg, *Painting in Italy: 1500–1600* (Harmondsworth: Penguin, 1970).

Goethe = Johann Wolfgang von Goethe, *Theory of Colours* [1810], trans. Charles Lock Eastlake [1840] (Cambridge, Mass.: MIT Press, 1970).

Góngora = Luis de Góngora, *Solitudes*, trans. Gilbert Cunningham (Alva, Scotland: Robert Cunningham and Sons, 1964).

Guinard & Baticle = Paul Guinard and Jeannine Baticle, *Histoire de la peinture espagnole du XIIe au XIXe siècle* (Paris: Editions Pierre Tisné, 1950).

Janson = H. W. Janson, *History of Art* (Englewood Cliffs, N.J., and New York: Prentice-Hall and Abrams, 1968).

Levey = Michael Levey, Introduction to *The Complete Paintings of Botticelli* (London: Weidenfeld and Nicolson, 1970).

Malraux = André Malraux, *Saturn: An Essay on Goya*, trans. C. W. Chilton (London: Phaidon, 1957).

Mandel = Gabriele Mandel, "An Outline of the Artist's Critical History," in *The Complete Paintings of Botticelli* (London: Weidenfeld and Nicolson, 1970), 9–13.

Monguió = Luis Monguió, "Rafael Alberti: Poetry and Painting," *Crítica Hispánica* 1 (1979): 75–85.

Navarro = Tomás Navarro, *Métrica Española* (Syracuse, N.Y.: Syracuse University Press, 1956).

Panofsky = Erwin Panofsky, *The Life and Art of Albrecht Dürer* (Princeton, N.J.: Princeton University Press, 1955).

Pedretti = Carlo Pedretti, *Raphael* (Florence: Giunti, 1989).

Pierce = James Smith Pierce, *From Abacus to Zeus: A Handbook of Art History* (Englewood Cliffs, N.J.: Prentice-Hall, 1968).

Pignatti, Terisio Pignatti, with Kenneth Donahue, *The Golden Century of Venetian Painting* (Los Angeles: Graphic Press, 1979).

Prideaux = Tom Prideaux, *The World of Delacroix, 1798–1863* (New York: Time Inc., 1966).

Rogelio-Buendía = José Rogelio-Buendía, *A Basic Guide to the Prado*, trans. Patricia S. Parrent (Madrid: Silex, 1983).

Roger-Marx & Cotté = Claude Roger-Marx and Sabine Cotté, *Delacroix*, trans. Lynn Michelman (New York: George Brasiller, 1971).

Rosand = David Rosand, *Titian* (New York: Abrams, 1978).

Sieber = Harry Sieber, "Alberti's Botticelli," *Kentucky Romance Quarterly* 4 (1969): 329–37.

Trapp = Frank Anderson Trapp, *The Attainment of Delacroix* (Baltimore: Johns Hopkins University Press, 1971).

Valsecchi = Marco Valsecchi, *Venetian Painting*, trans. Pearl Sanders (New York: Golden Press, 1962).

Venturi = Lionello Venturi, *Cézanne* (New York: Rizzoli, 1978).

"To Painting"

This introductory sonnet differs from all of the other sonnets in the collection. The first sonnet in the book proper, "To the Retina," sets up a pattern followed by all of the other sonnets (for information on the type of sonnet found throughout this work, see notes on "To the Retina" below). "A la pintura" does resemble the other sonnets in that it is hendecasyllabic and possesses an octave whose rhyme scheme runs *abba abba;* unlike the other sonnets, however, "A la pintura" possesses an unusual sestet rhyme scheme, quite difficult for the ear to follow: *cde cde.* Why does Alberti here forego the sestet-with-couplets that he uses throughout the rest of the book? I think the answer is that the *cde cde* scheme, effectively linking as it does the lines of the first stanza of the sestet to those of the second, creates a larger unity than would couplet rhyme, and Alberti finds this a more appropriate close to a poem that is saluting the coming together of disparate elements to create the single art of Painting.

As I explain below, throughout *To Painting* I have used Shakespeare's classic sonnets as models in shaping my English re-creations of Alberti's classic Spanish sonnets, employing both Shakespeare's meter and his octave rhyme scheme. In this introductory sonnet, however, while I do employ iambic pentameter, I have chosen a different octave rhyme: *aabb ccdd.* This rhyme emphasizes, better than would cross-rhyme, the semantic coupling of lines 1 and 2, 3 and 4, and 7 and 8.

In this sonnet, Alberti briefly introduces us to several elements of Painting.* Many are themselves subjects of later sonnets in *A la pintura;* all are the means by which the artist's vision, the "fictive reality of dream," is translated into the finished painting, the "real object, palpable, in place." "A la pintura" dwells on these concrete means, as Luis Monguió points out: "There is in this sonnet a clear emphasis on the material elements of painting—canvas, surface, brush, hand—upon which or with which other elements acquire also material substance—line, form, color, light, shadow" (Monguió 79). This is a poem based securely in the realm of the tangible and oriented toward praxis; the focus here is on the actual making of a work of art.

Notes on specific lines:

1–2: The fibers of the stem of the flax plant are spun into linen thread, which in turn is used to make canvas. Alberti begins his list of Painting's elements by naming a raw material—the first image is of a field of blue flax flowers—and then gradually moves us forward, metamorphosing the expanse of the field into the expanse of the canvas's surface, until he brings us to the point at which the eyes first meet the canvas, a moment of reciprocal recognition and expectation.

*All of the other sonnets in *A la pintura* celebrate only one element of painting; this element, often addressed metaphorically, is always saluted only in lines 1, 5, 9, and 14, each of which begins with the words "A ti" ("To you"). Note how far "A la pintura" diverges from this pattern: it is packed so full of subjects that it actually contains nine salutes.

6: "Wax or stone" immediately recalls sculpture (the modeling of wax, the carving of stone) and may also bring to mind lithography, which can be accomplished with a flat stone and greasy wax. Therefore, while these words, in the context of this passage, probably refer simply to the dual nature of the paintbrush—depending on what it is coated with, its tip can be soft or rigid—it is clear that they have been chosen carefully by the poet so that he might enrich his chosen art of painting by drawing into the orbit of its description other related arts.

9–11: Alberti is explaining how a painter depicts volume by placing a darker color next to a lighter one.

"Giotto"

Alberti's poems to painters are all written in different forms because each poem in some way imitates the style of the painter whom it is addressing, or is given a form particularly appropriate to him. "Giotto," with its litany-like repetition at the beginning of each stanza, takes the form of a *lauda*, an Italian verse form with religious content that developed out of popular adaptations of church liturgy. The oldest *laudas* are actually in Latin: the famous "Stabat mater" and the "Dies irae" are examples of this form. The earliest example in Italian, the language in which the form came to flourish, is St. Francis's "Laudes creaturarum" (lit. "The Praises of the Creatures," also known as "The Canticle of Brother Sun").

"Laudes creaturarum" is, in fact, the subtext of "Giotto." Like St. Francis's poem, "Giotto" is a devout song of praise in which aspects of the speaker's universe are addressed as "Brother" and as "Sister." Like St. Francis's poem, "Giotto" has traces of Latin.* We may well ask, however, why St. Francis's *lauda* is an appropriate form for a poem dedicated to Giotto. The answer is that Giotto, born only forty years after St. Francis died (and close to where he had lived), was much influenced by him. Giotto's earliest extant works are the frescoes he painted in the Church of St. Francis, in which he reverently depicts the saint's life and glorification. By choosing "Laudes creaturarum" as the subtext of "Giotto," Alberti reminds us of the influence of the one on the other, and furthermore, I think, suggests a profound similarity between the founder of the

*The reader can see just how close Alberti's poem is to that of St. Francis by putting the two side by side. I offer the following lines for comparison: one of St. Francis's stanzas runs "Laudato si, mi Signore, / per sora Luna e le Stelle: / in cielo l'hai formate clarite / e preziose e belle," while Alberti's final stanza begins, "Laude, Señor Dios mío / porque me armaste dulce, cariñoso."

movement that turned away from the hierarchies and ecclesiastical traditions of the Church to embrace the natural world and simplicity, and the painter who broke the bonds of Byzantine tradition and painted following nature.

My translation retains the refrain of praise at the beginning of each stanza but not the Latin in which it is partially written, because Latin evokes for most readers of modern English poems today a foreign strangeness it would not have evoked for Alberti's Spanish readers a few decades ago. Alberti's *lauda*, following tradition, has lines of varying lengths, though most are either eight or eleven syllables. The length of my lines is not regular either, though I have tried to keep them as compact as possible and have, to this end, taken the liberty of using an ampersand where appropriate. Finally, while not following a rigid scheme, Alberti does rhyme frequently. In order to preserve as much rhyme as possible, I have sometimes broken lines in different places, I have changed the order of items in a list (including those in lines 8, 22–24, and 32), I have created an internal rhyme where none existed in the original (line 32), and I have even gone so far as to fill out an existing image (line 28) and statement (line 37).

Notes on specific lines:

6–7: These lines refer to Giotto's frescoes, in which he applied watercolors to freshly lime-plastered walls.

17: The "human form" was very important to Giotto, who strove to create lifelike rather than stylized figures. His success in this endeavor helped to elevate the status of painting; indeed, art historians claim that it is Giotto who first made painting equal to the other arts. Thus is Giotto called "Painting's eldest brother" in the poem's last line.

26–27: In these lines, in order further to link the two men, the poet merges the voice of Giotto, who has been speaking throughout the poem, with that of St. Francis, who, according to legend, once gave a sermon to the birds at Alviano. This story was of course known to Giotto and served as the inspiration of one of his paintings.

"To the Retina"

This sonnet, like those that follow, takes the classic form of a traditional Spanish sonnet: it is composed of hendecasyllabic lines whose rhyme scheme runs *abba abba ccd eed*.* One English equivalent of this traditional form—and the one in

*Alberti's sestet rhyme is actually not as traditional as his octave rhyme, though it is certainly not without precedent. One example of such rhyme occurs in a series of Miguel de Unamuno's *Rosario de sonetos* (*Rosary of Sonnets*).

which I have chosen to re-create Alberti's sonnets—is the Shakespearian sonnet, with its slightly briefer iambic pentameter lines (which I have sometimes abbreviated still further to iambic tetrameter in order to keep the English as taut as its Spanish original) and its *abab cdcd* octave rhyme scheme, so much more suited to English, with its less abundant rhymes, than the more difficult Spanish scheme. While following the English form in the octave, however, I have retained Alberti's sestet rhyme because his final words never come in the form of a concluding couplet, as in a Shakespearian sonnet, but rather in a single line, whose rhyme, furthermore, links it to the third line of the sestet, thus tying the close of the poem to an earlier portion of it.

The retina is the perceptive structure of the eye. A sensitive membrane, the innermost layer of the wall of the eyeball, it receives the image formed by the lens and, transforming light to energy, sends the image to the brain by way of the optic nerve. The retina, curved and semicircular, is a network of nerve cells, notably rods and cones; the rods provide vision in dim light, while the cones respond best to bright light and provide color vision. Alberti's poem is both a celebration of this organ of sight and a poetic description of its qualities and workings.

Notes on specific lines:

1–2: My translation takes account of the fact that a native speaker of Spanish, reading the original, "donde mora / de par en par pintada la belleza" (lit. "where beauty dwells, painted wide open"), would most likely receive from "de par en par" (lit. "wide open") the image of a wide-open window, for this phrase is very commonly used in speaking of windows (also of doors). The translation also tries to take into account that "de par en par," when used figuratively, imparts a sense of clarity and openness, a lack of obstruction or opacity.

4: I have taken "rayo negro" (lit. "black stripe or ray") to be the first stripe on an imagined spectrum whose gamut is not the rainbow, but rather the "colors" of the night in the order in which they appear chronologically, from the darkness of midnight to the light of the dawn.

9: Alberti may be referring to the theory that it is retinal action that produces the splotches of color we see against a background of blackness when our eyes are closed. More likely, he is attributing to the action of the retina the images we see in our dreams.

10: Line 10 of the original, "torre del homenaje de la vida," reads literally, if every word is taken separately, "tower of homage to life." However, "torre del homenaje" is also a phrase that refers as much to a concept as to an architectural structure: the expression dates from medieval times and refers to a keep, or castle, in which a lord's governor, or chatelain, has sworn an oath to keep faith with him and to defend his fortress. Thus "torre del homenaje" evokes a distant time and code, and acts as a metonym for the notion of fealty. In Alberti's line we are brought to associate this idea of sworn loyalty with the retina; in this case, however, the oath has been sworn to life itself. In the translation, "chivalric" is meant to evoke the same complex of ideas (loyalty to a lord; medieval times; residence in a castle) as does "torre del homenaje," and "keep" was chosen in the hope that its double meaning would reinforce what is conjured by "chivalric." Finally, "chivalric" and "keep" act as "torre del homenaje" does with reference to line 11's "ajimez" (lit. "mullioned window"): they give it a context.

13: In his choice of "niña" (lit. "girl child"), Alberti has made a rich play on words, taking advantage not only of the fact that when "niña" is juxtaposed to "del ojo" (lit. "of the eye") it means "pupil," but also that "niña de los ojos" is an idomatic phrase whose meaning is equivalent to "apple of my eye."

"To the Hand"

"To the Hand" has been composed in loose iambic pentameter. The octave rhyme of its original has been converted into a rhyme approximating Shakespearian octave rhyme, but the original's sestet rhyme has been retained.

Notes on specific lines:

5, 8: Just as he does in line 1 with "tremor & steadiness," here, with "copula" and "disjunctive," the poet is playing with the opposing potentials of the hand. Further, he is playing with unusual vocabulary, bringing into poetry words more often found in grammatical discussions. Here, "copula" may be taken to mean simply "that which connects," and "disjunctive," "tending to disjoin."

11: "Ardent" is not in the original but was extrapolated from it for the sake of a rhyme.

14: A "tutelar god" is a guardian and also a personified spirit of place; tutelar gods are frequently denizens of gardens. "Tutelar god" is a more precise rendition of "alma" in this context than is its literal translation, "soul," which is less likely to register on a reader of English as a residing, guiding spirit of place than as an abstract theological concept.

"Botticelli"

As with all of his poems to painters, Alberti has created a style for "Botticelli" that is a particularly appropriate form in which to speak of that painter; to honor Botticelli, famous for his design, Alberti has created his own intricate design, an "arabesque." In an essay on Botticelli, Gabriele Mandel gives a brief critical history, excerpting the judgments of some well-known art historians, all of whom praise Botticelli for his use of line: Ruskin calls Botticelli's work "a play of pure line"; Mesnil remarks that in Botticelli's paintings "feeling is shown chiefly in gesture, in the moving line." Some critics speak of Botticelli not just in terms of line but also in terms of linear design, and more than once the painter's fluid, curving line recalls to them an arabesque: Venturi says of Botticelli, "His preference for line . . . is his strength, his glory. He is one of the greatest poets of line whom history records. . . . Botticelli dreams fantastic arabesques, slow and continuous dance-rhythms, the gracefulness of line"; Chastel writes, "He knew how to make outlines more precise, adjust folds, curve figures, interweave and loosen movements with the continuous effect of an arabesque" (Mandel 9–13).

The arabesque, then, seems to be a fitting form to link with Botticelli. Yet the arabesque is a form from the realm of the visual arts; how can this word, denoting "a complex circular design, a design with interlacing patterns," be applied to a poem? The answer is that in his "arabesque" Alberti has created a poem that circles back to its beginning, repeating, in its last lines, the first lines of the poem; moreover, there are smaller closed configurations within this larger one. Figure 1 plots the poem's design. With the exception of line 3, lines 1–8 are later repeated in the same order, appearing as lines 26–32 (although in beginning the circle again, Alberti reverses the order of lines 1 and 2). The end is not a total recapitulation, however, for the final line of the poem, line 32, does not repeat line 8, but varies it; the pattern is broken at the moment when Venus finally breaks into the poem. A smaller circle within the larger one is created by lines 13–17, which form their own closed pattern inside the greater pattern of the poem: the lines that follow line 13 soon circle back to it, and line 17 repeats it. The design created by this small circle is then continued, for the beginning of line 18 repeats a portion of line 14, thus compelling the poem to move from line 17 through line 14 before it reaches line 18; this is graphically represented by a double line between 13/17 and 14.

A different kind of repetitive pattern is that made not by the repetition of whole lines, or even of whole words, but of single sounds, creating rhyme. There is an abundance of rhyme in "Botticelli," and I have tried to create a poem equally rich in rhyme; indeed, the few alterations I have made in word order

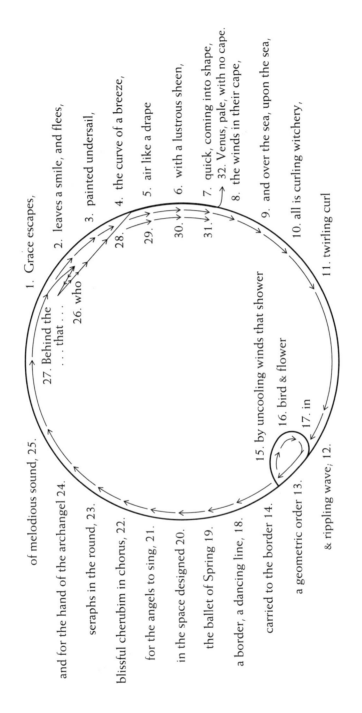

1. Grace escapes,
2. leaves a smile, and flees,
3. painted undersail,
4. the curve of a breeze,
5. air like a drape
6. with a lustrous sheen,
7. quick, coming into shape,
32. Venus, pale, with no cape.
8. the winds in their cape,
9. and over the sea, upon the sea,
10. all is curling witchery,
11. twirling curl
12. & rippling wave;
13. a geometric order
14. carried to the border
15. by uncooling winds that shower
16. bird & flower
17. in
18. a border, a dancing line,
19. the ballet of Spring
20. in the space designed
21. for the angels to sing,
22. blissful cherubim in chorus,
23. seraphs in the round,
24. and for the hand of the archangel
25. of melodious sound,
26. who
27. Behind the
28.
29.
30.
31.
. . . that . . . .

173

were effected in order to maintain rhyme. I have reproduced in my translation the internal rhyme present in the original, and I have tried to imitate the elaborate scheme of Alberti's end rhyme, although I do not reproduce it. This scheme underlines the five syntactic units in the poem: lines 1–8, 9–12, 13–17, 18–25, and 26–32. (Semicolons after lines 12 and 17 divide the poem into only three parts, but the repetition of lines 1–8 in lines 26–32, mentioned above, separates these two groups of lines from the larger groups in which they are found.) Alberti rhymes his first eight lines *ababacbb;* lines 9–12 are rhymed *dede;* lines 13–17, *ffggf;* lines 18–25, *hihjkjk;* lines 26–32, *babacbb.*

Because a circle is one continuous line, Alberti here, to duplicate its form, writes one long sentence whose flow is punctuated by frequent commas and briefly halted by the three semicolons mentioned above. This long, weaving sentence takes us back to Botticelli, both because of the arabesque its circular design creates, and because this design is created by a single line, for Botticelli often created parts of his designs with single lines. Michael Levey, praising the "master of marvelous line," points out that in Botticelli's most famous painting, *The Birth of Venus,* "one long memorable line indents the pale promontories" (Levey 5).

It is in fact to *The Birth of Venus* that "Botticelli" mainly refers. It is only in lines 18–25, as the poem reaches a section in which there are no lines or portions of lines that refer to any earlier lines or portions of lines, and no internal rhyme, that the poem moves away from its preoccupation with *The Birth of Venus* and alludes to three other paintings: *Primavera, The Mystic Nativity,* and *The Annunciation.*

The poem is about godbirth. It begins as Grace departs. What remains is the trace of a smile, which, as Peter Whigham has pointed out, is sometimes "the iconographic expression of an epiphany." Mention of Grace brings to our minds both the lovely, eponymic classical deity who with her two sisters so often accompanies Venus, and the notion of a free gift from God. The former association causes us to expect Venus, while the latter may put us in mind of the Annunciation. Thus does Alberti, in the first two lines of his poem, insinuate the idea of *The Birth of Venus.* Of the disappearing Grace and her smile, fading so soon, drawn in the wind, so to speak, there is soon nothing left but the wind itself, the curve of a breeze. In the pregnant emptiness, the poet notices the air, the blue backdrop of *The Birth of Venus,* which looks like lustrous cloth. Then there is a hint of something quickly forming, but what next appears before our eyes is not the shape of Venus, but only those of the Zephyrs, who occupy the portion of the painting that is to her left. The poet then becomes joyfully distracted by the bounty of curls and waves in the picture, from the rippling sea to the rippling tresses of the Zephyrs and of Hora (the figure on Venus's right). In lines 13–17 he celebrates Botticelli's geometric order with verses that create their own closed configuration, ending where they began; in these verses he mentions the Zephyrs' winds, and the carefully spaced flowers that fall from the top border of the canvas almost to the bottom.

The poem then moves away from *The Birth of Venus* as it progresses from borderline to dancing line, and we suddenly find ourselves in *Primavera*, another well-known painting by Botticelli. This painting is often referred to as a "ballet of Spring" because of the graceful disposition of the moving figures on the canvas and because of the dance the three Graces are performing in its left portion. It is a celebration of the birth of the new year and of the flowered season, and Venus, always associated with Spring, is at its center.

In the next line, the poet speaks of a "space" which, he continues, is "for" the bliss of cherubim in chorus, seraphim in round, and for the hand of the archangel. Harry Sieber contends that these images can all be found in Botticelli's less well-known *The Coronation of the Virgin* (Sieber 329–37).* While it is true that this painting does contain cherubim and seraphim (using these terms loosely, as I believe Alberti did, to denote two different groups of angels), the hand of the archangel is nowhere to be seen. More likely, I think, is that Alberti was referring to two different Botticelli paintings, each of which manifests the poem's theme of godbirth. The first is *The Mystic Nativity*, which shows in its center, above Jesus in the manger, a group of angels singing in a small choir and another group dancing in a circle above them. The second is the

---

*In "Alberti's Botticelli," Sieber speaks about "Botticelli" as an "ekphrastic" poem (one that, like Keats's "Ode on a Grecian Urn," is a poetic description of a pictorial or sculptural work of art). He mentions, among other things, that circularity is characteristic of this poetic genre. Sieber also throws some light on Alberti's own conception of the nature of a verbal arabesque. He offers a quotation from "Diario de un día" ("Diary of a Day"), a prose poem contained in *Poemas de Punta del Este* (*Poems of Punta del Este*), which Alberti composed during the years he was working on *A la pintura*. Here Alberti speaks of poetry that, arabesque-like, possesses a complex design, difficult to follow, which nevertheless by its close has revealed its pattern to the reader, to whom the windings of its intricate tracery have at last become clear: "El arabesco de mi poesía es barroco. La línea recta, escueta del comienzo, se me curva al instante, complicándoseme en un laberinto de vueltas y revueltas, sin salida aparente. Mas cada guía de esta difícil enredadera es clara, entramando un total de dibujo preciso que concreta lo oscuro, volviéndolo luminoso" ("The arabesque of my poetry is baroque. A straight line, plain at the beginning, suddenly curves, complexifying itself in a labyrinth of turns and returns, from which there is no apparent exit. But each vine shoot of this difficult climbing plant has a place in the framework of the precise design it is creating, whose whole makes what was obscure, concrete and luminous").

exquisite *Annunciation*, in which the hand of the archangel Gabriel reaches out toward the center of the painting. He is kneeling before Mary, whose hand reaches down toward his. There is a holy, palpitating space between the two hands; it is at the center of the painting.

This is the same space that Grace has impregnated and left in the evocation of *The Birth of Venus* at the beginning of the poem; it is the space occupied in *Primavera* by Venus, around whom Spring's ballet is being danced; it is the space reserved, in other paintings, for the bliss of the angels—cherubim in chorus and seraphs in the round. The hand of the archangel, placed before our eyes by the poet, is suddenly withdrawn from this space. Gabriel vanishes as quickly as did Grace, and his disappearance is described in the same words. We are led back to the beginning of the poem, where we are once more brought to the point of expectation. But this time we are not disappointed with a false manifestation, for this time it is not the Zephyrs who appear but Venus herself, finally occupying that rich and magical space at the heart of the painting, the space dedicated to the bliss of epiphany. This is the birth of Venus, and having brought us to this point, the poem ends.

Notes on specific lines:

7: Line 7 in the Spanish consists of the single word "concisa," meaning "concise, brief." When the poem doubles back on itself at its end, we read line 7 again in line 31. In each case, the line that follows speaks of a manifestation: in line 8 the Zephyrs appear, and in line 32 Venus herself finally appears. It is possible then that what is "brief" is the process of incarnation—that process which is at the heart of the poem. I decided to take this opportunity to emphasize this important point, while simultaneously providing a word that would chime in with "escapes," "drape," and "cape," in imitation of Alberti's own quadruple rhyme. It is thus that I came to render line 7 "quick, coming into shape," happily taking advantage, moreover, of the fact that "quick" means not only "swift" but also "live, animate."

25: I have left out the word "gregoriano" (lit. "gregorian"), which in the Spanish original modifies "arcángel" (lit. "archangel"), as does "canoro" (lit. "melodious"). It is not clear to me what Alberti meant by this: is the word an evocation of the Mass in which the Incarnation has been musically celebrated with Gregorian chant? Or are we supposed to understand "gregorian" as a metonym for "artistically simple, plain," and then apply this description to the manner in which Botticelli limned the archangel in *The Annunciation?* Certainly, Alberti's choice of this word enabled him to provide an important rhyme. Unable myself to rhyme on this word, and uncertain of the extent to which its sound alone determined the poet's choice of it, I opted to let this word go, concentrating instead on maintaining the rhyme and rhythm that are such an important part of this musical poem.

"To the Palette"

"To the Palette" has been composed in loose iambic pentameter. The octave rhyme of its original has been converted into Shakespearian octave rhyme, but the original's sestet rhyme has been retained.

Notes on specific lines:

7–8: When held by a right-handed painter, the palette rests in the palm of the left hand and is secured by the left thumb, which is inserted through a hole in the base of the palette. Lines 7 and 8 compare the palette, with its thumb hole, to the brow of the mythical Cyclops Polyphemus. Most readers of Western literature probably know Polyphemus from Homer's *Odyssey*, in which Odysseus blinds the Cyclops by ramming a pole into his single eye. Less well known, perhaps, is another tale about Polyphemus, that of his love for Galatea, told originally by Ovid and then by the Spanish Golden Age poet Góngora in his *La fábula de Polifemo y Galatea* (*The Fable of Polyphemus and Galatea*). Alberti's description in line 8 of Polyphemus as "enamorado" (lit. "in love"; excised from the English, in part because of our lack of familiarity with this particular strand of Polyphemus's story) affirms his acquaintance with Góngora's Polyphemus.

Interestingly, the poet once more brings Góngora to our minds in line 13, which, as Luis Monguió points out, "echoes in a conscious homage the famous one from Góngora's *Soledades* [*Solitudes*], 'en campo de zafiros pace estrellas' [lit. 'on a field of sapphires graze (the) stars']" (Monguió 83). Reference to Góngora is of course highly appropriate in the context of this classical sonnet.

"Blue"

Alberti's poems to colors are written in the form of numbered lists, each item of which is an association the poet has with the color. These associations are articulated in a form that might be called aphoristic. Now, the aphorism has no well-known analogue in the English lyric tradition;* indeed, a modern reader of English poetry would be hard-pressed to find much that is poetic in this form.

*A few modern English poets have experimented with this form. See, for example, W. H. Auden's "Symmetries and Asymmetries," as well as Wallace Stevens's *Aphorisms* and, even closer to Alberti's color poems, his "Thirteen Ways of Looking at a Blackbird."

In an attempt, therefore, to retain the form of these statements, but to render them simultaneously accessible as poetry, I have concentrated the statements as much as possible, in recognition of the fact that the telegraphic is an acceptable modern poetic mode. I have occasionally even made use of a kind of brevity made popular in modern English poetry by translations from the Chinese and Japanese.

Some of the associations that spring to the poet's mind come from the world of art; more come from the natural world. " Blue" is full of references to the sea and the sky; in "Red" Alberti is frequently thinking of the human body—its blood, its lips, its nipples. "Yellow" contains many items that speak of light in its various manifestations (while "Black" speaks of night and shadows), and "Green" is replete with allusions to the earth's myriad flora. It is only white, the subject of the last color poem, that more often evokes for the poet not a variety of images from the natural world, but rather a single image of an object of human design: the lime-whitewashed wall that appears with such frequency in Alberti's native Andalusia appears with a like frequency in "White."

Notes on specific items:

1: This is not a literal translation but a substitute offering. The original reads "Llegó el azul. Y se pintó su tiempo" (lit. "Blue arrived. And its time [or, its coming] was painted [or, painted itself]"). "Tiempo" here is ambiguous, evoking both the notion of time in general and the idea of a specific moment of arrival. The translation reflects my desire to give the English reader both these meanings. It also reflects my desire to give the English reader a sense of ambiguity similar to that experienced by the Spanish reader: "in time" creates an equivalent—though not at all an identical—moment of rich confusion.

6: The Virgin Mary has traditionally been depicted by painters as dressed in a robe of blue.

7: This item flows directly from item 6. Alberti is undoubtedly speaking here of the blue of Mary's robe in Fra Angelico's *The Annunciation*, one of the great treasures of the Prado Museum. In this painting, Mary's robe is so richly blue that the viewer easily believes the story told about Fra Angelico: that he made his blue by grinding lapis lazuli.

10: Perugino was a master painter to whom Raphael was apprenticed in his youth. In the third line of this item, I have extrapolated "like feathers" from the original image.

12: The words of this line imitate the melting and flowing of the colors reflected in the waters of Venice, Titian's home. The original line probably also evokes for Spanish readers "de oro y azul" (lit. "of gold and blue"), an idiomatic phrase meaning "splendidly attired," as are, indeed, all the subjects of Titian's paintings.

15: "Galena," the meaning (in this context) of the Spanish "alcohol," is a bluish gray mineral possessing a metallic luster.

16: The Sierra Guadarrama is a mountain range just outside Madrid. The mountains appear, blue and in the background, in some of Velázquez's paintings.

18: This synaesthetic statement is an allusion to the Prado's *Charon Crossing the Styx* by Patinir, a painting famous for the exquisite turquoise color of its waters.

25: In the third line, I have done a little unpacking and interpreting of the original, in which the blue voice is said to be "transparentada" (lit. "transparented") into lilac.

27: The Balearic Islands, of which the most well known is Mallorca, are a group of islands in the Mediterranean off the east coast of Spain.

"Raphael"

"Raphael" is not the poem we expect. Given that most of Alberti's poems to painters contain references to one or many specific works by the painters they are celebrating, we expect to see here specific evocations of some of Raphael's more famous paintings. Aside from the names in the penultimate line, however, there are none. Perhaps more importantly, we also expect to find that the poem Alberti has dedicated to this High Renaissance painter, so often called "perfect,"* is one possessed of a perfect form, classical and symmetrical. We find, though, that the opposite is true: the poem's stanzas are of irregular length, as are the lines that compose them, and the rhyme, too, does not hold to one consistent pattern. How can we explain this unexpected approach?

"Raphael" is perhaps best understood as a personal impression, a poem having less to do with Raphael Sanzio than with Rafael Alberti. Alberti seems here to have focused not on the objective achievements of the painter, but on his own subjective sense of Raphael. He may have chosen this approach because it allowed him the freedom to turn away from the religious content of Raphael's work, displeasing to our strongly secular and anti-Catholic poet, and to dwell instead on that quality of the painter which he seems to have most admired:

*The art historian Luciano Berti, for example, noting that Raphael died on his birthday, says that this exact life span "seems to symbolize . . . a completed perfection like that of a circle or sphere, such as was the ideal principle and the fundamental basis of Raphael's art" (Berti 117).

Raphael's effortless grace. Alberti, too, is a prolific, fluent artist, easy rather than tortured in his approach, and an advocate of spontaneous, unstudied creation. It makes sense, then, that he would have felt drawn to the seeming artlessness of Raphael's art, and drawn, too, to the myth of Raphael, who has appeared in fable as a youthful wonder, a boy artist, a natural from whom art gracefully flowed as from a fountain (note the poem's references to "fountain" and "source"), a painter ungoverned by rules and unconstrained. Focusing, then, on the impression he received from Raphael's art rather than on the art itself, Alberti created an ungoverned, unconstrained poem that moves spontaneously and is free, airy, graceful, and, above all, light, both in content and tone.

It was to bring over into English this sense of lightness, so central to "Raphael," that in translating this poem I have somewhat altered its form. Taking my cue from Alberti, who himself "dropped," or "stair-stepped," line 12, I have done the same thing with many of the poem's lines. This technique aids the movement and flow of the poem, mirrors the imagery of fountain, stream, and wellspring, and communicates to late twentieth-century readers of poetry— sensitive by now to the nuances of line placement and ready to learn from this placement something about the tone of the poem—that this is not a heavy, closed poem, but a light and open-ended one.

Besides spilling some of the lines out horizontally, I have also changed the margins for stanzas 2, 4, 6, and 10. I have taken this liberty for two reasons. First, this technique has much the same effect as spilling out the lines. Second, it subtly underlines the poem's structure, aiding readers in their grasp of this rather elusive poem. Careful study of the poem will show that it falls into three uneven parts: the first comprises stanzas 1–6 and celebrates the coming of Raphael, looking forward to the near future, which will see the birth of his art; the second comprises stanzas 7–9 and speaks of Raphael and his art in the pre- sent tense; the third comprises only the last stanza and, after the first line, speaks of the legacy of Raphael. Further observation will reveal that, in addition to the fact that it is oriented toward the future, the first section is structured so that each even stanza is an elaboration upon the odd stanza that precedes it. Thus, indenting the even stanzas underscores the secondary nature of these stanzas, while also visually distinguishing part 1 from the stanzas that follow it. Part 2 contains no stanzas of elaboration; thus, I have allowed it to remain flush against the left margin, where it forms, moreover, a completely different pattern than that of part 1. This visual diffference subtly underlines the temporal dif- ference articulated by these stanzas. Finally, the last stanza, where the poem makes one final movement, from the present of part 2 into the past of part 3, possesses, like stanzas 2, 4, and 6, a somewhat secondary nature. Thus, I have indented this stanza, giving it a position that not only sets it off from the stanzas that precede it but also communicates something about its nature—in this case, that it is "secondary" not because this stanza is elaborative, but because, rather than wrapping up the poem with a powerful summary statement, it echoes its own content and gently dissipates, floating off like the spirit it describes.

Notes on specific lines:

7: "Rain" has been added here to aid the rhythm of the English line, to help concretize the original's rather abstract notion of transparent refreshment, and to reinforce the connection with "fountain," out of which this stanza has flowed.

9: A burin is an engraver's tool. The workshop that Raphael ultimately founded was to become much engaged with the production of prints based on his drawings.

10: "Glint" has been added here to tie this line to the two preceding lines, which describe the banquet table set with (gleaming) utensils. The lines that follow riff off of "harmony," as the lines of stanza 2 riff off of line 4's "fountain." It is also interesting to note that both with "harmony" and with the earlier "magic," Alberti is employing words traditionally associated with Raphael. Here, for example, is Delacroix on Raphael's art: "In his simplest works as in his vast compositions full of majesty, his spirit . . . propagates . . . a harmony that enchants" (quoted in Pedretti 158).

13: This line has been filled out a little to provide a rhyme and to clarify Alberti's idea that the birth of this artist who will revive Greek classicism causes the sounds of space once again to be perceived, in the Greek manner, as the music of the spheres.

16–19: This stanza refers to the walls of the Vatican Palace, upon which Raphael painted some of his greatest works.

20–24: Like the above reference to the "music of the spheres," this stanza refers to Raphael's revival of classical art: he helped to bring back the classical principles of symmetry and proportion, excelling especially in the creation of human forms—both clothed and nude—as graceful as those in the sculpture of antiquity. In his art, what had been ancient was given fresh life and made new again.

25–30: This stanza, which makes the transition between the period of expectation and the period of creation, eases us gently from a first impression that it describes a scene of celebratory expectation to a revised reading in which the Cupids, doves, and trees are recognized as creations of Raphael, the products of his art. The stanza then re-forms in our minds as a general evocation by the poet of the many decorative borders that the painter and his helpers fashioned to surround his frescoes. I have added the word "willow" to line 28, particularizing the "little trees" so that the reader might more easily envision their "long hair."

31–36: The first half of this stanza names two of the qualities most often associated with Raphael, his sweetness and his grace, and then reminds us that his art, unlike that of Michelangelo, for example, was not surpassingly masculine and powerful but possessed elements both masculine and feminine. The second half alludes to the fact that Raphael also created, with his usual seeming effortlessness, architectural designs. "Golden section" is a geometrical term (for its definition, see the notes on "To Divine Proportion" below), a way of stressing the classical nature of Raphael's architecture. In the last phrase of the stanza, I have added "vibrant" and "invisible" to bring out more fully Alberti's lovely idea that Raphael gathered his beautiful architectural designs out of the air, which was as fecund for him as the form-enclosing stone was for Michelangelo.

37–40: In this last stanza in which Raphael and his art are spoken of in the present tense, Alberti names two more qualities possessed by his art: tenderness and beauty. He also alludes briefly to the popular perception of Raphael as an artist blessed by heaven.

41–42: Befitting its subject, the poem continues to move very gently from one section to another: here we are eased smoothly from Raphael's life to his death to his legacy.

44: In the original, Raphael's spirit is said to float "serenamente y pura" (lit. "serenely and pure"); "pura" serves the important function of providing a rhyme for the poem's last word, "pintura" (lit. "painting"). In order to follow Alberti and provide a rhyme for my own last word, "art," I have chosen a different descriptive pair, "free, apart," which also serves to emphasize Alberti's notion that the painter's spirit was not laid to rest with his body, but soared free of it to live its own posthumous existence in his art.

"Titian"

The most important collection of Titian's art in the world is in the Prado, and dominating this collection are the *poésies*, the first of which Titian created for Alfonso del Este and the latter of which were painted for Felipe II. These paintings depict scenes from the poetry of Ovid and Catullus, and bring to pictorial life the ekphrases of Philostratus; all of them portray characters from classical mythology. It was Titian, remarks one Renaissance art critic, who "gave the fullest pictorial realization to the poetic world sustained by court culture, with its evocations of classical antiquity and the pastoral tradition, its sensuality and allegorical elaboration" (Rosand 24). Of course, the subjects of these *poésies* were perfectly suited to the talents of Titian, who excelled at the new Venetian technique of painting with oil upon canvas, a technique that heightened the effects of light and color, and made for a softer and more sensuous presentation. David Rosand speaks thus of the particular style of Titian, whom he compares with Michelangelo: "In 'disegno' [lit. 'drawing'], Michelangelo was admittedly the unchallenged master, and in the expressive anatomy of the male figure was to be seen the demonstration of his mastery. Titian's 'colorito' [lit. 'coloring'], on the other hand, operated in a feminine mode and found its natural domain in the softer forms and substance of the female figure. No other painter of the Renaissance so thoroughly explored the expressive possibilities of carnal sensation or discovered in the sensuality of flesh such thematic variation. . . . Venus, of course, offered the proper iconographic context for his celebration of female sensuousness" (Rosand 33).

Is it any wonder then that it is *Venus and Adonis, Danaë,* and other *poésies* that Alberti focuses on in his tribute to Titian? These paintings are the most colorful, the most representative, and, for a Madrileño, the most accessible of Titian's work. Alberti also undoubtedly enjoyed writing a poem about paintings that possessed poetic subtexts! Finally, the *poésies* are much more in line with Alberti's secular nature and exuberant temperament than are any of Titian's portraits or religious works, all of which Alberti chose to ignore.

The poem's single tone is one of joyful fun and celebration. Titian is one of Alberti's favorite painters, and "Titian," the poet once remarked, is one of his favorite poems.* Clearly, the poet was enjoying himself here. Like the age of which it writes, the poem is itself "divinely disproportionate with gold"; indeed, the word "golden" or variations upon it occur nine times in the poem. The poem harks back not only to the Neoclassical Age of Titian, the fullness of the Golden Age of the High Renaissance, but also to that time captured by Titian's paintings, the mythological Age of Gold when the classical deities enriched the earth with their numinous presence. In order that his form might match his content, Alberti chose to compose this golden poem using *sexta rima,* a form initiated in Spain during its Golden Age and used throughout the Neoclassical era.

A poem in *sexta rima* employs hendecasyllabic sexains and uses an *ababcc* rhyme. As serendipity would have it, the English equivalent of *sexta rima* is the

*Titian is the very first painter whom Alberti lauds in his poetic tribute to the Prado, "1917," and in a conversation with me (July 6, 1984), he revealed that "Titian" was one of his very favorite poems.

"Venus and Adonis stanza," an iambic pentameter sexain with an *ababcc* rhyme. This Renaissance form was employed by Sir Philip Sidney in his *Arcadia* and by Edmund Spenser in the January eclogue of his *Shepheardes Calendar*, but derives its name from the poem with which it is most often associated: Shakespeare's *Venus and Adonis*. Happily taking advantage of the fact that the *sexta rima*'s English equivalent is a form that not only recalls the English Golden Age but brings to mind a poem based on Ovid's mythical tales, a poem imbued with a blend of richness and humor that is exactly consonant with Alberti's "Titian," I used the "Venus and Adonis stanza." Also, simultaneously echoing Alberti, who here creates a Spanish word out of a Latin one and uses a bit of inverted syntax, and underscoring the effect of this Shakespearian form on the reader, I employed some archaisms, notably "thee" and "thy." Finally, the exigencies of rhythm and rhyme caused me to change the word order in some lines, to drop a few modifiers in others, to make some substitutions, and occasionally to extrapolate from the existing words in order to create an additional word or two; however, no substantive changes were made.

The poem begins by naming several of the characters in the *poésies*, thereby locating us within that particular portion of Titian's oeuvre that Alberti has chosen to celebrate. Later, specific *poésies* are alluded to: the third stanza describes Titian's most famous painting, whose title it incorporates into its verse: *Bacchanal;* the fourth stanza describes the Prado *Danaë,* probably the most stunning of Titian's works; the first four lines of the fifth stanza seem to allude to *Bacchus and Ariadne,* while the last two lines probably refer to *Diana and Actaeon.* The other stanzas refer to more than one or two paintings in a generalizing way, although for me the seventh stanza specifically conjures up *The Worship of Venus (Cupids),* a canvas that shows a large convocation of Cupids; also, the final couplet of the sixth stanza utters its summary statement in such a way as to make a specific joking reference to the title of the painting *Sacred and Profane Love,* a serious and serene work that has nothing at all to do with the humorous image presented here.

Notes on specific lines:

1–2: These six names refer to characters out of classical mythology: each was painted by Titian in his *poésies* series. Bacchus, whose Greek name was Dionysus, was the Roman god of wine and revelry; he appears in Titian's *Bacchanal* and *Bacchus and Ariadne.* Diana (identical to the Greek Artemis) was a vengeful, virgin goddess of the hunt; Callisto was one of her followers. When Diana discovered that Jove (identical to the Greek Zeus) had impregnated Callisto, she angrily drove her former votary away, a scene Titian portrayed in

Diana and Callisto. Diana also appears in *Diana and Actaeon.* Danaë was a beautiful girl whose father, fearing a prophecy that his daughter's son would one day slay him, imprisoned her in a bronze tower, but Jove, who loved her, came to her in the form of a shower of gold, and she conceived Perseus. Titian depicts Jove's visit in two different works, each entitled *Danaë.* Adonis was a beautiful young man with whom Venus, the Roman goddess of love and beauty (identical to the Greek Aphrodite), fell in love; Titian paints them together in *Venus and Adonis.* Finally, Cupid (identical to the Greek Eros) was the son of Venus/Aphrodite; Cupid, in the form of a winged cherub, is found throughout Titian's paintings, usually at the side of Venus, but is especially to be remarked upon in *The Worship of Venus (Cupids)*,4 where, as I said before, his image is multiplied so that the canvas is crowded with a throng of Cupids.

3: For many years Titian was the official painter of the Venetian court.

4: The original of this line, "El ceñidor de Venus desceñido" (lit. "The girdle of Venus ungirded"), was used by Alberti in 1947 as the title of a small collection of poems, some of which later came to be included in *A la pintura.*

11: "Playful" is my translation of "lúdica," a made-up word which Alberti seems to have derived from the Latin "ludus" (lit. "play") and uses here to modify "edad" (lit. "age"). "Lúdica" lends the line a slightly archaic flavor, which I have not been able to reproduce here but have tried to create elsewhere in the poem.

19–20: In the Spanish these lines read "No ignoran las alcobas ni el brocado / del cortinón que irisa el escarlata" (lit. "Neither the bedrooms, nor the brocade of the large curtain that the scarlet cloth rainbows, are ignorant of"). It is not until the next line that we find out that what the bedrooms and brocade are not ignorant of is what is taking place on and above the bed: the impregnation of Danaë by Jove's golden shower. Since the literal translation of these first two lines is rather awkward and confusing, I decided to move away from it a bit, in the direction of greater clarity and precision, using as my guide the Prado *Danaë* (which shows two heavily pleated scarlet brocaded bed curtains shimmering in the light shed by the golden shower). I therefore conflated the bedrooms, brocade, curtain, and scarlet cloth, and identified at once what it is that the bedclothes are not ignorant of.

33: For the sake of creating a rhyme with "Dionysus," the original Spanish epithets for Mary, "la Madre de Dios, Nuestra Señora" (lit. "the Mother of God, Our Lady"), were changed to the epithet "pearl, pure and priceless," which both provides the needed rhyme and offers a rich resonance to those readers familiar with the medieval English lyric and narrative tradition.

43: Piave di Cadore was Titian's birthplace.

48: The poem ends in the same playful spirit that has marked it throughout: the joke here is based upon the fact that Priapus, in Greek mythology, the male generative power personified as a god, was the overseer and guardian of the penis.

"Red"

Notes on specific items:

12: It is possible, given this item's proximity to an allusion to Rubens, that the "snow" refers to the heavy white flesh of Rubens's women.

24: A reference to the paintings of Picasso's Rose Period, so many of which are filled with the marginalized human and animal denizens of the circus.

25: In the words of Luis Monguió, it is not clear whether the red of the flag is being set "against the blue of the sky or . . . opposed to the color of the Falangists' shirts" (Monguió 82). The fascist Falangists opposed the Republican Loyalists during Spain's Civil War.

26: Lost from the translation is the original's notion that it is the edge of an abyss that red reaches.

28: This item provides an extreme example of the concentration of language that I have tried to effect in the color poems (for an explanation of why I have tried to effect this concentration, see the note on "Blue"). The Spanish reads "Rojo de la bravura en las arenas / rojo español redondo de las plazas" (lit. "Red of the bravura in the arenas / round Spanish red of the plazas"). In translating it, then, I have not only dropped "arenas" and "plazas" for the single "bullring," which in this context is clearly the referent of these words, but I have also dropped the repeated "red," preferring to let the poem's title resonate in the open space created here.

29: "The matador's flipped cape" is my long translation of the single Spanish word "revolera," a technical term from the world of tauromaquia (bullfighting), which refers to a sticklike object called a "cape extender," by means of which the matador more easily flips the cape above his head.

"Tintoretto"

Appropriately, Alberti's poem to Tintoretto differs greatly from his poem to Titian, Tintoretto's predecessor in Venice. "Titian" partakes of its namesake's classical balance, golden tones, and slow, rich ease; all of this is gone in "Tintoretto." It is said that the master painter threw Tintoretto out of his studio when he realized the direction in which the young painter, briefly apprenticed to him, was headed. Tintoretto did indeed break away from Titian and the "High Renaissance," pursuing something more idiosyncratic. He became known, for example, for his innovative iconography (e.g., *his* Annunciation scene depicts Gabriel, on his mission to Mary, flying over a great broken wall). His work was considered novel and unorthodox, and not only because of his interpretation of traditional themes: Tintoretto was also deliberately asymmetrical; his canvases are strangely lit; the world he depicts is full of agitated movement. It is these traits that have led art critics to describe Tintoretto as "unmistakably Mannerist" and deeply "anticlassical" (Janson 376).

It is also these traits that have led Alberti to create for Tintoretto a poem whose form is anticlassical, asymmetrical, irregular in every way. His stanzas are of different lengths. His rhyme, too, is irregular, following no set scheme, differing in its pattern from stanza to stanza. Following the spirit of this rhyme plan, I, too, have rhymed according to no set scheme, even Alberti's (e.g., where he has rhymed *abcb* in the first stanza, I have rhymed *abbc*). Although I have not succeeded in rhyming as frequently as Alberti did, I have tried to rhyme wherever possible and where it is most important; to this end, I have added a phrase of my own (line 31, which merely expands on the previous line) to provide a rhyme, as did Alberti, for the poem's last word. In a similar move, expanding on the description presented by stanza 6, I have added the words "in commotion" to line 25 in order to provide a rhyme for this stanza.

Another feature of the poem is the brevity of its lines. Alberti's "Tintoretto" is mostly heptasyllabic, although there are exceptions, including the extremely short final lines of the first three stanzas and the very long final line of the last stanza, which prolongs itself in imitation of the very action it describes. We might well ask why Alberti has created such short lines to portray a painter known for his grand sweeps. I suppose that he has done this in order to echo the broken planes of Tintoretto, the choppy seas, the pieces of clouds. The poet was perhaps also thinking about how the viewer's eye keeps moving about because there is no center in a Tintoretto painting, because the canvases are so busy, because the eye, rather than lingering, is always drawn to follow the direction indicated by each leaning, pointing, twisting figure. These short lines, too, communicate something of the breathlessness and hasty movement of a Tintoretto.

In a manner befitting its subject, "Tintoretto" is organized in an unorthodox way. The art critic S. J. Freedberg has said, "Christian subject matter . . . had always been the stuff that most exercised Tintoretto's feeling and imagination and summoned his exceptional creativity" (Freedberg 362). Yet Alberti, hostile to Christianity because of what he viewed as the damage it had done to Spain, chose not to refer directly to any of Tintoretto's religious works, just as he does not refer to any of the religious works of Titian or Rubens in his poems to these painters. Instead, he summarizes these works in the first two stanzas of his poem and devotes the remainder to a description of a famous and typical secular work.

What Alberti is describing in the first two stanzas is what one critic has called the "lightning-and-thunderlike treatment of the lights and shades" in Tintoretto (DeWald 504–5). Tintoretto's canvases are often lit by lightning. Often, too, his figures are wraithlike. Marco Valsecchi, a critic of Venetian painting, says, "The pictorial invention of Tintoretto . . . is based on violent effects of light, on the play of shadows. . . . As in a great Baroque theatre, Tintoretto uses a vast human chorus to create myths of a magical, almost phantasmagorical vision"; he also speaks of the "spectral atmosphere created by the light" in Tintoretto (Valsecchi n.p.). Another critic speaks of Tintoretto's work as "eerie" and "phantasmal," noting the "atmosphere of hallucination" and "the illusory figures, like chalk drawings of disembodied spirits, that are a leitmotif of Tintoretto" (Pignatti 24, 106, 96).

There are many paintings by Tintoretto that are loosely described by these first two stanzas. Two paintings immediately brought to mind by the first stanza are *Christ at the Sea of Galilee* and *St. Mark Saving a Saracen*, both of which depict storms at sea with torn-up skies and waves, broken planes of shadow, and discontinuous and surprising light. The second stanza, a general evocation of much of the work of Tintoretto, also recalls the spooky, lightning-lit *Removal of the Body of St. Mark*, where on the left side of the painting several ghostly infidels are simultaneously set to flight. Their sudden motion visually echoes the clap of thunder that we imagine has just occurred and is the inspiration for their flight.

In the third stanza of his poem, Alberti turns to a painting prominent in the Prado and especially representative of the work of this painter called "il furioso": *Battle between the Christians and the Moors*. S. J. Freedberg has said that Tintoretto was one of those artists who is "charged with an extraordinary energy that requires to be expressed in movement, expansive and intense," one who "let form take shapes that seem determined by the pressures of propulsive rhythm" (Freedberg 354). One sees these artistic traits clearly in *Battle*, which depicts a furious fight at sea. Here are bodies falling, rolling, lunging intently toward each other, twisting away; here is an arrow about to fly, a lance being shoved into flesh, a sail's canopy collapsing; here even the background is a blur of battle motion. The painting is a whirlwind of violent movement frozen at a particular moment.

In the midst of this still storm, however, we notice one who has not been caught in the act of moving—a young girl who will move no more and lies palely floating in the water.

Notes on specific lines:

26: This is a reference to the biblical tale of the ascension of the Hebrew prophet Elijah, for whom, at the end of his life, God sends a chariot of fire. In it, Elijah "goes up by a whirlwind into heaven" (2 Kings 2:11). It is this last aspect of Elijah's ascent—the presence of the whirlwind—which, I believe, Alberti hopes to bring to the reader's mind with his phrase "carro de fuego" (lit. "chariot of fire").

"To the Paintbrush"

"To the Paintbrush" has been composed in loose iambic tetrameter. Unlike many of the other sonnets, whose octaves contain either quatrains of "semantic couplets," justifying couplet rhyme, or quatrains in which all four lines are wound together by a single idea, justifying cross-rhyme, this sonnet's octave contains quatrains in which the second line is set off from the first but connected to the third, which then spills into the fourth; neither the first two lines nor the quatrain as a whole form semantic units. Instead of the cross-rhyme or couplet rhyme into which I usually translate the octave, therefore, I have here retained Alberti's envelope rhyme (*abba*), which links the second and third line of each quatrain. Due to the difficulty of rhyming in English, however, and out of a desire that this sonnet be consistent with the others, I have employed different rhymes in the second quatrain of the octave, though the scheme remains the same—that is, the second quatrain rhymes *cddc*. Finally, I have, as always, retained Alberti's sestet rhyme scheme.

Notes on specific lines:

2: "Set" is my translation of "abre" (lit. "open"), and is used both in its usual sense of "fix in position" and in its nautical sense, "spread to the wind," in which latter sense it is always used with reference to sails.

9: The Spanish of line 9 reads "A ti, espiga en invierno y en verano" (lit. "To you, spike of grain in winter and in summer"). Here the poet introduces the image of the paintbrush as spike of grain, which sets up the lovely line that follows. The idea that the brush, unlike a real spike of grain, exists in all seasons has been dropped from the translation; the line ends instead with a less interesting phrase that merely extends the image but does provide a rhyme for the following line.

11: This line is an interpretation. The original reads "brasa de sombra o yerta quemadura" (lit. "burning ember of [or 'in'] shadow or stiff burn [or 'blight']"). After wondering how a coal or ember in shadow was like a paintbrush, and how this phrase was linked to the lines before it and the phrase following it, I finally decided that the poet might be referring to the tonguelike shape and liquid suppleness of the delicate, final flames that flare out of embers that have burned low and have been mainly reduced to shadows. The contrast referred to by the "o" (lit. "or") of this line, then, would be one of suppleness versus the stiffness that "yerta" describes; certainly, I reasoned, the concept of pliancy is applicable to a paintbrush. But then, did "quemadura" mean "burn, scar," or "blight, agricultural disease"? I decided that the poet wanted his readers to think of both meanings; after all, "burn" links the phrase to that which precedes it, and "blight" links it to the dominant image of the tercet, the spike of grain. It was through this logic that I ultimately arrived at "supple flame, or blight-burnt stalk, erect."

12: The image of the torch is not found in the original but was extrapolated from it for the sake of a rhyme.

14: It is hoped that for some readers the etymology of "architect" will resonate as they pronounce the phrase, bringing to their minds "chief artificer" and "master builder" with which to enrich "building designer," and bringing them thus closer to the Spanish original "albañil" (lit. "builder").

"Veronese"

Alberti wrote his poem for Veronese using the *silva*, a verse form in which the poet is free to use both seven-syllable (or seven plus seven) and eleven-syllable lines in any pattern. This is an apt form for this work because the alternately short and long lines create an ebb-and-flow effect, a swelling and a shrinking appropriate for a poem that begins by imagining rivers and ultimately reveals itself to be a male sexual fantasy. More importantly, however, the *silva* is appropriate because it is evocative of the poet Góngora, who used this form in his famous work *Soledades* (*Solitudes*). In evoking Góngora, Alberti first puts his readers in mind of a specific epoch, the Golden Age, during which both Góngora and Veronese lived. Second, he puts them in mind of Góngora's specific style, a rich, baroque, opulent, lavish, lush way of writing that is quite similar to Veronese's way of painting.

Veronese, however, was not the Góngoresque painter that Rubens was, and correctly, Alberti's "Veronese" is much less of a Góngoresque poem than is his "Rubens." "Rubens" begins with an epigraph by Góngora that helps readers to locate themselves and that shapes their expectations. In "Veronese," too, the title is followed by a phrase which is, in effect, a direction to the reader, but here the phrase is the title of one of Veronese's paintings, *Allegory of Spring*.

This may seem, at first, a puzzling reference, and readers may decide that the phrase is the same sort of offhand, glancing reference to the painting that the poem's form is to Góngora. After all, the painting contains no rivers, no Grace, no lovers, no hanging clothing, gold-lit doves, or balustrades, and no moon. What it does have, however, is Venus, voluptuously stretched across most of the foreground of the painting, and both raised slightly from a supine position and twisted a little, so that not only her shoulders, breasts, torso, and hips are displayed, but also her back. By naming this painting, then, Alberti is probably providing us with a full image of exactly the sort of goddess about which he is fantasizing.

The introductory phrase, however, also works as a subtitle; that is, it functions not only as a reference to a painting but also as a name for the poem. If we read "allegory" loosely, taking it to mean something close to "metaphor," then we can see that this wish-poem that speaks of the coming of love, of an explosion of sexuality, of a magical occurrence, of a genuine metamorphosis, might well be described as an allegory of spring.

Following the subtitle, the Spanish poem descends down the page in a stichic block. Loosening even more the already loose rules of the *silva*, which requires no specific stanza length or rhyme scheme, the poet abandons both stanzas and rhyme. I have gone even further and abandoned the stichic form; the translation retains the original's lack of a rhyme scheme and stanza pattern, but where Alberti has written the poem in one block containing long and short lines, I have stair-stepped the longer lines, and I have also created two breaks in the text. The stair-stepping was done so that, while retaining the original's long-and-short rhythm, the translation would not be weighed down by overly long lines. Fourteen-syllable lines are very uncommon in English poetry, especially in modern English poetry, and I feared that the heaviness created by long lines in a stichic block might prevent the reader from perceiving the tone of this poem, which is especially light, wistful, frivolous, and playful, in keeping not only with the subject but with Veronese, himself.*

---

*Many who like Veronese speak of him as lighthearted or whimsical; many who dislike him regard him as frivolous. These critics often point to a lack of spirituality and intensity in his work, and some complain that even his religious paintings are thoroughly secular and not without humorous detail. H. W. Janson, in his *History of Art* (Janson 382),

The other change in the original's form—the insertion of a break before line 21 and another after line 30—was made in order to emphasize the poet's creation of an interlude here. Study of the poem will reveal that lines 21–30, unlike those coming before or after, have less the air of a fantasy than that of a fantasy realized. Interestingly enough, these lines in which it seems as if the fantasy briefly becomes real, are the only lines in the poem composed of details from real paintings by Veronese. Several come to mind. We may think, for example, of both *Wedding of Cana*, in which Christ's table is set below balustrades above which the sky opens up to show gold-lit clouds and birds, and of the similar *Christ in the House of Levi*, in which His table is placed above balustrades and beneath arches through which a dramatically lit sky is visible. Perhaps we will also recall the well-known *Rape of Europa*, in which nude Cupids in the air throw blossoms down from above, or even the less well known *Allegory of Conjugal Virtue*, which also has nude Cupids and falling flowers, as well as blowing clouds. We may think of *Mars and Venus* too, in which clothes hang in the background, as well as any of the many Veronese paintings, including *The Coronation of the Virgin*, that show gold-lit doves, or any of the works of this very "architectural" painter that contain balustrades and arches.

Notes on specific lines:

1–2: The translation retains the original's ambiguity with regard to the identity of Love and Grace. Love and Grace seem to be at once goddesses who embody these qualities, to whom the poet speaks aloud his fantasy, invoking their names almost prayerfully, and the fantasized-about rivers themselves, already possessing in the poet's mind the identities they will attain after their metamorphosis, already identical with the goddesses.

8: I added "budded" to the original "open," preferring to offer a specific image rather than a less definite one, and thereby also avoiding the possibility, albeit slight, of the unwelcome intrusion of open-chest surgery into the poem!

28: "Beyond whose frame" is my expanded translation of the Spanish "donde" (lit. "where"), which is a bit inaccurate and confusing.

29: "Palms" is translated from the Spanish "palmas"; the words share the same

---

tells that Veronese, having completed a work later entitled *Christ in the House of Levi*, was summoned indignantly by the religious tribunal of the Inquisition on the charge of filling his picture with "buffoons, drunkards, Germans, dwarfs, and similar vulgarities" unsuited, it claimed, to its sacred character. Today we scorn the tribunal and all it stood for, and yet we may still be surprised and distracted by the begging dog, odd parrot, or leashed monkey that seem to find their way so frequently, along with their fellow creatures, into Veronese's most serious scenes.

double meaning. The present tense of "turns" is crucial here; it is part of what distinguishes this interlude from the passage that precedes it, whose imperfect subjunctive verbs indicate a contrary-to-fact situation, and the passage that follows it, rife with imperatives, as the poet's wishes, gaining urgency, become demands. To emphasize the different mood of this passage, created by the present-tense verb, I have taken two adjectives and turned them into two more present-tense verbs (line 23's "flit" and line 25's "hangs"). I have also taken the much greater liberty of translating as a possessive pronoun the definite article that begins line 24 in the original, thus definitively placing the narrator at the scene and thereby heightening the epiphanic quality of this passage.

33–34 and 37: The double entendre of "hard," "column," "come," and "die" exactly reproduces that which exists in the Spanish original.

39–40: These lines are my expanded translation of "despeinadora," an adjective modifying "moon" in the original. The word comes from the verb "despeinar" which the dictionary defines as "to undo, disarrange, ruffle the hair of," but which contains the Spanish word for comb, "peine," and provides any etymologically oriented Spanish reader with a picture of a woman taking the combs out of her hair to let it down. It seemed unfair to deprive the English reader of this same picture.

"To Line"

"To Line" has been composed in iambic pentameter. The octave rhyme of its original has been converted into Shakespearian octave rhyme, but the original's sestet rhyme has been retained.

Notes on specific lines:

5: The meaning of "arbitrary" in use here is "absolute; despotic." The original Spanish word is "tirana" (lit. "tyrannical").

6: Here the generic original, "flor" (lit. "flower"), has been specified to "roses" for the sake of a rhyme.

7. The original reads "imprescindible al sueño y la poesía" (lit. "indispensable to sleep/dream and poetry"). Part of this line is a pun: line may be seen to be indispensable to poetry and poets when it is taken to mean "verse." But how may line be indispensable to sleep/dream? I ultimately decided that Alberti was using "sueño" here to mean "a dream for the future." Line is indeed indispensable to this kind of dreaming, for line is an emblem of forward projection, of a casting from the present straight ahead into the future.

10: To my literal translation of the original "complejidad, araña, laberinto," I have taken the liberty of adding an *s* after "spider." This construction, because of the nature of the formation of the possessive in Spanish, was unavailable to Alberti. It seems to me to represent a good compromise, evoking a picture of a spider as Alberti obviously wanted to do, but also conveying more certainly the notion of "web." Given the context of "araña" in this line, as well as the fact that Alberti, throughout the poem, is describing the nature of line and naming various types of line, it makes sense to suppose that "araña" is working here as a metonym for "telaraña" (lit. "spiderweb"), which was perhaps too long a word to fit Alberti's eleven-syllable line. Certainly "web" is a better name for "line" than is "spider." In any case, the unobtrusive English possessive enabled me to preserve the original image while maintaining sense.

13: The original of "singing you" is "te canta," which can also mean "sings to you." I chose to read "te" as a direct object because it leaves the line a bit more open to interpretation and thus approximates more closely the ambiguous original, and because it invests with greater importance the poem's subject—line. "Sings to you" merely evokes line as the object of a celestial serenade, but "singing you" makes line the *subject* of the song, even as it has been the subject of Alberti's celebratory song here, and tosses out an array of possibilities: the burning heart of space is singing line into existence, creating it, defining it; the song of the flaming sun, which casts its light in rays, is a song about line; the brightest star in the night sky is singing the praises of that which links it, in the human imagination, to other stars, thereby creating forms, constellations about which myths and stories may be told; and so on.

"Bosch"

This poem refers exclusively to Bosch's famous triptych *The Garden of Delights*, whose panels are titled, moving from left to right, *The Garden of Eden and the Creation of Eve*, *Joys of the Senses*, and *Hell*. A traditional interpretation of the painting sees it as a cynical expression of man's fallen condition: because of Eve we are fallen and indulge throughout our lives in the joys of the senses on earth, whence after death we go straight to Hell. Lines 12 and 13 refer to a detail in the *Hell* panel; stanzas 3 and 5 refer to scenes in the middle panel; stanza 7 refers to a detail in the *Hell* panel; most of stanza 8 refers to the *Hell* panel. Basically, the poem moves gradually from reference to the middle panel to reference to the right panel. The poem's tone reflects this image shift and gradually grows darker and more ominous. The couplets describing the devil underline the movement from rowdy obscenity to horrific nightmare: first sexual jokes are made about the devil (lines 21–22 and 31–32), then the devil is associated with deception (lines 41–42), then the devil is said to be preaching (lines 66–67), and finally he is associated with the scything Grim Reaper (lines 77–78). I have slightly expanded the second lines of these couplets to make them conform to a common kind of English refrain.

The poem contains stanzas whose left margins are at three different distances from the left side of the page, composing three vertical columns. This structure may be in imitation of the triptych; certainly, it does cause the eye to wander back and forth over the page in a manner not unlike its action in viewing Bosch's painting. There is no correlation, however, between the contents of the left, center, and right panels of the painting and the contents of the left, center, and right columns of the poem.

There is no formal rhyme scheme, but the poem rhymes throughout. In order to preserve a rhyme I have sometimes changed the order of items in a list (in stanzas 1 and 3), and have, on two occasions, substituted words: first in lines 52–53, where it is probable that the author's main criterion for word choice was sound, and second in lines 58 and 60, where I made sure that the images I substituted could be found in the painting.

Finally, in accordance with his desire to imitate the style of the painter he is writing about, Alberti has here not only written in triptych form and given us patternless rhyme, chaotic and abundant; he has written a poem containing portmanteau words as well as nonsense words, many of which are grotesque, obscene, or humorous, as are Bosch's own creations in his painting. The following notes on specific lines explain my recreations of Alberti's extraordinary inventions.

Notes on specific lines:

3: "assholehipped" from "perniculimbrudo" ("trouser leg" + "ass" + the meaningless syllable "udo," which has an obscene ring to it for a Spanish-speaker)

4: "anus-eyed" from "ojipelambrudo" ("eyed" + "hair" + "udo")

6: "caprihorny" from "cornicapricudo" ("horn" + "Capricorn" + "udo")

7: "Beelzebuggering" from "mosquiconejea" (a verb made out of the words "fly," "mosquito," "rabbit," and "to dodge")

8: "cummingbirding" from "pajarea" (lit. "goes bird-catching"). "Pajarea" contains the root of the word for "bird"; the word also means "loiters about" and may have a vaguely obscene connotation, especially when juxtaposed to "zorrea," which contains the word "fox" and means "streetwalks, is a whore."

12: "fart-trumpeting" from "peditrompetea" ("fart" + "to trumpet")

21: "mandrake" from "mandroque" (a nonsense word close to the word for "mandrake")

32: "small pitchfork" from "garavijo" ("pitchfork" + diminutive)

41: "prickster, dickster" from "virojo, pirojo" ("tipped dart" + "red" + "strutting young man" + "fire")

44–46: "jackoffrabbit, packoffrabbit, fackoffrabbit" from "tiebre, notiebre, sipilipitiebre" (nonsense words that bring to mind the word for "hare")

49: "cuntery" from "sipilipitriva" (a nonsense word)

67: "puts on leeches" from "pilindrica" (a nonsense word rhyming with "predica" ["preaches"])

"To Perspective"

"To Perspective" has been composed in iambic pentameter; the octave rhyme of the original has been converted into Shakespearean octave rhyme, but the original's sestet rhyme has been retained.

Alberti is using "perspective" here in a general sense, letting it signify all those techniques by which painters represent three-dimensional objects on a two-dimensional surface, thus creating an illusion of depth. Two specific techniques evoked by the poem are "linear perspective," in which "all parallel lines and edges of surfaces receding at the same angle are drawn, on the picture plane, in such a way that they converge toward a single vanishing point," and "atmospheric perspective," in which "the spatial effects caused by the interposition of the atmosphere between the viewer and distant objects" are re-created by the painter through "a blurring of outlines, a loss of detail, an alteration of hue toward blue, and a diminution of color saturation" (Pierce 39, 6). Both of these techniques are used to create an illusion of distance.

Notes on specific lines:

5, 7: The words "feigner" and "iron lace" are my own; each helps in the composition of the English poem without departing too drastically from the sense of the Spanish original. The former aids the rhythm of the English line and merely specifies the nature of the relation between perspective and depth, while the latter provides a rhyme and may be viewed as merely an alternative way of bringing into focus the balcony, which Alberti describes as "close by."

9: The original Spanish of this line reads "A ti, aumento, valor de los valores" (lit. "To you, augmentation, value of values"). For the sake of rhythm, "aumento," which repeats the notion, articulated in earlier lines, that perspective provides a means of enlarging and expanding the picture space, has been dropped.

11, 13: "Música celestial, arquitectura . . . La línea con el número te canta" (lit. "Celestial music, architecture . . . Line, with number, sings you"). This concatenation of descriptive phrases links perspective with Pythagorean geometry.

14: My translation focuses on only half of the original epithet, in which Alberti hails perspective as both Painting's bridle and its helm ("brida y timón de la Pintura"), a description he attributes, in a footnote, to Leonardo.

"Dürer"

Alberti's poem to Dürer is composed of *redondillas*, quatrains that employ either an *abba* or an *abab* rhyme scheme. *Redondillas* are traditionally octosyllabic, but Alberti's heptasyllables are a standard variation on this form; indeed, heptasyllabic *redondillas* were in use on the Iberian peninsula as early as the thirteenth century.

It is a form, then, that was current during Dürer's time, and therefore one that is an appropriate choice for a poem about him. However, its appropriateness extends further: the seven-syllable line is a very short one, and the *redondilla* is a small, closed form; a poem composed of heptasyllabic *redondillas* is, thus, built of many small, discrete parts. The composition of this poem, then, was an act which imitated that of the engraver. Erwin Panofsky, in his biography of Dürer, explains how the engraver works: his strokes are short, thin, and numerous, and a design may be created from an accumulation of tiny, parallel hatchings (fine, inlaid lines). Moreover, the process of incision "is divided into two distinct stages. First, the engraver defines the contours; secondly, he fills in the details, working, however, not here and there as he pleases but undertaking and bringing to completion a limited area of not more than one or two square inches at a time, while the rest of the plate remains covered for protection. Thus he works much as a surgeon operates on a small portion of a body swathed in aseptic cloth. His work proceeds piecemeal, as it were, and proof prints show that an 'unfinished' plate is sharply divided into different sections, some completely elaborated, others containing only empty contours" (Panofsky 63).

The heptasyllabic *redondilla*, then, is an appropriate form in which to speak of a fifteenth-century engraver. One might argue at this point that Dürer was more than an engraver; however, it seems to be the case that Alberti thought of him primarily as such. Not only the form of the poem but also its words bear witness to this: nowhere in the poem is there a reference to Dürer's charming pastel watercolors of animals and landscapes, nor even to some of his better-known oil paintings. Of course, Dürer did only a fraction as many paintings as he did engravings; moreover, he is still recognized today as one of the greatest practitioners of the latter art, while he is considered a rather primitive practitioner of the former. Nevertheless, Alberti's single-faceted approach to Dürer is striking.

Moreover, the poem not only concentrates exclusively on engraving, but also alludes only to two specific engravings. In fact, we come to realize that it is the process of engraving itself that seems to interest Alberti here. This is fitting, of course, since Dürer helped to perfect the process. However, the poem is so composed that the reader perceives the process through a scrim of melancholy. Dürer's more somber works may be responsible for having inspired melancholy in Alberti, who in turn let this feeling tinge his description of the process of engraving. However, it may also be that Alberti found something depressing about the act of engraving itself, and let this tinge his presentation of Dürer. Perhaps he perceived the engraver's minimal hand movement (repeated, as I said above, in the minimal verses of the *redondilla*) as oppressively restricting, or felt his spirit sag at the thought of the repetitiveness involved and the patience and persistence required. Perhaps he was bothered by the notion of the graver's gauging instrument, so different from the soft and pliant paintbrush with which he himself was familiar. Or perhaps, somehow saddened by the starkness of the inevitably black-and-white print that is the result of the act of engraving, he transferred his emotion to the act itself. Whatever the source of the poet's gloom, however, the fact remains that melancholy is the dominant tone of the poem, and this near monotone combines with the restricted subject to create a very limited view of Dürer—one that is a good deal more idiosyncratic than those found in most of Alberti's other presentations of painters in *A la pintura*.

In this poem cum essay on engraving, in addition to the melancholiness of the practice, Alberti speaks of it in terms of the opposites involved. The first line, for example, speaks of darkness and light; the next lines, referring to the way in which an engraver neatly wreaks havoc upon the formerly smooth service of a plate, speaks of him "carefully . . . dishev'ling." In the penultimate stanza, the poet sets up a dichotomy between the cool calculation involved in the laying out of a design ("Pythagorean," "compos'd," "measure") and the intricacy of the design itself ("woof"), along with the agitated passion this intricacy arouses in the engraver ("unravel'd," "flame"). In the final stanza, this language of opposites even spills onto Dürer himself. I suggest that, in addition to the fact that he found it an insightful manner of speaking about his subject, Alberti chose to speak in terms of opposites because he found it a particularly appropriate way to discuss an art in which the artist must work in reverse, creating a design where everything faces in a direction exactly opposite to that in which it will face after the print has been made.

The translation was composed in loose iambic trimeter, this being the most minimal meter English provides that still allows for some discourse. Alberti's *abba* rhyme, which does not knit together syntactic units that would otherwise not be joined and is therefore not indispensable, has been changed, in order to facilitate the act of translating, to an *abab* rhyme, a scheme that is an acceptable alternate in a *redondilla* and thus, by extension, in a translation of one.

Notes on specific lines:

1: Readers should not forget the secondary meaning of "nocturne" ("a night scene"), more appropriate in this context than is its primary meaning.

3: From "dishev'ling" and "nocturne," each an exact translation of its Spanish original, I have extrapolated "undoes the night," which creates a rhyme, while underlining the poet's point. What is lost here is the word "domeña" which, in its context, tells us that the lancing light is controlled by the hand, a fact that I hope is made clear by the colon at the end of the first line.

6–8: The last two lines of this stanza go as follows in the Spanish: "a caballo la Muerte / por una selva oscura" (lit. "Death on horseback / through a dark forest"). It is possible, though I think not probable, that Alberti chose the last two words because of the resonance they possess due to their association, in the reader's mind, with the first tercet of Dante's *Divina Commedia*. In any case, the lines allude to Dürer's famous engraving *Knight, Death, and Devil*. Alberti refers to this engraving as an etching ("agua fuerte") in line 6, probably for the sake of the rhyme it creates with "Muerte." This inaccuracy is not carried over into the translation. However, I have done my own tampering for the sake of a rhyme, substituting for the two images Alberti uses to allude to *Knight, Death, and Devil* my own two images that similarly allude to this engraving. For another poetic view of this engraving, the reader is referred to Randall Jarrell's poem "The Knight, Death, and the Devil."

11: "Knife" here is used loosely to mean "a sharp instrument," just as Alberti is using "estilo" (lit. "stylus") loosely. Engraving is actually done with a burin, a small, sharp-pointed chisel whose mushroom-shaped handle fits into the palm of the engraver.

13: In the course of "Dürer," engraving is likened to surgery, to writing, and to weaving. The Spanish original of this line, "lenguaje lanzadera" (lit. "language shuttle"), brings together all three of these operating metaphors, for while "lenguaje" alludes to the world of writing, "lanzadera" brings in both weaving and surgery because its sound relates it to the Spanish words for "lancet" and "to lance." The translation, unfortunately, does not bring in surgery. It does, however, reinforce the weaving metaphor by describing the kind of movement this particular shuttle makes. I thought this a necessary precaution in view of the fact that for many readers today, "shuttle" immediately evokes a mental image of space rockets, a picture Alberti certainly did not have in mind when he thought of comparing the back-and-forth movement of the cross-hatching hand to that of the loom's shuttle.

14: Here I have taken "rúbricas" (lit. "rubrics"), which can also mean "flourish to a signature," "sign," "trademark," and "first letter," to be referring to Dürer's distinctive signature, lost in the heavily inked portions of some of his engravings (see, for example, *Melencolia I*).

16: The copper is that of the plates used in intaglio engraving; the wood is that of the blocks used in relief engraving. "Engraving," in its narrowest sense, refers only to the former, but is also used, more broadly, to include the latter. Dürer was a master at both, though he is probably better known for his copperplate intaglio engravings, and it is to the process of intaglio engraving that the poem seems mainly to refer.

17: For "Pythagorean," the English equivalent of the Spanish "Pitagórica," I think we may read "geometric," for the engravings of Dürer are "Pythagorean" only in the sense that they are strictly geometrical. (Since the Pythagoreans are credited with inspiring the first part of Euclidean geometry, "Pythagorean" is sometimes used in this loose sense.) Dürer was, in fact, extremely interested in geometry: for years he searched for a geometric formula for proportion in art, and attempted to use geometric principles to draw human figures; his woodcut *Geometrical Schematization of Human Movement* demonstrates his interest, as do, more substantially, his *Treatise on Human Proportions* and his *Introduction in the Art of Measurement with Compass and Ruler*, the latter of which deals with the problems of linear geometry, two-dimensional figures, three-dimensional bodies, and theoretical perspective.

18: Here I have added the word "skein" in order to make a rhyme, with the result that "compos'd/unravel'd," which might otherwise be assumed to refer only to the engraver's emotional and mental state, is tied back into the weaving metaphor.

19: This line is an unpacking of Alberti's concentrated "Todo es prueba de fuego" (lit. "Everything is trial by fire"), in which a Spanish reader would see the word "proof" ("prueba") in the expression "trial by fire," and would probably, given the context, remember that when an engraver desires to make a crucial test to see if his design is coming out all right, he is said to "pull a proof."

22: "Above folly," added for the sake of a rhyme, was extrapolated from "investigative" and "patient," as well as from "carefully," "compos'd," and the other words with which Alberti describes the "Pythagorean" face of Janus Engraver, an artist whom, as I said above, the poet conceives as dual, the precision of his hand movements being unmatched by his spirit, anxious and fretting, imagines Alberti, over the making of a design in which no error can ever be corrected. This view of the engraver as someone with two aspects is reinforced a final time by the penultimate line of the translation, which makes explicit what is only implicit in the original.

24: In this line Alberti is referring not only to Dürer himself, but also to an image in one of Dürer's better-known engravings, *Melencolia I*.

"Yellow"

Notes on specific items:

4: These lines are an indirect quotation from part 6 of Goethe's *Theory of Colours*, in which he speaks of "The Effect of Colour with Reference to Moral Associations": "766. In its highest purity [yellow] always carries with it the nature of brightness, and has a serene, gay, softly exciting character" (Goethe 307).

9: Because the English word "buckler" has lost its old sense of "a shield with a boss," I have found it necessary to add the word "boss" to the word "buckler" when translating the Spanish "rodela." "Boss," which evokes both roundness and protuberance, is too valuable to let drop out of this comparison between a breast and a shield.

24: "Me pone verde" (lit. "makes me green") also means "reduces me to ridicule," a sense unfortunately lost in the English translation.

25: This item, in the original, takes the form of a *piropo*, or street-corner compliment. To evoke this notion in English, I have added a few words to the first line.

"Rubens"

Alberti's epigraph perfectly prepares the reader for the poem that will follow. The words themselves indicate that the poem will partake of the burgeoning, flowering, fertile, celebratory spirit of springtime; even more important, though, is their author, whose name evokes a particular style of writing which Alberti found appropriate for his poem on Rubens.

Góngora was a poet of Spain's Golden Age; he lived between 1561 and 1627, a life span nearly matching that of Rubens (1577–1640). The two men also knew some of the same important figures in the Spanish court of that time, though it is unlikely that they ever met. It is not just the fact that they were contemporaries, however, that makes Góngora an appropriate voice for a poem on Rubens; with "Rubens," as with all of his poems to painters, Alberti sought a poetic style that would imitate the style of his subject, and in Góngora he found a virtual twin of Rubens. Góngora was a formal poet and a classic one who drew much of his material from Greek myth, especially as retold by Ovid in the *Metamorphoses*; Rubens, too, was formal and classic, and enjoyed depicting scenes from classical mythology. Their most striking point of similarity, however, is what Keats would call their "fine excess." Góngora's poetry, including *Soledades* (*Solitudes*)—a pastoral poem in parts, whose first line Alberti has taken for his epigraph, inviting readers to step into Góngora's world—is, to quote Keats again, "heaped with glowing hand." Góngora's poems heap metaphor upon metaphor, image upon image; they are lavish, abundant, extravagant. What better match could be found for Rubens? It is precisely his lushness, richness, and amplitude that strike a viewer of the magnificent Rubens collection at the Prado. Both men heap their beauties high.

There is an overflowing quality to the work of both. In Góngora, the images flow, one into another, in such a way as to carry the reader away from the original point; often he does not discourse upon or describe a single object to which he returns, but rather moves his full attention to each simile or metaphor, privileging it in turn, letting it evoke another, to which he then turns. Here, for example, is Gilbert Cunningham's translation of a few lines from the first of the *Soledades*:

> You kissed the kingdoms of the Dawn at last,
> Whose purple lap the clearest pearls contains,
> And from whose secret veins
> Comes precious ore to set their beauty fast.
> Then to the aromatic woods you passed
> Which, for the Arabian bird (whose track, though straight,
> Yet seems to emulate
> A rainbow in the sky . . .)

> (Góngora 37)

In Alberti's "Rubens," one finds the same sort of image trajectory, a movement I have tried to follow in my translation. The poet is seeking to imitate the richness and multiplicity of the images in the Rubens paintings that surround one in the Prado. Readers should not, at least at first, read the poem with the expectation that it will develop logically, but should let themselves be carried by the images. Like Góngora, Alberti also provides a loose formal underpinning for his lavish image-poem, and I have tried to follow him here, too. Góngora wrote the *Soledades* using the *silva*, a form in which the poet is free to use both seven- and eleven-syllable lines in any pattern; there is no set rhyme or stanza length. Following him, Alberti set himself no stanza length and, freer than Góngora, does not rhyme at all, except in the first line, effectively linking it with the epigraph, so that Góngora's poem flows into his. Alberti's lines are mostly fourteen syllables long, though some are shorter. I have tried to render this relaxed metrical regularity with a loose iambic pentameter beat. The rhythmic regularity of "Rubens" helps to balance the imagistically overflowing poem, and is, of course, consonant with the style of Rubens, whose lavish works were composed within formal bounds.

In order to stress the overflowing quality of Rubens, the excessive, lavish abundance he so admired in his paintings, Alberti, in addition to writing in an overflowing manner, also speaks of overflowing. Everywhere in the paintings of Rubens is an overflowing like that in his painting of Ceres, whose basket pours out a flood of fruit, spilling all over the ground. For Alberti, this superabundance, this rising up and spilling over, is best emblemized by *St. George and the Dragon*, in which Rubens depicts a magnificent white horse, rampant, infused with and radiating a spirit and power with which it, in turn, infuses its rider. This is the horse to which Alberti is referring at the beginning and the end of his poem when he mentions "el caballo que se eleva a hombre " (lit. "the horse that rises into man") and "ese caballo que se desborda en hombre" (lit. "that horse that overflows into man"). In the middle of the poem, Alberti also speaks of overflowing; here, it is in the context of a description of Rubens's flood landscapes, which include *Flood Landscape with Philemon and Baucis, Storm Landscape*, and *Shipwreck*.

I have mentioned that the poem begins and ends with a reference to the great horse. Actually, it is not just the beginning of the poem that is repeated at the end, but also key elements from throughout: the poem ends with a coda that neatly recapitulates its various subjects, naming them in reverse order. The final section of the poem begins with the vocative "Oh pintor" (lit. "Oh painter") (line 42), and a few lines later, moves into the coda (lines 47–55), which names "Amor" (lit. "Love"), "los cielos en orgía" (lit. "the skies in orgy"), "el mordido pezón flotante" (lit. "the bitten nipple floating"), "volutes de carne" (lit. "volutes of flesh"), and "ese caballo que se desborda en hombre." "Love" is another name for Venus, and it carries us back to that portion of the poem in which Alberti celebrates the gods and goddesses in Rubens's paintings, beginning with Venus (lines 27–41). "The skies in orgy" is a reference to the storm-landscape portion of the poem, which begins with the word "nubes" (lit. "clouds") (lines 17–26). Mention of the nipple reminds us of the quatrain directly above the "clouds" section (lines 13–16), in which Alberti alludes to the multiplicity of breasts in the paintings of Rubens. The "volutes of flesh" take us back to lines 5–12, in which Alberti gives us quick glimpses of the paintings: we see a rosy back, a taut muscle, and we get an impression of voluptuous white female flesh when we read of the spirit that carried the artist into production, the inspiring wave fetched up on the shore of his painting, an "espuma ebria siempre / rota en nácares blancas y venillas azules" (lit. "spume always inebriated / broken in white mother-of-pearl and tiny blue veins"). Lastly, the "horse that overflows into man" carries us back to the beginning of the poem (lines 2–4). Thus Alberti ends where he began, turning the flowing image-stream into a circle, unifying as he closes.

The different sections of the poem are, for the most part, set apart from each other by means of spacing. The first four lines, which speak of the great horse, are set apart from the next section by the space created when Alberti stair-stepped the fifth line, the single word "Era" (lit. "It was"). The following section on flesh, of which the "breast" quatrain is really a part, is similarly separated from the "clouds" section by the space surrounding the two short lines "Era además" (lit. "It was further") and " ¡Oh nubes!" Like the "clouds" section, the "gods and goddesses" section is preceded by space surrounding three short lines that title it ("¡Oh dioses, / dioses, / dioses!") (lit. "Oh gods, / gods, / gods!). The finale of the poem, however, the vocative quatrain and the coda, are not set apart, either from each other or the lines that precede them. Because this lack of separation tends, I believe, to make a difficult poem even more difficult, and because I think that contemporary English readers, already struggling with the unfamiliarity of this poem's formality, Góngoresque image-heaping, and classical references, should be given what aid can be extended to them, I have continued with Alberti's own system of setting apart the sections and have gone on to separate the last two.

Notes on specific lines:

1–2: "Era," the first word of the first two lines of the poem, and of many subsequent lines, can mean "he," "she," or "it" [was]. In the context of the first lines of this poem, it probably means both "he" and "it"; because of the flexibility of the Spanish word, Alberti can refer simultaneously to the artist and his work, something we often do when we use a painter's name. Certainly, by the end of the poem, Rubens and his work have become one, for when Alberti shifts into "Tú, el Amor, tú los cielos en orgía" (lit. "You, Love, you the skies in orgy"), naming the elements of Rubens's oeuvre, we are still understanding "tú" as referring to the painter, whom Alberti has just finished addressing ("Oh pintor . . . tu hermosura" [lit. "Oh painter . . . your beauty"]), although we have, of course, understood "your beauty" as the beauty of Rubens's paintings, thus facilitating Alberti's subsequent identification of the man and his work in the lines of the coda. Here I have even been able to underscore this identification by the addition of the copula "are" (line 47). However, in the first two lines of the poem (to return at last to these!) this sense of painter and paintings as one has been lost because an English translator must choose between "he" and "it." I chose "it" because I thought it was essential to maintain a continuity between Góngora's epigraph and Alberti's first lines, and in Góngora's line "era" can only be translated using "it."

I have, furthermore, added the words "all here" to create the rhyme by which Alberti links the epigraph to his poem. By means of this rhyme and the repetition of "it," the poem is made to flow out of the epigraph, and the reader moves more easily from the flowering season to that portion of the Prado that houses the paintings of Rubens.

15–16: These lines may be a reference to a little-known Rubens painting in the Prado, *The Origin of the Milky Way*, a stunning rendition of a theme that combines humor and sensuality: in it, the goddess Juno, in a chariot in the middle of the night sky, is fingering her nipple, from which milk spurts out into the mouth of the baby in her lap and into the sky beyond. The poet seems to be moving, in this quatrain, from a comment about the ubiquity of breasts in Rubens, to memory of Juno's breast in *The Origin of the Milky Way*, to the notion that other fingers, too, including, perhaps, those of the painter, are moved to alight here and "release . . . stars."

25–26: The Spanish lines here read "y la Belleza bella, en un despertar subito / verterse en los cabellos de Diana cazadora" (lit. "and beautiful Beauty, in a sudden awakening, / spills into the hair of Diana, hunting"). I know of no Rubens painting to which these lines may refer. They are preceded by the only negative mention in the poem of overflowing: everywhere else, Alberti celebrates the spilling profusion he associates with Rubens, but in lines 19–24 he seems to be warning the elements of the chaos they are capable of unleashing. In this context, lines 25–26 seem to be another instance (and one that offers a transition to the next section) of a negative overflowing—a boundary that should not have been transgressed—for here Beauty has spilled onto the goddess of Chastity, subverting the right order of things. Because I believe that a sense of the difference between Beauty and Diana is essential to an understanding of the passage, I have added "chaste" as a reminder of Diana's identity, and have replaced the somewhat redundant "beautiful" with "soft," thus further bringing out the contrast between the two. I have also regularized the meter of line 26, which describes Diana fulfilling her role, while I have made the preceding line about spilling transgress its rhythmic bounds. Amidst these efforts toward clarifying the contrast, however, the last phrase of line 25 was lost.

30–41: Unlike the "flesh" section, which mainly gives general impressions culled from Rubens's oeuvre, and the "clouds" section, all of whose lines refer to all of Rubens's storm paintings, this section on the gods seems to link specific lines with specific paintings. Lines 30–31 evoke both *Venus and Adonis* and *The Death of Adonis;* lines 32–33 evoke *Diana and the Nymphs Assailed by Satyrs;* lines 34–37 evoke *Drunken Silenus;* and lines 38–41 evoke the Rubens classics *Garden of Love* and *The Three Graces.* In this last painting, so luminous is their flesh that it is as if the bodies of the Graces were painted with light.

42–46: These lines try to reflect the ambiguity of the Spanish, which is poised between two propositions: Rubens's art is unwritten, his characters' exclaiming expressions are without corresponding linguistic signs, and his characters have no words to describe his beauty 1) because his art is not verbal and 2) because no one has ever produced the like before and it is simply ineffable.

53: I have added the word "whirled" here so that the English reader is in less danger of misreading "waterspout" as "drainpipe," and visualizes instead the natural phenomenon that is the second dictionary definition of "waterspout": "A funnel-shaped or tubular column of rotating, cloud-filled wind extending from an ordinary cumulus or cumulo-nimbus cloud down to a cloud of spray torn up by whirling winds from an ocean or lake." The image is crucial to the reader's understanding of this final, crescendo-like passage in which the poet brings together in a three-note chord the overflowing energy and power of the horse whose being rises into that of the man, the natural force of a waterspout, and the artistic inspiration that moved Peter Paul Rubens.

"To Composition"

"To Composition" has been composed in iambic pentameter. The octave rhyme of the original has been converted into Shakespearian octave rhyme, but the original's sestet rhyme has been retained.

"Composition" is usually defined as the organization or arrangement of the forms in a work of art. When one thinks of composition, it is usually in terms of the concrete act of plotting the design on a canvas, of diagramming the movements and placing the figures. In this poem, however, Alberti takes one step farther back, choosing to include within the notion of "composition" the abstract idea, or vision, that precedes the actual plotting. By taking this view of composition, Alberti endows it with a dual and dichotomized nature. It is thus that he comes to present it here in terms of paired contraries.

The translation of this poem, then, involved the preservation of Alberti's opposites, the careful reproduction of his oxymoronic naming. Sometimes the English is a literal repetition of the Spanish, as in "ideal net" (line 4), "premeditated fantasy" (line 5), and "wisdom's inspiration" (line 8). Sometimes, however, I have strayed from the literal in order to underline the nature of Alberti's presentation, or to enrich the resonance of a particular oxymoron. In line 1, for example, "cimiento" (lit. "foundation") has become "ground," not only to take advantage of that word's use as a painter's term but also to underline the latent earth/sky pairing that fills out the original. The two English words then begin to vibrate with suggestion, as do the Spanish, evoking both the lofty Mallarméan notion that a work of art is the concretization, the grounding, of an abstract idea seized from the azure, and the down-to-earth principle of landscape art that both earth and sky participate in composition's creation of harmony.

Other examples of lines where translation decisions were based on a desire to emphasize and preserve the original oxymoron include line 2, in which "trama" (lit. "tram, a silk thread used for the weft of the best velvets and silks") was translated "silken thread" rather than "tram" or "weft" in order to emphasize its contrast with "solid," and line 6, in which "avara de" (lit. "greedy for," and colloquially, "eager for") was translated by the colloquial expression "hot for," so that the reader might feel the full effect of the contrast between the verb and its coldly mathematical object.

The contraries appear a final time in the last line, which pairs something wild, untamable, and of the air with something that controls and directs. "Plans" was chosen to translate the original "razón" (lit. "reason," "the rational faculty") on the theory that since "plan" can suggest not only mental formulation but also graphic representation, it makes a better, more tangible foil for its partner, the invisible wind. "Plan" was put into the plural in order to draw into its net of representation the notion of future aspiration, which helps to shade line 13 into line 14. Finally, "sail-shaping" was created out of whole cloth to modify "wind" in order to convey a notion of the way in which wind might be linked with the act of composition; it was also hoped that "sail" would evoke "canvas," thus further tying "wind" to "composition."

Notes on specific lines:

1 and 7: The last word of each of these lines has no counterpart in the original. The words exist to provide rhyme and to clarify and emphasize by renaming.

3: In the original, line 3 reads "suma de acordes que entre sí aprisiona" (lit. "sum of musical chords which, between themselves, imprison"). Now, a sum of musical chords may be said to be a tune. I started, then, with this word, proceeding to define it in terms of "chord-dances blending" in order to enable the English reader to glimpse what the Spanish reader does in "acordes": the adjective "acorde" (lit. "in accordance"), which makes an important contribution to the stanza by reinforcing the notion of harmony.

"Green"

Notes on specific items:

3: "Branch-cups" is my rendering of "copa," which means both "cup" and "treetop."

8: "Ogival" is the adjectival form of "ogive," which is a "pointed arch."

9: Athena, in her capacity as peaceful protectress, is traditionally associated with the olive; Apollo, in his capacity as god of poetry and song, with the laurel.

10: The poet is playing with language here: he does not simply say, "un abrir y un cerrarse verde" (lit. "a green opening and closing"), but he adds the word "en," which brings to mind the common expression "en un abrir y cerrar de ojos," equivalent to our "in the twinkling of an eye," an evocation of speed. English will not accommodate this wordplay, but in order to communicate the phrase's full meaning I have added to "green opening & closing" the word "sudden."

17: "Veronese green" is the name of a certain shade of green paint. In his autobiography Alberti speaks of his excitement when, as a child, he received a gift of a box of paints with this color in it.

21: A harquebusier is a soldier armed with a harquebus (an obsolete kind of firearm). In Velázquez's *The Lances*, in the Prado, the beautiful shade of green worn by the harquebusier in the foreground is what first catches, then continues to hold, the eye.

30: An aquarelle is a drawing in watercolor.

"Pedro Berruguete"

In "Pedro Berruguete" Alberti uses *coplas de pie quebrado* (lit. "broken-foot stanzas"). These are stanzas normally comprising six lines, of which the first, second, fourth, and fifth are octosyllabic, and the third and sixth are tetrasyllabic. The earliest known *coplas de pie quebrado* date from the fourteenth century, but perhaps the most famous example of their use is in "Las Coplas de Jorge Manrique por la muerte de su padre" ("The Verses of Jorge Manrique on the Death of His Father"), written in 1476 and first published in 1494. Now, this is the precise time in which Berruguete lived. Moreover, Manrique and Berruguete share as a birthplace the same small town in Spain, Paredes de Nava, in Castile. *Coplas de pie quebrado*, then, evoking as they do a man born in Paredes de Nava who flourished in the latter part of the fifteenth century, are an appropriate form in which to speak of Berruguete, a form, incidentally, of which Alberti may have been reminded by his good friend the poet and scholar Pedro Salinas, who published in Buenos Aires, at the same time Alberti was composing *A la pintura*, an article entitled "Jorge Manrique, o tradición y originalidad."

However, *coplas de pie quebrado* are appropriate to this poem for another reason: they convey a sense of absence. Like the "missing-foot" stanza Keats employs in "La Belle Dame Sans Merci," the *coplas de pie quebrado* deliberately disappoint the ear, setting up a pattern only to break it, leaving the reader to feel that something is missing, and like the "missing-foot" stanza, the *coplas de pie quebrado* have been used in poems where the poet wants to communicate a lack of some kind. Manrique's poem, the supreme example of this form, speaks of the loss of his father, of life's transience, of the absence of permanence. Centuries later, when Ruben Darío wished to write "La Tristeza" ("Sadness"), it was the *pie quebrado* stanza that he chose in which to compose it; indeed, the noted prosodist Tomás Navarro specifically attributes to *coplas de pie quebrado* effects of sadness (Navarro 250).

Sadness, tragedy, loss, lack, absence—these are precisely what Alberti wished to convey in this poem which is neither a celebration of "the first real exponent of the Renaissance in Spain" (Bicchi 12), nor a description of the artistic achievements of the man who combined some traditional Castilian elements of painting with the newest Italian developments in perspective and in the depiction of light and space, but is rather a condemnation of Castile. Berruguete is best known for his painting *Auto-da-Fé*, a part of one of a series of panels he completed over a period of several years for the Church of Santo Tomás in Avila, whose vast decorative program was largely financed and encouraged by the infamous Tomás de Torquemada, the first Inquisitor General of the recently established Spanish Inquisition. Berruguete, then, is linked in Alberti's mind to the Inquisition, while the Inquisition seems to be linked in his mind to Castile, the main arena of its cruel activities, and, further, to a certain dearth in the Castilian landscape. The poet seems to link the absence of compassion and humanity in the one with the absence of fertility and fruitfulness in the other.

The poet's sense that the harshness of the land is bound up with the harshness of the institution that thrived there is largely communicated to us by his use of transferred epithets. Again and again, he speaks of the landscape and of Churchmen in terms of each other: in stanza 1 the flesh of the monks is said to be "sin agua" (lit. "without water"), while in stanza 3 the cypress is described as "en ayuno" (lit. "fasting"); and in stanza 2, ostensibly about the landscape but simultaneously about the monks who inhabit it, a reference to "yermos" (lit. "sterile, barren") robes is followed by mention of "desveladas" (lit. "sleepless, insomniac") grass bristles. The thrust of these transferred epithets becomes clearer in stanza 5, in which a description of the burning of the land by the sun is dramatically juxtaposed to a description of the burning of bodies by fire. Finally, in the last stanza, we find the key verb "se agavilla," an agricultural word meaning "to bind together in sheaves," which Alberti uses in his description of the things he sees as bound together in Berruguete's world: the painter's flame with shadow (perhaps the flame of Berruguete's talent with the shadow of his subject), life with death (probably the life of the Spanish people with the death carried out by the Inquisition), and living death and dying life with Castile; it is with this last instance that the poet's point about the desolating nature of Castile is finally brought home to us.

Also bound together in the sheaf of this poem are the men of the Church to the Church itself, and the colors of Berruguete's paints to both the Castilian landscape and Inquisitional torture. Using the same technique of which I spoke above, Alberti describes the churches depicted by Berruguete as if he were describing the latter's monks: the architecture is "pallid"; the bricks "mumble"; the golds are "anointed." Similarly, Berruguete's reds are said to be "enjutos," which can mean "dried out" or "sparse," while his whites are "óseos crujientes." Now, "óseos" means "bony," and "crujientes" refers to the sound made when something breaks or when two things rub together; thus, the imagination, knowing the context of the poem, leaps fairly easily from "óseos crujientes" to the thought of the tortuous bone-breaking performed in the service of the Inquisition. In this way does Alberti further tie together his poem.

The poem is structured so that it falls into two parts, each of which alludes to a different painting by Berruguete. The first part, beginning with the first word of the first stanza, "Aquí" (lit. "Here"), and continuing through the end of the third stanza, alludes to *Apparition of the Virgin to the Monastic Community*, a painting found in the Prado which depicts two rows of monks inside an exquisitely ornamented church whose side wall opens onto a courtyard where a solitary cypress can be seen. The second appearance of the word "Aquí," at the beginning of the fourth stanza, signals the beginning of the second part of the poem, which alludes to the famous *Auto-da-Fé*, also found in the Prado, a painting that depicts an ecclesiastical tribunal on one level and on another, beside a patch of hard, cracked ground, the burning at the stake of heretics. This second part smoothly segues into the conclusion of the poem, which may be seen as beginning with either stanza 6 or stanza 7.

In translating this poem I have retained the shape of the *coplas de pie quebrado*, but not their syllabic count; I have composed six-line stanzas in free verse, the third and sixth lines of which consist only of a word or two. In writing these short lines I have adhered, with a single exception, to the exact words with which Alberti composed his third and sixth lines, because the nature of the form is such that these words, set apart physically as they are and taking the place of whole lines, have enormous weight placed upon them. Moreover, since the poem does not rhyme, unlike most compositions of *coplas de pie quebrado* (absence on top of absence), we can be certain that Alberti, free of the exigencies of rhyme, used precisely the words he wanted. Looking at these words, one may even feel that they form a kind of summary of the poem. Leaving out the third line of the last stanza of the original, for a reason that I will explain later, they are: "laminados" (lit. "laminated"), "muerto el sueño" (lit. "dead the dream"), "amarillos" (lit. "yellow"), "silenciosas" (lit. "silent"), "y las piedras" (lit. "and the stones"), "solitario" (lit. "solitary"), "y los negros" (lit. "and the blacks"), "desmejora" (lit. "corrupts"), "mudas gredas" (lit. "mute marls"), "petrifica" (lit. "petrifies"), "consagrados" (lit. "consecrated"), "del tormento" (lit. "of the torture"), and "de Castilla" (lit. "of Castile"). Note especially the way the form enables the poet to "drop a bomb" with these words; examine, for example, the end of the poem, where "torture" and "Castile" come upon us as a surprise, and then are allowed to linger in our minds.

Notes on specific lines:

1–2: Berruguete is known for his frequent use of gold and silver, an ornamentation that was traditional among Castilian painters of his time.

4: "Facades" is derived from the Spanish "facies," usually used to refer to the faces of a crystal but also the term that designates the distinct alterations of the physiognomy in sick people. Alberti uses it at a point in the stanza when he is moving from a description of the ornamented walls of the church to one of the monks who are standing in it. The word draws the reader both backward to the glittering church and forward to the gazing monks. I chose "facades" hoping that it would function similarly, bridging the poet's leap from architecture to the human face.

7–12: Because stanzas 1 and 3 both describe details from the same painting, *Apparition of the Virgin*, and because the second appearance of "Aquí," at the beginning of a part of the poem where details from a second painting are mentioned, points to a two-part structure, each part of which has reference to a single painting, it seems reasonable to assume that stanza 2 also describes *Apparition of the Virgin*. However, there is no such landscape in this painting. Indeed, I have been able to find no such landscape in the extant work of Berruguete, into whose religious paintings a small bit of the natural world will at most occasionally obtrude. We must read these lines metaphorically, then, taking them as a description of the monks, bowed in rows like silent stalks. By choosing to speak of the monks in this way, Alberti not only communicates details about them and about Castile, but he reinforces his thesis about the equivalency between the outside and the inside, the link between the landscape and the men and activities of the Church that he communicates elsewhere in the poem (as well as in lines 10 and 11 of this very stanza) through his use of transferred epithets.

10: In translating "los yermos trajes quebrados" (lit. "the sterile broken suits") I have taken the liberty of expanding upon what is evoked by "quebrados" (lit. "broken") in this context of topography, hoping thus to keep the reader's attention on the equivalency being established here between the monks and the landscape.

22–24: In these lines I have stuck literally to the words of the original, whose reference to the dire effect of the celestial on the terrestrial is clearly symbolic.

34–36: Here I have imitated the collage syntax of the original, in which tool is piled on top of tool with no explanatory connectives. I have, however, turned "forma" (lit. "form, shape") into a verb in order to bring more clearly into focus what I take to be the relation between torture and the tools.

37–39: The adjective "melancholy," which modifies "flame" in the original, has been omitted in the translation for rhythmic reasons. More serious, however, is the change made in line 39, the only short line that does not stand as it did in the original. In Spanish, line 39 consists of the verb discussed above, "se agavilla" (lit. "to bind in sheaves"); it is an important word, and its sense has been retained in the stanza, though its position has been shifted. In the original, "se agavilla" rhymes with the final word in the poem, "Castilla." This is the only rhyme in the poem, and it acts to increase significantly the impact of the final word on the reader. Reasoning, then, that this rhyme should be retained at all costs, and knowing that the meaning of "se agavilla" should not be altered to achieve this rhyme, I shifted the verb and created a new image not found in the original: "the spokes & the space / in a wheel". These words provide not only the necessary rhyme but also a loose and paraphrastic translation of "concierta" (lit. "to compose, to harmonize, to make a whole"). Thus "tu melancólica llama / con la sombra que concierta / se agavilla" (lit. "your melancholy flame is bound in a sheaf with the shadow that makes it a whole") becomes "Your flame is sheaf-bound / to shadow: the spokes & the space / in a wheel."

40–41: It is interesting to note that lines 40 and 41, each beginning with "Aquí," seem to recapitulate, respectively, the first and second parts of the poem, each of which began with this same word, as I mentioned above.

"To Clothing"

"To Clothing" has been composed in iambic pentameter. As always, the original's sestet rhyme scheme has been retained, while its octave rhyme scheme has been altered to a scheme more suited to English. Here, as in the later "To the Nude" and "To Watercolor," however, this scheme is not Shakespearian octave rhyme, but an *aabb ccdd* rhyme, chosen because the octave contains "semantic couplets": both stanzas of the octave are divided by semicolons that clearly set off the first half of each stanza from the second half. Each stanza begins with a couplet describing a particular type of clothing (lines 1 and 2 describe a delicate gown, in such a way, moreover, as to insinuate femininity and sensuality into the passage, and lines 5 and 6 describe a heavy robe of the sort worn by monks in the paintings of Zurbarán, next to whose poem Alberti has placed this sonnet); each stanza ends with a couplet whose first line postulates a condition and whose second line postulates its opposite.

Notes on specific lines:

5: "Slow" and "restrained" cover both senses of the third term in the Spanish description, "pausado," which means both "slow" and "slowed down." The English line mimics the Spanish, which, in turn, deliberately imitates the qualities it is describing; it is a line that halts the tripping verse, slow and difficult to manage as the movements of one encumbered by heavy, inflexible clothing.

11: My translation slightly expands the original, which says only that clothing is skin that is "detachable" or "removable." This expansion enabled me to provide, for the poem's final word, a rhyme much in keeping with the light, humorous spirit of the poem.

12: This is a rather loose translation of the original, "Cantan su ley los campos de tu escudo" (lit. "The fields of your coat of arms sing their law"). The fields form the background of an escutcheon, or shield, on which heraldic bearings, or figures, are displayed, and beneath which the verses of the motto are blazoned; shield, figures, and verses are all included in the term "coat of arms." For the sake of rhyme and rhythm, I have switched some of the terms, but have retained the notion of a Clothing "family motto," articulated in a lyrical manner by a coat of arms.

"Zurbarán"

Alberti composed "Zurbarán" using *sexta rima*, or hendecasyllabic sexains with an *ababcc* rhyme. As was mentioned before, this was a form first employed in the Golden Age and is therefore evocative of that period, and hence an appropriate form in which to shape a poem about Zurbarán, a Golden Age painter. However, the form of the poem is appropriate to the subject in another way. This is not a liquid, flowing poem: not only does a period separate the first four lines from the last two in each sexain, but the sexains themselves do not flow together, instead remaining separate, self-enclosed. This poem is less like a moving stream than a series of still pools. The poem, then, is quite suited to its subject, Zurbarán, in whose paintings each object is discrete and each outline firm, whose still lifes depict fruits and vessels carefully set apart from each other, whose monks wear robes that hang in heavy, separate folds. Zurbarán's painted world is, moreover, one of solidity, and of stasis.

"Zurbarán" is composed of eight sexains, each of which is a separate meditation on an aspect, or a subject, of Zurbarán's painting; however, a few ideas do occur in more than one stanza. Some stanzas have reference to only one painting, while others make statements that are applicable to many of his works. The first stanza emphasizes the quality of clarity in Zurbarán's paintings, seeking first to describe it and then to account for it. The second stanza's first four lines might be titled "A Monk's Life": the details of Alberti's sketch are drawn from such well-known works as *The Vision of St. Peter Nolasco*, which depicts both the dreaming monk and his dream, and *The Miracle of St. Hugo*, which shows a group of monks at table. The last couplet of this stanza returns to the notion of thoughtfulness expressed in the first stanza's final couplet. This notion is then taken up as the theme of the third stanza, which looks at the objects in different paintings (the first two lines may be referring to *The Annunciation*, the second two to *The Miracle of St. Hugo*, and the third two to *Still Life with Oranges*), finding them so substantial that they are credited with consciousness. The fourth stanza very likely refers to a second still life, this one containing earthenware vessels and platters rather than fruit. This stanza, continuing the notion of cognizant objects, attributes piety to the tableware, thinking thus to account for the strong sense of spirituality this painting gives its viewer. Indeed, the art critic J. Rogelio-Buendía, remarking upon exactly the quality Alberti is emphasizing in this stanza, says that this painting always brings to his mind St. Teresa's reminder that "God may be found even among the cooking pots" (Rogelio-Buendía 204).

In the fifth stanza, Alberti refers to the typically Zurbaránesque practice of depicting two planes within his paintings, the terrestrial and the celestial. There are many paintings in which these two planes may be found, including *The Vision of St. Peter Nolasco, The Prayer of St. Bonaventura, The Vision of Blessed Alonso Rodriguez, The Annunciation, The Adoration of the Shepherds, The Battle of El Sotillo, St. Bruno in Ecstasy, St. Francis in the Portiuncula,* and *The Martyrdom of St. Andrew,* but perhaps the archetypal work of this genre is *The Apotheosis of St. Thomas Aquinas,* which does indeed depict a platform of cloud on which the saint stands (the platform, moreover, is hovering above the heads of a group of men who are praying in a room whose outer wall and ceiling are now filled with this bit of heaven that has descended to them). Through use of these two planes, Zurbarán seeks to depict the presence of the celestial in the lives of those on earth. In the final couplet of this stanza, Alberti swiftly changes tone and makes a joke about the frequent presence of hanging drapery in Zurbarán's pictures. The poet may be thinking in particular of *Fray Gonzalo de Illescas, Bishop of Córdoba,* which shows a huge and heavy drape hanging above the head of the bishop and nearly covering the opening in the wall behind him.

The subject of the sixth stanza is Zurbarán's paintbrush. The brush is compared to different things in the course of the stanza, but it is mainly the weight of its stroke that is emphasized: the brush is called a rough lover and then a clapping flame, but it is the metaphor that associates the brush with weaving which is the one that is eventually extended, and the stanza ends by linking the product of the brush with cloth. Following this stanza is one that is a religious meditation on earthenware; it most likely alludes to the still life spoken of in stanza 4. The poet describes how a contemplation of earthenware can inspire faith: its color is sublime and its shape reminds one of the Hand that shaped us in the Divine Image. The thought of mortal clay informed by a divine spirit leads, of course, to thought of Christ, and the last couplet, conflating *St. Bruno in Ecstasy,* which shows the saint looking upward in ecstasy, and *St. Francis Kneeling,* which shows, above Francis's kneeling form, the tiny figure of Christ flying upward, speaks of His Ascension and the joy that contemplation of it can evoke. Finally, the poem ends with a stanza that emphasizes the importance of form to Zurbarán.

Since, as I remarked in my note on "Titian," the English equivalent of *sexta rima* is the "Venus and Adonis stanza," an iambic pentameter sexain with an *ababcc* rhyme, I have adopted this form for the English "Zurbarán." I have, however, altered the pentameter to tetrameter, in accordance with my usual practice of trying to create shortened and tautened lines wherever possible. This practice is based upon the fact that our English monosyllables take longer to pronounce than do Romance polysyllables; therefore, in order to create an equivalent line in English, a translator from a Romance language must often create a shorter line (what must be counted is not the number of syllables but the time it takes to say them). The *ababcc* rhyme scheme of the *sexta rima* and its English equivalent is well suited to this poem because it helps to emphasize the semantic separation of the last two lines of each stanza from the four that precede them; accordingly, this rhyme scheme has been maintained in all the stanzas but one, stanza 4, where for the sake of a felicitous rhyme the scheme was slightly altered.

Notes on specific lines:

14: In the Spanish original, the vellum is thinking "del volumen que alumbra la madera" (lit. "of the volume which the wood illuminates"). Zurbarán has many paintings that show lighted volumes, but I could find none in which the light emanated from the wood on which the volume lay; often, in fact, the volumes lie on covered tables. In *The Annunciation*, however, a particularly still and thoughtful painting, there is a thin wall and a small wooden table upon which lies a closed vellum-covered book that is propping a volume illuminated by light emanating from heaven; it is this painting, I think, to which lines 13 and 14 refer. Therefore, when searching for a rhyme for line 16's "tablecloth," I came upon the word "prop," and thought it an entirely appropriate alternative to the original.

16: Here, as in a few other places, a word has been deleted for the sake of maintaining brevity of line. In the original, the tablecloth is said to be cloistering "arpillera" (lit. "sackcloth"); the phrase is probably a humorous reference to the meeting of the two cloths as the monks sit at table.

32: This line is a rather free rendering of the Spanish "recia llama / que blanquecinamente tabletea" (lit. "vigorous flame that, with a tinge of white [or 'in a somewhat white manner'] claps wooden clappers"). My line was composed after

I was told by a native speaker that "tabletear" is a word sometimes associated with the tapping rhythm of the flamenco dance.

33: I have untwisted a few threads here in order to make a little clearer Alberti's main metaphor of the paintbrush as an instrument of weaving. The line reads "telar del hilo de la flor en rama" (lit. "loom [or 'frame,' or possibly, by extension, 'pattern'] of the thread of the flower on the branch [or 'of the raw, unfinished flower']"). I have taken "en rama" to mean "unfinished," and have interpreted the line to be about a design not fully brought into being until it is realized by the thread on the frame.

39–40: The original speaks only of a magnanimous hand through whose power the human being finds himself parallel to what is divine; the words "gave a shape" are my own addition, employed in order to help the reader make the transition between the earthenware and the human being who discovers himself to be of a divine mold.

41: Missing from the English version of this line is mention of the "gloria abierta" (lit. "open gloria") of which the original line speaks. In Spanish, "gloria" is a term used by painters and art historians to denote a space at the top of a painting, like an opening in the sky, in which angels and resplendent light are depicted; the "gloria" traditionally represents heaven. Zurbarán's double-planed pictures are in effect extensions of, or variations on, the use of the "gloria." In line 41, mention of the "gloria" is juxtaposed to mention of the ecstatic monk, causing the reader to imagine the monk looking upward, toward heaven.

44: In the original, the fight for form waged by the painter from Extremadura (a region in the far west of Spain) is said to be a fight that both is "dura" (lit. "hard") and "se extrema" (lit. "is taken to extremes"). Unfortunately, only the latter pun on the painter's native region may be carried over into English.

47–48: The last two lines read "Gire en tu eternidad la disciplina / de una circonferencia cristalina" (lit. "May the discipline of a crystalline circumference revolve in your eternity"). It is both a wish for the painter's eternity and an expression that epitomizes the concerns of his life. The couplet's words mingle both a hope for heaven ("May . . . crystalline . . . revolve in your eternity") and a recognition of one of the painter's supreme values on earth: form ("the discipline of a . . . circumference"—for how can a circumference be said to possess "discipline" except that it holds the shape of a circle?). My translation seeks to communicate both parts of this double statement and to show how its second part links the couplet to the four lines that precede it.

"To Light"

"To Light" has been composed in iambic pentameter. The octave rhyme of its original has been converted into Shakespearian octave rhyme, but the original's sestet rhyme has been retained.

This sonnet is the only one in the book with a subtitle. This subtitle (Impressionism) is an economic way for the poet to make another statement about light: light was one of the most important components of Impressionism; the subtitle also helps us place some of the poem's images by giving them a context.

Notes on specific lines:

2–4: These lines read "ciega / para el pincel abierto que disgrega / la mancha de la mar y del celaje" (lit. "[light] blind for the open paintbrush which separates / the stain of the sea and of the twilit-colored clouds"). Here I have chosen to do a translation that is also an interpretation of these difficult lines. I have taken the light that is "blind" (or in darkness) "for" (or by means of) a paintbrush that is depicting twilit clouds to be light that becomes darkness by means of a paintbrush when the latter is painting a scene of dusk. In the original, the paintbrush is said to be "open" and separating the sea and clouds, because it is flattened against the canvas, drawing the line of the horizon, which is what separates sea and sky. In the translation, the modified substantives "stained sea" and "twilit-colored clouds" have been transformed into a verbal phrase in order to describe the action of the brush, which is effecting on the canvas what happens at dusk: all light gradually leaves the land and sea, and gathers, for a short while, in the sky.

11: "Denunciadora" (lit. "denouncer") is an extremely strong word in Spanish, bringing to mind the Inquisition as well as more recent scenes of denunciation and betrayal carried out by political informers. Thus, to the word "discloser" I have added, for emphasis, the words "causing fear."

"Velázquez"

Alberti's "Velázquez" is composed of thirty-one stanzas of varying lengths; some are merely couplets, while others are as long as eight lines. The lines themselves are also of different lengths. Finally, only a few of the stanzas contain rhyme. It should be clear, then, that Alberti has imposed no formal schemes upon his poem. Moreover, the stanzas themselves do not seem to be placed in any kind of rigid order, either logical or chronological. In all of this, Alberti imitates Velázquez, known above all things for his realism: Velázquez did not idealize, formalize, or make his subjects conform to a more shapely mold. Furthermore, since Velázquez did not impose a standard painterly notion of beauty on his subjects but painted them as they were, each seems individual. For this reason, I believe, Alberti lets many of the subjects and elements of Velázquez's paintings speak for themselves instead of describing them all in his own voice.

There are, then, many voices in the poem besides the poet's own, and besides that of Velázquez, who speaks only lines 84 and 85, and probably line 105. There are also many paintings described: some lines, of course, generalize about Velázquez's work, but many describe either several specific paintings or one particular painting. The lines about the nobility of Velázquez's dogs and horses, for example, may be said to apply to all of his many hunting scenes, as those that describe blue and those that describe black may be said to apply, respectively, to all of the paintings in which he used the Sierra Guadarrama as a backdrop and to all of the portraits whose subjects are dressed in black. Similarly, the stanza that mentions silver embroidery and rose, that in which the royal fool speaks, and that which alludes to Felipe's dazzlingly blond children all refer to more than one well-known painting by Velázquez. However, lines 28–31 refer specifically to *Prince Balthasar Carlos in Hunting Dress, with Two Dogs*, lines 60–62 refer to *The Lances*, lines 63–67 to *The Drunkards*, and lines 86–88 to *The Toilet of Venus*.

I have followed the poet's free-verse plan, imposing no formal schemes of rhyme or rhythm and using only occasional rhyme. In order to keep the free verse from sprawling, I have here, as before, tried to keep the lines as taut as possible; to this end I have used an occasional ampersand.

Notes on specific lines:

14–15, 21: El Pardo, outside of Madrid, is the site of a former royal palace, located by an oak wood; the Casa de Campo is a large park in Madrid and was for many years a royal hunting preserve; the Manzanares River flows through Madrid; the Sierra Guadarrama is a range of mountains outside of Madrid. All appear as backgrounds in Velázquez's paintings.

41: The poet quotes the phrase "luz no usada" ("uncommon light") from "A Francisco Salinas," a poem by the Golden Age poet Fray Luis de León. Alberti here wishes to link the skill of the younger Golden Age painter, Velázquez, to the skill of Francisco Salinas, the blind organist of Salamanca in whose hands, says Fray Luis de León, music became a power that caused the air to clear and clothe itself in beauty and "uncommon light."

59: In order to maintain rhyme, I have extrapolated "rush of wings" from Alberti's "pájaro suelto" (lit. "free bird").

70–71, 81: Velázquez lived from 1599 to 1660, largely under the reign of King Felipe IV (1605–65), whom he served as court painter. The Count-Duke of Olivares was for a long time Felipe's chief minister until his unsuccessful foreign policy led to his downfall. Velázquez not only painted numerous portraits of Felipe, but also painted Felipe's family, his chief minister, and many members of his court, including the royal buffoons, whom he accorded the same serious treatment he gave the king. It is this treatment to which the fool refers when, in line 71, he links his name to those of Felipe and Olivares: "Soy D. Bobo Felipe de Coria y Olivares." The joke is magnified by the addition of the words "de Coria" (lit. "from Coria," a small, out-of-the-way town in Spain) to the word "Bobo" (lit. "buffoon"), because a "bobo de Coria" is, proverbially, an extremely foolish person; thus the Spanish reads literally "I am Don Felipe Utterly Buffoon of Olivares." My translation eliminates "utterly," relieving the phrase of its awkwardness but also, unfortunately, of its second joke.

80: "Hound prince" is my own addition. Having deprived readers of one joke, I thought I should furnish another!

"Valdés Leal"

Valdés Leal, who has been called "one of the most curious personalities of Spanish painting" (Guinard & Baticle 135), and a man of "psychopathic temperament" (Rogelio-Buendía 55), is primarily known for only two paintings. These two paintings, executed in 1671–72 for the Hospital of Seville, are a macabre and horrifying pair, each of which depicts in a slightly different manner the themes of death and the vanity of life. They are called the *Postrimerías*, a term that refers both to the last days of man and to the "last things," as named by eschatology: death, judgment, immortality, and either heaven or hell. The first one, subtitled "Finis Gloriae Mundi" (lit. "The End of the Glory of the World") for a banner in the foreground bearing that inscription, is set in a charnel house and shows the bodies of a bishop and a knight of Calatrava, rotting in their coffins and covered with insects; in the background lies a more thoroughly decomposed corpse. The top of the painting shows the hand of Christ holding a balance; one scale holds the trappings of ecclesiastical success and bears the legend "Ni Más" (lit. "Neither More"), while the other holds the trappings of secular success and bears the legend "Ni Menos" (lit. "Nor Less"). The second painting, subtitled "In Ictu Oculi" (lit. "In the Blink of an Eye"), shows a skeleton extinguishing a candle with those words inscribed above it. The skeleton holds a scythe and a coffin, and is standing with one bony foot on a heap of rich debris (silken robes, books, swords, helmets, miters, etc.) and with the other on a globe.

"Valdés," say the art critics Paul Guinard and Jeannine Baticle, "pictures death in its role of decomposer of the flesh, but with the lack of measure that characterizes him, he represents a veritable charnel house where the worms and the enormous flies are painted with such a degree of realism that one shudders with disgust. He pushes horror into paroxysm" (Guinard & Baticle 137). The paintings are, indeed, repulsive.

They are also, however, the issue of a long-established tradition; the *Postrimerías* are not the aberrant result of a single diseased mind, but rather form a part of a large body of religious works whose theme is the mortification of the flesh. Perhaps it is because the *Postrimerías* are among the most theatrically baroque and strikingly repugnant of these works that Alberti chose them to represent their tradition, writing a poem about their creator that is really, as Luis Monguió points out, an expression of disgust at "the horrors of Spanish religious fanaticism." This poem is consistent with Alberti's beliefs, for he has long been opposed to the Spanish Catholic Church, not only in its role of enforcer of political oppression but also in its role of promulgator of an antilife attitude. "The dark and gloomy facet of Spanish religiosity," Monguió reminds us, "is an aspect that revolts and repels him" (Monguió 80).

Alberti composed "Valdés Leal" using *heptasílabo* verse, that is, lines of seven syllables; these he organized into *cuartetas* (quatrains) and *quintillas*. Although some of the rhyme is consonantal, most of it is assonantal, and although the five-line stanzas offer some variations, most of the rhyme is cross-rhyme (*abab*). None of this is very remarkable or very evocative of the figure of Valdés Leal, although Tomás Navarro does say that *heptasílabo* verse reached its highest lyrical prestige in the first third of the seventeenth century, and since Valdés Leal flourished at this time, this verse form may thus be said to be an appropriate one in which to compose a poem about him (Navarro 265).

What is interesting about the form of this poem, however, and what makes it a form particularly suitable to Valdés Leal, is its *estribillo*, or refrain. Only one other poem in *A la pintura* has a stanzaic refrain, the poem "Giotto," each of whose stanzas begins with the words "Laude, Señor Dios mío" (lit. "Praise be, my Lord God"). How different is the refrain of "Valdés Leal," which comes not at the beginning of each stanza but at the end, and which reads "Ni más ni menos. Nada" (lit. "Neither more nor less. Nothing"). If the refrain in "Giotto" helps turn the poem into a joyful prayer, the refrain in "Valdés Leal" does nearly the opposite, establishing a mood of bitter hopelessness and despair.

The refrain creates this mood not only through its message, but through the regular repetition of this message: no matter where each stanza takes us, it ultimately brings us round to these same depressing words; there is no way out, no exit. Claustrophobia is, indeed, one of the effects a refrain can have, and if its message is unpleasant the refrain is almost sure to create in the reader a sense of being shut in, a sense that may culminate in a feeling of panic, or even horror. One need only think of the effect upon the reader of the refrain "Nevermore" in Edgar Allan Poe's "The Raven" to begin to understand the power of a refrain to help create a horrifying atmosphere.

This sense of horror and claustrophobia is precisely what Alberti wished to create in this largely atmospheric poem that seeks mainly to convey to us the world created by Valdés: a closed world without hope or possibility, a world in which our noses are rubbed again and again in the stinking fact of the flesh's mortality, a world where no windows or doors open to show even a glimmer of anything our earthly lives may be but mortal, or of anything that may come to pass for us but death. It is a world which, like the poem that captures it, is morbid, obsessively singleminded, and spirit-depressing.

The images in the poem are derived mainly from the two paintings, especially from *Postrimerías (II)* ("In Ictu Oculi"). However, many of the images in the middle stanzas, stanzas 4 to 7, are not to be found in these paintings (nor in any other of the works of Valdés that I have come across) and were probably fabricated by Alberti to prolong and intensify the mood he was creating.

In my translation I have retained Alberti's quatrains and *quintillas* as well as his assonantal cross-rhyme, but I have changed his seven-syllable verse into iambic trimeter. Trimeter was chosen because, desiring to create an equivalent English line, I had to create a slightly shorter one (see the note on "Zurbarán" for an explanation of why this is so), and because lines of rhymed verse in English tend to have an even, rather than an odd, number of syllables.

The exigencies of rhythm and rhyme have required me at times to make some additions to existing lines, but I have done this by extrapolating from what already existed and by drawing from the source paintings. Perhaps a single example will serve to illuminate this process. The literal English translation of lines 33 and 34 reads "earth for the worm, / a frozen scythe." I felt that "frozen" was dispensable, since Alberti used it to make a rhyme and hence probably chose it primarily for its sound value. What is important here is that line 33 offers a brief evocation of *Postrimerías (I)* and line 34 of *Postrimerías (II)*; the lines are a kind of summary. Keeping my eyes on the paintings, then, I changed "frozen" to "skeleton-held," which provides both the necessary syllables and a fuller reference to *Postrimerías (II)*. Then, working backward to obtain a rhyme for the key word "scythe," I chose "writhe," since this word, rather than adding something new to line 33, merely expands upon the notion of earth and larval creatures, in addition to being a word that preserves the tone of the poem.

Notes on specific lines:

4: The first four words of the refrain, "Ni más ni menos" (lit. "Neither more nor less"), come from *Postrimerías (I)*, where, it will be recalled, the first two words are inscribed on one scale of the balance and the last two on the other. In the context of the painting, the words mean that the various contents of each scale are worth neither more nor less than the contents of the other scale; that is, neither ecclesiastical success nor secular success is worth more than the other, for both are mere earthly possessions of which man is soon stripped when his ephemeral life has come to an end. Alberti adds the word "Nada" (lit. "Nothing") to the first four words as a kind of abbreviated gloss: nothing earthly is worth more or less than any other earthly thing because all are worth nothing.

If "Nothing" serves as a gloss on Valdés's lesson, however, it also, I believe, serves as a negative comment upon that lesson and the worldview behind it. It may, I think, be seen as Alberti's summary statement of what is contained in Valdés's art, and what that art can offer us. Heard ten times in the course of the poem, "Nothing" is perceived by us as its keynote; thus, we come away from the poem associating Valdés with this word, and with what it implies of emptiness and worthlessness.

The literal translation, "Neither more nor less," has been shortened to "No more; no less" to accommodate the trimeter line.

"Black"

Notes on specific items:

3: The voice of black is referring here to the amphorae of classical times, on which mythological scenes were painted upon a black background.

4: The last image in this series was created with the vocabulary of etching, during the process of which acid, poured into a groove originally etched by a needle, is said to "bite" the groove. The ink that then fills the bitten groove creates a deeply black design.

6: This item contains a reference to Rembrandt's *The Night Watch*, in which the illuminated lieutenant, who shares the center of the painting, bears a gold scabbard that looks as if it were carved with black figures.

7: "Black as a wolf's mouth" is a figure of speech so common in Spanish that, upon hearing it, most Spaniards probably no longer register the image at all, perceiving it only as an intensifier. I might more accurately have translated it "black as pitch," but this would have destroyed the poet's imagistic progression from one mouth to another. In the last line, "silhouette" is my addition; it is, I think, what the poet is referring to when he writes "como agujero / que recortan los cuerpos en algunas / determinadas claras superficies" (lit. "as [the] hole / that the bodies cut into some / specified clear surfaces").

18: "Tenebrae" is the Latin word for shadows and darkness; it has come into English bearing its original meaning, but is usually used to refer to the matins and lauds sung in Roman Catholic Church services during Holy Week to commemorate the Crucifixion. It is my translation of the Spanish "tinieblas," which is commonly used to mean "darkness" but also refers to the above-mentioned matins and lauds of Holy Week. Because it brings to the phrase the notion of a church service, "tenebrae" also manages to help translate the preceding Spanish noun "oficio" (lit. "holy office or service"), thus freeing the space for a word more specific than "service" that could help to convey the mournfulness of this brief evocation of Carreño; I chose "lament," whose alliteration with "long" imitates Alberti's own alliteration at the beginning of item 18.

22: In the original, "mass" is qualified by "black." Here, as in other items (e.g., item 20), I have left out the word "black" for a more concentrated effect, letting the poem's title provide the name for these descriptions, letting it serve as the tacit half of each metaphor articulated by these items. In this case, however, "black" was also left out because its juxtaposition to "mass" might have created, in the minds of some English readers, an unwanted association between Zurbarán and Satanism.

"Goya"

Following his practice throughout *A la pintura*, Alberti has here chosen a form for his poem that reflects the nature of his subject's work. Goya's work embraces two extremes: walking through the Goya rooms in the Prado, one passes from the most lighthearted pastels—here are children at their games and a pretty young woman holding a pink parasol—to some of the most horrific paintings imaginable, the "Black Paintings"; named both for their color and their mood, they are depictions of nightmare and despair. Goya, says the critic María Asunción Mateo, perceived as few others ever have "la España de sol y sombras" (Alberti, *Antología* 87). It is this combination of sun and shadows, light and darkness, this dual thrust of Goya's oeuvre as a whole, that not only informs the content of Alberti's poem, but is also that aspect of Goya's work that Alberti has chosen to emphasize through his choice of form: deliberately echoing the essential duality of Goya, Alberti has presented us with a poem that possesses both two different left-margin settings and two different attitudes about rhyme.

Unlike most of Alberti's other poems to painters, "Goya" contains both stanzas that rhyme with a vengeance, frequently employing triple rhyme, and stanzas that do not rhyme at all. More significant, however, than this particular reflection of Goya's duality is the other way in which Alberti has chosen to echo Goya's two sides, for the double margin setting allows the poet to speak in two different voices. It is possible, of course, to argue that the poem contains but one voice and that the double margin setting has only the symbolic significance mentioned above. I believe, however, that the poem makes more sense if the stanzas whose margins begin on the far left side of the page (stanzas 1, 4, 5, 6, 7, and 9) are understood to be spoken by the poet, and the stanzas whose margins are indented (stanzas 2, 3, and 8) are understood to be spoken by the painter. This interpretation gains cogency when it is discovered that, with the exception of its last two lines, stanza 8 is a compilation of various titles that Goya himself gave the set of prints he called his *Caprichos*.

If we now look at the poem bearing in mind that it expresses the duality of Goya's work and that its second, third, and eighth stanzas may be seen to be spoken by Goya himself, we notice two things. First, the poem does not present the clear trajectory from light to darkness which we might expect to find if we consider that the colorful Royal Tapestry Cartoons were done near the beginning of Goya's career and the Black Paintings near the end. Upon closer examination, however, we discover both that Goya's early work contains more than a few images of suffering (e.g., *The Poor at the Fountain, Winter, The Injured Mason*) and that his latest work makes at least a few excursions back into the realm of color and beauty (e.g., *The Milkmaid of Bordeaux*). Thus, while it is true that Goya's work, in general, becomes darker and darker, reflecting the increasing anguish that he felt both as a result of his own serious illness and his country's terrible political fate, it is not entirely accurate to see Goya's career as a straightforward journey from the sun to the shadows, and the poem's structure reflects this truth.

Second, we see that while the poem as a whole, like Goya's work as a whole, contains both light and darkness, those stanzas which we may read as spoken by Goya himself contain only darkness: stanza 8, as I have said, is basically a compilation of titles from the nightmarish *Caprichos*; the lines of stanza 2 all contain references to the Black Paintings; stanza 3 refers to the living death that is the fate of the witness of atrocities. The other stanzas in the poem contain at least a modicum of light; these do not. Why?

The answer may be that while a perusal of Goya's work shows many examples of both the bright and the murky, he was most influential as an artist of the darkness, and it is the voice of this Goya whom later generations of artists heard speaking to them. The writer and art historian André Malraux, in his *Saturn: An Essay on Goya*, speaks of the particular legacy of Goya to modern artists. He claims that Goya recovered "the subterranean element" that Italian art had denied. The style of Renaissance Italy, he explains, was "the expression of a world where the Devil does not exist," but Goya acknowledged the Devil and the Devil's realm of nightmare, horror, torture, and useless suffering. In the midst of the great age of the rational, conscious Enlightenment, Goya turned to the irrational, the unconscious, the dark, and many artists since have followed him down this path. Malraux's perception of Goya is of one who moved "in the lost domain where we think we discern the source of our bondage." Goya, concludes Malraux, "heard welling up inside him a message which was nothing but the never-ending song of darkness" (Malraux 91–92, 141–42).

As may be concluded from the above passages, Malraux saw Goya as a revolutionary, as someone who broke with the conventional and gave us the unexpected. Indeed, Goya's oeuvre does give us one strange, surprising shock after another. Alberti's form for "Goya" tries to imitate this aspect, too, of the painter's work, for here is a poem that moves unexpectedly, surprisingly, changing tone, voice, and style from one stanza to another. The poem progresses, for example, from stanza 1, where we hear the objective voice of the poet giving a kind of summary statement composed of paired opposites, to stanza 2, in which we hear the deranged-sounding voice of the painter himself speaking as a torturer, addressing the subjects of his Black Paintings; and from stanza 7, which quickly, smoothly, reels off images from many different works of Goya—including some pleasant, pretty images from his early work—to stanza 8, which focuses only on the frightening *Caprichos*, gives us no pictures at all, and is constructed by juxtaposing certain titles of that series, giving an impression of raving, disconnected speech.

Because the poem is so full of specific references, I have devoted a great portion of the following section to linking particular lines of the poem with the particular paintings or etchings to which they refer. Most of Alberti's Spanish readers, of course, would probably have no trouble at all identifying the poem's references, since Goya's works are so well known in Spain.

Notes on specific lines:

7–15: Because the construction of the original lines emphasizes the object rather than the subject (e.g., line 7, "De ti me guardo un ojo" reads literally "Of you I keep the eye"), I have tried to stick with this emphasis rather than shift to emphasize the subject, as a more literal translation (e.g., "I keep your eye") would require.

8–9: Cf. *Saturn Devouring His Children*.

9–10: Cf. *Two Old Men*. Some critics think that one of these old men is shouting into the ear of the other; Alberti obviously sees something more repellent going on here. In any case, the painting can definitely be seen as a reference to Goya's ear trouble: in middle age, Goya was struck by an illness that caused him to experience great pain in his ears; he also said that he was tormented by strange noises. The illness eventually left him deaf.

11–15: Cf. *Drowning Dog*.

16–18: Here Alberti shifts into rhyme; in order to preserve this music, contained only in particular stanzas, I have changed the line breaks.

19: Cf. *Courtyard with Lunatics*, *Madhouse*, and *Plague Hospital*.

20: The original reads "Ruedo tuerto de la alegría" (lit. "One-eyed [or cock-eyed] circle of gaiety") and may refer both to Goya's famous *Blindman's Buff*, a colorful early painting depicting children at play, and to *Gay Folly*, a later, bitter etching of a cockeyed circle of grotesque and graceless adults that parodies both *Blindman's Buff* and another early painting, *Dance on the Banks of the Manzanares*.

21: Many works in Goya's *Disasters of War* series depict people in the exaggerated poses into which great anguish can strike human beings. Luis Monguió suggests, however, that this line and the two that precede it may refer to Goya's series on bullfights, and that Alberti may be thinking here of the infirmary that exists in the bullrings to take care of the wounded bullfighters, the bullfight ring of false gaiety where so many tragedies occur, and the histrionic agony of the performing bullfighters (personal correspondence, 9 February 1992).

22: For the sake of a rhyme, I have doubled Alberti's single utterance "se cae" (lit. "to fall down").

23: During Goya's lifetime, Spain regressed from an age of enlightenment under Charles III, to a period of invasions under Charles IV, to a time of terrible political splintering under Ferdinand VII.

24: This line introduces Goya's theme of witchery and offers a transition into the next stanza, in which we may be seen to be "flying" (on the broomstick of one of the painter's witches or devils?) down the halls of the Prado, past Goya's most famous works.

27–30: Cf. Goya's paintings of these two toreros, or bullfighters, and his etchings depicting the death of Pepe-Hillo.

31–32: Cf. the famous *Dressed Maja* and *Nude Maja*, Goya's frontal views of the Duchess of Alba—with and without her clothes.

33–34: Cf. *The Family of Charles IV*. The word I have translated as "grotesque" is "esperpenticia/o," an adjective created by Alberti from the noun "esperpento," a word employed by the playwright Ramón Valle-Inclán to describe the technique of systematic distortion by which he grotesqueified reality so as to portray its essence more truthfully. Thus, Alberti is here not only describing the king and queen of Goya's royal portrait as grotesque, but also saying that Goya deliberately portrayed them this way in order to give us a truer picture of them.

36: One of the Black Paintings bears these words as an alternate title. The "Holy Office" is that of the Spanish Inquisition, still strong in Goya's lifetime. He was persecuted by the Inquisition, and depictions of some of its horrors can be found in his work.

37–39: Cf. *The Third of May, 1808*. Alberti often uses the noun "scarecrow" (and other parts of speech he creates out of it) to express his disgust, a reaction appropriate for a viewer of this painting, which depicts the bloody execution by a Napoleonic firing squad of a number of Madrid's citizens. In this case, however, the word also vividly evokes the figure of the victim at the center of the canvas, whose arms are stretched out wide and whose face wears a pathetic expression.

41–42: Cf. *Cardinal Bourbon*. Here Alberti echoes the wordplay of the Spanish poet Quevedo. The spirit of this poet, known, among other things, for the bitterness of his satire, is not inappropriately evoked by Alberti in the midst of this poem about Goya.

43: Cf. *The Meadow of San Isidro*.

44–45: Cf. *The San Isidro Pilgrimage*.

51–54: Cf. possibly *The Burial of the Sardine*.

57: The "nightly round," besides being a general description, may also refer, more specifically, to the nightwatch (the police of that time).

59: Cf. both paintings entitled *The Witches' Sabbath* (the later painting bearing this title is one of the Black Paintings). The image of the long-horned goat carries Alberti into the next stanza, although there he is referring only to the creature in the earlier painting.

61: The original Spanish reads "De dónde viene tú, gayumbo extraño, animal fino" (lit. "Where do you come from, strange *gayumbo, fino* animal"). "Fino" can mean "thin" or "delicate" or shrewd"; I chose the latter meaning because of the expression on the face of this "He-Goat Devil." "Gayumbo" is an obscure word from the realm of tauromaquia, referring to a bull who is fought while being restrained with ropes. Since the reference here is not to a bull, and most

North American readers are unlikely to come up with the specific image that these words evoke, I chose (as I did in line 59, whose Spanish original reads literally "the big-horned one") to add the word "goat," thus also gaining a rhyme.

66: The Spanish noun here is "disparate," which means "nonsense, folly, absurdity," and in the plural, is the title Goya chose for a late set of etchings.

67–68: Neither the word "nonetheless" nor the word "etchings" has a Spanish counterpart. "Nonetheless," however, merely provides a transition to "true," and "etchings" merely supplements "sketchings," naming a second type of work that Goya produced. I made these additions because each provides a rhyme, thus enabling me more closely to duplicate Alberti, who has here created a stanza dense with rhyme. It should also be noted that while I translated "real" as "true," it might also be translated as "royal," in which case "irreal / disparate real" might be seen to be speaking of the "unreal royal nonsense" of the Spanish sovereigns.

71: I added the word "milk" to this cloud description in order to gain a rhyme.

75: "Blithe as breeze" is my translation of "jubilosa" (lit. "jubilant"), a translation which is probably too much of a distortion, but which I settled on not only because it provided a rhyme but also because it conveys something of the carefree insouciance of the painting evoked by lines 73–75, *The Parasol*. *The Parasol* is a colorful, sunny, outdoors scene, representative of much of Goya's early period. In evoking it here, Alberti may be synecdochically evoking Goya's whole youthful period, thus providing a very dramatic contrast with the lines that immediately follow, which plunge the reader suddenly into a state of dark and paranoiac anxiety.

81–82: These are ironic titles, and the etchings they name are as nightmarish as the rest of the *Caprichos*. *Bon Voyage*, for example, depicts a monstrous winged creature flying through the darkness; on its back are visible four heads, whose faces are distorted by fear.

84–85: These are the only lines in the eighth stanza that do not name one of the *Caprichos*. It is possible that the lines refer to *The Burial of the Sardine*, in which the landscape itself really does look terrified: the trees' arms are outstretched, and the clouds are reeling. However, these last lines may also refer to a number of the etchings in a series that followed the *Caprichos*: *The Disasters of War*. Here are depicted many scenes having to do with burial, including one of a mass grave, and everywhere are the terrified faces of the victims.

"Delacroix"

Delacroix was a quintessential Romantic: we see this in his choice of dramatic subjects, in his flamboyant and colorful style, and in his philosophy. He believed, with the other Romantics, that art should be expressive of passion and born of inspiration. Indeed, passion and inspiration are frequently mentioned in his journal. On the former subject, he wrote, "Fine works of art never age because they are marked by genuine feeling. The language of the passions, the impulses of the heart, are always the same; what inevitably gives the stamp of age . . . are the formulae which were fashionable at the time of creation" (Prideux 176). On the latter, he wrote: "In painting, execution should always be extempore" (Prideux 177) and "Let those who work coldly keep still; do they know what it means to work under the spell of inspiration? What fear, what terror there is that you may awaken the sleeping lion whose roars shake your being to its very foundations" (Roger-Marx & Cotté 83).

For his poem about this high Romantic, Alberti has chosen the hendecasyllabic *cuarteto*, which Tomás Navarro has said was the stanza most often used in Romantic poetry (Navarro 341). I have followed Alberti in his creation of four-line rhyming stanzas, although my rhyme pattern differs from his (the *cuarteto* allows many rhyme variations), and I have further shortened the lines so that they might retain the tautness of their originals.

In addition to the fact that this form was favored by the Romantics, making it an appropriate one for Alberti's poem on Delacroix, there is, I believe, a second reason for the poet's choice of it: it is likely that he also chose this form because its very short lines convey exactly the sense of breathlessness and hurry that Alberti sees as one of the salient traits of Delacroix's oeuvre. Remember that while the poet begins his last stanza with the key word "passion," he goes on to add "in movement," and it is these words taken together that most clearly name Delacroix's work for Alberti. Remember also that Alberti originally paired this poem with his sonnet "To Movement."

"Delacroix," then, both names and manifests movement. There are a few other poems in *A la pintura* that share the form of "Delacroix," but they do not share its movement. Alberti achieves this sense of movement, we have already noted, through his use of short lines, but also, it is important to see, through the fashioning of lines that are not end-stopped, but instead flow onward, creating forward movement rather than containment. Yet a third way in which Alberti achieves a sense of movement is through a structural trick: he links the last word(s) of one stanza with the first word(s) of the next, so that the reader does not pause and then leap to the next stanza, but rather is carried smoothly along from one to another.

Let us examine how the poet effects this movement. The last line of the first stanza clearly evokes Delacroix's famous *The Abduction of Rebecca*, with its background of flaming blood-red towers, an image that carries us right into stanza 2. There it is followed by a glimpse of sky, possibly from *Christ on the Lake at Genesareth*, and then by an evocation of *The Massacre at Chios*, with its burning cities on the horizon and its piles of dead. The stanza also manages to evoke *The Boat of Dante*, in which one sees fire in the background and dead in the foreground.

The "muertos," or "dead," in the final line of stanza 2 then carry us directly into the battle imagery of the first lines of the third stanza, which may evoke for us any number of Delacroix's battle paintings, including the famous *Battle of Taillebourg*, in which, at the center of a darkly colored battle raging all around it, is a luminous white horse. If the lines do in fact bring into our minds *Battle of Taillebourg*, then its horse prepares us for, then merges smoothly with, the one Alberti mentions in the next line, which, again, may remind us of many horses painted by Delacroix, but is especially evocative of the white horse in *Tam O'Shanter*, racing madly along the coast with all its limbs spread out.

The moving flow of images from Delacroix's paintings continues to propel us forward: having just been given the image of a horse in stanza 3, we progress easily into stanza 4, which begins with mention of reins and a harness. The horse quickly drops away, however, as we are presented first with an image of the moon, and then with the name of Liberty, mention of whom finally identifies this stanza for us as an evocation of Delacroix's great *Liberty Leading the People*. In this painting the personification of freedom is shown, a goddess with her pale white breasts exposed, leading a charge. Notice that once again, through his choice of words, Alberti not only propels us from the horse of stanza 3 right into stanza 4, but also keeps us moving smoothly and quickly along here, as the white horse bare of harness blurs into an "unharnessed," or "bare," or "undressed" white moon, which blurs into bare-breasted Liberty, "risen" like the moon and now riding a "crest," or "swell," or "surge." This image of a mighty surge then carries us directly to the first words of the last stanza: "Passion in movement."

Notes on specific lines:

1: It is no accident that "color" is the first word in the poem. Delacroix is famous as a colorist. Baudelaire is known to have remarked specifically on Delacroix's color, often almost electric, which he called "scientifically supernatural" (quoted in Trapp 300). Delacroix was full of admiration for the great colorists Titian and Rubens, and he followed their lead in the value he placed on color. In his journal, he often wrote on color. Here are a few examples of his thought on the subject: "Contrary to common opinion, I would say that color has a more mysterious and perhaps more powerful influence: it acts, as one might say, without our knowledge. . . . Color is nothing if it is not suitable to the subject, and if, in imagination, it does not add to the effect of the painting. . . . Gray is the enemy of all painting. . . . Owing to its oblique position in daylight, a painting will always appear grayer than it really is: banish therefore all dull colors" (Prideaux 177).

1–3: Alberti surprises us here, where we would expect the painterly elements of color, light, and line to be grouped together, in rhetorical opposition to the human motions and emotions they express; that is, just as vehemence is said to take the form of light and urgency the form of line, so we expect to read that drama takes the form of color. Instead, Alberti pulls a switch here and says that color takes the form of drama. By doing so, he gives us both readings, since most readers will first read all of the painterly elements together before they go back and correct their initial reading. Thus he succeeds in saying not only that drama is expressed by color, but also that color is the drama, or a part of the drama, in Delacroix's paintings, a statement that further underlines for us the importance of color in Delacroix.

4: Only here, with "flight," and in line 11 with "limbs," have I added words to the original—here to gain a rhyme, and in line 11 to fill out both the image and the rhythm. Both words were suggested by the paintings these lines evoke.

18: The original reads "pintor [painter] en arrebato." "En arrebato" is more violent than "in a spin"; it means something like "in a fury." "In a spin," however, does convey a sense of whirling frenzy, the movement implicit in which not only ties in with the rest of the poem, but also leads to the poet's beautiful final image, for which, most important of all, it provides a rhyme.

"To the Nude"

"To the Nude" has been composed in iambic tetrameter. Here, however, the traditional Shakespearian octave rhyme has yielded to a different scheme (*aabb ccdd*) because in "Al desnudo" each quatrain is divided into couplets. Semicolons at the ends of the second and sixth lines mark the semantic division between the first and second couplet of each quatrain. In the second quatrain, the division is especially noticeable, for here the first couplet is a quick, breathless one, evoking an image of a fleeing nude, like the one running across the panels of Botticelli's *The Story of Nastagio degli Honesti*, prominently displayed in the Prado. The second couplet, in contrast, is calm and almost languorous, evoking an image of a nude in repose.

In this poem, notably in lines 1–4, 11, and 13, Alberti addresses the nude not as a naked female body but as flesh covering bones. Thus is the nude a "skeleton embellished," and thus can the brush, busy fleshing out the bones, be said to be simultaneously "clothing" and "unclothing."

Notes on specific lines:

3–4: "Revocada" in this context most likely does not mean "revoked" or "recalled," but here takes on its secondary meaning, "newly plastered or painted." In this sense, the verb is always used to describe the brightening of the exterior walls of a building, an action that Alberti saw performed with whitewash many times in his native Andalusia. Hence my translation, "newly / whitewashed," which captures for the English reader the sense of something dazzlingly standing out from its background, which is, in fact, exactly what the bather's white flesh does against the dark background in which Renoir has set her in the painting that illustrates "Al desnudo" in the 1968 edition of *A la pintura*.

8: The line reads "sueño palpable de la forma plena" (lit. "palpable dream of the full form"). Here I have capitalized "form" to bring out the latent reference to the Platonic notion of ideal Forms, and have used "expressed" to emphasize the nude's act of reification—her flesh reifies the doubly abstract "dream" of the "form"—which is the heart of the line.

11: The "tram" is the silk thread used for the weft in the weaving of the best fabrics.

"Cézanne"

Cézanne's biographer Lionello Venturi says that the painter's work was "conceived as if meant to be seen from a distance" (Venturi 60). This is true of many Impressionist works: up close the paintings can seem chaotic and formless, but from a distance the painted images emerge and become clear. Alberti, as is his way, has imitated this quality in the construction of his poem on Cézanne. In the midst of reading it, one feels that it does not cohere: like the brushstrokes of a closely viewed Cézanne painting, the stanzas all seem to be going in different directions; however, having finished the poem and stood back from it, so to speak, one realizes that a solid impression of the subject has emerged.

Alberti's poem is also like Cézanne's work in that it abjures conventionality. Although there is much rhyme, no single rhyme scheme is followed, and neither the stanzas themselves nor the lines within them possess a uniform length.

The translation has duplicated this irregularity, imitating Alberti's imitation of a painter whose effects were achieved not through a reliance on classical forms, but rather through the creation of his own harmony.

In Cézanne's work, this harmony which does not arise out of regularity is partially created by tonal unity. So it is in Alberti's poem. Here, though the verses may be irregular and the stanzas may be pursuing different subjects, a single tone binds the poem together. This tone emerges from the consistent presentation of Cézanne as one for whom painting was a struggle; who, in Venturi's words, never "surrendered to the joy of painting" but "who thought, and thought profoundly, about his art"; who worked out and amplified a vision of his own "through hard work and perseverance" (Venturi 73). Gustave Geffroy, who in 1894 prepared the first serious and important study of Cézanne, wrote that "the works of Cézanne . . . tell of the straining towards reality, of patience, long exertion, artistic integrity, and a scrupulousness not easily satisfied" (quoted in Venturi 36). This is precisely the view of Cézanne given us by the poem, whose stanzas, despite their varying subjects, all contribute to our sense of the laboriousness of Cézanne's toil. It is, if we may judge from biographical sources, an accurate picture of the painter that we are given here; it is also one that articulates a relationship to art which Alberti, himself a fluent, prolific, and often playful artist, must have found fascinatingly alien—which perhaps accounts for his poem's emphasis on the artist's attitude toward his art.

Notes on specific lines:

4: "landscape": As a young man, Cézanne wrote to his friend Émile Zola, "None of the pictures painted indoors, in the studio, will ever equal the things painted out of doors. . . . I see some superb things, and I must resolve to do nothing but open-air painting" (quoted in Venturi 30). Cézanne did come to spend most of the days of his mature years planted humbly in front of a landscape, translating his sensations to images. He died as the result of pneumonia, contracted after having become thoroughly chilled while painting out in the Aix countryside in late October.

5: In line 5, "La plástica, diaria, muda vida" (lit. "the plastic, daily, mute life"), "plástica" means both formative (fashioning, creative) and that which is capable of being formed (malleable); thus, the line points to both the artist and the work of art. Since the English word "plastic," currently associated in our minds primarily with what is fake, cheap, and junky, may not be relied upon to communicate the double sense of the Spanish "plástica," I used "still life," whose pun enabled me to refer both to the artist's process and to his product.

13: The words "of coloring" are my addition; with them, I hoped to shed some light on Alberti's invocation of Cézanne as a "primary god" and to add the richness of a pun to the word "primary."

18–27: Though this stanza, too, speaks of attitude and process, it also gives us one of the few descriptions we receive of what a Cézanne canvas actually looks like. It is an accurate and knowledgeable description. Cézanne's most learned critics have pointed out the same things about his work. Venturi, for example, writes that Cézanne's colors were "applied in short, separate touches, running in different directions" (Venturi 74), and he speaks thus of Cézanne's *The Card Players* (1890–92): "From the infinite gradations of [his] colours arise the volumes of figures and things. . . . Continuous outlines would have isolated the figures; instead, they hold together because, like the table and the background, they are built up with zones of colour. By means of this rhythmic composition of colour zones, he substitutes modulation for modelling" (Venturi 126). Alberti's description is also noteworthy because the particular disposition of the words on the page, in its last six lines, reinforces what the words are saying.

28, 36–38: Cézanne's single most famous pronouncement on painting is contained in a letter to his friend Émile Bernard: "Treat nature in terms of the cylinder, the sphere, and the cone, the whole being put into perspective, so that each side of an object and a plane is directed towards a central point. The lines parallel to the horizon give breadth. . . . The lines perpendicular to this horizon give depth. But nature for us men is more depth than surface. Hence the necessity of introducing into our vibrations of light, represented by reds and yellows, a sufficient amount of bluish tones in order to give the feeling of air" (quoted in Venturi 117–18).

30: From his middle years onward, Cézanne became more and more interested in form. A contemporary critic had this to say about his later work: "Of nature he gives a version all his own in which the juxtaposition of hues and the arrangement of lines make his so forthright painting a kind of synthesis of colours and forms in their intrinsic beauty. It is as if he wished to restore to each object its original form, intact, not devitalized by art practices, its true and essential lustre" (quoted in Venturi 40). The other Impressionists also became increasingly interested in form, and their work began to lead them into new artistic territories, but it was Cézanne who made the major contribution to twentieth-century art. His decision to work toward a new organization of forms in which the structure of the images became more volumetric and abstract, and his experiments with multiple perspective, in which objects were shown from different angles in order to convey the fullness of their volume, contributed much to the development of new trends in art, including that of Cubism.

33: "Clavada" is the adjective Alberti used to describe what the sky-aspiring paintbrush/thorn does to the hand holding it. It means, literally, "pricking, stabbing," and I have translated it as "tearing" to convey a sense of its movement. "Clavada" is also a form of the verb "clavar," and there is a popular expression in Spanish that contains this verb: "clavar los ojos en" (lit. "to fix one's eyes on, to gaze"). I think that the poet expected many readers to think of this expression, thereby associating the idea of gazing with the wounding motion described by "clavada," and that this was one of the reasons he chose "clavada" rather than another adjective. Because this connection between the painter's suffering and his gaze is an important one, and one that dovetails with the last two lines of the stanza, I have incorporated it into my translation of lines 34–35, "doblado / mártir de la retina" (lit. "bent [or 'bowed, stooped'] martyr of the retina"), offering to the English reader "martyr to a retina, gaze-worn."

34: The poet perhaps picked Saint Sebastian rather than another martyr because Sebastian was killed by arrows, and the shape of an arrow is similar to that of a paintbrush.

35: In addition to expressing the idea that Cézanne was a kind of victim of his gaze, a martyr to its intensity and duration, and to the uniqueness of his vision, just as he was the prisoner of his own conceptions of painting, "mártir de la retina" probably also alludes to Joris Karl Huysmans's famous comment on Cézanne: "A revealing colourist who contributed more than Monet to the Impressionist movement, an artist with diseased retinas who in the overwrought apperception of his eyesight discovered the foretokens of a new art—thus we may perhaps sum up this too much forgotten painter, Monsieur Cézanne" (quoted in Venturi 35). In the introduction to her book on Cézanne, Anna Barskaya notes that, affected by this criticism and cognizant of the originality of his particular vision of the world, "Cézanne himself was very near to believing that his sight was defective and ascribed to it the fact that 'the planes overlap each other' while 'absolutely vertical lines seemed to me to be falling'" (Barskaya 44).

36–38: See note to line 28. Alberti's "cubo . . . cilindro y . . . esfera" has been changed to conform to Cézanne's language. As a final thought, it is interesting to note that just as Cézanne's art theory lies outside of an oeuvre that exists whole and complete without it, and was articulated at the end of his life, so Alberti's stanza on Cézanne's theory comes at the very end of a poem that would have been complete without it.

"To Grace"

"To Grace" has been composed in iambic pentameter. The octave rhyme of its original has been converted into Shakespearian octave rhyme, but the original's sestet rhyme has been retained.

This sonnet may be said to belong to that class of poems in the European tradition that are portraits of a lady. Here, the lady is a personification of the quality of grace; indeed, she is probably one of the Graces of Greek mythology, who were themselves but simple personifications: "With you," Pindar says to them, "all becomes sweetness and charm." With reference to the fact that Alberti addresses her as "fino relámpago" (lit. "fine lightning"), it is interesting to note that the most celebrated sanctuary of the Graces was at Orchomenus in Boetia, where they were worshipped in the form of meteors.

In making his portrait of the lady, Alberti describes her breast in the first stanza, her back in the second, and her smile in the third. At the same time, the stanzas each describe different aspects of grace: stanza 1 speaks of its loveliness, stanza 2 of its fleetingness, stanza 4 of its lack of self-consciousness and self-indulgence. Stanza 3 speaks of a less considered aspect of grace: its quickness, dazzle, witty aplomb. Spanish dictionaries actually list "wittiness" and "amusing quality" as definitions of grace. For English speakers, however, the connection between grace and funniness is more recondite, and therefore line 11 ("burladora, inefable travesura"), which reads literally in English "trickster, ineffable prank," presented a problem: how could I translate "burladora" so that an English speaker would link it with the notion of grace? It is the sprightly, graceful trickster Puck who provided the bridge between "burladora" and "grace." Moreover, with Puck in mind, an English reader, I hoped, would understand how a prank could be raised to the level of art, which is, I think, the meaning of "inefable travesura."

Notes on specific lines:

1: Here I have departed from the original and named the addresssee, thus creating a rhyme. The addressee, however, is ambiguous: Alberti is speaking in this poem both to the quality of grace itself, and to this quality embodied, that is, to a Grace. In order to preserve this ambiguity, therefore, I have not placed "grace" immediately after "embodied," for this would call to mind only "a Grace"; instead, I have dropped the line, thus allowing the reader to perceive "grace" on its own, as well as linked to "embodied."

6–8: The lines read "sal que aletea / y . . . en vuelo delinea / tu fugitiva . . . espalda, diosa" (lit. "charm that flaps its wings and in flight delineates your fleeing back, goddess"). I have taken these lines to mean, first, that her charm is connected with her fleetingness, and second, that her own flight is like a bird's flight, but I have also tried to preserve the sense of metamorphosis suggested here: charm → bird in flight → fleeing goddess.

"Renoir"

Alberti's "Renoir" is a soft, flowing composition. The poem slips easily from line to line; there are only a few genuinely full stops in it. The liquid sounds of the poem augment the reader's sense of its fluidity. It is, furthermore, a light poem: no heavy or harsh sounds or images weigh it down. All this is, of course, in imitation of the painter, whose light, airy, graceful compositions contain no sharp edges: all is soft and flowing.

In order to preserve these qualities, I have, in translating "Renoir," made two major changes in its form. First, I have taken it out of its "block" form and spilled it into horizontally cascading verses, because, for the reader of English in this post-Pound and post-Williams age, stichic poetry daunts the eye, and certainly does not communicate a sense of loose, flowing movement. Second, in a very similar action, I have created five stanza breaks, while the poet created only one; this was another way of unclotting the poem. The breaks have been made after each of the full stops I mentioned; thus, they merely underline pauses the poet already wanted us to make.

The poem has no formal rhyme scheme, but is full of verbal music, containing rhyme, repetition, alliteration, and assonance. My translation has only one end rhyme, but I, too, have employed repetition, alliteration, and assonance. The original's line lengths are irregular; so are the translation's.

"Renoir" celebrates the beauty of the colors in Renoir's paintings, and the ubiquity of rose. Rose is found frequently in Renoir, especially in the dresses worn by his subjects (see, for example, *Children on the Seashore, Dancing at the Moulin de la Galette,* and *The Music Lesson*), in the flowers of his still lifes, and in the faces of his women, themselves so much like flowers. Here, Alberti celebrates even the rose of the heels and buttocks painted by Renoir! English fortunately shares with Spanish its double sense of "rose" as both a color and a flower, a double meaning that informs the whole poem.

238

Notes on specific lines:

17: "Bougainvillea" has replaced "carnation" as the dream of deep red because North America, unlike the South of Spain, has few fields of deep red carnations. Indeed, if "carnation" brings to the North American mind any particular color at all, it is probably the pale flesh tone whose name is "carnation" in most of the crayon boxes manufactured in this country; for those who know Latin, the link between "carnation" and flesh is even stronger. "Bougainvillea," on the other hand, does evoke a deep vermilion color and is, moreover, a flower that also grows in Spain.

20: "In its sleep" has been added to the original to make gentler a line that would otherwise strike too harsh a note: the rules of English syntax require that the translation of "¿Se murió el color negro?" (lit. "Did the color black die?") end with the word "die," though the original (closing instead merely with the word "black") does not end this way. In addition to preserving the tone, moreover, "in its sleep" ties in thematically with the previous lines, reinforcing the poet's evocation of sleeping, dreaming colors.

27–29: Perhaps more than any other lines, these manifest the effect upon my work of Ezra Pound's maxim that a translation must remain essential, that it must wring out all excess like water is wrung out of a sponge.

38–40: I have taken this out of the passive—a less acceptable form in English than in Spanish—and have attributed the action to the eye of the painter (mentioned in line 33).

"White"

Unlike the other poems to colors, "White" repeats a single image several times—that of the lime-whitewashed wall, ubiquitous in Andalusia. Clearly, Alberti's first fifteen years in Puerto del Santa María, outside Cádiz, so firmly imprinted this image in his mind that it is his major association with the color white.

Notes on specific items:

1: This translation is an interpretation. I have taken the original, "soy / la imprescindible sangre para el justo / clarear de la luz en los colores" (lit. "I am the indispensable blood for the just clarification [or 'illumination'] of light in the colors") to be referring to the fact that it is white that lightens the colors sufficiently for them to be differentiated from each other. For example, dark green, dark purple, and dark blue may, in their paint jars, all look like almost identical blackish pigments, but add white to them and, as if lit from within, they reveal their separate identities.

13: I have added the image of the hand, implicit in the Spanish.

14: Here Alberti is using "nocturne" in both its musical and its painterly sense—that is, as a term that denotes both a musical composition evocative of the night, and a painting that depicts a night scene.

16: The precatory language and the reference to "Brother Indigo" recall Alberti's earlier poem "Giotto," and therefore suggest that Alberti may intend for us to understand that white is speaking here of the kind of work which the poet imagines it to have performed for Giotto, who created special shades of blue and rose.

19: In the middle of the center panel of Uccello's *The Rout of San Romano* is a huge white horse, rampant. Uccello (whose name means "bird" in his native Italian) is best known for this painting, but he is also remembered for his study of perspective, which became an obsession with him. Indeed, art critics suggest that Uccello never realized his full potential as a painter because he was always distracted by problems of perspective. Giorgio Vasari's *Lives of the Most Excellent Italian Architects, Painters, and Sculptors* is the source of the well-known and highly illustrative story that tells how Uccello, having spent the entire night in his study working out the vanishing points of his perspective, when finally summoned to bed by his wife, replied only, "How fair a thing is this perspective!"

22: "Dawn's light" is from "alba," which has an additional meaning in Spanish that Alberti undoubtedly hoped to evoke: "alb," the pure white linen vestment worn at the Eucharist.

25: This item refers to Brueghel's famous snow scene, *The Return of the Hunters*.

27: White neckruffs and white flames are everywhere evident in El Greco's masterpiece *The Burial of Count Orgaz*. The lack of punctuation here is in imitation of the Spanish original.

28: There are many white-cloaked monks and much white crockery in Zurbarán's paintings, but Alberti may be thinking here of one painting in particular, which includes all of the familiar elements—white habits, white plates, and a white cloth: *Saint Bruno and the Miracle of the Uneaten Meat*.

29: In Spanish, "blanco" ("white") is also another word for "target," and the phrase "dar en el blanco" means "to hit the mark." Thus, when Alberti has white say that it is "dispuesto a dar / en el blanco" (lit. "disposed to hit the mark"), a Spanish reader, seeing "white" in "target," understands that white is saying it is drawn to itself. It can only be hoped that readers of the English translation will picture to themselves that type of target whose bull's-eye is white!

"Van Gogh"

One of the most striking things about this poem is that so many of its lines are composed of single words: thus does the poet imitate Van Gogh, whose brush-strokes each stand out separately, discrete, isolate. Another way in which the poem imitates some of Van Gogh's paintings is in its lack of balance and order: not only are the stanzas of all different lengths, but the poem does not progress logically; the reader receives from the rapid progression of images in the poem a sense of richness, but also a sense of confusion and even, at one point, of hysteria.

As has been noted before, in addition to conveying to the reader an overall sense of the oeuvre of the painter being addressed, many of the poems to painters also contain references to specific paintings. In "Van Gogh," some of the allusions are quite clear: stanza 2 refers to *Starry Night*, stanza 4 to the more repellent of his sunflower paintings (Paris, 1887), and stanza 5 combines a reference to one of his wheatfield paintings with a reference to *Gaugin's Armchair*.

While Alberti's "Van Gogh" has no formal rhyme scheme, every end word rhymes with another in the poem, even if the two rhyming words are not in the same stanza. The poet has rhymed wherever possible; so have I.

Notes on specific lines:

1: Van Gogh painted in the blazing Midi sun hatless, and suffered from the light and heat.

25: Van Gogh often applied paint not with a brush, but with a palette knife.

31: "Weld," the literal translation of the Spanish "gualda," is a yellow dye from Holland.

37: In the original, the grammatical stop comes one line later: a period separates the humble chair from the yellow candle and flower. By placing a colon between the nightmare and the chair, I have made a clearer distinction between the two different paintings referred to here (the wheatfield painting and *Gaugin's Armchair*, the latter of which contains a chair, a candle, and a flower), yet have kept the link between them that Alberti clearly wanted. This link is ambiguous. Is the poet suggesting that the nightmare occurred as Van Gogh sat in this chair? That it was brought on by the violent end to his friendship with Gaugin, here associated with his chair? In any case, the nightmare is a "mortal" dream, an intimation of mortality. The words "knife," "gore," and "violent" in the previous stanza help to prepare the reader for this intimation, just as "mortal" here prepares the reader for the death alluded to in the stanza that follows.

51: After the colon, the original reads "alta, / la estela." "Alta" may be translated as either "high" or "superior," and "estela" as either a "wake, track" or a "monument." Moreover, "estela," when combined with the notion of height in "alta," brings to a Spanish reader's mind the common word "estrella" ("star"). Bearing all this in mind, I have translated "alta, / la estela" as "starry wake," hoping that "starry" will remind the reader of *Starry Night*, and that this allusion to a painting that is certainly a superior and lasting monument to its creator will bring to the line the requisite richness.

"To Watercolor"

"To Watercolor" has been composed in iambic tetrameter. As always, the original's sestet rhyme scheme has been retained, while its octave rhyme scheme has been altered to a scheme more suited to English. Here, as in "To the Nude," however, this scheme is not Shakespearian octave rhyme but an *aabb ccdd* rhyme, chosen because the octave contains "semantic couplets." In this case, the first two lines of each quatrain, separated from the last two by a period, name and describe watercolor, while the last two lines of each quatrain tell what watercolor is from the point of view of the watercolorist's materials.

In order to maintain the rather short tetrameter lines, a few changes have been made. First, the standard "To you" at the sestet's beginning has been changed to "through you" and moved down a line. I have also twice telescoped words: line 9's "acequias y atanores" (lit. "irrigation ditches and drains") has been changed to "irrigated tracts," and lines 12–13's "creces, / . . . te agotas" (lit. "you expand, you expend yourself") has been changed to "you . . . become diffused." In order to maintain rhyme, I have slightly altered the order of items in lines 1–2, and have transformed "you dawn" into "you . . . : dawn's sun" in line 13.

In the octave, Alberti addresses watercolor itself—that is, that kind of paint whose liquid is a water dispersion of the binding material contained (as opposed to oil paint). In the sestet, he also begins to address a nymph who is the embodiment of the art of watercolor. It is thus that he can say in line 12, addressing both the nymph and the watery paint, who are each "watercolor": "Wept from your own eyes, you run. . . . "

Notes on specific lines:

3: "Wetted" is from "abrevadora," a word often used in connection with the watering of cattle. Thus, a Spanish reader might understand not only that the watercolorist's paper is like a wetted brow, but might receive also an image of the paper's brow drinking up the water, as do cattle at a trough.

7: Two meanings of "cabellera," "long hair" and "comet's tail," have been brought together here to create an image of tailed hair, or "hair, close-tied," a phrase applicable to a paintbrush.

12–13: In order to reinforce the meaning of "you run," the image of the wept and running watercolor, here, as in the original, is deliberately made to run into the next image, in which the watercolor, now joyfully spreading, is seen to be a dawning sun.

"To Divine Proportion"

"To Divine Proportion" has been composed, for the most part, in iambic pentameter. Here, as always, the original's sestet rhyme scheme has been retained while its octave scheme has been altered to one more suited to English. For the first time, however, I have employed two different types of rhyme within the octave: the first stanza uses cross-rhyme (traditional Shakespearian octave rhyme) and the second uses couplet rhyme. This unusual mid-octave substitution was provoked by my discovery of two couplet rhymes that very accurately convey the meaning of the Spanish original. The reader may reflect that a sonnet dedicated to Divine Proportion is hardly the place in which to create unmatching quatrains. However, I was, in a sense, following Alberti's lead, for he has already made this sonnet different from all the others in *A la pintura:* here, he deliberately does not conclude with the words "de la Pintura" (lit. "of Painting") as he has in each sonnet throughout the book. This moment of asymmetry in a poem about proportion is probably more than an ironic joke; Alberti is probably trying to remind the reader that certain disproportions within a work do not necessarily create a disharmonious whole. It is, in fact, precisely this point that Alberti wishes to convey through his pairing of "To Divine Proportion" with "Picasso."

We understand proportion not just as a relationship between parts, but especially as a harmonious or symmetrical relationship between parts. During times such as the Classical Age and the Renaissance, proportion, like other sorts of harmony, was often said to be "divine" or "golden" because its existence seemed to point to an ordered universe. There actually exists a work called *Divina Proportione*, written in 1498 by a certain Luca Pacioli, who, moreover, in his dedicatory letter, mentions a newly completed treatise on painting by Leonardo, a fact crucial to historians in their attempt to date Leonardo's *Trattato della Pittura*. This famous treatise contains a whole section on the proportions of the human figure and is a classic source of our information about proportion. It seems likely, then, that Alberti chose to modify "proportion" with "divine" not only because it is a fitting adjective and one traditionally associated with proportion, but also because "divine proportion, through Luca Pacioli, is associated with Leonardo's definitive work on this subject.

Notes on specific lines:

2: The original reads "media, extrema razón de la hermosura" (lit. "mean, extreme reason for [or, ratio of] beauty"). The English line loses the mean/extreme contrast, choosing to concentrate instead on "razón," offering both of the meanings this word would evoke for a Spanish reader, each of which is relevant in this context.

2–5: Here Alberti is playing with the paradox that the rigid set of rules which govern proportion may give rise to voluptuous beauty, that within the narrow confines dictated by mathematic formulas, fluid life abounds.

6: The "golden section" is known to students of geometry; it is created when a line so bisects another as to create two uneven line segments (A and B) whose ratio to each other (A to B) is equal to the ratio of the entire line to the longer segment (A + B to A). "Squaring up to scale" is my translation of "cuadratura," known to painters as the process by which a design occupying a small space may be copied onto a larger space while maintaining the original proportions; this is achieved by dividing both the small design and the large space into the same number of quadrants and then transferring the content of each small quadrant into its corresponding quadrant in the larger space. English-speaking painters often simply call the process "squaring up."

10: The "five regular forms," also known as the "five Platonic solids," are the tetrahedron, the octahedron, and the icosahedron (each of whose faces is an equilateral triangle), the hexahedron (each of whose faces is a square), and the dodecahedron (each of whose faces is a regular pentagon). In the light of the fact that the dodecahedron is traditionally listed as the last of the five regular forms, it can be seen that the poem moves smoothly from line 10 to line 11, just as it later does from line 11 to line 12, where it moves from "arc" to "compass."

12: The Spanish reads "Luces por alas un compas ardiente" (lit. "You light [or, light up, show] by means of your wings an ardent [or, burning] compass"). The line is evocative, but difficult to pin down. With "wings," the poet may be alluding to the quality of soaring beauty possessed by divine proportion, and "compass" may be a synecdoche for geometry and drawing, disciplines "set on fire" by the articulation of the principles of proportion.

13: It is interesting to note that, while line 14 is not consistent with the last lines of the other sonnets in the collection, line 13 does recall at least two other penultimate lines (line 13 of "To Line" and line 13 of "To Perspective") and one antepenultimate line (line 12 of "To Clothing"), each of which is about singing.

14: The words Alberti substituted for his traditional sonnet-ending "de la Pintura" are "de oro." The entire Spanish line reads "A ti, divina proporción de oro" (lit. "To you, divine proportion of gold"). The appearance of "gold" here is appropriate because, as I have said above, "golden" has been traditionally linked with "proportion," as it has been with many symmetrical constructs, including that named in line 6, the "golden section." The reader will note, however, that the translation expands a little on the poet's association of "divine proportion" with "gold": I have added the words "from dark." This addition secures the important final rhyme. Thus the poem ends with a phrase not originally in it but extrapolated from it, linking "divine proportion"—in a manner inspired by all those who, like Alberti, have celebrated it—with the emergence of beauty and order from chaos, gold from dark.

"Picasso"

"Picasso" is a special poem for Alberti because he not only loved and admired the painter's work, but also knew him personally. Indeed, he dedicated the whole of *A la pintura* to Picasso. At the time the book was first published in 1948, however, Alberti was not yet a close friend of Picasso; it was later that a lasting friendship developed between the older and the younger man. Eventually, Alberti came to write four different works on Picasso, which he ultimately drew together under the title *Lo que canté y dije de Picasso* (*What I've Sung and Said about Picasso*) (Barcelona: Broguera, 1981). This collection includes: his book of poems *Los 8 nombres de Picasso* (*The 8 Names of Picasso*) (Barcelona: Kairos, 1970), in which *A la pintura*'s poem on Picasso has been included, although its title has been changed from "Picasso" to "De azul se arrancó el toro" ("Out of Blue Charged the Bull"), a line from the first section of the poem; *Visitas a Picasso* (*Visits to Picasso*), a record of some of his visits to the painter between 1968 and 1972; "Picasso en Aviñón" ("Picasso in

Avignon"), the introduction to a book of that title published by Le Cercle d'Art (Paris, 1970); "Picasso, o el rayo que no cesa" ("Picasso, or The Ray Which Does Not Cease"), the introduction to *Le rayon ininterrompu* (*The Interrupted Ray*; Paris: Le Cercle d'Art, 1972). In addition to all these works, Alberti also composed a special painted poem for the frontispiece of the 1968 edition of *A la pintura*, inscribing it to "the poet, Pablo Picasso." It is accompanied by a design by Picasso, which he in turn has inscribed to "the painter, Rafael Alberti."

"Picasso" strives to be true to the spirit of the painter it honors: abjuring classical tradition, it has no set pattern of rhythm and rhyme, although there is much rhyme throughout the poem. Rather, it is "modern": that is, first, the reader is unable to place it within a tradition and cannot use his or her knowledge of the tradition in order to reach an understanding of the poem, but recognizing that the poem is a world unto itself, must come to an understanding of it through a study of its internal patterns and repetitions, of the rules it has created for itself; second, it is at times somewhat disorienting, both semantically, when it is fragmented or elliptical, and spatially, due to the irregular pattern it makes on the page, the result of dropped lines, stair-stepped lines, varying margins, stanzas of all different lengths, and spaces between letters. The poem is also like Picasso's work in that it puts together things that are ordinarily not found side by side. Just as Picasso's Collage Cubism juxtaposes on the same canvas a painted representation of an object and an actual object, such as a piece of wood or linoleum, so Alberti's poem juxtaposes on the same page a stanza of heavily metaphorical poetry and a list of titles of paintings (lines 30–43). The feature of the poem that is most reminiscent of Picasso's work, however, is its structure, for "Picasso" is a poem that moves through many different phases, each of which has its own rhythm and inner coherence. The transitions between these phases are often quite abrupt as the poem keeps changing, moving forward, occasionally taking up a previous theme again, until finally everything is brought together in the climax of the Guernica section.

The poem moves chronologically. Its one hundred lines take us from the birth of Picasso to 1937, the year in which his work culminated in *Guernica*. The first four stanzas evoke Picasso's Andalusian background, generally forgotten but of great importance to Alberti, who is himself an Andalusian. Here the poet links the deep blue of the sky and sea of the painter's birthplace, the popular seaport town of Málaga, with the blue that charges so many of the painter's works. He also links the perpetual presence of the guitar in the oeuvre of Picasso with its omnipresence in Southern Spain, and finally, most important, he introduces here the theme of the bull, ancient symbol of Spain, and in this poem, a symbol of the painter as well.

It is interesting to note at this point what Alberti later chose to observe about Picasso's roots: "Toda esa claridad, locura, gracia, pasión, arrebato, arbitrariedad, esa chufla y burla violenta se las debe Picasso sin duda . . . a su infancia malagueña. Como yo . . . le debo al mar de Cádiz toda la sustancia de mi poesía" ("All that clarity, craziness, grace, passion, fury, arbitrariness, those violent taunts and jokes—Picasso owes them without doubt to his childhood in Málaga. As I owe to the sea of Cádiz all the substance of my poetry") (Alberti, *Lo que canté* 143). Alberti also speaks of the importance of the guitar, "este instrumento profundamente arábigo-andaluz" ("this profoundly Arabic-Andalusian instrument"), and of the "rasgueos y ayes de cante jondo para aquel niño que en los patios profundos de Málaga lo escuchó entre los limoneros y el cercano vaivén de las olas mediterráneas" ("guitar-strummings and moans of the Cante Jondo for that child who, within the deep patios of Málaga, heard it all, among the lemon trees, beside the ebb and flow of the Mediterranean waves"). Finally, noting playfully that "en Andalucía todos nacemos toreros" ("in Andalusia we are all born bullfighters"), Alberti later goes on to speak of what the bull has often come to mean for Picasso, for himself, for many Spanish artists: the bull, he says, becomes "el símbolo de la bravura del pueblo español, de su potencia creadora" ("the symbol of the bravery of the Spanish people, of their creative power") (Alberti, *Lo que canté* 238–39, 142, 226).

Picasso's earliest known painting is a bullfighting picture, *The Picador* (1889–90). In his early years, and indeed throughout his career, Picasso depicted many aspects of the spectacle of the bullfight. Art historians, however, usually begin their histories of Picasso's career with mention of his turn-of-the-century Blue and Rose periods. Alberti, too, having spoken of Picasso's background and formation, and then mentioned his name for the first time, makes his first specific reference to Picasso's work in his "blue and rose" stanza. Here he alludes to the well-known *Woman Ironing* (1904) of Picasso's Blue period, and conflates different images from the paintings of his Rose period, drawing particularly from *Young Female Nude and Nude Child with a Goat* (1906).

The next section, beginning with line 30, speaks of Picasso's Cubist period, which spans the next decade of his life. It wonders at its conception, names several crucial titles from that period (or approximations of titles!), and speculates over what is lost and what is gained with Cubism. The poem then mentions "upheaval," "stiff shrouds," and "abysses," which John Walsh has interpreted as a reference to Picasso's transition to Collage Cubism, at which time his canvases began to be three-dimensional, to have lacquered objects mounded on them, to appear like flat maps that had suddenly become topographical, complete with rises separated from each other by dipping abysses. The verses of this section then list the most frequently used elements of Collage Cubism, and finally bring the section to an end by naming the artistic phase it has been describing.

The poem then speaks of Picasso's departure from Cubism, taking up again the strand of its story in which the painter is a bull. Here the bull/painter sees a way out of his trap by envisioning scenes outside of the arena in which he finds himself. The scenes named here are from the very paintings Picasso created at the time he was breaking away from strict Cubism, the paintings of his Monumental period: *Bathers* (1918), *Three Bathers* (1920), *Three Women at the Spring* (1921), and *Women Running on the Beach* (1922). The following stanza (lines 69–75) underscores the link that has already been made between the painter (born a bullfighter, as Alberti said, because he was born an Andalusian) and the bull.

The next stanza covers that phase of Picasso's work in which the studio is one of his favorite subjects, and in which the various anatomical parts of his studio models are deliberately displaced. Lines 79–82 refer to the painting of this period entitled *The Dance* (1925).

Line 83, the single word "Monsters" (as well as the two dropped lines following it which modify it), is a transitional line which most likely refers both backward, to the grotesque women of *The Dance* and to other paintings of that period mentioned just above, and forward, to lines 86–88, which may be loosely descriptive of Picasso's creative ventures into artistically foreign territory, but which probably also allude to the next phase of his work, in which he became involved with the theme of the minotaur. It is possible that Alberti is thinking in particular of the *Vollard Suite* (1934), four prints on the theme of a blind minotaur, guided on a magical expedition by a young girl. The last three lines of this stanza are probably a reference to a new creative development in the career of Picasso: the writing of automatic poetry. It was toward the end of 1935 that Picasso's association with the Surrealists led him to compose a quantity of automatic poetry joined to illustration; the illustrations were sometimes just colorful, curving marginal doodles.

The subject of the final section of the poem is what, for Alberti, writing in exile in 1948, and for many still today, is the culmination of Picasso's work: *Guernica* (1937). Here the poet uses to great dramatic effect that link between the Spanish bull, the Spanish people, and the Spanish painter Picasso that he has already forged in the reader's mind. Alberti then ends the poem with a brief statement about the power of *Guernica*. It is clear that as far as he is concerned this work is both a high point and a turning point. Many years after *Guernica* was completed, responding to Picasso's declaration that he had painted many works that spoke out against authoritarianism and violence, Alberti said, "El

grito más agudo lo diste con *Guernica*" ("You cried out most sharply in *Guernica*").
He also spoke of *Guernica* to Picasso as a "síntesis suprema de todos tus anhelos,
tus deseos de paz, de libertad" ("supreme synthesis of all your yearnings, your
desires for peace, for liberty") and as a work that gives "el alerto cada día, cada
aurora del mundo" ("the alert each day, each dawn of the world") (Alberti, *Lo que
canté* 243–44). Finally, Alberti has always valued *Guernica* as the first mani-
festation of Picasso's political awakening, the first product of a new awareness,
jolted into being by the horror of the Fascists' war on Spain, an awareness that
was to guide Picasso's actions throughout the remaining decades of his life.

In my translation of "Picasso," I have tried to duplicate the changing rhythms
and the ample, schemeless rhyme. In pursuit of the latter, I have occasionally
even privileged sound over meaning where such a choice was necessary and,
less radically, have changed the order of items in a list; a few times I have extrap-
olated from the original text. In accordance with my usual practice, I have also
tried to keep the poem as tight as possible, and to this end have employed
ampersands where appropriate, and have abbreviated "ed" to "'d" in those cases
where the "e" is silent. Finally, I have adhered strictly to the spatial presentation
of the original, imitating the varying margins and the dropped lines, and main-
taining the poet's particular distribution of the lines into stanzas.

Notes on specific lines:

4–6: Here I have tried to make up for the loss of the ambiguity of the orig-
inal (in which "de azul" can mean "out of blue," "from blue," or "made of blue,"
and can modify "bull" as well as give an indication of whence the bull is charg-
ing) by making use of the possibilities offered by English: I capitalized on the
existence of our phrase "out of the blue," and on the double meaning of our verb
"charged."

9–20: In the original, lines 10, 11, 12, and 13, and lines 17, 18, and 19 rhyme
with "España." Except for line 10, "fina tela de araña" (lit. "delicate web of the
spider")—which, given the word "guitar" in line 7 as well as the distinctive
sound of this stanza, may be a reference to Lorca's lovely image of the guitar-
strumming hand creating in the air a pattern like a spiderweb—the lines of the
first stanza have little semantic value and appear to have been constructed with
the sole purpose of providing rhymes for "España." Similarly, beyond conveying
a somewhat cloudy notion of influence, constraint, and then freedom, the sec-
ond stanza, too, is largely sound-poetry. John Walsh has found in this sound-
poetry, these repeated "ñ" sounds, the music of the Cante Jondo, or "Deep
Song," the ancient voice-and-guitar flamenco music of Andalusia, and has sug-
gested that Alberti is here evoking Spain not only by naming it and rhyming on

it, but also by re-creating the sound of its traditional music. I puzzled over how to translate these lines, realizing the difficulty of conveying the sound of Cante Jondo with English words while simultaneously rhyming on the word "Spain," and suspecting that not many readers of English poetry would recognize the Cante Jondo sound even if I were able to duplicate it! I finally decided that I must take a less oblique approach than Alberti did: I would not "evoke" Cante Jondo, I would name it; I would not allude subtly to the Lorca line, I would incorporate it; and so on. I also decided to employ the rhyme words semantically, hoping, in the first stanza, to fill out "Spain" a little in the reader's mind, and in the second, to sharpen Alberti's suggestions about the nature of Spain's influence on Picasso. These stanzas, then, were more transformed than translated; in fact, one line was even shifted from the first stanza to the second.

22: "Maternités," a French translation of the Spanish original, "maternidad," is the word most art historians use to denote the series of paintings from Picasso's Blue period that depict a mother and child.

84–85: The original Spanish lines, "¡Oh monstruos, razón de la pintura, / sueño de la Poesía!" (lit. "Oh monsters, reason of painting / dream of poetry!"), allude to words by Goya, a painter not inappropriately evoked in a description of Picasso's work at this time: "The dream of reason produces monsters."

92–98: At this point in the poem the reader already knows to identify the bull with both Picasso and the Spanish people. The poet then goes a step farther and conflates the fate of the bull in the ring with the fate of the Spanish Republicans during the Civil War: the ritualized stages of the bullfight are associated with the course of the war through April 26, 1937, the day on which Hitler's *Luftwaffe*, in collusion with Franco's Fascist forces, bombed the small Republican town of Guernica for over three hours, reducing it to rubble and killing or wounding a large number of its civilians. Now, a bullfight may be said to be like a play with three acts: the first is the act of the pica (the "i" here is pronounced like a long "e" in English and the word rhymes with the last syllable of "Guernica," pronounced with an accent on the "i"), in which the bull is first played by the torero's (bullfighter's) assistants, then by the torero himself, who displays his grace and courage by means of the passes he makes with his cape, and in which the bull is finally beset by the mounted picadors, who stab him with picas (long lances); the second is the act of the banderillas, during which three pairs of banderillas (brightly decorated darts) are thrust into the bull's shoulders, weakening him still further; the final act is the act of death, in which the bull, fighting for his life, makes his last rallies against the torero, who plays him until his strength is broken, and then squaring off against him, kills him with a final thrust of the sword. In the poem, the word "Guernica" stands for both the town (and, by association, its destruction) and the painting. As the former, evoking the event that took place on April 26, 1937, it is associated with the culminating actions of the bullfight, the last blows the bull is able to sustain after having already received in his flesh the picas and the banderillas; as the latter, it is a response of the artist to the wounding of the bull that is his country— it is his "sally." Similarly, the white-hot pain is simultaneously that of the bull/nation in one of the last stages of its fight, that of the painter who feels its pain and represents it, and that of the witness who views this representation.

PRAISE FOR *PAT AND DICK*

"A complicated picture of the Nixons . . . [a] largely sympathetic examination of one of America's most mysterious political couples . . . the distance from Watergate—and access to new personal documents—gives *Pat and Dick* a freshness to a much-considered chapter of history."

—*USA Today*

"Will Swift's sympathetic but rigorous examination of their marriage upended [my] long-held assumptions and left me deeply moved by the end. This president and his first lady left such a deep mark on their times and our history that it is important to come to understand, in reading *Pat and Dick*, the intricate personal drama that was going on behind the public upheavals."

—Kate Buford, author of *Burt Lancaster: An American Life*

"[A] fair-minded and thorough attempt to trace the long, jagged arc of the Nixons' marriage . . . highly intelligent and far more sophisticated than the decades' worth of quick takes . . . Swift's psychological paradigms serve him well."

—*The New York Times*

"The daunting challenge in writing a dual biography, particularly one about a president and First Lady, is composing the subjects in a comfortable balance, so that one does not eclipse the other. Swift meets this challenge brilliantly, and his Nixons—equally fascinating—illuminate each other. The result is an insightful and engaging book."

—Daniel Mark Epstein, author of *The Lincolns: Portrait of a Marriage*

"The marriage of Richard and Pat Nixon undergoes sharp analysis by Swift . . . a model of well-documented revisionist history."

—*Kirkus* (starred review)

"Will Swift's deeply researched Pat and Dick . . . [is] balanced, treating matters like Watergate seriously, but also giving Nixon and his considerable achievements the credit they deserve. . . . Swift, a historian and psychologist who writes strong, clear prose, has no apparent ideological or political axes to grind. However, he doesn't hesitate to blow the whistle when he sees political piling-on."

—*The Washington Times*

"Swift has formed an absorbing depiction of Richard and Patricia Nixon. . . . He provides one of the best, if starkest, descriptions of Richard in love and politics."

—*Publishers Weekly*

"A joy. It is smart, thoughtful, poignant, and insightful. Will Swift sensitively renders two of the most caricatured and pilloried Americans of the late twentieth century in all their multi-dimensionality and complexity. *Pat and Dick* offers readers a guided tour of America, illuminating its politics, the American family, the White House, and the American home."

—Gil Troy, author of
Mr. and Mrs. President: From the Trumans to the Clintons

"A useful insight into the Nixons as individuals and as partners. . . . Crack[s] wider the window into a marriage that has interested and puzzled this country for a long time and doubtless will continue to do so far longer."

—*The Washington Post*

"[Swift] gives us among the most nuanced portraits of these two complex individuals that we have yet seen . . . for all biography buffs, presidential history buffs, and those who study profiles of marriage."

—*Library Journal* (starred review)

"This intriguingly fresh and lucid portrait of these two epochal figures will be the standard reference work for many years."

—Irwin Gellman, author of
The Contender: Richard Nixon, The Congress Years 1946–1952

"Presidential biographer Swift focuses on the spousal team of Pat and Dick Nixon, zeroing in on the incredibly strong marriage that sustained them through both personal and political triumphs and humiliations. . . . This intimate portrait into their marriage not only humanizes their carefully constructed and often maligned public image but also illuminates the strong ties that irrevocably bound the private couple."

—*Booklist*

"The most humanizing portrait of the Nixons we're likely to have. Based on first-rate research, clear writing, and smart analysis, *Pat and Dick* triumphantly sets the historical record straight in these illuminating pages. Highly recommended."

—Douglas Brinkley, author of *Walter Cronkite*

"Will Swift has given us a true joint biography . . . in a highly readable narrative. We come to see how Pat Nixon had an impact on the administration that was ignored or not perceived during their White House years. The book also merits by giving serious analysis to their post–White House years when there was a sense of redemption and even deeper love and understanding between them."

—Carl Sferrazza Anthony, National First Ladies Library Historian
and author of the two-volume *First Ladies*

"Will Swift's deeply moving and nuanced portrait of the Nixon marriage sheds new light—and brings a fascinating layer of human emotion—to the most controversial president of the 20th century.

This is not just a book for scholars, but for anyone who has ever wondered about the real lives behind the scandal of the Nixon era."

—Amanda Foreman, author of
A World on Fire: Britain's Crucial Role in the American Civil War

"Thorough, fair-minded, and evidence-based. A compelling and eye-opening portrait. Swift gives us an incisive lens to understand the politics and psychology of late-20th-century society."

—Evan Thomas, author of *Ike's Bluff*

"With an eye for the telling detail, Will Swift deftly revises our view of the Nixon marriage, showing that the reserve the couple displayed in public masked a deep love and abiding respect. . . . Even readers who thought they fully understood 'Plastic Pat' and 'Tricky Dick' will be enlightened by Swift's perspective and delighted with his vivid descriptions."

—Betty Boyd Caroli, author of
First Ladies: From Martha Washington to Michelle Obama

"*Pat and Dick* does exactly what a biography should do: show its subjects with empathy, insight, and critical acumen. We see Richard and Pat Nixon as they saw themselves, beleaguered and under-deserving of the bad press they often received. . . . Swift does not minimize their failings, especially their vindictive and petty efforts to punish their critics, but he also shows why the pressures of office made them behave, at times, with such animosity. In *Pat and Dick* the personal and political merge in a narrative that makes Swift's book one of the must-read biographies of the age."

—Carl Rollyson, author of *Amy Lowell Anew: A Biography*

"[This] excellent . . . biography . . . should be read by anyone interested in the Nixon presidency or more broadly about marriage in postwar American society. . . . [I]t humanizes Richard Nixon in a way that will surprise his detractors and clearly establishes the importance of Pat Nixon to him throughout his political career and beyond. This splendidly researched and very well written book is a pleasure to read."

—Iwan Morgan, Commonwealth Fund Professor of American History at University College London and author of *Nixon*

"In analyzing the Nixon's marriage, Will Swift provides new insight into two of the most complex political actors of the twentieth century. Swift further erodes the 'Plastic Pat' image, giving her a place of prominence beside, not behind, her husband."

—Mary C. Brennan, author of *Pat Nixon: Embattled First Lady*

"Will Swift brings his keen insights as a clinical psychologist and his considerable skills as an historian to explain the always fascinating and complex relationship between two very private public figures. Moreover, he perceptively describes their enduring relationship in the context of evolving attitudes toward marriage in postwar America."

—Melvin Small, author of *The Presidency of Richard Nixon*

Pat and Dick

The Nixons, an Intimate Portrait of a Marriage

WILL SWIFT

Threshold Editions

New York   London   Toronto   Sydney   New Delhi

Threshold Editions
A Division of Simon & Schuster, Inc.
New York, NY 10020

Copyright © 2014 by Wayne Swift

First Threshold Editions paperback edition August 2014

THRESHOLD EDITIONS and colophon are
trademarks of Simon & Schuster, Inc.

For information about special discounts for
bulk purchases, please contact Simon & Schuster Special Sales
at 1-866-506-1949 or business@simonandschuster.com.

The Simon & Schuster Speakers Bureau can bring authors
to your live event. For more information or to book an event,
contact the Simon & Schuster Speakers Bureau at
1-866-248-3049 or visit our website at www.simonspeakers.com.

Designed by Ruth Lee-Mui

Manufactured in the United States of America

1   3   5   7   9   10   8   6   4   2

Library of Congress Cataloging-in-Publication Data

Swift, Will, 1947–

Pat and Dick : the Nixons, an intimate portrait of a marriage /
Will Swift. — First Threshold editions hardcover edition.
    pages cm
1. Nixon, Richard M. (Richard Milhous), 1913–1994. 2. Nixon, Pat, 1912–1993.
3. Presidents—United States—Biography. 4. Presidents' spouses—United States—
Biography. 5. Married people—United States—Biography. I. Title.
    E856.S95 2014
    973.924092'2—dc23
        [B]
                                                    2013024650

ISBN 978-1-4516-7694-5
ISBN 978-1-4516-7695-2 (pbk)
ISBN 978-1-4516-7696-9 (ebook)

For my grandchildren,
who bring me joy:
Piper, Cole, and Emerson Swift,

and for their delightful parents,
Dylan and Brittany

God will not look you over for medals,
degrees or diplomas, but for scars.
—Elbert Hubbard

What counts in making a happy marriage
is not so much how compatible you are
but how you deal with incompatibility.
—Leo Tolstoy

Contents

Prologue   1

Part One:
An Ambitious Young Couple

1. "Will You Think of Me Sometimes?"   9
2. Going Places   24
3. Married, Happily   32
4. Love After Pearl Harbor   45
5. Giant Slayers   58
6. The Faces of America's Future   74
7. Crises on the Home Front   84
8. Safeguarding the American Home   98

Part Two:
Cultural Leaders and Private Citizens

9. "Heroes" and "Housewives": Dick, Ike, Pat, and Mamie   115
10. A Turbulent Ascent   138

11. Enduring Defeat   153
12. Darkness   171
13. Your Turn, My Turn   182

Part Three:

White House Dreams and Nightmares

14. Adjusting to the White House Fortress   207
15. "We Had Held Our Own"   226
16. A Private Marriage in the Public Spotlight   243
17. Love in the White House   266
18. The Zenith   283
19. Falling Apart   309

Part Four:

Affliction and Recovery

20. Renewal in Exile   341
21. A Peaceful Twilight   357
    Epilogue   378

    Acknowledgments   383
    Notes   387
    Index   449

Pat and Dick

Prologue

September 1952

The finest steel has to go through the hottest fire.
—Richard Nixon

When the *Nixon Special* train pulled out of Pomona, California, on the balmy evening of September 17, 1952, Pat and Dick Nixon were looking forward to a friendly whistle-stop tour up the West Coast and into the Rocky Mountain states. The Republican ticket, headed by World War II hero General Dwight D. Eisenhower, was favored to win the election that fall, and the thirty-nine-year-old Dick and his tenacious forty-year-old wife, Pat, were determined to help ensure victory by bringing youth, vigor, and momentum to the campaign. But the following day, Nixon was confronted with a firestorm of criticism that threatened his place on the ticket and his very future as a public man.

The *New York Post* had published a sensational story claiming that Nixon was the beneficiary of an $18,000 expense fund that "millionaire" Republican businessmen had raised for him. The article's subheading, "Secret Rich Men's Trust Fund Keeps Nixon in Style Far Beyond His Salary," made Nixon sound corrupt. It also implied that the Eisenhower-Nixon campaign pledge to clean up the scandals in Harry Truman's Washington was hypocritical.

By Friday the *Nixon Special* had become an isolated and oppressive prison for Dick and Pat. They were surrounded by a storm of attacks on Dick's integrity—attacks that threatened to derail the entire presidential campaign. The jittery Nixons and their staff members could contact the outside world only by making quick phone calls at each campaign stop to assess the latest reactions to the story, and by gleaning information from local reporters. As the train inched its way through California's Central Valley and into Oregon, Dick and Pat learned stop by stop how quickly their political support was ebbing. Newspapers across the country were printing increasingly distorted accounts of the expense fund; Democratic National Committee chairman Stephen Mitchell had told the UPI, "Senator Nixon knows it is morally wrong," and had called for Nixon's resignation from the ticket. Nixon campaign headquarters was being flooded with calls for him to resign, and Eisenhower, on his own train whistle-stopping through the Midwest, faced protesters with signs saying "Donate Here to Help Poor Richard Nixon." The political and social standing the Nixons had worked toward for years was falling apart.

At two o'clock in the morning of Saturday, September 20, 1952, in Medford, Oregon, Dick Nixon, battered by fatigue and struggling to fight off a black mood, slipped into the bedroom on the *Nixon Special* and woke up Pat. He had been informed that the *Washington Post* and the pro-Republican *New York Herald Tribune* had published editorials calling for him to offer his resignation to Eisenhower.

Normally tough and resolute, Dick was losing confidence. He told his wife about the latest newspaper verdicts. "Maybe I ought to resign," he said, testing her resolve.

Pat did not brook this idea. "You can't think of resigning," she said.

"If you do, Eisenhower will lose." Her voice grew more vehement. "You will carry the scar for the rest of your life. If you do not fight back but simply crawl away, you will destroy yourself."

Dick equivocated, but Pat knew how she could quash all discussion of quitting. "Your life will be marred forever and the same will be true of your family, particularly your daughters," she told him. Dick calmed down and regained his steely determination to succeed. The 1952 fund crisis was neither the first nor the last time Pat would have to steady and toughen her besieged and ambitious husband at a critical moment in his career.

Amid the avalanche of criticism, the GOP national committee was panicking, and some of Eisenhower's advisors were urging him to remove Nixon from the ticket. By the time the Nixons' train stopped in Eugene, Oregon, Pat and Dick faced protesters' signs: "What Are You Going to Do With the Bribe Money?" and "No Mink Coats for Nixon—Just Cold Cash." Dick defiantly told the crowd he was "proud of the fact that Pat Nixon wears a good Republican cloth coat, and she's going to continue to." That Saturday night in Portland, after a dispiriting and chilly parade through the sparse crowds, the Nixons drove to their lodgings at the Benson Hotel. Agitators from the local Democratic headquarters threw pennies into their car. Wearing dark glasses, sporting canes, they carried tin cups and waved signs saying "Nickels for Poor Nixon." An angry mob obstructed the entrance to the hotel and jostled Pat and Dick as they pushed their way into the hotel. By the time they reached their bedroom, Pat looked, according to her friend Helene Drown, "like a bruised little kitten." Stunned and appalled at the treatment they had received from the crowd and the press, Pat said, over and over, "It can't be happening. How can they do this? It's so unfair. They know the accusations are untrue."

Finally, his candidacy and career at stake, Dick resolved to respond to the charges against him. The fund had been audited and was legal. The national GOP organization raised $75,000 to pay for him to speak on national television. On Monday afternoon, September 22, on the flight back to Los Angeles, Dick took Pat aside and told her that in order to answer the charges he would have to reveal all of their personal finances. He had scheduled a talk for the next day. As a child of poverty, Pat found the idea humiliating. "Why do we have to parade how little we have and how much we owe in front of millions of people?" she demanded. "It seems to me that we are entitled to at least some privacy."

On Tuesday, September 23, before the broadcast, as husband and wife waited in a dressing room at the El Capitan Theater, the NBC studio in Hollywood, Dick faltered, sinking into a despair born of rejection and exhaustion. "I don't think I can do it," he told Pat.

"Yes, you can," Pat countered as she took his hand and led him up to a set decorated as a "GI bedroom den." She watched as he positioned himself behind a desk. Then Pat, wearing a dress sent to her by supporters who had hand-sewn it for her, took her place on a chair next to him. As the camera panned in and Nixon began speaking, Pat kept a tight smile. Cameraman Ted Rodgers had told her that he might zoom in on her at any moment. Maintaining a silent, nearly motionless demeanor was her only option. "The *best* I was able to do was sit like a wax figure," she said later, "afraid if I made one move I might show too much emotion, my control might give way on the screen."

Nixon would not have been able to make the speech successfully without her presence beside him. He delivered a remarkably personal and hard-hitting defense of their financial integrity—a kind of political response never before seen in American politics. His recitation of parental loans, his and Pat's struggles to pay the mortgage, their lack of life insurance, their eighty-dollar-a-month apartment, and Pat's soon-to-be-famous "Republican cloth coat" evidenced their kinship with middle-class American families. And when he delivered his pièce de résistance—declaring that his daughters had received as a gift a dog they named Checkers, "And you know, the kids, like all kids, love the dog and I just want to say this right now, that regardless of what they say about it, we're gonna keep it"—he and Pat entered the annals of American political theater. At the time and throughout his life, Dick's critics would deride the speech for what they called its calculated sentiment, and mock Pat as the robotic political wife. Yet his "Checkers speech" struck the majority of the American public as authentic; it won them over. It also convinced Eisenhower to keep him on the ticket. "You're my boy," Ike declared when they met in Wheeling, West Virginia.

Nixon disproved the allegations about his expense fund, but the victory would prove a problematic one. Although Dick and Pat were to remain central characters in the American drama for another forty years, this cruel and mortifying episode would forever darken their view of politics and the power of the press. It would tinge Pat's emotional depth of engagement with her public role and reinforce a naturally secretive and retributive aspect in Nixon's character that, post-Checkers, made it more difficult for his wife to know about and, thus, temper his worst vindictive instincts. It was one step toward the White House and also away from it, eventually leading them both into the wilderness of political exile.

The Nixons have been caricatured ("Plastic Pat" and "Tricky Dick") for so long that many readers will be surprised by the relentlessness of the pressure the Nixons faced for nearly half a century and by the resilience they demonstrated under the scrutiny of the press and the hostility of part of the public. Given that they would be tested by political attacks and crises throughout their public lives, their decision to maintain a strong bond was crucial.

When Americans remember the Nixon marriage, they focus on the highly publicized conflicts of the White House years. But the Nixons' recently released love letters and other documents challenge the prevailing narrative that the Nixons' partnership had been a dreary compromise tolerated by two disaffected partners. In fact, in many ways their bond fit the pattern of many midcentury American marriages. Few, if any, long partnerships consist of one unbroken spell of mutually sought intimacy; instead they stall and progress, with a couple's closeness waxing and waning as one or the other copes with career disappointments or ventures out toward personal and professional goals that set them at some distance from each other, or forges new friendships that fulfill the emerging aspects of their characters. From the complex and unbalanced courtship (with Dick chasing a reluctant Pat) in California, through some of the most dramatic political crises in American history, to their final thirteen years of rehabilitation, intimacy, and relative privacy on the East Coast, this book follows these two pivotal twentieth-century figures and shows why the Nixons attracted fervent admirers and vociferous critics.

A new understanding of the nation's thirty-ninth First Lady is central to this biography portrait of their marriage. Her newly available letters, keepsakes, and First Lady's press-office materials in the Nixon archives, as well as interviews with Nixon family members, friends, and associates, reveal Pat Nixon as a woman who was both vivacious and astute, and explain why she was rated as one of the most admired women in the world for many years. Dick Nixon's complex character—his strong points clarified and his defects placed in a new perspective—is more accurately seen through the humanizing portrait of his wife and his marriage.

Written by an historian and clinical psychologist who counsels couples, this book is a psychological portrayal of a bond with many flaws and strengths. *Pat and Dick* casts a fresh light on political marriages and on the stresses, problem solving, and satisfactions of any long-term union.

Part One

An Ambitious Young Couple

Find a purpose to serve, not a lifestyle to live.
—*Criss Jami*, Venus in Arms

You must do the thing you think you cannot do.
—*Eleanor Roosevelt*

It is not a lack of love but a lack of friendship
that makes unhappy marriages.
—*Friedrich Nietzsche*

1

"Will You Think of Me Sometimes?"

At the beginning of January 1938, twenty-five-year-old Dick Nixon found his native ambition blocked. He was living in a small room over his parents' garage. He was working in a job he had been reluctant to take, he did not have a girlfriend, and he was back home in the town he had tried to leave behind. After placing third in his graduating class at Duke Law School, he had been bitterly disappointed when prominent East Coast law firms had turned down his job applications. Even worse, his mother, Hannah, had to find him a position. She had pulled strings to have her friend Tom Bewley offer Dick a job as an associate at Wingert and Bewley, Whittier's most reputable law firm. Dick had ignored Tom Bewley's phone calls for a month while he waited to hear about a possible job in Los Angeles with the FBI, which ultimately rejected his application—claiming, oddly, in an internal memo, that he was "lacking in aggressiveness." It would be the last time in Richard Nixon's life that anyone would charge that he was insufficiently aggressive.

The previous November, when Dick finally showed up for work at Wingert and Bewley, he was resolved to put in grueling hours to advance himself. But the firm, which specialized in probates, divorce cases, and estates, barely had enough business for a third attorney. On December 7, a month after he began work, Dick had the distasteful task of representing the Garrett party in a default divorce hearing, but he did not like listening to the complaints of warring spouses. To supplement Dick's income and workload, Tom Bewley arranged for Dick to be named an assistant city attorney, a position in which he prosecuted cases in the police court and supervised Whittier's law enforcement. When the Boston Café, a greasy spoon across Philadelphia Street from his office, defied a city ordinance by selling liquor, Dick arranged for the chief of police to station an officer in front of the café to arrest drunken customers whom Dick could prosecute on charges of drunkenness. The café soon closed. Sitting in his tiny office on the top floor of the tallest building in the city without enough meaningful work to do, Dick had to recognize that everyone in the conservative and inward-looking Quaker stronghold of Whittier was aware he had not yet succeeded at law or love. Casting his eye toward the hills above the town, from the back side of the sixth-floor offices, he could see the homes of many of the upper-middle-class families whose wills and estates his firm handled, and he knew all too well how they looked down upon those with less impressive homes below—including Hannah and Frank Nixon. He could also gaze out at the Spanish Revival architecture, rustling palms, and eucalyptus trees that covered the hillside of Whittier College, his alma mater, where his future had looked so promising just three years before. There he had been a student body president, a star debater, and a promising scholar, if not the kind of football hero the campus more readily celebrated. Now he functioned as an entry-level lawyer.

When Dick looked north past the central part of the city, which was dotted with fragrant groves of orange, lemon, and walnut, interspersed with avocado and olive trees, the Whittier hills rolled out in patches of desert green and forest, encasing part of his hometown of twenty-five thousand people. To the south of those hills sprawled the gritty Santa Fe Springs oil fields that in 1922, back when Dick was nine, had employed his father, furiously trying to recover from decades of economic hardship in Yorba Linda, an even more provincial part of the Southern California basin.

On a clear day he could discern from his office window, in the west, the glittering blue of the Pacific Ocean and the ocher strands of beaches where, once in a while, he went to have fun. Twelve miles off to the northwest, dreamily, hazily visible from his office, stretched the metropolis of Los Angeles and the promise of a life among the rising young professionals pursuing dynamic careers, prominent politicians priming themselves for ever-greater electoral success, and sleek and ambitious men and women gallivanting around nightclubs and theaters. Although his town was only twelve miles southeast of the racy parts of Los Angeles, in Whittier when women went shopping, they still wore gloves and hats. They left calling cards to invite each other to elaborate teas. Drinking and smoking were not encouraged in public.

Whittier sits eighteen miles from the Pacific Ocean in the southeast corner of Los Angeles County, which is bordered to the north by the many high peaks (some up to nine and ten thousand feet) of the San Gabriel Mountains. Stretching for sixty-eight miles, this mountain range shields the Southern California basin from the intense summer and winter temperatures and the harsh land of the Mojave Desert. Protected as it is, Whittier thrived in the distinctive balmy, sweet-scented air and bright sunshine that had come to exemplify the American dream of an easy and comfortable Southern California lifestyle.

There Frank Nixon broke a spell of business failures that had dogged him his entire life: His Nixon Market and gas station thrived in the local economic boom. Upper-crust Whittierites saw the Nixon Market as a place for a quick stop on the way home from a round of golf. Dick's father and his fellow citizens were content in such dire times to remain in what local lawyer Merton Wray called "an eddy on the stream of life." But for Richard Nixon and other young people who longed to plunge into that stream and see how far it could take them, Whittier was a stagnant enterprise, with little opportunity for risk, excitement, or extraordinary achievement. Even romance was a matter of parlors, wary parents, and familiar faces. A duchy of fearsome propriety amid a West that was still wild in places, Whittier was as suffocating to a young man as any New England village.

Dick Nixon may have loved and hated his hometown, but, nearby, Pat Ryan entirely relished the practice and promise of her professional life in Whittier. In January 1938, she was midway through her first year teaching business courses at Whittier Union High. The school was located on Whittier Avenue, just a short walk from Dick's office and easily visible from his office window. When Miss Ryan first took charge of a study hall, the boys had great fun snapping metal clickers at one end of the study hall and then the other as she marched from side to side attempting to quell the commotion. "You could kid around with her," Virginia Endicott remembered, "but there was always that fine line that you did not cross." For all her no-nonsense resolve as a teacher, Miss Ryan was a sophisticated, modern woman. Lithe and graceful, she wore fashionable skirts with bright blouses and sweaters that set off her luxuriant red-gold hair, her fresh-complexioned face, and her high cheekbones. And she wore lavender perfume. Student Robert Blake remembered that "Miss Ryan was quite a dish."

Each weekday morning Pat showed up early in Room 120 and deposited her papers on the green steel desk in front of the blackboard. She taught bookkeeping, shorthand, and typing. When the students began pouring in, she greeted them by name at the door to the classroom, expecting to be called Miss Ryan in return. Inside the thirty-foot-square room, the tables were lined up neatly in rows, each one topped with a typewriter. Windows covering one wall of the classroom faced onto an attractive grassy area, but Pat Ryan was much too busy to daydream. Miss Ryan ran a tight ship, even if a charming and friendly captain was at the helm. "She expected clockwork punctuality from us," student Jean

Lippiatt recalled. "She allowed no compromises, no second-rate job."

Through relentless work and self-improvement, Pat had prevailed over her arduous circumstances as an orphan in a poor truck-farming family in the dusty village of Artesia, California, during the worst of the Depression era. She had put herself through the University of Southern California and obtained the equivalent of a master's degree in merchandising. At the age of twenty-five, after years of working several jobs to survive, she was grateful to be released from privation and strain, with one steady position that now paid all her bills. Beneath her accommodating demeanor lay a steely fortitude, forged from years of hardship, toil, and unstinting effort to better herself. The young teacher was compassionate toward struggling students—she would even venture into the citrus and avocado groves to convince migrant workers that their children needed to stay in school—but she was determined that they would absorb the perseverance, industry, and perfectionism that had brought her to the front of their classroom. They, too, could achieve advancement beyond their station, a profound alteration in the terms of the lives they were born into.

Suddenly junior and senior boys were becoming interested in learning to type. Many teenage boys in her class developed infatuations, while female students acquired schoolgirl crushes on her. Young Pat Ryan was discovering the price of glamour in a dull community: She was being wooed to the point of harassment by her many admirers, including her students. Some of the boys in her class placed a small query in the student paper asking where she lived and were able to locate her apartment. They followed her to the one-story stucco "bungalow court" where she lived on Hadley Street, across from a bowling alley. Summoning up the nerve to knock on her door, they received a mighty cool reception from Miss Ryan, who was not only intent on maintaining her professional demeanor but preternaturally guarded, even secretive. Groups of girls staked out her apartment, eager to flesh out their fantasies of her exhilarating life. One evening, in an eerie harbinger of the intrusive attention that would become commonplace in the public life of Mrs. Richard Nixon, Pat returned home from a date and walked to her door in the glare of headlights fixed upon her from a car full of young admirers.

On Tuesday, January 18, 1938, Dick acted on his resolve to change the terms of his life in Whittier. If he was going to be stuck in his hometown until something better came along, he would see what he could do with it. At the end of another day of small-bore legal labor, he left Wingert and Bewley and walked for several blocks, with his trademark preoccupied, slumped-shouldered gait, to the grounds of the Spanish-style St. Mathias Episcopal Church. In the parish Sunday school room, the Whittier Community Players were holding auditions for a Little Theater production of George S. Kaufman and Alexander Woollcott's drawing room mystery *The Dark Tower*, a romantic and comedic play centering on a devious murderer.

As the world at large would later discover, Dick Nixon was never a man entirely at ease in public. His dark hair and features, appealing at certain times and moods, made him at other times appear brooding, intense, a beat behind, as if he were fiercely taking mental notes about how the rest of humanity performed, then diligently applying those lessons to his own behavior. Acting on the stage seemed as likely an activity for Richard Nixon as monasticism would be for the cosmopolitan rogue John F. Kennedy, a scion of a privileged and political family, a young man who in January 1938 was in his undistinguished junior year at Harvard. But Dick was long experienced at mastering tasks that didn't come to him naturally. With characteristic resoluteness, he had told himself he would socialize with his fellow young people, garner some business contacts, have some fun, and not incidentally attempt to meet a woman he could learn to love, and who could learn to love him back.

Two blocks away from Dick's office, Pat Ryan, Whittier High's likable yet all-business business teacher, was having dinner with her new friend and fellow teacher, the veteran Little Theater actress Elizabeth Cloes, at the Hoover Hotel on Whittier's central Greenleaf Avenue. Elizabeth intensely lobbied Pat to audition for *The Dark Tower*. Behind Pat's cheerful persona, Elizabeth saw hints of a mysterious darkness or melancholy—suggesting that she might be perfect for the role of mercurial Daphne, described by the playwrights as a "dark, sullen beauty . . . wearing an air of permanent resentment."

Even though Pat had enjoyed acting in college productions and had earned money by taking bit parts in Hollywood films, she was not sure she should devote her energies to an amateur production. Pat, accustomed to meeting other people's needs, allowed Elizabeth to pressure her into trying out for the play. After dinner, the two women walked under the dark green ficus trees that framed the downtown streets and headed over to St. Mathias Church. In the rehearsal room, as Pat studied the script, Dick Nixon was successfully auditioning for the part of Barry Jones, "a faintly collegiate, eager, blushing youth" who had written the play *The Dark Tower* and was waiting for it to debut on Broadway. The moment he saw the beautiful newcomer look up from her script to notice him, Dick fell in love. "I found," Dick later said, "I could not take my eyes away from her."

The Nixons' first meeting has taken on a mythic quality—such that their fellow actor Grant Garment seems to have a "slight recollection"—perhaps even, he admits, a "wishful recollection"—that he was the one who first presented Pat Ryan to Dick Nixon. His account is contradicted by Elizabeth Cloes's more believable recollection in her Whittier College oral history. Elizabeth, who knew Dick casually from the Nixon Market, introduced the two of them. According to Cloes, Dick "was most attentive all evening."

For Dick, twenty-five-year-old Pat had the charisma of a movie star and the elusiveness of a woman who was out of his league. She was, indeed, a fun-loving and lively young woman "with titian hair." Adding to her allure, he learned that she had done several successful screen tests and had been given small parts in the movies *Becky Sharp* (where her lines had ended up on the cutting-room floor), *The Great Ziegfeld*, and *Small Town Girl*. By contrast, Dick, at the age of twenty-four, was intellectual, adventurous, yet socially unpolished. His college friend Hubert Perry thought that Dick was "always kind of serious—not laid back like the rest of us." They were both members of the college glee club. When the group went on trips, Dick would go to the back of the bus and pepper the other members of the club with sober questions. "He wanted to know what you thought about everything," Perry recalled.

Living at home in cramped quarters with his parents, Dick was not meeting any young women he fancied or who fancied him. Hubert Perry recalled that Dick "did not have social graces and did not go out on many dates. He was too busy studying." In the winter of 1937 Dick did accept Hortense Behrens's offer to escort one of her pretty friends on a double date with Hortense and her companion to the Los Serranos Country Club. Hortense, the director of *The Dark Tower*, had her version of why romance was eluding Dick. She found him to be a dull dinner companion, and, when she had a chance to dance with him, regretted it. Dick never offered his own version of that evening wherein his sense of humor, his brilliance, and his curiosity were not appreciated.

After their tryouts for the play, Dick offered Pat and Elizabeth a ride home in the brown 1935 Chevy that he shared with his younger brother Donald. Perhaps already sensing Dick's laser focus on her, Pat sat on the far side by the passenger window. Elizabeth settled in between them. Pat later told the author Earl Mazo that she thought Dick "was nuts or something." An emotionally reticent woman raised by a reserved father, who offered her only rare bursts of affection, Pat could not fathom a man being so impulsive in matters of the heart. When Dick boldly told Pat, "I'd like to have a date with you," she replied, "I'm busy." A few nights later, Dick carefully chauffeured them to a second rehearsal and brought them home. "And the third time as we came out the door," Elizabeth recounted, "I said, 'Pat, you sit next to him. He doesn't want to sit next to me.' . . . And she said, 'I don't want to sit next to him.'" Elizabeth once again positioned herself between them. Dick leaned across Elizabeth and asked Pat, "When are you going to give me that date?" And she laughed. Pointing his finger at her, "Don't laugh," he blurted out. "Someday I'm going to marry you." Pat guffawed. In his memoir Richard Nixon reported, perhaps defensively, that they all laughed.

During rehearsals Dick saw further evidence that Pat might appear easygoing but had a mind of her own as well as a powerful stubborn streak. Backstage on opening night, Pat, overwhelmed with shyness at the singing part of her role, wriggled her long red hair, shook her head, and said, "No, I'm not going to do it." She mouthed the words of her song "Stormy Weather" during the performance. Behrens did not consider either Pat or Dick to be particularly distinguished actors, but the writer for the *Whittier Daily News* said that Pat nailed "a role which called for temperament—and did she have it? Plenty! She did some fine acting as she wheeled in and out of the room, always in a semi-rage." The reviewer praised Dick for carrying "out his assignment well."

In mid-February, Dick invited his parents to the Whittier Woman's Club House to see the play's opening-night performance. Dick's mother, Hannah, was born a Milhous, one of the highest-and-mightiest Quaker family clans in Whittier, and not naturally inclined to enjoy the frivolity of theater. Dick's cousin Jessamyn West, the writer, recalled that the Milhouses thought "it rather a pity that for biological reasons there had to be admission of non-Milhous blood into their family line." Frank Nixon had eventually stopped attending Milhous family get-togethers because he tired of being treated as a second-class member of the tribe. Dick idealized his mother as a moral exemplar and wanted her to approve of Pat. But inevitably Hannah would confuse the character of Pat Ryan with the shocking role she played onstage. As Daphne Martin, an angry and abandoned mistress, Pat described men as "sons of bitches" or "pansies." This was not the kind of language that usually sat well with the pious Nixons. After the performance, when Dick eagerly queried his mother about Pat, Hannah told Dick only that "she did her part nicely." Hannah was ambitious for all her sons. To her, young Miss Ryan, with her impoverished background, her status as an orphan, and her lack of Quaker heritage must not have seemed like an ideal match for her gifted son, whom she had taught to strive for excellence in all endeavors.

As the play ended, Pat raised Dick's hopes by agreeing to join him at the Kiwanis Young Professionals Club ladies' night. Viewing the evening as their first date, he was unnerved. Pat was drawn to Dick, but rattled by his relentlessness. "He was handsome in a strong way," Pat later told her daughter Julie. "He had a wonderful quality in his voice which I have never heard in another man." Pat also consented to spend a Sunday afternoon at his parents' home. As Hannah served coffee and her special strawberry shortcake, Pat sought to charm her, to prove to the Quaker matron that she was no Daphne Martin. But there would never be any deep resonance between the two women. Hannah was too cloistered in her Quaker world for Pat, who liked to think of herself as a modern vagabond. At the age of nineteen Pat, in a not uncommon paying arrangement for that era, had driven an elderly couple three thousand miles across the country in their old Packard, braving hazardous roads, several flat tires, a cooling system breakdown, and brake failure—in order to deliver the couple from Southern California to Connecticut. Pat then arrived in New York City without a job, but found work in a hospital for tuberculosis patients in the Bronx—a world away from Southern California.

Springtime in Whittier was accompanied by the delicious fragrance of orange blossoms. For Pat's twenty-sixth birthday in mid-March, Dick sleuthed out her address and sent her roses. A few days later she accompanied him to Bird's restaurant in Laguna and they watched "the sun set over the water from our favorite point," he wrote her during the war.

Dick had long since learned that to get what he wanted required persistence. Although his peers had esteemed him for his accomplishments, he had been neither popular nor beloved by them. He was hurt by their coolness toward him. In 1929 Dick was humiliated when he lost an election for president of his high-school class to an easygoing and popular fellow, who represented all Dick lacked in gregariousness and grace. Dick was quietly determined never to lose again. Indeed, he maneuvered cleverly and judiciously behind the scenes for three years in order to win an election as president of his Whittier College student body in 1933.

As he would do in convincing Americans to elect him seven times to public office, Dick, out of a deep wellspring of need, would think harder and work harder than anyone else. Dazzlingly, he would consider every angle and seize every opportunity, directly or surreptitiously, to advance his cause. He would win, not from being loved, but from being inevitable. Pat loved to go ice-skating with her friends. Dick forced himself to try to master the sport, which he had never enjoyed and for which he was not suited. Kenny Ball, a local acquaintance, entered a local rink and was shocked to see Dick, "the worst ice-skater in the world," trying to stay upright as he fell and bloodied himself over and over again. The incident would be a metaphor for his entire career: Bloodied, discouraged, self-pitying, even despairing after inevitable setbacks, he would lift himself up through sheer will, redouble his determination, and charge with guile toward his goal.

Always adventurous, Pat was looking forward to spending some of her extra cash on traveling during the summer of 1938. The past fourteen years of her life had been, for the most part, grueling. At the age of thirteen, she had nursed her mother as she died of cancer, run the household for her father and two brothers, and garnered honors grades in high school while being a member of the Filibuster Club that debated parliamentary law, served as vice president of Les Marionettes, the drama club, taken the lead role in the senior play *The Rise of Silas Lapham,* and held the position of secretary of the student body—all roles that suggested she might be destined for a career in politics herself—even if people did not think that way about women, with the exception of Eleanor Roosevelt, in the late 1930s. Four years after her mother died, she cared for her father while he succumbed to silicosis—the product of his work in the mines of the state of Nevada where Pat had been born. In order to get through junior college and college, Pat worked as a janitor sweeping floors in a bank, a typist, a pharmacy manager, a telephone operator, and a sales lady at Bullock's Wilshire Boulevard department store in Los Angeles. There was no job she wouldn't do to get ahead. At the age of twenty-five she was ready to have some unencumbered fun. Far away from morally vigilant Whittier, she spent weekends at her married half sister Neva's apartment in Los Angeles, where she could savor the attention of handsome and sophisticated young men.

Dick pursued Pat out of a profound need for love and personal fulfillment—which Pat was already experiencing in her daily life. Having lost her parents at an early age, Pat was not yet open to romantic love. Dick filled his days with legal work he did not relish and his evenings with club meetings and speaking engagements that might advance his career but left him bereft of intimacy or a feeling of achievement. The students adored Pat because she made them feel, as Sherril Neece recalled, like "*you* were the most important 'Cog in the Wheel.'" For her, the students were a large extended family whom she nurtured and from whom she received love in return. After years of living mostly on her own, this new family meant everything to her.

Dick persisted—a moonstruck suitor who threatened her freedom and her peace of mind. That summer, he wrote her notes and, worse, composed poems and songs for her. He would show up at her apartment on school nights, asking her to go for a drive or to join him on walks around the hillside areas surrounding the college. His frantic lunges at her partially walled-off heart appeared to her at times to be overwrought. "He's a bit unusual," she told a friend. Pat used every trick she could conjure up to fend Dick off. She was a gypsy and a vagabond, she told him, someone incapable of settling down. Far from being deterred, he turned the words of her warning into terms of affection—nicknaming her "My Irish Gypsy" or "Miss Vagabond." He gave her a clock that reminded him of "that vagabond within you makes you want to go far places and see great things." She could be a vagabond if she liked, but he would travel with her. Pat's thank-you note was amiable, but not overly encouraging: "I like it [the clock] ever so much! Its new name is Sir Ric," she wrote him. Her postscript left him hope: "P.S. Sir Ric has the nicest face—I like him so very much." When turning down Dick's requests for dates did not work, she set him up with her roommate Margaret O'Grady, but he spent that evening singing Pat's praises. Miss Ryan knew she had to take more drastic steps. Little did she realize that her resistance meshed with Dick's deeper needs: It fueled his lifelong belief that he had to work harder to get what he wanted, to fight to prove his worth.

Acting "like a rat," as one of her friends said, she locked the door to her apartment on several occasions and refused to answer his insistent knocking. He went for a romantic walk by himself ("a star fell right in front of me"), came back, and slid under her door a maudlin note telling her "Yes—I know I am crazy . . . and that I don't take hints, but you see, Miss Pat, I like you." One evening she threw him out of her apartment. When she tried telling him directly that she did not share his feelings, he was peeved and hurt. Dick lied, saying that he did not have feelings for her. A few days later he wrote her to apologize. He was still fond of her, he said, even though she had hurt his pride by her failure to be candid. He would never give up.

Pat kept too busy to take much note of him. Faculty consultant to the high-school pep committee, which performed rallying skits at halftime, she also taught night school. And on weekends she escaped Whittier and the watchfulness of the town gossips. "I never spent a weekend in Whittier," Pat later boasted to her daughter Julie, "the entire time I taught there."

Unaccustomed to dealing with someone whose willpower equaled or bested her own, she made him a humiliating deal: If he promised not to make any more marriage proposals or avowals of love, she would allow him to drive her up Whittier Boulevard into Los Angeles on Friday evenings and to pick her up on Sunday afternoons after she had enjoyed her weekend dates. When one of her weekend dates lasted later on a Sunday evening than he expected, Dick paced around the city lest he imagine what he was missing. He tried to settle himself down by reading in a hotel lobby. On other occasions he would go to movies to eat up the long hours. He played along, hoping that the time he spent with her, even in such mortifying circumstances, would cause her to see how much more she had in common with him than she did with those fancy city boys. In later years Pat would be embarrassed by the trials she had put Dick through. But at the time, she still put more roadblocks in his way.

In his 1938 datebook Dick scribbled cryptic notes about the progress of his courtship. On the Friday of Memorial Day weekend he took her to Bullocks department store in Los Angeles, and wrote down what appears to be part of their discussion that evening: "Don't know whether I like or not [presumably Pat speaking] . . . will you think of me sometimes [Dick speaking]?"

*   *   *

In July 1938, Pat traveled by bus to Michigan to buy a car, which she drove home. In an effort to slow Dick down, she did not contact him upon her return. She moved apartments and gave Dick a strong message that she did not reciprocate his feelings—she did not give him her new address. For Pat, the summer interval provided a break from having to contend with dating Dick, keeping up appearances for Whittier's vigilant matrons, and juggling a busy schedule. For the better part of two long months Dick did not hear from her. He sent a letter to her at her school. "I'd like so very much to see you," he implored her, "any time you might be able to stand me. . . . I swear you'll not be bored if you give me a chance." Pat relented after several months and saw him again.

Even as he renewed his courtship of Pat, that fall Nixon harnessed some of his prodigious energy and his gift for leadership into social and business-building interactions, and politicking. He led a public discussion of a ballot measure on veteran housing reimbursement and chaired the Inter-Service Banquet, where he could mingle with three hundred members of the Kiwanis, Lions, 20-30 Club, Rotary, Progress, and Junior Chamber of Commerce organizations. He also starred for the Little Theater as a district attorney in the play *Night of January 16*, which had had a successful run as an audience-participation drama at the Ambassador Theater on Broadway. All of these activities garnered Dick coverage in the *Whittier News*. At the same time, Dick seemed to have made progress in his campaign to win Pat. His enhanced status as a successful professional and his growing self-confidence had aided his cause.

Did her awareness of a thinning field to choose from also make a difference? Pat never said. His veiled scrawls in his December 1938 appointment book read like a record of trinkets of affection he had received from her. She probably accompanied him to the Browley Dance on December 10, after which he wrote "Awful Life Saver." Five days later is the notation "6:00–2:00 Christmas Tree, Italian Village"; he surprised Pat by placing a small decorated Christmas tree in her apartment. At the bottom of his December 18 diary page, he jots down what might have been the most heartening news of all, in what must be Pat saying: "I was lonesome for you—glad you came." On the twenty-third he mentions going "To L.A. Wiltshire" and hearing "Like you this morning." Later that evening, during "dinner and shopping in Hollywood," he writes, one of them said, "Don't want you to hate me." Under his Christmas tree Pat had placed a package of encouragement, if not certainty.

2

Going Places

For Dick, 1939 began on a particularly promising note. Like many of Whittier's young people, he and Pat were big football fans; in fact, Dick was crazy about the game. On January 2, because their two former schools were squaring off, she accompanied him to Pasadena on a comfortable seventy-three-degree day to watch the Rose Bowl. Dick's team, Duke, undefeated and unscored upon in nine games that year, was heavily favored to beat Pat's USC. The final minutes of the game were so exciting that even a woman as reserved as Pat might grab her date's hand. Duke led 3–0 until the final minute of the game when backup Trojan quarterback Doyle Nave threw a winning touchdown pass. Pat's team won 7–3, but for Dick the game was a victory. He later told interviewer Frank Gannon that Pat felt sorry for him, and he claimed Duke's loss helped him win her over.

On his twenty-sixth birthday—January 9—Pat sent Dick a clock. He was excited by this first gesture signifying that the feelings between them might be mutual. In his thank-you note, he included one of his law firm's promissory note forms on which he pledged to pay her "four billion dollars when I'm fifty, or before if you'll let me." He explained that he had "an uncontrolled impulse" to send this note, "so here it is—crazy—but fun." He ended exuberantly, "You're sure tops, Miss Pat and I just have to tell you."

He also expressed his intense romantic feelings in letters that revealed his fears that he would "bore her with his thoughts," and his view of himself as an unaccomplished suitor. "There was something electric in the usually almost stifling air in Whittier. And now I know," he wrote her. "An Irish gypsy who radiates all that is happy & beautiful was there. She left behind her a note addressed to a struggling barrister who looks from a window and dreams. And in the note he found . . . a great spirit which only great ladies can inspire. . . . And though he is a prosaic person, his heart was filled with that grand poetic music, which makes us wish . . . she might be forever happy."

By the spring of 1939, as the orange trees once again unfurled their yearly blossoms, he felt particularly encouraged about his relationship with Pat. At one point Pat invited him to supper: "[W]hy don't you come Early Wednesday (6)—and I'll see if I can burn a Hamburger for you." She sounded on the brink of romance: "Did you see the sunset? A new picture every few minutes. Well? Yes, Pat." At another time— perhaps on her birthday in March—she accepted a gift from him with greater enthusiasm than she had the clock he had given her the previous year: "Gee, Dick. Guess I am a pretty lucky Irishman! . . . Best of all was knowing you had remembered."

Still, there were hindrances to his courtship. Every time he wanted to take her out on a date, he had to haggle with his brother Donald over the use of the brown 1937 Chevrolet coupe they shared. Dick ordered a brand-new black Oldsmobile, which he picked up at the Oldsmobile factory in Lansing, Michigan, in March. He did not feel that he could afford the frill of a car radio. He delighted his brother

Eddie, almost nine years old, by taking him along on the thirty-nine-hour train trip to Lansing.

Back in Whittier, when he discovered that Pat liked his dog, King, an affectionate Irish setter, he cleverly included the dog on their outings. Sometimes they brought Eddie along on their trips to destinations like their favorite beach in San Clemente. Pat took a motherly interest in the frail boy, making him laugh, chasing him on the beach to build up his stamina, and buying him adventure books to interest him in reading. Pat occasionally drove Eddie to Huntington Beach by herself and the two of them would run to see who could reach the sand first. Although Pat was barely taller than Dick's nine-year-old brother, who had long legs, she could still beat him. Eddie was impressed.

By summer, Pat began to indicate she was taking the courtship seriously. She resolved to get better acquainted with Hannah Nixon. Instead of taking the older woman out to tea or even attending church with her, Pat chose to prove herself the kind of woman Hannah would respect: the hardworking, self-sacrificing kind. She rose at 5:00 a.m. and went over to the Nixon house to help Hannah bake pies, which were a profitable and dauntingly numerous staple of the Nixon Market. Hannah needed to make fifty pies six mornings a week. Hannah, with typical understatement, called Pat's action "unusual for a busy girl." Although Mrs. Nixon had initially seen Pat as fragile, she had come to realize that Pat was, like herself, a woman of stamina. Wisely, Pat never tried to compete with her by baking pies from her own recipes; she would instead perform the role of the dutiful potential daughter-in-law. Yet the young woman's gesture backfired: Hannah convinced herself that Pat was aggressively pursuing her son, not the other way around. The matrons of Whittier agreed with Hannah. After all, wouldn't it be just like an orphaned working-class girl to chase such an eligible boy, and from such an upstanding family?

Pat developed a playful relationship with Frank Nixon. He spared her the bitter anger his sons had endured and never lashed out at her. As Pat grew closer to Dick and his family, she became increasingly direct with him. One day she boldly confessed to him how much the gold-rimmed cap on his front tooth—the result of a basketball injury—bothered her. Off went the cap. Anything to be appealing.

By the middle of 1939 Dick had become preoccupied with a wide variety of legal projects, and he often worked at his desk through lunch, sipping pineapple malts and eating the hamburgers his secretary Evlyn Dorn brought him from an adjacent drugstore. Nixon had started out focusing mainly on family law, but after eighteen months of practice, he had worked on at least nine civil trials in local courts and in the Superior Courts of Orange and Los Angeles. His salary crept upward. While Nixon was paid an average of $75 a month in his initial six months with the firm, he made a total of $1,480, or almost $125 a month, in the year of 1938. In 1939 he doubled his previous year's income.

In August 1939, hoping to capitalize on some local Nixon family connections, he set up a one-lawyer branch office of Wingert and Bewley in La Habra, a quiet crossroads of three thousand inhabitants, surrounded by citrus, walnut, and avocado groves southeast of Whittier. He spent midday in the La Habra offices, in the back of a run-down drugstore, drumming up business that was not always forthcoming. The glacial pace of business in the new office had one advantage: It gave him the opportunity and the motivation to insinuate himself into the local political culture, hanging out at the local coffee shop, where he built connections with key businessmen and city officials. At the same time, he began reaching out beyond his profession to build a larger public identity for himself, partly by becoming a popular luncheon and after-dinner speaker. Dick was considering running for a seat in the California Assembly and hoped that the connections he made on the banquet circuit would help him win his first political contest. Herman Perry, a local banker whose office was in the same building as Wingert and Bewley, became a mentor to young Nixon. He dissuaded Nixon from making a run in 1939 because he recognized that his protégé did not yet have enough experience to convince voters he was right for the job.

Dick was also obsessed with a new get-rich scheme, his first immersion in the Southern California boom mentality that had survived the discouragements of the Depression era. A number of citrus growers and wholesalers believed that the technology was now available to convert the surplus citrus from the 1938 crop into frozen juice, which could become a profitable, national, mass-market venture. Several of the law firm's clients talked Dick into forming a corporation, named Citri-Frost, and raising money from local businessmen. Two big shipping companies showed interest in buying large quantities of their product when they figured out how to package the juice. Experiments with cellophane bags, cartons, and cans all failed. Hoping to survive until they could develop the right container, Nixon and his business partners cut costs by going out into the orchards to pick and squeeze the fruit. After his legal office hours were done for the day, "Dick worked his heart out on the thing," Tom Bewley remembered. "He worked like a dog. He was out there cutting oranges day and night." In 1939 the company squeezed more than twenty-one thousand gallons of juice and sold less than two-thirds of it. They lost money and eventually gave up. Other entrepreneurs would later succeed in similar ventures by freezing not the juice but its concentrate, which could be more easily packaged.

Putting less pressure on a relationship with Pat as a means to define himself, he created the room for her to experience her own investment in their courtship. On fall weekends Pat and Dick went to Whittier College and University of Southern California football games. At other times they skied in the mountains on the edge of Los Angeles and muddled their way through ice-skating at the newly opened Hines rink in Whittier. Afterward they gathered up a few couples for a home-cooked spaghetti dinner. Pat and Dick also loved movies, including such soon-to-be-classic films as *Jezebel, You Can't Take It with You, Gone with the Wind, The Young Mr. Lincoln,* and *Mr. Smith Goes to Washington.* They attended the local cinema near Dick's office on Greenleaf Street in Whittier or watched films at the big movie theaters in Hollywood. Afterward they sometimes went to an ice-cream parlor. When they felt flush, they went to concerts at the Hollywood Bowl, which featured celebrated singers like Ella Fitzgerald and Nat King Cole as well as great conductors and pianists.

In August 1939 "the vagabond," her friend Virginia, and her

roommate Margaret took a sightseeing vacation, driving up the Pacific Coast to Vancouver in British Columbia. By the time they got to San Francisco, Pat found she missed Dick. She felt "so sorta' lonesome," she wrote him, because she did not have a chance to say a proper good-bye. When they reached Vancouver she sent him at his law office a scenic postcard with the cryptic message "Love from Mother." This time she was not pushing him away, but hiding her growing feelings from the local gossips at home. Pat knew that Hannah Nixon would not be alone in her suspicion about a bond between a Nixon and a Ryan. Whittier's prominent local boys were not supposed to marry outsiders, and particularly not those below their station. "Some people felt," Judith Wingert, the daughter of the senior partner in Nixon's law firm, recalled, "that he should have been going with a girl from, you know, a better family . . . one that didn't work." Pat was neither part of Whittier's pious inner circle of Quakers nor a member of its upper-middle-class country club and bridge set.

After receiving Pat's romantic missives, Dick might have expected more encouragement from her, but when she returned home, she did not relent in her insistence that they postpone discussion of marriage. He persisted; she explicitly prohibited any such talk for three months. In October, when the interval had passed, he wrote her a note: "Seriously, little one, let's go to Arizona . . . we could still have fun!" Assuming that he was suggesting they indulge in a sexual escapade, she rebuked him. He shot back a note celebrating her virtue: "You have the finest ideals of anyone I have ever known."

In 1939, Tom Bewley and Jefferson Wingert made him a partner in the law firm. "Now for the first time," he wrote in his memoir, "I was no longer Frank and Hannah Nixon's son—I was Mr. Nixon, the new partner" in Wingert, Bewley, and Nixon. He still helped buy vegetables for his parents' market, he still taught the Quaker young people's class at the East Whittier Friends Church on Sundays, and he still lived with his parents, but he was newly confident, having won small-town success by dint of his industry.

In the winter of 1940, he honored the second anniversary of their first meeting by writing Pat a letter trumpeting how madly he was still in love with her. Now calling her "my dearest heart," he let her know in Quaker terms that "nothing so fine ever happened to him or anyone else as falling in love with Thee." Gone were the goofy and exaggerated love letters of the man-boy; they were succeeded by adult letters from the heart.

If there is truth to the adage that we marry our parents, Dick and Pat are its exemplars. Beneath her glamour and verve, Pat was surprisingly similar to Dick's standoffish, pious, and unglamorous Quaker mother, Hannah, whom he professed to revere. Both women were proper and emotionally self-contained rescuers. Hannah had nursed tubercular patients (including Dick's beloved older brother Harold, to whom she was devoted, who died in 1933 at age twenty-three). So had Pat. Dick, though perhaps not as immediately attractive as Pat's father, resembled him in his typically reserved nature, his uneven temperament, and his restless ambition to move beyond the world he lived in.

Young and forward-looking, they did not rehash their harsh early years on farms, dwell on their angry fathers, or bemoan the deaths in their families. They shared an outsider's mentality—born of their emotional shyness and their distrust of fancy people in fancy places. They also shared an underlying, no-nonsense melancholy. As optimistic as he was about the future, Dick could be moody—and not only when his romantic hopes were being dashed. Pat liked to cheer people up, but Dick had detected an underlying sadness behind her "lovely smile." Neither of them liked to unbutton their emotional vests, and as they grew closer they still kept many secrets. Dick did not learn how Pat's father died (from silicosis), nor did he share much about the loss of his brothers Harold and Arthur. He did not know her real name (Thelma) until he applied for a marriage license.

Dick promised her adventure. Slowly he convinced her that "he was going places." Pat was impressed, as she told her daughter Julie, that Dick "always saw the possibilities." He "believed that life could be good and that problems—well, if you could not solve them, you could make things a little better." Other men might have been more appealing and easy, but she was finding herself drawn to his vitality, his stability in his profession, and his openness to a wider world. He could offer her not just the promise of his career but his emerging yet intense sense of purpose. "From the first days I knew you, you were destined to be a great lady," he declared in a letter. "I want to work with you toward the destiny you are bound to fulfill. . . . It is our job to go forth together and accomplish great ends and we shall do it too." Although Dick and Pat would later claim that they did not discuss politics often in the early days, Pat told several of her best friends that Dick was "going to be president someday."

In March 1940, Dick took Pat in his black Oldsmobile for an hour-and-a-half drive down U.S. Highway 101 into southern Orange County halfway between Los Angeles and San Diego. He pulled into a dirt road leading to the Dana Point promontory, a sandstone cliff with a precipitous face, overlooking Capistrano beach and the San Clemente coastline. The promontory had been a navigational landmark for ships and migrating whales for centuries. In the early part of the nineteenth century, Richard Henry Dana, in his book *Two Years before the Mast*, had described the spot as "the only romantic cove in California." Parked by the edge of the cliff, he waited until the blaze of the Pacific sunset to make a bold proposal.

3

Married, Happily

As the sun eased into the ocean off Dana Point, Dick once again asked Pat to marry him. Their daughter Julie tells us that, even as Pat accepted, she still felt conflict about giving up her freedom. For a woman whose parents fought and died young, and who had to care for her orphaned brothers, intimacy was associated not only with love and endurance, but also with uproar and loss.

In the era of Pat Ryan's young adulthood, women usually married when they were in their early twenties. Surely Pat had come to love Dick, but did she also consider that in her twenty-eighth year, she was on the verge of becoming an old-maid schoolteacher? Pat had defied convention by giving herself the years of adult independence she always wanted. She did not feel completely ready for the commitment marriage entailed, but she resolved to make it work. She told Dick yes.

In his exuberance Dick made an ill-advised decision to drive Pat to his parents' home to tell them the news. They crept into Hannah and Frank's bedroom and woke the couple, who had gone to bed earlier. Stunned, Hannah reacted with her typical reserve, and Frank with his characteristic enthusiastic bluster. Their sleepy reaction "broke the romantic spell of the evening," Pat would tell Julie, leading Pat to wonder if her future in-laws had reservations about the match. Pat likely knew that other matrons in Whittier would look down upon their union, because Dick came from a hardworking local family while Pat's provenance appeared less certain but definitely more hardscrabble. Hannah's less than joyous reaction at the news, however, had more to do with being confronted with a situation that required of her an immediate emotional reaction. Like most Quakers, she preferred to sit with her reactions and consult her own inner light before responding.

Pat's family had a full night's sleep before the young couple told them of the engagement, but they appeared initially no less ambivalent. Only her brother Tom was enthusiastic about Dick, who shared his love of football; he found his sister's fiancé an easy conversationalist. Tom gave Pat a big hug, but her twenty-nine-year-old brother Bill became tearful at the thought of losing his sister. Half sister Neva, whose home had been the base for Pat's dates with fancy city boys, was concerned that Dick was not exciting enough—"too quiet," she thought. Dick was far more adventurous than she realized.

Now that he had won his campaign for Pat's hand, Dick became obsessed with deciding what ring to put on her finger. This public symbol of their very private match had to deliver the right message. During a business trip to Northern California with Don, Dick kept his brother up a good part of the night debating the benefits of diamonds and other gems and their settings. "A man only buys a ring once in his lifetime," Don recalls him saying gravely, "and that should be a ring his wife would always be proud to wear."

Dick brought his fiancée to look over his choices. Pat, always understated in her tastes, preferred a simple gold band that would not draw attention, but she liked or pretended to like the ring Dick wanted her to wear—a diamond set between two smaller gems on a band sparkling with diamond chips. Pat depleted her savings to pay for her share of the $315 cost (approximately $5,000 in today's terms); a copy of the bill of sale is preserved at the Nixon Library. Dick's Citri-Frost venture had been designed to provide extra funds for luxuries like a wedding ring, but he was struggling to keep his business afloat while helping his parents out financially and paying off college loans. It was important, as would so often be the case, for Dick to make a grand gesture—to celebrate his big triumph in a life not yet replete with successes. Was he embarrassed that he could not afford to pay the entire bill himself? Was this one of the many small humiliations that helped stoke his ambition?

That spring, as they prepared to wed, Dick left work each after-noon to pick up Pat after school and drive her home. Seventeen-year-old students Helen Noll and Barbara Gose would accompany them on the ride to Pat's room in Barbara Gose's home in the 200 block of North Bright Street. "Everyone was so happy," and "we all had a lot of fun," Helen recalled seventy years later. She and Barbara thought Dick was handsome and smart, if not gregarious: "it wasn't like he rushed over and gave you a big hug." They adored Pat. Helen remembers how comfortable the engaged couple seemed to be with each other.

In the months before they married, Dick made only one misstep. Pat was grading papers after classes when an employee of the Nixon Market scuttled in with a May basket, which he shyly placed on her desk. When she saw the ring hidden amid the flowers and straw in the basket, she pushed it aside. This was not the romantic moment she had surely envisioned. Alice Koch, a teacher in an adjacent classroom, entered her room, saw the ring, and slipped it on Pat's finger. Her fellow teachers gathered to celebrate, but her fiancé was still missing. Could he not have waited to give the ring to her in person? Dick was at best exhibiting an ignorance of social codes, and at worst he was giving Pat a warning signal that his work would remain a much higher prior-ity than his wife.

However the couple worked out this conflict, Dick soon formal-ized his proposal in a letter that called upon them both to strive to make a significant contribution to the world around them. His "dear heart" was, in his opinion, an extraordinary woman. "You have always had that extra something," Dick wrote, "which takes people out of the mediocre class." Dick encouraged Pat by seeing in her a nobleness of spirit, a gallantry, and a fine intelligence that she was not prone to acknowledge in herself. These qualities would infuse her remarkable public performance during Nixon's tumultuous public life, giving her a steadfastness that led her to become, in the words of Nixon biographer Conrad Black, "one of the unjustly unsung heroines of American political history."

Pat was committed to backing Dick's outsize ambitions, but it is not likely that she expected herself to assume a role beyond that of supportive spouse. The era's emphasis on wifehood and motherhood consigned most women to the domestic sphere. Pat's modesty, tendency toward self-criticism, and attachment to privacy precluded her from imagining herself willingly entering the spotlight. Although both the Nixons would later deny it, Pat had plenty of evidence that her husband was drawn to politics, starting at least with his aborted plans for a campaign for the California State Assembly in 1939. Dick's mentor Herman Perry brought him into the Young Republicans Club, where he promptly became the group's president. In the winter and spring of 1940, just before his engagement, Dick drove throughout Southern California delivering a stump speech attacking FDR for trying to "pack" the Supreme Court with additional appointees who would support the New Deal. He had hoped to build a campaign base in case Gerald Kepple, a fellow Republican Quaker, chose not to run for another term in the California State Assembly, but Kepple had decided not to step down. By the time of her engagement, Pat was well aware that she could become a politician's wife, even if neither she nor Dick yet had an idea of the commitment and sacrifice that public life required.

As for Dick, he already felt indebted to Pat. She had transformed him into a more open and happy young man. "I someday shall return some of the benefit," he wrote, "you have conferred upon me." Whatever life brought them, he promised, "I shall always be with you— loving you more every hour and attempting to let you feel that love in your heart and life."

Whatever the dynamic of power and influence would be between husband and wife in the long term, in the spring of 1940 Pat took charge of planning their June wedding. Not a regularly practicing Christian, she vetoed a church ceremony, but to satisfy her in-laws, she did become a Quaker. Uncomfortable with grand occasions, she arranged for a small wedding. She didn't want the event to create financial burdens for her husband, her brothers, or her in-laws. Dick chose the least expensive room—the two-level, serendipitously named Presidential Suite—at the Spanish-style Mission Inn in Riverdale, California. The inn, a mecca for tourists, featured a spiral staircase, bell towers, colonnades of arches, stained-glass windows, fountains, mosaics, and other quirkily ornate features. Pat and Dick had often had dinner dates there.

Dick's aunts Olive Marshburn and Edith Timberlake gave a tea and shower for Pat, and the couple was feted at a dinner dance at the Town House in Los Angeles. The prewedding festivities and the wedding itself occurred against a somber backdrop that surely tinged the events for the young couple and their family and friends: Dispiriting news had arrived regularly that spring and summer from the European war that was increasingly preoccupying America. By June 1940, Hitler's Germany had routed the Allied forces near Dunkirk and was already proceeding with its conquest of Western Europe. One week before their wedding, Pat Ryan and Dick Nixon would have turned on their radios to hear that the Nazis had marched up the Champs-Élysées in Paris to celebrate their conquest of France. The day after their nuptials, France would officially surrender to Germany, leaving Great Britain alone and vulnerable to invasion. In less than a year and half, the war would envelop the young couple and profoundly alter the direction of their lives. On Friday afternoon, June 21, Don Nixon drove Pat from Whittier to Riverside. At the inn Pat changed into a simple light blue suit, pinned an orchid to its lapel, and donned a dark rose hat adorned with blue roses. Dick bought himself a dark suit for the occasion. When he accidentally bumped into Pat in the hallway, violating the tradition that the groom not see the bride before the ceremony, he pretended that his eyes were closed.

For Helen Noll and the other twenty-five or so guests, this was "not just another wedding." At the end of a decade of economic hardship and austerity, and with war swallowing Europe, it was considered a major event to hold a marriage ceremony in such an exotic setting. Noll remembers flowers massed in the Presidential Suite and Pat walking in the suite's side door to take her vows. Facing each other on a red Oriental rug, Pat and Dick were married in a Quaker ceremony in front of a grand piano. William Mendenhall, the new president of Whittier College, read the service.

At a reception in the inn's Spanish art gallery, family members and friends listened to organ music and ate a several-tiered cake—"with a veiled bride and a groom in white tails atop the crown"—baked by Dick's mother and carried carefully on her lap in the car from the Nixon home to Riverside. There are no photographs recording the start of their fifty-three-year marriage.

During Dick's relentless pursuit of her, Pat had come to recognize that he was a crusader. She did not yet know that their entire marriage would be a crusade of one sort or another, or that she would have to rescue him many times along the way. Nor could she know that the one time she looked away and trusted him to handle a crisis on his own, he would falter in an inglorious fashion that would haunt the rest of their lives.

In their first years together, by grounding themselves in their union, the Nixons would help each other surmount some of the sadness of their difficult childhoods. Driven people, Pat and Dick would, nevertheless, find ways to relax and cultivate a circle of friends. Pat and Dick started out their married life as a spontaneous and fun-loving pair. Feeling what they called "really splurgy," with $200 in their pockets and a trunk full of canned goods—the labels had been pulled off as a wedding prank, leaving them to eat grapefruit for lunch and spaghetti for breakfast—Pat and Dick took off for a Mexican honeymoon, without an itinerary.

In what would be a rare event for them, the Nixons enjoyed an extended, unscripted period together. Heading in the general direction of Mexico City, they stopped to tour churches, temples, small villages, pyramids, and archeological sites. They attended, but quickly left, a gory bullfight in Mexico City. At a concert by the Mexican Symphony they encountered anti-American sentiment—the mention of U.S. composer Aaron Copland's name drew copious boos.

"That's what we still like to do," Pat said in the 1960s, "to get in the car and ride off just to be going, without any particular destination. It is always a lot of fun." Such trips were the perfect antidote for the compulsive and perfectionist aspects of their personalities.

Honeymoons can be difficult for young couples who have not lived together or who have not had sexual relations. The collision of expectations and fantasies with the realities of a new spouse's idiosyncratic behavior can lead to disillusionment or even despair. For Dick and Pat, though, the honeymoon seems to have been a time of fresh closeness. On their way home they stopped off at the magnificent, recently built Boulder Dam, where Mrs. Bell, the mother of one of Pat's junior college friends, spotted them. When Pat revealed that she was on her honeymoon, Mrs. Bell was struck by Pat's happiness.

Endeavoring to save some of the $200 they had brought with them, Pat and Dick drove through the night on the way back to California. Prone to superlatives, Dick later said, "We probably got more out of our honeymoon while spending less than any couple in history." With $22 still in their pockets, the newlyweds arrived back in Whittier on the evening of the Fourth of July as firecrackers burst in the evening air.

Pat and Dick spent the summer living in a rented apartment in Long Beach, near the ocean. On Sunday mornings Pat baked fresh biscuits and set out Dick's favorite jams and honey. In the afternoons they went hiking or drove to the beach. Sometimes they went to the movies. "Our life was happy and full of promise," Dick said in his memoir.

To accommodate everyone who had been left out of the small wedding in Riverside, Frank and Hannah threw a reception at their Worsham Drive estate, perched on a hillside above Whittier College. Complete with a turret visible from the front, the house had three levels, set on a slope that dropped steeply into the backyard. Hannah and Frank Nixon had recently surmounted their lower-middle-class status by buying the lavish property from the Stoody construction family, the builders of the fancy homes from which Whittier Hills matrons had long looked down upon the Nixons. The party for the young Nixons took place in the backyard's attractive hillside gardens, laced with a stream and fishponds and filled with exotic South American plants and monkey trees. Ed Nixon remembers that "Strauss waltzes filled the air."

When Pat returned to teaching in the fall, the Nixons moved back to the Whittier area, living first in an apartment over a garage, then in a duplex, and later in a small house on Walnut Street. In the evenings, Dick, who was becoming increasingly political, would often travel to speak at venues like the Lions Club in Long Beach or the Kiwanis Club in San Clemente, to build up his law practice and spread his name among the influential Orange County gentry. During the 1940 presidential campaign, he campaigned for Wendell Willkie and attacked FDR with hard-hitting speeches.

Pat busied herself working with the high school's pep committee, holding some of their meetings in the terraced backyard of the Nixon Worsham Drive home, working with the students on their chants and gestures. Pat went to great lengths to rouse her students' school spirit. One day each school year, students and teachers reversed roles. According to Whittier student Eloise Hilberg, Pat enjoyed herself going "the whole route to play the part of the student," dressing in "bobby sox and a school sweater." "It always seemed like Pat was just one of the students," recalled one pupil. During her years teaching at Whittier High, Pat experienced something of the carefree adolescence she had missed, even as she upheld her authority as a rigorous, even rigid teacher. Despite her intense involvement with her students, according to her friend Marion Burdlong, Pat maintained "an aloof friendliness" and was "never one to disclose her inner feelings, nor did she talk about her sentiments and ambitions" with anyone.

With money tight in the waning years of the Depression, most struggling young American couples entertained at home. Evlyn Dorn, Nixon's first legal secretary, and her husband attended the Nixons' first dinner party. Pat cooked up a pot of spaghetti with meat sauce. Dick made the salad and mixed the drinks. He was always "the highlight of the party because he had a wonderful sense of humor," Pat later recounted. "He would keep everybody in stitches." He also pitched in to help prepare the rest of the meal. "Remember the time when you even made the chop suey?" Pat wrote him during the war. "I never shall forget how sweet you were . . . the night I had the teachers for a wiener roast—you carted, helped with the salad, bought the pies."

The Nixons found plenty of cost-free ways to amuse themselves, including at-home theatricals. "I will never forget one night when we did 'Beauty and the Beast,'" Pat recounted to biographer Earl Mazo. "Dick was the Beast, and one of the other men dressed up like Beauty. This sounds rather silly," but "we used to put on funny shows. It was all good, clean fun, and we had loads of laughs."

In a late-1960s interview with biographers Earl Mazo and Bela Kornitzer, Pat expressed frustration that people "think he has never had a good laugh in his life. . . . Sure, he is sensitive and restrained, but he can be lots of fun." Perhaps she was exaggerating to counter Dick's stiff reputation. But during the war she would write her husband that "you always make people have a good time. Our parties have always been your successes." Dick may have felt like a loner and an outsider, but he could perform like a born extrovert.

Pat and Dick drew close to Helene and Jack Drown, who would become lifelong confidants. Helene, an effervescent fellow teacher at Whittier High School, was Pat's assistant faculty advisor on the high-school pep committee. Jack, who had played football with the 1936 Stanford Vow Boys, a squad that had famously pledged never to lose to their rivals the University of Southern California, was attending USC Law School when the couples first met in September 1940.

Sharing a keen sense of humor, Pat and Helene bonded quickly. Helene thought that Pat was a rare beauty—"a really outstandingly beautiful" woman, filled with "gaiety, and a love of life, and a sparkle in her eye that just was very radiant and contagious." By contrast, she saw Dick as a "very clean cut, good looking man," and was drawn to his expressive eyes, which were "very twinkly and very kindly."

Pat and Helene shared the challenges of being newly married

wives—which included improving their cooking skills. They exchanged their first recipes, and when they ran late at school supervising student extracurricular activities, they walked home together and "pooled our resources—as poor as they might be" to "have a gala evening together of good conversation." Helene marveled at how efficiently her friend used every spare moment of her time: Pat did not leave her dishes undone at night, repaired her clothes before putting them away in the closet, and got up early to organize her apartment for ten minutes before she left for school.

On their first double date the Nixons and the Drowns, who loved Spanish and Mexican food, went out to a Spanish restaurant. Dick took charge of ordering for everyone, as he often would when the couples went out. After dinner they went to the Philharmonic Auditorium in Los Angeles to see the Oscar Straus operetta *The Chocolate Soldier*, which was based on a play by George Bernard Shaw. They had seats behind a post, but they enjoyed the music.

Even though Dick was "jovial" that night, Jack could tell there was something bothering him. The two men went to retrieve the car because it was "raining pitchforks." While they were driving back to the theater to pick up their wives, who were waiting under the protection of the marquee, Dick confided some of his anxieties about his law practice. Describing one of the day's cases, Dick said, "I just don't know why those people had to get that divorce. I did everything I could to talk them out of it." Jack teased him that lawyers should be happy because divorce cases can make them a lot of money. "No, I think it's the other way," Dick told him. "We should do everything we can to keep people together." His conservative values and his Quaker background did not always mesh with the world he encountered at work. Yet at this point in his life Dick could alleviate the rigor of that work with a private life that was enjoyable and sustaining.

Jack recalled that Dick was an easy man to befriend. "He liked to exchange. He certainly was a good listener," Jack said in a Whittier College oral history. The young lawyer had definite interests outside his work. "He was extremely interested in athletics," Jack remembered. "He seemed to know every football player in the United States and maybe Canada . . . he had apparently heard my name." Dick also loved music. Buying the cheap seats they could afford, the two couples often went to performances at the Los Angeles Civic Light Opera. Surprisingly, when he was socializing, Dick usually did not seem interested in talking about the law or his job. He liked "situation humor . . . something funny that had happened," Jack said. "I don't recall that he ever came out with 'Well I heard a great one today.'" He didn't tell "what you call off-color jokes."

The Drowns and the Nixons had some rowdy adventures together. One night Dick Perdue, one of Nixon's law school classmates, and his wife joined them for the blue-plate special at the supper and theater club of Broadway showman and impresario Earl Carroll, on Sunset Boulevard in Hollywood. The cost of admission was a steep two dollars and fifty cents, but the young couples got their money's worth. Beautiful girls performed on an enormous stage that had a "wide double revolving turntable and staircase plus swings that could be lowered from the ceiling," Jack recounted. During one of the acts each of the dancers lay down, put one leg up, and "then they'd call some [of] us out of the audience and we had these hoops and we'd throw them . . . the one who could put the most hoops on the legs won the champagne." Jack wasn't sure whether the future president or Dick Perdue won the prize, but they celebrated their victory with a fine bottle of champagne.

Pat loved to dance. On rare occasions she and Dick would treat themselves to one barely affordable drink and dancing at the flashy Cocoanut Grove nightclub in the Ambassador Hotel, an establishment frequented by presidents from Hoover to Nixon, on Wilshire Boulevard in Los Angeles. Adding to its allure for Pat and Dick, who were both movie buffs, the 1939 Academy Awards ceremony, hosted by Bob Hope, was held in the nightclub in February 1940. Errol Flynn, Clark Gable, Carole Lombard, Spencer Tracy, Katharine Hepburn, Gary Cooper, Marlene Dietrich, or Lana Turner could be seen partying regularly amid the palm trees from which stuffed monkeys hung under the blue ceiling covered with sparkling stars. Dick was drawn to Hollywood celebrities. The Cocoanut Grove, Hollywood's top club, provided a heady counterpoint to the provincialism of Whittier.

Intent on enjoying traveling while they were young and unencumbered, the Nixons visited British Columbia and Yosemite Park and took many shorter trips around California and Arizona, venturing as far as Indiana. For their first wedding anniversary, which would be June 21, 1941, they drove through the desert in the middle of the night on their way to New Orleans, where, allowing themselves an extravagance, they dined on French-Creole cuisine (including Oysters Rockefeller) at the world-renowned Restaurant Antoine, a favorite of Presidents Franklin Roosevelt, Calvin Coolidge, and Herbert Hoover. Next they boarded the *Ulua*, the United Trust Company Steamship Service Company liner, for a round-trip cruise to Panama, with stop-offs in Port Limón, on the eastern coast of Costa Rica, and Central America's most important seaport, Puerto Cortés in Honduras.

Shortly after the ship left port, on the evening of June 22, their steward told them the sobering news that had come over the ship radio: Hitler had invaded Russia. Pat and Dick, who engaged with current affairs simply as citizens rather than public figures at this early stage, not public figures, were alarmed that Hitler had betrayed his August 1939 pact with Stalin, and, according to Nixon's memoir, hoped that the Nazi leader was overreaching in a manner that would undermine his grandiose designs.

When the ship docked in Havana, Dick, not one to stop working completely, spent part of his time exploring whether he could set up a law practice in Cuba. Their visit to the Canal Zone took them to what Pat noted was "often called the most immoral spot in the world," populated with American soldiers prowling through cabarets and bars looking for women in the raucous, narrow streets.

The Nixons had selected the cheapest cabin, which turned out to be next to the engine room; Dick, already seasick, became ill from the smell of oil. Nonetheless, they quickly bonded with a new group of couples on board, who took bets on how long Dick could last in the dining room before he would turn green. He did participate in some of their riotous parties, which included a "vice-versa" evening where everyone cross-dressed. According to his daughter Julie, Dick came "as a Grecian lady, draped in costume—sheet, turban, brooch, bosom etc."

Pat felt let down when they returned to Whittier, noting in her diary that she was "just a gypsy at heart." She did not go back to teaching that fall, seeking instead to stretch herself in a world wider than a provincial California village. But before she could look for another job, a life-changing job opportunity arrived for Dick. In October, the general counsel of the Office of Price Administration (OPA) wrote Dick asking him to interview for a position in Washington, D.C., with the recently formed agency, whose mandate was to prepare the country for the likelihood of war. While the yearly salary of $3,200 was less than the two of them made together in Whittier, it was enough to support them in taking the first of many ambitious steps toward the center of the nation's political heartbeat. As the Nixons would learn, the world of politics and government changes those who venture into it. And, as they would soon discover, so does the world of war.

Love After Pearl Harbor

On Sunday, December 7, 1941, Pat and Dick left a movie mati-
nee in Hollywood to discover that the world around them
had been immutably transformed. As the Nixons exited the theater, a
newsboy held up a paper with the headline JAPS BOMB PEARL HARBOR.
"We're at war, mister," the boy told them. What shock, outrage, fear,
and uncertainty they must have felt. Having bonded effectively as a
couple in their first eighteen months of marriage, they would soon
confront the first of myriad challenges in their long union. How could
they negotiate their relationship amid the strain, separation, and en-
forced personal independence of wartime?

The war soon summoned them from Whittier to Washington, D.C.
After Dick received confirmation of an appointment in the Office of
Price Administration personnel section, Pat and Dick (by now veterans

of long-distance car trips) drove across the country, taking turns at the wheel, braving snowstorms and icy conditions in Tennessee to arrive in the capital on the afternoon of January 9, Dick's twenty-ninth birthday. They went straight to the OPA's makeshift offices on Sixth Street and Independence Avenue. Immediately after Dick was sworn in as a government official, they began looking for an affordable apartment in the overcrowded Washington area. The "City of Magnificent Intentions," as Lafayette described it, would see its population double in the following couple of years, as citizens, particularly women, streamed into the hub of hectic effort to win a two-fronted world war.

In a stroke of remarkable luck, they drove across the Potomac, perhaps noticing the antiaircraft defense batteries recently erected on the outskirts of the city, and came upon the as yet unfinished Beverly Park apartment complex in Alexandria, Virginia. The landlord, a fellow Californian, took a liking to the couple—perhaps he was attracted to Pat—and, ignoring a waiting list, rented them a small one-bedroom. Pat considered it "a miracle!" as she wrote in her diary. Washington, full of the peril of war, might offer them something like home.

Both Dick and Pat plunged into the war effort, with Dick intent on learning how the government operated. The mission of the Office of Price Administration was to protect citizens from unscrupulous businessmen who would use the cover of wartime as an excuse to overcharge consumers. Dick would work for eight months in the OPA's tire-rationing division, where, as a lawyer, he helped explain and modify the complicated rules that the government had prescribed for policing the automobile industry. He found the work tedious, but applied himself with his usual industry. By March 1942 he had been appointed informally to a deadly dull–sounding position as the acting chief of interpretations in the sub-branch of the Rubber Branch.

Pat did her part for the war effort by volunteering as a secretary for the Red Cross. By August she obtained a $2,600-a-year job for herself as an assistant business analyst at the OPA. She soon, however, grew impatient with the OPA's rigid rules, which she believed interfered with providing real economic assistance to people. Pat and Dick would be short-lived believers in big government; Dick later claimed that his

OPA job soured him on bureaucracy and taught him the limited value of government intervention in the private sector.

Based on his OPA work, Dick could have had a draft deferment, but in wartime Washington smart and ambitious men realized that serving in the theater of war was a crucial step toward a high-level professional or political career. After much reflection, and with Pat's support, Dick put aside his Quaker reservations about fighting in a war. He enlisted in the U.S. Navy—a surprising choice given his propensity for seasickness, but he had heard that the navy was seeking lawyers for administrative work on aircraft carriers and other large ships.

Facing a wartime separation, Pat and Dick took a brief retreat together that would create memories to savor during the lonely days to come. They spent a long weekend in Cape Porpoise near Kennebunkport on the rocky coast of Maine. Many of the hotels and restaurants along the coast had been forced to close because wartime gas rationing ruined tourism. The Nixons were the only guests in a small clapboard hotel. They took tranquil walks along the shore, read, and kept themselves warm together during the cool coastal nights. In the afternoons they picked blueberries on their two-mile walk to the Porpoise Restaurant, where they ate a full lobster dinner for a dollar. The Nixons bought a painting of a small lobster boat beached on a curving shore of purplish-blue water, which would hang in the master bedroom of most of their homes.

On Monday, August 17, 1942, in what would be the first of many partings over the next years, Pat saw her husband off at Washington's Union Station. Dick endured a gloomy train ride to Rhode Island for two months of rigorous officer training at Quonset Point, the first week of which, Dick wrote Pat, "was the longest I've ever known." He disliked studying naval science and ballistics and was no fan of the arduous physical training in the summer humidity. He found solace in his correspondence with his wife.

The Nixons' wartime letters are extraordinary documents, offering vivid evidence of the couple's strengthening bond and the evolution of their individual characters. Their separation allowed these emotionally straitened individuals the space to discover and express their profound feeling for each other. At the midpoint of Dick's training, they met up for a weekend in New York City. As she recounted to his parents later, when Pat first spotted him in the crowd at Pennsylvania Station, Dick looked "so different: younger, real tanned, thinner, and of course very handsome in his blue uniform with all the braid and the blue cap." Dick, she said, wanted to dine "where we can sit with real silver, on a real tablecloth with someone to serve." They splurged on a meal at the Rainbow Room in Rockefeller Center. Dick felt all the more lonely on his train ride back to Quonset. At the base he wrote her that "this weekend was wonderful. Coming back I looked at myself in the mirror and thought how very lucky I was to have you . . . I was proud of you every minute I was with you." Acknowledging his reticence ("I am certainly not the Romeo type"), Dick explained, "I may not say much when I am with you—*but all of me loves you all the time.*"

Pat also felt a keen sense of loss. After one late-night phone call, she wrote him what may be one of her first romantic missives: "It's two o'clock but I just had to write you to say *how very much I love you.*" Her pet name for him was Plum. After telling him about a movie she had seen, she wrote, "I miss Plum's hand very much." In a comment that, in her concern for her husband's burdens, foreshadows her feelings in later years in the White House, Pat wrote, "I hope I said nothing to worry you—when you are working so hard, etc. it would be awful to add to the load."

After Dick was appointed as a lieutenant junior grade in the U.S. Naval Reserve in October, he and Pat received an unwelcome shock. Dick had requested "ships and stations" as his first choice for active duty, with the expectation that he would be assigned to a battle fleet in one of the war zones. Instead he was sent to a naval station at an air base in Ottumwa, Iowa, amid the cornfields in the southeastern corner of the state, eighty-five miles from Des Moines. Dick discovered that the naval air station was not even fully built. "Its uncompleted runway stopped abruptly in the middle of a cornfield," he later wrote. Pat happily quit her frustrating OPA job and took a bus to the hinterlands to join him. Although Dick put the best gloss on his Iowa stint in his memoirs, claiming that they were pleased with the midwestern hospitality they received, the Nixons were bored and restless. Being a navy couple in the landlocked center of America was not their definition of adventure.

After serving as a communications officer at the base, by December Dick was transferred to a position as an administrative aide to the executive officer at the flight training center. According to her daughter Julie, Pat's experience working for the OPA led her to obtain a job at Ottumwa's Union Bank, which hired her to develop the complex bookkeeping program needed to keep track of the government's new point-rationing system. Pat also worked as a teller. Bitterly cold and snowy, Ottumwa made Whittier look like a state capital. Pat was not fond of a social life in which the highlight was "coffee socials with navy wives." At Christmas their mood brightened, but they also felt homesick as they received boxes of expensive (for Iowa) oranges, grapefruit, tangerines, Pat's favorite fudge, walnuts, dates, and cherries from his parents in California. After attending a Christmas Eve service at the Presbyterian Church, the couple invited six officers for Christmas-night dinner and showed off the bounty in their fruit bowl. That December Dick spotted a listing on the mess announcement board asking officers in his age group to apply for immediate sea duty; he jumped at the opportunity. When a posting came through for the island of New Caledonia, they hightailed it out of Ottumwa. By early May they were in San Francisco.

Pat decided to stay in the Bay Area, which had the best job opportunities, while Dick was overseas. She located a job as a correspondence clerk with the Office of Civilian Defense. After scouring the newspaper, she found a cheap bedroom and bath in a garage attached to a house at the top of a hill at 2829 Divisadero Street, an address Dick would soon come to know by heart. He wrote her there every day.

Pat and Dick returned to Whittier to store their car. After a brief visit, his family and a group of friends went to Union Station in Los Angeles to see the couple off. His parents and his ninety-three-year-old maternal grandmother Alvira were heartsick at his assignment to a war, and not just because they worried about his safety. By joining the navy, Dick had ignored his family's Quaker heritage of pacifism. Nixon was not, however, a pacifist, and never considered being a conscientious objector. Joining the effort to defeat Germany and Japan "wasn't a move I made because I was a real brave fella," Dick later told biographer Jonathan Aitken. "It was just simply an innate inner feeling that it was vitally important to be where the action was." Nixon found a moral imperative for combat that would allow him to join a war effort uniting him with his fellow citizens in a larger cause, position him for a postwar role in public life, and provide him with a new maturity and a broader range of human experience.

The parting was not easy. The family had breakfast at Union Station's Harvey House restaurant, which Dick remembered as a "painful meal full of sad silences" amid the chitchat. The Nixons, like parents all across America, knew that this might be the last time they saw their son, and their distress was exacerbated by their moral objection to the war their son would be fighting in. As Pat and Dick stepped up onto a wooden block to board the train, they turned and saw that Frank Nixon had begun to sob. Evlyn Dorn remembered how Frank's sorrow unnerved the group. Dick Nixon and his young wife, who both detested displays of emotion in public, cringed. To cover his own feelings, Dick pointed to his youngest brother and loudly proclaimed, "Eddie, you take care of your mother."

Pat was as emotionally torn as any young American wife—fearful that she might lose Dick, but proud of her husband and supportive of his patriotism. "I would have felt mighty uncomfortable," Pat told Nixon biographer Bela Kornitzer, "if Dick hadn't done his part." She was able to derive satisfaction from supporting the war effort by making a sacrifice of her own—living frugally and with little socializing. On May 31, 1943, the day he left for the war zone, Dick undertook the somber task of writing his will—a task his legal practice left him well prepared to do—leaving all his property to Pat, appointing her "executive without bond" with "absolute discretion" in settling his estate. Asking for as "simple and inexpensive a funeral as possible," he concluded the brief document by telling Pat to remarry, should he die, and by making clear that remarriage would have no effect on her rights under his will.

Dick headed overseas on an unpleasant seventeen-day voyage crammed in with three thousand fellow servicemen on the converted ocean liner SS *President Monroe*. Pat and Dick would be apart for fourteen months, during which time they wrote each other every day. "Your letters are my only happiness now," Dick wrote her. On their third wedding anniversary (June 21, 1943), Dick penned her letter on his knee in a Quonset hut, while "wishing that you and I could be riding down the coast of Monterey to spend a month at the beach." He spent an hour in a local cathedral "thinking of our years together and loving you every minute of the time . . . I think of our last few days in S.F.—our walks up Market [St.]—and into the stores. I really get a big bang out of shopping with you—and I hope you buy *everything* you want always." Reminiscing about the day they met in February 1938, he could not resist tweaking her. "Remember how you treated me then?"

Dick claimed that her job with the OPA was far more important than his had ever been there. "I'm really *very* proud—as I have always been. I like to tell the gang how smart you are as well as being the most attractive person they'll ever see. Dear Heart you are the tops! Small wonder that I have no other interest than you."

His separation from his wife, combined with his frustrating and ultimately undistinguished role on the outskirts of the real war, brought up old feelings of inadequacy, heightening his attachment to Pat. In a letter replete with the sentiment of his 1938 infatuation with Pat, he wrote, "The only thing that matters is that I love you more every day," his postscript describing her powerful impact upon his mood: "When I feel blue—I think of our times together—and it has a miraculous effect. You are a real tonic for me." Because wartime delivery was erratic and undependable and letters would arrive in batches, they agreed to number and date their missives.

Dick did not have with him a good photograph of his wife. He badgered Pat for nine months until she set aside her reservations about doing something self-indulgent and dragged herself to a portrait studio. The beautiful picture left Dick ecstatic. Now he had something tangible to brag about with his wartime buddies. "Everybody raved—wondered how I happened to rate! (I do too)," but the image of his absent wife intensified his loneliness amid the tedium and tension of war.

Dick served with the South Pacific Air Transport Command in General Douglas MacArthur's Southwest Pacific Theater, supporting ground operations on New Caledonia, Bougainville, and Green Island. He prepared flight plans for the cargo and transport planes, ordered supplies for the troops, and helped evacuate the wounded and dead. Later he became head of an air transport operation.

His first base was in the capital of New Caledonia, Noumea, a crucial seat for the Allied forces that had fought off Japan's advances toward Australia, New Zealand, and the Solomon Islands. The city was set on a hilly peninsula in the southeast end of the island. One Sunday Dick and several friends rode a jeep into the lush, stream-filled mountains that surrounded the base, amid shining blue butterflies and exquisite flora. "You rode along with me all the way," he wrote Pat. "I think of you when I see beautiful things." To bring her closer, he enclosed in his letter samples of some of the attractive and unique vegetation and the red berries he found along the way.

In September 1943, flying at ten thousand feet overlooking the South Pacific islands and the ocean, he did not have time to complete a full letter, but wanted her to know that "I love you just the same up here as down below." The next morning when the sun came up, he flew above the clouds and saw a spectacular sunrise. He missed her then, but assured her, "We will see sunrises from the air together—and I hope very soon."

With dull work and too much time on his hands, he was often miserable. He did not want her to suffer as he did, and he urged his wife to "get good dinners, see lots of shows, buy nice clothes, have your hair fixed—and anything else you want or need," hoping that she could "make up for me here." "It will make me feel swell to think of you having some enjoyment." He knew how the separation hurt her. As much as she appreciated his loving gesture, she felt she should share his sacrifice. There would be plenty of pleasure in their future, she thought.

On August 24, from his post on the island of Vella Lavella, Dick complained to Pat about how "the damn central office" seemed to thwart his attempts to get closer to the action. He yearned to move to a "less civilized place, where I would feel I was doing more." In a request certain to scare a wartime wife, he added, "I am working on an angle. . . . Keep your fingers crossed and wish hard!" Pat wanted her husband to do worthwhile and rewarding work, but that didn't mean she wanted him closer to Japanese bombing.

Restless, in January 1944 Dick wangled a post in Bougainville, the biggest of the Solomon Islands, where, not long after his arrival on the island, the Japanese attacked. "One night it was pretty close," he remembered. "This plane . . . had come in very low. We heard the bombs dropping as they came down the runway. We dived out of our tent into the foxhole. As soon as we got out, we saw that our whole tent had been sprayed with bullets. It was a close one." Downplaying the danger for his edgy wife, he wrote, "It isn't really as bad as it sounds and the danger is very small. The only casualties are among those who refuse to get up and go in a foxhole and there are few people like that."

Now styled "Nick" Nixon by his comrades, the thirty-three-year-old lieutenant felt loosed from the restrictions of his previous sheltered civilian life. Living in close quarters with a wide variety of working-class mates, he took up drinking, swearing, smoking cigars, and poker, which he mastered. Dick learned that he was a good bluffer, a skill he would later find useful in politics. On July 4, 1944, he wrote Pat that at poker he had "won over a thousand to date."

In one letter that foreshadowed the isolation and self-absorption of his years in the White House, Dick wrote Pat, "I'm anti-social, I guess, but except for you—I'd rather be by myself as a steady diet rather than with most any of the people I know. . . . I like to do what I want when I want. Only where you are concerned do I feel otherwise—Dear One."

Outwardly affable, he was popular with his fellow servicemen of all stripes, but he still had the heart of a loner. At the same time, Dick felt at home operating in a community of men. Biographer Stephen Ambrose points out that the rigid structure of the navy hierarchy temporarily freed Dick from the urgency of his ambition, allowing him an easier sociability than he had previously enjoyed: No one "below him was a threat and no one above him was a block to his advancement." He formed a close friendship with Lieutenant James B. Stewart, with whom he spent hours relaxing while sitting on a veranda overlooking the ocean. Dick confided to Stewart about his relationship with Pat (revealing that she was the only woman he ever slept with), his feelings about the conduct of the war, and his thoughts about the future of the country.

Dick used his connections as a navy supply officer to procure food and drink that his fellow combatants sorely missed. A "first rate scrounger," as he called himself; he would swap anything with other units to obtain supplies for his men. He endeared himself to them by opening "Nick's Hamburger Stand," also known as "Nick's Snack Shack," where fighter pilots passing through the island could stop for a free, rejuvenating Australian beer, fresh, cold pineapple juice, good old American hamburgers, and a bit of much-needed camaraderie. According to air force fighter pilot Chandler Worley, "It meant so much . . . just a few minutes' satisfaction." Dick wrote Pat that he had gone to a Cary Grant movie with several pilots, who appreciated the "Snack Shop, etc. We have had toasted hamburger sandwiches for them for the past two weeks—with cold juice or coffee. That's making a big hit as you can imagine."

Fantasizing about the future with Pat soothed him. "Dear one—what fun we could have on a farm!" he wrote her. "Dogs, horses, snow—and somebody to do the work! Whatever it is, whatever you do, it will be wonderful to be with you again. I love you so *very very* much right this minute." On March 17, 1944 (her thirty-second birthday), he happily remembered that it was the sixth anniversary of the first time that he had sent her flowers, and that a few days later they had traveled together to have dinner at a restaurant called Bird's in Laguna, California. "For all the years to come—your birthdays will be reminders of our happiness and my love for you." He would indeed honor her future birthdays.

Both Dick and Pat fretted over the constant possibility that Dick would die in war. The previous December, Pat had felt particularly unsettled. She had not heard from Dick in nearly a month and she did not know what kind of danger he faced. She turned down several invitations from married friends to join them for Christmas dinner. Instead, she spent Christmas Day circling San Francisco in a ferry, until the lights of the city brightened the gloomy dusk. When she got home, she re-read all of her husband's letters.

Insecure about the love he had so recently won, it would have been natural for Dick to wonder whether Pat, alone in a big city, might turn to fancy big-city men for companionship, as she had done during their courtship. Dick asked her to write at the beginning of each letter that she loved him—"I always look first for that," he told her. Such reassurance was a balm to a man who would never perceive any victory as permanent.

Dick need not have worried. Pat embraced the identity of the model wife, left behind, while her husband fought overseas. "With her husband in the South Pacific," Pat's friend Gretchen King recalled, "she [Pat] felt she should not be participating in social events." Pat also stayed close to home to save money. She was "very frugal and . . . she made a lot of her clothes and hats," according to King. Pat focused on her work ambitions, leaving her job at the Office of Civilian Defense to join the Committee for Congested Production Areas, and finally landing a good job as a price economist for the San Francisco division of the OPA. She was pictured in the *San Francisco News* with several colleagues looking over new government orders granting her office price-fixing authority on a variety of civilian goods. At the OPA she worked alongside Gretchen King, who had moved to San Francisco in 1940 when her husband, Robert, was appointed by the FBI to monitor activities by Soviet and homegrown communists. Gretchen was immediately drawn to Pat, who knew how to make a friend. "She seemed a well-disciplined person," King later said, "with great poise and presence, with an ability to handle any situation that might arise." For her, Pat had "the most beautiful eyes I've ever seen—clear, alert, intelligent. She impressed me as such a warm, happy, sparkling person. There were times when we must have seemed like a couple of high school youngsters, laughing, giggling, and thoroughly enjoying each other."

The Kings' social life consisted of dinners and outings with the other FBI agents and their wives. Since Pat "seemed so alone," they often invited her to join them. Although she turned down invitations for dinner parties, Pat did dine alone with the Kings on Saturday evenings or share a Sunday brunch. The Kings found her "always interested and contributing to whatever subject was under discussion."

Before returning home in early August 1944, Lieutenant Nixon was awarded two battle stars and a commendation from his commanding officer "for meritorious and efficient duty." Halfway through his fourteen months of service in the South Pacific, Dick had imagined his reunion with his wife. "I'm going to walk right up to you and kiss you—but good. Will you mind such a public demonstration?" Certainly, after so long apart, even a public display of affection would please his normally reserved wife. Nixon flew from the South Pacific to Hawaii and then sailed to San Diego, calling Pat the moment he arrived and arranging to meet her at the airport. When Pat, dressed in a bright red dress (his favorite color for her), spotted Dick standing behind the airport fence, "her eyes lighted up," Nixon remembered, "and she ran about fifty yards at breakneck speed and threw her arms around me." It was no doubt the biggest and most joyful embrace of their married life, and one of the few occurring in public. But their exuberant hug was a signal that if their romantic feelings had not been completely mutual before Dick left for war, they were now.

As was true for many reunited couples, it might have been difficult sometimes for the Nixons to reconcile their new identities. Lieutenant "Nick" Nixon, who now swore, drank, and smoked cigars, and civilian Pat Ryan Nixon, his self-denying and independent wife, might have needed to recalibrate their intimacy—finding a healthy balance between their new habits and their old patterns, their alliance and their individual autonomy. While he was away, Pat had gently reminded Dick of her gift for finding happiness on her own—a trait that allowed the Nixons comfortably to spend significant periods of time apart—and one that many White House observers would later misread when they labeled their marriage as loveless. "I will have to admit that I am pretty self-reliant and if I didn't love you I would feel very differently" about living on her own in the big city, she wrote during the war. "In fact these many months you have been away have been full of interest, and had I not missed you so much and had I been foot loose, could have been extremely happy. So, sweet, you'll always have to love me lots and never let me change my feelings." Offering both a warning that she needed to be loved intensely and an appeal for Dick to provide that kind of love, Pat was setting forth what she wanted from her marriage in the future. Once their lives became hectic with politics, she would have less opportunity to receive that from her husband.

From late August through the end of the year, Pat and Dick were reunited, as he was stationed at the Alameda Air Station on the east shore of San Francisco Bay. As a first lieutenant with Fleet Air Wing Eight, he performed mostly menial work: "I was the chief janitor," he would tell his daughter Julie. Pat and Dick threw a dinner party in their small apartment for Gretchen, her husband, Robert, and another couple. The Nixons "seemed so right for each other," Gretchen King remembered. Robert King found it easy to develop and maintain a friendship with Dick: "He was a little on the quiet side, but still fun, not outgoing or ebullient . . . but . . . a warm and genuine person who was very easy to talk with." The war had reinforced Dick's serious bent of mind. But Dick also impressed Robert as an "idealistic dreamer," even though his war experiences had toughened him, honed his sense of bureaucratic politics, and made him more deft at social interactions. Now that his role in the war zone was over, he was ready to talk about the America that would emerge from victory to command the globe. How would the country function within the international community? Would the nation become a force for peace? "He seemed to be dreaming about some new order that would make wars impossible," Robert King thought. Nixon did not choose to discuss his ambitions with his new friend, but he showed great interest in talking with Robert about the multitude of communist espionage activities in the San Francisco area. Shortly, Dick's campaign against communism would animate the first public venture in the life of the Nixons, as they worked together to elect Dick to political office.

5

Giant Slayers

*I*n the fall of 1945 the Nixons were living near Baltimore while Dick worked at Middle River, Maryland, terminating naval contracts with private corporations. Pat was pregnant—she was due to deliver in February. Dick's navy colleague James Cobey, who socialized with the couple, found them to be "very conservative, very conventional, but on the way up—happy and optimistic." Pat and Dick had every reason to be sanguine about their prospects: they were well-educated, hardworking, essentially personable people who in the rush of postwar prosperity were primed to prosper. They just needed the right break. One day that October, an airmail letter arrived that would change the Nixons' lives completely. Dick opened it to find that Herman Perry, his political mentor in Whittier, was asking the young naval officer if he would like to interview to run against the popular, well-financed, five-term incumbent Democratic congressman Jerry Voorhis on the Republican ticket in 1946.

For the Nixons, just now recovering from a wartime separation, a political campaign would present the second great challenge of their marriage. Over the next two days Pat and Dick debated the pros and cons of accepting Perry's offer. Serving in Congress would be an honor as well as an extraordinary break for a young man with no experience in public office, yet to realize the opportunity meant returning to Whittier, a small town they had purposely deserted five years before. Dick remembered keenly how a lack of gas money had hindered his failed run for the Assembly in 1940. They would have to spend most of their savings on a race against a popular incumbent and endure the rigors of a campaign even as Pat would be taking care of a new baby. The Nixons had saved $10,000 (from their salaries and from Dick's poker winnings) to buy a home where they could raise a family. A congressional bid, especially when both the candidate and his marriage were relatively young and untested, would be an enormous risk. After two tense days of juggling insecurities, fears, and aspirations, they decided to gamble on their future. Although they both had reservations about spending their savings, Dick told his biographer Jonathan Aitken that he convinced Pat that "we're not starting off with a lot in any event and we won't be much worse off for losing." Pat Nixon valued money and the security it represented, but she took a chance that supporting her husband's ambitions would have a better long-term payoff. They planned to invest half of their savings in the campaign. In 1960 Pat gave a *Time* magazine reporter her account of why she supported his run for Congress: "I could see that it was the life he wanted, so I told him that it was his decision, and I would do what he liked." Her decision converged with the expectations that were then being established for women in the postwar era: They should subordinate themselves to their husband's ambitions and desires.

Having made a bold decision, they sought a quick and positive response from their supporters. But when Dick called Herman Perry, after midnight East Coast time, Perry threw them a curve. Dick would not be handed the nomination; he needed to audition along with five other potential candidates before the Committee of 100—local Republican businessmen, bankers, ranchers, community leaders, and wealthy conservative matrons. With no choice but to follow Perry's dictum, the Nixons went west.

In early November Pat made the first of thousands of appearances as a candidate's wife, this one at a luncheon with Republican women in San Marino. She barely passed the test. One Republican matron carped, "Why, this girl doesn't even know what color nail polish to wear." Pat was a quick student—she softened her nail color right away— even though she resented the attitude of these upper-crust ladies, none of whom had worked as hard in their lives as she had already. They reminded Pat of the prima donnas she had ambivalently served at Bullock's department store in Los Angeles. Dick, dressed in his naval uniform (because he did not own a decent suit), appeared before an open meeting of the Committee of 100 in the William Penn Hotel in Whittier. Intense, earnest, he radiated conviction that he could win, employing an "aggressive and vigorous campaign on a platform of practical liberalism," a term he used to contrast his Main Street beliefs with what he saw as the extravagant, government-sponsored ambitions of the New Deal. One committee member called him an "electrifying personality."

Back in their small Maryland apartment on November 29, Pat and Dick were awakened by a call around 2:00 a.m. Answering the phone with middle-of-the-night trepidation, Dick heard Roy O. Day, the chairman of the Twelfth District Republicans, shouting exuberantly over the gravelly long-distance line, "Dick, Dick, the nomination is yours!" Pat and Dick were too excited to get back to sleep. That morning Dick was in touch with Massachusetts congressman Joseph Martin, Jr., the minority leader in the House of Representatives, and other Republicans, to plot strategy.

In 1946 Pat and Dick would burst onto the national scene as one of the first political couples campaigning together in American history—the Pat and Dick team—a feat made possible by the large role of women on the home front during the war.

Pat Nixon would be a pioneer of the type of activist political spouse who unstintingly supported her husband, took a prominent role in his campaign and stood by his side, and sacrificed her privacy and much of her own autonomy for the sake of the marital team. She was not interested in enduring the calumny that Eleanor Roosevelt had faced for her outspokenness. Instead, she would later come to understand how polarizing her husband's personality and politics could be and realize that she could benefit him most by being a warmer, uncontroversial, and positive presence. She guarded what she said and did in public for the rest of her life. Within half a decade of her first campaign, she would come to personify the engaged and devoted postwar political wife—an association that would often be intended not just to describe her but to undermine her husband, deemphasize her influence, and wound her personally. And she would pay a high price for her contribution to the Nixons' success.

In January 1946, after Dick received his discharge from the navy, he and Pat returned to Whittier and the Twelfth Congressional District that the young Republican lawyer sought to represent. The district was fluid and had been changing over the past year since Voorhis had been back to visit. Constituting more than four hundred square miles in the California basin southeast and west of the San Gabriel Mountains, it was a daunting territory for an untested politician to master—especially one with minimal funding. While its three hundred thousand constituents consisted mainly of conservative middle-class and lower-middle-class folks like the Nixons, the district also had wealthy and sophisticated denizens of the larger communities of San Marino, South Pasadena, Alhambra, and San Gabriel. Its citizens had been contentedly represented for ten years by Democrat Jerry Voorhis, who had a measure of power in Washington.

Dick and Pat moved in with his parents, surrendering their hard-won independence for economy and bowing to the exigencies of the postwar housing shortage—just the kind of problem Dick would decry on the campaign trail. Swinging into action to support their prewar colleague, Dick's old law firm renamed itself Bewley, Knoop, and Nixon and put him on the payroll—without expecting any real work from him—so that he could devote himself full-time to his campaign.

From the start, the campaign would be a family affair. Dick and

Pat set up their campaign headquarters in an abandoned storeroom in an old downtown storefront, just down the block from Nixon's law firm in the Bank of America building. The Nixons paid the rent out of their savings and scrounged around town for used furniture they could borrow. Hannah Nixon lent them a worn leather sofa, and Don Nixon and Pat's high-school friend Marion Burdlong found some mismatched chairs, a battered desk, an old typewriter, and a throw rug to furnish the makeshift office.

Pat's dedication to the campaign was resolute and wholehearted, even as the due date for her baby's birth grew increasingly near. She sold part of her inheritance—her one tangible asset, a share of a property she owned with her brother Tom—for $3,000 and invested the bulk of the proceeds in six-page illustrated pamphlets that introduced the unknown Richard Nixon to the public as a future leader who had fought to defend the country in the "jungles of the Solomons" and was "One of Us." Using the effectively cutting language that would become a Nixon campaign trademark, the pamphlet contrasted the war hero Nixon to Voorhis, who had "stayed safely behind the front in Washington."

Twenty-six years later, at the time of the Watergate investigation, Pat would angrily wonder to her daughter Julie why no one had been outraged back in 1946 when some member of the enemy camp broke into Nixon's headquarters and stole a huge batch of these precious pamphlets. Historians are divided about whether the Nixon headquarters was actually vandalized or whether the First Lady was confusing incidents in which Voorhis supporters had come to the office to ask for piles of Nixon pamphlets and then promptly thrown them away. There is no evidence to confirm Pat's memory. But even if all the Twelfth District Democrats did was to take and trash the pamphlets in which she had invested her inheritance, the incident was Pat's first encounter with political mischief, and it clearly caused a trauma she never forgot or forgave. She felt as if her last dollars had been swiped from her purse. It would be the first of many disillusioning political moments for a woman who had entered the political arena with her youthful idealism intact. Dick, on the other hand, was by birth and breeding a man who saw politics as war; the incident with the pamphlets no doubt encouraged his conviction that the best defense against deviousness was a good offense.

Money was extremely tight. Pat appreciated when other citizens contributed to the campaign and the financing wasn't all up to the Nixons alone. As Pat typed correspondence and paid bills at her battered desk in their office on Whittier's main street, she was heartened when Whittierites came in bearing their own small contributions to the cause. "I've known an indescribable kind of emotion," Pat told the *Saturday Evening Post* in 1952, "that comes when men and women obviously in poor circumstances stop to shake hands and press a half dollar or perhaps a dollar into my hand for a campaign in which they believe just as sincerely as we do." One woman, nearly blind with no money to give, came in daily to do the only thing she could—lick stamps and affix them to envelopes. For Pat such altruism was repayment for the "inevitable periods of despondency" of an underfinanced, hardscrabble campaign.

In speech after speech over those four hundred square miles, in house parties where the Nixons' smiles could never sag as they gripped the hands of strangers, in exhausting house-to-house canvassing during which Democrats or the disgruntled could slam the door or shirk the doorbell, Pat and Dick fought vigorously to prove the viability of his candidacy. Wealthy Republicans were not sure that Nixon could topple Voorhis, who had beaten other candidates the Committee of 100 grassroots Republican supporters had put forth in the past. Local contributions did not offset the serious shortfall in their coffers. Republican supporter Charles Cooper remembers how upset Pat was by their tenuous situation: "One morning Pat came into my office almost in tears. She said they were running out of money for the campaign and did not think they could finish it unless they could get more money . . . we got hold of the right people and raised money in a hurry." Bankers, ranchers, and small businessmen began contributing.

Pat worked for the campaign until February 17 and the final days of her pregnancy. Early in the morning of February 21, Dick was eating breakfast when Pat suddenly screamed for him from the back bedroom. Her labor had begun. She was prepared, her bag packed and ready to go. Dick scooped her up, carried her down the front steps, and set her gently in their Oldsmobile. Shortly after 9:00 a.m. her doctor at Whittier's Murphy Memorial Hospital examined her. He told Dick that the birth was not imminent and that a woman who was approaching her midthirties and having her first child, he believed, could expect a long labor. The newly declared candidate rushed off to attend a key campaign strategy luncheon at the Los Angeles Athletic Club, expecting he could return in time to see Pat through the birth, leaving Helene and Jack Drown to keep watch in the waiting room.

Pat's labor was complicated by a breech delivery, and the infant emerged with a broken shoulder. Despite the complications, the baby arrived only four and a half hours after Pat arrived at the hospital. The seven-pound daughter, soon to be known as Tricia, had penetrating blue eyes, fair skin, and black hair that would soon fall out and grow back blond. Dick was not present. No doubt Pat urged Dick to go to Los Angeles, but might she have later regretted her focus on his needs to the exclusion of her own? Pat was used to tolerating pain and handling it on her own. Maybe she did not need an anxious husband complicating matters. However she felt about her husband's absence, within hours of Tricia's birth Pat was sitting up in her hospital bed reading magazine articles and papers to research the various sections of the Twelfth District.

The announcement of Tricia's birth and photos of the young family were a boon to the campaign, generating coverage in the district's newspapers. The *Whittier News* fawned over "the perfect young lady" and her "lovely mother." The *Monrovia News Post* reported Dick's first public comment on his daughter, which not so subtly proclaimed his own independence from political special interests: "She is the only boss I recognize." He declared that "when the time comes she will register and vote Republican." In coming years, the more private Tricia and her more gregarious sister, Julie, would frequently be called upon to help sell the Nixons as an exemplar of the squeaky-clean postwar American family.

Within three weeks of the baby's birth, Pat was back on the campaign trail, leaving Tricia in the care of Hannah as she confronted an overwhelming backlog of administrative work to support the initial primary campaign. She served as the campaign office manager, taking charge of typing and mimeographing the campaign materials, getting them printed, mailed, and distributed throughout the area. Pat, sometimes accompanied by Dick, walked door to door to deliver brochures to shops and private homes. Pat brought in many volunteers and urged them to build momentum for the campaign by ringing as many doorbells as they could.

At night Pat tended to Tricia and slipped away when she could to do more typing for the campaign. For Pat, during that first hopeful campaign, "it was a very exciting life," Evlyn Dorn said, "to be in the center of things." She was enamored of her husband's brilliance and convinced of his potential. According to Georgia Sherwood, whose husband helped set up the candidate's schedule of radio addresses, Pat could talk about little but Dick and her new daughter.

In April Herman Perry found them a small Spanish-style stucco house on Walnut Street several blocks south of the campaign headquarters and an equal distance from Whittier College. They rented the poorly furnished one-bedroom house from a local barber. Pat put the baby's crib in the living room—with its lone couch—so that Dick could sleep. But the house overlooked a yard where neighbors raised minks, which squealed throughout the night and smelled twenty-four hours a day. The whole Nixon family suffered. Dick found an old radio to drown out the howling, but that did not put a dent in the stench. Pat had to display remarkable stamina to endure the strenuous daytime campaign schedule and new motherhood after having so little rest at night.

The lack of sleep and money, the unremitting work, and the looming possibility of failure left the Nixons overwhelmed at times. The stress of risking everything on an underfunded and understaffed campaign sometimes led Pat to weep or carp, and made Dick moody or snappish. Pat later recalled that at one point early in the campaign, she burst into sobs when she discovered that they had run out of money to buy stamps for the flyers she had bought with part of her family inheritance.

Other people witnessed the effects of stress on the couple. An incident at a radio studio where Dick was preparing to give an address offended Georgia Sherwood and her husband, Tom Dixon. When Pat walked into the studio, according to Dixon, "Nixon flared at her like a prima donna" and "ordered her out with as little ceremony as he would have a dog." After incidents like this, Pat learned that it was better to leave him alone when he was absorbed in his work. This stratagem accounts for part of the public distance observers noticed between the Nixons on plane trips and other occasions during the presidential and vice presidential years.

Pat elicited a pledge from Dick that she would not have to give speeches, but she undertook almost everything else. An anxious person, Pat pushed through her discomfort to attend meetings with women's civic groups, hospitals, children's centers, and "coffee klatches" in homes throughout the district. At the home events, neighbors provided coffee and dessert while Pat's husband talked about the issues before moving on to his next venue. Pat would stay to give brief remarks and charm the attendees with her personal warmth. She performed this public role while eschewing the solace of smoking cigarettes—a real sacrifice for her—as she did not want to give anyone the opportunity to criticize her as less than a model candidate's wife. Although Pat had anticipatory anxiety about going to campaign events, she loved people and warmed to the task more easily than she expected once she was among the voters.

According to Dick, Pat offered him "thoughtful and sometimes quite persistent critiques" of his performances at the house parties. His use of the word "persistent" suggests that her perfectionism, while often valuable, was sometimes more judgmental than he could comfortably tolerate. Pat would have noticed, for instance, that Dick had trouble looking women directly in the eye while talking to them about campaign issues. The well-known national political reporter, novelist, and screenwriter Adela Rogers St. Johns, who traveled with the Nixons, told biographer Fawn Brodie: "God, she made it rough for him. She would say, 'That was a disaster' or 'Well, I've heard you make lousy speeches, but that was the worst.'" Whether or not the tone of her advice might have alienated Dick as much as its content assisted him, Pat matched her rigorous professionalism with a warmth that ultimately aided her husband by winning over voters.

Perhaps Pat's most important contribution to the campaign came in the form of what is today called "opposition research." During the primary and the general election for this first campaign for Congress, Pat attended the rallies of Dick's political adversaries and wrote down their remarks in shorthand. She used this inside information to great advantage in helping her husband counter the rhetoric and political positions of his opponents as he prepared his speeches, which she scrutinized. Dick spent the winter and spring of 1946 traveling throughout the district giving speeches with a populist message that celebrated the "forgotten man" who did not need government interference in his life. He often worked twenty hours a day. Pat accompanied him whenever she could, with a ready smile and an eagle eye, judiciously passing out the precious Nixon flyers, sitting at his side at rallies, and taking shorthand notes on his presentations.

The Nixons were close to having no funds in the bank until the *Los Angeles Times* endorsed Dick in mid May and he won the Republican primary in June. Under California's election rules, both Nixon and Voorhis could cross-file and run on the Republican and Democratic tickets. If Voorhis won both the Republican and Democratic primaries, he would have both party nominations, which was tantamount to victory. In the June 4 primary, Nixon won the Republican nomination, but he was disheartened that Voorhis received 12 percent more of the overall vote. The young navy veteran would start out as a considerable underdog in his one-on-one effort to unseat a longtime incumbent, but Voorhis was increasingly seen as inimical to business interests in the district. In the late hours of the first nights after the primary, Pat watched wearily as Dick paced and fretted in their scruffy downtown headquarters, his agitation edging into resentment that his effort had not been better rewarded. As his wife and his devout believer, Pat had her work cut out for her.

Having depleted their physical and emotional energies, Pat and Dick treated themselves to a two-week vacation in the Canadian Rockies, where the snowcapped mountains around Banff and Lake Louise cooled the heat of campaigning. They had three months to overcome Voorhis's lead. As they contemplated the fall campaign, Dick yielded to self-doubt and dark moods, but Pat, who tended more toward anxiety than despondency, focused on the progress they had made in a few short months and the length of time they had to surmount the remaining obstacles. She was proving herself to be the backbone of the relationship, the one who could be relied upon to stand strong.

Pat's optimism proved accurate. As the campaign heated up and Dick began vigorously attacking Voorhis for having labor sympathies, significant contributions started flowing into the Nixon campaign. With their new funds the Nixons purchased and passed around twenty-five thousand white plastic thimbles cleverly labeled "Elect Nixon and needle the P.A.C." The PAC was the Political Action Committee of the labor group, the Congress of Industrial Organizations (CIO).

Nixon's focus on Voorhis's union leanings was part of the overall Republican congressional strategy in 1946 to regain control of Congress after sixteen years out of power. The GOP was determined to regain national political clout by any means necessary, and that meant tarring the Democrats for representing socialistic values at home and capitulating to communists abroad at a time when the Soviet Union was becoming America's primary foreign adversary. The GOP national chairman had set the tone in June by declaring that the fall elections would provide voters a choice between "communism and Republicanism." The uproar over labor strikes fanned a national hypersensitivity to the dangers of a communist takeover at home.

Taking his cue from the national GOP, Dick began to add an aggressive antilabor stance to his populist message. In foreign affairs, Dick disdained the penchant for isolationism that was still prevalent among some Republicans, urging that the United States should vigorously push back against communism so that democracy could flourish.

After Voorhis returned from Washington to Southern California at the end of August, he handed Nixon a gift by foolishly agreeing to debate his relatively unknown challenger. In their first encounter Nixon promptly pigeonholed Voorhis as a socialist who believed in big government. Pat was impressed; by the end of that debate, she was sure Dick had proved himself "the better man," but she wondered whether the audience agreed. She became convinced of Dick's success "when time and again, a poorly dressed man or woman would slip a coin or a crumpled bill in my hand and say, 'Use it to buy a little gasoline,' or perhaps just, 'God bless you.'"

Suddenly on the defensive, Voorhis agreed to four additional debates, which drew increasingly large crowds and generated a progressively more electric atmosphere that would come to resemble critical end-of-season football games. As the candidates entered the hall, bands played and battalions of their volunteers cheered. Pat sat attentively through them all. Whatever criticisms she had of his public style seem to have dissipated the more he practiced. Moreover, in this kind of forum her husband—a champion college debater—was in his element. She was fiercely proud of his debating skills, and found his "delivery terrific."

The final debate was held in an overflowing San Gabriel Civic Auditorium as several hundred people stood outside the building and listened over loudspeakers as the candidates sparred. Nixon's supporters and the partisan Republican newspapers played up Nixon's victories for all they were worth. Acknowledging the power and precision of Nixon's dramatic verbal parries, Voorhis later wrote, "I can't say I was exactly 'ready for the fray.' But the 'fray' was certainly ready for me."

During this last debate Dick Nixon summarized his constituencies, who not surprisingly were people like himself, or at least like the man and the boy he had been growing up in Whittier without the advantages that the elite enjoyed: "the person on a pension trying to keep up with the rising cost of living . . . the white-collar worker who has not had a raise." His voters were the people who wanted to shake off the hand of government and make their own success and ensure their own and the nation's abundance. Dick was elaborating on the 1946 national Republican election slogan: "Had Enough?" Americans were fed up with shortages of meat, cars, liquor, housing, and jobs. His voters had had enough of having too little and believed that after nearly three decades of deprivation they deserved more.

Pat relished the opportunity to participate in a substantive battle of beliefs. She continued to take notes on his speeches and help him refine his message. Surely, as a woman who had endured and surmounted her own deprivation, her husband's message personally resonated. In the final six weeks of the campaign she sat smiling through six or seven speeches a day—all of them tailored to the particulars of the crowd by Dick, who had a gift for extemporizing. Pat claimed that she was never bored. Polls were showing a strong positive trend for Nixon. Pat was heartened by the upsurge in campaign contributions. "Huh Boy!" she would say during the last days of the campaign. "These people must really believe we're going to win with the way donations are coming in." By the end of the campaign the Nixons had recouped the money they had invested in the primary.

On election night, November 5, after leaving a restaurant, Dick and Pat listened to the vague early election returns on their car radio. Because the ballots were counted by hand, the returns seeped in with torturous slowness. Initially Dick had a small lead, and then Voorhis did. The exhausted Nixons felt grim, but with her greater optimism, Pat bolstered Dick when he despaired of victory. By 9:00 p.m. Dick began to pull ahead. Pat and Dick waited until the early-morning hours to learn that Nixon had triumphed by a margin of greater than 15,000 votes out of more than 114,000 cast. Their relentless campaigning had paid off in a year when a Republican tide swept the country.

"I think today my greatest satisfaction . . . is not for myself but for my wife and my parents," Nixon told the *Whittier News* and other district newspapers: Of the seven electoral victories that the Nixons would enjoy, this was Pat's triumph as much as Dick's—if not more so. He was the savvy strategist, the shrewd debater, and the keen extemporaneous speaker, but he knew he would not have won without her. Pat made an enormous contribution with her stouthearted efforts when the odds were against them, her strong support at his moments of despondency and doubt, her crucial feedback, and her warmth and charm.

Kyle Palmer, the political editor of the *Los Angeles Times* and one of Nixon's champions, invited the Nixons to come to the *Times* building on election night to make a victory statement and to celebrate. Afterward, Pat and Dick went to a rowdy Committee of 100 party at the Huntington Hotel in Pasadena, where Dick played the piano, and then on to Jack and Helene Drown's house in Rolling Hills for a final celebration. Thoroughly exhausted, the Nixons declined the Drowns' offer to share an expensive bottle of sherry. Helene had a better idea: "Let's save it for a day when we will be able to crack it over a mantel of the White House." She was not alone in expecting Pat and Dick to end up in the Executive Mansion. Herman Perry told a group of his banking buddies that they would be guests of the Nixon White House long after Perry himself had died.

The Nixons went to bed that night in a state of jubilation. "Pat and I were happier on November 6, 1946, than we were ever to be again in my political career," Dick recalled in his memoir. The next morning, the young congressman-elect wrote in big letters in his datebook for November 5 an exultant "VICTORY!" Yet there was a shadow looming over their triumph. Voorhis, other Nixon election opponents and political adversaries, as well as certain journalists and historians would later charge that Nixon's win was marred by dirty campaign practices and virulent, unjustifiable antilabor attacks that went beyond the prescriptions that the national GOP had given its congressional candidates.

Nixon undoubtedly outcampaigned, outspent, and outdebated Representative Voorhis and was more effective in garnering the support of key newspaper editors from the *Los Angeles Times* and most of the thirty newspapers in the district. While Nixon biographers Irwin Gellman and Jonathan Aitken argue that dirty campaigning did not play a large role in Nixon's eventual victory, Nixon biographer Conrad Black calls the campaign "mischievous." Nixon and his staff misrepresented Voorhis's record to emphasize his labor associations and socialist values and to suggest that he was ineffectual in Congress.

Dick Nixon did not need to distort his opponent's record in order to win. The GOP took control in the House of Representatives for the first time since 1931 and captured the Senate as well. Pat, who was herself as partisan as he was and a true believer in the values and policies propounded by Republicans, would not have run a campaign as divisive as her husband's. For all Dick's brains and talent, perhaps she would have ultimately been the better candidate, but she surely would not have won.

Their victory drew attention to the Nixons in the national media, but Pat's role was, not surprisingly, underreported. *Newsweek* saluted the "husky ex-footballer" for his upset victory and quoted Voorhis saying that Nixon had a "silver tongue." *Time* praised the "dark, lank Quaker attorney" who triumphed over long odds to defeat the "high-powered, high-minded" incumbent and declared blithely that he had "politely avoided personal attacks on his opponent."

The Nixons spent the weeks following what the press and radio outside the Twelfth District called their "giant-killer act," responding to hundreds of congratulatory letters and telegrams, visiting their supporters throughout the district to thank them, and attending parties and dinners in their honor. The businessmen and professionals of the Southern California basin believed they now had an assertive representative who would help California achieve a balance of power with the eastern elite. Their candidate would also challenge the power of the unions. His backers celebrated his victory as a first step toward a Nixon presidency. The silver-tongued Quaker attorney might have blushed at such talk but did not discourage it. Wallace Black, a lawyer colleague of Nixon's, remembers Dick confiding that "someday he would be president."

A week after the election, when a reporter from the *Temple City Times* asked Nixon about his plans for the future, Dick chose to portray himself only as an avid family man. He and Pat had to "start getting acquainted with our pride and joy," eight-month-old Tricia, which they did for several weeks before leaving her with his parents for approximately a month while they drove their new 1946 Ford to Mexico for a brief vacation and then on to what they saw as their bright future, in Washington, D.C. The Mexican leg of the trip became an ordeal when U.S. customs officials made them completely unpack the car that Frank Nixon had so artfully crammed with luggage and boxes of household belongings. He had created an intricate arrangement that took Pat and Dick hours to reduplicate. As heady as they were about their recent victory, they did not pull rank to try to circumvent the inspection.

The Nixons would not shy away from surmounting obstacles. The real story of this 1946 campaign—for good and for ill—was the gutsy resolve Pat and Dick brought to bear on a difficult electoral challenge and the awful campaign that Voorhis ran. The Nixons fought bravely, resourcefully, and at times ingloriously to push past every impediment that blocked their path. For the most part, they would not shrink from this pattern for the rest of their lives. There were times, however, when Pat seemed less inclined to battle in the White House.

The Faces of America's Future

As they arrived in Washington in December 1946, Pat and Dick entered a challenging new phase in their marriage: They would have to forgo the kind of intimate political teamwork they had enjoyed during the 1946 campaign and work at a greater distance from each other, with new and sometimes dissimilar goals. Like many couples who had quickly begun having children after reuniting at war's end, they would have to negotiate the loneliness and separation inherent in pursuing their dual ambitions. Husbands in this era would devote themselves to their careers, off on their own in their gray flannel suits, while their wives focused on raising a young family that could prosper in the emerging world of affluent consumerism.

Dick cannily made himself stand out in the large class of GOP congressional freshmen by casting the Nixons as a prototypical young family struggling with postwar realities. The Washington area was suffering from acute shortages of affordable housing, partly due to the lack of construction during the war years. The Nixons could not find a reasonably priced apartment. Publicizing their housing choice, they took a room at the Mayflower Hotel while they waited for Frank and Hannah Nixon to bring ten-month-old Tricia to Washington in early January. By their own standards the Nixons were now flush with cash and did have some money for rent; they had replenished their wartime savings of $10,000, which they had expended for the campaign, and had accumulated an additional $3,000. The young congressman's salary would be $12,500 a year. But Dick rarely shied away from an opportunity to play the underdog.

In mid-December, a *Washington Post* article featured the Nixons as an appealing young congressional couple in a quandary. With "time . . . growing desperately short," and with their recent electoral "luck . . . gone into a tailspin," young Mr. and Mrs. Nixon were searching diligently and a bit desperately to find a home before their young daughter arrived. Dick told the reporter that there was "no proper place" for young children at the hotel. The Mayflower would eventually make an exception to its rules and provide a crib for the baby. It would take Pat until March to find a two-level, two-bedroom apartment at 3538 Gunston Road in a recently built housing complex in Park Fairfax, an area of northern Virginia that was being cleared of forests. According to biographer Lance Morrow, the "Virginia countryside [of the late 1940s] was abruptly and surprisingly rural, with that sense of sultry, vaguely menacing remoteness one sometimes feels at night deep in the Mississippi or Alabama countryside." Having grown up in the farmlands of the California basin, neither Pat nor Dick was intimidated by desolate areas. Their apartment in Virginia was twenty minutes by car from the center of Washington, and it had the advantage of being located in a neighborhood with many young families.

On Friday, January 3, Hannah, Frank, Pat, and Tricia gathered in the visitors' gallery of the House of Representatives. They looked down into a chamber imbued with majesty: It was adorned with relief portraits of twenty-three of the most famous lawgivers in history, including Thomas Jefferson, Moses, Pope Innocent III, and King Edward I. A quotation etched into the marble of the chamber from the nineteenth-century statesman Daniel Webster exhorted the representatives to "perform something worthy to be remembered" in "their day and generation."

The day would be unique in the annals of the House of Representatives. The three men who would serve as president in the 1960s were all being sworn in that day, all of them determined to take Daniel Webster's challenge seriously. Dick and his fellow Republican congressmen sat in the semicircular seats on the right side of the Speaker of the House, while the Democratic representatives, sitting across the wide center aisle, included John F. Kennedy and Lyndon B. Johnson. At noon the Nixon family watched as, at the command of the Speaker, all 435 representatives stood, raised their right hands, and repeated the oath of office. Members of John F. Kennedy's dynastic family were seated near Pat in the visitors' gallery. The Nixons and the Kennedys represented entirely different worlds: one working with striving and resentment, and the other permeated with entitlement and a fresh sense of noblesse oblige. The out-of-place, lower-middle-class Nixons might have seemed no match for the glamorous, wealthy Kennedy clan, but both families were possessed of a drive and ambition that would make them converge as adversaries over the next fifteen years.

"In the late forties, Washington seemed like a cross between ancient Rome, and Athens, Georgia—the headquarters of postwar world power, it is true, but provincial, [and] oddly unsophisticated," writes biographer Lance Morrow, whose father ran the *Saturday Evening Post*'s Washington bureau. The capital lacked a clear system for integrating new congressional families into its established community, nor did it educate them about Washington protocol or the opportunities the city offered them. While the John F. Kennedys, who lived in elite Georgetown with a housekeeper and a valet, had entrée to the city's prominent social circles, the Nixons were adrift. As the excitement of being sworn into Congress gave way to the exhausting diurnal duties of legislating and living as a family, Pat and Dick felt lost in the mazes of government and in the insecure and competitive social world that surrounded it. The Nixons encountered a city that Washington journalists Robert S. Allen and William V. Shannon aptly described as having "the graceless, vacant, strictly utilitarian, and almost featureless character of a huge waiting room, where all the seats are taken but everyone sits alone."

According to Donald Thompson, Nixon's assistant campaign treasurer, Pat felt "like a fish out of water." She no doubt missed her California friends and felt the absence of a significant role outside the home, without the means of integrating herself into circles where she could make new friends and assist her husband in advancing his career. Neither Pat nor Dick enjoyed attending the ubiquitous Washington cocktail parties where aspiring Washingtonians built their networks; Congressman Nixon was also uncomfortable at intimate Washington dinner parties with people he did not know well. His brilliant mind moved so rapidly that he was often impatient with the people around him—he could finish their sentences in his own head before they had gotten one-third of the way through expressing them.

Recognizing the estrangement the Nixons felt, Donald Thompson contacted Catherine Rippard, the wife of a Washington savings and loan executive, and asked her to guide Pat through the capital's murky social waters. Rippard connected Pat to the Congressional Wives Club, whose members were spouses of a sitting or former member of Congress, a Supreme Court justice, or a member of the president's cabinet. Pat soon, however, discovered the truth of Allen and Shannon's pronouncement that "Washington society is like lemon meringue pie without the filling: all fluff and a lot of crust." Pat was disappointed to discover that the Congressional Wives Club's activities consisted mainly of bridge lessons and assembling an annual cookbook of spouses' recipes. She had hoped that the group of women did substantive charity work or had educational programs.

The Nixons might have felt sophisticated back in Whittier, but it was hard for them to maintain that self-image in Washington. One of the first dinner parties they attended that winter would underscore their provinciality and cause them deep embarrassment. Massachusetts Congressman Christian Herter, one of the Brahmins of the

House, had sent them an invitation to dine at his home. The dress requirement was listed as "informal." Hoping to fit in, Pat bought "a teal-blue cocktail dress" that complemented Dick's dark blue suit. As they entered the Herter mansion, they were shocked to see that the male guests were dressed in black suits and sported black bow ties, while the women were wearing full-length evening gowns. It was a quick and painful lesson—"informal" meant black tie.

According to Richard Nixon, he and his wife had "scarcely a moment to themselves" during their first years in Washington. Adjusting to spending less time with her husband was a wrenching change for Pat, but she was an adaptable woman. As she had shown during the war years, Pat had a propensity for independence—born of her solitary and loss-filled childhood. Dick came home in the evenings for dinner and a brief bout of play with Tricia, but then often went to his study to work. "He can keep right on thinking about and working at politics," Pat noted, "from the time he wakes up until he goes to sleep." At night when Dick read position papers in his study, she read or sewed in her bedroom; she would take a hat-making class that year. Even though they did not spend much time together during the work week, they appeared to have found a center of contentment. "They would always solve their problems without arguments," Mrs. Clifford Moore, their maid and babysitter for ten years, told the *Washington Post* in 1972. "I've never seen them unhappy or dissatisfied." But then again, they rarely expressed their resentments in front of others.

Without a doubt, Pat garnered immense satisfaction from Dick's political position. She viewed the sacrifices she had to make as her way of contributing to his career and to her country. Yet like many of the women of her generation who were defining themselves in domestic terms, she felt lonely and overwhelmed at times in her new postwar role as a wife, homemaker, and mother. Ambitious husbands did not give their wives much assistance raising children. But Pat was not a complainer. Her letters to her close friend Helene Drown reveal her to be both philosophical about her husband's absences and political obsessions and occasionally resentful of his failures to cut the lawn or otherwise spend time at home with his family.

In the late 1940s, bright, competent American women, formerly animated and enriched by their wartime work outside the home, had to find creative ways to challenge themselves intellectually and to satisfy their longing for adult stimulation. Pat met some of these needs by creating a new family at her husband's office in Room 528 on the top floor (known as "the attic") of the House Office Building. When Pat was not busy caring for Tricia or cooking, shopping, cleaning, or repairing their apartment, she found a way to reinclude herself in Dick's political life by volunteering at his office—particularly when she was needed to answer his increasingly voluminous correspondence. She helped out whenever she could spare the time. Pat forged an indelible bond with Dorothy Cox, a secretary from California, who had joined the inner Nixon circle. "We were like a family," with an "esprit de corps that is so important in a family," Dorothy Cox remembered. "We were all in it together pulling for the boss because he gave us the feeling he was going places." She loved working with Pat.

The Nixons would be tested by having to manage their often incompatible domestic and career ambitions while at the same time presenting a unified presence in Washington's merciless social and political spotlight. They knew that their performance could radiate through national Republican circles. Pat and Dick arrived in the capital with a reputation as the attractive but unpolished middle-class California couple who had overcome hopeless odds to slay the wealthy, liberal Voorhis. Reporters and fellow congressmen were curious about the pair, and not all of the initial coverage was kind. Early on, the *Washington Post* tagged Nixon as "the greenest congressman in town." But others were more enthusiastic. In January 1947, reporter Elizabeth Oldfield of the *Washington Times Herald* boosted Dick's regular-guy image ("He is as typically American as Thanksgiving") and declared him to be representative of a new wave of politicians: "Serious and energetic, he is indicative of the change in political trends, the increasing emphasis on youth, and a genuine desire to serve the country." She had high hopes for him: "If he bears out his promises, he will go far."

Others also saw the Nixons as avatars of the era. An Associated Press wire service photographer decided that the rising young Nixons would be perfect subjects for a photograph epitomizing the young and fresh Republicans of the Eightieth Congress. The photographer rented bicycles. He posed the couple amid the blooming cherry trees that surround the Jefferson Monument at the Tidal Basin. In the photograph Pat stands beside a bike at the edge of the water, reaching ambitiously with her right hand to touch the branch of a large, arching cherry tree. To her left, Dick, wearing a white shirt and tie, sports a bike with a basket mounted across its handlebars, in which sits one-year-old Tricia, wearing a white bonnet that matches the blossoms. Dick is smiling and gazing beyond Pat and across the basin, as if surveying a glorious scene from his future. Pat later told Julie that the staging of the photograph had been a nerve-racking experience for her. Dick had not ridden a bike in more than fifteen years. His wife feared that he would fall off, tossing Tricia into the waters of the basin.

This nationally syndicated photograph was the perfect vehicle for establishing the Nixons, and by extension the new Republican congressional families, as the faces of America's future. Fellow congressional couples had to bite their lips at the missed opportunity. The upstart Nixons were becoming a couple to court. The grand dames of Washington, President Truman's friend Perle Mesta (known as the "queen of Washington society") and Alice Roosevelt Longworth ("the other Washington monument"), may well have noted the quick ascent of the young congressional couple from California, but they did not yet rush to welcome the young Nixons into their dining salons. California was not yet taken seriously as a center of power.

The radical transformation in the Nixons' marriage, from the private bonding of equals to an alliance between a political man and a helpmate whose public role was to provide support from home, became underscored in the late summer and fall of 1947 by Dick's first official trip abroad. While he had tea with British prime minister Clement Attlee at 10 Downing Street—a heady proposition for a young politician who had, one year earlier, been scrambling to raise enough funds to compete in a primary election—Pat stayed home, caring for a daughter who had "a rather tough time adjusting herself to the heat" of a Washington summer. Dick had joined Republican Christian Herter as a member of the Herter Commission for a six-week European mission focused on assessing the viability of Secretary of State George Marshall's plan to provide U.S. aid to reconstruct a continent socially and economically devastated by war. Pat, Hannah, Frank, and young Eddie had accompanied Dick to New York City, where they saw the Broadway sensation *Oklahoma!* and toured the *Queen Mary* before the ship departed from New York Harbor.

Pat, who had longed to go to Europe despite her devotion to Tricia, understood the importance of Dick's trip, but during those hot and solitary six weeks she surely wished at times for the tonic of foreign travel. She kept herself engaged by participating even more fully in the operation of his office, which was burdened with work during the congressman's absence.

Before he left, Dick had hired, he wrote a political friend, "a very satisfactory colored woman" to assist Pat with eighteen-month-old Tricia. The elder Nixons had moved that spring to a sixty-acre farm they had purchased near Menges Mills, a Mennonite village, in York County, Pennsylvania. It was only eighty miles from Washington, which meant her mother-in-law could give Pat breaks on weekends.

The guilt and loneliness Dick felt being away from his family for six weeks in Europe he addressed, as he had during the war, by writing Pat daily letters. Unfortunately for all of us, Pat's letters to Dick during this time have been lost, and with them has vanished her perspective on her life and the burden of her husband's absence. Writing to Pat from the *Queen Mary*, Dick said he was impressed that even the ship's least expensive tourist-class section had a nursery, with toys, murals, and "nurses in attendance." He mused about how easy it would be to bring Tricia along if they could arrange a similar trip the following summer. "I sure do miss you," he wrote her.

Skirting over the grim conditions he encountered in a shattered Europe, Dick kept his missives upbeat and encouraging. He did not write to her about meeting a young Greek woman whose breast had been amputated by communists or about witnessing a young protester being blown up by a grenade hurled by a left-wing insurgent. Nixon would be forever marked by witnessing the advance of communism in countries weakened by the war. He realized that without U.S. food and money, "Europe would be plunged into anarchy, revolution, and ultimately communism." Combating the specter of communism would come to define his world outlook and make him famous.

On Sunday, September 14, Dick stayed at the Excelsior Hotel on Lido Isle in Venice. "This place is another we must see together," he wrote Pat. He and his delegation arrived in Milan in time to attend a performance of *Manon* at La Scala, the renowned opera house, which had been recently repaired of its wartime damage. Mindful not to rub in his adventures to a housebound wife, he wrote, "This might sound like a junket! But it has been a hard, tough trip + we are really learning things. The pleasure will have to wait until we can come together!" He ended his letter by telling her, "I miss you every min[ute]." When Dick arrived home in the second week of October, he presented Pat with four or five pairs of long black Italian gloves, as well as elegant Italian placemats, which she thought too expensive to use.

Nixon became a firm supporter of the Marshall Plan. Polls showed that 75 percent of Dick's constituents in the Twelfth District strongly opposed U.S. foreign aid to Europe despite the clear possibility that communist inroads there might threaten the United States. He would need Pat's support as he mustered his energy to garner the support of his district for the plan. The stakes were high. If they were successful in convincing his constituents that a war-weary country should once again invest itself in the fate of Europe, then the young congressman would be seen as helping protect his country, a stance that would also advance the chances of his re-election effort in 1948. With Pat at his side, Dick went on a lightning-fast tour of the district, giving fifty speeches in a several-day period. Playing smart politics, he made sure to tell his constituents that oranges would be included in any food parcels sent overseas.

When the Nixons came back again to Whittier for the 1947 Christmas holidays, they had much to celebrate. Pat was pregnant with their second child, who was due in July. Nixon had refined the larger cause in which he would immerse himself and his marriage for more than forty-five years: creating security at home and fostering world peace through American leadership abroad. They had established themselves in the public arena as a quintessentially American family, happy and prosperous, grounded by a loving wife whose husband looked out toward a future of promise.

7

Crises on the Home Front

$\mathcal{D}$ick proved prescient about the escalating national worries about communist subversion of democracy at home, and eagerly sought out a position on the House Committee on Un-American Activities (HUAC), whose job was to identify and remove extremists (communists or fascists) from the government payroll. For most of the year Dick devoted himself to long workdays on the HUAC special legislative subcommittee, which was stirring controversy with its investigation into alleged communist infiltration of the American government. He was coauthoring the Mundt-Nixon bill, requiring communists to register with the government. Reporters had begun to speculate about his darker motivations (curtailing civil liberties while amassing power) and question his agenda as a public figure.

Almost every long marriage is tested by periods of discord or extreme duress. In 1948, the stress of Nixon's new committee assignments, along with raising a young child and having another baby on the way, brought about the first fissures in Pat and Dick's bond. Now in the first trimester of her second pregnancy, Pat was wearing herself out handling all the household chores and childcare so that Dick could focus exclusively on his increasingly arduous and increasingly significant congressional duties. What little free time the Nixons shared was devoted to driving eighty miles each way on weekends to look after Dick's elderly parents at their Pennsylvania farm. Dick appreciated the break from the intensity of the capital, but Pat was exhausted by her in-laws, who were lonely in the Gettysburg countryside and were coping with Frank's poor health. As a woman who never allowed herself the luxury of whining about her own difficulties, Pat was irked, according to her daughter Julie, to hear Dick's parents vent their grievances. She also was angry because she needed Dick to understand she felt neglected, which was the unintended consequences of his obsession with work. Pat had taken care of Tricia alone while Dick was in Europe; he was busier than ever when he returned.

Over nearly eight years, the couple had already endured and surmounted great tensions and trials. Their painful wartime separation had allowed them to develop their own autonomy and reinforce their love for each other; the travails of the 1946 campaign had cemented their effectiveness as a political team. Despite their intense public obligations, the Nixons now wanted to give their young family a stable home life that would be anchored by a mother who, like the majority of middle- and upper-class mothers in the postwar era, would stay at home to rear her children. Dick knew how essential Pat was to his efforts to advance the Nixons' prospects in the world beyond their suburban Virginia neighborhood. Her confidence, her humor, and her steadiness grounded him, especially during his emotionally precarious moments. Yet now, in the winter of 1948, as they managed a demanding domestic life and increasingly controversial and arduous political roles, the Nixons found themselves in the middle of a power struggle over their conflicting priorities.

A further disruption aggravated the tension between them. Dick had an accident and injury of the kind suffered by people whose lives are harried and distracted. On Wednesday morning, February 11, Dick was carrying two-year-old Tricia down the icy front steps of their apartment building as he hustled to get her to nursery school and arrive on time to chair a meeting of the HUAC special legislative subcommittee. He slipped and crashed hard onto the steps and the ground. While he deftly managed to save Tricia from injury, he landed flat on his back and elbows. In intense pain, he yelled for Pat, who summoned their neighbor, Nixon's congressional assistant William "Bill" Arnold. Arnold drove Nixon to Bethesda Naval Hospital, where X-rays showed that he had suffered fractures to both elbows. The doctors were able to manipulate his elbows into alignment without having to do surgery. His heavily damaged left elbow remained in a cast for almost three weeks.

His injury meant more work for Pat; she had to drive Dick around. Much to the consternation of his wife, Dick did not view the icy accident as an admonition to slow down and focus more on his life moment to moment. He took one week to recuperate at home before returning to his customary frenetic pace. Within a few years, such heedlessness of his mental and physical well-being would lead him to develop a serious stress disorder. At this point in his career, however, his compulsive office routine worked in his favor. Dick was empowered by a press corps that now was giving him the positive attention he sought. After news spread about his accident, he won plaudits for protecting his daughter. For Pat, Dick's accident, her isolation, her pregnancy, exhaustion, the daily demands of motherhood, as well as a lifetime of subordinating her needs to those of others, converged into a breaking point. When she finally vented her misery to Dick, he was taken by surprise. In her biography of her mother, Julie Nixon offers no more details than that Pat told him "how deep her discontent was."

One reason that the Nixons are fascinating is that they embody marital ambivalence—that is, Pat and Dick were drawn to certain parts of each other's characters even as they were unhappy about other aspects. Part of Pat's chemistry with Dick involved her fascination with his intellectual prowess and his ability to speak well extemporaneously.

At the same time, she was dismayed by his single-minded focus on politics to the exclusion of a more relaxed lifestyle. She admired his dedication, but not his obsession. For his part, Dick was drawn to and grounded by Pat's discipline and her ability to structure their home life. He also rebelled against it. He loved her dignity and her righteousness, and yet he chafed at her distaste for public life and its ethical compromises.

The previous year, when they were newcomers to Washington, Pat was too busy getting settled in an unwelcoming town to give much thought to her marriage. Now that she was adjusting to Washington, her mixed feelings about her role as a wife came to the fore. Magazines like *Woman's Day* and radio programs offering the advice and gossip of talk show hosts Alma Kitchell and Nellie Revell told her that her main job was to free her husband from household obligations so that he could create a prosperous life for his family. A woman was supposed to set the emotional tone of the home; her goal was harmony. The postwar era put American wives in a difficult position: They were asked to carry a backbreaking burden and be happy about it. They were not supposed to argue about their domestic role or to augment it with a job outside the home.

When people become more assertive, they often start by building up resentments and then exploding. Gradually, when they see early signs that their legitimate needs are being ignored, they learn to negotiate. Pat was bucking social norms by indicating her unhappiness to her work-obsessed husband, but she likely had more complaints than most ordinary wives, whose spouses could at least spend weekends relaxing with their families. In asking Dick to focus more on her and the children, Pat exhibited a new maturity of character. She was no longer willing to be merely an extension of her husband's ego. In her book *Hidden Power*, Kati Marton said of the partnership between Dick and Pat in 1948, "Eight years into their marriage, her role as equal partner was over." Marton does not consider the possibility that Pat's lower profile was her choice. The congressman's wife was still an equal partner in their joint endeavors, with a different sphere of action that she would define more completely than she had before—and one for which she would demand more support and respect. Richard Nixon, like most emotionally tight-lipped men of his generation, did not publicly acknowledge how difficult it was to balance time with his family with his need to distinguish himself in Congress.

Dick, utterly ensnared in his legislative and political work, had not noticed how much he had taken his wife for granted. Chastened, he wrote his unhappy wife a letter promising her "his abiding love" and committed himself to pay more attention to her and the family. He could not keep these promises.

For the Nixons, the birth of their second child not only completed their family but eventually altered the dynamics of the marriage. On an oppressively humid Fourth of July night, Pat went into labor. It took Dick twenty minutes to drive her from their apartment in Park Fairfax, Virginia, to the Columbia Hospital in central Washington. He arranged (perhaps he pulled rank) to get Pat a corner room where she could have the benefit of a breeze while her labor intensified. Keenly aware by now of Pat's recently expressed dissatisfaction and feeling some guilt over his missing Tricia's birth, Dick stayed at the hospital to await the arrival of their new child. Fathers did not typically join their wives in the delivery room in that era; Dick waited in the lounge until the sweaty and grinning obstetrician came out sometime after 4:00 a.m. to tell him of the birth of his second daughter, Julie, who weighed a hefty nine pounds and six ounces. She had missed being an Independence Day baby by only four hours.

Pat remained in the hospital for five days and might have benefited from staying there longer to rest, given what awaited her at home. Hannah Nixon, who had agreed to care for twenty-eight-month-old Tricia, was ill, and that left Pat to juggle an unsettled toddler, a needy newborn, and a sick mother-in-law. To cushion Tricia against the immediate shock of knowing she had a competitor for her mother's affection, Pat had swaddled Julie for her homecoming, even though it was still swelteringly hot. Tricia pointed at the bundled-up baby and demanded, "What's that thing?" Julie developed a rash from the heat, and a mood to match. Like many stay-at-home mothers of her era, Pat sometimes felt despondent that "the camaraderie and carefree time of her early married years were a thing of the past."

Pat and Dick sought ways to refresh their bond. When they could, they went dancing at the Shoreham Hotel in Washington. On Labor Day weekend that year, they took a too-brief family vacation at a resort on the Delaware shore. But a few days off was not a long enough time to recover from what remained an extraordinarily stressful period in their marriage.

During the summer of 1948, with victory in war three years past, Americans were feeling a renewed sense of crisis in a world that appeared more threatening than the one they faced in the years before World War II began. Now the menace was not the bellicosity of the Axis powers but the aggressive designs of the Soviet Union. The two-year-old Cold War competition between the communist and Western worlds was fast intensifying. In February 1948, Czechoslovakia fell to a communist coup; that June, a Soviet East German blockade cut off railway and road access to the Allied sectors of Berlin, necessitating an airlift to bring supplies to the citizens of West Berlin. Inside America, what would become known as the Red Scare (of the late 1940s and 1950s)—the belief that communists were undermining the nation from within—was now a national preoccupation. Many Americans feared the "unseen malignant forces at work on the wholesome body of America." Richard Nixon was passionate about rooting out what he believed to be these hidden political infections in the American system.

The riveting and melodramatic congressional inquiry into Alger Hiss and Whittaker Chambers would be the first battlefield in the war against supposed communist influence within the nation's borders, and the first-term congressman would be in the thick of it. The hearings he so thoroughly dominated in August and December 1948 would have long-lasting effects on the passions and ideologies of the nation, establish Nixon as a central and controversial American public figure, and singe the Nixon marriage.

Investigating the possibility that a large communist spy ring had operated in the United States before and during World War II, the HUAC subpoenaed Whittaker Chambers, a pudgy, short, and disheveled senior editor at *Time* magazine. Chambers testified that he had been a communist spy in the 1920s and 1930s and that State Department official Alger Hiss, who had been part of the American delegation in the Yalta talks with Roosevelt and Stalin, had been his contact person. This was a shocking accusation. Alger Hiss was an elegant, well-connected, and articulate former high-level State Department official and had been secretary-general of the United Nations Charter Conference. A Harvard Law School graduate, he was an archetypal member of the East Coast establishment that Republicans so disdained.

Hiss, the president of the Carnegie Endowment for International Peace, appeared at his own request before the committee to deny he was a communist. But Hiss made a fatal mistake: On August 5, in his first hearing before the committee, he was condescending to Richard Nixon about his interlocutor's less-than-Ivy-League education, presuming that Nixon had gotten his law degree from a second-rate law school. Nettled by Hiss's insolence and struck by the vast differences in the testimony of Chambers and Hiss, Dick carefully studied the transcript of the session and concluded that Hiss, who had appeared so cocksure, had consistently hedged in his testimony, qualifying many of his statements with the phrase "to the best of my knowledge."

That same day Hiss testified, President Truman held a press conference in which he agreed with a reporter's statement that the HUAC hearing was a "red herring" designed to divert attention from the failures of what Truman called the "Terrible Republican Eighty," meaning the Eightieth Congress, controlled by the GOP and intent on thwarting Truman. The Republican majority on HUAC, wary of political fallout in an election year, wanted to drop the case. A dogged Nixon persuaded them to pursue it.

Nixon made a career-defining bet on the unprepossessing Chambers, a man whose mouth cultural critic Lionel Trilling described as "a devastation of empty sockets and blackened stumps." Might Dick's investigative agenda have been unduly influenced by his resentment of the condescending Hiss? At this pivotal decision point in his career, as he had to unpack his motives and make a cool and measured assessment of the road before him, Dick would have certainly benefited from the counsel of Pat, who had terrific intuition about people. Through the crisis that would challenge Dick that August, Pat remained, in the historical record at least, a tantalizingly silent partner. Without a doubt she was affected by her husband's single-minded investigation. She was enduring the sleepless nights that come with tending to a month-old baby, while Dick "immersed himself in the case," as Pat later told Julie, "with an absorption that was almost frightening." Her husband said that he had many reservations about pursuing the case. He was risking his career by opposing the president of the United States and the convictions of most of the press, and by aligning himself with a former communist against a respected public servant. Nixon was once again imperiling the reputation of the Committee on Un-American Activities, which had continuously been attacked as an unfair group out to curtail civil liberties. He neither wanted to destroy an innocent man's life nor go against his own conscience for fear that he might be wrong.

In his memoir *Six Crises* Nixon described his "period of doubt, of soul-searching, to determine whether to fight the battle or flee from it." It was a time when "almost unbearable tensions build up," he wrote. "Crisis can indeed be agony," Nixon declared. "But it is the exquisite agony which a man might not want to experience again—yet would not for the world miss." A woman like Pat Nixon, however, might not have romanticized crisis the way her husband did. She went through her own period of soul-searching when she decided whether to take on her husband with complaints about the misery he was causing her. Should she be tough enough to stay out of the battle? Or strong enough to take it on? She had to face the fear of upending the stability of their marriage (with the well-being of their children at stake), while she skirmished for the health of their union. As a political wife, Pat had to evaluate the importance of her personal needs when they nettled her husband, who believed he was fighting not only for the future of his family, but, more gravely, for the welfare of the country. This was never an easy decision.

August 1948 proved to be the toughest month in the Nixon mar-
riage until August 1974. Dick had promised to take Pat on a vacation
she sorely needed, after a month of attending to a toddler and now
a newborn infant. Her mother-in-law had gone back to her home in
Pennsylvania. Yet the monumental challenges of the HUAC investi-
gation left no room for a real getaway. It was difficult "back in 1948
before the scope of the Communist underground movement had
become generally known," Nixon wrote, "to believe a man like Cham-
bers over a man like Hiss," which meant that Nixon worked "round
the clock" to search for evidence that would back up Chambers's
story. When Dick was home, he was often tense and slept little. He
was determined not to let the country down by deciding to retreat
from the battle and let a communist off the hook while forfeiting
a once-in-a-lifetime chance to establish a reputation on an issue of
white-hot national interest. As a result, he acknowledged that he was
"quick-tempered," and easily lost his appetite. In his memoir *Six Crises*
he admitted to being "mean to live with at home and with my friends."
As would always be the case, Pat was strongest, Dick acknowledged,
when the going was rough. She spent little time with her husband that
month, and what time she did have was surely spent shoring him up.
Dick worked through his own doubts about who was telling the truth
in the case while Hiss and Chambers vied for credibility and exculpa-
tion in the hearing chamber and in public opinion.

The *Washington Post* regularly attacked Nixon and HUAC, suggest-
ing that its activities were violations of civil liberties on a number of
grounds. The committee's hearings functioned like court proceed-
ings, but they did not offer the rights guaranteed to the accused in
criminal trials. The committee was able to make vague charges against
witnesses based on their past political associations, without giving
them the chance to provide evidence on their own behalf or to cross-
examine the witnesses testifying against them. A Herblock cartoon in
the *Washington Post* portrayed an innocent man being attacked by a
tiger (labeled *Smear Statements*) while Richard Nixon and other HUAC
members watched from the stands. The same paper decried "the entry
of our society into the twilight zone between government by law and

government by lawlessness," and in another editorial suggested that "it is the Committee which is subject to the most serious indictment of all." The *Boston Herald* and the *Baltimore Sun* also wrote scathing editorials denouncing the foolhardiness of HUAC.

Pat read "voraciously," according to Dick, about the case and Nixon's role in it. She "spotted every vicious cartoon, or negative biased column or news report." Convinced that her husband was fighting honorably to protect the country (and the future of his family in that country), she was incensed by any criticism of what he was doing. "She knew we were on the right side," Dick wrote in his 1990 memoir *In the Arena.* "This certainly strengthened her, but it did not make the cruel barbs hurt any less." For her, Hiss was "the press's fair-haired boy," backed by Washington power brokers. Dick maintained that Pat was more bothered by political attacks against him than he was, but as a thoroughly political individual who came of age in an era when men admitted little vulnerability, he could never admit how thin-skinned he was. Eleven years after the Chambers-Hiss case concluded, he did confess to biographer Earl Mazo that "the terrible attacks from the press, nasty cartoons, editorials, mail" made it all "as difficult an experience as I've ever had."

At the dawn of the television age, on August 25, 1948, Nixon seized the opportunity to showcase himself in what would be the world's first televised congressional hearing. He displayed his interrogation skills and anticommunist fervor before the cameras. Americans—mainly on the East Coast—owned a total of 325,000 television sets that summer, and many of them were watching this gripping hearing. As the two antagonists faced off, Nixon offered proof (a motor vehicle certificate) that Hiss had at one point turned his car over to a communist operative—as Chambers had testified. As Hiss ducked and tried to slide around Nixon's questions during nine hours of intensive interrogation, reporters realized that they had been too quick to champion a man who seemed an imperturbable and incorruptible figure of the American establishment.

Given his new national prominence, based on his television performance and newspaper coverage of it, Nixon found the 1948 election an easy race. Early that year he got a head start when the U.S. Junior Chamber of Commerce chose him as one of the nation's Ten Outstanding Men of 1947. Unchallenged in the Republican primary, he cross-filed on both the Republican and Democratic ballots. He won both the Republican and the Democratic primaries. Fortunately for Pat, Dick did not need much support from her on the campaign trail that fall. She and the children flew with him to California in late September for a couple of weeks of campaigning against unknown Independent party candidate Una Rice. Nixon felt confident enough of victory to take time off from his own campaign and embark on a nationwide tour for the Republican presidential candidate, New York governor Thomas E. Dewey, during which he focused on attacking the ethics and competence of President Truman, who had not endeared himself to Nixon by saying that the HUAC was "more un-American than the activities it is investigating."

In November 1948, on the night after Dick's re-election, the Nixons and Jack and Helene Drown celebrated with an evening at the Cocoanut Grove in the Ambassador Hotel in Los Angeles. Performing that night was the famous cabaret singer the Incomparable Hildegard, best known for her song "Darling Je Vous Aime Beaucoup." Jack, fortified with a lot of champagne, went up before the show to tell Hildegard that "there was a great statesman in the audience that night—Congressman Richard Nixon." Hildegard was familiar with Nixon because of the Hiss case. As the show began, she appeared to the sound of a "great blast of trumpets," and summoned the "great statesman" up onto the stage. "Of course all the people were laughing because he was a Republican," Jack recounted, "and the room was filled with Hollywood Democrats. . . . But I'll never forget" what he said: "'You're all having so much fun, I almost wish I was a Democrat.'" The crowd loved it. Ushering Pat up onto the stage to join him, Dick added, to further applause, and with more affection than accuracy, "I'll tell you this, my lovely wife Pat was a Democrat when I married her." Pat later revealed she had voted for Franklin D. Roosevelt in 1932 and 1936.

*　　*　　*

Parents of young children sometimes forget that they require time alone together. Politics can itself be like a young child—incessantly demanding an adult's attention to the exclusion of everything else in life. As December approached, Pat and Dick recognized that they needed to do more to revitalize their marriage. Dick's exhausted wife needed time away after an unrelenting year of tending to children and to a tense and intense husband, and Dick needed to recuperate from his grueling year. After his re-election, he bought tickets for a Caribbean cruise with several other congressional couples. "This time," he told Pat, "absolutely nothing is going to interfere with our vacation." She gave him a wry smile, telling him, "I hope you are right, but I still have to be shown."

On December 1, while Pat was doing last-minute packing for the cruise, which was to leave the next day, Nixon read newspaper articles that suggested the Hiss case was about to take another turn. After learning that Chambers had reportedly hidden a batch of crucial new evidence, Dick pondered postponing the vacation, but, as he recalled in his memoir *Six Crises*, he didn't "have the heart to tell Pat the bad news." He told the House doorkeeper William "Fishbait" Miller, "I'm going out to sea and they are going to send for me. You'll understand when I get back." Dick was well aware that being summoned home to handle a communist conspiracy would make riveting press copy.

On Friday afternoon Pat and Dick boarded the SS *Panama* from Miami for what she, at least, thought was going to be a well-earned week of rest sailing through the Canal Zone. At the Friday night dinner Dick told their companions that he and Pat were taking the cruise to avoid being interrupted by telephone calls. Pat did not count on the radiograms that began arriving on Saturday. While they were dining at the captain's table that night with fellow congressmen Mike Kirwin of Ohio and Sterling Cole of New York and their wives, a radiogram from Stripling announced the new evidence that Dick had seen hinted at in the newspaper reports:

```
SECOND BOMBSHELL OBTAINED BY SUBPOENA CASE CLINCHED
INFORMATION AMAZING. HEAT IS ON FROM PRESS CAN YOU
POSSIBLY GET BACK?
```

*   *   *

When Dick read the cable aloud to his tablemates, Pat cried out, "Here we go again," and threw her hands up in anger. Yet again work had trumped play. She would have been even angrier if she had known that her husband had been expecting the summons. With no newspapers aboard, the Nixons had no way of knowing that while they were having their first dinner at sea, Chambers was leading HUAC investigators into his moonlit vegetable garden and retrieving five rolls of incriminating microfilm from his hollowed-out, homegrown pumpkins. The film contained fifty-eight pages of confidential State Department documents, proving Hiss was a Soviet agent.

Dick decided he needed to return to Washington. Bidding Pat good-bye, Dick traveled to a Coast Guard flying boat that brought him back to Miami, where he was badgered by reporters who wanted to know what he thought of the Pumpkin Papers. Having not yet been briefed on Chambers's garden walk with reporters, he had no clue what they were talking about. After being updated, he exclaimed, "Oh my God, we really have a lulu on our hands this time."

According to Dick, Pat was "hardly able to believe that their chance had been thwarted." Flying home early from Jamaica, the next port of call, Pat was entitled to have very mixed feelings—anger at the loss of a well-earned vacation and yet perhaps some feeling of satisfaction that her sacrifice might help safeguard the country. Dick, after looking at the documents, hyperbolically told the press he had seen "conclusive proof of the greatest treason conspiracy in this nation's history . . . puncturing the myth of the 'red herring' President Truman created."

Hiss was later indicted for perjury because the statute of limitations for charging him with spying had run out. He was sentenced to five years in prison. His guilt was hotly debated for several decades, but scholars now overwhelmingly concede that he was a spy. His conviction ratified HUAC as a legitimate communist-hunting committee and gave the Republicans the imprimatur as the party most competent to root out communist subversives. The Hiss case did not save America from any calamity, but it brought about greater concern about the intentions of the communists in America. It also ushered in the overreaction of the McCarthy era in America—a grim episode of red-baiting that Nixon would eventually be asked to address by giving a national speech condemning the kinds of techniques McCarthy used.

Thanks to the Hiss case and the publicity that surrounded the young congressman in 1948, the public image of Richard Nixon and his stalwart wife was forever altered—for good and for ill. Dick and Pat were elevated to the status of national heroes by conservatives, but his relentless investigation of Hiss earned him the eternal enmity of liberals. After Hiss was convicted and jailed, his supporters blamed Nixon, saying he had railroaded an innocent man. Quick to feel victimized, Dick despised those reporters whose previously glowing articles about him curdled into sour and harsh attacks on his work and his character. Pat was enraged that her husband was scapegoated for proving that the press was wrong about Hiss. In the 1980s, Pat vehemently said, "He did what he felt was right, and from the time this became apparent in the Hiss case, he was a target." She absorbed the full brunt of the darker side of politics at the expense of her previous political high-mindedness. When she wrote about the Republican Party in her letters to Helene Drown, she would continue to refer to the GOP as "we," and she often traded gossip with Helene about what was happening in Republican circles nationwide. But she no longer loved politics or public service with the same passion that her husband did. Pat was so wounded by the Hiss episode that she could barely speak about it to her daughter some thirty years later.

Whatever her feelings about the domestic sacrifices Dick made in his pursuit of justice in the Hiss case and the advancement of his career, Pat Nixon would continue to be a politically unquestioning supporter of her controversial husband. The first crisis of Dick's career would also be the first crisis of their marriage. They would surmount both trials, but the scars they bore would reopen as painful wounds in the years to come.

8

Safeguarding the American Home

*I*n 1948 the Democrats took a whopping seventy-five seats from Republicans in the House, and won nine more in the Senate—gaining majorities in both houses of Congress. Not only did President Truman, who resisted the Republican investigation of Alger Hiss, win a surprise re-election, but Richard Nixon would now be a junior congressman in a minority party. This position was not the best launching spot from which to jet-propel a political ascent. Friends and associates discussed whether he should stay in the House and play it safe or run for statewide office, but Pat had already decided. She encouraged him to run because he would have a better opportunity to enhance his political aspirations in the U.S. Senate. Dick tended to agree; he was not a cautious man, and he would rather take a risk and recalibrate later if he failed.

Nixon, almost overnight, had become a prominent voice in the Republican Party. In the 1948 campaign, one advertisement for Nixon had proclaimed him "America's Greatest Enemy of Communism." After the Soviet Union detonated an atomic bomb, and the People's Republic of China took over the mainland in 1949, Americans increasingly feared communist aggression and subversion—worries that escalated in June 1950 when North Korea crossed the thirty-eighth parallel and attacked South Korea. In January 1950, Klaus Fuchs, a theoretical physicist, admitted to selling atomic secrets to Russia. He was convicted of espionage later that year. In February 1950 Senator Joseph McCarthy of Wisconsin infamously claimed in a Wheeling, West Virginia, speech that he had discovered a vast network of communists engaged in espionage from within the federal government. Nixon deftly kept a distance from McCarthy, who had little use for careful research and facts and would become the standard-bearer for Red Scare zealots in the fall political season, but saw that fanning the anxieties of voters, fueling their resentments, and offering scapegoats could all be powerful tools for winning votes and gaining national attention.

After Congress recessed in August 1949, Pat and Dick took the girls on a "leisurely" driving trip home to California, where they could also introduce three-and-a-half-year-old Tricia and one-year-old Julie to the beaches they had enjoyed during their courtship. During the past months Pat had supervised from afar the decoration and color schemes for a $13,000 home they had bought at 14033 Honeysuckle Lane in the southern part of Whittier. There were only three neighboring houses on the lane. Until Dick began campaigning, the Nixons shared a local telephone line with thirteen other families. Neighbors could listen in on each other's troubles. Ruth Haroldson, who also lived on the lane, overheard Pat Nixon telling Dick about a fight between their daughters: "Julie just bit Tricia on the ear—it's bleeding."

Before they knew it, the 1950 Senate campaign was under way, pitting Richard Nixon, a well-funded and highly organized congressman—one who had developed an exceptionally intuitive grasp of the national mood, a penchant for executing precise long-range strategy, and a gift for knowing how to put his opponent on the defensive—against a well-known congresswoman, Helen Gahagan Douglas, who was a leading far-left, New Deal liberal. She spoke out passionately about rights for women and African Americans, about safeguarding American workers, and about affordable postwar housing. Instead of mastering legislative processes, Douglas used her celebrity and her dramatic skills to promote her agenda. In 1948 she had marched onto the House floor with a bag of groceries to showcase the diminished buying power of housewives after the government lifted wartime price controls. In contrast to Richard Nixon, she opposed the Taft-Hartley Act, a federal law that restricts the powers and activities of the labor unions, and believed that the House Un-American Activities Committee was unconstitutional.

Helen Douglas was a supporter of liberal causes, but she was not a communist. She was so sure of herself she felt no need to soften her stand that communism posed no genuine threat to America's lifestyle or its safeguards. In 1946 she had said, "The fear of communism in this country is not rational. And that irrational fear of communism is being used in many quarters to blind us to our real problems." She made herself vulnerable to attacks from conservatives by voting against the Truman plan to aid Greece and Turkey and against the McCarran-Wood bill requiring the registration of communists. This underestimated the nation's rising fear of communist intrusion. As a woman running for the Senate in an era when only Margaret Chase Smith of Maine had won election on her own account and the prevailing national mood was a fearful belligerence, she faced an uphill battle. She had also not been adequately collegial in the House of Representatives and she had not endeared herself to President Truman, who did not offer her his enthusiastic support.

Douglas ran a sloppy and unsophisticated campaign; she had no strong financial backing and was out of touch with the moderate and conservative views of her fellow Californians. After former California senator Sheridan Downey backed her opponent Manchester Boddy, the conservative publisher of the *Los Angeles Daily News,* in the Democratic primary, Douglas refused to try to appeal to Senator Downey to get back in his good graces for the regular election. While Douglas alienated the big-money businessmen and oil interests with her positions on local issues, Nixon garnered their support and the endorsements of most of the key California newspapers, including the *Los Angeles Times.* In this election Nixon would attract national attention for the second time in his career and would—for good and for ill—become a permanent part of the national conversation about politics.

From the day Dick announced his candidacy in November 1949, he put a stark choice to voters—either freedom or "state socialism." For a man who had once written his wife, "I like to do what I want to do when I want to do it," socialism had a deeply negative psychological resonance, suggesting personal subjugation and constriction. Nixon pledged to his supporters that he would run an inexhaustible "fighting, rocking, socking campaign" that would crisscross the state.

The California Senate election featured two prominent politicians and their spouses vying against each other in what became both a vicious class battle and a fight about ideologies. Dick and Pat, presenting themselves as an average American couple with working-class roots, contrasted themselves with the glamorous, well-connected and leftist Democratic representative Helen Gahagan Douglas—a beautiful actress of Broadway, light opera, and Hollywood, and a friend of Eleanor Roosevelt's—and Helen's husband, the movie star Melvyn Douglas. Pat and Dick would pour their contempt for Douglas into driven campaigning against her.

After the Great Depression and World War II, American voters longed for stability and a "return to normal living" as symbolized in domestic images and consumerism. In 1950 women were voting in increasing numbers. A candidate's wife who represented traditional family values increased his chances of winning. Pat positioned herself as a domestic but politically engaged woman, in a time before feminists championed women being seriously engaged outside their home. Contrasting Dick's wife implicitly with Douglas, the Nixons put out a campaign flyer describing Pat as an ideal homemaker and mother, but also as someone "seriously interested in national affairs and problems of government." "Glossy middlebrow magazines," historian David Greenberg pointed out, "displayed photographs of the Nixon family sitting together in their cheerful living room or on their idyllic front lawn." The Nixons sent out a postcard showing a photograph of Dick hugging Pat, Tricia, and Julie in front of an inflatable cowboy "Bop Bag" toy. Historian Gil Troy aptly characterized the Nixon persona and its battle plan: "Dick Nixon fought communism with an arsenal of postwar domestic artifacts: blond children, a slim wife, toy cowboys, and lawn furniture."

Helen Douglas threw open the door to negative campaigning by saying that Nixon's voting record matched that of the Republicans' favorite far-left bogeyman, East Harlem congressman Vito Marcantonio. Douglas's primary opponent Manchester Boddy had put out a flyer titled "The Douglas-Marcantonio Record," a sheet that implied that Douglas voted the Communist party line with Marcantonio. After Douglas tried to tie Nixon to Marcantonio, Nixon revived Boddy's accusations that Douglas voted for Marcantonio's communist positions. It was famously called the "Pink Sheet" because it was printed on pink paper. Nixon's campaign distributed five hundred thousand copies of that same "Pink Sheet." According to the Douglas camp, Nixon was a "pip-squeak" and a fascist who ran with the "back wash of Republican men in dark shirts." She compared Nixon to Hitler and Stalin. Douglas repeated the disparaging label "Tricky Dick" that publisher Manchester Boddy had originally pinned on Nixon. It was an understandable epithet, given his subtle, effective, and lawyerly misrepresentations of her record, and it outlived him.

Douglas and her associates badly miscalculated by throwing insults at Nixon—a man who was exquisitely sensitive to humiliation—and his wife, who was easily angered when barbs were directed at her, at Dick, or at any of their hardworking constituents. Nothing motivated the Nixons more than arrogant and wrong-headed opponents. According to her daughter, Pat "recoiled from the shrillness" of Douglas's attacks on her husband. Pat, who helped research and critique Dick's speeches, could get very snarky about criticism aimed at him. Nixon aide Richard St. Johns remembered that Pat "could be waspy" while scolding her husband at home or at campaign headquarters, but when the opposition did that, she lit into Dick, demanding, "How could you let them do that?"

Pat and Dick campaigned throughout the state in a secondhand wood-paneled station wagon with big NIXON FOR SENATE signs attached to each side. By June they had already logged ten thousand miles; they would be on the road constantly in the sixteen weeks that preceded the election. A speaker on top of the car blared out music announcing their arrival at every new location. At each of the ten to twelve daily stops, Nixon stood on the street or hopped up on the station wagon's tailgate to speak. Pat mingled with the crowd, passing out red Nixon thimbles with the provocative inscription "Safeguard the American Home." By the end of the campaign Pat had given away more than sixty-five thousand thimbles.

A Nixon staffer explained that Pat and Dick underwent periods of struggle in their marriage as well as times when their marital life was relaxed and positive. "They were all over the map like any couple in that kind of political position." The Nixons found the twelve-hour days on the road enervating. Inevitably there were irritations, harsh words, and flare-ups between them. During a previously mentioned incident in the 1946 campaign, when Nixon was rehearsing a speech at a small radio station in northern California, he barked at Pat, who was sitting nearby, "You know I don't want ever to be interrupted when I am working." She walked out, but when she returned to suggest that it was time for him to leave, too, he snapped, "I'll go when I'm damned well ready."

As the campaign rhetoric grew more vitriolic, leftist hecklers began to show up regularly wherever the Nixon station wagon stopped at a rally. In San Francisco, at the end of a cold day, an opposition sound truck appeared and heckled him via a loudspeaker, drowning out Dick's speech to a tiny crowd. Dick began answering the questions blared at him. Suddenly, "a curious thing happened," Pat Nixon remembered. A large crowd, drawn by the unusual loudspeaker debate, gathered and outshouted the hecklers. The experience of being heckled rankled Dick, and he became more reluctant to stop in the big cities, where his opponents could taunt him.

Sometimes Pat and Dick brought four-year-old Tricia and two-year-old Julie along with them. But when they left the children at home, Pat remained anxious about them, calling home several times a day to check on them. Hannah Nixon and a black maid cared for the children. Neighbor Helen Daniels remembered that "the girls missed their parents a lot while they were away campaigning."

Murray Chotiner adroitly managed the campaign, usurping some of Pat's role as a sounding board. Nixon, however, was his own chief strategist and did not always listen to Chotiner's advice. Julie would later circumspectly describe her father's outlook on politics and electioneering: "Politics was a harsh, even hurtful battle, a man's world," Nixon felt, "and he had difficulty thinking of women making political strategy and decisions." Nixon, a man of his time in terms of his view of the role of women, refused to allow his savvy, informed, and emotionally intelligent wife a larger role in decision making. He may also have had difficulty tolerating her perfectionism and her discomfort with the rough-and-tumble tactics he believed were necessary to win. "Pat still had advice and criticisms, but her recommendations were no longer a matter exclusively between her and her husband. Rather, they were weighed along with the seasoned views of an entourage. And her advice was not always taken." She advised him on the style and substance of the campaign and shared her perceptive observations about the people they encountered. She would have to contend with Murray Chotiner, who would be the first of a group of men who would form a wall around Nixon, insulating him from the influence of his wife and other aides and politicians whose opinions they found contrary to their own agenda.

In a provocative phrase that would forever tar Richard Nixon, in the last stages of the campaign, chroniclers reported that the candidate called Douglas "pink right down to her underwear," but, as Nixon aide and historian Frank Gannon has pointed out, there is no compelling evidence that Nixon ever uttered those words in public. In fact, Dick did express it privately to his aide Bill Arnold. Douglas herself was no stranger to red-baiting her opponent. "You Pick the Congress-man the Kremlin Loves," read one of her flyers. As the campaign rhetoric became more vitriolic on both sides, leftist groups continued to send hecklers to disrupt Nixon's speeches. Jack and Helene Drown, who ran the Long Beach Nixon campaign office, helped with a counterattack. They painted the sides of their Plymouth sedan with NIXON FOR SENATE signs and put up their own roof loudspeaker to drown out protestors, at one point playing the tune "If I Knew You Were Coming I'd 'Ave Baked a Cake."

In this first election of the modern media age, television played an important role. On the eve of the election Pat and Dick decided to soften a last-minute television appeal by including their daughters in the broadcast. Pat spent thirty nerve-racking minutes struggling to keep their two antsy girls from disrupting her husband's hard-hitting message. Dick's insistence on talking about the dangers of communism on the campaign trail meant that he received a boost when Mao Tse-tung sent Chinese volunteers into the Korean War a few days before the election.

Dick, weakened and tense from the hard-hitting battle, could not allow himself to feel optimistic. On Election Day, November 6, Pat packed a picnic lunch. They decamped to a Los Angeles beach on a brisk and gloomy day to rest and prepare themselves for the election results. They set up an umbrella, but they were miserable. Shivering by the ocean, they waited for the voters' decision; he was despondent by the time he arrived home. Dick often felt an emotional letdown after he met a challenge or surmounted a crisis. His insecurity about his electability and popularity dominated his exhausted thoughts. In the end Nixon received more than 2,100,000 votes, winning by a margin of 680,000 votes. It was the largest margin of victory in any national Senate race that year. "Dick was so exuberant," Pat remembered. "We hopped from one victory celebration to another far into the night." Dick played "Happy Days Are Here Again" on every piano he could find.

Douglas would later admit in her memoirs that she lost because "there was the United States fighting Communism, and I was the person who said we should limit the power of the military and try to disarm the world and get along with Russia." The *Los Angeles Daily News* did a postelection analysis, excoriating both candidates for running the "dirtiest" campaign in California's history. For the first time since the Hiss case Nixon received harsh criticism in the national press: He was lambasted for "brazen demagoguery" in the *New Republic* and tagged as "a dapper little man with an astonishing capacity for petty malice."

California senator Sheridan Downey retired early, and Dick was sworn in at the start of December. With Christmas approaching, Pat and the girls stayed home in Whittier and missed the ceremony.

Pat had endured a bruising, dispiriting, and exhausting year helping Dick achieve his goal. For the first time, she found herself criticized in the media. Pat, who had to scrimp to afford reasonably priced outfits for formal events, was hurt when columnist Drew Pearson wrote that she had to wear costly dresses because her long neck and bony shoulders made it impossible for her to wear regular sizes. Dick told writer Eleanor Harris, "I thought that was the height of viciousness." Pat wrote Helene that when Drew Pearson later entertained at a Sulgrave Club dinner, "they had the nerve to invite us." No one crossed Pat Nixon lightly, nor did she forget a slight against her husband—in her mind, an attack upon him was an attack upon her. In her letters to Helene, Pat writes with delight about shunning the opposition: "I had a wonderful opportunity to snub Giggs Donahue (remember his campaign against us!)." During the vice presidency, the Nixons would not entertain hostesses who had ignored them during their congressional years.

During the 1960 campaign Pat told another pool reporter, in front of UPI's Al Spivak, how politics had taken "quite a rough toll on her daughters." It had not been easy, Pat told them, for Tricia and Julie, who were teased at school ("Your father stinks"). Herbert Block's (Herblock's) cartoons in the *Washington Post* portrayed their father looking like an evil monkey.

By February 1951 Pat and Dick could afford to buy a $41,000 two-story, three-bedroom, white brick home with a small backyard at 4801 Tilden Street in the affluent Spring Valley section of northwest

Washington. They hired a decorator to help give it a "bright California look with cheerful aqua walls, peacock blue draperies and a touch of spring green in the furniture covering." Self-sufficient and financially prudent, Pat went to sewing classes and made all the slipcovers, draperies, and curtains, as well as a quilt for their bed.

To help finance their new residence, the Nixons sold their Whittier home in May, making a profit of $4,000 after less than two years. In 1951 Dick made an extra $7,000 from speaking engagements on top of his $12,500 Senate salary, and that went toward renovation. Pat shouldered the whole burden of moving, but not without resentment: "I have moved so many times and the process has always been gruesome," she wrote Helene. "Dick is always too busy, at least *his* story, so I do all the lugging, worrying, cussing." But she was enthusiastic about her new "electric kitchen with *dishwasher* and disposal." In September, Pat told Helene Drown how happy they were with the house and their neighbors: "What a luxury to have s-p-a-c-e. The children . . . have never been as happy as here with their space to dig, their Sears-Roebuck swimming pool." The entire family "fell" for the new medium of television: "Tricia likes cowboys or horror stories so Julie has little chance."

Pat took Julie to a neighborhood nursery school where each mother helped out every ten days. She needed the break from full-time childcare. Pat did not feel they could afford full-time help, but she hired a cleaning lady who came twice a week. As the wife of a senator, Pat now had more time for herself and her demanding social obligations.

In contrast to his carefully honed image as an ideal 1950s husband, Dick was not handy around the house. "If a nail has to be driven around our house—campaign time or not," Pat told the *Saturday Evening Post,* "I'm the one that has to swing the hammer." Nor did he tend to the grounds. Dick will "mow the lawn when I put on enough pressure, but it has been difficult to catch him." For Pat, Dick's lackadaisical attitude toward the lawn epitomized his willingness to place too much of the household burden on her. She vented her feelings to Helene: "Our lawn is 2 ft. tall. . . . However, our colored man hasn't shown up so Dick said he'd take another try at it. I'll telegraph you when it happens." A year later Pat highlighted his passive-aggressive attitude: "I even got Dick to mow the lawn last Sunday and he's been complaining of sore hands ever since."

Pat was irritated, but she tried to put her frustration in a context that muted it. "The important thing," she told the *Saturday Evening Post*, "is that Dick is doing the thing he wants to do in the way he believes he can best serve his country, and that is the kind of life I want the Nixon family to live." She politicized her situation, adding: "Perhaps we both felt this strongly because we come from typical, everyday American families." Pat was becoming adept at marketing the family. She did not tell reporters how difficult it was to manage the home and the children with scant help from her husband.

When Nixon reached the Senate, he went into an overdrive mode; he was already chasing the next challenge. Dick became a popular Republican Party spokesman, their most successful fund-raiser, and, in historian David Greenberg's account, "the vessel for hopes of a conservative revival." He crisscrossed America by plane and by car, averaging three speeches a week, appearing in twenty-five states. He was on the road more than he was in the Senate chamber. As a result of this hectic schedule, Dick developed stress-related neck and back pain. Pat confided to Helene that "Dick is more tired than I have ever seen him. The doctor told him that he would have to get away and also take it easier." Pat, independent since the early deaths of her parents, felt more tolerance than most wives might about Dick's impossible schedule, but at times she felt obliged to make light of her loneliness: "Yes, Saturday night and all alone again!!" she wrote Helene. "I am accustomed to it now." Pat worried about the effect of his absences on the children. In her biography of her mother, Julie claims, not altogether convincingly, that she and Tricia had no problems with their father's frequent absences from home. In the Pat Nixon collection at the Nixon Presidential Library there is a poignant WELCOME HOME DADDY sign that Pat and the girls created. They might have kept it up all year.

He was often due home. Pat was a dedicated mother and likely went out of her way to make up for her absent husband. Dick, when he was in attendance, did his best to be an attentive father. He indulged his daughters, leaving their mother to discipline them.

Consumed by ambition, Dick did not give proper attention to his health or his marriage. He was having trouble sleeping, was experiencing neck and back pain, and was chronically exhausted. After reading the bestseller *The Will to Live* by Dr. Arnold A. Hutschnecker, a self-styled expert in psychosomatic medicine, Dick met with the physician at his office at 829 Park Avenue in New York City, and then informally in Dick's suite at the Waldorf Hotel. Speaking to friendly Nixon biographer Jonathan Aitken, Hutschnecker claimed to have helped Nixon by dispensing "sensible non-medical advice." (In his 1974 book, *The Drive to Power*, Hutschnecker explained that he helped his patients with their "emotional conditions," including "misery, tension, unhappiness.") The physician told Aitken that he had concluded that the primary source of Nixon's pain was his tendency to cover his insecurities by overwork. Although there is much debate in the Nixon literature about Hutschnecker's role, the doctor seemed to function as at least a wise mentor.

Dick reduced his schedule and began to take more vacations. In November 1951, Dick and Pat spent what she called "a glorious ten days" in Sea Island, Georgia, where they swam, bicycled for five miles a day "on wooded paths" or "hard sand," and played golf. Pat asked Helene to assure her husband, Jack, that the Nixons took lessons before hitting the links. They ate at night in the dining room, where they were "unrecognized!!" Pat excitedly noted. "The only thorn was that hurricanes blew off the coast for part of the time," she wrote Helene, "so we didn't have the beach weather we had hoped for." "It was a real rest for Dick," Pat wrote, "but not long enough."

The Nixons wanted a vacation in California with the Drowns, but they didn't feel they could "swing it financially." So Dick went off on his own trip, with Pat's encouragement. Senate colleagues were also worried about Dick, and at the end of November, George Smathers, the Democratic U.S. senator from Florida, arranged for him to vacation in Vero Beach and Miami, where he consulted an osteopath. Smathers recommended "a secluded beach where they wouldn't be bothered." Dick played golf by himself every morning on a public course, swam daily, and then reported to his wife that he was exhausted and had to go to bed early. Playfully, Pat wrote Helene: "I wouldn't vouch for that last part!"

Smathers asked his high-school friend Charles "Bebe" Rebozo to take Dick out for long, quiet outings on his boat. Rebozo, a former Pan Am airline steward and self-made business enterpreneur, was a generous, funny, and warm Cuban American who saw through Dick's shyness. Nixon and Rebozo shared working-class backgrounds and an aggressive approach to success. Although he initially complained to Smathers that Nixon wasn't a stimulating companion because "he doesn't drink whiskey; he doesn't chase women; he doesn't even play golf" (a real crime in Florida), he saw him as "a kind of genius." Bebe liked his depth and sincerity. Dick returned from Florida in a better frame of mind. He took a long Christmas hiatus with his family. He then bought some used golf clubs and took up golf as a form of relaxation.

Bebe and Dick developed an intense brotherly bond. They engaged in adolescent hijinks. Nixon could kid around with him. There are rumors that Bebe was possibly bisexual, but, if he was, he knew how to compartmentalize that fact so that it did not embarrass his friend. Dick Nixon could relax with Bebe; that meant everything to a man who was awkward and anxious around most people.

Bebe was a great raconteur, but he also knew when to allow Nixon solitary time for making notes on his omnipresent yellow pads. Dick grew to trust Bebe's discretion and relied upon him for advice about his personal finances. They invested in real estate together. Without offering convincing proof, Anthony Summers and other authors have speculated that Rebozo was linked to the Mafia through his banking and real estate enterprises, and that Nixon made money directly or indirectly through his connections to the Mafia.

For his part, Bebe saw Nixon as a powerful man who legitimized him. Their mysterious and powerful connection sometimes provoked jealousy in the women they married. Rebozo's second wife, Jane Lucke, once said, perhaps partly in jest, "Bebe's favorites are RN, his cat, and then me." Pat had her own ambivalence about Rebozo's friendship with her husband. She once carped that "Bebe's like a sponge. He soaks up whatever Dick says. . . . Dick loves that." But Pat also realized that Dick benefited from spending time basking in the warmth of Bebe's personality and in his Florida home—an environment similar to the one he experienced growing up in California. Over the next thirty years, Bebe became an affectionate "uncle" to Julie and Tricia and a prominent and intriguing third party in the Nixon marriage. Julie fondly called him "Beebes."

Every Tuesday Pat put on a Red Cross nursing cap and joined her fellow Senate wives in rolling bandages for the Senate Ladies group. She still helped out at Dick's office where longtime Nixon secretaries Loie Gaunt, Rose Mary Woods, and Marje Acker, who would become lifelong protectors and friends to Pat and Dick, had joined the staff. Pat worked for fourteen hours responding to some of the approximately six thousand telegrams and thirty thousand letters that came pouring into Nixon's office after Dick, in his maiden speech in the Senate, lambasted Truman for firing General Douglas MacArthur, leader of UN forces in Korea, for insubordination. Nixon also critiqued the president's "failed Asian policies . . . that resulted in the birth of Red China." Pat decided to attend a Senate wives' luncheon at the White House because it was her first invitation to dine there. She worried, "I'll probably be cold-shouldered by Bess" because of Dick's political attacks on the president. It was becoming increasingly clear to Pat that being the wife of such an outspoken and combative crusader could be socially awkward, even troublesome.

The young senator and his wife were required to attend many social engagements—congressional receptions, embassy dinners, and elegant parties at the swanky Sulgrave Club. In May 1951 they went to a dinner at the club in honor of Washington doyenne Mrs. Perle Mesta, the U.S. ambassador to Luxembourg, and "Mr. and Mrs. Joe

Pew of Sun Oil." Pat, with tongue in cheek, wrote Helene, "some combination! I will . . . tell you what Luxembourg has done for her." Pat felt guilty leaving her daughters with babysitters. She had been raised in a close-knit family; leaving her children at home went against the maternal habits that had been instilled in her. Pat tolerated the guilt because she believed that "a wife's first duty is to help and encourage her husband in the career he has chosen."

On occasion Pat and Dick left the children at home with sitters while they spent a weekend alone together. On a Friday night in February 1951, Pat met up with Dick, who had been traveling, in New York City. They saw the musical *Call Me Madam*, "which was a riot." The next evening they attended conservative journalist and author Ralph de Toledano's cocktail party, where they conversed with Hede Massing, a former communist spy. Afterward, they went to Mrs. Theodore Roosevelt, Jr.'s, dinner. Among the guests were playwright Clare Boothe Luce, financier Winthrop Aldrich, author William L. White, Rockefeller Center designer Peter Grim, and several former ambassadors. It was, for Pat, "as impressive as a group as we have ever 'broken bread with.'" On Sunday a wealthy supporter called for them in a chauffeured car and took them to a luncheon at the Piping Rock Club on Long Island. Then a millionaire brewer threw a party for them at his country estate. Pat "could hardly stumble back to Washington," she wrote Helene. "It was all so fantastic and fun." At times Pat and Dick could surmount their lower-class resentment of wealthy elite easterners to mingle with the upper-crust Republicans who could advance Dick's career goals.

Pat was delighted in April 1952 when Dick took her on a second honeymoon in Hawaii with their closest friends, Jack and Helene Drown. They danced every night, swam sometimes twice a day, and took hula lessons. Unfortunately for all us, there are no photographs of this for Nixon's fans and detractors to contemplate. It would be, Pat said, "the last carefree vacation I ever had."

Part Two
Cultural Leaders and
Private Citizens

Anxiety is the handmaiden of contemporary ambition.
—*Alain de Botton*, Status Anxiety

The secret of life, though, is to fall
seven times and to get up eight times.
—*Paulo Coelho*, The Alchemist

A man is not finished when he is defeated;
he's finished when he quits.
—*Richard Nixon*

9

"Heroes" and "Housewives": Dick, Ike, Pat, and Mamie

Right before 4:00 p.m. on Friday, July 11, 1952, just as Pat was biting into a bacon, lettuce, and tomato sandwich with Helene Drown and Murray Chotiner's wife, Phyllis, at Chicago's Stock Yard Inn restaurant, a news bulletin interrupted the televised film they were watching. "Ike Chooses Nixon," it announced. Pat's sandwich popped out of her mouth and fell onto her plate. "I was speechless," Pat told reporters. "I couldn't take another bite." Pat rushed to the Republican Convention hall and was escorted to a box in the balcony, telling the reporters who flocked around her that she was "amazed, flabbergasted, weak."

Pat might have been shocked, but not entirely surprised.

Responding to rumors that Dick might be offered the Republican vice-presidential spot, she had stayed up with him most of the previous night debating whether he should accept. Dick was ambitious to rise to a national rostrum, but he also knew that he would have to do the hardscrabble campaigning, and he worried that, if the ticket lost, he would be blamed for bringing down a formidable candidate who was a popular national hero. Dick needed his wife's support in his decision. Pat did not look forward to another campaign; her injuries from the grueling, vituperative 1950 senatorial race were unhealed. In addition to campaigning alongside him, she would have to face losing whatever semblance of private life they still possessed. Vaulting to the center of the national arena, one step away from the presidency, might entail many tedious social and ceremonial duties that she and her ambitious husband found enervating. Despite Ike's promises of an increased role for Dick, Pat did not find the "surface glamour of the idea" of the vice presidency compelling. Dick and Pat—especially Pat—also worried about the damage that their absences to campaign and to engage in public duties, as well hostile press coverage, might inflict on their young daughters.

At 4:00 a.m., the Nixons called aide Murray Chotiner into their bedroom to provide a third perspective. Chotiner, sensing that Pat had been arguing against running for the vice presidency, reminded the couple that if the Republican presidential ticket lost, Nixon would keep his Senate seat. If he were to leave public office, his national prominence would ensure that he could launch a lucrative career in law. If he did not accept the invitation to run with Ike, Nixon would remain an obscure senator for years awaiting his chance to wield national influence. "The junior senator from California doesn't amount to anything," Chotiner said. "There comes a time when you have to go up or out." After he left their room, Pat continued to argue against taking the position and thought she had talked Dick out of accepting it. But, if he ran, she wanted him to know she was with him: "I guess I can make it through another campaign."

Dwight Eisenhower let his advisors choose his running mate. Ike's advisors recommended Nixon partly because he was a young westerner who balanced the ticket in age and geography. The "Old Guard" conservative wing of the Republican Party trusted Nixon's anticommunism, while the liberal bloc approved of his strong internationalism and his moderate views on domestic issues. After the convention nominated him by acclamation, Nixon summoned his wife to join him on the convention podium. Pat gave him an exultant kiss. Caught up in the euphoria of the moment, Pat and Dick bussed each other again for the photographers, who captured a rare personal moment in the Nixons' public life. Eisenhower, in his acceptance speech, told the American public he had chosen in Nixon a partner who had "statesman-like qualities" and a "special talent, an ability to ferret out any kind of subversive influence wherever it may be found and the strength and persistence to get rid of it." Powered by a potent swirl of adrenaline and fatigue, Dick and Pat joined the hero of D-Day and his wife on the convention stage to accept the applause of the delegates.

Soon enough, attacks on Pat and Dick's integrity made the accusations of the California Senate race look tame by comparison. During the 1952 election campaign, the Nixons would be charged with having a slush fund, gambling in Havana, engaging in income tax fraud, owning a wealth of real estate, and of taking $52,000 from the oil industry during the 1950 campaign—this last charge was based on letters that proved to be forgeries. The ordeal that Dick and Pat would undergo as they fought against the charges would begin to change the Nixon partnership. Pat became more estranged from the tumultuous world of politics, while Dick grew to be even more the righteous, resentful gladiator, with the wounds of combat a price he was willing to pay. The contrast between their overachieving public personas and their complicated private feelings would become ever more dissonant over time. Pat's image as the exemplary wife, mother, and public helpmate diverged further from the truth of her emotions. Even as she yearned for a more substantive mission, she also craved unguarded domestic peace.

Pat's fears about the campaign materialized immediately. Hannah Nixon called to tell her that newspaper reporters camping out in front of Dick and Pat's home had barged inside. They rang the doorbell, pushed past the scared babysitter, woke up Julie and Tricia, and asked them to pose for photographs. Frightened by the rude awakening and the flash of the cameras, the children started to sob. "I want my mommy," Julie cried out. Pat hurried home from Chicago to soothe their trauma. Hoping one photo session would satiate the press, Pat allowed a *Washington Post* reporter into the backyard of their Tilden Street home to snap a photograph of her with her daughters sporting large "I Like Ike" buttons. Six-year-old Tricia opined that she was "tired of photographers and reporters." Shortly after Nixon was nominated, Jacqueline Bouvier, a twenty-four-year-old reporter for the *Washington Herald-Times* and a future First Lady, interviewed Tricia for her "Inquiring Camera Girl" column. Jackie asked Tricia, "What do you think of Senator Nixon now?" Tricia replied, "He's always away. If he's famous, why can't he stay home?" Neither child relished the attention. Julie asked reporters who came to the house, "When are you going away? Soon?"

Pat effectively played two roles, that of contented, stay-at-home wife, like Mamie, and that of full partner to Dick, working to win women's votes. During the campaign, Pat Nixon and Mamie Eisenhower put themselves forth in the traditional roles as housewives, effectively symbolizing the American way of life, while their husbands campaigned as protectors of it. Pat and Mamie helped the Republican Party fight for women's votes by highlighting the prosperous American home as a symbol of the security of democracy and the superiority of the capitalist system amid the uncertainties of the Cold War era. Pat also portrayed herself as interested in the big issues; she emphasized that she and Dick "always work as a team." She claimed disingenuously that a future in politics "terrifically thrilled" her, but made sure to minimize her role to that of the standard political wife: "I go around with him and talk to the women." Learning to be a saleswoman for herself and her husband, Pat stressed their humble beginnings, their arduous political journey, and their similarity to ordinary Americans "who still believe in the American dream."

Not everyone was willing to buy what she and Dick were selling. Some critics derided the Nixons for mythologizing themselves, calling them "Mr. and Mrs. Horatio Alger, Jr.," but others embraced them. Their social mentor Alice Roosevelt Longworth referred to them as "those darling Nixons." The *Chicago Daily Tribune* called Pat the "political Cinderella of the election campaign."

The Eisenhower-Nixon ticket promised not only to clear Washington of communists but to clean up the Truman administration's corruption—a campaign promise that made the attacks on Nixon's ethics all the more dangerous. Without thoroughly checking the facts, the *New York Post* accused Nixon of living in luxury by drawing on a secret $18,000 political expense fund raised by wealthy supporters. Pat and Dick were traumatized by how quickly the nation's press corps banded against them to disseminate the accusations. What they saw as the sloppiness, indifference, and vengeance of the press appalled the Nixons.

Eisenhower was aboard his "Look Ahead Neighbor" train conducting his own whistle-stop campaign, stopping at six or seven cities a day to make phone calls and check mail in cities in Iowa and Nebraska. Sherman Adams, Eisenhower's chief of staff, recalled that "there was a great deal of hue and cry about Nixon resigning from the ticket," and that Eisenhower had received "messages and advice from all over the country." He discussed the issue with Eisenhower "immediately after the bomb burst," and Ike told Adams that if Nixon left the ticket, they would lose the election. When one hundred newspapers published editorials on September 20, running two to one with the suggestion that Nixon resign, Ike began to fear the growing controversy would derail his chances of winning the presidency.

Eisenhower's advisors and close associates were not totally comfortable with Nixon's awkward social style and his anticommunist rhetoric. The general amplified the pressure by proclaiming that both he and his running mate had to be "as clean as a hound's tooth." When Eisenhower and Nixon spoke by phone late on the night of September 20, Ike endorsed a plan for Nixon to explain the fund, provided by his backers to pay his political expenses, in a televised appeal, but stopped short of giving his running mate his full endorsement. Nixon told Eisenhower that he needed to make clear his unequivocal support for his VP candidate. Spouting off to a five-star general as if he were an errant underling, Nixon shouted, "There comes a time in matters like these when you have to shit or get off the pot!" Eisenhower replied that he would decide in his own time, after hearing response to the broadcast. He closed the telephone conversation with a neutral "Keep your chin up." Now Nixon had to prove the charges false.

While Dick holed up in a hotel for thirty hours, sleeping little and polishing his speech, Pat spent a day with the Drowns at their home in Rolling Hills. On the afternoon of Sunday, September 21, after Eisenhower's call, New York governor Thomas Dewey phoned Dick to pass on Eisenhower's alleged request that Nixon, at the end of the speech, proffer his resignation for consideration. Nixon stubbornly objected and hung up.

As Pat and Dick walked down the hotel corridor on their way to the El Capitan Theater in Hollywood, where he would deliver his speech, "It seemed like the last mile," as Dick later wrote. He placed himself behind a desk and Pat seated herself on a divan next to him on a set decorated to look, as Nixon's television advisor Ted Rogers said, like a "GI bedroom den." Nixon later called it a "flimsy-looking, nondescript room." Pat watched him with a fixed gaze, unwilling to betray emotion that might undermine or distract from her husband's words. Not knowing exactly what her husband was going to say, she listened as he engaged in what commentators called a "financial striptease," presenting the American public with stunningly intimate details of their family's circumstances.

A wide swath of American voters identified with the Nixons' financial struggles: living in a cheap apartment to save money, straining to make mortgage payments, borrowing from parents, making do without a portfolio of stocks and bonds to provide security, and driving a two-year-old Oldsmobile. "Well, that's about it," Dick said as he moved toward the climax of his speech. "That's what we have and that's what we owe. It isn't very much but Pat and I have the satisfaction that every dime that we've got is honestly ours." With that statement—with his entire speech—he won the allegiance of many voters who disdained the corrupt and arrogant elitists who had attacked the Nixons. He added, "I should say this—that Pat doesn't have a mink coat. But she does have a respectable Republican cloth coat. And I always tell her that she'd look good in anything." And to help throw down a gauntlet to Eisenhower, he said, "I don't believe I ought to quit, because I am not a quitter. And, incidentally, Pat is not a quitter. After all, her name is Patricia Ryan and she was born on St. Patrick's Day, and you know the Irish never quit." With that statement he played on his wife's background to ally himself with Roman Catholic voters.

This attack on his campaign financing was neither the first nor the last smear that would be thrown at him, Nixon told the public. Dramatically, he stood up, walked out in front of his stage desk, and made his final case: "And as far as this is concerned, I intend to continue the fight. . . . Why do I feel . . . the necessity . . . to come up here and bare [my soul] as I have? Why is it necessary for me to continue this fight? And I want to tell you why. Because, you see, I love my country. And I think my country is in danger. And I think that the only man that can save America at this time is the man that's running for president on my ticket—Dwight Eisenhower." He boosted Eisenhower even while trumping him with the dog and the cloth coat.

After asking viewers to contact the National Republican Committee to say whether he should stay on the ticket or resign, Dick ran out of time and forgot to mention where to write or wire a message. When the camera clicked off, he tossed down his notes and mopped his face with the stage curtain. The speech was a failure, he told Pat. She embraced her husband and reassured him that she was delighted that he "had not stayed on the defensive, but had needled Stevenson" about his own financial history. Dick's carefully staged "fund scandal speech," as he would call it, transformed a humiliating ordeal into a career-making victory, but one that made the Nixons national celebrities who would thereafter be diligently scrutinized.

Mamie Eisenhower cried while watching the program with her husband in the private offices of the manager of a public auditorium in Cleveland. Fifteen thousand supporters chanted "We Want Nixon" as they waited for Eisenhower to appear in the auditorium. Dick's speech that night had garnered a television and radio audience of almost sixty million people—a record not rivaled until the Kennedy-Nixon debates in 1960. Eventually more than three million letters, telegrams, and phone calls running 350 to 1 in favor of Nixon flooded into the Republican National Committee. Eisenhower summoned him to a dramatic reunion in Wheeling, West Virginia, and gave him his blessing.

Thirty-nine-year-old Dick would write that the "fund crisis made me feel suddenly tired and old." This fourth trial in the Nixon marriage exacted an enormous personal toll on both partners—reinforcing and heightening a cynicism and mistrust that would permeate the rest of their public lives. Before the Watergate scandal, Dick called the ordeal of September 1952 the "hardest" and "sharpest" of his life. It also created a crack in the couple's unity as a team. "It kills me," Pat said to Julie about the fund crisis. "It makes me so exasperated, so tired—the unfairness." As Dick recalled, the controversy went beyond previous political crises in costing Pat her "zest" for "political life." Dick, on the other hand, often celebrated the anniversary of his Checkers speech. He founded the Order of the Hound's Tooth, its members the aides, news people, and party officials who had lived through that awful week with him. The group met for years to celebrate Nixon's harrowing victory. Although he denied the impact the fund scandal had on his view of politics and the press, Dick grew increasingly cynical and suspicious.

The Checkers speech also proved to Pat and Dick, and the nation, the effect of television, which eclipsed the traditional media, and the power of family sanctity projected on a large scale. During their years in the White House, Dick would press Pat to use television, as he did, to reach the American public and refurbish an image under siege from the media. Pat would reluctantly comply by participating in televised interviews.

One consequence of the speech was that the Nixons felt an underlying wariness in their relations with the Eisenhowers. Ike and Mamie did not seem to be aware that they had done anything that the Nixons would find hurtful or inappropriate. When, after the speech, General Eisenhower questioned Dick and Pat about rumors that the fund had paid for their home decorator, Mrs. Nixon was quietly infuriated—her home and her integrity were sacrosanct territory. Dick reminded Ike that their enemies were fabricating this smear to tarnish the Republican ticket's integrity. That Ike even raised this question with them was a disloyalty Pat Nixon did not easily forget. It probably took her a while to forgive Eisenhower, if she ever did. Pat developed a stiff neck and retired to her bed. This was not the last time she would develop a psychosomatic response to political stress.

The Nixons endured six additional weeks of relentless speeches and whistle-stop appearances in 214 cities, over forty-six thousand miles, before Election Day. Protecting his avuncular persona, Eisenhower requested Nixon be the campaign hatchet man, with his boss's full blessing. Still smarting from the fund furor and employing the kind of rhetoric he had used in previous campaigns, Dick launched fresh vituperative attacks on his opponents, assailing Democratic presidential candidate Adlai Stevenson's "fancy striped pants language" and depicting him as a man of "more veneer than substance," one who held a Ph.D. degree from Secretary of State Dean "Acheson's College of Cowardly Communist Containment." *Time* magazine called Nixon the "Fighting Quaker," and Dick appeared to relish maligning his opponents, while earning further enmity from liberals. Pat, meanwhile, was winning general admiration. She loved connecting to people on a one-to-one basis, and all across the country, voters could feel it. "We Like Nixon" banners were changed to "We Like Nixons" streamers.

Five days before the public voted, Pat and Dick were outraged when their longtime nemesis Drew Pearson wrote a column accusing them of falsifying their tax returns. He asserted they had claimed that their California house's value was less than ten thousand dollars in order to qualify for a veteran's exemption on residential taxes. Infuriated, Nixon did research to show that a different couple with the same last name had received that tax break. Pearson eventually printed the truth. Despite Pearson's initial column, the Republican ticket won a resounding victory over Stevenson and Sparkman. The Eisenhower-Nixon team garnered thirty-four million votes—55 percent of those cast. In the 1952 election, for the first time, women voted in equal numbers to men. Although men and women gave the Republican ticket a majority of their vote, women were 5 percent more likely to cast their ballots for Eisenhower and Nixon. Pollster Lou Harris concluded that women blamed the Democratic Party more for the Korean War, inflation, and corruption in Washington.

As a veteran of a long military career, Dwight Eisenhower considered Nixon an experienced junior officer who could help represent him in a wide range of political and legislative situations. Eisenhower preferred to appear to be above the fray, but he actually worked in a hands-on manner. No one else in Eisenhower's cabinet could match the young vice president's political skills or his ability to communicate effectively with the regulars of the party, some of whom deeply distrusted the president. With Eisenhower's approval, Richard Nixon broadened the role of vice president by becoming a partisan spokesman and by serving as the administration's broker with Congress. In August 1953, Ike made Dick the chairman of the president's committee on government contracts, which emphasized African-American education and employment issues. From that moment on, contrary to current historical opinion, Nixon became the chief spokesman for his boss on civil rights issues.

In the fall of 1953, the president deputized Pat and Dick to be ambassadors through nineteen Asian countries, during a crucial new phase of the Cold War. Eisenhower set the trip up as a goodwill mission to hide his underlying goal of using the Nixons as forward observers on a political and intelligence-gathering mission. Russian dictator Joseph Stalin had died that spring, and the Korean War, which had claimed fifty-five thousand American lives, had ended in July. Although the United States had wrested a stable South Korea from the conflict, communist advances elsewhere in Asia were endangering U.S. power and influence. The Nixons went on a seventy-day, forty-five-thousand-mile goodwill tour ("one and a half times around the world!" Pat wrote in her diary) through Asia. She and Dick scoured the State Department briefings on the countries and leaders they were visiting. Pat's remarkable ability to absorb facts and figures meant, according to a member of the traveling group, "We suddenly discovered that she was our walking encyclopedia." Nixon's task was to advocate for American values and interests with U.S. allies, reassure them of

America's commitment to the region, and assess their perspective on the emerging presence of a newly communist mainland China. Pat Nixon would temper and augment her husband's diplomacy and serve as an exemplar of American values: showing compassion for the ill and downtrodden, demonstrating Americans' genuine interest in the people of other countries, and encouraging women to strive to support themselves and bolster their self-confidence.

Departing for Asia on October 5, Pat and Dick were embarking on the most significant mission of their lives thus far, even as they felt guilty about leaving their children for ten weeks. The day before they left was "dominated and saddened," Pat wrote in her diary, by "the thought of leaving Julie and Tricia." To justify her separation from her daughters, Pat fell back on her commitment to duty: "But a job had to be done—so full force ahead."

Pat chafed at the limitations of what was expected of her. She would later write Helene that she would like to work "rather than all the useless gadding I am expected to do." During their diplomatic tour Pat and Dick presented themselves in a way that provided Pat a meaningful role as an international advocate for women's rights. During their tour Pat challenged men's traditional attitude that women's place was in the home. Pat accompanied the vice president to gatherings that women did not normally attend with their husbands. This expanded role allowed Pat to recognize that she had more to offer than a static advertisement of American domestic values.

Ignoring State Department pressure to maintain a traditional ceremonial role that included shopping and women's social gatherings and teas, Pat advocated for women in Australia, New Zealand, and a large swath of the Asian world, where females were disempowered and often prevented from assuming any public prominence. While Dick met with governmental officials and heads of state, Pat visited several hundred hospitals, schools, and public institutions to learn about social and educational conditions that affected women. Her conscious and articulated agenda was to foster women's rights. When Pat went to the ultra-private Auckland Club in New Zealand, Kiwi women were admitted for the first time in its seventy-six years. In Sydney, Australia, both sexes were included in luncheons and dinners—a rare event. In Melbourne, women made history by attending a luncheon in the state parliamentary building where the male members honored the vice president.

In Malaya she was the first woman to dine at what had been an exclusively all-male club. She appeared at events with her husband in Muslim countries like Indonesia, Afghanistan, Iran, and Pakistan where Pat knew that "Wives had never been invited to official functions before." She created the conditions for change: "Naturally, the ladies rejoiced. It meant a precedent had been established."

U.S. News & World Report noted that Nixon was touring Asia "with the energetic enthusiasm of an American Congressman stumping his home district." Often during the trip, including an impromptu visit to a slum area in Hong Kong, Pat and Dick spontaneously stopped their car and shook hands with crowds that the Nixons called "inspiring." Despite extreme heat, almost no air conditioning, poor sanitary conditions, overly exotic food in some locations, and the strain of an official working agenda crammed with hundreds of culturally unfamiliar ceremonies and state dinners, Pat and Dick showed Asians the attractive face of democracy and exemplified its willingness to stand up to communists by directly confronting their propaganda.

After her return to the United States, Pat proudly told reporters, "Everywhere I went it helped women," even as she retained a sense of awe and modesty, saying to a reporter from *Redbook* magazine, "Imagine me—a farm girl—consorting with kings and queens." In his memoir *RN* Dick acknowledged that Pat's public events "gave great impetus to the respect for women that was slowly developing" in that part of the world. She was the first woman of her generation to balance being a dutiful wife with advocating for the public prominence and valuation of women. In this regard her forerunner was Eleanor Roosevelt, almost thirty years her senior. The former First Lady was more outspoken about human rights, but Pat followed in her path, demonstrating through her attentions to others the values that Mrs. Roosevelt spoke about explicitly. Pat's actions had an effect. Foreign leaders and reporters noticed she fulfilled the protocols of her position in a way that suggested a warmer and more humanistic side of power. Her friendly demeanor, her subtle understanding of the complexities of international politics, and her genuine curiosity about the people and cultures she encountered were qualities that made her a terrific goodwill ambassador—a role that would suit her in years to come.

For Dick, this tour was the genesis of his role as an influential diplomatic advisor. Now that Americans were learning about the world through the medium of television, Pat and Dick Nixon's diplomatic missions helped them create a recognizable berth for themselves as the nation's "Second Couple." When the Nixons returned to Washington's National Airport, they were greeted as celebrities by an array of State Department officials, ambassadors, and senators. At the White House, Eisenhower publicly praised Dick for his thorough and competent work, and, demonstrating his growing affection and admiration for Pat, added, "But the reports on you, Pat, have been wonderful." Pat then rushed home to see both daughters, who had temperatures. She later told reporter Isabella Taves of *Redbook* magazine that Tricia had been sick most of the time her parents had been abroad.

In 1955, Pat, accompanying her husband on a monthlong goodwill mission to Central America and the Caribbean islands, expanded her diplomacy to include more humanitarian endeavors. Pat sought to influence public attitudes about leprosy by making an unprecedented visit to the Pale Seco Leprosarium that served 116 patients at a leper colony in Panama Bay. When she shook hands with some of the lepers who had almost been cured, she was moved. Other patients—some with no feet or toes—sang and danced for her while she tapped her feet to the rhythm of a carnival band. She smiled and spoke to many patients, while others hid behind newspapers or placed their hands over their faces. She was featured in headlines in the Panama newspapers, but her efforts were not well publicized in the U.S. press until well after they had occurred. Mrs. Aida Hurwitz, who ran the leper colony, wrote Pat, "The Patients are still talking about your visit and often mention how charming and friendly you were with them." The patients asked Hurwitz to inform Mrs. Nixon they had seen a picture of Julie and Tricia in *Life* magazine and "found them adorable."

President Eisenhower, who had been posted to Panama in the early 1920s, was delighted to read an enthusiastic editorial about Pat's visit in the Panama papers, and to receive updates from Nixon about the current conditions in Panama. Upon his return to the United States, Richard Nixon told a *Los Angeles Times* reporter Pat's visits with the lepers "made a greater impression than anything I did or said in Panama."

Throughout the vice-presidential years, Pat also played a significant role behind the scenes. She joined the small staff in the vice president's office and helped them organize her husband's schedule and draft his public correspondence. She still gathered material for his speeches and edited them even as she responded to her own increasingly voluminous fan mail—up to 150 letters a week.

Eisenhower relied on Nixon to keep the conservative faction of the party united behind him. On March 13, 1954, Dick, in a televised address, successfully challenged Joseph McCarthy's menacing anticommunist campaign without using the senator's name. Nixon warned of the dangers of politicians "shooting wildly" and making themselves "the issue" by their "reckless talk and questionable methods." Eisenhower thought it was a "magnificent" speech. Pat kept her strong political views hidden, but, according to her profile in the National First Ladies' Library, she intuitively mistrusted Senator McCarthy. She did, however, support his efforts to uncover State Department employees with communist leanings. In late 1953 McCarthy had begun to undo himself by investigating communist infiltration of the army, in hearings that fully exposed his bullying tactics and would lead to his censure in the Senate that December.

Eisenhower feared that if the Republicans lost control of Congress in the 1954 midterm elections, the Republican right wing would commandeer the party's leadership in the belief that more conservative policies would win over voters—a move that the president feared would destroy the party's reputation and influence. The president asked Dick Nixon to campaign vigorously while he stayed on the sidelines until the second half of October. Pat provided encouragement while Dick, against a backdrop of increasing unemployment in which businesses were shutting down, highlighted the Eisenhower administration's anticommunist record and pummeled the Democrats, whose left wing, he claimed, wanted to socialize American institutions. While conservatives praised his pugilistic style, his patriotism, and his regular-guy persona, Nixon's vociferous attacks led liberals to call him a demagogue and a liar. According to the *New York Times*, Nixon's charges that Democrats had a blueprint "for socializing American institutions" involved making "sweeping generalizations of sometimes dubious quality" while "planting the dark and ominous reference." In the midst of the campaign, *Washington Post* cartoonist Herblock depicted Dick Nixon crawling out of a sewer. Pat canceled their subscription to the *Washington Post* lest their children see such cartoons.

Despite the fierce opposition attacks on Nixon and the negative press he generated, the Republicans lost only two seats in the Senate and sixteen in the House—better than the average number of losses the party in power endures during most midterm elections. The Democrats took control of both houses of Congress. Five days before the end of the campaign, the president wrote Dick praising him for his effective and exhaustive efforts and emphasizing the appeal of Pat ("the most charming of the lot").

Dick promised Pat a European vacation after the election, but by now she was wise to his schedule, writing Helene Drown, "You are probably laughing at this yearly farce." The Nixons went to Florida instead. Pat was becoming increasingly cynical about the likelihood that she could ever share a normal family life with her work-obsessed husband. If she, like many American women in the 1950s, compared herself with television wives like Harriet Nelson in *The Adventures of Ozzie and Harriet*, Pat had to realize that she was sacrificing more for her family than most wives were. During the demanding vice-presidential years, Pat replenished herself by visiting with Helene Drown in California and Washington. "How I do enjoy your letters!" Pat wrote Helene in 1959. "I just light up, sit back, and devour." Both Nixons released the tensions of their high-strung marriage by having companions in leisure; Pat had Helene Drown, and Dick snuck away with Bebe Rebozo and Jack Drown to Key Biscayne.

*　　　*　　　*

Despite the Nixons' mistrust toward the Eisenhowers, engendered during the fund crisis, and the common belief that Eisenhower was ambivalent about Nixon's hard-hitting partisanship, the Nixons and the Eisenhowers had a warmer interpersonal relationship than most historians portray. Pat and Mamie grew increasingly fond of each other during the 1950s. Two days after the 1953 inauguration, Mamie invited Pat to be one of the hostesses at an enormous White House reception for four thousand representatives of the Daughters of the American Revolution. "She was most friendly," Pat wrote Helene, reporting that the First Lady took her up to the private living quarters. The Eisenhowers broke tradition by inviting "Dick and [me] to receive with them at the reception for the diplomats. The usual procedure is to entertain separately. So they have been extremely friendly." In January 1954, President and Mrs. Eisenhower invited eighty guests to a formal White House dinner for the Nixons, an honor not regularly given by presidents to their seconds in command. In the receiving line that evening, Mamie introduced Dick and Pat "as two of their best friends." The Eisenhowers' gestures were especially reassuring to a vice-presidential couple who had been left hanging for days during the fund crisis.

Nixon met at a minimum three times a week with Eisenhower in national security, cabinet, and legislative meetings. After Dick and Pat's successful tour of Asia and Dick's effective confrontation of McCarthy, Ike began to trust him implicitly. Eisenhower, whose intellect had been minimized and belittled by columnists and historians, increasingly valued Nixon's intelligence and competence. As early as 1954 Ike began telling Dick Nixon that "we should meet regularly for breakfast or lunch." They did so throughout 1954. On January 7, 1955, the president wrote Nixon, "It has been much too long since we have had a chance for a quiet talk." He spoke with Nixon days later and suggested that they meet once a month or every three weeks. They kept to Ike's plan. On May 2, 1955, they played golf together at the Burning Tree golf course outside Washington.

President Eisenhower esteemed Pat as an intelligent dinner companion, a politically savvy wife, and a skillful diplomat at home and abroad. He saw that Pat was genuinely interested in international affairs and did her homework before meeting foreign officials. By 1960 he was sending her clever birthday letters. In 1961, in an unusually lively manner, he wrote, "My crystal ball tells me that you and St. Patrick have something in common today, and I want to join with the leprechauns in sending congratulations."

Still, the relationship between the Eisenhowers and the Nixons was complex for many reasons. That the president and First Lady were not as physically robust as their younger partners created tensions. Mamie suffered at times from shortness of breath, fatigue, and heart palpitations—stemming from a bout of rheumatic fever in childhood—and Ike had a heart attack in 1955, had stomach problems, and underwent an operation for ileitis in 1956. His infirmities meant that Nixon, as a divisive and still-green politician, loomed as a potential president, and a problematic one. The difference between Nixon's and Eisenhower's backgrounds and health created ripples of ambivalence in Ike's generally positive attitude toward his vice president. Mamie, on the other hand, was grateful for how effectively Pat substituted for her whenever she or the president was ill. Pat and Mamie shared a warm personal style; both were perfectionists who appreciated competence. In 1956 after visiting with the Nixons, Mamie wrote them that it was "wonderful fun being with you all at luncheon yesterday." She was "deeply touched" to receive a gift of "the lovely Brazilian jade amulet and shall long cherish it as a token of our friendship." She also admired the "clever . . . amusing jingles" Pat composed to accompany the gifts.

During the 1950s, as historian David Halberstam observed, a family was supposed to be a "single perfect universe—instead of a fragile mechanism of conflicting political and emotional pulls." The "perfect" Nixon marriage endured fierce pressures during the vice-presidential years, leaving little time for the joint parenting of young daughters and less private time for the couple to nurture their bond. Pat had to cope with the social coercion that demanded she exemplify perfection. That meant being an unerring hostess and guest. Mrs. Nixon received the wives of administration officials and foreign diplomats who made courtesy calls to her home. Seventy-six foreign missions in Washington were required by protocol to entertain the vice-presidential couple. As a result, Pat and Dick were obligated to dine out as many as four nights a week. The Nixons returned the hospitality by holding formal dinners at establishments like the elegant and private 1925 F Street Club. Women's magazines like *McCall's*, *Redbook*, and *Ladies' Home Journal* encouraged housewives to suppress their unrealized ambitions or their conflicts about their husbands' devotion to their work. After telling Helene there were four White House dinners in one week, Pat added, "Oh, joy, I can hardly wait."

Dick agreed. He told *Collier's* magazine that "two, three and sometimes four formal parties a week are a chore. Washington social life is very unattractive and extremely boring. The difficult part is that you can't allow your boredom to show." Dick went on to say that "the best test of a man is not how well he does the things he likes, but how well he does the things he doesn't like." By that standard Pat and Dick were exemplary.

For all her reservations and frustrations, Pat relentlessly polished her persona as the ultimate competent housewife—the embodiment of the American dream. She told reporters that despite her hectic schedule she did most of the cooking, shopped twice weekly, set out all the family's clothes, sewed draperies, and made her daughters' dresses. Amid her public duties, she made sure to be home to give the girls a bath and read them a bedtime story before going out again. In a gesture that inspired Middle American housewives and annoyed others, Pat opened her closet on a Saturday morning and showed *Collier's* reporter Helen Worden Erskine an orderly assemblage of outfits.

Pat Nixon was named Outstanding Homemaker of the Year in 1953, Mother of the Year in 1955, and the "nation's ideal wife" by the Homemaker's Forum in 1957. In order to cope with the demands of being the vice president's wife, she hired a full-time housekeeper in 1953 and paid a man to come in each week to clean the windows and floors. Every bit as much as her husband, Pat sought to control and promulgate her image. She allowed photographers to snap pictures of her vacuuming or pressing her husband's pants, but she made sure that there were no photos of her staff. When Dick was listed among the best-dressed men in the nation, Pat told her friend Louise Johnson, "That's my steam iron!"

But there was a dark side to presenting themselves as a perfect couple: Pat and Dick could not control being observed. The image they strove so hard to maintain victimized them. The Nixons were irked that their carefully marketed lives were examined by busloads of tourists and other gawkers who looked into their Tilden Street home from the road. People rang their bell to ask for autographs. But Pat and Dick did enjoy a sense of community with their loyal neighbors, which offered some semblance of normal community. On July 4, 1954, the Nixons entertained dozens of them with a fireworks display in their yard. That night Dick earned his daughter's admiration for being the "hero of the lighting performance." Contrary to myth, the Nixons did take many vacations, which Dick sometimes cut short to return to Washington. In August 1954 Pat wrote Helene that she was "again enjoying (?) a manless vacation" in Ogunquit, Maine. "Perhaps not quite as the governor has assigned a *very handsome* State Trooper to 'guard' us," Pat added.

That summer, in a rebellious mood toward the intrusive press, Pat made a public relations mistake that would haunt her for years. She offered *Collier's* reporter Erskine an obvious, and obviously untrue, piece of public relations propaganda: "We've never quarreled. Dick and I are too much alike. We don't even differ in our opinions." This remark set the stage for later accusations that she was inauthentic. The Nixons also convinced Erskine to describe them both as "unfailingly even-tempered, slow to anger," a characterization that their public and private history clearly belied.

With the pressure they endured, and with Dick's melancholic tendencies, there were tense and fractious times in the marriage. In his dark portrait of Nixon, author Anthony Summers cites observers who claim that Pat was moody, that she kicked her husband out of their home and lost her temper at him in front of visitors. Nixon's cousin Jessamyn West asserted that at one point Dick asked Hannah Nixon to fly from California to Washington to help resolve a quarrel he was having with his wife. Julie Eisenhower avers that her parents avoided confrontations with each other. Whatever the truth of their conflicts and how they handled them, like most wives who cheerfully accommodate their spouses most of the time, Pat surely reached her limit on occasion and vented her fury. She often eased her resentment by spouting off to Helene.

Pat felt increasingly trapped by her competing obligations and considered the vice presidency to be a dead-end job. Eisenhower received credit for the 1954 electoral victories while Dick was attacked for the hard-hitting campaigning Eisenhower sanctioned. Dick felt pleased at some points and unappreciated and discouraged at other times about the feedback he received for the backbreaking work he had done for congressional candidates. In February 1955 Pat convinced Dick to sign a private agreement with her that he would serve for only one term. He probably complied to assuage his wife's stress about the burdens the Eisenhowers placed on both of them, putting off the inevitable re-evaluation of that decision for more than a year, when the issue would truly be joined both with his wife and with the president. But for Pat, having an exit strategy from a painful situation made the pressures more bearable.

After the harsh anti-Nixon press during and after the 1954 midterm elections, both the Nixons and the Eisenhowers were privately re-evaluating their political alliance. Ever the general, Eisenhower did not let fondness or respect for his staff interfere with his decisions about what officers he could best deploy to help him win his battles. He kept his options open until he had determined the best strategy for winning the 1956 election. Pat despised the fact they "were not in control" and that their political relationship with Eisenhower "remained so delicate and tenuous." Dick was worn out and felt unappreciated. He yearned to be one of Eisenhower's few intimates. During his days as a supreme military commander, Eisenhower learned to separate work and friendship. He played cards with old friends and was not interested in fostering that kind of intimacy with his underlings. Richard Nixon was one among many (including chief of staff Sherman Adams) who felt excluded from Eisenhower's emotional inner circle. Taking personally what was Eisenhower's overall management style, the vice president fell into one of his periodic bouts of despondency.

The dynamic between the president and vice president shifted profoundly on Saturday, September 24, 1955. After the Nixons returned home from attending the wedding of his secretary Drusilla Nelson, Pat went upstairs to change into casual clothes while Dick read the *Evening Star* newspaper downstairs. The phone rang and Dick answered. White House press secretary James "Jim" Hagerty told him that the president had suffered a heart attack while visiting his in-laws' home in Denver. Dick sat mute in the living room for ten minutes, absorbing the potential enormity of the news he had heard, before he called deputy attorney general William Rogers, Nixon's closest confidant in the administration, and asked him to rush over to the Nixon home. Then Dick went upstairs to tell Pat. She was speechless. Pat gently informed their daughters. Tricia came downstairs, crying. "The president isn't going to die, is he, Daddy?" she asked. He reassured her and then, seeking to elude the reporters and camera people who had surrounded his house, slipped out the back door, where Rogers's wife had parked her car. The next day, to make a public show of the administration's stability at a time of uncertainty, Dick and Pat attended Westmoreland Congregational Church, where their children went to Sunday school, then invited a small contingent of friendly reporters to their home for a bland, reassuring interview.

"I just wish there were some way I could lighten your burdens," Pat wrote Mamie. But now the Nixons themselves were taking on heavier burdens. Pat allowed dozens of press men to camp out in the maid's room in their basement so that they could avoid being uncomfortable in the chilly fall weather. "They visit and prowl at night which is a little hard on light sleeper me," she wrote Helene. Dick presided over cabinet meetings (sitting in his own seat, not the president's) and meetings of the National Security Council. For seven tense weeks, as Eisenhower recovered, Nixon swam in what he later called the intoxicating "great stream of history." His judicious and nonself-aggrandizing method of handling the crisis rehabilitated his image, which, in turn, rehabilitated his mood. Pat and Dick took on the added responsibility of officially hosting the visits of the presidents of Italy, Guatemala, and Uruguay.

Returning to active duty after his heart attack, Eisenhower thought deeply about who could most effectively take over the presidency should he die in office. Beyond his dislike of the idea that anyone would replace him, Eisenhower was concerned that Nixon lacked the executive experience needed to run the government. Ike was not sure whether Dick was ready to win an election on his own. Ike decided to run for a second term. Now that McCarthy's excesses had diminished anticommunism as a national preoccupation, the president and his advisors asked themselves if Nixon's harsh rhetoric suited the changing times. In a meeting on the day after Christmas 1955, Ike encouraged Dick to consider not seeking a second term as his vice president and to instead take a cabinet post before running for the presidency later on. At a press conference on March 7, 1956, when reporters asked the president about reports that he had asked Nixon to take a cabinet post, Eisenhower explained that "I have asked him to chart out his own course, and tell me what he would like to do." Eisenhower did not realize that Dick would find the option of a cabinet post humiliating— partly because the press would see it as a clear demotion. The president carefully conserved his prerogatives until he needed them; he was not aware that his failure to give Nixon a full public endorsement would motivate the Republican base to champion his vice president.

Pat knew how often Dick had undertaken the tough politicking in Washington and on the campaign trail that the president demanded of him, and she saw how much physical wear and tear and emotional turbulence he had endured in the process. As a result, Pat was disturbed when Eisenhower did not publicly endorse her husband for a second term as vice president, even if she had secured a decision from her husband not to run again. As secretary Dorothy Cox told biographer Jonathan Aitken, he was "dreadfully wounded and hurt." According to Nixon biographer Irwin Gellman, from December 1955 until April 1956 Nixon was depressed and had difficulty sleeping. He saw at least eight different physicians, some of whom prescribed barbiturates. Pat was protective of him and wanted the agony to end. In

Eisenhower's diary of March 13, 1956, he recorded that Nixon told him that "his most serious problem" was that Pat wanted to leave the capital. Eisenhower wrote that he "did not want her to be upset. VP said that if she feels in August as she felt now, he would have difficulty in saying he would do *anything.*"

But then Pat changed her mind after Dick returned home on April 9, in a healthier state of mind, from a Key Biscayne vacation with Rebozo. "No one is going to push us off the ticket," she told Helene. On April 26, Dick told the president that he wanted to run again. Eisenhower told Nixon that he was glad, but asked Nixon to announce the news himself. After a brief debate, they agreed that Eisenhower's press secretary James Hagerty would inform the press that Eisenhower was "delighted by the news" that Nixon would seek the vice-presidential nomination. But then, out of the blue, in July, when Nixon already had nine hundred Republican Convention delegates pledged to vote for his renomination, former Minnesota governor Harold Stassen—Ike's disarmament advisor—threw a wrench in Nixon's plans by touting Christian Herter, who was now the governor of Massachusetts, as a vice-presidential candidate. Eisenhower firmly believed that it would be inappropriate for a president to influence the vice-presidential selection until after he was renominated. Ike did not reassure the Nixons. The president never fully understood how partisan politics worked and, thus, never realized that Pat and Dick would find his lack of overt support ungracious and uncouth. The Nixons misinterpreted Ike's behavior as a slight. As fond as Pat and Dick were of Ike, they could not yet feel totally safe that he was unequivocally on their side. In August 1956, Pat would tell a reporter, "In politics you can never count on anything."

A Turbulent Ascent

During Dick's second vice-presidential term the Nixons excelled as international super-ambassadors. Time and again, they faced down protesters, challenged bullying communist leaders, and faced physical injury, even death, while enhancing America's prestige on three continents. By doing so, they refurbished Dick's political standing, which had been diminished by charges that he was a political flamethrower at home. Their international successes were a key reason Dick would win the Republican presidential nomination in 1960. Their global popularity was not matched at home, where Pat was often seen as a dull homebody and Dick as a nitpicker and bully. Comedian Mort Sahl captured another aspect of their controversial personas when he joked that the Nixons sat home at night, "Pat knitting the American flag and Dick carefully reading the Constitution, looking," Sahl said after pausing a moment, "for loopholes."

During the 1956 Republican Convention in San Francisco, Pat shared the attention paid to her husband. She held her own press conference at the Mark Hopkins Hotel, patiently answering inane questions about how many kittens her daughters had (seven) and how many hats she brought to the convention (six). Later, when she received a loud ovation as she took her seat in the convention hall, she stood up, blushing while acknowledging cheers. The *San Diego Union* reported she reacted "with mixed pleasure and confusion." Dick told state delegates, "I have been cussed and discussed—but everybody pretty well agrees that Pat's all right."

Nixon was easily renominated, but he nearly missed delivering his acceptance speech. The very day Dick was nominated, his seventy-five-year-old father was dying. His abdominal artery ruptured, causing a rapid deterioration and drawing Pat and Dick to Whittier. Frank Nixon insisted that Dick and Pat return to the convention. "Dick, you keep fighting," his father told him.

The Republican Party presented Nixon far more unequivocally than it had in 1952, marketing their presidential team as "Ike and Dick, All American Partners" and prominently featuring Mamie and Pat. Appealing to concerns about personal and national security, the party's campaign advertisement urged, "For you, your family, your future—vote Republican." Nixon caught influenza and struggled with laryngitis while hustling to cover thirty-two states in fifteen days. Pat set aside her belief that wives should not talk politics and gave a political speech for her husband to Oklahoma Republicans.

The Nixons' turbulent ascent toward the presidency encountered the first of several major setbacks when Dick became the main target of opposition attacks during the campaign. Democratic candidate Adlai Stevenson skewered the vice president, claiming he was creating a divided America ("Nixonland"), "a land of slander and scare . . . sly innuendo, the poison pen . . . the land of smash and grab and anything to win." One of the major themes of his campaign was that Nixon would take over during a second Eisenhower term, and the nation could not afford that. In a nationally televised speech on election eve, Stevenson—sounding like the man he lambasted—asked if

Americans wanted Nixon to be "a guardian of the hydrogen bomb." But Dick Nixon was not enough of a bogeyman to scare away American voters. They trusted Eisenhower and gave the Republican ticket 57 percent of their votes on November 4, 1952.

Stevenson had asked Americans if they wanted to elect as their future vice president a man "who takes the low road," and one who "spreads ill will instead of good abroad." For Pat Nixon, those were highly provocative charges. She would do her utmost to refute them and propagate a positive portrayal of her husband and her country.

The following spring, the Nixons made an eighteen-thousand-mile, three-week-long official vice-presidential visit to Africa and then briefly to Italy, centering their travel on the ceremonies marking the independence of the former British colony of the Gold Coast as the nation of Ghana. As Pat and Dick crisscrossed the continent, visiting six African countries, Pat again focused her efforts on supporting women with events that implicitly elevated their status. When Sultan Mohamed V of Morocco offered Mrs. Nixon a formal audience, he broke his country's practice of isolating women from mixed-sex gatherings. Liberian female political leaders, who accompanied her on visits to orphanages, marketplaces, and schools, were impressed with how much Mrs. Nixon accomplished in encouraging women as she shook their hands and kissed their babies in full view of the cameras. She wanted to help build their self-confidence. In temperatures of over one hundred degrees, she dodged rats and rotting fruits and vegetables in marketplaces. She won over aides and local citizens alike with her graciousness. When Pat was presented with the eye of a big fish in a Khartoum market, she popped it in her mouth and "took it like a pill," said Nixon's new aide Donald "Don" Hughes, who had been detached from the military and was starting out by assisting Pat on this trip. He learned from her about the demands of diplomacy; swallowing that delicacy was, according to Pat, simply part of "how you do it," Hughes said.

Pat Nixon's positive reviews counterbalanced the lingering aversion toward her husband. International correspondent Ruth Montgomery

called Pat "a phenomenon of our times" who had "made as much im-
pact as any man who has ever represented America abroad." Journalist
Earl Mazo, who accompanied the Nixons to Africa, was impressed as
he watched Pat charming "peasants by the thousands and potentates
by the dozens." She showed genuine interest in everyone she met and
in their customs. She greeted them in a casual and winsome manner.
Mazo was astounded by her stamina (she was the only person in the
traveling delegation who did not get sick) and her apparently genuine
interest and enjoyment in everyone they met. In an article titled "Mrs.
Nixon as Ambassador," in the *New York Herald Tribune,* he proclaimed
that "Pat Nixon has become a top-rung personality—a woman of con-
siderable importance at home and abroad simply by being herself. . . .
That may be a novel achievement in Washington where . . . women
normally assume an aura of power by shining as party givers, promot-
ers of causes or makers of profound or witty observations on foreign
or domestic matters." Nixon's friend Senator George Smathers read
the Mazo article into the Congressional Record, adding, "I think all
of us will agree that much of what the Vice President is doing . . .
could not have been done without the help of his most lovely wife, Pat
Nixon." As for Dick, he earned plaudits from the African-American
daily the *Pittsburgh Courier,* whose reporter, Alex Rivera, accompanied
them through Africa. Watching Nixon at close range, he concluded
that the vice president was not only well prepared for every event, but
was genuinely "a warm, engaging, sincere personality."

When the Nixons returned from Africa, they moved into a large
stone English Tudor with eight bedrooms—two of which became
Pat and Dick's first home offices. They had purchased the house
in January 1957 in order to accommodate their increasing social
responsibilities, their need for privacy, and Pat's aspirations to be a
model homemaker. Their house was situated in a cul de sac at 4308
Forest Lane, on more than half an acre of grounds adjoining Glover-
Archbold Park, in the Wesley Heights area of Washington. While
the Nixons were in Africa, their friend Louise Johnson led a group
of friends in supervising the refurbishing of the house, moving and
unpacking the family's belongings. The Drowns and friends Ray

Arbuthnot and his wife bought California redwood furniture and a grill and set them up on a flagstone terrace overlooking the park. "We didn't realize what a favorite spot it would be," Dick wrote the Drowns, "until we walked in and saw it all set up."

In late November 1957 President Eisenhower suffered a mild stroke. Richard Nixon met with more than one hundred reporters and cameramen for a news conference that was unprecedented—the first and only time the vice president held such a press conference at the White House. Nixon's job was to reassure the nation and the world that President Eisenhower was recovering quickly and the administration's work did not have to be curtailed. During the president's convalescence, Nixon made clear he had not assumed any new duties. He had consulted with the cabinet to "clear away nonessentials" to lighten the president's burdens. As he had in 1955, Dick would preside over cabinet and national security meetings while Eisenhower recovered. The president and his wife further curtailed their schedules, which added to the Nixons' obligations, including the hosting of a state dinner for King Mohamed V of Morocco.

After five years working under Eisenhower, Nixon had figured out how much Ike wanted him to work independently. On December 3, 1957, Dick wrote in his private diary that "Ike apparently prefers the kind of operation in which his subordinates carry the ball and do not take things up with him unless they feel it is absolutely necessary to do so."

Mamie increasingly called upon Pat to fill in for her, often on short notice, at White House functions. By the spring of 1958, the heavy workload felled Pat. Her body was weakened by the chronic stress she endured. She badly sprained her back while lifting Julie up to see a bird's nest. Days of bed rest did not help; she was hospitalized. Helene Drown flew from California to take care of the girls. "It did hurt me to know that you were in such pain," Helene wrote Pat, "but at least it prevented you from going to the usual teas, luncheons, presentations, etc. and gave me a chance for a real visit." Exacerbating the stress on Pat was the question of whether Dick would run for president in two years' time. Helene urged Dick to stop avoiding a conversation with Pat about his plans to run. He resisted this entreaty, averse as he was to both ambivalence and confrontation. It is not clear how long it took before the issue was joined between them.

Pat's back had not yet fully healed by the time the president asked the Nixons to make an eighteen-day diplomatic trip to South America in May 1958. The centerpiece of the trip was the inauguration of Arturo Frondizi, the first democratically elected Argentinian president in twenty years. While Dick inspected industrial plants, talked to government officials, and sold businessmen on American investment in Argentina, Pat, more or less recovered, toured schools, orphanages, and hospitals. The Nixons went on to be greeted warmly in Paraguay, Uruguay, Argentina, and Bolivia. Then, on a solo visit to the University of San Marcos in Lima, Peru, Dick was pelted from a distance with fruit, bottles, and stones by leftist demonstrators. One stone ricocheted off Nixon's shoulder and struck his Secret Service agent Jack Sherwood in the mouth, breaking a tooth.

At the Caracas airport, Pat and Dick faced more peril. According to Don Hughes, the State Department did not place the Nixons' automobiles next to the planes, nor did the State Department officials guard them. As Pat and Dick stood at attention in front of the terminal listening to the Venezuelan national anthem being played, the shrieking crowd above them on an observation deck hurled insults, garbage, and "tobacco-brown" spit on them. "At first the spit looked like giant snowflakes," but, as it landed on the Nixons, it turned into revolting, lurid stains. Although Pat's red suit was darkened with brown splotches and her face was covered in spittle, the Nixons endured the abuse without flinching. Pat and Dick walked briskly hand in hand along the red carpet toward their cars. Along the way, they were assailed with fruit, other objects, and more spittle from the loud-mouthed crowd on the observation deck and the strident demonstrators behind the fences at the border of the runway. When Pat and the Venezuelan foreign minister's wife reached their open car, Don Hughes opened the door for them. Pat "took out a big white handkerchief to wipe up a big glob of spit on the seat," Hughes remembered.

As their motorcade traveled into Caracas, Pat was riding behind her husband in a car with Hughes and the foreign minister's wife when protesters pulled a vehicle into the street to block it off. More than five hundred enraged demonstrators quickly emerged out of side streets and alleys and attacked both of the Nixons' cars with pipes, rocks, clubs, and fists. "I have never seen such hate on people's faces," Hughes recalled. A rock smashed into Pat's window. A hefty demonstrator struck the car with a club. "I felt we were going to die," Hughes recalled. "I would have put money on it." He was struck by how calmly Pat put her arm around the distraught foreign minister's wife. "She was one tough lady. She was as brave as any man I have ever seen." Pat kept an eye on her husband's limousine to determine whether protesters had been able to shatter his windows. Dick also glanced protectively at his wife's car, but focused mainly on calming himself and his Secret Service agents. He did not want them to overreact by pulling out their guns and inciting the violent crowd.

When a rock splintered the shatterproof window in Nixon's car, a sliver of glass flew into the foreign minister's eye. He bled profusely. An agitator beat Nixon's window with an iron pipe. Slivers also flew into the vice president's face and that of his Secret Service agent. The crowd began rocking Nixon's car in an effort to turn it over and set it on fire. Meanwhile, six Secret Service agents had left their cars, but without drawing their weapons, an act that might have further incited the crowd. After twelve terrifying minutes the agents were able to maneuver a press truck to block oncoming traffic, giving the Nixon party a chance to speed past the roadblock and find safety in the American embassy. Pat, angry that the protests were dominating their goodwill visit, finally allowed herself to realize how much danger they had been in only after they arrived at the embassy. Dick was so exhausted by the ordeal that he fell asleep in midafternoon.

The demonstrations, which marked the most violent protest against high-ranking Americans in the Cold War period, were primed to cause a diplomatic conflagration. The incident was widely covered in the national and international press. The U.S. ambassador wanted to have the damaged cars removed from sight. "The Boss," as Hughes and other staff affectionately called Richard Nixon, was adamant that the cars be left in front of the residence so everyone could see what had happened to them; he felt that reporters and Venezuelans alike needed to appreciate the magnitude of the affront to America's goodwill ambassadors. The next day, as Hughes left with the Nixons for a luncheon that the members of the Venezuelan governing junta had begged them to attend, the press studied the damaged cars and began clapping for the Nixons. Pat welled up with tears. The junta had given Hughes grenades and handguns for protection. When Pat stepped into the car, she had to step over a hand grenade that Hughes had left in the car. She gingerly picked it up with her thumb and forefinger, saying, "I believe this belongs to you," and handed it to him.

Pat and Dick returned to Washington, D.C., as national heroes who had stoically endured a violent insult on behalf of America. The Eisenhowers met them at the airport, bringing Julie and Tricia with them. Half the members of Congress, the full cabinet, and a crowd of fifteen thousand also were present. Eisenhower gave the civil service half a day off, and many of them were among the hundred thousand cheering as Pat and Dick drove to the White House with Ike and Mamie in an open-topped car. Echoing the sentiments of many Americans, Helene Drown wrote Pat: "You should get purple hearts and a citation from the armed forces. It was a great victory for our way of life . . . when they [the communists] acted like savages it turned the tables upside down on them." J. Edgar Hoover sent Pat a transcript of radio commentator Paul Harvey's comments saluting her poise and courage and told her she had "stayed in the front lines of the political wars without respite"; she had shared her husband "with the ungrateful and the avaricious" while keeping "so little for herself." The *Los Angeles Times*' Washington bureau chief, Robert Hartmann, opined that the riots had increased Nixon's stature. By demonstrating physical courage, readiness to take decisive action, and remarkable self-control and judgment under "supercharged circumstances," he showed the qualities of a true American.

*　　　*　　　*

Dick spared Pat the dreary task of accompanying him for most of his fall campaigning as he sought to build chits with party regulars and stave off Democratic gains that November. But she joined him on a brief stopover in Indianapolis and on an intense three-day visit to California at the beginning of October. The American public had begun to perceive the Eisenhower administration as tired and old; they blamed it for that year's severe recession. Gearing up for a presidential run, the man the press had dubbed the "new Nixon" sought to project a temperate presence, but his efforts to motivate flagging Republicans floundered without the partisan attacks he was known for. Frustrated, Nixon once again resorted to slashing rhetoric. The election results were more devastating for the Republicans than many had expected. The Democrats picked up forty-seven seats in the House and seven in the Senate. Although he received many appreciative letters from Republican partisans, some members of the media blamed Nixon. Already the national goodwill that Pat and Dick had engendered in South America was being put in question.

Continuing a pattern of polishing Dick's tarnished image through foreign travel, the Nixons went abroad once more. This time Eisenhower sent them to London to honor the American servicemen who died while serving in England during World War II. Pat and Dick accompanied the queen at a ceremony for the dedication of the American Chapel in St. Paul's Cathedral. Ruth Buchanan, a friend whose husband, Wiley, was Eisenhower's chief of protocol, accompanied Pat and Dick to the Guildhall, where Nixon talked to the English Speaking Union in front of the queen's cousin Lord Mountbatten, the last viceroy of India, and other British notables. Ruth Buchanan's dinner partner turned to her and said, "I feel sorry for your vice president. Everyone here is a fabulous orator. It must be frightening." Ruth told him she was not worried. When Dick spoke, "He was sensational," Ruth remembered. "You could have heard a pin drop. He mesmerized them for a moment."

His British hosts, who had known of him mainly as an anticommunist crusader, were surprised that he spoke passionately about the need for increasing aid to the developing nations of Africa and Asia:

"We should adopt as our primary objective not the defeat of Communism, but the victory of plenty over want; of health over disease; and of freedom over tyranny." After an appearance at the Oxford Student Union in which Nixon vigorously responded to confrontational questions about his political style and his anticommunist stance, and a final press conference, his reputation in the British press shifted from that of an "uncouth adventurer" to a man whose visit left him "trailing clouds of statesmanship and esteem."

Pat met the women of the Fleet Street press in U.S. Ambassador John Hay Whitney's London mansion. The reporters opened the interview by querying Mrs. Nixon about her marriage. "This might sound exaggerated," Pat said, "but I am just as much in love with my husband as I was on the first day." The ladies of the British press did not know enough about her life story to catch the unintended irony—she had not fallen in love right away—in her statement. Her comments were sincere and served their purpose. Pat won affirmative reviews from the British press for her gracious manner and her attractive wardrobe. The left-leaning *Spectator*, however, carped that she was a "doll that would be smiling when the world broke." Nixon had reestablished that he was a politician of presidential timber and Pat had demonstrated that they were a formidable couple.

During their first six years in the White House, Ike and Mamie had dined out in private homes on only four occasions, but on December 19, 1958, they brought their son Major John Eisenhower, his wife, Barbara, and their bridge-playing friends George Allen and his wife to an informal roast beef dinner at Pat and Dick's Tudor home. The Eisenhowers were grateful to the Nixons for pinch-hitting for them so often and now, with the contest for the 1960 Republican nomination looming, the president and his wife knew it would help Dick's chances to highlight the bond between the two couples. Ike and Mamie stood with Pat and Dick on the Nixons' steps, in front of a door decorated with a big spruce wreath and a red bow and rimmed with lights. Photographers snapped away.

Over the next three days the future presidential candidate and his wife held a series of Christmas parties, as they also would in 1959, for important members of the congressional, diplomatic, and journalistic communities "with over a hundred at each," as Pat told Helene. "So the days are humming here, but it is exciting too." Pat, as always, carried most of the burden: "Dick always amuses me when he thinks all there is to a party is to announce the day." Their daughters also kept them busy. Twelve-year-old "Tricia had a gala New Years party and dance for a mixed group," Pat told Helene in 1958. "Seems a little early to start but 'it is being done down here.' Julie [age eleven] had a Christmas party for sixteen."

Pat and Dick functioned most effectively as a political team during their foreign missions, advocating for the United States and its democracy among peoples whose political systems were still being established and could become hostile to American interests. The Nixons' performance in the Soviet Union in the spring of 1959 further enhanced their credibility as a pair worthy of the White House. It was an uneasy visit and Pat would play a key role in relaxing the tensions between hosts and guests. The vice president and his wife were officially representing the United States at the first American trade exhibition in Moscow just as the forty-year freeze in cultural relations was beginning to thaw between the two superpowers. Still, Cold War attitudes meant they were met with coolness from the Soviets. Arriving at Moscow's airport, they received only "correct treatment." There was no honor guard, no national anthem, and no crowds.

The Soviets were unhappy about the recent Captive Nations resolution in Congress attacking Soviet suppression of the subjugated countries of Europe. The Nixons took a brief stroll along one of Moscow's main shopping avenues and startled bystanders on Tchaikovsky Street by shaking everyone's hand and by practicing simple Russian phrases. Traffic grew snarled as women "gathered to stare at Mrs. Nixon's fashionable pointed shoes," her attractive, brightly patterned attire, and her bouffant hairdo.

Nixon burnished his reputation as a savvy and tough international politician while he toured the American National Exhibition in Moscow with Soviet leader Nikita Khrushchev. Photographs of Nixon shoving his finger into Khrushchev's chest during an impassioned argument played well at home, as did televised versions of their "kitchen debate" over the merits of the communist and capitalist ways of life. A bold *New York Times* headline read NIXON AND KHRUSHCHEV ARGUE IN PUBLIC . . . ACCUSE EACH OTHER OF THREATS.

While the two leaders stood in front of an American model home exhibit, Nixon kept his cool in a blustery debate, but he was not sure he had prevailed over the premier. Nixon focused on the value of a free exchange of ideas and information, and he challenged Khrushchev for never conceding a point or even pausing long enough to allow a sustained rejoinder. "I felt like a fighter wearing sixteen ounce gloves and bound by Marquis of Queensberry rules," he wrote in his memoir *Six Crises,* "up against a bare-knuckle slugger who had gouged, kneed, and kicked." For Don Hughes, the skirmish was "like a fight between a man with a meat cleaver and one with a fencing foil." Most reporters, however, thought that Nixon had won the confrontation by keeping his temper in check and by making cogent arguments while Khrushchev attempted to dominate him. Some observers cringed at the undiplomatic tenor of their arguments, but Nixon felt the Soviet leader would have had contempt for any sign of weakness.

Pat would make a case for America not by argument but by action. She believed her job was "to carry good will into channels which the vice president may be unable to reach." Accordingly, she handed out dozens of lollipops and a whole box of chewing gum at a Moscow kindergarten, presented two dogwood trees for the botanical gardens, and visited hospitals, pioneer camps, and the large department store GUM. At the farmers' free market, one old shawl-covered lady bought her roses and said, "We must be friends so we can have peace for everyone." Pat was surprised that neither Mrs. Khrushchev nor any of the wives of Russian officials were included in the banquet welcoming the Americans. She prodded Khrushchev until he relented and invited Nina Khrushchev and other leaders' wives to official events. During meetings with these women, Pat encouraged them and their fellow Soviet women to assert themselves and to understand that women can have an ameliorating effect on diplomatic exchanges.

On the fourth day of the visit, Khrushchev insisted that the Nixons join him twenty minutes outside the city at his lavish stone dacha overlooking the Moscow River. Beneath lofty birches and pine trees, Khrushchev presided over a five-hour lunch at a table set up on the lawn, haranguing the Nixons about a Berlin divided between east and west, the nuclear weapons test ban, and disarmament. "On matters of substance he conceded nothing and demanded everything," Nixon wrote later. "He could not have been more unreasonable." Khrushchev was also noticeably agitated, and at several points his wife had to calm him.

At the luncheon the Soviet leaders encountered an outspoken Pat Nixon. When First Deputy Premier Anastas Mikoyan, seated across from Mrs. Nixon, initiated a conversation with her, Khrushchev became possessive of her and intervened, saying, "Now look here, you crafty Armenian, Mrs. Nixon belongs to me. You stay on your side of the table." He drew an imaginary line down the middle of the table. "This is an iron curtain," he said, "and you don't step over it." When the tension peaked between the Soviets and the Americans, Pat pressed her advantage. When her husband stated that the United States was ahead in the development of fuels that facilitated missile mobility, Khrushchev atypically declined to discuss the subject, to Pat's good-natured amazement. "I'm surprised that there is a subject you're not prepared to discuss, Mr. Chairman," she told him. "I thought that with your one-man government you had to have everything firmly in your own hands." Mikoyan rescued Khrushchev, saying that the Soviet leader could not be informed about everything.

The Soviet leaders granted Nixon a historic opportunity to make a radio and television address from Moscow to the Russian people, a speech that *Life* magazine called a "masterpiece—a tough, but sympathetic statement" in which he debunked Soviet propaganda without appearing hostile. Afterward, Pat and Dick traveled for five additional days outside Moscow, visiting Leningrad, where Russians stood and applauded them at the Kirov Opera House, and Siberia, where Dick was heckled by Soviet workers and Pat danced the polka with a small Russian girl at a camp for young pioneers. Russian children in the Urals threw flowers into the Nixons' car and cried out, "friendship, friendship." Nixon underscored Eisenhower's invitation for Khrushchev to visit the United States. That fall, the Soviet leader undertook a grand American tour, a thirteen-day visit during which he shed none of his belligerent pride in his nation's system. Riding in a car with Ruth Buchanan, the wife of Eisenhower's chief of protocol, Khrushchev told her, "Your grandchildren will be raised by communists."

After departing the Soviet Union, the Nixons made a four-day visit to Poland. The Polish government, worried about offending the Kremlin, did not announce the visit beforehand, but Radio Free Europe, the Voice of America, and the Roman Catholic Church did. Hundreds of thousands of Poles gathered in the streets to blow kisses, shout pro-Nixon and pro-American slogans, and throw innumerable bouquets of flowers into the Nixons' car. Pat's face was scratched by roses. Dick stood in the car "catching them like a baseball player." The motorcade stopped eight times "to clear out the piles of flowers." Nixon cabled Eisenhower that it was "one of the most moving experiences I have ever had." Outside Warsaw, Pat stepped carefully through a damp forest in her spike heels and went on a "hugging and kissing spree" at a steel mill.

Dick performed at his best when he had to recover from a professional failure or from criticism about his overzealous partisanship. Pat and Dick arrived home to generally ecstatic reviews. In a cover story, *Life* called the Russia trip "A Barnstorming Masterpiece." The often caustic *New York Times* reporter James Reston thought Nixon had picked the "perfect way to launch a campaign for the U.S. presidency." Reston credited the vice president for "keeping the spirit jovial and generally improving the ambience." Ronald Reagan, the president of the Screen Actors Guild, sent congratulations. Journalist Ralph de Toledano, a Nixon enthusiast, went overboard in *Newsweek*, saying that the vice president "might have changed the course of history" in Moscow.

Pat received praise as well. Calling Mrs. Nixon a "Diplomat in High Heels," the *New York Times* declared that her shoes might be her "trademark around the world": Her "pencil slim heels have clicked across the pavements of America, plodded through mud puddles in Vietnam, sunk in the snow in Alaska, and now they are in the Soviet Union." Dorothy Roe of the Associated Press opined that Pat "probably did more to convince the Russians that Americans are a nice people than could years of diplomatic exchanges."

But the Nixon daughters provided their parents with the best reception. Julie and Tricia made them a pink-frosted angel food cake with green letters proclaiming "Welcome home, mommy and daddy." The girls invited neighbors to the family's recreation room for a special homecoming premiere of their own version of *Cinderella* with handmade costumes and stage sets.

That December, as part of a continuing effort to promote their image as a likable Norman Rockwell family, the Nixons allowed the *Washington Post* to cover their Christmas Day celebrations. Julie and Tricia got up early to open their presents. Pat's Christmas morning tradition was to cook a late breakfast of waffles and country sausage "for leisurely eating after the excitement of opening gifts subsided." After a traditional turkey dinner with all the trimmings, the family gathered around the piano to sing while Nixon played. Wouldn't the American people want to see more of this happy family in the White House?

11

Enduring Defeat

*A*successful long-term marriage can surmount the many small and large defeats that inevitably scar a union. Couples who remain contentedly married handle their disappointments without becoming so distant from each other that their partnership becomes a cold and permanent standoff. If nothing else, the Nixons are exemplars of such perseverance. In the early 1960s they lived through two enormously painful electoral defeats, both of them rife with bad luck, poor judgment, and self-doubt. Pat bore the hardship of two political campaigns she did not relish, and Dick submitted to a restless interim year out of the political arena. Confronted with irresolvable problems, a couple must find a way to negotiate around difficult issues without creating rancor that undermines the relationship. The Nixons struggled—sometimes in anger, sometimes through compromise—to balance their radically different attitudes toward public life. By 1958, Dick and Pat had still not openly discussed the conflict between Dick's impending presidential campaign and Pat's hopes for a more peaceful life beyond whistle-stops, public smiles, and innumerable hands to shake. She wanted a life without endless contention. Dick was aware that whenever he articulated his desire for the White House, he risked inciting Pat's anger. In 1956 she had almost thwarted his run for a second vice-presidential term by her strenuous objection to it. Her acute ambivalence about politics, fine-tuned over more than a decade of public insults and injuries as well as inequities in their relationship, threatened his ambitions. She wanted privacy and he needed politics. Perhaps he hoped that as he positioned himself as an inevitable presidential candidate, she would acquiesce to his decision. She usually did, and perhaps that is what happened this time. By 1959, she appeared as committed to a Nixon presidential campaign as her husband was. She would do all that was asked of her, summoning a smile and extending her hand to all who would grasp it.

Dick would need all the help she could offer. In 1960 Dick won the Republican nomination easily. Although both he and the Democratic nominee, John F. Kennedy, had maintained cordial relations since they entered Congress in 1946, Dick had an admiration for Kennedy's persona that his opponent did not share. Kennedy respected Nixon as a political strategist, but after he decided privately to run for the presidency in 1956, JFK made derisive statements about Nixon's sentimental and divisive style. Dick believed that his opponent had been a lazy and lightweight senator, but he developed a compassion for Jack Kennedy in 1954 when Kennedy was hospitalized for severe back pain that required a potentially fatal spinal-fusion operation.

The year 1960 marked the first American election in which the "candidates" for First Lady played a prominent and possibly decisive role in the choice of president. Although Pat Nixon, forty-eight, and Jacqueline Kennedy, thirty-one, were almost a generation apart in age and could hardly have been more different in background and upbringing, they shared striking physical and psychological similarities that are often minimized, but that are key to understanding both their competitiveness and the subtle connection between them. They were alluring counterparts. With her high cheekbones, auburn hair, and slim silhouette, Pat looked like she was in her thirties; she was a woman of austere, regal, yet maternal beauty. Broad-shouldered Jackie had a boyish beauty, a soft, sexy voice, and a precocious fashion sensibility. Pat and Jackie, both reserved women wounded by politics and bruised by their husbands' ambitions, were wary of statecraft, partly because they had a fierce desire to protect their children, and partly because they valued privacy. In truth, Pat, fully seasoned, had far more interest in political issues than Jackie did, but neither one wanted to give speeches. Both were perfectionists who deeply valued beautiful objects, antiques, and interior design. Pat was far more of a home-maker than Jackie, who had been born with servants and still relied on them to manage her household.

Pat Nixon and Mrs. Kennedy perceived their husbands as uniquely gifted men who deserved their loyalty, but they could despair about the single-minded commitment to political ambition of their men, and their adherence to the hard-nosed cadre of aides who surrounded them. Both wives would ultimately prove themselves to be exemplars of what Kennedy called grace under pressure, but Pat was ultimately the warmer of the two women, and the one who resonated more deeply to the call of duty.

Reporters tried during the campaign to stir up a fashion competition between Pat and Jackie, but both spouses resisted. When Pat was asked whether she would consider debating Jackie on television about clothes, Mrs. Nixon firmly replied, "I would be willing to debate on something of value, not clothes." Pat was not about to advertise her small collection of ready-to-wear, conservative, American-made dresses; Jackie, who wore designer fashions, was focused on her pregnancy. When asked about rumors that she spent thirty thousand dollars a year on clothes, Jackie winningly reported she could not do that "unless I wore sable underwear." Having already suffered one miscarriage and one stillborn child, Mrs. Kennedy had a good excuse not to accompany her husband on his campaign tours. With the exception of a few carefully selected appearances, she campaigned by holding press teas in their Georgetown home, giving brief talks at neighborhood political rallies, and conducting a charm crusade from the pages of newspapers and women's magazines.

Pat waged her own battle in the glossies, but she accepted the necessity of campaigning in person, alongside her husband, all around the country. In terms of electoral effectiveness, Pat's grit outpaced Jackie's wit. The American public had not yet fallen in love with Jacqueline Kennedy, as they would once she entered the White House. But Pat Nixon was as familiar to them as television actress Donna Reed, and as much admired. Women would vote in greater numbers for Richard Nixon than they would for John F. Kennedy.

Yet Pat Nixon was well aware that she had her detractors. A February 1960 *Time* magazine cover story captured the views of critics, that she was "too serene, too tightly controlled; that she smothers her personality with a fixed smile and a mask of dignity." Making light of such coverage, she told the reporter Christine Hotchkiss of the *Los Angeles Times,* "I've . . . been called the super-efficient wife and mother—a machine that walks like a woman—almost!" Pat readily acknowledged her stoicism ("I may be dying, but I certainly wouldn't say anything about it"), but she spoke only occasionally about her fear of making a mistake that would hurt her husband—a fear that left her tense, curtailed her spontaneity in public, and allowed her detractors to caricature her.

The campaign was fierce and frustrating. On Friday, July 15, at the Los Angeles Coliseum, as John F. Kennedy accepted the Democratic Party nomination for president, he signaled Nixon and his wife that the cordiality of their Senate days had ended, attacking his opponent as a candidate who would "invoke the name of Abraham Lincoln . . . despite the fact that his political career has often seemed to show charity towards none and malice for all." This kind of attack enraged Pat, who already did not respect Kennedy for his womanizing. The Democratic nominee, calling on Americans to be "pioneers on the New Frontier," set up a dichotomy between "national greatness and national decline, between the fresh air of progress and the stale, dank atmosphere of 'normalcy.'" The Nixons were accustomed to being the fresh young faces of the Eisenhower administration. By marketing his youth, Kennedy suddenly boxed them in as representatives of a tired era. By the time of the Republican Convention in Chicago in late July, Kennedy was enjoying a ten-point lead in the polls and the Nixons were in a familiar one-down position.

On July 28, Nixon gave what Kennedy speechwriter Ted Sorensen termed a "brilliant" acceptance address matching his opponent's feisty, even bellicose rhetoric. "America will not be pushed around by anybody, anyplace," Nixon declared. "When Mr. Khrushchev says our grandchildren will live under Communism, let us say his grandchildren will live in freedom." Challenging Kennedy's "New Frontier" theme, Dick claimed the Democrats "promised everything to everybody with one exception: they didn't promise to pay the bill." He did not, however, attack Kennedy personally. In their convention speeches the two candidates presented their new 1960 personas to the nation: a tougher Kennedy and a more gentlemanly Nixon. As his running mate, Dick chose United Nations ambassador Henry Cabot Lodge, Jr., a Massachusetts Brahmin and indifferent campaigner. Kennedy's choice, Senator Lyndon B. Johnson, was a dynamic and effective vice-presidential candidate.

On the strength of Nixon's powerful acceptance speech, polls showed that Nixon had regained the lead by six points. Yet in a nation where Democrats outnumbered Republicans fifty million to thirty-three million (with seventeen million independents), the Nixons would have to find a way to appeal beyond party identity to a nation that felt the start of a fresh new decade required an exciting, risk-taking leader. Pat and Dick began on the defensive, associated as they were with the status quo, and privately agreeing with Kennedy that it was "time America started moving again."

President Eisenhower, who could have boosted Nixon as a dynamic successor, did the opposite. Ike made a slip that gave the Democrats leverage on their weakest issue—Kennedy's relative lack of experience. Dick emphasized the fact that he had chaired twenty-six National Security Council meetings, presided over nineteen cabinet meetings, and had 173 meetings with President Eisenhower during the past eight years. "I have sat with the president when he made those lonely decisions," Nixon said. Eisenhower did avow that his vice president had indeed been a full participant in every major administration decision, but then, baited by the press and sensitive to criticism that he was not fully in charge of his own administration, when asked for an example of a major idea that had originated with Nixon, the president replied in an offhand way as he was leaving the podium, "If you give me a week, I might think of one." Nixon never revealed his feelings about Eisenhower's mistake. Ike, who rarely apologized, quickly called Nixon to do so. But reporters and political adversaries pounced on the president's comment as proof of Eisenhower's disdain for Nixon and Nixon's tendency to overinflate his role.

Dick pledged he would campaign in all fifty states—a promise he would regret. As he and Pat made a mid-August trip through North Carolina, Dick bumped his kneecap while getting into a car. Within twelve days he was hospitalized for a serious staphylococcal infection. For two weeks, when he should have been checking off seven states, Nixon lay in a hospital waiting for antibiotics to take effect. Pat and the girls visited him every night. Using the rare opportunity to spend extended time with their father, Tricia and Julie introduced him to their favorite television programs. Mrs. Nixon, feeling the pressure of the campaign calendar, hated seeing her husband sidelined. "Pat, who seems to feel that Dick is having a wonderful, jolly time in the hospital," Jim Bassett, the planning director for the 1960 campaign, wrote his wife, Wilma, "is in one of her 'moods,' . . . nobody else in the U.S. would believe it, would they?" Pat could be ill-humored under intense pressure. Already anticipating two months of separation from her children during a punishing, uphill campaign marathon, Pat seemed to suffer more than her husband. The Nixons watched helplessly as Dick's postconvention poll advantage disappeared in the first weeks of September. Kennedy moved into a two-point lead. It was maddening. Dick left the hospital early, determined to work doubly hard to neutralize Kennedy's ability to inspire enthusiasm among voters.

Pat, every bit as stubborn as her husband, mistakenly sided with

Dick against advisors who recommended he set aside his fifty-state pledge. The Nixons had powered through exhaustion on many previous campaigns and foreign trips, but now they were approaching their fiftieth birthdays, and they erred in believing their willpower could trump their physical limitations. One of the greatest ironies of the 1960 election is that Richard Nixon, a healthy man with great stamina, appeared less physically robust than Kennedy, who suffered from a painful chronic back condition and Addison's disease—a weakness of the adrenals that could have killed him. Kennedy, thanks to massive doses of pharmaceuticals and the cover of physical grace, appeared to outstrip Nixon in vigor. Kennedy also exhausted himself in the campaign, traveling to forty-five states.

With the goal of garnering as much local television news coverage as possible, Dick and Pat covered twenty-five states in the two weeks leading up to the historic first televised presidential debate. On September 12, they started a five-day, fourteen-state sprint, flying nine thousand miles from Baltimore through the Midwest to the West Coast. During the day they drove from one campaign stop to another; at night they flew to the next city. As 1960 campaign chronicler Theodore H. White pointed out, the battle "flung them . . . into such physical exertion day after day, night after night as would sap the energies of a trained athlete."

After three days on the road, Dick developed a 103-degree temperature and chills. Goaded by the prospect of defeat, the Nixons soldiered on. John Lungren, Dick's personal physician, worked furiously to bring down his fever. Pat, who kept to her schedule whether or not she was ill, might not have encouraged him to slow down until he was healthy. Yet if he rested, he would probably fall further behind; if he pushed himself, he risked making deadly mistakes. Suffering from night sweats, Nixon slept poorly. Partly as a result, he was prone to rages. Nixon's friend and appointments secretary Don Hughes had served in three wars, but for him "nothing was as draining" as accompanying Nixon during the entire 1960 campaign. "You get short-tempered." In a famous incident that occurred while driving through Iowa, Dick, "in a blaze of fury," kicked the seat in front of him so hard that Hughes smacked his head against the dashboard. Hughes fled the car. One of Nixon's advance men, H. R. "Bob" Haldeman, had to run after Hughes, calm him down, and convince him to return to the vehicle.

Pat responded to the brutal pace and the unraveling tempers by summoning her stoicism. She became calmer as Nixon and his men grew more frenetic. Hughes did not ever recall seeing her in a mood "where she took an aggressive approach on an issue. She was a quiet and reserved person. She was her own boss and did her own thinking." However, Dick used aide Dwight Chapin as a go-between with Pat when he wanted to cancel dinners with her in order to attend an additional political event or write a speech. Dwight recalled that she was often furious with her husband and asked Dwight to convey her feelings to him. Pat drew support from her bond with Dick's secretary and her frequent companion Rose Mary Woods.

Richard Nixon made numerous mistakes in his first presidential campaign—not the least of which was his decision to debate his less-well-known challenger. Eisenhower had advised against it, but Nixon had great confidence in his ability to win such a contest—particularly since he thought he had bested Kennedy in a Pennsylvania debate in 1947. Nixon, however, did not underestimate Kennedy's campaigning skills. The first televised presidential debate was an enormous cultural event: Pat was one of approximately seventy million viewers who watched it on what author David Pietrusa described as the era's "flickering, often snow-speckled, cathode-ray screens." Kennedy prepared carefully for this crucial appearance: He got a tan, practiced assiduously with aides, and rested. The Nixons stayed out late touring street rallies the night before the debate. Dick further depleted himself by giving a speech to a hostile union audience the following morning. It is difficult to know whether his judgment was altered by illness, overconfidence, or both. Dick spent little time preparing. A few minutes before airtime, he rode to the studio of the WBBM-TV station in Chicago, where Henry Cabot Lodge called him and encouraged him to "erase the assassin image." Nixon followed that advice to a fault—Dick had already told Ike that he was going to be less confrontational in this campaign.

Stressed, gaunt, with a one-hundred-degree temperature, Dick had the bad luck that follows a man who is pressing too hard. He banged his knee once again—on the door of the car that brought him to the studio. His face turned "white and pasty." Instead of choosing to use makeup, Dick, who thought makeup was for sissies, covered his often-shadowed jaw with a faint powder "beard stick." On television Nixon looked tense, pallid, and sweaty. In Theodore H. White's famous description, Nixon appeared "almost frightened, at turns glowering and, occasionally haggard-looking to the point of sickness." He had lost ten pounds from his illness; his shirt fit too loosely around his neck. In the glare of the studio lights, Dick looked less a president than a shady character. "As he half-slouched," his eyes were "exaggerated hollows of blackness, his jaw, jowls, and face drooping with the strain," White wrote.

Pat had helped her husband prepare for many debates in California during their years in the House and Senate; she knew that he was a shrewd and tough debater. But instead of remaining in Chicago to support her husband and offer last-minute guidance, she returned to Washington to watch the contest with Julie and Tricia. This suggests that either the Nixons were too sanguine about Dick's debate prospects or Dick was not relying heavily on Pat for feedback. Pat noticed that her husband looked worn out, but she atypically underestimated the importance of appearances.

John Kennedy opened the debate with a statement that even author Rick Perlstein, who faulted Nixon for dividing America, called a "sucker punch." Violating the candidates' agreement to focus solely on domestic affairs, John Kennedy showed off his foreign policy credentials before promising to "get the country moving again." ("And they called Dick Nixon the dirty one," Perlstein wrote.) Nixon's response was surprisingly reactive and defensive, but what bothered Pat most, according to Julie, was a question from NBC news correspondent Sander Vanocur. The correspondent, who had a cordial relationship with Kennedy, asked a fair question about Eisenhower's press conference gaffe, which undermined voters' confidence that Nixon surpassed Kennedy in experience. There is no evidence to back up the myth that radio listeners thought Nixon had won while television viewers gave the edge to Kennedy. However, that night, columnist Russell Baker wrote, "Image had replaced the printed word as the natural language of politics."

At first, Dick thought he had performed well. Although his press director Herb Klein said, "None of us disillusioned him that evening," Dick claims in his memoir *Six Crises* that Rose Mary Woods and other advisors told him that he looked pale and tired. Pat said that she "couldn't imagine why he looked that way." Telling reporters that she "had no comment" on the debate, Pat flew immediately to Chicago to debrief him. A perfectionist, she could be very critical of his performances, but now she had to be careful not to alienate him at a time when he needed her. Fortunately for him, she thought he had won on substance—or at least that is what she told him. She could focus on this success while helping him realize that he needed to build his strength and gain weight.

If Nixon brought more gravitas and experience to the 1960 contest than did JFK, the latter's emotionally intelligent and seductive manner with the press helped neutralize his disadvantage. Over the course of the next three debates, Nixon bested or held his own with Kennedy. The polls were essentially deadlocked as the candidates and their wives headed into the last weeks of the campaign.

In 1960, women outvoted men for the first time. Recognizing how popular Pat Nixon was with women, the Nixon campaign declared the week of October 3 "Pat Week." Pat was uncomfortable being in the spotlight, but she recognized her starring role would boost the election effort. The campaign sent out flyers listing "Eleven Reasons Why We Should Elect Nixon President," the final one being "Because we want Pat for First Lady!" Every day that week a "Pat-mobile" led a caravan of attractively decorated cars into high-visibility precincts. The Republican National Committee Women's Division issued a news release highlighting Pat's experience in order to rally women behind her. The First Lady's "job is more than glamour," they reminded voters. "She represents America to all the world." Teams of precinct workers sporting "Pat for First Lady" buttons rang doorbells in all fifty states. Pat attended some of the many neighborhood coffee klatches, events in supermarkets, and women's club appearances. At rallies all across the country Nixon touted his wife as "the stronger one" in the marriage who "should be the one running rather than me." He wouldn't say "who ought to be president," he told the crowds, "but I'm for Pat as First Lady."

Now in full campaign mode, Dick moved past a recent and embarrassing marital mistake—one that Pat had uncharacteristically spoken up about: He forgot their twentieth wedding anniversary, on June 21, 1960. "Dick didn't give me a thing," Pat told a reporter, "but the Jaycees gave me a spray of red roses, so I guess my flowers will have to do." Atypically, Dick apologized to her in public.

Entering the final week of the campaign, Nixon had been hurt by the nation's recession, which deepened in October—330,000 Americans had lost their jobs. By the following May, the unemployment rate peaked at 7.1 percent. Kennedy may have won support among black Americans when he called the wife of Martin Luther King, Jr., to express his support when the civil rights leader was jailed after an Atlanta sit-in. Then Pat and Dick were stung and their campaign damaged when columnist Drew Pearson asserted that Richard Nixon had helped his brother Don obtain a $205,000 loan from business tycoon Howard Hughes, whose companies won government favors in return. Stories about Dick's alleged untoward assistance to his brother would gain traction over the years.

Nixon had plotted a major television blitz in the last week of the contest while he and Pat engaged in nonstop campaigning in a final effort at victory. On November 2 the Nixons campaigned in New York City with Eisenhower, Lodge, and New York governor Nelson A. Rockefeller. Five hundred thousand people watched their parade proceed through a snowstorm of confetti and ticker tape from Wall Street to Herald Square, where Dick spoke in front of Macy's. The *New York Times* reported that there was "little of the near-hysteria" and fewer of the teenagers who had greeted Kennedy in the city a week before. In this Democratic stronghold, the Nixons faced signs saying "We Like

Ike, but get no kick out of Dick," and "Ike's O.K., but it is Kennedy all the way."

Theodore H. White revealed in his memoir that he portrayed Nixon as a devil and Kennedy as a heroic character to enhance the drama of his book about the election. White, who rarely mustered more than pity for the Nixons, wrote about their fatigue. He noted Dick's unusually rapid pattern of speech, his "fluffing of a phrase" and "the drawn, almost wasted face of Mrs. Nixon, who followed her husband everywhere and whose quiet charm, never ruffled, bears its exertions with a stoic weariness and tired sweetness that, to some who followed her, was close to tear-provoking." Even when covered with rotten eggs, as she was in Muskegon, Michigan, Pat remained calm. Dick claimed in *Six Crises* that Pat never "lost her dignity or her poise in the face of even the greatest provocation." Her physical stamina, coupled with her ability to detach herself from pain, he recognized, was greater than his own—she could shake hands long after he had faded. During the campaign Pat's weight dropped from 115 to 103 pounds, making her five-foot-five-inch frame look wraithlike.

Pat and Dick brought Julie and Tricia along with them for the last week of their marathon. While Kennedy focused on the big northeastern and midwestern states with large electoral counts, the Nixons and their daughters made a long detour to fulfill their fifty-state pledge. A woman whose life was defined by the obligation she felt toward service, Pat thought of herself as a political volunteer. Pat had long valued direct and authentic connections with her fellow citizens, in a way that pushed past the mercenary conventions of campaigning. In a June interview with Christine Hotchkiss of the *Los Angeles Times,* Pat told her that "I value the sense of connection that comes from even the fleeting glimpse into the personality of another human. It is exciting to me and I like to be there, completely present, so as to give my entire attention to the person momentarily before me." The force of her comments transcends political bromides. Pat believed that "It's very important to be a team and to meet the voters, because . . . you can only truly represent them by knowing them."

After three days of barnstorming across the country, sleeping just a couple of hours a night, Pat and Dick flew with their daughters back to California for a final campaign rally at 2:00 a.m. on Election Day in the Ontario-Riverside area, in front of fifteen thousand supporters. Dick had traveled sixty-five thousand miles and given 180 scheduled speeches; Pat accompanied him much of the time, but also made separate trips to broaden their reach. It is difficult to imagine how utterly depleted Pat and Dick were at the end of their final sprint—they were beyond numb. At almost 4:00 a.m. Pat and Dick arrived at the Ambassador Hotel in Los Angeles. They slept for two hours before driving to vote in Whittier, the site where their courtship had begun just twenty-two years earlier, and where Dick had sprung to national office just fourteen years before.

As the nation voted and the candidates and their families waited in exhausted suspense, Pat distracted herself by taking her daughters to a Beverly Hills hairdresser. Pat expected victory that evening. As she told Julie, "I knew Kennedy too well to think that the country would elect him." Pat had listened to Washington rumors about Kennedy for twelve years. Dick, Don Hughes, and his Secret Service agent Jack Sherwood eluded reporters and drove to Tijuana, Mexico, a world far from American politics. Prone to pessimistic thoughts and self-doubt on an Election Day, Dick told Don Hughes that there would be "no talk of elections or politics" on their trip to Mexico. After consuming margaritas and enchiladas at the Old Heidelberg restaurant, they headed back to Los Angeles while Dick napped in the car.

Nixon headquarters was situated in the Oriental-themed, purple, blue, red, pink, and violet Royal Suite in the Ambassador Hotel. Pat, Dick, and their daughters gathered with Bebe Rebozo, Murray Chotiner, Hannah Nixon, and Don and Ed Nixon and their wives. They agreed not to turn on the television until 6:00 p.m. California time, when significant voting patterns would start to emerge from the East Coast precincts. Over the next five hours, the Nixons and their team experienced excitement, uncertainty, and near despair. Kennedy took an early lead of 1.7 million votes, based heavily on the initial returns from the East Coast. Between six and seven West Coast time, Eric Sevareid of CBS and John Chancellor of NBC had begun to talk about a Kennedy victory, but the Democrat's lead narrowed as the western and midwestern states reported. The advantage shifted perilously back and forth in key battleground states like Texas. To add to the drama, reports filtered in suggesting that there were voting irregularities in both Illinois and Texas, where Kennedy had begun to maintain narrow leads.

The Nixons had agreed that it would make more sense for Pat to watch the early returns with Julie and Tricia in a separate hotel suite, while Dick kept abreast of the incoming results in the Nixon headquarters, riotous with constantly ringing telephones and aides rushing in with fresh dispatches. By 11:30 p.m., when Kennedy's lead began to look insurmountable, Pat joined Dick downstairs. When Dick told her that he would signal their supporters that Kennedy might be elected if the current trends continued, Pat said, "I simply cannot bring myself to stand there with you while you concede the election to Kennedy." Her reply was blunt, but it arose from her growing incredulity that the Massachusetts senator might win. Two weeks before the election, when polls showed Kennedy running even with Nixon, Pat had become visibly distraught. She asked speechwriter Bryce Harlow, "How can we let the American people know in time what kind of man Kennedy is?" It was the first time Harlow had seen Mrs. Nixon lose her composure. Pat was appalled by Kennedy's campaign shenanigans, which, she believed, based on the conviction of Republican operatives, included preparing to engage in voter fraud, and placing a story with columnist Drew Pearson about a large loan that millionaire Howard Hughes had purportedly made to the Nixon family. As Chris Matthews wrote in his book *Kennedy & Nixon,* Pat, well acquainted with Washington stories about Kennedy's womanizing, was "especially frustrated by what seemed a media conspiracy to package their opponent as a devoted husband."

On election night, faced with rumors that Kennedy was stealing the election, Pat was apoplectic. She charged back upstairs to her suite with Helene Drown, fiercely unwilling to lend her presence to a surrender to what she saw as election fraud. Helene convinced her that she had to make an appearance with Dick out of respect for their supporters.

Returning to Nixon headquarters, Pat told Dick, "I think we should go down together and tell them how much we appreciate what they have done." In his memoir *RN*, Dick said of her, "I do not know which quality I loved more—the fight or the warmth."

Pat and Dick entered the ballroom of the Ambassador Hotel to the prolonged cheers of their supporters. As Dick declared that Kennedy would win if the current trends held up, Pat began to cry. Dick put his arm around her. As they left the ballroom and walked back up to their suites, she sobbed. This Election Day, she later told Dick, was "the saddest day of my life."

Her anger and frustration also indicate how much she had come to invest herself in the prospect of being First Lady and to believe it was a role she had earned through hard work and considerable sacrifice. Late on election night, as Jim Bassett's wife, Wilma, walked past Mrs. Nixon's room in the Ambassador Hotel, Mrs. Bassett recalled "a long bony arm reaching out from an open door" and grabbing hers. It was Mrs. Nixon. Pat threw herself on her bed and cried. As Wilma rubbed her back in a vain attempt to comfort her, Pat told her, "Now I'll never get to be First Lady."

Kennedy won the election by a paltry total of about 40,000 votes— a winning margin that takes into account inaccurate accounts by UPI and AP about the confusing results in the state of Alabama, where voters chose electors. Eventually Kennedy won Texas by 46,257 votes and Illinois by only 8,858 votes (out of 4,757,404 votes cast). He would have a more significant majority in the Electoral College (301–219). Along with many Republican stalwarts, Dick and Pat became convinced that they had been cheated out of the presidency by voter fraud. "Kennedy's organization approached campaign dirty tricks with a roguish relish," Dick wrote in his memoir, "and carried them off with an insouciance that captivated many politicians and overcame the critical faculties of many reporters." Political historians would debate for decades the extent and significance of illegal behavior and voter fraud in the 1960 election.

In a decision that was both statesmanlike and self-serving, Nixon declined to demand a recount. Dick realized that even if he won "in the end, the cost in world opinions and the effects on democracy in the broadest sense would be detrimental" across the globe. Asking for the ballots to be recounted would make him look like a sore loser, and he did not want to hinder his future political aspirations.

Pat and Dick disagreed on what had happened. He believed he had lost "because I spent too much time . . . on substance and too little time on appearance," and because the media favored Kennedy. And she still thought it was a simple story of a stolen election. Pat was stunned that the vast majority of the American public and press blithely accepted what she saw as Kennedy's crimes against her husband. She never fully recovered from the trauma of the 1960 election. "Nineteen sixty disillusioned her beyond redemption," her daughter Julie wrote. Toward the end of his life, Nixon jokingly told his assistant—and now pundit—Monica Crowley that "Mrs. Nixon still says we should order a recount."

For an extended period of time after the election, Pat fell into a "state of numbness." She had no desire to think or talk about politics. She wrote to her friend Helene that her "faith in the right" had been "shaken to the point" that she could not discuss the situation anymore. Helene Drown shared Pat's feelings about the election. The Drowns were moping, she wrote Pat, because they were so bothered by "the fact that it was stolen. . . . And we are so helpless. . . . All we can do is stare at a lot of broken ideals and wonder if it is worth it to try to mend all the pieces. . . . If I sound downcast, believe me—I am!" Some reports suggest that Pat vented her rage at her husband, but there is no direct confirmation of that. More likely they pulled apart from each other, as they often did, to soothe their wounds in private.

Nixon sequestered himself in Key Biscayne for a few weeks. His press secretary Herbert Klein, who spent time with Nixon there, found him to be so "completely depressed" that he "found it difficult to speak." Pat and the girls joined Dick in Florida for a few days right after the election and then again for Thanksgiving. At Christmas the family sought out the distractions of New York City. Pat and Dick treated the girls to Broadway musicals; at the musical *Fiorello!* the audience gave them a standing ovation. But there would be no truly satisfying diversions for a couple who had fought so hard and come so close to victory. It would take time for them to mourn the demise of what had become their mutual dream. In some ways they could not help each other—except by avoiding aggravating each other's pain.

On January 20, 1961, John F. Kennedy was inaugurated as the thirty-fifth president of the United States on the steps of the Capitol. As the wife of the departing vice president, Pat Nixon stood less than five feet from Jacqueline Kennedy; *New York Times* reporter Joann Lynott noticed that Jackie smiled constantly and held her head high, while Pat appeared to be on the verge of tears as she watched Kennedy assume an office she believed he had stolen. Reporters did not emphasize the fact that Jack Kennedy did not kiss *his* wife after the ceremony. In a 1964 interview with Arthur Schlesinger, Jr., Jackie remarked that, like Dick Nixon, Jack "would never hold hands in public or put his arm around me . . . because that was naturally distasteful to him."

Pat's biographer Lester David claims that Pat had snubbed Jackie that day, when the Nixons and the Eisenhowers greeted the Kennedys at the traditional White House coffee before the swearing-in ceremony. Pat nodded a brief hello, but then turned away from Mrs. Kennedy, who was seated next to her on a couch. Pat talked to someone else. According to David, Pat got up and left Jackie by herself. While unconfirmed by other sources, the story is plausible; Pat had developed a visceral dislike for the entire Kennedy family. And in several of Pat's letters to Helene Drown, Pat shares her pleasure in snubbing enemies. Jackie snidely told Schlesinger, "You could see she [Pat] could really be rather New York chic when she wanted, in sort of a black Persian lamb coat and hat." Kennedy, Jackie thought, rarely focused on his image: Otherwise "he would have made me get a frizzy little permanent and be like Pat Nixon."

Dick told his wealthy friend Elmer Bobst, the chairman of the board of a pharmaceutical company, that the inauguration marked "one of the most trying days of my life." The Nixons had lost what would have been their best and brightest opportunity to inhabit the White House. It was their tragedy that they were denied that chance in 1960 and, instead, won the White House eight years later when they were more embittered and the country was embroiled in war at home and abroad—not the right conditions for a traumatized couple to lead with positivity, flexibility, and generosity.

If the bitterness that fueled Nixon during the Watergate crisis had been first sown during the Hiss case and stoked during the slush fund crisis, then it was inflamed beyond all measure by the loss of the presidency in 1960. He had made more of an effort to be a gentleman than in previous campaigns, but pulling his punches got him nowhere. "From this point on I had the wisdom and wariness of someone who had been burned by the power of the Kennedys and their money and by the license they were given by the media," Nixon wrote tellingly in his presidential memoir. "I vowed that I would never again enter an election at a disadvantage of being vulnerable to them—or anyone— on the level of tactics."

Immediately after the inauguration the Nixons and their friends Roger and Louise Johnson flew to Eleuthera in the Bahamas, where Bebe Rebozo awaited them. They planned to stay a month, but Dick could tolerate only two weeks of the languid pace. "As much as I enjoyed it at the outset," Dick wrote in *Six Crises*, "after a few days of shallow talk, the lack of interest in subjects of importance grew more and more boring." Dick was too exhausted to relax deeply; he needed to soothe his depression with work. They cut their vacation short.

Echoing Pat's need to retreat, Helene said, "I am not fit company for anyone." Pat turned down almost all social and political invitations for the final six months she remained in Washington. She had attended enough political dinners and events to last a lifetime, though she would soon discover she had another lifetime of politics ahead of her.

Darkness

*I*n a dark period in the Nixon marriage, Pat and Dick spent their longest interval apart since World War II. Dick moved to California to earn a living and to retreat from the Washington political scene, rented a small apartment on Wilshire Boulevard, and served himself TV dinners. Pat stayed in Washington so that Julie and Tricia could finish the school year there. She made several trips to Los Angeles to look for a new home with a husband who was lonely and depressed in his new bachelor life. He joined the law firm of Adams, Duque & Hazeltine as a partner doing individual and corporate civil cases for insurance and construction companies, but found it "difficult to concentrate" and "to work up enthusiasm" for his work. In his sixth month of mourning, he began to feel some relief when Pat and the girls joined him in early April for an Easter vacation in Santa Monica.

The girls loved the beach, and as he wrote in his memoir *RN*, "their enthusiasm about California began to rub off on me."

When the rest of the family joined Dick in California that June, they lived amid the movie stars they had once ogled at the Cocoanut Grove nightclub. Pat and Dick rented a movie producer's home in Brentwood near the residences of actors Fred MacMurray and Cesar Romero. Soon, unable to find a suitable house to buy, they built a four-bedroom, seven-bathroom ranch-style home, with a swimming pool, at 410 Martin Lane in Trousdale Estates, a new development in Beverly Hills. Harpo and Groucho Marx were their neighbors. After nearly fifteen years of the Washington suburbs, this new house offered Pat the respite she craved. She indulged her passion for gardening. Pat told the *Ladies' Home Journal* that she found in private life "a miracle of peace, friendliness, and good will," which contrasted sharply with the vitriol of political life. Indicating how wary and tense she had felt as part of a public couple, she said, "We were enjoying a breathing space, no longer leaders of a crusade for which we must be prepared to fight. An inadvertent word or misunderstood gesture or normal mistake by one of us need not cost our candidate far beyond common sense."

Pat hoped that her daughters would find some respite, too. "The people who lose out are the children," Pat told a *Time* magazine reporter. "Any of the glamour or reward in it comes to the grownups. It's the children who really suffer." Pat was now a car-pool mother of daughters who lived normal teenage lives. That fall the Nixons enrolled Tricia and Julie in the private and chic Marlborough School in Beverly Hills. The girls had begun to show more interest in politics and history; the following summer they worked at the local Republican headquarters.

Pat Nixon reconnected with old California friends and had extensive correspondence with acquaintances from her and Dick's travels to fifty-five countries during the vice presidency. Pat and Dick entertained visitors from across the country and around the world who came to talk about trade relations or improving foreign relations. Pat and her daughters hoped that Dick would be satisfied writing a memoir and working as a lawyer, but as she told *Ladies' Home Journal* in

November 1962, "probably in our hearts we always knew better." Out of politics, Dick was as restless as Pat was relieved. Dick had difficulty mustering enthusiasm for his job as a lawyer and, as he wrote in his memoir, "Virtually everything I did seemed unexciting and unimportant by comparison with national office."

Dick had wanted to relocate to California partly to spend more time with his family, but during their first year in California he would, by his own admission, see them less often than he did when he lived in Washington. Dick could not stop working: He wrote columns for the *Times-Mirror* syndicate, kept up with political correspondence, engaged in fund-raising, went on speaking tours, and developed his memoir *Six Crises*. He spent the better part of the summer and fall of 1961 working intently on the book, editing five ghostwritten chapters on the Alger Hiss case, the fund crisis, Eisenhower's heart attack, the near-death experience in Caracas, and the Moscow Kitchen Debate; he himself wrote the final section about the presidential election. In telling the stories of these crises Nixon celebrates his qualities of diligence and persistence as key components of success. He sets himself firmly in the tradition of American heroes who help America fulfill its destiny to be a shining example (a city on the hill) to other nations. In the book Dick acknowledged that part of him wanted to flee from crises; he revealed his fears of failing, of being indecisive, and of losing control. This self-analysis drained him. By the end of 1961 he claimed to be more tired than he had been at the end of the 1960 campaign. "I was almost ten pounds underweight from the strain and fatigue, and I became short-tempered at home and at the office."

When *Six Crises* was released in 1962, Dick was criticized for dedicating the book to "Pat Who Also Ran," an acknowledgment so brief as to seem a sign of coldness toward his loyal wife. Dick, however, saw the dedication as a tribute. In the run-up to the campaign in March 1960, Pat had told a reporter from the *Chicago Daily Times* that if she ever wrote a memoir, it would be titled "I Also Ran." Dick took her words and made them a public compliment. Yet no matter how much the American public sought to hear him express direct affection for his wife, and no matter how much such expressions would have benefited him, he could never bring himself to share those private feelings in the public arena.

His well-written book—fascinating for its intended and unintended insights into his psyche and his moral character—sold more than three hundred thousand copies, earned him $250,000, and won good reviews. It also, as John Kennedy had predicted, when he met with Nixon after the 1960 election, renewed his stature and reinforced his prominent position in the Republican Party.

By the fall of 1961, Eisenhower, the former Republican national chairman Leonard Hall, and Murray Chotiner were urging Nixon to jump into the California gubernatorial race. Polls showed that the former vice president had a twenty-point lead over Democratic governor Edmund "Pat" Brown. When Nixon had campaigned for Republican senator William F. Knowland against Pat Brown in the 1958 gubernatorial race, Dick thought Knowland had run a poor race. Nixon felt that Brown was beatable by a strong candidate like himself. Nixon was intrigued but uncertain; he was far more passionate about national issues and foreign affairs than he was about such state-level business as highways, irrigation systems, school budgets, and smog, but he was drawn to the arena. As governor he would have a political base; as a new governor, he would also have cover to pass on a 1964 rematch with the increasingly popular president.

Dick, in his memoir *RN*, Pat (in articles in the *Ladies' Home Journal* and in *Good Housekeeping*), and Julie (in her biography of her mother) published detailed versions of the stressful family debate over the merits of a race for governor. Their characterizations of the process give us an inside look at the decision-making dynamics in the Nixon marriage, which, as in many marriages, allowed each partner to assign the role of villain and assume the role of victim, each one consciously or unconsciously working to induce guilt in the other, until one spouse prevailed. In his memoir *RN*, Dick acknowledged that this decision created "a major new crisis for me and my family." The crisis was born of the stress between what Dick thought was right for himself and what he owed to his wife and daughters. He understood that Pat "has always been one of those rare individuals," he wrote in his memoir, "whose ego does not depend on public attention." His own gladiatorial nature yearned to be "in the arena," as he would title a late-in-life memoir. He also knew that Pat believed that politicians were "the most vicious people in the world," as she told producer Samuel Goldwyn, Jr., at a dinner one night at this time.

On September 25 the family dined at home that night in front of a roaring fireplace. After dinner Dick discussed the pressures on him to run, and the pros and cons of entering the race. "Why you?" thirteen-year-old Julie asked. "Can't somebody else carry the ball for awhile?"

"It doesn't look like it right now," her father told her. "The consensus is that my experience could be of value now in California."

Pat was firmly against the race. "As nearly as I can define my attitude," she frankly told *Ladies' Home Journal* in November 1962, it was "let's not. Let's stay home. Let's be a private family. Let's take a vacation trip when we want to. Let's not be leaders, but instead make our contribution in other ways." Pat went so far as to insist that she "would not be going out campaigning with you as I have in the past." That campaigning would be difficult, she knew; Brown was a formidable candidate and the Republican Party of California a petulant group of factions ready to ensnare Dick in a nasty primary fight.

Julie declared, "All I want is for everyone to love everyone and be happy. I can't study or do anything when one of us is not happy." Although Dick Nixon does not mention it in his own writings, author Earl Mazo has reported that Julie found this kind of family tension destabilizing. Eager to bridge the dissent between her parents, Julie told her father that she would support whatever decision he made.

People recalling the same stressful situation often contradict each other's account, and that happened among the Nixon family. Pat, interviewed by Julie in the mid-1980s for a biography, told her daughter that Tricia was initially opposed to the run, but in Dick's memoir *RN* he recalls that Tricia said, "I am not sure—but I kind of have the feeling you should just to show them you aren't finished because of the election that was stolen from us in 1960!" If Dick's memory is accurate, he would have had two votes in his favor, but his actions that night suggest he was outvoted three to one. "Well . . . that is life. You don't always win," Dick told them, in a manipulative act guaranteed to make the others feel guilty. He withdrew to his study to prepare a no-go speech. Tricia saw how unhappy he was. "If it means so much to Daddy," she told her mother, "maybe we should change our votes." Pat felt bad. Tricia went upstairs to tell her father about her change of mind.

According to Dick, Pat eventually came to his room and sat on the sofa, away from the light of his desk lamp. Dick could detect, in her voice, her struggle to hide her disappointment at his determined desire to run. "I am more convinced than ever that if you run, it will be a terrible mistake. But if you weigh everything and still decide to run, I will support your decision. I'll be there campaigning with you just as I always have." Dick, exacerbating Pat's guilt, told her again that he was opting out, but she insisted he make his own decision. She did not want to be blamed for vetoing a decision that might be good for her husband, the country, and the state. At least at this point in their marriage "the good of the country" and the health of Dick's psyche weighed more favorably on his side than "the good of the family" weighed on hers. According to Nixon's account, they sat in silence for a while before she approached him, placed her hand on his shoulder, gave him a quick kiss, and left him alone to decide. Relieved, he threw his notes in the wastebasket and started over. Pat's inability to stick to her instincts at this moment of crisis was one of her biggest mistakes in the marriage. At a press conference on September 27, Dick announced that his heart was not in private life but public service. He would run. After the conference, Pat had dinner with Carol Finch, the wife of Robert Finch, one of Nixon's 1960 campaign directors. "I'm trapped," Pat told her. "Which way can I go? He can't help it. He must always have a crusade." She told the reporter from *Ladies' Home Journal* that she felt it was her duty to allow a "great man" to run because "it is necessary to the future of his country and the world that he be elected." Her statement sounds platitudinous but she believed it—at least when she wasn't exasperated with her husband. Pat deeply valued loyalty to a cause and to a man; they surpassed the importance she placed on personal happiness. She told the reporter she looked at her dog and said, "Well, Checkers, here we go again."

Right on cue the accusations against Nixon rolled in—just as Pat had feared. On the day Dick announced his candidacy, reporters asked Nixon at his press conference why he had paid only $35,000 for a Hoffa Teamsters' Fund lot—Hoffa had invested a significant amount of his Teamsters Retirement Fund in Trousdale Estates—that was worth $42,000. Nixon claimed that he had merely paid the asking price. California Democrats resurrected the 1960 campaign charge that Nixon secretly arranged Howard Hughes's $205,000 loan to his brother Donald. Pat's keen bitterness about political attacks grew more pungent. On October 17, 1961, during a "Chat with Pat" reception in Sacramento, "her lips quivering with anger," Mrs. Nixon told newsmen that living through the "smears" against her husband was the most difficult part of campaigning. Asked about the Hughes loan, Pat replied, "There's the 6-year-old smear. There's also the 11-year-old smear. There have been smears since the Hiss case. They don't seem to invent any new ones."

Besieged once again, the Nixons distanced themselves from each other during this campaign. "We never have fights," Pat later told the *Los Angeles Times,* "we just move away from each other." With the exception of a joint initial tour of the state, Pat campaigned separately from her husband. She did not have to listen incessantly to Dick's speeches in a race she doubted he could win, and Dick did not have to be distracted by subtle indications of her underlying disenchantment.

Pat's increased distance likely also resulted from her awareness that she had become a less integral part of Dick's team. Her husband had surrounded himself with a cadre of younger advisors (John Ehrlichman, Bob Haldeman, Ron Ziegler) who did not seriously challenge him or second-guess his strategy or his motives. They were more cowed by his anger than longer-term professional team members like Robert Finch and Leonard Hall. In 1962 Dick also brought back Murray Chotiner, who had managed his campaigns for the Senate in 1950 and for the vice presidency in 1952. Pat had not changed her dim view of his chicanery. Working as an unpaid advisor to Haldeman, Chotiner found underhanded ways to suggest that Brown was a communist sympathizer. Nixon was not pleased when the normally friendly *Los Angeles Times* exposed the Nixon campaign for mailing fake "Committee for the Preservation of the Democratic Party" circulars claiming that Brown was under the influence of left-wing extremists. Brown went to court and got a restraining order.

The campaign officially kicked off on the morning of September 12, 1962, at the Los Angeles County Fairground in Pomona—where the Nixons had launched two previous successful congressional campaigns. Blitzing the state with typical thoroughness and determination, they lunched in San Diego, dined in Sacramento, and held an evening rally in Oakland. Her counterpart as a political wife in this campaign was Bernice Brown, a gray-haired grandmother who, fifty-three to Pat's fifty, looked ten years younger than her age. Seemingly apolitical, Bernice, an avid golfer, was no Jackie Kennedy—she was the daughter of a San Francisco police captain—and she was feisty. Mrs. Brown had announced back in June that she would be willing to debate Mrs. Nixon on television. Pat, with her experience, political aptitude, and articulate manner, might have performed well in such a debate, but she would have dreaded and despised every spotlit second of it. Interest in Mrs. Brown's political theater faded, and reporters moved on to more interesting skirmishes.

Suppressing her misgivings, Pat assumed her beneficent, game-on campaign persona. Republican and independent women loved her; at events she outdrew Bernice Brown. Reporter Tom Wicker wrote that Pat was often told "by gushing ladies with what must have been maddening frequency how wonderful she would have been as First Lady." Her fans had no idea how painful, not just maddening, their compliments were to her.

Pat remained the conscientious, dutiful campaigner she had been in six previous elections. After a fund-raising tea in Santa Barbara she worried whether she had done enough; she had shaken the hands of a thousand women and autographed six paper plates. "People paid to get in," she said. "All they did was meet me. Maybe there should have been some entertainment. . . . If there was a microphone, I would have made a little talk." At the beginning of October Pat Nixon slipped on the floor of her bathroom in a San Francisco hotel and cracked three ribs. Concealing her intense pain, she went on to shake hands with thousands more voters because, an anonymous source told the *Hartford Courant*, she "didn't want to ask for pity."

Brown, untainted by any scandal, hammered home the idea that Nixon, like Senator William Knowland before him, was more interested in using the governorship as a stepping-stone to the presidency than he was in addressing California's local issues. After President Kennedy addressed the nation following the successful resolution of the Cuban Missile Crisis toward the end of October, Nixon and other Republicans knew they had little opportunity to make inroads on a popular incumbent. "We had to play the dreary drama through to its conclusion," Dick wrote in his memoir.

On Tuesday, November 6, Pat and Dick Nixon and his staff monitored the election results in the gold, white, and beige Presidential Suite in the Beverly Hilton Hotel. By midnight, when it appeared Dick had lost a California election for the first time, Pat, according to reporter Jules Witcover, removed herself to a separate room to grieve another loss. Dick lost by nearly three hundred thousand votes out of the six million cast.

Dick initially refused to meet with the press. He watched on television as his press secretary Herb Klein went downstairs to read his concession statement. "The boss won't be down," Klein announced. "He plans to go home and be with his family." The press protested. Their reaction triggered Dick's exquisitely ingrained resentment of the media. They had been after him, he believed, ever since the aftermath of the Hiss case, and for "the next twelve years of public service in Washington, I was to be subjected to an utterly unprincipled and vicious smear campaign: Bigamy, forgery, drunkenness, insanity, thievery, anti-Semitism, perjury, the whole gamut of misconduct in public office, ranging from unethical to downright criminal activities." When a CBS reporter asked Klein whether Nixon was afraid to meet with them, Dick became enraged.

Klein was in midsentence when Dick appeared, gaunt and un-shaven, and abruptly forced him aside. "Good morning, gentlemen," he began in an uneasy voice. "Now that all the members of the press are so delighted that I have lost, I'd like to make a statement of my own." In a rambling fifteen-minute peroration, he was gracious to his campaign volunteers and to Governor Brown and vitriolic to those who had opposed him. He alternated between praising and criticiz-ing the stunned reporters, and finally ended by venting years of rage: "And as I leave the press, all I can say is this; for sixteen years, ever since the Hiss case, you've had a lot of fun—a lot of fun—that you've had an opportunity to attack me, and I think I have given as good as I've taken . . . just think of how much you're going to be missing. You won't have Nixon to kick around anymore because, gentlemen, this is my last press conference."

He stalked away from the microphone and into what seemed like political oblivion. After sixteen years of political triumph and failure, why had he cracked open on this occasion? A number of his aides claimed that he had had a couple of scotches that night and a watered-down drink in the morning, but that he was relatively clear headed. John Ehrlichman believed that Nixon, who had a chronic problem with insomnia, sometimes mixed barbiturates and alcohol. Regardless of what he had imbibed, Nixon was triggered by a volatile mixture of exhaustion, self-pity, discouragement, and humiliation.

Pat was not present. She could not tolerate standing at her hus-band's side for another concession speech, having felt humiliated after seeing replays of herself crying in the Ambassador Hotel ball-room on Election Night two years before. This time, accompanied by Julie and Tricia, she watched the television coverage of her husband's press conference in their den at home. Still bitter about press cover-age of her husband, Pat yelled "Bravo" when Dick attacked the press. According to Julie, when Dick arrived home, Pat blurted out, "Oh, Dick," as he rushed past her, heading to the backyard to weep. That af-ternoon would be the first time Dick and Pat broke down emotionally in front of their daughters. Pat lay on her bed in a darkened room and cried while Julie and Tricia sat on the floor beside her and wept. The

Nixons' angry despair was so powerful that Helene and Jack Drown took Tricia and Julie home with them for several days.

When Julie and Tricia returned home, Dick drove the girls to school. As they left the car, Dick offered them his prescription for handling defeat: "You just go on. You go on with your head held high." As a couple, Pat and Dick would go on, but over the next years the terms of their marriage would shift. Pat was no longer as willing to cater to Dick. She would insist on the private life that she had barely glimpsed that summer of 1961 in California. She had correctly assessed that the gubernatorial campaign would damage them as a family and temporarily corrode her husband's reputation; now her judgment merited more respect. As they struggled to reclaim some of the closeness they had forfeited during the two losing campaigns, "There was a sadness," Tricia remembered, "and the sadness went on for years."

13

Your Turn, My Turn

As part of the Nixons' effort to resuscitate their spirits and their union after three harrowing years of political campaigning and two electoral defeats, the Nixons planned a six-week sojourn in Europe for the summer of 1963. This would prove one of the happiest seasons in their marriage. Pat and Dick went to the top of the Eiffel Tower, took a gondola ride through Venice, explored the pyramids, and toured the remnants of the Forum and the Parthenon. They were accompanied by Julie, Tricia, Jack and Helene Drown, and the Drowns' twenty-year-old daughter, Maureen—this was the fulfillment of a desire the couples had shared since their early days in Whittier. But Dick's all-consuming political work had thwarted their plans over the years. Now at last they could travel on their own terms. During this trip and the next four years, both of the Nixons worked to balance the summons of politics with the pleasures of being private citizens and a married couple.

They cobbled together a compromise itinerary for the trip that balanced their conflicting needs. Dick soothed his ego and refurbished his reputation by holding press conferences in foreign capitals—his "last press conference" in Los Angeles had quickly proved not to be that at all—and having diplomatic tête-à-têtes with European leaders. In between, Pat enjoyed a "normal family" tour of Europe with her husband, daughters, and friends.

According to Maureen Drown Nunn, all across Europe that summer, the travel industry "pulled out all the stops" for the famous couple and their traveling companions. Dick and Pat first declined the offers of free cars they received from hotels, but then changed their minds and decided to accept these courtesies. Pat and Dick started every morning with an intimate ritual. They rose early, went to a small restaurant, sipped coffee, and read the newspapers. Dick would ask, "Pat, have you seen this article?" They took turns reading passages to each other. On several occasions, Maureen, who would arise late, remembers sitting outside the door of a restaurant savoring "what a beautiful thing it was" that her parents' friends enjoyed such companionable time.

In Paris President and Mrs. Charles de Gaulle unexpectedly summoned the Nixons to the Élysée Palace for an impromptu luncheon with U.S. Ambassador Charles E. Bohlen and his wife. During a two-hour alfresco lunch on a patio behind the palace, Nixon expounded on his ideas about the Atlantic Alliance, while de Gaulle spoke about the importance of negotiations with the Chinese, and of détente—a new idea—with the Soviet Union. Pat relished meeting the dignitaries and the geopolitical tenor of the conversation. After lunch, President de Gaulle, whom Richard Nixon revered, toasted the American couple. "I realize that you have been checked in the pursuit of your goals," he said to the former vice president. "But I have a great sense that . . . you will serve your country again in an even higher capacity." His gesture heartened Dick, even as it reminded Pat how difficult it might be to remain in exile from the realm of politics.

Their interlude abroad was only one component of a larger realignment of their lives. Pat now dictated how the couple would live their lives. The Nixons and their daughters loved the home they had built in Southern California, but they did not want to be surrounded by people who looked upon them as also-rans; Tricia and Julie were often teased at school. Dick made good on his promise to break from politics, by leaving the West Coast and moving to Nelson Rockefeller's turf in New York. Pat supported this change. At a time when many Americans were making a mass exodus from metropolitan areas and moving into the suburbs, she sought the anonymity and engagement of big-city life. To rebuild the family's depleted finances, Dick accepted a partnership with a firm on Broad Street in lower Manhattan. In December 1963, after Dick obtained his license to practice law in New York State, the firm would reconfigure itself as Nixon, Mudge, Rose, Guthrie and Alexander. Its marquee partner would soon attract a distinguished international corporate clientele and double the firm's income.

Ten days before embarking for Europe, the Nixons moved into a twelve-room apartment they had purchased at 810 Fifth Avenue, at the corner of Sixty-second Street in Manhattan. With its views of Central Park and the Plaza Hotel, and with neighbors like Nelson Rockefeller and William Randolph Hearst, Jr., the apartment was a suitable residence for a law partner making $250,000 a year. Mrs. Nixon supervised remodeling the apartment and furnished it "in French provincial with a preponderance of pastel yellows and golds." Fina and Manolo Sanchez, a Cuban refugee couple who had worked for the Nixons since 1961, moved into an enlarged room off the kitchen and became part of the family.

Every dream, of course, has its shadows. As much as Pat loved her new life, she missed the California climate and the outdoor barbecue. Pat and Dick yearned for their garden and its lime tree, from which they had made their own limeade. Although Pat cultivated friendships in New York City, none of them was as close as her bond with her best friend, Helene, whom she missed. Nonetheless, within two weeks of moving into their new home, Pat told Dick over a home-cooked meal that "I hope we never have to move again."

At first, the Nixons dove enthusiastically into New York's social and cultural life. Pat and Dick enrolled their daughters at the Upper East Side's Chapin School, the alma mater of Jackie Kennedy. They enjoyed theater and often took Julie and Tricia, especially, to musicals, including *How to Succeed in Business Without Really Trying*, *110 in the Shade*, *Hello Dolly*, and Mary Martin's first Broadway flop, *Jennie*. They also introduced the girls to Carnegie Hall and the Metropolitan Opera. Pat and her daughters enjoyed window-shopping along Madison and Fifth avenues and strolling Central Park with Dick and their dogs, Checkers and Vicki (a young poodle). At times they were pestered by strangers who wanted their autographs. On Sundays the Nixons sometimes worshipped at nationally known preacher Norman Vincent Peale's Marble Collegiate Church on West Twenty-ninth Street. At this transitional period in their lives, the Nixons were drawn to Peale's philosophy of facing obstacles directly, looking for the seeds of a solution in every problem, while never focusing on defeat, but, instead, on "the power of positive thinking."

The Nixons joined the elite Metropolitan Club, located only a few blocks from their apartment, and took Julie and Tricia to dinner there or at the Edwardian Room in the Plaza Hotel, a grand Spanish Renaissance Revival–style room, with paneled oak wainscoting, an elaborate trussed ceiling, stenciled decorations, and mirrors. When Dick and Pat went out alone, they liked to dine and dance in the Edwardian Room.

Initially, they accepted invitations to charity balls and social events, but they quickly grew weary of that circuit, which reminded them too much of their hectic life in Washington. Pat and Dick attended small dinner parties at 21, Le Pavillon, The Colony, and Delmonico's restaurants. Over their years in New York, the Nixon family developed a holiday tradition of having a pre-Christmas meal at Luchow's famous steak house before seeing the Rockettes at Rockefeller Center.

Pat and Dick entertained friends in their apartment's turquoise and gold dining room, and Dick entertained business friends at private clubs on Wall Street. Pat dashed across the street for violin-serenaded luncheons in the elegant Palm Court in the Plaza Hotel with her lively neighbor Kathleen Stans, the wife of Dwight Eisenhower's budget

director, and other friends. To escape the city on weekends, Pat and
Dick joined two posh and beautiful country clubs—Blind Brook in
Purchase, New York, and Baltusrol, in northern New Jersey.

The Nixons' Christmas party became a popular event during their
five years in New York, with powerful and famous invitees including
prominent members of the clergy, judges, admirals, ambassadors,
lawyers, businessmen, politicians, *Reader's Digest* editor-in-chief Hobart
Lewis, and their wives. Actors Arlene Dahl, James Stewart, and Ginger
Rogers, along with Harry Winston jeweler Don Carnevale, listened to
Richard Nixon play Christmas carols on the piano while former New
York governor Tom Dewey sang in his deep baritone voice. Nixon's Re-
publican operative Victor Lasky, an anticommunist writer and former
public relations expert for the CIA, who had accompanied Nixon to
the Soviet Union in 1959, former television producer William Safire,
a 1960 campaign aide who had been working in Moscow as a public
relations agent for the American National Exhibition, and their wives
brought a touch of conservative political intrigue to the party.

On November 20, 1963, Richard Nixon visited Dallas to attend the
Pepsi-Cola Company's board meeting. Dick held a press conference,
but luckily for his reputation and good conscience, he told local jour-
nalists that he hoped that the city would give Kennedy a "courteous
reception" upon his arrival that day. Dick flew out of Dallas on the
morning of November 22. On the way home from LaGuardia Airport,
when his taxi stopped for a red light, a man rushed over to the cab
and told them that Kennedy had been shot. When Dick arrived home,
the doorman rushed out in tears and told him, "It's just terrible.
They've killed President Kennedy."

Dick found his wife and daughters watching the events unfolding
on television. Pat was all too aware that the world was infused with
hatred; from the vitriolic leftist hecklers of the Senate 1950 campaign
to the anti-American agitators who threw rocks at her limousine in
Caracas, Venezuela, she had encountered threatening violence first-
hand. Dick feared his electoral comments about Kennedy had incited
a right-wing lunatic to kill his rival. He was relieved when he called

FBI director J. Edgar Hoover, who told him that the assassin was a deranged communist.

Nixon conveyed his condolences to Mrs. Kennedy. "While the hand of fate made Jack and me political opponents," he wrote her, "I always cherished the fact that we were personal friends from the time we came to Congress together in 1947." Dick praised Mrs. Kennedy fully for the "indelible impression" she made as First Lady.

A few weeks later, once the nation had mourned and buried its assassinated leader, his widow replied in a letter striking for its forthright acknowledgment of Nixon's ambition and its risks. "We never value life enough when we have it," Mrs. Kennedy cautioned him. "I know how you must feel—so long on the path—so closely missing the greatest prize—and now for you the question comes up again—and you must commit all your and your family's hopes and efforts again . . . if it does not work out as you have hoped for so long—please be consoled by what you already have—your life and your family."

In the turbulent days following the assassination, Kennedy's staff forgot to invite the Nixons to the funeral. Dick asked Congressman Pat Hillings to arrange for an official invitation. On Monday, November 25, a brisk and sunny autumn day, Pat and Dick walked respectfully behind Mrs. Kennedy and her family in the procession to the funeral Mass at St. Matthew's Cathedral in Washington, D.C. For the one million mourners who lined the route and the millions more who watched on television, the Nixons' presence was unremarkable amid a sea of 220 foreign dignitaries, heads of state, and members of royal families.

At the Requiem Mass, in the procession to Arlington National Cemetery, and at the burial service, Pat and Dick would have had the opportunity to reflect on seventeen years of conviviality, rivalry, fondness, bitterness, and, finally, sorrow that had inextricably intertwined the two couples. It was also a time to reconsider their priorities. Dick could not help but wonder how the president's death would affect the impending 1964 presidential campaign and his career. For Pat, being in Washington was a reminder of the exhausting obligations that had burdened her life there.

During the winter of 1964 Dick often acted as if he had taken Mrs. Kennedy's advice to heart. He devoted himself to spending more time with his wife and daughters, who would soon head off to college. Dick brought Rose Mary Woods home from his Wall Street office for dinner with Pat and the girls. Entering the apartment, he often put on a record of classical music or a Broadway musical like *Carousel* and lit a fire. "He tries hard to have a fun, family life," Julie noted in her diary.

Pat and Dick had long since become fatalistic about the physical perils of political life, but they were shocked to learn that Kennedy's accused assassin, Lee Harvey Oswald, had seriously considered targeting Nixon. Dick told biographer Jonathan Aitken that, according to testimony Marina Oswald gave the Warren Commission about her husband, Oswald showed a gun to his wife and told her he was going to use it on Nixon; she prevented him from carrying out his plan by locking her husband in the bathroom.

The new president, Lyndon B. Johnson, quickly consolidated his power, capitalizing on the nation's grief to pass Kennedy's landmark civil rights bill, announce a War on Poverty, and foster the social programs that would become the Great Society. The Nixons knew that Johnson would be a formidable opponent in the 1964 presidential election. The Republican nominee, Arizona senator Barry Goldwater, honored Nixon by asking him to introduce him at the Republican Convention in San Francisco. Pat at first refused to go; attending a contentious political conclave in California meant a return to an arena that she never wanted to re-enter. Eventually her loyalty to party and husband won out over her aversion. In the Cow Palace that July, she listened to her husband legitimize Senator Goldwater to the nation as "Mr. Conservative" and "Mr. Republican." But both she and Dick were appalled by the combative, right-wing tone of the nominee's acceptance speech. Breaking ranks with liberal and moderate Republicans, Goldwater ringingly declared, in words that would reverberate throughout the fall campaign, "Extremism in the defense of liberty is no vice . . . moderation in the pursuit of justice is no virtue."

Nixon knew Goldwater could not win. Hoping to prevent a

massacre of his splintered party and to re-establish his bona fides with the Republican base, Nixon made 150 appearances in thirty-six states that fall. He stumped for Goldwater and for House and Senate Republican candidates, many of whom valued his support. As a positive presence for his party, he could shoulder past the prevailing caricature of himself as a bitter loser, and thus present himself as a logical, even inevitable presidential candidate for a party aching for unity. But beyond the calculations of ambition, practicing politics kept Nixon alert and alive. Dick knew that a career in law, however challenging, would ruin him: "I would be mentally dead in two years," he wrote in his memoir, "and physically dead in four."

As the first whiff of the fall campaign swept through the Nixon apartment, Pat and the girls hightailed it out of town for a monthlong vacation in Scandinavia, the Low Countries, Scotland, and Ireland. When they returned, Pat faced a milestone in her life as a mother: Tricia, while still living at home, matriculated at Finch College in Manhattan. For a woman who placed such a high value on motherhood—and one who suffered guilt about balancing politics and parenting—she felt considerable emotional turmoil. Like many women of her era, at the age of fifty-one, Pat had defined herself as the consummate wife and mother. Now, with her daughters nearly grown, with a husband who did not need her to be a full-time political helpmate, and lacking a financial imperative to take on a job outside the home, she had to ask herself how she could live a life rich with meaning and value. Nationwide, women who came of age in the postwar period were beginning to ask themselves this question, which would roil the nation for the rest of the 1960s and beyond.

Pat responded to the looming empty nest by taking on a role familiar to her: She helped Rose Mary Woods run Nixon's law office. Pat wrote Helene that she was "slaving 14 hours a day" answering the phone, typing replies to the mail—often staying until 10:00 or 11:00 p.m. Moreover, belying her reputation as a woman who despised politics, Pat volunteered during the 1964 campaign. Reassuming her persona as "Miss Ryan," she fielded calls from "panic-stricken campaigners who want *help*," as she put it, fending off a Democratic rout in the 1964 elections.

Her political work, however peripheral, helped her cope with the first stirrings of midlife crisis. Pat was aware time was growing shorter: "The years fly so fast—a good sign of age," she wrote Helene, "those rocking chairs are beckoning." By the winter of 1965, she had become increasingly unsettled. While Dick hustled around the world as an international legal consultant/foreign policy expert or sold his political expertise across America, Pat lacked the purpose that came from participating in a larger cause. "After you have been in political life," she told her friend Carol Finch, who visited her in New York, "at first you try your hand at charity work, but it is not the commitment of politics. You know I do get restless."

Her friend Helene Drown might have detected restlessness in Pat when she wrote her in February 1965 to say, "If Dick is going to be away and you haven't any hot dates for Sat. Mar. 3, maybe we could line up a few boys at some local bar and have ourselves a whirl." Yet the anomie that both Dick and Pat experienced in the mid-1960s did not seem to manifest itself in an urge to seek romantic renewal outside their marriage. For a modern politician—and especially one who traveled around the world so frequently—there were remarkably few rumors that Richard Nixon was less than faithful in his marriage. In 1976 the *New York Times* reported that beginning in 1967 J. Edgar Hoover's FBI had investigated the possibility of an affair between Nixon and Marianna Liu, a hostess at the Hong Kong Hilton, during three visits to Asia between 1964 and 1967. Richard Nixon had had top secret briefings on the People's Republic of China and the FBI was concerned that his contacts with Liu could be damaging to national security. In 1967, when Liu was in the hospital recovering from an appendectomy, Dick sent her a bouquet of flowers, a get-well note, and a card with his New York address. According to Liu, Nixon offered to help her relocate to the United States, but she never asked him for assistance. That 1967 note was, she claims, the last time she heard from him. When the *National Enquirer* concluded that they had an affair, Liu forcefully denied the claim, sued the paper, and settled out of court. J. Edgar Hoover may have hoped to use this information to gain a hold over Nixon. But the FBI never found any evidence that Liu was a foreign intelligence agent, that Nixon had an intimate connection with her, or that their friendship compromised national security.

In June 1965 the Nixons took a second honeymoon of sorts, in the company of their daughters and Bebe Rebozo, a twenty-fifth-anniversary trip to revisit haunts from their 1940 honeymoon. They stayed at the Reforma Hotel, situated on the fashionable Paseo de la Reforma in Mexico City. The art deco hotel had beautiful views of Chapultepec Castle and its park. Twenty-five years before, Pat and Dick could barely afford one night at this elegant venue, but this time they ensconced themselves there for a week. According to Julie, Dick planned all the events for their June 21 anniversary, including a lunch at a restaurant they remembered from 1940, a shopping excursion, and dinner at the Normandie restaurant, which featured rounded mahogany banquettes, painted tableaus of seventeenth-century French mansions set against brooding skies, and an orchestra—a flourish Pat loved. Dick and Pat danced to the romantic theme song "More," from the 1962 movie *Mondo Cane*: "More than the simple words I've tried to say / I only live to love you more each day."

Pat as a private citizen was as solitary a figure as when she was a politician's wife. From the end of the 1964 Republican election disaster (in which Johnson won by a landslide) until the beginning of the 1966 campaign, Nixon traveled incessantly, making four hundred appearances in forty states in an effort to rebuild the shattered Republican Party and the Nixon brand in anticipation of another effort for the presidency.

Pat made clear her ambivalence about his cause—much to her husband's chagrin. In January 1966, Dick did what parents of teenagers sometimes do, but should avoid: He confided to Julie about the tension with her mother. "We all have to contribute and try if we want to be happy," he told Julie. Referring to Pat, he said, "You must learn to accept things as they are and forge ahead." As usual, he had difficulty being direct with her about his desire to run for president again. This was not the last time he would lean on Julie to vent his marital stress and to buffer his relations with his wife—this would occur again most famously during the Watergate crisis.

Pat's priority was to spend time with Tricia and Julie before they left home permanently. In the fall of 1966 Julie matriculated at Smith College. David Eisenhower was studying at nearby Amherst College. Julie became reacquainted with David, whom she had known earlier, and they fell in love. Tricia lived at home while attending Finch College in Manhattan. As their daughters began their separate lives, Pat wanted Dick to slow his pace and reconnect with her, but that did not happen. Helene gave her advice about how they could divert themselves and relax as a couple, but Pat wrote her that "Dick keeps scheduled up to the ears so there is no possibility for 'involvement' for such frivolous activities."

Pat felt guilty about her unwillingness either to traipse around the world as the wife of an international lawyer or to slog through the country with Dick campaigning for congressional candidates. She did not see a necessity to help him collect political debts and refine his knowledge about foreign affairs. Bebe Rebozo and other cronies could accompany him abroad. But, as the 1966 congressional elections loomed, she asked her daughters for reassurance that she was not failing her husband. Like many women in the late 1960s, Pat felt caught between her loyalty to her husband and her awareness of her own emerging needs.

As Americans became increasingly divided by Johnson's conduct of the Vietnam War, the nation's still-fraught race relations, and the deepening reach of certain Great Society legislation, Republicans gained many congressional seats in 1966. Nixon worked energetically for the GOP cause by appearing on behalf of more than 104 members of Congress in thirty-five states, expecting they would not forget their debt to the former vice president if he ran for president in two years. After the elections, Dick decided to take a six-month hiatus from partisan politics in order to tamp down his image as a partisan crusader. From March through June 1967, he made four trips throughout

Europe and the Soviet Union, Asia, Latin America, and then Africa and the Middle East. He traveled partly as a "goodwill ambassador for Pepsi Cola," where he was a board member, and partly as a prospective presidential candidate showcasing, and strengthening, his expertise in foreign affairs.

Hiatus or not, Pat knew what his intentions were. During their traditional year-end Key Biscayne vacation in 1966, on an atypically dreary and cold Florida day, Pat, bundled up, sat on the beach with Tricia and Julie. Her mood matched the weather. She told them "flatly, almost tonelessly" that she did not want to endure another presidential race. The humiliation of 1960 was still real and raw.

When Pat spent a three-week vacation in August 1967 with the Drowns in California, Helene served as a sounding board for Pat's emotions. As staunch Republicans, the Drowns had been disturbed by Goldwater's defeat in 1964 and were ambitious for Richard Nixon. Like the Drowns, Pat believed in her husband's leadership and wanted him to realize his presidential ambitions, but she dreaded the hardships of a political campaign and the combative and invasive nature of life in the political floodlights. Helene reminded Pat that she had not left Whittier, California, to live out a destiny as a housewife. Her well-earned reservations about the dark side of politics competed with her desire to play a significant role in a larger mission. Pat also thought it was more important for her husband to do meaningful work than it was for him to advance in a career that held more money than meaning. Pat began to prepare herself for a campaign she saw as inevitable, but she did not openly encourage her husband.

By December 1967, Dick found himself grappling with his own readiness to take the electoral plunge: "I was not sure that I still had the heart," he wrote in his memoir. He knew, as few did, how punishing a presidential campaign could be. He was now almost fifty-five years old. On Christmas Day, Nixon surveyed his family's opinions. According to his memoir *RN*, Tricia and Julie supported another presidential run because they knew how passionate he felt about returning to power. Julie thought he was depressed by being out of politics and appealed to his sense of duty: "You have to do it for the country." Tricia recognized how important the race was to her father's sense of self and personal mission. "If you don't run, Daddy," Tricia said, "you will have nothing to live for." Before he left New York for Florida to mull over his decision, Pat told him, "Whatever you do, we'll be proud of you." She knew she could not stop his impetus to run.

Dick spent ten days in Key Biscayne with the Reverend Billy Graham and Bebe Rebozo. He knew well the pitfalls of political life, as he defined them to a *Good Housekeeping* writer: "It's like living under a magnifying glass. Jealousies are spotlighted. Friendships take on a political cast." As he walked on the beach, he weighed his concerns about hurting his family and ruining his rebuilt reputation, and his insecurities about being acceptable to the American people, against his belief that he was the man to manage America's wars against dissidents at home and communists abroad.

Bebe Rebozo felt protective of the Nixon women and was less ambitious than he had previously been for his friend. Graham encouraged Dick to run; otherwise, he thought, Dick would wonder whether he could have attained the presidency. In early October, Graham had presided at the funeral of Nixon's mother, Hannah, who had been incapacitated by a stroke two years before. Dick was distraught and Graham was a significant comfort. Dick associated the evangelical minister with Hannah and her resolve and idealism, qualities he felt he would need to sustain him in the uphill battle for the White House.

On the evening of January 15, 1968, Dick invited Rose Mary Woods and Fina and Manolo Sanchez to join the Nixon family in their New York apartment for a discussion formalizing his decision to seek the White House. He wanted Pat to think that, despite her reluctance, she was part of a team that had been integral in the decision-making process. "I have decided to go," he told them. "I have decided to run again." According to Dick, Pat paused before giving her reluctant blessing: "I know what you are asking us to do, and what you are asking of yourself. Now that the decision is made, I will go along with it." But she would not love it. Pat acknowledged to *Good Housekeeping* that she doubted whether he "should go through it again." Pat did not "care about politics one way or the other," but she was convinced that a loyal wife should endorse her husband's decisions.

Pat refurbished her wardrobe and plunged both solo and in the company of her husband into the cold and snowy primary precincts of New Hampshire and Wisconsin. When she was not campaigning, she helped run his law office, work on his correspondence, and arrange his travel. Once she committed herself, Pat was formidable. Eating little (and dropping over the course of the campaign from a dress size ten to a size eight), she marched through shopping centers, schools, and factories. More than in the 1962 election, she traveled alongside her husband, listening to his stump speech hundreds of times. Journalist Tom Wicker noted that she was attentive "with an only slightly glazed expression of awe and admiration." The Nixons took weekend rest breaks in Key Biscayne, but Pat used that time to write up to fifty letters a day to important players in the campaign.

She dusted off and redonned her 1950s persona as a cheerful housewife. When she was asked, "What is your greatest contribution to your husband?" she claimed, "I don't nag him. The best I can [do] is cheer him up." She maintained her breastplate of privacy throughout the campaign, even as she recycled a few pet stories that emphasized her difficult childhood. "If people work, they can have what they want," she told reporters. "People dream what they can achieve. It is possible." Amid the anxiety, conflict, and displacement now roiling the country, with uncertainty and anger rife in every aspect of American society, Pat sought to have mainstream Americans identify with her and draw inspiration from her life.

In a nation so divided about everything from America's role in the world to the role of women in society, no candidate's wife could shape her presentation in a way that would appeal broadly and rescue her from criticism. She was damned by some if she was Plastic Pat, and damned by others if she presented herself as a New Woman. Many campaign reporters castigated Pat for her bland answers to questions and her unshakeable smile, while others, like Louise Hutchinson of the *Chicago Times* and Marie Smith of the *Washington Post*, believed that Mrs. Nixon had evolved into a more confident woman than she had been in 1960. However, underneath her gracious persona, Pat shared Dick's anxieties regarding social class and his hostility toward the press. She famously vented her irritation to Gloria Steinem, when the feminist journalist pushed Mrs. Nixon to talk about her personal life and challenged Pat's refusal to admit that she disliked critical articles in the press. When Steinem asked her what she wanted to do as First Lady, and whom she admired most in history, Pat unleashed her underlying resentment: "I never had time to think about things like that—who I wanted to be, or who I admired, or to have ideas. I never had time to dream about being someone else. I had to work . . . I'm not like all you . . . all those people who had it easy." (Ironically, Gloria Steinem had told this author that she grew up in a trailer park.)

During the first six months of 1968 the Nixons were staggered by an avalanche of dizzying events, some of them traumatic and tragic for the nation. As Nixon won three-quarters of the votes in the New Hampshire and Wisconsin Republican primaries in March and April, the campaign of Democratic antiwar candidate Eugene McCarthy garnered surprisingly strong results against President Johnson. In mid-March Senator Robert F. Kennedy of New York, evoking a ripple of fear in the Nixon camp, dove into the race for the Democratic nomination his brother had won eight years before.

When riots erupted at Columbia University, Pat spoke out vehemently against the college students who "think the world owes them a living and it really doesn't." Pat recalled, "We pulled pranks when I was in college, but what they're doing is really destructive." Then at the end of March, Johnson stunned the nation by withdrawing from the presidential race. On April 4, two days after the Wisconsin primary, civil rights leader Martin Luther King, Jr., was assassinated in Memphis, leading to riots that started in Washington and New York and fanned across the country. Tanks surrounded the White House. Amid this escalating national conflict, Nixon gained a resounding win in the Oregon primary, but sat out the California Republican race, knowing that favorite son Governor Ronald Reagan would win it easily.

*   *   *

In the early-morning hours of June 6, Dick woke up in his New York apartment to a somber voice: "Mr. Nixon, Excuse me, sir. Mr. Nixon." When Dick opened his eyes, Julie's fiancé, David Eisenhower, was standing by him. "What is it?" Dick mumbled. "They shot Kennedy," David said. "He's still alive, but he is unconscious. He was shot right after his victory speech." Robert F. Kennedy had won the California Democratic primary. The following day Pat entered Dick's study and interrupted his work. "Dick, that poor boy just died," she told him tearfully. "It's on the radio." Despite his political differences with Robert Kennedy, Nixon recorded in his memoir that he was "saddened and appalled by such tragic human waste." Several days later, Pat and Dick sat in St. Patrick's Cathedral in New York and listened to Edward M. Kennedy eulogize his assassinated brother. When Pat was asked whether she worried about her husband's safety, she acknowledged "the safety factor is a problem," and it weighed on her "to an extent," but she claimed to campaign with faith that everything would work out right, "instead of fear." Candidates had to be seen in person, and not just on television, if they were to create a country "where you're not stalked by fear every moment."

When Pat and Dick arrived at the Republican Convention in early August in heat-struck Miami Beach, Dick had in his pocket the full support of former president Eisenhower, who had, after an in-person appeal from Nixon, broken with his policy of not giving preconvention endorsements. On Wednesday evening, August 7, the new CBS program *60 Minutes* filmed the Nixons in their penthouse suite at the Hilton Plaza Hotel as they watched Maryland governor Spiro T. Agnew, who would become the vice-presidential nominee, give the nominating speech for Nixon. Dick sat in an armchair tracking the delegation roll call votes on a legal pad while his wife and family (which now included Tricia's boyfriend, Edward F. Cox) were gathered around him on sofas. At 11:00 p.m. Wisconsin gave Nixon enough delegates to secure the nomination. The family and an entourage of staffers "just screeched and clapped and grabbed each other. We all felt humble, proud, and happy," Pat told Frances Lewine of the *Los Angeles Times*.

The next evening Pat and Dick were greeted with a "deafening" roar when they walked toward the podium in the Miami Beach Convention Center. Nixon told the national television audience that he was buttressed by a "courageous wife and loyal children [who] stood by him in victory and also defeat." In a country that felt at times as if it was on the verge of chaos, Nixon pledged to provide fresh leadership for Americans whose cities, he said, were "enveloped in smoke and flame" with "sirens in the night," and for his countrymen who were "dying on distant battlefields abroad" and "killing each other at home." Signaling his newly emerging constituency, Nixon saluted "The voice of the great majority of Americans, the forgotten Americans, the non-shouters, the non-demonstrators. . . . They're decent people. . . . They work in American factories, they run American businesses," citizens who "give lift to the American dream." He memorably ended his acceptance speech by styling himself as the personification of that American dream: "A child . . . hears a train go by in the night and he dreams of faraway places where he would like to go. It seems like an impossible dream." Nixon asked his fellow citizens to "help me make that dream come true for millions of Americans."

As Nixon spoke, former Pennsylvania governor William Scranton sat next to Pat on the platform. "And every time he said anything and they cheered," Scranton told author Jeffrey Frank, "she'd turn to me and say, 'Now why do they do that?' She wanted someone to tell her something all the time."

During the last week of August, when the Democratic National Convention met in Chicago to nominate Vice President Hubert H. Humphrey as their presidential candidate, the world watched on television as Chicago mayor Richard J. Daley's police force used tear gas and clubs on antiwar protestors. Nixon made brilliant political capital out of the Democrats' convention chaos. A week later, Pat and Dick, showered by a squall of confetti partly arranged by their advance men, audaciously rode in a motorcade through the Loop in downtown Chicago—their daughters and David Eisenhower followed in cars behind them—in front of four hundred thousand peaceful onlookers. Contrasting themselves with Democratic candidate Hubert Humphrey and his wife, Muriel, the Nixons showcased themselves as a couple who represented domestic stability in a city and country that had spiraled out of control.

Nineteen-sixty-eight was heralded as the year of the "New Nixon"—a candidate reporters described as "calmer, more reflective, and more at ease with himself." But there was also a "new" Pat Nixon who seemed "more outgoing, and less reserved." She wore a chic hair-style in a lighter shade. Additionally, there were the "new Nixons," rebranded as a traditionally hierarchical couple—with Pat as the de-voted wife and Dick as the boss—to appeal to conservative and inde-pendent voters concerned about social change and what they viewed as the deterioration of social mores. The Nixons promised to stabilize a frightened country divided in nearly every way. Pat styled herself as a campaign volunteer and not the full partner she had been in 1960. When Marilyn Goldstein of *Newsday* asked her if she missed her star billing as an equal partner with Dick from 1960, Pat laughed, and told her, "I'd rather be his right-hand man. I always have been." She was "the eyes and ears of women voters," she told reporters. "I fill him in on what women think," she said, noting that women wanted peace at home and abroad.

Countering the counterculture, Julie and Tricia represented those clean-cut young adults who valued their elders and eschewed the youth revolution sweeping certain sectors of the population. They fo-cused on courting young voters; David Eisenhower served as the head of Youth for Nixon. Everywhere these paragons of clean Republican living campaigned, they, like the Nixons, were faced with protesters who screamed obscenities and waved clenched fists. These demonstra-tors saw Nixon as a proponent of an oppressive and unjust society and as a war hawk with no plan to disentangle the nation from the Viet-nam War.

An old-fashioned definition of the Nixons' public roles suited Dick, because he was now relying on a strong political team composed nearly entirely of men (H. R. Haldeman, John Ehrlichman, Dwight Chapin, Raymond Price, Pat Buchanan, John Mitchell), some of whom were drawn from the world of advertising. Pat Nixon, partly by choice and partly in response to the dictates of her husband's inner circle, backed off from helping helm a political world she increasingly distrusted.

There was, however, a downside for Mrs. Nixon. Bob Haldeman, Nixon's future chief of staff, brought no warmth to his domination over the Nixon staff, exerting strict control over access to Nixon and underestimating Pat's value to her husband. According to Julie, soon after he took charge, Haldeman failed to instruct local Republicans to introduce Mrs. Nixon at several rallies. Nixon ordered Haldeman to pay more respect to his wife. Pat Nixon and Bob Haldeman did see eye to eye on one crucial element of the campaign: They did not want to end up with a candidate as exhausted and ill as the Nixon of 1960. Dick needed more free time to replenish himself and strategize. He would travel to fewer states (twenty-seven) and would refrain from presidential debates—which would have benefited his challenger more than himself. Pat admitted to the press that her husband "gets very tense when he is on a heavy schedule" and "sometimes [blows] his stack."

Mounting the most expensive presidential campaign to that point in history, Nixon reached voters through controlled appearances in the media: televised town hall meetings with representative citizens, radio addresses, and radio and television commercials. His main claim was that the nation had regressed since 1965 and strayed from its traditional sources of strength and value. While offering purposely general comments about his proposals, Nixon promised to work to end the war in Vietnam and "win the peace in the Pacific." He pledged he would crack down on lawless behavior and violence, and that he would restore order to cities and colleges where demonstrators and rioters appeared to have lost all respect for authority. He reached out to liberals by saying that he would eliminate the military draft.

Dick expected President Johnson to manufacture a fall surprise to aide Humphrey's underdog campaign, and Johnson obliged. On October 31, five days before the election, the president went on television to announce a bombshell compromise: The North Vietnamese government had agreed to participate in peace talks in Paris and to stop bombing South Vietnamese cities. This announcement lifted an already advancing Humphrey in the polls. Two days later, however, President Nguyen Van Thieu of South Vietnam, sensing he might obtain a better deal from a Republican administration, announced that his government would not participate in the talks, throwing the advantage back to Nixon. President Johnson and his Democratic colleagues were convinced that Nixon and his Republican cronies had engaged in treasonous back-channel communications to convince Thieu not to come to Paris. Nixon in turn was convinced that President Johnson and his Democratic operatives ordered the FBI to bug Spiro Agnew and Nixon's campaign planes.

Pat and Dick voted by absentee ballot so they would not have to endure a sleepless night at the end of a brutal campaign. On the morning of Election Day they flew from Los Angeles to New York on their campaign plane, *Tricia*. Polls showed that this presidential contest would be close, just as it had been eight years before. Although Dick felt more confident about their chances than he had in 1960, he decided to inoculate the family against a possible defeat. Gathering Pat, Julie, Tricia, and David in his private office compartment on the plane, Dick told them that there was a possibility of an electoral "stalemate" that would throw the election into the hands of the heavily Democratic House of Representatives for a decision. "Even though it will be extremely close, we can win," he said. "In fact, I think we probably will. If we don't win we'll simply go on to other projects. . . . And we won't have the spotlight of the world on us and every movement we make." His comments were meant to console Pat in advance, because she hated to lose.

The Nixons settled into adjoining suites on the thirty-fifth floor of the Waldorf Towers on Park Avenue in New York City. This evening, like that of the 1960 election, was another wrenching all-nighter. Nixon maintained a small lead in the popular vote, but it evaporated by 10:00 p.m. An hour and a half later, Humphrey gained a lead that grew to six hundred thousand votes by midnight. But by 12:30 a.m. Nixon had won 231 electoral votes of the 270 he needed. A win in California would put him over the top. He won Ohio and Missouri.

In his memoir Nixon claimed he did not communicate with his family during the long night because he did not "want them to keep up a cheerful front for my sake." If Nixon was accurate, he was exhibiting the kind of behavior that garnered him a bad reputation as a husband. Tricia's boyfriend, Ed Cox, remembers the evening differently: "He would come out into our suite at key moments and bring us up to date. He was optimistic about the outcome." In the early morning hours when CBS anchor Walter Cronkite was discussing the voting returns in Illinois, Cronkite analogized back to 1960, because Mayor Daley of Chicago was holding back the upstate vote. Eight years before, Daley had waited to see what the downstate totals were so that he could add in whatever he needed from the Chicago "graveyard vote" of deceased voters.

Highly stressed, Pat eventually took a small nap in the middle of the night. Dick was leading in the key state of Illinois by one hundred thousand votes, but Mayor Daley was withholding voting returns in some precincts in Cook County. At 6:00 a.m., when Pat heard rumors that Daley was interfering, the traumatic memories of 1960 came flooding back. She vomited in the bathroom.

At eight-thirty in the morning, aide Dwight Chapin burst into the room and told Nixon, "You got it. You won." ABC had declared Nixon the winner. Dressed in his bathrobe, Dick walked down the hall to the suite where Pat, Julie, Tricia, David, and the Drowns were waiting. They kissed and embraced, but they were so spent that "there wasn't the elation one would normally expect," as Dick recalled. Pat and Dick spent a few minutes alone. After recounting what a difficult night she had endured, Pat said, "But Dick, are we sure of Illinois? Are we completely sure?" "Absolutely," he told her. According to the account in his memoir, Dick then held Pat while "she burst into tears of relief and joy." In a three-man race that included Governor George C. Wallace of Alabama, Nixon garnered 43.4 percent of the vote and beat Humphrey by half a million votes.

After Dick dressed, the Nixons and David Eisenhower made a triumphant appearance in the Grand Ballroom of the Waldorf Astoria. A huge throng of supporters had stayed up throughout the night in order to celebrate Nixon's comeback from the political wilderness. The president-elect told the American people that he had been deeply moved when a teenager in a small town in Ohio held up a placard saying "Bring Us Together." This, he said, would be the major objective of his administration: healing the split between the races and the generations.

Back at home at 810 Fifth Avenue, the family scrounged up a luncheon of bacon and eggs. Afterward, Richard Nixon retreated to his study, placed Richard Rogers's triumphal *Victory at Sea* on the record player, and turned up the volume. Having won the presidency, he readied himself for combat on a far grander scale. "My fellow Americans, the dark long night for America is about to end," Nixon had promised in his acceptance speech in Miami Beach. He had hyperbolically declared that he would usher in the "glory of the dawn of a new day of peace and freedom for the world." In his own mind he had big dreams, but did he have the vision and emotional resilience to realize them?

Pat told reporters, "This comeback for Dick is the story of the century—don't you think?" Pat's jubilation, however, soon faded to worry. Anxious about new vexations and challenges that might be in store for them in Washington, Pat withdrew emotionally. She needed to gather herself for the overwhelming task of being First Lady of a country at war with itself. As one of the most experienced political teams to win the White House, Pat and Dick were professionally equipped for the challenge of helping Americans rebuild their fractured sense of community, but they would also bring with them more than twenty years of wounds, scars, and strains that would test their resilience and commitment to the welfare of the nation and to each other.

Part Three

White House Dreams
and Nightmares

Ambition is a drug that turns its addicts into potential madmen.
—*Emil Cioran*

Being first lady is the hardest unpaid job in the world.
—*Pat Nixon*

Courage is not having the strength to go on; it is
going on when you don't have the strength.
—*Theodore Roosevelt*

Adjusting to the White House Fortress

*B*efore they entered the White House, the prospective First Couple celebrated the American equivalent of a dynastic wedding. On December 22, Julie married Dwight David Eisenhower III, at Marble Collegiate Church in New York City. Julie and David chose a private ceremony, with no press coverage inside the church, and a nonpolitical guest list. As the organist played the "Trumpet Voluntary," Richard Nixon walked his daughter down the aisle of the scarlet, white, and gold sanctuary, decorated with pine boughs and green balsam wreaths, with red and white poinsettias flanking the altar. When Nixon gave her away to David, Julie turned to kiss her father. Her parents became teary. The Quaker service, conducted by the Reverend

Norman Vincent Peale of the Reformed Church of America, featured Quaker plain speech—"thee" and "ye" replaced "you" for their vows—and a modern sensibility: Julie promised to love, comfort, and honor her husband, but not to obey him. Former president and Mrs. Eisenhower listened over a closed-circuit monitor to the ceremony from Walter Reed Hospital, where Ike had been hospitalized for another heart attack, and Mamie had a respiratory infection.

Richard Nixon was also sick with the flu on his daughter's wedding day. At the reception at the Plaza Hotel, he managed to dance with his wife and the bride. For the parents of the bride, the event was a keen marker of the passage of time, bringing with it not only joy but sadness. Dick, happy to see his daughter join the family of the patriarch he had served as vice president, regretted that he had not spent more time with his daughter as she grew up.

The Nixons used the presidential interregnum to prepare for new jobs, new lives, and new living quarters. When they visited Lyndon and Lady Bird Johnson in the executive mansion in mid-December, Pat was appalled by the shabbiness of the White House; the carpets and curtains were worn and the walls needed paint. She made several visits to the White House to assess what she could do to brighten up the family quarters and make the rooms "above the store" feel more like a home. When she and Dick took a weeklong vacation in Key Biscayne, they continued to work. He finished his inaugural address and chose members of his cabinet, and she made lists of decorating changes she wanted to instate.

As the inauguration drew near, President Johnson sent *Air Force One* to Florida to deliver the Nixons back to Washington. Pat and Dick showed a rare exuberance. He hugged her, then lifted her up and twirled her around. The Nixons were not aware that the young press secretary Ron Ziegler was already on board and had observed them. The Nixons may have shared such intimate moments often enough in private, but their rare, semipublic expression was an instance of uninhibited delight in what they had achieved and what awaited them. Their trials in the White House—what Harry Truman called the Great White Prison—would be manifold, more

This rare photograph of Pat with her friends is believed to have been taken at her wedding shower. *Courtesy of Whittier College Special Collections & Archives, Wardman Library, Whittier, California*

During their courtship and early marriage, Pat and Dick enjoyed hiking in the California mountains. Here, they join Dick's brother Donald and a group of friends sitting on a log in the early 1940s. *Courtesy of Whittier College Special Collections & Archives, Wardman Library, Whittier, California*

Dick's first public comment on the birth of his daughter: "She is the only boss I recognize." *Nixon Presidential Library and Museum*

By 1949, Richard Nixon wanted to run for the Senate. To garner national publicity, the young family posed for the *Saturday Evening Post.* *Nixon Presidential Library and Museum*

On July 11, 1952, after Pat Nixon heard the stunning news that Eisenhower had chosen Nixon as his running mate, she rushed to the convention hall. Swirling with adrenaline and exhaustion, the couple exuberantly took the podium together after his nomination. *Corbis BE030444*

ABOVE LEFT: Six-year-old Tricia, holding up a "Welcome Home Daddy" sign, and four-year-old Julie greet their father upon his return from the Republican convention. Nixon would often be away from home during the vice-presidential years. *Getty 149935245* LOWER LEFT: While planning the presidential campaign, Ike gives Dick a lesson in fly-fishing on July 29, 1952, at Eisenhower's rest haven in Colorado. *Nixon Presidential Library and Museum* ABOVE RIGHT: In August 1952, the Nixons publicized themselves as a wholesome American family by showcasing their love of music. Here the family, with Tricia in the foreground, sings along with Dick while he plays. *Corbis BE030439*

After the success of the Checkers speech, Pat and Dick campaigned across the country on the *Nixon Special* during the rest of the fall campaign. Pat struck a prototypical supportive pose—straightening Dick's tie at the Penn Harris Hotel on October 9, 1952. *Historical Society of Dauphin County*

LEFT: Here, Nixon, who was decidedly not domestic, donned a chef's hat as "Chef of the Week" and looked into a stocked refrigerator as if he were about to prepare a meal. *Nixon Library and Foundation* RIGHT: Pat Nixon and Mamie Eisenhower enjoy an intimate conversation at a formal event. As Mamie's health declined in the 1950s, she increasingly called upon Pat to stand in for her as First Lady at important White House and diplomatic events. *Nixon Presidential Library and Museum*

During the early 1950s, the Nixons tried to take their daughters away for brief vacations (Dick would often arrive late or be called home early). Here the vice president and his family enjoy a rare private moment at the New Jersey shore.
Nixon Presidential Library and Museum

LEFT: On their August 1953 New Jersey shore vacation, the Nixons and their dog, Checkers, pose for a family portrait on a driftwood log. *Nixon Presidential Library and Museum* RIGHT: Holding Checkers, Dick Nixon demonstrates a tenderness that contrasts with his public image as a ruthless politician. *Nixon Presidential Library and Museum*

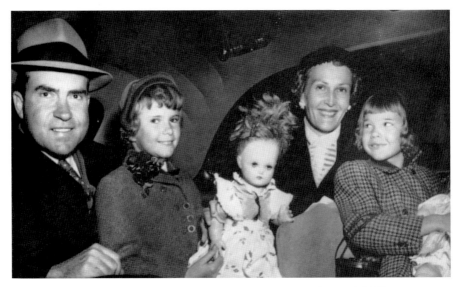

The Nixons travel in a car during a family vacation in the mid-1950s. *Nixon Presidential Library and Museum*

LEFT: *Life* magazine captured Pat Nixon shopping for groceries with Julie and Tricia. Pat Nixon was named Outstanding Homemaker of the Year in 1953, and the "nation's ideal wife" by the Homemaker's Forum in 1957. *Getty* RIGHT: Dick Nixon was passionate about football. On December 4, 1955, he and Pat watched the Washington Redskins lose to the New York Giants at Griffith Stadium. *Corbis U1299187INP*

The Nixons and the Drowns on a vacation in Nassau, 1954. Helene Drown and Pat Nixon were best friends who met in 1939 when they were teaching at Whittier High School. The Drowns were loyal political supporters—Jack Drown worked on Nixon's political campaigns—and lifelong friends who went through "good and bad times together." *Nixon Presidential Library and Museum*

Dick and his best friend Bebe Rebozo in a golf cart at Riviera Country Club, Coral Gables, Florida, September 1958. Rebozo became a permanent member of the Nixon family, accompanying them on the thirtieth wedding anniversary trip to Mexico. Julie nicknamed him Uncle "Beebes." *Photofest*

The Nixons' daughters (eight-year-old Julie is yawning) stayed up late to attend the inaugural ball with their parents after Eisenhower was sworn in for a second presidential term on January 20, 1957. *Nixon Presidential Library and Museum*

Dick and Pat watched a solo dance by a tribesman near Accra, Ghana, in March 1957, during their three-week-long official visit to Africa and then briefly to Italy. *Photofest*

LEFT: On a brief visit to Rome where they met Pope Pius XII, Pat and Dick looked relaxed waving to photographers in front of the Trevi Fountain. *Corbis 42-19075698* RIGHT: The windows in Nixon's limousine were shattered by protesters on May 13, 1958, in Caracas, Venezuela, during Pat and Dick's eighteen-day goodwill visit to South America. This incident was the most violent protest against high-ranking American officials in the Cold War era. *Nixon Presidential Library and Museum*

The Nixons returned from Caracas as national heroes. President Eisenhower, aware of an extraordinary political opportunity, made an exception to his policy that he would only meet officials at the White House. He brought Julie and Tricia to Washington's National Airport to welcome their parents home. *Corbis WL002646*

Pat at tea with women of the Fleet Street press at Ambassador John Hay Whitney's London mansion, November 1958.
Nixon Presidential Library and Museum

Dick wears a "Pat for First Lady" button as the Nixon family gathers for the 1960 Republican convention. The Republicans declared the week of October 3, 1960, "Pat Week." *Nixon Presidential Library and Museum*

LEFT: Pat talks to a boy with polio during the 1960 campaign. *Nixon Presidential Library and Museum* RIGHT: Campaigning for governor of California, Nixon greets a man in a Kennedy mask and sombrero during the Mexican Day parade on September 16, 1962. *Nixon Presidential Library and Museum*

President-elect Richard Nixon smiles as he escorts his daughter Julie to her marriage to Ike's grandson David Eisenhower on December 22, 1968, at the Marble Collegiate Church in New York City. *Nixon Foundation*

LEFT: Richard Nixon dances with Tricia to the strains of "Thank Heaven for Little Girls," in the East Room of the White House following her wedding to Edward Finch Cox on June 12, 1971. It rained for most of the day and stopped only long enough for the guests to be quickly seated, watch the ceremony, and rush back to the White House when it started raining again. *Photofest* RIGHT: Dick dances with Pat at Tricia's East Room reception. *Nixon Presidential Library and Museum*

On May 31, 1970, an undersea earthquake caused a landslide that led to an estimated twenty thousand fatalities in remote areas of the Andes Mountains in Peru. The president sent Pat on a goodwill mission there. Pat trudged through the rubble for five hours, teaching Peruvian First Lady Consuelo Gonzales de Velasco, the wife of General Juan Velasco Alvarado, how to comfort the survivors. *Nixon Presidential Library and Museum*

In January 1972, Pat made an eight-day multinational trip to Africa, centered on the inauguration of William Tolbert as the president of Liberia. Here, she is pictured wearing elements of a traditional native costume at the inauguration ceremony with President Tolbert, surrounded by tribesmen. *Nixon Foundation*

LEFT: A worldwide television audience watched as the Nixons arrived at Beijing's gray Capital Airport outside Beijing on the morning of February 21, 1972. Here Nixon greets Premier Chou and other officials on the tarmac as Pat looks on. Pat Nixon made her own bold statement by wearing a fur-lined red coat signaling her openness to the Chinese people and her attention to their culture. *Nixon Presidential Library and Museum* RIGHT: Pat Nixon found the prime minister "charming," and he appeared to reciprocate her feelings. *Nixon Presidential Library and Museum*

The Nixons standing up in a car surrounded by large crowds during their visit to the Soviet Union in May 1972. *Nixon Presidential Library and Museum*

On a cold and dreary January 20, 1973, Pat held the Milhous family Bible as Richard Nixon took the presidential oath of office for the second time. *Nixon Presidential Library and Museum*

In one of the last grand White House evenings before the Watergate crisis intensified, on March 1, 1973, the Nixons held a state dinner for Israeli prime minister Golda Meir, a key Nixon Middle East ally. *Nixon Presidential Library and Museum*

On August 8, 1974, the night he resigned the presidency, Richard Nixon embraced his daughter Julie in the family quarters of the White House. Ed Cox put his arm around his grieving wife, Tricia. Days earlier, Dick had told them, "Well I really screwed it up good, real good, didn't I?" *Nixon Library and Foundation*

Pat and Tricia, near tears, listen to Richard Nixon say good-bye to the White House staff and the cabinet in the East Room, August 9, 1974. When Pat learned that her husband was going to speak in front of television cameras, she told her husband, "Oh, Dick, you can't have it televised." Nixon disagreed. "That's the way it has to be," he said. "We owe it to our supporters. We owe it to the people." *Corbis UT0003844*

(from front to back) Presidents Ford, Bush, Reagan, and Nixon and First Ladies Betty Ford, Barbara Bush, Nancy Reagan, and Pat Nixon stand in front of Nixon's birthplace at the ceremonies for the opening of the Nixon Library and Museum, on July 19, 1990. It was the first time that four living presidents had attended a public event together and was also Pat's first official public appearance in eleven years. *Nixon Foundation*

LEFT: Dick and Pat lived in their seven-bedroom home in Saddle River, New Jersey, from 1981 until 1991—longer than they lived in any other residence. For exercise, they enjoyed taking their dogs on walks around the neighborhood. *Nixon Presidential Library and Museum* RIGHT: The Nixon family celebrated Pat and Dick's fiftieth wedding anniversary in Saddle River on June 21, 1990. Back row: David and Julie Eisenhower, the Nixons, Tricia and Ed Cox. Second row: Jennie and Alexander Eisenhower, Chris Cox. Front row: Melanie Eisenhower. *Nixon Foundation*

On June 26, 1993, a grieving Richard Nixon walked into Pat's funeral service with Reverend Billy Graham. On this occasion he could not hide his vulnerability or contain his sorrow. He would never recover from her death, passing away ten months later. *Corbis*

Tricia, Ed, and Christopher Cox lead the Nixon family into Pat's funeral service. Julie and David Eisenhower, and then their three children, Jennie, Alex, and Melanie, follow behind the Coxes. Richard Nixon, standing on the right side, covers his face with a handkerchief. *Nixon Foundation*

than they could ever have imagined. But they began in a moment of ebullience.

On a bitterly cold and dreary January 20, 1969, Dick, dressed in a black suit and silver tie, and Pat in a rosy double-breasted coat walked separately, as is tradition, from the top of the Capitol steps to take their places on the inaugural platform. Upon his arrival, the president-elect stood at attention for the traditional four ruffles (on drums) accompanied by four flourishes (by trumpet) leading into the presidential anthem "Hail to the Chief." Incoming chief of staff H. R. "Bob" Haldeman studied his boss with a sense of awe: "Expression on his face was unforgettable, this was the time!" Haldeman wrote in his published diary. "He had arrived, he was in full command . . . someone said he felt he saw rays coming down from his eyes."

Pat held the 1828 and 1873 Milhous family Bibles, their pages open to the sky, and Dick placed his left hand squarely on a passage that he had carefully chosen from the second chapter of Isaiah ("They shall beat their swords into plowshares, and their spears into pruning hooks: nation shall not lift up sword against nation, neither shall they learn war anymore"). Chief Justice Earl Warren led him through the oath of office that made him the thirty-seventh president of the United States. After President Nixon finished the oath, he guided Pat to her front-row seat and solemnly bowed low to her.

Mrs. Nixon listened to her husband, in his inaugural address, propound the ideals that represented himself and his wife at those times when they could lift their eyes from their daily conflicts and contentions and focus on the bright goals they sought to achieve. To a nation riven by the past five years of America's involvement in the Vietnam War, the new president spoke of reconciliation ("We cannot learn from one another until we stop shouting at one another—until we speak quietly enough so that our words can be heard as well as our voice") and peacemaking ("The greatest honor history can bestow is the title of peacemaker. . . . This honor now beckons Americans. . . . If we succeed, generations to come will say [that we] mastered our moment. . . . This is our summons to greatness"). To a country enduring the greatest racial upheaval since the Civil War—with divisions that

Nixon had profited from politically—he called for racial unity ("[We must] go forward together. This means black and white together as one nation, not two"). Dick echoed the call to greatness that he had put to Pat nearly thirty years before when they were courting ("It is our job to go forth together and accomplish great ends").

The president's call to bind the nation's wounds and move ahead on a new agenda met its first test a few minutes later as the Nixons rode in their bubble-topped limousine from the Capitol to the White House. Their car was pelted with stones, sticks, empty beer cans, and firecrackers by antiwar protesters, bringing to the streets of Washington the furious activism that for more than three years had divided a nation ensnared in war. Pat and Dick had faced violent demonstrators before, most ominously in a traumatic ride through Caracas, Venezuela, in 1958. But now they were on U.S. turf, in a city they knew well, and they watched in horror as the small American flags the Boy Scouts passed out were burned by protesters. A Vietcong flag was lifted high and then pulled down. When the limousine turned onto a peaceful zone on Fifteenth Street, the new president and First Lady decided to defy Secret Service orders and display their mettle to a polarized country. Dick ordered the bubble top removed. They stood and waved at as many onlookers as they could. There were 250,000 Americans lining their route.

That night Pat accompanied Dick to six crowded inaugural balls, wearing a mimosa yellow silk satin bell-shaped gown with a matching embroidered collar and cummerbund and a jacket embroidered with "byzantine scrolls of gold and silver bullion." Most presidential couples dance, if only briefly, at these celebratory events, but the Nixons did not, an omission that would reignite questions about the nature of their marriage. They stood around, talked, and joked with the crowd.

At 1:30 a.m. the new president and his wife returned to the White House for a family party. Walking through the eerily dark corridors, switching on lights, the Nixons, their daughters, and Ed Cox and David Eisenhower gathered in the West Hall, at the far west end of the family quarters on the second floor. While everyone else relaxed on comfortable skirted and patterned 1960s-style couches, Dick sat down at the piano and played "Rustle of Spring" and a song he had composed for Pat during their courtship. If the two of them acknowledged the bond between them that undoubtedly had made this day possible, it would be in the notes of that song. "It's good to be home," Pat announced—shocking the family with the realization that they would indeed be living in the White House. She suggested that they turn on all the lights in the White House and "make it cheery." At the president's command, the Executive Mansion glowed with light.

The new First Couple would face myriad challenges in the president's first term. Living in a fishbowl for the nation to scrutinize, they would have to navigate the isolation inherent in managing two impossibly demanding and infrequently intersecting jobs. They were perfectionists, and that made their challenges even more consuming. To appeal to their middle-American supporters who felt increasingly threatened by the decade's rapid social changes and discord, they sought to present themselves as a traditional couple, while endeavoring to avoid alienating the growing number of activists who were pushing at the boundaries of conventional male-female roles and other societal norms.

Their enterprise as a presidential couple was made more difficult by their unhealed wounds from more than two decades of political combat—injuries they still felt keenly. Having long believed that they had been unfairly assailed by the media, they assumed the press was bent on destroying them. Their belief was powerfully reinforced by a Republican Party that had held an inherent bias against the media as far back as 1947. Yet they would have to court both friends and adversaries if they were to succeed at garnering national support for Nixon's conduct of the war in Vietnam, his Middle East negotiations, and his dealings with the Soviet Union and ultimately with China. The president would also need backers for his plans to combat crime, subdue race conflicts, and reform welfare. Their mistrust of the press was not totally misplaced—many press people, such as Drew Pearson, felt genuine hostility toward them. Richard Nixon, having narrowly lost one presidential election and barely won a second, was eager to employ all public relations strategies at his disposal. For all his soaring inaugural words, he presided over a country furiously divided over its future course and tentative at best in its support for a leader with a history as a polarizing figure. He needed a helpmate who would soothe the country's fevers and smooth its perceptions of its president.

With a society in flux over the public roles of women, Pat Nixon, as First Lady, was confronted with an almost impossibly contradictory role. Her immediate predecessors were Jacqueline Kennedy, who had matchless glamour, and Lady Bird Johnson, who was renowned for her environmental activism. Following Jackie's White House restoration and Lady Bird Johnson's beautification project, Pat was pressured by the press to announce an overarching national project. She declined to be rushed. A battle-scarred consort entering a war presidency, she would take her time to figure out how she could meld her passions with her husband's policies. In the meantime, working from her natural strength, she would concentrate on personal diplomacy within the White House and beyond.

She began as homemaker and host, arranging for rooms on the second and third floor of the White House private quarters to be painted. Pat redid its long, dark green Center Hall in a deep yellow that she thought brought "a bit of sunlight into the hall" and helped decorate it with antique furniture from the White House storeroom.

She had plenty of help from her husband. Dick poured out waves of memos commenting on and exerting control over every aspect of their presidential life. In early February he sent a formal memo to his wife recommending that she and Tricia engage a professional decorator to oversee the refurbishing project. Pat chose Sarah Jackson Doyle, whom she had used before in selecting antiques for the Fifth Avenue apartment. Doyle's assignment at the White House was huge: In addition to the family quarters, she had to update the Oval Office and Nixon's private hideaway in the Executive Office Building, where he retreated to take naps and write memos and speeches on yellow legal pads. In the Oval Office, Doyle and the First Lady added a rich blue carpet with a gold presidential seal at the center and reupholstered the sofas and chairs in yellowish gold fabric that, with the blue carpet, suggested the state colors of California.

Pat prepared separate bedrooms for herself and her husband. She told head usher J. B. West, "*Nobody* could sleep with Dick. . . . He wakes up during the night, switches on the light, speaks into his tape recorder or takes notes—it's impossible." Mrs. Nixon took over Lady Bird Johnson's dark bedroom on the southwest side of the White House. To the east of Pat's room, off the Center Hall, she set up Dick's bedroom, which had been Lyndon Johnson's. Pat removed LBJ's grand canopied four-poster bed and brought in a more modest bed from White House storage that had been used by Truman and Eisenhower. When Dick found out, he quipped, "Politics had literally bred strange bedfellows." The Nixons removed from the bedroom Johnson's three-television console, his two wire-service printers, and his taping system.

The Nixons took great pleasure in using the formal rooms on the second floor for private dinners and official entertaining. On the Truman Balcony, the Nixons enjoyed candlelit dinners and a view looking south to the Washington Monument, and the memorials to Lincoln and Jefferson. Before formal dinners on the first floor, the Nixons greeted heads of state in the elegant Oval Room, furnished with Federal American and French furniture and graced by a fireplace with a Federal mantel and a dentil molding.

Whenever they were in Washington, Julie and David stayed in the Queens' Bedroom, where five British and European queens had slept. Twenty-three-year-old Tricia, a graduate of Finch College, chose Luci Johnson's former East Bedroom on the second floor. Tricia shared her mother's love of privacy, and initially she coped with the stress of living in the heavily staffed White House by shutting herself in her room, lying on her bed, and reading. According to Nixon staffer John Ehrlichman, neither of her parents could lure her out. On orders from Nixon, who did not think he could accomplish anything constructive by confronting his daughter directly, Ehrlichman invited Tricia to lunch in the White House mess to encourage her to participate more fully in White House life. Tricia, dressed "all in pink-and-white angora," had a sandwich with him. When Ehrlichman began to discuss how she spent her time, Tricia told him that the president's staff members "were not about to run her life . . . what she did and when, she would decide." She stood up abruptly and returned to her room, leaving him to eat the rest of his lunch by himself. She was her mother's daughter.

Pat Nixon soon discovered how easily every move she made could be cast in partisan political terms. Lady Bird Johnson had named the White House flower garden the "Jacqueline Kennedy Garden," in honor of her predecessor, but Pat, who loved gardening and deplored self-promotion, changed the name to the "First Lady's Garden." Tampering with the Kennedys' fingerprints in the Executive Mansion was a far more incendiary decision than removing LBJ's ubiquitous telephones, wires, and television sets. The Committee for the Preservation of the White House, under Lady Bird Johnson, had decided in 1968 to replace a mantelpiece the Trumans had placed in the First Lady's bedroom with a marble mantelpiece designed by White House architect Benjamin Latrobe. The installation took place during Pat's tenure in early 1969. The Trumans' original mantelpiece bore two plaques, one indicating that Lincoln had slept there and the other installed and chosen by Mrs. Kennedy: "In this room lived John Fitzgerald Kennedy and his wife Jacqueline during the two years, ten months, and two days he was President of the United States." Although Pat had renamed the garden, she had nothing to do with the changing mantels, but journalists accused her of obliterating the Kennedys from the White House. One Washington newspaper headlined an article ERASING WHITE HOUSE HISTORY. According to her correspondence secretary Gwen King, "It really upset Mrs. Nixon at the time. . . . Things like that always upset her because she tried very hard. She was careful to 'steer the right course' as she would say." Such early criticism reinforced Pat's fear of making a mistake that would harm her husband.

While Pat was undertaking a relentless schedule of social entertaining, Dick reorganized his office to funnel information more efficiently in and out. The new system left him added time to strategize about foreign and domestic policy and reduced interruptions from officials who felt they deserved his time, but it also limited the variety of people and opinions he encountered. Nixon created a fortress within the White House, marshaled by chief of staff Bob Haldeman, who fostered a bunkerlike mentality with the power Nixon had given him. Staff members called Haldeman and his assistant Ehrlichman, the chief aide for domestic affairs, "The Berlin Wall," because of their German family names and their ruthless manner of restricting access to the president. Haldeman was said to have "a gaze that would freeze Medusa" and the bearing of a "Prussian guard." He savored his role as what he called "the president's son-of-a-bitch." Critics derided both his arrogance and his fierce attention to detail.

Nixon's ascent to power led him to make big plans to advance world peace through winding down the Vietnam War and fostering more open relations with the Soviet Union and China, but it also widened and deepened his vindictive streak, the result of a lifetime of perceiving himself as an aggrieved outsider. Haldeman later claimed that he sought not only to protect the president from anyone who might waste his time, but also to safeguard Nixon from his darker side. The president gave Haldeman orders to fire staff members for small infractions, to cut off members of the press (by barring them from the presidential plane and restricting their access to stories), or to punish legislators for disagreeing with him ("Put a 24-hour surveillance on that bastard").

Haldeman often ignored Nixon's impulsive orders, assuming his boss would forget about them. Speechwriter Raymond K. Price remembered Nixon as being possessed by "a sense of and a desire for accomplishment in a historic sense, yet a deep-seated insecurity and fear of failure," a combination that created strong internal conflict and anxiety that he coped with by "strik[ing] out at others." According to Dwight Chapin and Bob Haldeman, Nixon did not apologize for blowing up at them over things like "schedule deviations, people allowed to get too close, [and] flaws in the programming." Chapin described Nixon as "fair and considerate," while Haldeman told biographer Jonathan Aitken that the president tended to ignore insiders and failed to thank them for their efforts. Haldeman did, however, find that Nixon had "a marvelous sense of humor" and "had a lot of fun with him."

*   *   *

With so many years of public service, Pat and Dick Nixon were as prepared to be president and First Lady as any modern presidential couple up to that time—yet no pair is ever entirely primed to be the presidential couple. All long-term marital relationships are multifaceted, but as they adapt to the new roles a presidential couple's relationship must stretch out to incorporate many new layers. There were essentially three different marriages in the Nixon White House. The first, their private union, was mostly hidden from view—leaving lots of room for negative speculation; the barricade the president erected around his relationship with his wife was as formidable as the fortress around his office. The second Nixon marriage was between two partners in the same joint professional venture, one that was enacted on the first floor of the White House and in its two wings. There, the Nixon marriage branched out to include the president's staff in the West Wing and the First Lady's team in the East Wing, who had to integrate and adjudicate their inevitably competing and sometimes contradictory ambitions and agendas. The third Nixon marriage was the public relations version of their union. It was shored up by the president and First Lady's personal staffers and their press offices.

The Nixons' White House partnership was defined by their characters and their personal histories. Throughout Pat's difficult early years, people usually found her likable, if inscrutable. As a young child and an adolescent, Dick was wounded by his perception of himself as unpopular, which left him persistently uncertain about where he stood in the regard of others. Haldeman thought that Nixon tried to compensate for his insecurity "by imposing a rigid self-discipline to shield him from mistakes. That self-discipline was so tight it was *unnatural.*" Although Nixon could be wonderfully personable with larger groups, Haldeman found that he was often "stiff, artificial, sometimes even embarrassing with individuals." Pat had the opposite problem. In front of large groups her strict self-discipline, born of an innate caution against saying or doing something that would harm her husband, sometimes led her to appear forced, tense, and shy. In a one-to-one encounter she was usually spontaneous, warm, and emotionally present.

Although they shared a genuine sensitivity to the struggles of work-ing and lower-class families, Dick often compensated for his early sufferings by associating with powerful people. Pat possessed a more natural affinity for the common person. Penny Adams, the White House radio and television coordinator and later Mrs. Nixon's deputy press secretary, called Pat "a great equalizer" who expressed "interest in everyone she met and found something special in each." According to veteran White House reporter Helen Thomas, Pat "was the warmest First Lady I covered and the one who loved people most." She "never forgets her days of poverty," said Thomas, and "goes that extra mile to shake a hand and greet a stranger."

Pat had long been irritated, as First Lady expert Carl Sferrazza Anthony pointed out, that access to the White House and to the First Couple was reserved mainly for the "wealthy and famous." At a recep-tion for a thousand campaign volunteers in the East Room in their first days in the White House, Pat mounted the podium and, casting aside her usually cautious persona, declared, "We're going to invite our *friends* here and *not* all the big shots." Nixon, demonstrably un-comfortable, felt she had made a gaffe. He tried to cover for her by saying, "Of course, *all* our friends are big shots."

The Nixons' differing attitudes toward people emerged around the Sunday church services they instituted in the White House. The wor-ship services were held in the East Room, which was wired to accom-modate an electric organ and altered to allow a raised platform for a choir. The Sunday services appealed to the Nixons' conservative sup-porters, provided an opportunity for congressional and local Washing-ton families to come to the White House, and allowed the Nixons to avoid all the commotion and the complex security and logistical prob-lems involved in attending a church. Yet Pat and Dick did not always see eye to eye about the composition of the congregation. In Septem-ber 1969, Haldeman wrote a memo to Rose Mary Woods, copying Pat's social secretary Lucy Winchester, indicating that the president "feels that we have too many non-VIPs" at the Sunday worship service. The previous Sunday the president had determined that about 40 percent of the guests were not people important to his politics and policies. He wanted the balance to be "80% VIP and no more than 20% non-VIP." Pat could not have been pleased when Lucy told her about the memo, but she went along with the decision.

According to Bob Haldeman, Richard Nixon, in contrast to his modest wife, adored "pomp and ceremony." On the evening of January 31, 1969, at a white-tie East Room reception for foreign diplomats, a color guard preceded the president and First Lady down the stairs from the family quarters, to the sound of trumpets. Haldeman observed that the president was "trying not to look as tickled as he obviously was . . . [he] really ate it up. . . . He loves being President."

Nixon was dismayed by the pedestrian uniforms of the White House police; he wanted to bring to the White House a touch of the splendor he had witnessed in European capitals. He asked John Ehrlichman to design new uniforms. Mrs. Nixon hated the pompous new "Student Prince" outfits with "white tunic, gold braid, and pillbox hats." The White House police wore them for only a week. The press lambasted them mercilessly until the president had them revert to what they previously wore. For the tour guides, Pat ordered simple uniforms—gray trousers and blue blazers. Recalling how excited she was touring the White House in the summer of 1933 (when she was working in New York at a tuberculosis hospital) and, a few months later, mingling with Franklin and Eleanor Roosevelt at a hospital conference dinner, Pat wanted to share the White House with as many regular folks and civic groups as it could accommodate.

Her own working quarters were unpretentious and comfortable. "When I get into my own room," she told a *Life* magazine reporter, "I feel at home and that's where I really live." She spent much of her private time working at her desk in a dressing room adjoining her bedroom in the southwest corner of the second floor, a space drenched with light from two corner windows. It looked southwest with a view of the White House rose garden. Jackie Kennedy had given the room its ambience by installing French wallpaper featuring images of flowers and birds.

Pat's workspace was a pool of light in a house that otherwise felt to her dark and defended. "We are shut up in this house," Pat told Helen

Thomas. Nixon special counsel Charles Colson said "it was like living in a bunker. . . . You'd look out on the streets and you'd see thousands of people protesting. You were literally afraid for your life." Pat's correspondence served as her link outside the fortress, diminishing somewhat her sense of isolation. She liked to read letters from voters, summarizing the contents for her husband. On average, Pat spent four to five hours each day supervising her correspondence staff, editing and signing the responses they had composed, and selecting letters to answer personally. "When a letter from the White House arrives in a small town," Pat said, "it's shown to all the neighbors, and often published in the local paper. It's very important to the people who receive it."

Like Eleanor Roosevelt, and other First Ladies dating back to Lou Hoover, Pat Nixon took action on behalf of certain of her correspondents: arranging for psychiatric treatment for a suicidal drug addict, assisting an unemployed shoplifter who needed a job, and arranging for a young girl to have successful emergency heart surgery her parents could neither afford nor navigate. (Pat and her staff called the National Institutes of Health and the American Heart Association and asked them to intervene.) One correspondent informed the First Lady that a little girl had been pushed off her bicycle and beaten up as a "nigger lover" after she gave away her Christmas money to buy a present for a black child. Pat Nixon wrote the child a letter commending her and made sure it was published in newspapers where the girl lived.

Pat and Dick had difficulty adjusting, Nixon wrote in his memoir, to "the paradoxical combination of loss of privacy and sense of isolation" of the White House. They were surrounded by staff members, Secret Service agents, medical personnel, communication specialists, transportation assistants, ubiquitous photographers, and reporters. During the vice-presidential years, the Nixons had returned home to a residential neighborhood after their workday was done; they could do their own shopping and go out with friends for dinner without press coverage. Now that they were living in the White House, and did not enjoy the same freedoms, everything they said and did could quickly become news, and be misinterpreted.

The president's 1969 daily diary reveals how frequently the Nixons escaped the capital. During his first full year in office President Nixon spent only six months in the White House. Mrs. Nixon was in residence for about seven and a half months. In addition to Camp David, Dick and Pat established two other retreats, one near Bebe Rebozo in Key Biscayne, and another in San Clemente, California (soon to be christened La Casa Pacifica, "the Peaceful House"). Pat supervised the furnishing and decorating at both sites. As the pressures of their professional marriage and their hectic schedule of social entertaining in the First Mansion impinged upon the marriage, their sixteen visits to their southern, western, and northern retreats were essential for restoring their partnership. The First Lady accompanied the president on five of eight vacations he took in Key Biscayne, and for eight weekends out of the twenty-one quick working trips he made to Camp David. The Nixons spent a month and a half in San Clemente in 1969. They made three separate visits there, including a four-week working vacation at the end of August. The president and his wife also spent more than a month out of the White House on domestic and foreign presidential trips.

For all the demands and distractions of his new office, the president made one day of the year special. In early March 1969, he enlisted Lucy Winchester, Pat's press secretary, to help plan a surprise fifty-seventh-birthday party for Pat on the eve of St. Patrick's Day. Winchester was struck by how excited he was, and by how thoroughly he had visualized the event. He was very specific about what he wanted: Winchester was to bring Pat to the north end of the East Room, where she would be greeted by a band playing "Happy Birthday." He was so caught up in depicting his plans to Winchester, he sang the entire "Happy Birthday." On the night of March 16, Pat entered the East Room to say a brief hello to what she had been led to believe was an evening for male friends and colleagues. Instead, many of her friends were lined up to greet her. Dick had arranged for a celebratory dinner to be served at round tables in the State Dining Room. The Strolling Strings—musicians who would go throughout the room and who had first been employed by the Eisenhowers—serenaded the First Lady during dessert. After the birthday cake was brought in, Pat interrupted the president's toast. She wanted to blow out her candles and make a wish. What might she have wished for? Peace, perhaps—in Vietnam, across her country, and outside the White House, where the Nixons awoke and went to bed every day to the chants of antiwar protesters, who sometimes were so loud the president had trouble falling asleep.

Staff members saw the Nixons' marriage as a blend of playfulness, affection, and conflict. The First Lady's East Wing staff director, Connie Stuart, thought that the Nixons were "delightful as a couple. I thought they were pretty funny." They nagged each other, and joked about it. In January, as a fifty-sixth-birthday present, the press gave the president a six-month-old Irish setter, whom he named King Timahoe. Nixon let the dog lie on the brocade sofa in the family quarters. Seeing dog hairs on the fine furniture sent a shiver up Pat's spine. The furniture was in peril not only from the dog but from the president: When he forgot to use a towel to protect his silk ottoman from his shoes, he heard about it from Pat.

Dick was punctual to a fault. When she was late, he was annoyed. Once at the Western White House, Nixon had to wait for Pat and Tricia at the helipad. Secret Service agents radioed that "President Nixon . . . is waiting at the ramp and looking at his watch." Pat heard their appeal, but took her time. The president tapped his foot.

Finding official dinners tedious, on their own the Nixons ate quickly. Dick allotted five minutes for lunch (often pineapple and cottage cheese brought in from Knudsen's Dairy in Los Angeles) while Pat and Tricia frequently shared a simple sandwich and salad for lunch. When a crisis or an official event did not intervene, Pat, Dick, and Tricia dined in the elegant Family Residence Dining Room, which Mrs. Kennedy had decorated with antique wallpaper murals of colorful battle scenes from the Revolutionary War. They rarely spent more than half an hour eating. Nixon, conscious that a president must "maintain a certain figure" of dignity, always wore a jacket and tie at dinner. Pat wanted the evening meal to be a relaxing family time; she made conversation that took the president's mind off politics and policy. After eating, Nixon liked to work in his Executive Office Building hideaway or in front of a fire in the Lincoln Sitting Room, where Pat and Tricia sometimes joined him.

When former president Dwight Eisenhower spoke to the delegates at the 1968 Republican Convention by a televised feed from Walter Reed Army Hospital, where he was being treated for heart problems, he gave Richard Nixon his wholehearted endorsement as the Republican presidential candidate. The next day he suffered a heart attack. By late March 1969, he had been diagnosed with congestive heart failure, and he resigned himself to dying. His last words on March 28 were "I want to go. God take me." Just after noon Nixon was meeting in the Oval Office with Defense Secretary Melvin Laird when Walter Tkach, the White House physician, and Bob Haldeman came to tell Nixon that Eisenhower was dead. "I knew that he had been sinking fast, but the news hit me so hard that I could not speak," Nixon wrote in his memoir. Nixon turned away from his staff and walked to the large Oval Office windows overlooking the White House gardens. He started to cry, retreating to his private bathroom to sob. Then he called Pat to tell her. Pat, Dick, and Tricia quickly dressed in black and made their way to the hospital to pay their respects.

At the funeral at the National Cathedral, Nixon eulogized the president he had served. In his testament to Eisenhower's accomplishments he reiterated his goals for his own presidency: "He restored calm to a divided nation. He gave Americans a new measure of self-respect. He invested his office with dignity and respect and trust. He made Americans proud of their President, proud of their country, proud of themselves."

In limning Eisenhower's virtues, he inadvertently pointed to what would prove to be his own flaws, traits that would lead to his tragedy. "Oh, he could be aroused by a cause, but he could not hate a person," Nixon told the nation. "He could disagree strongly, even passionately, but never personally. When people disagreed with him, he never thought of them as enemies. He simply thought: 'Well, they don't agree with me.'" When it came to an attitude toward one's enemies,

Nixon would model himself after Eisenhower mainly on the last day of his presidency, when he spoke wisely, but belatedly, about the dangers of hating those who hate you.

The Nixons accompanied the late president's body to Abilene, Kansas, where he was interred in a small chapel on the grounds of his presidential library. Pat and Dick mourned Eisenhower as an assured and brilliant mentor, a demanding boss, an enthusiastic and occasionally ambivalent supporter whose attentions warmed them and whose detachment unnerved them, and finally as a friend and family member.

If the legacy of Dwight Eisenhower's paternal authority shadowed the Nixon White House, so did the ghost of John F. Kennedy. Pat and Dick contended with Americans' worship of the late president and his wife, and their reverence for the Kennedys' grace and charm. The Kennedys had set a standard of excellence in White House social events that the Nixons hoped to match or, in the president's case, surpass. On April 29, 1969, Pat and Dick, in a memorable White House evening, threw a seventieth-birthday party for jazz icon Duke Ellington, to whom Nixon gave the Presidential Medal of Freedom, America's highest civilian honor. Among the guests were musical legends Richard Rodgers, Cab Calloway, and Mahalia Jackson. After some of America's greatest jazz musicians performed Ellington's most celebrated music, Dick played "Happy Birthday" at the piano, as the jazz musicians jived alongside him. At the end of the program Ellington sat at the piano. After a moment of intriguing silence, Ellington announced that he would like to improvise a melody. "I shall pick a name—gentle, graceful—something like Patricia," he declared. He created a tune that was "lyrical, delicate, beautiful—like Pat," as Dick called it in his memoir.

Pat instituted her own brand of social entertaining called "Evenings at the White House," a series of performances by artists in varied American traditions—from opera to comedy to bluegrass and Broadway musicals. In December 1969, comedian Bob Hope inaugurated the series. That winter the evening event featured Red Skelton cracking jokes, and on February 22, the cast of the musical *1776* performed a complete Broadway show—another first—at the White House. Three days earlier, the Nixons had held a dinner for Andrew Wyeth, the American regionalist painter whose work was, according to *Christian Science Monitor* reporter Christopher Andreae, immensely popular with the "silent majority" of Americans to whom Nixon had appealed for support over the war in Vietnam. Wyeth arranged for his close friend pianist Rudolf Serkin to play selections from Chopin and Beethoven. Toasting Wyeth, the president and First Lady noted that the evening celebrated "two historical firsts," a world-class painter being honored with a White House dinner and an exhibition of a major American artist's paintings in the First Mansion.

On February 24, entertainer Peggy Lee sang in the East Room after a State Dinner for President and Mrs. Pompidou. Miss Lee told the press that she was asked to perform because she was "a non-political, non-prejudiced person." Washington's East Wing reporters concluded "that some of Peggy's numbers had been embarrassingly sexy, and that she had broken the sacred rules of protocol by kissing President Nixon after her 45-minute act." She denied kissing the president, but told a reporter, "If I'm sexy, I can't help it." However sexy she was, her performance did not win the plaudits from White House observers that Kennedy's cast of characters had.

By mid-January 1970 the Nixons had entertained more than forty-five thousand people in their first year in the White House, besting by seventeen thousand the number of people the Johnsons had entertained in 1968. There were 116 receptions and 64 official and state dinners. *U.S. News & World Report* called the Nixons' first year of entertaining "unprecedented."

In August 1969, half a million people attended the Woodstock Music Festival (billed as "An Aquarian Exposition: 3 Days of Peace and Music") in Bethel, New York. This festival, a high point of the 1960s countercultural movement, offered sex, drugs, rock 'n' roll, and plenty of mud. In this context, the Nixons' social events seemed out of another era. Perhaps sensing that President Nixon was trying too hard to make an impression and present a solid if stolid version of American cultural life, reporters and Washington's opinion-makers failed to acknowledge how hard the Nixons worked to offer creative events. Only *U.S. News & World Report* called Pat Nixon's soirees "elegant and gay."

In early March 1970, the *New York Times Magazine* panned the Nixons' parties and declared that the couple had ruined Washington social life. In an article titled "Washington Society Isn't Exactly Swinging," reporter Thomas Meehan recalled that in the Kennedy years the parties often "swung" until four in the morning. "Nowadays," he opined, "the social scene in Washington is dominated by a single fact: Richard Nixon does not like parties. Nor, significantly does his wife. Parties are said to make them nervous and uncomfortable." Condescendingly, he declared that the Nixons preferred to bowl or watch TV. Meehan criticized Mrs. Nixon for not having interest in being "much of a hostess" and quoted a Washington doyenne's opinion that the First Lady was "as bland as they come." A Washington society writer called the city "Dullsville-on-the-Potomac." The so-called Beautiful People—fun, sophisticated, and creative types—had left Washington and were replaced by Nixon's corporate and legal supporters, whom Jack Anderson dubbed the "Square Society." There was some truth to the criticisms, but they were also unkind. Pat and Dick had been typecast as inelegant 1950s squares. An intense wartime president and his cautious wife would find little tolerance within the capital for their presentation of the best possible version of their vision of America.

"We Had Held Our Own"

Richard Nixon was eager for Pat to begin her program of encouraging volunteerism as soon as possible. In early February 1969, he wrote a memo to John Ehrlichman, asking for a game plan within a week: "This is a time the program for volunteer action could well be launched or at least some substantial progress made on it."

Mrs. Nixon, however, was not eager to inaugurate a national agenda of her own; she was still organizing her East Wing staff, making the private quarters of the White House more livable, and scheduling events to welcome the congressional and diplomatic communities to the White House during the early days of the new administration. She was happy to defer the kind of solo activities outside Washington that would place her in the spotlight, especially at such a contentious time, when every mistake she made would be magnified and pounced upon.

She had received little criticism so far. Dick monitored her press coverage, and noticing that the *Houston Chronicle* had declared, "Mrs. Nixon is off to an excellent start," he passed the article along to Ehrlichman, with instructions to disseminate it to reporters.

On the recommendation of Herbert Klein, the head of White House communications, Pat hired Gerry van der Heuvel, a lively, charming, and popular former reporter for the Washington bureau of the *New York Daily News*, as her press secretary. For social secretary, she chose Lucy Winchester, a powerhouse Nixon fund-raiser who had been based in Lexington, Kentucky. Pat Nixon did not like working with a large staff. She wanted to deal as directly as possible with individuals and organizations, as she had in the vice-presidential years, and she expected, wrongly, that such a model could work in the larger sphere of the White House. Although the president's staff was set up as a hierarchy under Bob Haldeman, the First Lady's staff consisted of two equals (Winchester and van der Heuvel) reporting separately to their boss. In what Connie Stuart, who later served as Mrs. Nixon's chief of staff, called an "age-old tug-of-war," the two secretaries fought. "The social secretary wants to do everything nicely," Stuart explained, whereas "the press secretary wants to make sure the press can cover the event and that makes it tacky." As a result, Pat Nixon had to spend time resolving disputes between her two secretaries, women she didn't know well and had not worked with before.

The Nixon marriage absorbed the friction from within the East Wing as well as the stresses inherent in the typically tense relationship (in most administrations) between East Wing and West Wing staff members. The president and his staffers sought to maintain control over parts of the First Lady's domain in the Executive Mansion, and her staff fought back. Those staff conflicts reverberated into tensions between the president and First Lady. Managing complicated travel schedules and speaking commitments and clearing them with each other were bound to generate conflicts. Pat would often be irritated at Dick for pushing her people around, and he would often be irritated at her because her people were not doing it the way he thought they should.

The president and Haldeman carefully monitored White House events and entertainment at state dinners to make them opulent spectacles, showcasing Pat and Dick's conservative values, patriotism, and sociability. Nixon "absolutely hated the large formal dinners that he constantly had to host," Haldeman wrote in his memoir. "Nevertheless he would throw himself headlong into the preparations, driving everyone, from the chef to the household staff, to his own wife, crazy." He pored over minute details of dinner menus and evening programs. Winchester received innumerable memos from Haldeman with the president's critiques and directives. Service was "way too slow" at the Governors' Dinner on July 16; the waiters needed to start clearing away dishes as soon as the president and First Lady finished a course.

In September, Haldeman informed Winchester that henceforth the president wanted a person assigned to him, the First Lady, the guest of honor, and the guest's wife or husband "to make sure that none of the principals get trapped by one guest for an undue length of time." "Key people we want to give attention to" should have an opportunity to talk with the hosts and main guests. State dinners were also opportunities to settle scores. Before the Medal of Freedom dinner in April 1970, the president told Haldeman to place *Washington Post* publisher Katharine Graham, not an admirer of the Nixon administration, "as far from our table as possible and preferably at one where there is no VIP whatever." Even the White House church services were not safe from the president's meddling. Haldeman wrote Winchester a pointed memo ("I know it is none of my business") asking her to consider rebalancing the flower and mantel arrangements. They were based on an "east-west balance" rather than the "north-south balance" the president considered appropriate.

Pat Nixon had yet to establish and feel comfortable with her own power as First Lady. By August 1969 Nixon realized the "PN thing is a real problem," as Haldeman wrote in his notes. East Wing reporters were complaining that the First Lady's press office was disorganized. Reporters griped that Gerry van der Heuvel was late with press releases, played favorites with journalists, and was chronically unavailable on deadline. Worst of all, a *Newsweek* article in late May panned the "badly organized" East Wing operation for a "closed-door policy" that was keeping reporters from "humanizing" the Nixons: The article quoted a reporter saying, "They are shutting the door in our faces." Van der Heuvel was accused of being "so protective of the Nixons that she is choking off legitimate information."

In mid-September, the Nixons went to New York, where the president spoke at the United Nations about the Vietnam War. On the flight back to Washington, Bob Haldeman and Pat Nixon discussed her East Wing office. Haldeman noted in his diary that the First Lady was "determined to run her own operation," but that "she will *have* to have better staff to do it right." He was encouraged by the First Lady's "increased interest" in making changes. Pat Nixon reassigned her controversial press secretary, sending her to be the special assistant to the U.S. ambassador in Rome. Her replacement would not be so thoroughly under Pat's control.

Dick frequently used Haldeman as a messenger and enforcer around Pat's professional duties, in a dynamic many long-term couples employ: They find a go-between. At first, adding a third party can help dispel tensions, but over the long term communicating through an additional person usually increases stress and complicates a marriage. In the first nine months of 1969, according to Connie Stuart, who became the First Lady's chief of staff, "Mrs. Nixon would initiate [discussion of issues], the president would absorb [it], he'd go down and discuss it with Bob, and sometimes he'd say, 'Bob, you call Mrs. Nixon and work it out.'" Not surprisingly, the First Lady and Haldeman continued to mistrust each other. She was put off by his arrogant manner and his desire to isolate the president. Haldeman disdained her preference for tackling her pile of correspondence over taking a more active public role in supporting the president's programs. He dismissively called her Thelma (her given first name) behind her back. The president himself was also frustrated by his wife's devotion to her correspondence and dispatched domestic advisor John Ehrlichman to talk to her about that. A wary Pat agreed to a late-afternoon meeting in the Oval Room. When he revealed his agenda, Pat "bristled." According to Ehrlichman, she "icily" explained that members of the American public merited a personal response from her, or at least a personal signature. When he told her that her friends worried she was too thin, implying that she was under stress and not coping well, and that she needed someone to talk to, Pat did not bother to reply. The president's aide was encroaching on personal territory. Their talk was over.

The triangle among the Nixons and Bob Haldeman became increasingly dysfunctional. The president's chief of staff served more as an irritant than as a buffer in the Nixons' overstretched marriage. The three of them eventually agreed that Pat's East Wing staff needed to synchronize its activities with the president's team and that Mrs. Nixon needed to hire an East Wing chief of staff. Ehrlichman asked his assistant Charles Stuart to make a plan for reorganizing the East Wing. Pat hired as her staff director *and* press secretary his wife, Connie Stuart, a vivacious thirty-one-year-old with four years of public relations experience. As a new First Lady, Pat did not yet have enough confidence to reject a candidate whose husband worked so closely with Ehrlichman, whom Pat intensely disliked.

In concert with Nixon's reorganization and expansion of the White House staff, the East Wing staff was enlarged to thirty employees, complete with a flowchart showing the chain of command. Haldeman and Ehrlichman were officially positioned under Mrs. Nixon in the East Wing hierarchy. Connie Stuart became the "official spokesman for the First Family," became the overall supervisor of the East Wing staff, and monitored their cooperation with their counterparts in the West Wing. The First Lady's appointments staffers, who were responsible for scheduling and calendars, coordinated with Dwight Chapin in the West Wing appointments office. Stuart and her assistant Helen Smith coordinated with Dick's press secretary Ron Zeigler and his assistants. Lucy Winchester reported to Stuart, but worked for the president when he held stag events.

The new structure was more effective, but it created its own tensions. Lucy Winchester was accustomed to reporting directly to Mrs. Nixon, and Winchester, according to Stuart, initially resented having to go to her. According to Lucy Winchester, Pat "rolled her eyes at me when Connie, whom she had not initially chosen, was foisted on her." Pat held in her negative feelings and then expressed her displeasure by procrastinating about following through on the West Wing's agenda for her (going on the road to tout a national agenda like volunteerism) and by obstructing their attempts to streamline her East Wing operation. At times she avoided discussing staff problems with the president when she should have tackled them head-on, but at other times her noncommunication was productive. "If you ignore some of the petty tensions, they become less," Stuart explained.

On Stuart's third day on the job, the president called her into the Oval Office. "What have I done wrong?" she wondered. In a thirty-minute meeting, Nixon stressed what a remarkable woman his wife was and asked Stuart to study everything that had been written about her new boss so that she understood the First Lady well enough to represent her best interests. His wife deserved excellent press and staff support. "She's important, she matters. She matters to me. She matters professionally, and you work hard, young lady," he told her. Stuart soon disarmed sixty-five disgruntled East Wing reporters by meeting individually with each of them. To address complaints about lack of access, Stuart held two press conferences a week, on Mondays and Thursdays.

After Stuart was integrated into the Nixons' communication channel, the dynamic between husband and wife and between East and West wings was considerably calmer. When an issue arose, Pat talked to Dick, who talked to Bob; Bob talked to Connie, and then Connie talked to Mrs. Nixon. Stuart and Haldeman worked out a functional professional relationship, resolving a problem "before it became a husband and wife issue."

The president and the West Wing still did not totally trust Stuart, however. Within a month of taking over, Stuart was frustrated by the "volumes of memos and phone calls" she was getting from Haldeman and his staff regarding "bad press" about the sociability of the White House. Advising Haldeman to "tell the President not to worry," Stuart launched a press campaign highlighting the Nixons' diverse entertainment programs and that they had entertained four times as often as the Kennedys and twice as often as the Johnsons.

The criticism from East Wing reporters was particularly disappointing to Pat and her staffers, as well as to the West Wing, because she and the president had made an effort to court the media within a month of taking office. On February 18, 1969, Pat surprised the East Wing press corps (all of whom were women) by inviting them to a breakfast with the wives of cabinet members. She even held an impromptu press conference with them—something no First Lady had done since Eleanor Roosevelt. The president stopped by to announce that the breakfasting reporters were the first guests to dine in the Nixons' State Dining Room. Although Pat would not be accompanying him on a fast-paced, weeklong trip to meet with top European leaders, the president said that his wife was his "greatest asset." Their breakfast, the president asserted to the roomful of women reporters, was an indication of the importance he would place on women during his administration.

In February 1969 Nixon announced a program he called the New Federalism, which focused on returning to the states some of the power that the Democrats had removed from them and transferred to the big-government programs of the Great Society. In his inaugural address Nixon had asserted that the country's greatest current need was "to reach beyond government and to enlist the legions of the concerned and the committed . . . we need the energies of our people— enlisted not only in grand enterprises, but most importantly in those small splendid efforts that make headlines in the neighborhood newspaper instead of the national journal." He concluded, "Until he has been part of a cause larger than himself, no man is truly whole."

Speaking to *U.S. News & World Report*, Pat soon emphasized her commitment to her husband's goals: "The Government has taken over too much already. I believe, as my husband does, that the responsibility must begin flowing back to the States and to the local level, to the people." At the February press conference Pat responded to the urgings of Nixon and Ehrlichman that she adopt a public cause, announcing she would focus on volunteerism and initiate a "national recruitment program" to engage thousands of volunteers to become involved in organized efforts to enhance the quality of life for all citizens.

For Pat, a key part of the American heritage was the story of early settlers banding together to help build each other's homes, churches, and schools. She believed that America could benefit from a revival of that pioneer spirit. As her husband had wished, Pat's program allowed her to complement Dick's domestic goals: It highlighted the administration's compassion for the disabled and for elderly citizens, and its interest in helping youth, while showcasing an emphasis on individual rather than government enterprise. Pat's volunteerism agenda focused especially on engaging women who did not work outside the home—as was still the case for a majority of American women—and yet wanted to contribute to their communities.

However much she would like to have stayed close to home even as she promoted volunteerism, Pat had no choice but to acknowledge that Lady Bird Johnson's activism and her travel on behalf of her husband's programs had expanded the role of the First Lady and made touring the country an expected part of her job. Some reporters carped that it was not until mid-June that Pat, with Julie in tow, undertook her first domestic foray as First Lady. She visited ten "Vest Pockets of Volunteerism" in Portland, Oregon, and Los Angeles. Accompanied by forty members of the press, and often heckled by demonstrators, the First Lady and her daughter toured the Foundation for the Junior Blind and a social service center in Los Angeles; in Portland they visited an adult literacy center, the Green Fingers Agricultural community project in the inner city, a black arts community, and a Braille Center.

Washington Post reporter Marie Smith cited other journalists' increasing appreciation for Mrs. Nixon's trip because it shifted the focus from "violence and destruction" in America to "good and constructive things." Nan Robertson of the *New York Times* thought Pat was "warm as always, but seemed dutiful and lacking in spirit until the very end," when she began to enjoy herself. After her return to the White House, Pat and her staff reviewed newspapers from across the nation and sent letters of "commendation" to volunteer organizations, which were often printed in the local newspapers. Over the next few years, she would hold frequent White House receptions to honor volunteer organizations that had responded to local needs.

Nixon and his West Wing lieutenants carefully monitored the press coverage of his wife. According to Herb Klein, White House communications director, they devoured "the so-called women's pages as avidly as they read political columns." They were disturbed they had not convinced the press to provide what they believed was a respectful and fair depiction of the First Lady and the Nixon partnership itself. A staff member contacted NBC and proposed that the network film a special program featuring Mrs. Nixon. The White House dangled an irresistible incentive: The First Lady would grant NBC her first televised interview. NBC reporter Nancy Dickerson recalled that the network did not refuse the White House's entreaties for fear it would be cut off from future access to important White House stories. NBC agreed to follow Mrs. Nixon on the presidential couple's first round-the-world trip to eight countries in Southeast Asia and Europe, and to air a special titled "Mrs. Nixon's Journey." On the morning of their departure, the president made a last-minute appeal for the traveling press to give full coverage to Mrs. Nixon's activities during their twelve-day journey.

On July 20, 1969, just four days before the Nixons' departure, American astronauts Neil Armstrong and Edwin E. "Buzz" Aldrin, Jr., became the first space explorers to set foot on the moon. Four days later, when the Nixons embarked on their diplomatic trip, Dick flew on *Air Force One* from San Francisco to the mid-Pacific, one thousand miles southwest of Hawaii, for the splashdown of Apollo 11. Federal regulations did not permit the First Lady to travel to the landing site; Pat took *Air Force Two* to Hawaii, where she watched the event on television with reporters and friends.

Pat and her daughters had watched the moon landing on their television in the West Hall of the White House, while Nixon viewed it with Haldeman and Apollo VIII astronaut Frank Borman in Nixon's private sanctum in the Executive Office Building. As Nixon spoke to the astronauts from the Oval Office, Pat, Tricia, and Julie could see him from their West Hall windows and watch as he congratulated the astronauts on the phone—the same scene unfolding on their television. Richard Nixon told Armstrong and Aldrin, "Because of what you have done the heavens have become part of man's world . . . it inspires us to redouble our efforts to bring peace and tranquility to earth."

In early August the president greeted Armstrong and Aldrin aboard the recovery ship USS *Hornet*, saying, "This is the greatest week in the history of the world since the Creation"—an overstatement that his friend Reverend Billy Graham in particular found hard to accept. On the evening of August 13, after their return from their diplomatic trip, the Nixons held an official state dinner at the Century Plaza Hotel in Los Angeles to honor the crew. Nixon and Vice President Agnew presented them each with the Presidential Medal of Freedom. The moon landing and the astronauts' safe return were a highlight of the Nixons' first White House year.

Late in July, on the day after the astronauts' return, Nixon, on the island of Guam, outlined what would come to be called the Nixon Doctrine—the policy that the United States would provide arms and military aid, but not military forces, to Asian allies who were fighting communist offensives with their own troops. The political purpose of the trip was to reassure Asian allies that the United States was not going to pull out of the Pacific arena even as the administration began to institute the process of "Vietnamization," a painfully slow withdrawal of U.S. troops from South Vietnam that would occur alongside an American commitment to provide military equipment and financial aid to support the South's own fight against North Vietnam. The Nixons made a surprise visit to Saigon, where Nixon met with President Nguyen Van Thieu. For the first time, a president and his wife traveled in a war zone together; no previous First Lady had toured an active combat zone. Eleanor Roosevelt had visited U.S. troops and surveyed the home-front efforts in Great Britain in 1942 and in nonactive combat areas in the South Pacific in 1943.

NBC reporter Dickerson and a film crew covered Mrs. Nixon's public activities at each stage of the trip. While her husband conferred with President Thieu and government officials, Pat visited an orphanage filled with children who had lost their parents in the war. Then, accompanied by heavily armed agents, she made a risky trip eighteen miles north of Saigon to Long Binh, a major command center for the U.S. army, in a military helicopter. Pat later acknowledged having "a moment of fear going into the battle zone," but she forwent a tour of the facilities and insisted on being taken directly to the wounded soldiers in the Twenty-fourth Evacuation Hospital. "I came to see the boys," she told officials. Blandly, Mrs. Nixon told Dickerson that "all of them really felt that they were helping to preserve freedom for this country." As Eleanor Roosevelt had when she visited in the South Pacific during World War II, Pat took down the wounded soldiers' names and addresses so that she could write to reassure their families at home. She represented herself to Dickerson as an ambassador who wanted "to see the people and let them know that we are thinking of them at home."

Dickerson traveled through all eight countries with Mrs. Nixon, waiting for an interview that ultimately was filmed in Bucharest, Romania. Dickerson and the First Lady were exhausted by the trip and vexed by the difficulties in setting up the lighting, electrical outlets, and background for the interview. Behind her politic, cooperative manner Pat appeared drawn and strained. Even under the best of circumstances she did not relish the cold eye of the camera. As the interview "droned on," Dickerson felt like she was "slowly dying" from Mrs. Nixon's laconic manner. "Pat seemed to have no thoughts or opinions of her own, or else she was scared to voice them," Dickerson wrote in her memoir, which was published after the Watergate scandal had driven the Nixons from the White House. Did she experience Pat as so mousy at the time or was her memory colored by the filter of Watergate? It is hard to know.

The Bucharest interview was a manifestation of the larger issue Pat experienced in her first year in the White House. Having long been accustomed to a subordinate role as Dick's wife, she appeared to be overwhelmed by pressures to define her own unique identity as First Lady. She was stymied by her own perfectionism, her fear of making mistakes, and her uncertainty about how she could carve out an independent role that would not conflict with her husband's policies and his need to be in charge. Dickerson's observations about the First Lady raise the question of whether Pat Nixon might have struggled with depression at times during 1969 as she endeavored to resolve these strong internal and external conflicts. Pat was not generally prone to depression—in fact, she was more likely to feel anxious under stress—but in this period she was burdened by the immense responsibilities she faced on a daily basis and her doubts about her own ability to be a leader. Pat appeared to feel hopeless at times about her ability to meld her passions with her role in a way that would serve herself and her country. In 1969 she did not seem to want to be First Lady.

Dickerson asked in the Bucharest interview whether she and the president exchanged any private jokes. "Yes," Pat said, adding that whenever they entered their living quarters in a new country "the first thing we do is say hello to the four corners." U.S. security officials prevailed upon Dickerson not to air the comment. She was, however, fascinated that the Nixons were both "preoccupied" by the "possible presence" of electronic bugs or tapes.

In order to make the broadcast appealing, NBC superimposed Pat's pleasant voice over footage of Pat's visits to an orphanage welfare project, a workshop for mentally disabled children, a school for the blind, and a floating market tour. Nancy put aside her frustration with the First Lady's banal comments and lack of facial expression, and ended the broadcast with a statement conveying a positive view of her. Mrs. Nixon, she said, is "often portrayed as a disciplined and somewhat passive figure," but on this trip "she gave of herself unsparingly, effectively, and with good humor and she enjoyed doing it." Countering the attitudes of reporters hostile or indifferent to Pat Nixon, Dickerson added, "We have often underestimated our first ladies, but Mrs. Nixon should not be underestimated."

The Nixons watched the broadcast from their new home in San Clemente. Pat called Dickerson immediately after the broadcast ended and told her that throughout the program, the president "kept pounding the table in front of him saying, 'That's right! That's right! That's the way you are, and that is how people should see you.'"

According to Mrs. Nixon, she was proudest of the president "when he speaks extemporaneously and from the heart," a speaking ability she felt she lacked, while he was proud of her warmhearted diplomacy, partly because it was a gift he did not possess.

But some reporters continued to attack Pat Nixon as a passive First Lady. They were not directly attacking the Nixon marriage yet; that would happen later, as a broad conflict further escalated between the postwar vision of the American nuclear family and the 1960s alternative that its proponents believed would better empower women. In 1963, the year the Nixons moved to New York and Pat relinquished her duties as a political spouse to take care of her household and family full-time, Betty Friedan published *The Feminine Mystique,* the book that is often credited with igniting in the United States what became "second-wave feminism," in contrast to the women's movement of the late nineteenth and early twentieth century that focused on gaining legal rights for women. Friedan claimed that male editors of women's magazines promoted the idea that women can be fulfilled solely by being mothers and housewives. She asserted that women needed to have a meaningful work life in order to experience satisfaction. In response, *Ladies' Home Journal* and other women's magazines slowly began to change their tone and posit that the "contemporary woman—better-educated, longer-lived, more involved in the community and the world—has a great opportunity to change the society around her." These magazines, however, still printed articles that supported women who continued to stay at home.

Second-wave feminists and some East Wing female reporters who echoed their views perceived Pat as the quintessential Cold War homemaker and someone out of step with the emerging roles of women. Dorothy McCardle, a reporter for the *Washington Post,* labeled Pat "a dutiful wife in the old-time sense." Some East Wing reporters, attuned to the cultural uproar about the roles of women and eager for the conflict that makes good stories, expected a contemporary First Lady to respond to the society around her, embracing an independent persona engaged with politics and issues outside the realm of the home— even as she carefully avoided the appearance of grasping for power.

Other less prominent newspaper reporters, echoing the public's high approval of Mrs. Nixon, maintained a second narrative about the First Lady—she was doing a superb job in a difficult role.

Despite the Nixons' concerted effort to reposition Pat, they faced new criticisms that hurt her and rankled him. In September 1969, Marie Smith, in a "Profile of Pat" in the *Washington Post,* made a case against the First Lady. She had not fully taken up a big project, nor did she project a dynamic presence with a fresh voice and a compelling narrative. "She speaks in platitudes," Smith wrote. "It sounds like she's reading lines that someone wrote for her." That same month *Ladies' Home Journal* writer Lenore Hershey asked painful and provocative questions: Would Pat Nixon, "that almost tragic epitome of the captive political wife, finally come into her own in the White House?" Or had her "feminine spirit been burned out by that long climb beside Dick Nixon to 1600 Pennsylvania Avenue?" In an era when "Let it all hang out" was the slogan of the counterculture, Pat's "carefully controlled, ladylike tautness" did not resonate. But Hershey saw what she considered hopeful signs as she followed Pat's "Vest Pockets of Volunteerism" tour in June. Mrs. Nixon, she wrote, had discovered "the power of compassion, and its dynamism not only gave radiance to her role but also seemed to nourish her inner sense of involvement and adequacy. A spirit so long imprisoned seemed to stir and flutter before our eyes." Hershey concluded that the First Lady "is discovering the right to her own reactions and is enjoying them . . . [Pat] has broken the plastic barrier."

The Nixons and their staffers were heartened by polling results suggesting that the prominent line of press criticism was out of sync with the views of the American public. In the summer of 1969 Gallup polling found that 54 percent approved of the way the First Lady was conducting herself, while only 6 percent disapproved. Amazingly, her nine-to-one approval rating outranked those of both Lady Bird Johnson and Jackie Kennedy at their most favorable. But a cynic would note that a large percentage expressed no opinion—that is, didn't care. Richard Nixon enjoyed a 56 percent approval rating, but 22 percent disapproved of him.

Continuing his campaign to promote Pat, the president asked speechwriter William Safire to develop a public relations program for the First Lady. In response, Charles Stuart wrote a twenty-four-page memo to John Ehrlichman detailing what respondents to a Gallup poll considered Mrs. Nixon's strengths ("shuns the limelight, not a show-off, dignified, ladylike, good taste") and weaknesses ("lacks flair, square, wooden, unreal, just plain folks"). Stuart noted that the nation "has grown to expect their First Lady to be an active public personality and busy with newsworthy affairs." He said that in domestic affairs, Pat could focus on shoring up perceived weaknesses in the Nixon administration's reputation by meeting with youth, the aged, and inhabitants of areas that were impoverished or recovering from natural disasters.

To show her role on the home front, Pat should have been featured decorating the Nixons' new homes in Key Biscayne and San Clemente and picking out furniture for them. "Untold pages in *House Beautiful* and *Home and Garden* have literally been thrown away," Stuart opined. The First Lady should be presented as someone who has fun—going to sporting events (she did love bowling and baseball games), shopping, taking a vacation at a resort with friends, holding a fashion show in the East Room, or screening movies with friends. She could define her relationship with culture by going to an occasional opening night of a Broadway show in New York, touring art galleries, and taking the president to the theater and musical events in Washington.

The Nixon administration put into place most of Stuart's recommendations, and they would bear fruit over time, but in the short run the criticism escalated. The *New York Times* published an article, "A Starring Role Is Not for Mrs. Nixon," in which reporter Nan Robertson asserted that the First Lady was taking a "traditional and limited view of her role." Adding her voice to the chorus of other critiques, Robertson asserted that Mrs. Nixon was a "throwback" to Mamie Eisenhower and compared poorly with Mrs. Johnson. Robertson faulted Pat for her "ostensible lack of impact on the nation," her minor role in advising her husband, and her excessive focus on answering the thousands of letters she received each week. But many Americans deeply admired Mamie Eisenhower and considered it a compliment for Pat to be compared to her. Republican journalists were happy with Pat Nixon's warm persona as First Lady and her thoughtfulness toward ordinary citizens.

"She has been found on occasion," Robertson sniffed, "even stuffing envelopes and putting in the cardboard backing for photographs she has signed." While Dick hated the criticism, he agreed she spent too much time on her letters. But for Pat, no amount of castigation was going to create a wedge between her and her correspondents—the "little guys" whom she was determined to help by answering their letters and inviting them to the White House.

The president fought back on his wife's behalf. He wrote to Stuart to suggest she put a press pack together for the wire service reporters that would bolster Mrs. Nixon's image, including reports of the First Lady's well-received performance on the Southeast Asia trip and a listing of all "the firsts Mrs. Nixon" had brought to the White House: the Thanksgiving luncheon for elderly citizens (225 District of Columbia citizens from nursing facilities and homes for the aged ate in the State Dining Room and the East Room); the programs for disadvantaged children, using the presidential yachts for the first time for that purpose; and the special Christmas parties and Halloween parties. "I know it is hard to get the press to cover any of these positive items, but we have to try to keep selling them," Nixon said.

As 1969 progressed, opponents of the Vietnam War grew increasingly angry with Nixon for failing to end the war quickly. Violence escalated across the nation. More bombs exploded on college campuses. In October, in Washington, D.C., 250,000 antiwar protesters held a Moratorium to End the War in Vietnam on what they called a national day of protest. They threatened to hold monthly protests until Nixon terminated the war. Inside the White House, there was what Julie Nixon called "a tenseness in the air so sharp that it was almost tangible." By midfall the Nixons felt that it would be impossible to attend Julie's graduation from Smith College in June 1970 without inviting disruptive demonstrations. "It will be necessary for me to plan some sort of trip out of the country," Nixon wrote

Haldeman. He thought the family could travel to Mexico or North Africa to justify their absence.

On November 3, Nixon made a televised address to the nation to explain his plans for forging a peace in Vietnam. He famously asked the "great silent majority of my fellow Americans" to support his decision to continue the war until the North Vietnamese leaders negotiated a "fair and honorable peace" or until the South Vietnamese people could defend themselves. He reiterated his policy of "Vietnamization." By the end of December, Nixon was thinking about how his administration could continue "to mobilize the silent majority . . . to keep this very real asset from wasting away." But he would soon decide to invade Laos and Cambodia, an unpopular decision that would accelerate its wasting.

Despite the country's troubled attitude toward him and the war, the president believed that he and his wife had helped the nation begin to rise out of the turbulence that had dominated the 1960s. At the end of 1969, Nixon wrote in his memoir that in a difficult year, "We had held our own." He was referring to his administration, but he might as well have been speaking about his marriage.

A Private Marriage in the Public Spotlight

The divisions caused by the Vietnam War ruptured the Nixon presidency during the second year of Dick's term. As he said in his 1971 State of the Union address, the war was "a long, dark night of the American spirit." Pat and Dick stepped carefully out of the White House to try to smooth some divisions, advance the Nixon agenda in Vietnam and at home, sharpen other conflicts to prepare for the 1972 elections, and do the political work of building a permanent Republican majority of voters. Their efforts were complicated by what some Americans, originally during the Johnson administration, had dubbed the "credibility gap"—the contradiction between the words and actions that didn't jibe, leaving those people mistrustful of both. Dick promised to end the war, but then escalated the bombing. Pat presented a persona as a perfect human being without fears or weaknesses, but for the majority of the voters, this was nonsense.

Violent campus disturbances escalated in the spring of 1970. The Nixons reached out to those students who were not protesting against the Vietnam War or the administration. During the first week of March, Pat, serving as the president's emissary to students, visited college volunteer programs working with impoverished, blind, mentally disabled, and aged citizens in Kentucky, Missouri, Colorado, Michigan, and Ohio. She traveled with heavy security and visited spots where angry student demonstrations were unlikely. Nonetheless, she encountered protesters chanting "kill for peace," a sarcastic reference to Nixon's policy of bombing his way to a peace settlement. One dissenter held aloft a placard: "Killing for peace is like raping for chastity." At a day care center in Colorado, a bearded youth shouted at Pat, "How many of these little kids are going to be soldiers?" Pat ignored the protests and shrugged off a death threat against her at the University of Colorado at Boulder.

In Cincinnati, Pat addressed students right after William Kunstler, the radical lawyer who defended the Chicago Seven, the alleged disrupters of the 1968 Democratic Convention, spoke to them. She received as vigorous a round of applause as he did. One of the students told reporters: "She wanted to listen. I felt like this is a woman who really cares about what we are doing. I didn't expect her to be like that." Students at her other stops warmed up to her in similar ways.

During her trip, Pat held four news conferences with student volunteers, some of whom sported "peace" buttons carrying the ubiquitous antiwar slogans. Covering over her discomfort, she told the press she was not perturbed by students who carried signs of protest because she believed that young people are "all idealists" trying to change the world. The *Chicago Tribune* reported that the White House had screened the students appearing with her at the press conferences, but the presidential staff was "smart enough to include the peace pin wearers, the blue jean clad and the long of hair." Pat told the press that she reported back to her husband daily by phone and that the president "has great faith in young people and he's glad I'm out advertising the fact." Reporters noted how well students responded to Pat's willingness to listen to them.

Kandy Stroud of *Women's Wear Daily*, who had coined the phrase "Plastic Pat" during Pat's first year as First Lady, remained a skeptic. She viewed the tour as "smoothly oiled professionalism, top-notch public relations, and a slick and careful packaging job . . . to sell the President's wife." But the *Washington Post*'s Marie Smith, an occasional Pat Nixon detractor, appreciated "her ability to face with poise and assurance a roomful of reporters and to express with ease and articulateness her interest in and concern for people." *Time* asked, "Whatever happened to the matron in the Republican cloth coat, the silent partner in the Nixon marriage?" She had acquired, in *Time*'s view, "sufficient self-confidence to face pickets, skeptical reporters, and ordinary citizens with the same aplomb."

While some of the negative feelings about her were tied to reporters' visceral dislike of her husband, she suffered from her own unfortunate timing. Many perceived that she had hidden behind White House walls while she figured out her role. Then she had emerged just as America's debate over the role of women in society peaked. Pat Nixon entered the White House as a subordinate woman who professed she wanted to go down in history solely as the wife of a president. But she found herself facing a debate over "self-actualization" and feminists who thought that every woman should focus on defining a distinctive identity and her own personal ambitions. The *Mary Tyler Moore Show*, which had its premiere in the fall of 1970, featured a young, unmarried career woman, and it quickly became one of the country's most popular television shows—even in middle America. To be a First Lady managing competing expectations from the Silent Majority and the emerging feminist movement required exceptional skill; Pat could not hope to please everybody. After fourteen months of ignoring or pegging Mrs. Nixon as an uptight 1950s housewife trapped in a bad 1970s marriage, reporters saw glimmers of a more engaged First Lady, more attuned to the times.

*   *   *

In November 1969, investigative reporter Seymour Hersh broke the story that U.S. soldiers had killed 504 women and children in the Vietnamese village of My Lai the previous spring. News of this massacre, as well as reinstatement of the draft in December, aggravated the bitterness and disillusionment that a growing number of Americans felt toward a war that was not winding down as the administration had led them to expect. Nixon, in an attempt to curtail North Vietnam's ability to attack the South, announced on April 30, 1970, that his administration had sent U.S. troops into Cambodia and had bombed key North Vietnamese–controlled areas of that country. Students nationwide immediately protested. Walking through the Pentagon the next day, Nixon denounced "the bums blowing up campuses," a reference to a few violent episodes among more than two hundred antiwar protests that month, but students assumed he was demeaning all young protesters.

On May 4, 1970, a confrontation at Kent State University between students protesting the incursion of U.S. troops into Cambodia and members of the Ohio National Guard escalated into violence that would reverberate across the country. Students threw rocks and chunks of concrete at guardsmen, who fired their weapons, killing four young people and injuring eleven others. A photograph of an anguished fourteen-year-old runaway, Mary Ann Vecchio, kneeling over the dead body of student Jeffrey Miller became emblematic of the era. In the following week student or faculty strikes shut down 450 colleges. Antiwar leaders organized a National Day of Protest in Washington for Saturday, May 9. D.C. transit buses were parked bumper to bumper around the White House by nightfall on Friday. Inside the cordon of buses, helmeted army troops in riot gear protected the presidential mansion. National Guard troops were placed on alert within the Executive Office Building. Nixon dispatched Pat and his daughters to safety at Camp David.

Anxious about the escalating conflict and its potential for violence and worried about how the protests could undermine public support for his conduct of the war, Nixon slept only a few hours on Friday night. At 4:00 a.m. his valet Manolo Sanchez discovered his boss listening to Rachmaninoff's Second Piano Concerto in the Lincoln Sitting Room. Nixon looked broodingly out the window and noticed small groups of students gathering near the Washington Monument. Driven by the Secret Service, Dick took Sanchez by car to the Lincoln Memorial, arriving before 5:00 a.m.

Petrified Secret Service agents, who were concerned that Nixon might be attacked and injured, dispatched Nixon's personal physician, Dr. Walter Tkach, to the scene. Dick quietly spoke to a small group of students who were shocked to see him. The president told them he shared their goal of stopping the killing and ending the war in Vietnam. He went on to say that he didn't want their antipathy toward the war to "turn into bitter hatred of our whole system." While he appreciated that they thought he was "an SOB," he said he understood their position, confessing that as a young man, he had been a supporter of British prime minister Neville Chamberlain's pacifism toward Hitler's Germany. The press later exaggerated how much he talked about sports and travel with the bleary-eyed students who had camped out and were just waking up.

As the group around him grew to thirty or so, including "more leader types," as Nixon reported later, the president told them that "we were trying to build a world in which you will not have to die for what you believe in." He spoke about a universal "spiritual hunger" that could not be satiated, Nixon asserted, by ending the war or cleaning up the environment—a concern he shared with the protesters. In his 1970 State of the Union address he had said, "the great question of the seventies is, shall we surrender to our surroundings, or shall we make peace with nature and begin to make reparations for the damage we have done to our air, to our land, and to our water?" That hunger, he told the protesters, has been "the great mystery of life from the beginning of time." Sanchez, increasingly unnerved by the growing crowd, tricked his boss into departing, telling him he had a phone call in the car. As the first rays of dawn spilled over the Washington Monument, Nixon's car pulled away. A bearded student approached the car and gave the president the finger. Nixon returned the gesture. "That S.O.B. will go through the rest of his life telling everybody that the

President of the United States gave him the finger," Dick told Sanchez. "And nobody will believe him!"

Haldeman and other staff members caught up with Nixon early that morning and joined him for breakfast in the Rib Room of the Mayflower Hotel. His chief of staff found the president in a state of nervous exhaustion, rambling, tightly wound. Dick wanted to walk back to the White House through Lafayette Park, where the protesters had gathered. He seemed to think he could personally defuse the demonstrations by talking the activists out of their rage. A staffer forced the president back into his car. For Haldeman, "the weirdest day so far" in a presidency would only grow stranger.

When Pat woke up that morning at Camp David, she decided to return to the White House to join her husband. Her Secret Service agents were worried about conveying her safely by car from Camp David in Maryland down Washington streets swamped with hundreds of protesters, chanting, singing, some waving homemade peace signs, many carrying Vietcong flags. Using an ambulance as a wedge against potential roadblocks, and a black limousine as a decoy, the agents placed Pat, Julie, Tricia, and her boyfriend Ed Cox in an unmarked sedan. Julie felt as if she was in a "play removed from reality" and had a "sick, hollow feeling" in her stomach by the time they arrived at the White House, which was barricaded and darkened, with all the window shades drawn.

Once she was inside, ignoring the raucous chants of the protesters and the whining of their sound equipment, Pat caught up on her mail in her dressing room. Dick, meanwhile, isolated himself in his office. By dusk, as the protests died down, the Nixons felt what Julie called "the numbness that comes from an intense assault on the senses." For both Pat and Dick, the threatening car rides, as well as the sense of being under siege, were another painful assailment in a career that had been full of them. Yet the Nixons did not use this dark period to learn more nuanced strategies for coping with barrages of protests against them and their ideas. Instead, when pressure on them escalated, they retreated further and further into an "us versus them" mentality that increasingly justified Dick's punitive and secretive ways of handling dissent. Neither did the antiwar activists develop a more nuanced understanding about how to deal more effectively with the president.

Nixon announced to the country on June 30 that the Cambodian incursion had precipitated what he declared to be a big victory; the United States had captured 40 percent of the enemy's arms in Cambodia. This would lead to greater reductions in U.S. troops in the area that fall, he said. He went on to decry what he declared to be an epidemic of antiwar violence at home. According to Nixon, in his first year and a half in office a deeply threatening "urban underground of political terrorists urging murder and bombing" had emerged. From January 1969 through April 1970 there had been "at least 40,000 bombings, attempted bombings and bomb threats," he claimed. With so much public anger directed at them, the Nixons continued to agonize over attending Julie's graduation from Smith College as well as David Eisenhower's ceremonies at Amherst.

In May, Pat was uncharacteristically short-tempered when a reporter asked if she would be attending the graduations. "Why do you keep asking those questions?" she snapped. "You sound like a broken record." According to Haldeman's unpublished diary entry of March 3, 1970, Nixon was leaning against attending, but then reversed himself after Vice President Agnew advised him that "he was wrong in not going." The president decided that he "should just go and sit in the audience and take the heat if there's a demonstration or a bad speaker."

In April, however, the Nixons learned that Rennie Davis and Jerry Rubin, members of the Chicago Seven who had disrupted the 1968 Democratic Convention in Chicago, were teaming up with the radical group the Black Panthers in the Western Massachusetts area. They recruited demonstrators from several local colleges to protest the president's visit. At one preliminary rally, members of the Chicago Seven led ten thousand students in a chant of "Fuck Julie and David Eisenhower." Julie herself recognized that her father's attendance at graduation would be a provocative event, writing John Ehrlichman that "the Smith girls are furious at the idea of massive security precautions." In early May the president announced that the Nixon family would not be able to attend because "lawless elements threatened to disrupt the events." The president's language was intended to encourage the Silent Majority to resent the coercive tactics of the protesters.

The Nixons held their own, jocular version of graduation that June at Camp David, with a family party at which Bebe Rebozo—wearing Notre Dame faculty robes borrowed from labor secretary George Schultz—read a humorous address coauthored by speechwriter Pat Buchanan. The president toasted the young couple, but none of them could forget that frightening campus protests had forced their festivities into retreat. Deeply disappointed, Pat was quiet and detached at the party. Forgoing a family graduation was a harsh penalty for the family of a wartime president, but there were deeper deprivations to come.

In late September and early October Pat and Dick traveled to Europe for state visits with President Josip Tito in Yugoslavia and Generalissimo Francisco Franco in Spain, and for consultations with the president of Italy. The Nixons had an audience with Pope Paul VI in the Vatican and went on to Britain, where they met for an informal lunch with Prime Minister Edward Heath at Chequers, the official country retreat of the prime minister. The Nixons finished their trip with a state visit to Ireland, where they met with Prime Minister Jack Lynch. For the first time Pat met some of her Ryan relatives in County Mayo, where her grandfather was born. Pat and Dick also visited Nixon family sites in County Kildare.

As Pat and Dick prepared for that European trip, the *New York Times,* no friend of the Nixon White House, took a powerful swipe at their marital partnership. On September 13, journalist Judith Viorst ridiculed the Nixons' marriage in the *New York Times* Sunday magazine, in an article, "Pat Nixon Is the Ultimate Good Sport." Demeaning as the title was, Viorst's description of their union hurt more: "There are many who would describe the Nixons—as one long-time observer has—as people who have lost whatever they once had between them." She added that many critics call the Nixons' marriage "dry as dust." The nationally syndicated article gave credence to rumors that had circulated in Washington for years; stories that the Nixons had an unhappy marriage. One friend told the reporters that she hoped Pat did not see the Viorst story because it "might kill her," but that was not a realistic expectation. Lyndon K. "Mort" Allin, who worked for Patrick Buchanan, presented the president extensive daily surveys of what was covered in the media. White House press monitors picked up the attack on the Nixon union.

In an article likely instigated by outraged Nixon friends and staffers, reporters Vera Glasser and Malvina Stephenson counterpunched with a newspaper article, claiming that the Viorst attack was, as their headline termed it, MUCH ADO ABOUT NOTHING. The Nixons' friends and associates refuted "hints of strain," and found the accusations to be "incredible." They argued that Pat and Dick were not "show people"—like Ronald and Nancy Reagan, former actors who ostentatiously showed affection for each other in public. The Nixons were sentimental, friends claimed, but did not "parade it" because observers "might find it [a public display of affection] phoney." While Adele Rogers, the wife of his secretary of state, was recovering from an accident, the article recounted, Dick autographed her leg cast and quipped, "This is the first and only time you will see my hand on another woman's knee."

One of the biggest myths about Richard Nixon is that his public treatment of his wife revealed how he felt about her and how he treated her in private. Many observers (including staff and friends) were struck by his unwillingness to touch his wife in public. Reporter Helen Thomas, who maintained that the Nixons were a close couple in private, acknowledged that their public togetherness was "definitely on the undemonstrated side." Susan Porter Rose, the appointments secretary to the First Lady, told an interviewer that "from time to time, we would wish that he would be overtly more beckoning to her—with more public displays of affection." Secret Service agents wondered why the Nixons did not talk to each other on the presidential helicopter or when they walked on the White House grounds. Speaking to a group of nine female reporters who interviewed him at the White House on

March 11, 1971, Dick offered a partial explanation of his taciturn connection with his wife. Dick told the reporters that he felt that the most important aspect of a marriage was "an emotional, chemical, almost mystical relation." His comment suggests that he and his wife could be content with a silence that outsiders might not appreciate.

Some onlookers noticed that Dick could be callous and forgetful of Pat—particularly while they were campaigning. He was aware of the value of portraying a warm public relationship with his popular wife, but he was ruled by his powerfully conditioned behavior, reserved Quaker heritage, and ingrained belief that the public arena was a gladiatorial place with no room for intimacy or vulnerability. For a man obsessed with public relations, this was a signal failure. Some of his presidential staff agreed. Roger Ailes, Nixon's television advisor, wrote Haldeman that "the President should show a little more concern for Mrs. Nixon." In one of twenty-one bullet points recommending how the Nixons could improve their television image, Ailes suggested that Dick talk to Pat more frequently and smile at her more often in public. "Women voters are particularly sensitive to how a man treats his wife in public," he wrote. "The more attention she gets, the happier they are." Dick's failure to take this advice, despite his fierce commitment to countering negative portrayals of his presidency and of his family, suggests the depth of his inhibitions.

Others saw Dick's behavior not as specific to him but as common to men of his generation. Connie Stuart, the East Wing chief of staff, believed that when Nixon walked away in a crowd and Mrs. Nixon had to run to catch up, "he was [being] a rather typical male. . . . He simply got wrapped up in the moment and he'd be off doing his thing . . . they always said it was his fault . . . [but] she was usually involved in a conversation and was busy doing something." Connie also recalled moments of intimacy between them. "Frankly, I saw them, at times, in public when they'd sneak a little pat, or a little whatever." Dwight Chapin watched the Nixons hold hands when they went for walks. He often saw Dick put his arm around Pat and touch her affectionately before they got off elevators at public events.

From reporters to Nixon staffers, observers extrapolated their assessments of the Nixon marriage from how they witnessed the couple behave in public settings. Journalist Ben Bradlee thought Nixon "had that sort of dingy marriage; I have a feeling they never touched each other in any way." Presidential aide Alexander Butterfield said "the president didn't speak to her much." Washington insider and Senate deal-broker Bobby Baker believed that "she gave eighty and he gave twenty percent." Diane Sawyer, who worked in the White House and later helped Nixon write his memoirs, called their marriage "this dance of unhappiness."

Those who had witnessed the pair in private described a couple who faced extraordinary pressures, but maintained a warm, intimate connection, however frayed it might become at stressful times. Stuart told the *Hartford Courant* in September 1970 that the Nixons had an affectionate and close bond. Nixon, Stuart declared, was a man "who compliments and observes what she is wearing." He also shared "in family jokes" with his wife and his daughters. Pat's press secretary Helen McCain Smith reported that "He wrote her perfectly darling notes . . . affectionate notes, tucked in beside her pillow." "He might say she'd done a wonderful job." He knew "what a tremendous asset she had been."

A close friend of Julie Nixon Eisenhower, retired law school dean Cynthia Milligan, spent a lot of time with the Nixon family during the Watergate crisis and in their retirement years. She often saw the president and Mrs. Nixon during her White House visits with Julie. When Milligan and her husband, Bob, went to the third floor of the White House to pick up Julie and David for an evening out, the elevator often stopped on the second floor, and she spotted Mr. and Mrs. Nixon sitting together in companionable conversation in the family quarters. Often all three couples would chat before going out. "I never picked up any signs of tension from Julie's parents or from talking intimately to Julie and Tricia about their parents," Milligan said. "My husband and I shared quite a few meals with the Nixon family over the years and I was always impressed by what good parents and grandparents they were. They always showed great interest in what we all were doing."

Haldeman, who was highly critical of his boss on other matters, asserted that Nixon spent a significant amount of time with his family at Camp David, where they did not have to worry about intrusions from the large and omnipresent White House staff. The Nixons bowled, swam, walked, went sledding in winter, and watched movies together. Pat sometimes read alone while Dick rewatched his favorite movies. Marje Acker, a secretary to Nixon whom the pair considered part of their family, remembered many late-afternoon gatherings with Pat and Dick Nixon relaxing by the pool at Camp David followed by dinners and movies with popcorn. At the White House Pat and Dick watched football and baseball on television and bowled in the Executive Office Building.

Alexander Haig, who would become Nixon's last chief of staff, believed that "he worshiped Pat. I knew this when I worked for him. Their relationship was not ostentatious or phony." Aide Frank Gannon described Dick as "the guy with no game who couldn't believe that he got the hot girl." When Pat modeled for the cover of *Ladies' Home Journal* and for six pages of high-fashion photographs in January 1972, Nixon sounded like a starstruck fan: "She looked like a young model in her twenties, and every picture was really a knockout." At a dinner he told the members of the cabinet and their wives that they should look at the article to see why "in a few years you'll be hearing people say, 'How can that old man be married to such a vivacious, beautiful, young woman?'"

For her part, Pat told reporter Frances Lewine, "He's very dear personally. . . . I don't think I would have stayed with him otherwise." A year later, during the 1972 campaign, when reporters asked her if she was happy, she told them, "Yes. Completely. I have the best man in the world. I love him dearly." Julie Nixon believed that her mother often tried to protect her father because she knew how "very vulnerable" he was behind his tough persona. Frank Gannon observed Pat needling her husband. Frank remembers Dick playing "Irish Rose" on the piano in San Clemente. Pat told Dick, "Let Frank play."

Other people who knew them in either professional or personal capacities present a tempered but positive view of their relationship, one that often benefits from the perspective of time. Susan Porter Rose told authors Gerald S. Strober and his wife, Deborah Hart Strober, in the early 1990s, "I know how close they were. There may have been some periods when they were out of phase, but there is no question about the depth of that relationship." When they were under stress, they withdrew from each other, but they rallied during crises, at least until Watergate. Pat herself corroborated Rose's comments. In February 1969 Pat told reporter Eugenia Sheppard of the *Los Angeles Times* that she and Dick did not have grand arguments, but when confronted with major disagreements gave each other some distance. When they had a chance to unwind, as when they retreated to San Clemente or Camp David, Dick and Pat became more relaxed with each other.

While John Ehrlichman would later say Nixon treated Pat as "a respected, but limited partner" who was "not a heavyweight," and was seldom included in campaign strategy meetings, Herb Klein believed that Mrs. Nixon "was never hesitant to discuss issues with her husband" and often offered feedback on "the efforts of the [campaign] day ranging from small details to the effect of the candidate's view on the issues. When she spoke out, everyone from the President on down listened." Stuart believed that she advised him "on the atmosphere" of the country, its concerns, and the "strategic, stylistic approach." Pat told journalists covering her in 1972 that she might not be in the "Big League in the final decisions," but the press should not be concerned about her influence because "I was there on the basic ones." She wouldn't name what she had done or say how she had influenced her husband, but "don't worry," she said. "He gets my opinion constantly." In his diary the president revealed his sensitivity to those opinions, writing that "her criticisms from time to time are not intended to hurt, and she usually does understand the problems we have."

In March 1971, as the president accelerated his re-election plans, he knew his image as a husband, father, and man needed refurbishing. In an hour-and-fifteen-minute interview with nine women reporters in the Oval Office, he submitted to unusually personal questions about himself and his wife, who was celebrating her fifty-ninth birthday in five days. Nixon said he did discuss national issues with Mrs. Nixon, but that he did not ask her opinion on things like "troop withdrawals." Nor did he poll the cabinet, much less his family, on important decisions. His wife generally shared his views, he said, but had strong opinions that did not always agree with his own. Pat did not speak out often in public because they agreed that they could not have "two official voices in one family." Mrs. Nixon, he said, was "a very good critic . . . if we have a press conference, a speech or something of the sort." Her "sensitivity about people" was one of her greatest strengths. He appreciated her attunement to the younger generation, and her awareness about "what people understand and what they don't." Nixon also said, disingenuously, that he was *never* concerned about "criticism and opinion."

He offered the reporters some morsels about Pat's insecurities and her overall character. Given her "great passion for privacy," he wished Pat could spend time at a secluded beach walking along the water without anyone observing her. In his view, she was overly sensitive about looking her best at all times. Too often, when he asked her to go for a walk on the beach with him, she told him, "I can't go looking like this. . . . There's probably a camera." But private as she was, Dick believed Pat loved being First Lady because of what she could accomplish—and not for the glory of the position per se, he told them. Pat went on to corroborate that positive view of her present role in a cover story interview with Winzola McLendon for *McCall's*, denying that she would have preferred any other type of life: "I don't think anything could be more important" than politics, she said. She was happier in the White House than she had been at other points in her husband's political career. "Dick confides in me," she said, "and he knows I keep his secrets."

In the interview with the women reporters, Dick compared Pat to Yvonne de Gaulle, the wife of his idol Charles de Gaulle, the late French president. Madame de Gaulle "had an enormous influence" on her husband by "giving him a sense of security, stability." Dick described Pat as being "the stronger partner of the two," a woman with "great strength of character" and possessed of physical and emotional stamina, a unique combination. "She does not blow easily under stress," he said. He described her in navy lingo as a "sundowner"—a strong disciplinarian with their children and a woman who liked to keep the White House in "ship shape." She ran "a very taut ship" and was, in his view, too tough on their daughters. In May 1971 the Nixons further airbrushed the image of their marriage by cooperating with Winzola McLendon of *McCall's* magazine on her cover story: "The Nixons Nobody Knows—A Surprising Private View of a Public Marriage." The article included photographs of Pat and Dick petting their dog King Timahoe and pictures of the couple walking together on the beach on a dismal, rainy afternoon.

Dick Nixon focused to an unhealthy degree on the mundane details of the running of the White House, the management of his public image, and the perception of his marriage. His hypersensitivity to minutiae and his obsessive focus on the negative press reports about him and Pat—while taking the positive press accounts and feedback from his myriad devoted supporters for granted—caused him to be a far less effective president than he could have been. All these behaviors were maladaptive attempts to cope with his view of himself as an unpopular outsider—a fixed perspective he developed early in life. Despite his superior intelligence and his extensive preparation for the presidency, it was hard for him to succeed while he worried about what his wife was saying to the press or what she was wearing. Nixon further damaged his presidency by overburdening his rigid chief of staff, Bob Haldeman, with petty details that included power conflicts with the press, with opponents, and with his wife. Nixon did not allow himself, Haldeman, and other members of his inner circle enough opportunity to focus on the important matters of domestic policy and building goodwill with Congress.

Whether he was doing the talking about his marriage or other people were doing it, Nixon would orchestrate the responses he wanted to an extravagant extent. The Pulitzer Prize–winning conservative author Allen Drury interviewed Pat Nixon for his book *Courage and Hesitation: Notes and Photographs of the Nixon Administration*. Before she met with Drury, Nixon sent his wife a memo with a script to use that advertised his thoughtfulness, generosity, and sense of humor. For the most part, Pat kept to that script because she believed that the press had underreported these aspects of her husband's character. She might have gritted her teeth while sticking to some of these prescribed remarks. "He is so thoughtful of all of us. He is always planning little surprises and little gifts for us," she dutifully told Drury. "He is not a cold man. I have never seen anyone more thoughtful than he is . . . he does the little things that mean so much." Often, she pointed out, he told jokes at the start of his speeches, but "some people just don't want to write about it because they think it makes him seem more human and likable." When he played Christmas carols on the piano at a White House Christmas party for children, "The children gathered around him and put their arms around him. Children know."

On Sunday, June 21, Pat and Dick celebrated their thirtieth wedding anniversary with a meal of tacos that recalled their honeymoon. Dick presented Pat with the traditional thirtieth-anniversary gift—a strand of pearls. It was also Father's Day. Julie and Tricia gave their father a pink surfboard, which he declined to use on the beach at San Clemente. At a White House ceremony that day, the Mexican ambassador presented the Nixons with a silver box commemorating their anniversary. Pat was surprised when Dick mentioned offhandedly that they were going to a "beautiful resort" in Mexico in early September to celebrate thirty years together. But Dick gave her a more important present: Bending with the times, he signaled his openness to a less traditional marital relationship and a more active role for the First Lady. Responding to her concern about a humanitarian disaster, he sent her abroad to represent him.

The assignment, a trip to Peru, was not an easy one. In October 1968, the left-leaning General Juan Francisco Velasco Alvarado took over Peru in a coup and became president. He severely strained relations with the United States by nationalizing U.S. oil fields and sugar plantations, befriending the Soviet Union, firing on U.S. fishing boats off the Peruvian coast, and expelling U.S. military attachés. After an earthquake—the worst in the history of the Americas—erupted on the ocean floor in May 1970, its shock waves causing catastrophic land-slides in the Andes, the United States promised $10 million in aid. Pat had been disturbed by the paltry news coverage of the disaster and the extent of the devastation. "I just wish there was something I could do to help," she told Dick. Soon Nixon decided that his wife could be a far more effective representative in Peru than Vice President Agnew, who had been slated to visit. A tour by Pat would help repair relations between the United States and Peru and held "no possibility of unfa-vorable reaction," he told Haldeman, while the "VP could get some bad stuff."

The trip was a perfect opportunity for his wife to reclaim a more equal footing in the marriage by demonstrating her independent strengths, revive memories of Pat and Dick's joint effectiveness in the 1950s, confound critics who described her as passive and old-fashioned, and gain international stature as a dynamic First Lady. As he often did, Nixon asked Haldeman to "handle anything real touchy with her" instead of having any such difficult conversation himself. He wanted the press coverage of her visit oriented toward television rather than the written press, telling Haldeman to "take only friends—be coldblooded and tough." He asked Pat Buchanan to write up twenty minutes of talking points so Pat would not have to "wing it" during interviews or visits.

On the weekend before Pat's departure, people dropped off cash and checks at the gate to the Nixons' home in San Clemente, part of a charitable contribution that included two planeloads containing ten thousand tons of donated medical supplies, food, and clothing. She also brought with her an official relief check for $30,000, a small dona-tion from her husband, checks sent by American private citizens that ranged from $5 up to $10,000, and cash.

Once in Peru, Mrs. Nixon turned down the safer option of flying to a fishing port 250 miles north of Lima and being transported by land from there. She insisted on taking the more dangerous flight directly into the interior of the country. Mrs. Nixon and Peruvian First Lady Consuelo Gonzales de Velasco traveled in a small cargo plane high into the snowcapped Andes Mountains, bringing relief supplies to a devastated area now referred to as the Valley of Death. Pat sat on an improvised seat—a kitchen chair bolted to the floor of the plane—and Mrs. Gonzales de Velasco was strapped into the copilot's seat. Their plane made a dangerous landing on a narrow dirt airstrip at the bottom of a deep valley surrounded by tall mountains.

As they visited earthquake survivors, Pat took the lead in talking in personal terms to the victims and indicated to Mrs. Juan Gonzales de Velasco how she could interact in a similar way. For five hours the two First Ladies trudged through the rubble, hugging small children and comforting grieving mothers. UPI reported, "Sometimes Mrs. Nixon grabbed up little children and kissed them on their mud-stained cheeks." Pat became the symbol of the Nixon administration's compassion for the peoples of the Americas. After her return, Pat gave a full report to Mrs. Eleanor Taft, who chaired the Peru Earthquake Voluntary Assistance Group. Mrs. Nixon believed that her mission had helped address the first phase of the crisis—the need for medical aid and supplies—but that a need for reconstruction and rehabilitation still existed. "The greatest need is for permanent shelter building supplies and the related tools," Pat wrote in her report.

"To have President Nixon send his wife here means more to me than if he had sent the whole American Air Force," President Velasco Alvarado announced. *La Prensa*, a newspaper in Lima, opined that the American First Lady "had radically improved previously strained U.S.-Peruvian relations." Peru awarded her its highest honor, the Grand Cross of the Order of the Sun, which was formally presented to her at a ceremony in Washington a year later. This mission was the first turning point in presenting Pat as a modern First Lady representing a visionary president.

White House staff members, monitoring the press reports, were delighted with the "incredibly wide photo play" she received for three consecutive days. Nixon and his men were encouraged to read effusive praise in newspapers that were frequent critics of the administration. The *Manchester Union-Leader* declared the mission was carried out by a First Lady with "leadership, imagination, and energy." The *Atlanta Constitution* said that Mrs. Nixon's efforts personified "a liberated woman's best qualities . . . the president can be proud."

During the mission to Peru, Pat gave her husband new reasons to respect her competency at a time when his staff often excluded or disparaged her. Even so, what Stuart would call the "spirit of détente and cooperation" between the East Wing and West Wing staffs began to deteriorate again. Pat may or may not have taken her concerns directly to her husband over meals in the Family Dining Room or during walks along the beach at San Clemente, but in any case, the Nixons also dealt with each other as leaders of different realms of the White House and continued to deal with each other via staffers, go-betweens, and memorandums.

Dick tried to avoid being the direct recipient of Pat's anger. An overly confrontational father, who felt no compunction about expressing anger at his children or being belligerent with customers in his family store, raised Dick. Although Frank loved his children, his rage scarred Dick. Within his own home, Nixon modeled himself more after his mother, who worked indirectly to achieve her goals within the family. Pat understood Dick's sensitivity to personal conflict and believed that the presidency placed an impossible burden on her husband. She was stressed by creating additional tension for him, even though she lost her temper at times.

Mrs. Nixon was frustrated because she often received last-minute memos informing her of a presidential trip. Her staff was fed up with being shut out of the planning process. The president's men in turn were irritated because the East Wing staff was late with schedules, but Pat's aides complained they had not been given adequate notice to make preparations. Through Stuart, Pat indicated that she did indeed want to travel with Dick, reminding the president that her presence "enhances the 'dynamic family' image, and inspires superb local press coverage." She was eager to hold local events that publicized the president's programs. Stuart told Haldeman that when the president was in Chicago discussing the environment and the issue of water pollution,

Mrs. Nixon had reinforced his message by visiting projects dealing with thermal pollution, land reclamation, and conservation. Similarly, when he was in Denver conferring with law enforcement officials, the First Lady visited a home for young offenders and juveniles with drug problems. Haldeman did not reply to the memo, but Nixon aide Chuck Colson did, telling Stuart to address her concerns not to the chief of staff but to him—a response that left her more frustrated at how hard it was to navigate the maze of power.

Pat Nixon and Bob Haldeman were, in John Ehrlichman's estimation, "unfailingly courteous to each other," even though they still battled behind the scenes through their staff members. Pat realized that Haldeman was an essential aide to the president, but she did not trust his judgment, his skills at managing and connecting with people, or his estimation of her role. For his part, Haldeman was annoyed by how often she interfered and altered his plans for the president. He failed to confer with her on issues she felt were important. When Nixon's team ordered a new presidential plane, for example, Haldeman, at Nixon's direction, created a floor plan without consulting the First Lady. When Pat discovered that her sitting room had been placed at the back of the jet and that she would have to walk through a large staff compartment to reach her husband, she made clear her displeasure. Whether Nixon approved the floor plan to put some space between himself and his wife is not clear, but nonetheless, his failure to consult her about the plan was inconsiderate. The next time the plane was out of service for maintenance, workers reconfigured it, at a cost of $750,000.

Mrs. Nixon had far more respect for the press than the president or his chief of staff did. She canceled Haldeman's orders limiting the number of reporters covering White House social events, and vetoed his plan to keep them behind velvet ropes, even though both of those directives either came directly from the president or had his tacit assent. She did not approve of the tiered bleacher-type seating Haldeman ordered, without her approval, for East Room events, and rarely allowed it to be used. Pat also countermanded Haldeman's decision to allow country-western singer Johnny Cash to record his White House concert and sell it commercially. Pat believed allowing such a recording would cheapen the White House.

Haldeman did not understand the dynamics of the household in terms of who was in charge in the East Wing and the social entertaining. He "would go stiff all over" when Lucy Winchester challenged one of his actions and once, evidencing insecurity about his social skills, told her, "You and Mrs. Nixon do not think I know which knife to lick first." When Haldeman wanted to move furniture around in the White House, the social secretary reminded him it was not his house. "He couldn't tell Mrs. Nixon what to do and he didn't," Winchester said later. When Mrs. Nixon heard about some of Haldeman's plans she would say, "That is just plain hokey." To be fair to Haldeman, he was usually acting on direct orders from his boss or inferring, based on their many conversations, what Nixon wanted. Haldeman's job was to absorb the criticism. Pat understood that Haldeman was acting on behalf of her husband. Sometimes, however, when Pat told Dick about some of Haldeman's actions, Nixon was infuriated at his chief of staff. When Haldeman eliminated Herb Klein's job as communications chief, Pat asked Dick why he had done it. Nixon discovered that Haldeman had lied to him about Klein's desire to leave. The president was enraged.

If Haldeman exasperated Pat, Helene Drown irritated the president and his aides. At least that is how Ehrlichman, bitter about his experience working with Nixon, recollected it in his 1982 memoir *Witness to Power*. Drown, Pat's frequent companion, at the White House and at San Clemente, became Pat's "conduit for complaints to the staff, a role she undertook with undue enthusiasm." Ehrlichman, without acknowledging that the president had used him and Haldeman as blunt instruments in the same role Drown took on, harshly described her as "a waspish woman who managed to translate Pat's low-key requests and suggestions into mean-spirited demands." Ehrlichman felt Helene's antagonism affected Pat's mood. Riled up by Helene, Pat would complain to Dick.

In April 1971 Nixon hid out in his office at La Casa Pacifica to avoid contact with Helene, who would happily bypass his aides to make her opinions known directly to him. Nixon strategized with Bebe Rebozo, Rose Mary Woods, and Ehrlichman about how to remove Helene from La Casa Pacifica. Nixon rehearsed with Ehrlichman a call the president had asked him to make to Helene's husband: "Tell Jack it is for the good of the country that Helene Drown gets out of my house." Dick's decision—and it is not known whether he discussed it directly with Pat—did not balance his wife's needs with his own. Perhaps Pat acquiesced temporarily because she recognized the stress it caused Dick to face personal confrontation in his private realm. Ehrlichman made the call and Drown left immediately, but several months later Pat convinced Dick that she needed her friend's company, and she was readmitted to the Nixons' home. If Pat had to tolerate Haldeman, then Dick had to make room for Drown.

When Helene saw an excerpt of John Ehrlichman's book in *People* magazine, she wrote a furious letter to John challenging him about his story. It was a lie, she told John, that Nixon called her husband, Jack, and asked him to make her "leave at once and stay away." Helene acknowledged that in the Drowns' forty-two-year friendship with the Nixons, "We have gone through bad times and good with each other. . . . We treasure our friendship."

On Wednesday, November 4, the day after Republicans had achieved mixed results in the off-year elections—a gain of two Senate seats, but a loss of nine seats in the House of Representatives—Pat, Dick, and Haldeman flew back to Washington from San Clemente and had a showdown of sorts on the plane, in one of the few documented occasions on which, in the presence of other people, the First Lady confronted the president. According to Haldeman's diary, Pat "blasted me and P [Nixon] about West Wing interference in social operations." She was angry that they were countermanding press secretary Lucy Winchester and slowing down East Wing decision-making. Pat demanded the East Wing keep control over all its operations. The men said they would comply. Haldeman and Nixon designated Dwight Chapin and later Alexander Butterfield as intermediaries with Mrs. Nixon. Pat was no longer willing to let her husband or his aides run her life as completely as they had. She had gained enough confidence as First Lady to stake out her own territory, defend it, and clarify her own role in the White House. This confrontation may not have ended all the guerrilla fighting between Pat and Dick and their lieutenants, but Pat had made a good start toward putting the East Wing in a better position with its West Wing counterparts. She had also insisted on receiving renewed respect as wife and First Lady.

For all the open and subterranean disputes between Pat and Dick and their staff, the First Lady still sought gestures that would sweep away the shadows between them. With the White House clouded by conflict within and without, she decided to create a surprise for her husband. Over a year's time she worked quietly with National Park Service engineers to figure out how to light the White House at night. On an evening in August 1970, as the Nixons approached the White House in a helicopter, Pat gave the signal to activate its new outdoor lighting. According to Julie, the president was so elated that he asked the pilot to circle the White House three times. Three months later, in a November 25 ceremony, as the Marine Band played "America the Beautiful," Pat pushed a button that would light the house and grounds every evening. Ever since, the White House has been lighted at dusk, and an illuminated flag flies all night from its roof. About three weeks later, Pat called Haldeman at home, disturbed to have heard of plans to light the Commerce, Justice, and Archives buildings at night. Mrs. Nixon thought that only national monuments should be illuminated. Nor would lighting of additional public buildings, in her view, set a good example for the public during a time when energy conservation was beginning to become an important issue. She prevailed. That Christmas, the Nixons inaugurated the first public candlelight tours of the White House. Nineteen-seventy may not have been the easiest year, but at least the White House glowed with light against the darkness that often engulfed it.

Love in the White House

As the 1972 election year approached, Pat and Dick fought against their reputations in some quarters as uninspiring and retrograde leaders by going over the heads of the print media to reach the American public on television. Their attempts to create alluring White House social events were only partially successful, but their extensive public relations efforts began to pay dividends in a revitalized view of the First Lady, the Nixon marriage, and the president's strengths. While Richard Nixon pursued a somewhat progressive domestic agenda and endeavored to wind down the Vietnam War, the presidential couple also reverted to a strategy that had worked before—going abroad to refurbish their standing at home.

In February 1971 Pat and Dick quietly pulled off a social coup that had eluded Lady Bird and Lyndon Johnson during their five years in the White House: Pat convinced Jacqueline Kennedy Onassis to bring her children back to the White House for the first time since their father's assassination. Painter Aaron Shikler had completed portraits of the Kennedys, and it was traditional to have a formal unveiling ceremony. Pat wrote Jackie asking what she would like to do. The former First Lady, who had married the Greek shipping tycoon Aristotle Onassis in October 1968, replied that she felt a public ceremony would be too difficult; she preferred a private viewing. Jackie knew she could count on the Nixons' discretion because they valued privacy as much as she did. The president's pilot flew on a secret mission to New York to bring Mrs. Onassis, thirteen-year-old Caroline, and ten-year-old John to Washington. The White House corridors were blocked off so staff members could not intrude upon the family's tour.

Given Jackie's exalted reputation for White House restoration, Pat and Dick had every reason to be on edge about showing her the changes they had wrought. On the evening of February 3, the Nixon family welcomed Mrs. Onassis and her children in the Diplomatic Reception Room, which Jackie had turned into a drawing room of the Federal Period (1790–1820). Pat showed Jackie the English Regency chandelier and the antique furniture she had added to the room.

Near the entrance to the Diplomatic Reception Room, the Nixons pointed out the former First Lady's spectral full-length portrait, in which she wears a finespun peach gown set against a brown background, and then took her into the Grand Hall to see the contemplative rendering of the late president. Jackie said little when she saw President Kennedy's portrait—she was in a battle with the artist who had sold a reproduction of the painting to a magazine without her approval. While Tricia and Julie took Caroline and John to the Solarium to see Washington's nighttime views, Pat and Dick gave Jackie a tour of several rooms that White House curator Clement Conger had helped Mrs. Nixon renovate. They had transformed the Map Room into a handsome reception area with American Chippendale furniture; the China Room now had an 1800 English Regency chandelier, a new carpet, and additions to the china collection; and the Vermeil Room was refurbished with draperies, rugs, and antique furniture.

The Nixons also escorted Jackie through the formal rooms on the first floor. Pat had plans to redo the Red Room in the American Empire style, add Duncan Phyfe American Sheraton furniture to the Green Room, and wallpaper the Blue Room, which Jackie had covered in striped cream-colored silk satin, while refurnishing it in James Madison's French Empire style. "Every family should put its own imprint there," Jackie told the Nixons. "Don't be afraid to change, always upgrade."

The two families had drinks in the West Hall on the second floor. During dinner in the Family Dining Room, young John spilled his milk on the table—an accident that relaxed everyone, as did their mutual recollection that Alice Roosevelt Longworth, the daughter of Theodore Roosevelt, had her appendix removed in this very room. They reminisced about their experiences during the 1950s. At one point, Jackie looked at Dick and told him, "I always live in a dream world," a remark that encouraged the Nixons to steer the conversation away from any topic that might disturb the former First Lady. After dinner the president took John Junior into the Oval Office to show the boy a desk like the one he, as a toddler, had once hidden beneath—the subject of a famous photograph. John remembered.

Mrs. Onassis appreciated all that her husband's former rivals did for her. "You were so kind to us yesterday," she wrote the Nixons. "Never have I seen such magnanimity and such tenderness." She cited the Nixon girls as exemplary young women. "It was good to see her [Caroline] exposed to their example and John to their charm! You spoiled us beyond belief. . . . I have never seen the White House look so perfect. . . . It was moving, when we left, to see that great House illuminated, with the fountains spraying. . . . Your kindness made real memories of his [John's] shadowy ones. . . . The day I always dreaded turned out to be one of the most precious ones I have spent with my children."

While the First Lady and the president were graciously hosting Jacqueline Onassis in her former home, that same Dick Nixon was working clandestinely to undermine her onetime brother-in-law, Senator Edward M. Kennedy, a potential 1972 contender for the presidency.

In December 1970, Nixon arranged for his aide Charles Colson to leak to the *National Enquirer* a photograph of the married Kennedy dancing with a European princess. In May 1971, Nixon ordered nearly round-the-clock surveillance on the Massachusetts senator. Colson had one of his clandestine lieutenants, former CIA agent Howard Hunt—wearing a red wig, nerdy glasses, and a voice-altering device—tail him.

Even as Nixon used underhanded stratagems to ensure that a Kennedy would not again defeat him in a bid for the presidency, he and Pat strove to bring Kennedyesque glamour to the White House. In early February 1971, renowned opera singer Beverly Sills performed at the year's first "Evening at the White House." For Sills the event was "an opera singer's nightmare." She couldn't hit the last note of *The Barber of Seville.* Later, as she hit a high note in the mad scene from *Lucia di Lammermoor,* she popped a hook in her dress, causing its zipper to slide down the back. Nonetheless, the three hundred guests loved her performance. The UPI headlined their report of the evening WHITE HOUSE FALLS FOR OPERA SINGER: HOOK, LINE AND ZIPPER.

In November 1971, the Nixons invited the New York City Ballet to perform at a state dinner in honor of India's prime minister Indira Gandhi. One of the accompanying musicians was a hairy and bearded guitarist, who became the subject of a mild skewering by *Washington Post* reporter Sally Quinn. Connie Stuart found Quinn's article "quite funny and no reflection on the White House," but the president was not amused; he had previously bragged that his musical performers "make the Johnson years almost barbaric, and the Kennedy years very thin indeed." Haldeman sent off a harsh memo to Stuart complaining about the East Wing's judgment in selecting a musician whose grooming made him stand out. Stuart wrote back pointedly, "the unknown looms menacingly when dealing with the entertainment profession. It's kind of like dealing with politicians."

The Nixons also relied on visits from British royalty to bring glamour to the White House. In July, Tricia and Julie garnered major headlines when Prince Charles and his sister Princess Anne visited Camp David, cruised by boat from Washington to Mount Vernon, and attended a supper dance for seven hundred on the South Lawn. The

Nixons also entertained Prince Philip, the Duke of Edinburgh, the Duke and Duchess of Windsor, and the queen's cousin Lord Mountbatten at separate events.

Pat and Dick did not bring in the classiest crowds or the chicest entertainers, and the parties ended too early when the Nixons went to bed—but they did their best to make their social mark. As early as the end of their first year in the White House, Marie Smith of the *Washington Post* saluted them for having replaced their early, dull state dinners with "innovative" entertainments that had "a new sparkle added" thanks to the personal interest taken by the president.

On March 11, 1971, television correspondent Barbara Walters interviewed President Nixon in the Blue Room and pressed him about Pat's upcoming birthday. "Do you think there will be anything else to celebrate that evening?" she asked. Dick tried to brush her question aside, but when she persisted, he told her that a lot of their friends would be there "and I can only say that it will be a very interesting evening. Could we just leave it that way?" The birthday celebration had an Irish theme, thanks in part to a serendipitously occurring state dinner for Prime Minister John Lynch of Ireland. Singer Dennis Day performed "When Irish Eyes Are Smiling," accompanied by actor Fred MacMurray, on saxophone.

After dining, as the Nixons gathered with three hundred guests in the East Room, Dick said, "I understand I am supposed to make a surprise announcement. The difficulty is every time I try to make a surprise announcement, it's leaked. This is no exception." The news was something of a birthday gift to Pat: Their strong-willed, twenty-five-year-old daughter Tricia was now formally engaged to a handsome, resolute, twenty-four-year-old Edward Ridley Finch Cox, a second-year law student at Harvard. A scion of a prominent New York Republican family, he had a decidedly liberal streak, having worked in 1968 for consumer advocate Ralph Nader as one of the first Nader's Raiders, investigating government corruption in the Federal Trade Commission and other agencies. He and his fiancée did not always agree on the issues—but their personalities and their backgrounds meshed.

Kandy Stroud, the Nixons' nemesis at *Women's Wear Daily*, temporarily ruptured the festive mood at the White House with an article titled "That 'Terrible-tempered Tricia'—fact or rumor?" She pointed out that Tricia could perform flawlessly: attending the investiture of the Prince of Wales, organizing the White House visit of Princess Anne and Prince Charles—where reporters floated rumors of a royal romance between Tricia and Charles—and giving a poised, televised tour of the White House. But Stroud also suggested that the Nixons' elder daughter was temperamental, sometimes unreliable, vindictive, and elusive. "They call her the 'phantom' of the White House," Stroud wrote. What Stroud did not report—though she would have been delighted to, had she known about it—was that Tricia's White House tea for Finch College alumnae that April had almost become a hallucinogenic experience. As a fellow alumna, Grace Slick of the rock group Jefferson Airplane was invited to the event, and she brought along the Chicago Seven radical Abbie Hoffman. Slick had planned to slip LSD, hidden under her fingernails, into the punch, but she and Hoffman had stupidly told a journalist of their plans. Their confidant tipped off the White House security guards in time for them to intercept the duo and eject them.

Tricia's very public engagement, and the announcement of her intention to hold her wedding in the White House, focused greater attention on the size and influence of Pat's East Wing operation. Columnist Harriet Van Horne of the *San Francisco Examiner & Chronicle* wrote that Mrs. Nixon is surrounded by the "largest, costliest public relations staff ever assembled," a team that cost taxpayers $150,000 a year. Van Horne quoted an anonymous source who declared that "Pat's press is a computerized, Madison Avenue snow job. She comes out like a statue of the Holy Mother." However sharp the criticism, Pat's team was indeed growing worthy of Madison Avenue, and its efforts were slowly paying off in flattering images of the Nixons and their family.

If their "Evenings at the White House" did not enthrall reporters, Dick and Pat recognized that their daughter's wedding could exemplify the elegance, class, and power they sought to project in their public life, while presenting them—just as the 1972 election campaign was beginning—as a wholesome American family that valued unity, stability, and commitment. Several days before the engagement announcement, Nixon had assigned Haldeman to "ride herd" on the East Wing's planning of the wedding. Haldeman ordered his deputy Alexander Butterfield to keep close watch "on all the handling of events and publicity." Pat and her daughters, aided by Stuart, were making most of the arrangements, but with so much at stake in terms of the president's re-election, the president wanted to control decision-making, from a distance.

Tricia's wedding day, June 12, 1971, was one of the most joyful days in Dick and Pat's marriage. "All of us were beautifully, and, simply, happy," her father would say of it later. But the day still had its share of complications and tense moments, along with a small undertow of melancholy. Dick told reporters that Pat was "a little sad at her last daughter leaving." He felt the same. "It's a little difficult to lose your last daughter and moving to the White House doesn't change the feeling of a mother or a father." After spending most White House evenings dining with at least one of their daughters, Pat and Dick would need to adjust to dining alone.

Tricia was the eighth presidential daughter married at the White House, but the first to wed in the Rose Garden. This was a risky choice: It rains frequently in Washington in June. Three previous White House brides attended: Alice Roosevelt Longworth, who had married Representative Nicholas Longworth in the East Room fifty-five years earlier, Lynda Johnson Robb, and Luci Johnson Nugent. Tricia and Julie enjoyed Mrs. Longworth's sense of humor. A year earlier, Longworth had dined at the White House with their parents, and the girls stopped by to ask how she was feeling. She replied, "Absolutely venomous," and "they loved it," Pat reported. Reporters asked Longworth whether Tricia's wedding brought back reminders of her own nuptials: "No," she answered with her trademark crustiness, "it doesn't bring back one goddamned memory." She added, "I was married twenty years before Hollywood. This wedding was quite a production."

The wedding day dawned muggy and partly cloudy; a steady drizzle soon started. Dick wanted the ceremony to remain in the Rose

Garden, but by noon the more cautious Pat and Julie were urging Tricia to move the wedding to the East Room. After talking with the bride-to-be, the president supported her because he realized that, as he told reporters, "She's determined to have a Rose Garden wedding." At four-fifteen, when Nixon called the air force for an updated weather report, he learned a fifteen-minute clearing was due to move through at four-thirty. Nixon ordered the plastic covers removed from the gold chairs, and four hundred guests were quickly seated—although Longworth later sniped that her chair was still wet. Among the attendees were performers Art Linkletter, Ethel Waters, and Red Skelton, J. Edgar Hoover, Chief Justice Warren Burger, Ralph Nader, the Reverend Billy Graham, and Attorney General John Mitchell and his flamboyant and volatile wife, Martha (who wore an orange sashaying garden dress and sported a matching orange umbrella). Congressmen were not invited. Members of the radical May Day Tribe had threatened to hold wedding day demonstrations near the White House, but the twenty protesters who showed up were limited by the government to an hour of standing at the Washington Monument and waving what the *New York Times* called "limp Viet Cong flags."

Pat Nixon looked resplendent in a white dress covered with pale embroidered flowers. After she was seated, three bridesmaids (including Julie) in lavender and green preceded the bride to the altar. As the Army Strings played "Trumpet Voluntary," Richard Nixon, wearing a morning coat and striped pants, escorted Tricia, in an "embroidered white organdy dress with a sleeveless fitted bodice," down the staircase from the Blue Room balcony and along the white carpet. The aisle was bordered with lilies, white chrysanthemums, and snapdragons on plinths interspersed with topiary rose trees. The president kissed Tricia before giving her away.

Ed and Tricia were married under a twelve-foot-high white wrought-iron gazebo entwined with white flowers. The Nixons had arranged with ABC News to film parts of the wedding for a broadcast later that evening, in a program hosted by correspondents Virginia Sherwood and Frank Reynolds. The cameras were turned off for the private, eleven-minute, ecumenical marriage ceremony itself—a liturgy blending Methodist, Episcopal, and Catholic traditions—conducted by the Reverend Edward Gardiner Latch, D.D., the chaplain of the House of Representatives. Tricia and Ed wrote their own vows, which described a marital union as "most precious" and offering a life "of great and unreserved giving of self." The new couple quickly kissed their parents and led the rest of the guests down the aisle, scrambling through a sudden downpour.

At the reception in the East Room, Nixon tapped his new son-in-law's shoulder to cut in and dance with his daughter to the tune "Thank Heaven for Little Girls." To the applause of the crowd, Dick later cut in on Pat, who was dancing with the bridegroom. Pat threw her arms around her husband and he twirled her around the floor. Reporter Helen Thomas thought they looked "happier than I have ever seen them before." Dick exuberantly took to the floor, dancing in turn with his daughter Julie, Mamie Eisenhower, and Lynda Bird Johnson. He later said that he would henceforth adhere to his Quaker principles and not dance in the White House again. He kept his word. While munching on wedding hors d'oeuvres on the Truman Balcony, Pat, Julie, and Bebe Rebozo convinced Dick, who did not like the sight of himself on TV, to watch the ABC wedding special in the West Hall. He was pleased to see that he was "standing pretty straight," as his family had asked.

Sixty million people watched the television coverage of the event. *Life* magazine thought that the wedding brought viewers something "akin to American royalty," and CBS reporter Dan Rather agreed: "It may be the closest thing Americans have, or want, to a royal wedding." As Pat and Dick had hoped, the intensive television coverage of the stately wedding provided valuable, humanizing publicity for the Nixon family. At a time when the nation was still racked by war abroad and unrest at home, it was a unifying event.

Unfortunately for the Nixons, the next day the *New York Times* shared first-page coverage of the wedding with an article based on excerpts from the top secret Pentagon Papers. The publication of the first of the papers, a series of classified documents obtained by former defense contractor Daniel Ellsberg and leaked to the *New York Times*, detailed the history of the Kennedy and Johnson administrations' involvement in Vietnam, including deceptions around both presidents' intentions and policies.

Two days later an infuriated Nixon ordered Haldeman to make sure that no one connected with the White House gave an interview to a staff member of the *New York Times* without the president's permission. Nixon had hoped Tricia's wedding would at least temporarily elicit what he considered more balanced treatment of his administration from the press. In May, he had played, he thought, the "good sport" at the annual White House Correspondents' Dinner, but in his next press conference, reporters, Nixon thought, "were considerably more bad-mannered and vicious than usual." For Nixon that behavior confirmed his theory that treating the press "with considerably more contempt is in the long run a more productive policy." When Nixon gave a press interview about his wife in the spring of 1971, he ordered Haldeman to make sure that there were no reporters present from the *Washington Post.* He believed its coverage of his family and his administration had been far too harsh.

In the aftermath of the Pentagon Papers disclosures, administration officials tried to calculate how those revelations might have weakened the U.S. "position with the North Vietnamese and the Soviets." National Security Advisor Henry Kissinger convinced the president that this release of classified documents was a threat to national security. The administration went to court to try to prevent further publication of the papers, but the Supreme Court eventually ruled against it. Later that summer, a special operations unit secretly sponsored by Ehrlichman—which called itself the "plumbers" and was focused on stopping leaks in the Nixon organization—broke into Ellsberg's psychiatrist's office to find evidence that could discredit him. The burglary was the beginning of a downward slide into abuses of power that would imperil the reputation of the president, undermine all that Nixon had accomplished in office, and place oppressive strains on Pat and Dick's marriage.

In his State of the Union address the following January, Nixon laid out an ambitious set of programs he called the New American Revolution, centering not only on improved health care, revenue sharing with the states, and welfare reform, but also on environmental transformation. The president's main environmental interest, however, was in parklands, and he planned "to expand the Nation's parks, recreation areas, open spaces, in a way that truly brings parks to the people where the people are." Between 1971 and 1976 the "Legacy of the Parks" program transferred from the Federal government to state governments eighty thousand acres of undeveloped public lands.

Pat used her growing personal popularity to garner newspaper coverage that would promote this and other environmental initiatives taken by her husband. Ignoring protesters whose signs read, "Nixon Speaks with a Forked Tongue" and "I Want My Brother back from Vietnam," Pat conducted ceremonies transferring land to the states at sites in Virginia, Minnesota, Michigan, Oregon, and California. She cooperated with ABC News on a documentary, called "A Visit with the First Lady," because they offered to show significant coverage of her "Legacy of the Parks" tour. ABC filmed her five-state journey that culminated at Border Field, six thousand feet of oceanfront land on the border between the United States and Mexico.

As Pat spoke at the transfer ceremony, she noticed hundreds of people standing behind a barbed-wire fence in Mexico. Mrs. Nixon complained about the fence to the mayor of Tijuana, who was seated beside her. In a historic move, she asked the mayor to have the fence pulled down because "we're such good friends with Mexico. We don't need a border." Despite protests from her Secret Service agents, she walked into Mexico. She picked several children up, carried them in her arms across the border, and embraced surfers on the beach there.

In September 1971 ABC aired its television special on the First Lady. Virginia Sherwood interviewed Pat at the White House and in San Clemente, where she was far more relaxed and playful than she had been in the 1969 documentary with Nancy Dickerson. Sherwood portrayed the Nixon marriage at its best.

True to form, Dick was not sentimental about his wife in front of the camera. Pat, however, did her best to sell the Nixon marriage. She told

Sherwood that at the end of a long day she and Dick sat together in front of a fire in the Lincoln Sitting Room and chatted. They dined together with greater frequency in the White House than ever before. "Dick is a wonderful dancer. He is my favorite partner," she said, but he was too busy reading official papers to linger at social events and dance. She revealed—in a comment that may have appeared more poignant to viewers than she realized—that she sometimes danced by herself in the hall. She repeated her theme, "We've always been a team," and added, "I've helped him in many ways." The woman who had recently been described as "a paper doll, a Barbie-doll, plastic, antiseptic, [and] unalive" now came across as engaged and engaging, a First Lady who could serve a volleyball, putt on a golf course, and expertly swing a polo mallet. An article about the documentary by Louise Hutchinson of the *Chicago Tribune* was titled "Pat a Political Bonus for Nixon."

The Nixons and their handlers were doing a better job of portraying their marriage as a warm and mutual partnership, but Pat had a sharp reminder that even though Dick listened to her advice, he did not always take it. In September 1971, after Supreme Court Justices Hugo Black and John Harlan announced their retirements, Pat broke her rule against commenting in public about political issues. Asked during the opening of the Eisenhower Theater at the Kennedy Center whether she thought a woman should be appointed to one of the U.S. Supreme Court vacancies, she replied, "I think it will be great to get a woman on the court. And if Congress doesn't approve her, they'd better see me." When reporters followed up to ask if her husband agreed with her, she said Dick was "all for me," and announced that she was working on her husband to make that happen. Nixon tried to oblige her and make history.

With two spots to fill, Nixon wanted to locate two strict conservatives who would counter the liberals on the Court, but he had trouble finding women who fit his criteria. After he announced his intention to nominate Mildred Lillie, a little-known intermediate California state appellate court judge, to fill Harlan's seat, the American Bar Association rated her as "unqualified." On October 21, when he chose two men, Lewis F. Powell, Jr., and William Rehnquist, as his nominees, Pat was upset. "Boy is she mad," Dick told Haldeman. The First Lady had made a public declaration because she believed that she had a commitment from her husband and she was furious about his change of mind. During dinner that night, Pat argued with him about his failure to choose a woman. She did not buy into the "argument of the bar turning her down." Pat did not think it was sufficient reason to scuttle the nomination. Frustrated by her opposition, Dick cut off the discussion by saying, "We tried to do the best we could, Pat."

As her own confidence as First Lady increased (despite her setback on the Court decision), and as she caught up to the changing times, Pat was increasingly willing to take strong public stands on women's issues. "I'm liberated," she told the *Los Angeles Times*. She claimed that her husband never stopped her from doing the things she wanted to do, that "In fact, he's proud of me." During an impromptu press conference on a flight during her "Legacy of Parks" tour, Pat avowed that the National Women's Political Caucus sounded "pretty wild" to her. She was distancing herself from liberal feminist leaders like Gloria Steinem and Bella Abzug. Pat wanted to see more women run for political offices because "women can do a lot for politics" and said, in striking contrast to most of her fellow Republicans, that she would be willing to campaign for a Democratic woman as she has "always believed in supporting the person, not the party."

She was concerned women did not vote for other women. Women had to be educated to do so, Pat thought. In January 1972 she told the *Ladies' Home Journal,* "I am for equal rights and equal pay. But I don't believe in parades or things like that. I believe the way for women to achieve is to be qualified." Pat was discovering how to be a conservative, yet "liberated" wife who could appeal to her husband's Sunbelt constituency and to the media she felt plagued her husband.

Nixon, prodded by Pat, was himself evolving on women's issues. He ordered all his executive departments to make plans to attract more qualified women to appoint to the top positions. He also established a presidential Task Force on Women's Rights and Responsibilities.

*   *   *

On January 3, 1972, Pat attended the inauguration of William Tolbert, the grandson of a South Carolina slave, as president of Liberia. Tolbert had been a personal friend of the Nixons since they met on their vice-presidential trip to Liberia in 1957. Pat received unprecedented public notice for her multinational trip to Africa, visiting not just Liberia but Ghana and the Ivory Coast. To prepare for the trip, she gave a dinner for African ambassadors, rekindled friendships with representatives of the countries she was going to visit, and received briefings from the president and Henry Kissinger. During her eight-day trip, Pat conferred with the presidents of the three countries and discussed U.S. policy on Rhodesia and South Africa—both countries were run by whites and were the object of increasing international pressure to hand over power to their black majorities—as well as human rights issues across the continent, the future of U.S. economic assistance, and the president's upcoming trip to China.

Arriving in Liberia, Pat was welcomed with honors usually reserved for a head of state. After receiving a nineteen-gun salute, she reviewed the honor guard. On the forty-mile motorcade ride to the Liberian capital of Monrovia, she sat next to Tolbert in an open car. Thousands cheered her along the route. At the inauguration ceremony, held in one-hundred-degree heat, in a small Baptist church, the new president called her a woman of "courage, strength of character, and fortitude of spirit." At the inaugural ball, he presented her with Liberia's top honor, the Grand Cordon of the Most Venerable Order of the Knighthood of Pioneers of African Redemption. Atypically, at the end of a long day that followed a sleepless night, Pat allowed herself to acknowledge the demands of her role, telling a news conference, "Being First Lady is the hardest unpaid job in the world."

In Ghana, when the president of that country whispered to Mrs. Nixon that she should bow to members of the National Assembly before addressing them, she told the group, "I'm taking orders from headquarters. He says to bow." The legislators laughed and applauded her. She told the legislators that the U.S. congressmen "don't have so much fun" as their Ghanaian counterparts. In the Ivory Coast she stood in an open car in the rain and waved to crowds estimated at seventy-five thousand—including men wearing feathers and "fiercely painted tribal masks"—who greeted her with shouts of "Vive Madame Nixon." When Pat announced that her husband would run for re-election as president and said she supported the run, she garnered new headlines, including FIRST LADY SPILLS BEANS; SAYS DICK TO RUN AGAIN. When a reporter requested additional revelations and news-worthy tidbits about her trip, she declined, saying, "I want to cash in on my diary when I write it."

Pat's enthusiasm, her affection for the African people, and her re-spect for Western Africa's culture came through in the worldwide news coverage of her trip. The president, their daughters, and the White House staff carefully monitored the coverage, with aides noting that 85 percent of all U.S. daily newspapers covered the story of her arrival in Liberia. They showed the president headlines saying PAT EMBRACES TOLBERT: CROWD ROARS APPROVAL and PAT A HIT AS LIBERIAN PRES. SWORN IN. The day after the inauguration in Liberia, Dick cabled her what amounted to a professional love note: "The TV coverage, particularly by CBS, was outstanding. *New York Times, Washington Post* and *Los Angeles Times* all had front page stories. . . . Everybody here believes sending you on the trip was a ten strike. Tricia, Julie and I are saving all the good clips for you. Love, Dick." This cable is remarkable because it is the only extant public note to his wife that the president signed with "Love."

In his diary, Dick crowed, "Pat had press conferences in each coun-try, had conversations with presidents of each country, and carried it all off with unbelievable skill. . . . As Julie put it, what came through was love of the people of the countries she visited for her, and, on her part, love for them." Even the *New York Times* acknowledged, "They loved her in Monrovia . . . they loved her in Accra, too."

Charles Colson sent the president a seven-page memo admitting that the White House team had failed in their quest to add color and humanity to the president's image, but "Mrs. Nixon has broken through where we have failed . . . men and women identify with her, and in return with you." The "warm and appealing" image of the First Family is "maybe one of the most important political developments of your Presidency." Julie and Mrs. Nixon had "'caught on' big: I don't think we have yet realized the full political implications," Colson continued. ". . . Men often judge other men by the character of their wives. Mrs. Nixon's character has come through magnificently." Women were again interested in the family side of the Nixon administration.

Doug Hallett, who worked under Chuck Colson and often criticized the administration for overemphasizing public relations and for the gap between its words and actions, saw that in Africa Pat "was credible as a liberated woman." "She is an enormous asset. She can do the things you can't do; her moves will not be instantly labeled political, as yours would; she has the ability to project warmth and create empathy." The "warmth of the First Family and the public affection for Mrs. Nixon" could make the difference in the election. Pat sent a copy of the memo to Helene Drown with a note attached: "Thought you would be amused by the late recognition."

Dick was impressed when his wife returned home looking hearty and revitalized despite her draining schedule. Pat felt invigorated by re-experiencing her love of foreign cultures, her competence as a goodwill ambassador, and her memories of the earlier, career-advancing trips she had made with Dick during his vice presidency. She was, however, disappointed by the reception accorded her by the West Wing staff. Pat was "very put out," Dick noted in his diary, that neither Ehrlichman nor Haldeman spoke to her about her trip. When Dick told her that Haldeman believed that her trip was the only administration event to garner "universal approval," Pat replied, "Well, at least, they should tell me." To capitalize on the interest in her African trip, Pat agreed to do a television interview with Barbara Walters. But Walters irritated Pat by diverging from the agreed-on topic. In addition to talking about Africa, Walters raised questions about the need for day care centers in the United States. She mentioned the president's "old-fashioned attitudes about women," and queried Pat about whether she would support a woman for president. Walters inquired about the happiest and most stressful times in Pat's marriage and whether people had exaggerated her sense of privacy. Noting that the president sent Pat two cables stressing the superb press coverage she had received, Walters demanded to know if the trip was intended as much to improve his public image as to foster foreign relations. Pat sensed attack in Walters's questions, and she told Dick afterward they were "vicious."

Dick immediately went to his wife's defense. He instructed his press secretary Ron Zeigler and the First Lady's chief of staff to confront Walters and ask her why she took "such a cheap shot" at Pat. Did Walters want to kill all her chances for future cooperation from the White House? Nixon ordered Stuart to block all coverage of the First Lady unless she cleared it with the West Wing. But Pat had ideas of her own. Her husband had set up a White House Television Office in January 1971, and he directed two of its principals, producer Mark Goode and television advisor Bill Carruthers, to help Pat. She wasted no time telling Stuart to keep them away from her: She did not want their advice. She relied on her own experience with Walters to decide whether to decline future televised interviews. But she knew showcasing herself was crucial to her husband's strategy for winning a second term.

~18

The Zenith

*I*n early 1972 the Nixons made historic trips to China and the Soviet Union—interludes that gave them a respite from the incessant hostility that was directed at their White House fortress by liberals and antiwar activists. Occasionally the anger could penetrate, as it did on the evening of January 28, 1972. In honor of the fiftieth anniversary of *Reader's Digest*, the president had conferred the Presidential Medal of Freedom on its founders, DeWitt Wallace and Lila Acheson Wallace. Just as the Ray Conniff Singers began to entertain the Nixons' dinner guests, Carole Feraci, a Canadian who had filled in for one of the singers, pulled out from under her dress a banner that read "Stop the Bombing." She went on to read a statement castigating the president for "bombing human beings, animals, and vegetation" in Vietnam. "You go to church on Sunday and pray to Jesus Christ. If

Jesus Christ were in the room tonight, you would not dare drop another bomb. God Bless the Berrigans and Daniel Ellsberg." The guests booed. Some cried, "Throw her out." Martha Mitchell, wife of the attorney general, suggested Feraci "ought to be torn limb from limb." Although Conniff fired Feraci on the spot, the president did not think she had done the administration much harm. According to Haldeman, she might have generated sympathy for the Nixons. But Pat was angry because she judged any protest against the president in his own home an unforgivable breach of decorum, and as a staunch defender of her husband's war policies, she particularly resented this one.

In February 1972 the Nixon marriage reached its professional zenith when the couple made their trip to China, the climax of years of diplomacy. There had been little or no direct dialogue or trade between the United States and the People's Republic of China since the communists had taken over the mainland in 1949. During this mission to China, Pat and Dick gave their finest performance—marking their most memorable moment on the world stage—as forty million people watched them on television. The First Lady played a starring role beside her husband, without upstaging him, in a remarkable diplomatic transformation that Dick had hoped for since he assumed the presidency.

For more than a decade, long before he became president, Dick Nixon had been intrigued by the possibility of a global opening to China. In conversations with Charles de Gaulle in Paris in the early 1960s, the French president challenged Nixon to ponder the importance of reintegrating China into the international community. Dick's thinking about China evolved during his international fact-finding trips, starting under the Eisenhower administration and continuing into the mid-1960s. In a 1967 article in *Foreign Affairs*, Nixon argued that the international community needed to bring China back out of "angry isolation" into "the family of nations." From the start of his presidency, he directed National Security Advisor Henry Kissinger to convince the xenophobic and isolationist Chinese to open to the West. China's recent frosty relations with the Soviet Union, including border clashes between the two communist powers, encouraged the country to respond to overtures from the United States. During Kissinger's secret trip to Beijing in July 1971, the Chinese invited Nixon to make a state visit. Premier Chou En-lai (now more often referred to as Zhou Enlai) and Kissinger mapped out the contours of the trip and negotiated the main components of an agreement between the two former enemy states.

Pat lobbied privately and publicly to accompany her husband on the trip, telling reporters, "I'm putting my name on the sign-up list." When Nixon told a news conference that the American delegation would be "a small working group," she joked that she would go to Ireland by herself if she was not invited to China. According to Haldeman's unpublished diary notes, the president did not initially plan to take the First Lady with him. He relented, but he still did not want to be upstaged: "The P's [president's] now concluded that PN's [Pat Nixon's] got to go on the trip because of the way Henry's set things up [Kissinger accepted Premier Chou En-lai's request that the president bring Mrs. Nixon along]." Dick did not want her to bring any staff, "But she has to have an advance man to handle her activities. She should be separately scheduled, take no women's press along with her, should not ride with the P." After he thought more about it, he realized Pat's presence would save him from having to take up valuable negotiating time mingling with the Chinese people for the television cameras and that "people contact is more important than meetings, in terms of public relations" in the United States. In a comment that reflects a sexist view of women's public roles that was common at the time, Nixon bluntly told Haldeman, "If Pat goes, she goes solely as a prop." He didn't want Secretary of State William Rogers's wife to join them, or anyone else who would diminish focus on negotiations that could dramatically affect the geopolitical balance of power.

On February 17, several thousand supporters attended a departure ceremony on the White House lawn. Nixon, who juggled pessimism and realism, called the mission "a journey for peace," but he had no illusions about sweeping away decades of hostility. The trip was the most stressful and uncertain of all that the Nixons had taken; Pat had been "sick to her stomach" throughout the previous weekend, worried that the Chinese had not given her a specific schedule of events, and tense about doing anything that might harm Dick's diplomacy. She told reporters, "Of course I wouldn't say anything to spoil the good work Dick has done." She and Dick and their advisors knew little about the attitudes they would encounter in China. Dick was chancing a highly visible international failure. He was risking U.S. relationships with Taiwan and the Soviet Union and jeopardizing his own political support from intensely anticommunist elements in his own party, but Dick viewed the risk as worth taking because he felt a U.S. rapprochement with China would calm the region and perhaps motivate the Soviets to help the United States wind down the Vietnam War.

The Nixons had quieted their nerves by doing intense preparation. They learned basic Chinese phrases, Chinese history, and culture, studied *Quotations from Chairman Mao Tse-tung*, known in the West as the Little Red Book, learned something about Chinese philosophy and the structure of the Communist Party, and studied sketchy biographies of the main leaders. Pat read some of Mao's poetry. Speechwriter Pat Buchanan prepped the First Lady on how to answer reporters' questions as she toured sites in China. Nixon spent more than forty hours discussing the trip with Kissinger. On the flight to China Dick read four-foot-high briefing books. Ramping up the stakes for Pat, the State Department reminded her that she had an "unprecedented opportunity . . . to influence the way in which Americans view the Chinese, Chinese women, and the social order." On the morning of February 21, the worldwide television audience watched as the presidential plane, renamed *The Spirit of '76* for this occasion, landed at the dull, gray Capital Airport outside Beijing.

Premier Chou created a dramatic tableau by standing alone on the tarmac to greet Nixon. The president ordered Secret Service agents to barricade the plane's door after he exited so that no other government official, particularly Kissinger and Rogers, could share the glory when Nixon shook the premier's hand. "That handshake was over the vastest distance in the world, twenty-five years of no communication," Chou purportedly said at the time. The Chinese claimed the phrase had come from Nixon. Columnist Hugh Sidey described the moment for readers of *Life* magazine. Nixon "came in vast silence. It [the small greeting party] was the only such welcome for a president in history and it was stunning. . . . The panoply of presidential power that has brought whole cities into the street cheering was shrunken to a few people."

Pat Nixon made her own bold statement. Wearing a fur-lined red coat, she followed her husband down the stairs. Her coat matched the airport's red banners with their revolutionary slogans and signaled her openness to the Chinese people and her attention to their culture. Set off against the dark outfits of Communist Party officials, the coat was one of the fashion masterstrokes of the era. It looked as if she was personally bringing color and hope into a gray world. Pat knew that the color red meant good luck to the Chinese; she wore bright red coats and dresses at many of the settings she visited in China. In that moment and in the remaining days of the visit, she was catapulted into diplomatic stardom.

Pat and Dick stood at attention as they listened to a Chinese band play "The Star-Spangled Banner" on the windy and cold runway—a groundbreaking moment in the center of the communist world. The Nixons rode into central Beijing in curtained limousines along eerily deserted streets. They traveled through Tiananmen Square, the city's main and most historic plaza, which was nearly empty, to their official guesthouse. Shortly after their arrival, Nixon and Kissinger were whisked away for a secret one-hour meeting with the ailing, epochal figure Mao Tse-tung, who pointedly grasped Nixon's hand for a full minute. Photographers recorded their talks. Nixon was enthralled with Mao's power and his philosophical bent. The president was not displeased that Mao complimented him on his book *Six Crises*. The president brought Mao a friendship gift, sculptor Edward Boehm's porcelain group of white swans, which symbolized peace and was valued at more than $250,000. As this was a state gift, the State Department paid for it. In China the president spent fifteen hours in meetings with Chou, seeking to forge a stable relationship between the two countries and working out principles of territorial integrity—the United States seemingly acknowledging Taiwan was a part of China, mutual nonaggression in Vietnam, and noninterference in each other's internal affairs.

On their first evening in Beijing, Pat and Dick attended a banquet in the Great Hall of the People in Tiananmen Square. Television networks carried it live, without commentary, for four hours. Nixon noted that more people viewed the banquet via television than had seen any previous historic event. In the background a Chinese band played a medley of Chinese and American music, including "America the Beautiful" and "Turkey in the Straw." Echoing Lincoln's Gettysburg speech, Nixon declared that the world might not remember what words would be said that evening, but that the events of the trip would be supremely memorable; he went on to quote Mao, saying, "Seize the day, seize the hour." At the banquet Nixon walked amiably from table to table to offer respectful toasts to his hosts.

While her husband was sequestered in private meetings with Premier Chou, television film crews followed Mrs. Nixon as she introduced Americans and the rest of the world to China. According to her aide Jack Brennan, the Chinese were wary of authority figures, but they were drawn to Pat's warmth and grace. Helen Thomas, one of three female reporters allowed on the trip, remembered that when young Revolutionary Committee guides attempted to involve her in discussions of Communist Party dialectics, Pat would smile politely and say, "Yes, I am acquainted with the philosophy."

Pat emphasized how much she enjoyed the sights, her own connections to the people and places she visited, and singled out similarities between the American and Chinese people. She trudged through the dusty gray Evergreen People's Commune, a large community labor and living collective with its own government, in a snowfall, observed acupuncture treatments at a clinic, turning away at first, saying, "I think it's sort of rude to watch," hugged children at the Beijing Children's Hospital, and visited math and art classrooms, telling them she was a schoolteacher, and passing on a "hello from the children of America." While she petted the commune's pigs, she recalled she had once "raised a prize winner—second prize" during her 4-H years. When she asked about the breed of pigs she was seeing and Helen Thomas declared them to be "Male chauvinist[s]," Pat joined in the laughter. At the Beijing Glassware Factory she focused on some small green elephant figurines: "Ah, the elephant," she declared, "the symbol of our party." In the kitchen of the Peking Hotel, with its staff of 115 cooks, she gamely tasted a goldfish and a "fiery stuffed pickled squash," claiming it was delicious. Wickedly, she offered a bite to a reporter, who grew pale upon tasting it.

While shopping, Pat cracked up Jack Brennan when she chose a pair of pajamas for Dick, held them up to Brennan, approximately the same size as her husband, and asked if he thought they would fit "Ricardo." Brennan and other members of the official party were less amused with Barbara Walters, who tried to stand next to Pat at every opportunity. CBS's Walter Cronkite and ABC's Harry Reasoner were also in hot pursuit of television photo opportunities at Pat's side. Even conservative political journalist William F. Buckley, who had come along on the trip although he had initially opposed the president's overture to China, recognized that "Pat Nixon was the only show in town."

When Pat and Dick went together to the snow-covered courtyards of the Forbidden City, they saw a royal reception room where child-emperors had managed the affairs of state with "prompting from their mothers who had hid behind screens." Nixon joked, "It's the same today. The women are always the back seat driver." On their second night Pat and Dick sat alongside Mao's grim, vengeful wife, Chiang Ching, who had avidly purged the Communist Party and spearheaded the burning of books during the Cultural Revolution beginning in 1966, a social and political movement designed to enforce communism and eradicate capitalist elements in Chinese culture and society. It was only now abating. The Nixons watched the interminable proletarian ballet Ching had created and staged, *The Red Detachment of Women*, which told the story of a peasant who was tortured by a landlord, ran off to join communists, and came back with her colleagues to kill her tormentor. Correspondent Bernard Kalb quoted another correspondent who said it "took revolutionary patience to sit through the first act."

In the key public moment of their visit, on a cold, sunny day, the Nixons traveled to the Badaling section of the Great Wall of China, begun three centuries before the birth of Jesus and stretching from the Yellow Sea to the Gobi Desert—a stretch of more than three thousand miles. For Pat, the most exciting moment of the trip was standing on a wall that was "so graceful winding up the mountain like a dragon's back." According to historian Gil Troy, photographs of the smiling Nixons standing "on the enduring symbol of Chinese xenophobia" symbolized their historic "breakthrough." Reporters, starved for commentary from a president who had been sequestered mostly in private meetings, asked him what he thought about the wall, and most of them quoted him, "The Great Wall is a great wall," without adding his final comment that the wall was representative of a great people. Although he had erected barricades both real and metaphorical around and within his own White House, the president went on to say, "We do not want walls of any kind. . . . As we look at this wall, what is most important is that we have an open world."

Chou En-lai and his wife, Deng Yingchao, captivated Pat, who described him as "a charmer" with a "delightful sense of humor." Sitting beside Chou at a dinner, Pat mentioned her visit to see the giant pandas at the Beijing Zoo. She picked up one of the packs of Panda Cigarettes set by each place at the table. "Aren't they cute? I love them," she said, referring to the drawings on bright pink paper of two pandas cavorting with each other. Chou responded, "I'll give you some." She thought he meant the cigarettes, but he was offering her pandas. Less than two months later, on April 16, 1972, Pat officially welcomed two giant pandas (Ling-Ling and Hsing-Hsing) and the Chinese delegation that brought them to Washington. The two pandas caused what Pat called "panda-monium," attracting hundreds of millions of visitors over the years, until their deaths in the 1990s. In return, the United States government gave the Chinese people two North American musk oxen named Milton and Matilda. These shaggy beasts with curled tusks—native to North America and the arctic region—developed mange and did not attract the same level of adulation in China.

On the last afternoon of the weeklong visit, the Americans and

Chinese issued what became known as the Shanghai Communiqué, declaring a mutual desire to normalize relations and a joint opposition to any other country "seeking hegemony" in the Pacific arena— a reference directly to the Soviet Union. Additionally, Nixon promised Chou and Mao that he would move against the Soviet Union if they attempted to dominate the Asia Pacific area militarily.

In the trip's final negotiations Kissinger exerted himself to create a document expressing both sides of the most contentious issue between the two countries—relations with the island of Taiwan, where Nationalist Chinese, exiled from the mainland by the communists in 1949, still declared themselves the legitimate government of all China. The United States acknowledged there was "one China," of which Taiwan was a part, agreed to "a peaceful settlement of the Taiwan question by the Chinese," and acknowledged an ultimate objective of U.S. military withdrawal from Taiwan.

But by tying China to the United States, Nixon circumscribed its ability to attack Taiwan. At a banquet on February 28, Nixon hyperbolically called his visit "the week that changed the world." The Nixons' trip contributed to the eventual Westernization of China and shifted the balance of power, placing the United States in a cardinal position between China and the Soviet Union, at least until Watergate diluted Nixon's diplomatic influence. It may also have helped the president resolve the Vietnam War. U.S. editorial responses to the visit were cautious, but generally positive. "A smiling dragon is a big improvement over one spitting, but it is still a dragon," opined an editorial in the *Los Angeles Herald Examiner.*

The trip may not have permanently altered doubts about the vitality of the Nixons' private marriage, but it certainly proved them to be one of the most powerful couples on the world stage. Kandy Stroud of *Women's Wear Daily* was struck that Nixon "seems to have taken a second look at his wife." The man who had ignored or sniped at his wife in public suddenly seemed "genuinely attentive and gentle." Stroud noticed that he coaxed her to his side when she fell back to let him garner the attention.

No one was trendier that year than Pat Nixon in her red wool coat on the far side of the world. *Chicago Today* wondered in a February 24 editorial whether historians might conclude that while Dick conducted business, Pat did "the important work," establishing "direct and friendly contact with the Chinese people on a normal human level" through her "unfailing warm, gracious conduct." White House correspondent and columnist Robert Thompson editorialized that Pat had achieved a perfect balance between playing "a vital role in world affairs" and maintaining a "feminine manner."

In the diplomatic arena Pat had become a woman truly of the early 1970s—someone who balanced significant achievement with a domestic and family focus.

The president's staff fully appreciated Pat's public relations triumph and sought ways to capitalize on it. Pat Buchanan prepared a memo for the First Lady suggesting that in interviews she should praise the noncommunist aspects of Chinese society (the food, the historic sites, the friendliness and pride of the people) while expressing reservations about the "enormous price the Chinese people have paid for the material gains which free people take for granted." The president and his aides wanted her to participate in a prime-time television special they would propose to ABC or CBS to give viewers a broader perspective on China. The staff offered to write a script, for Pat to read in a voiceover as background for television footage from the trip. But Pat Nixon resisted, telling the West Wing she had nothing new to say except "obvious generalities and superficial comments." They pushed a second time; she did not budge.

With the presidential election looming, Dick escalated efforts to plant stories that highlighted him as a good man and a masterly international negotiator. Upon his return from China, Nixon enlisted Kissinger's aid in strengthening the president's image as a world leader. Kissinger, Nixon thought, was the best-qualified person to emphasize the president's extensive preparations for foreign trips, the toughness that never became belligerence, his ability to treat fellow leaders with respect, his superb discipline, his stamina, and his candor. Nixon felt he had to advance his own cause via his national security advisor, but he had to monitor Kissinger's comments carefully, because he did not trust Kissinger not to go beyond glorifying himself in the press and using his position to advance his own reputation.

When it came to foreign policy, Dick thoroughly trusted Pat's discretion, her ability to act properly and to make acute observations, as he told Frank Gannon during a series of interviews in 1983, so much so that he was able to use her as an envoy to the Soviets when relations between the two countries grew delicate. In March 1972, North Vietnam, armed by the Soviet Union, invaded South Vietnam where U.S. troops were stationed. This offensive jeopardized Nixon's plans to visit the Soviet Union that spring. Dick briefed Pat on the difficult situation and asked her to meet with Irina Dobrynin, the wife of the longtime Soviet ambassador to Washington, Anatoly Dobrynin. Nixon told Pat to discuss her previous visit to Moscow in 1959, and what she might do during the Nixons' planned trip to Russia, but to express concern that the current situation in Vietnam might jeopardize the mission to Moscow. She had tea with Mrs. Dobrynin at the Soviet embassy and told her, "We do not want anything like Vietnam to interfere with the summit." Irina took Pat's hand and reassured her that the trip would not be canceled. According to Nixon's memoir *RN*, Pat "showed great skill and subtlety" in her discussion with Irina Dobrynin. Pat returned to the White House and confirmed for Dick that the plans for the summit were intact. Nixon promptly called Kissinger to say how much the Russians were counting on a presidential visit.

Beginning their trip on May 22, Pat and Dick received a cool and formal welcome at Moscow's Vnukovo Airport. While in the Soviet Union, Nixon engaged in cordial but tough-minded talks on strategic arms limitation and Vietnam with Soviet leaders, including the general secretary of the Communist party, Leonid Brezhnev, President Nikolai Podgorny, Premier Aleksei Kosygin, Foreign Minister Andrei Gromyko, and Dobrynin. On May 26 in the Kremlin, Brezhnev and Nixon signed the ABM Treaty, limiting antiballistic missile systems, and an Interim Offensive Agreement, which froze the number of ballistic missiles at the 1972 level while prohibiting development of more land-based ICBM silos. These agreements, emphasizing diplomatic restraint and a commitment to avoid military confrontations, were the first step in arms control and the abatement of geopolitical tensions known as détente. Pat asked to sit in on the ceremony. None of the Russian leaders' wives was invited, but Dick told Pat to slip in and watch from behind a column so as not to attract attention, as she was the only spouse allowed to witness the signing of the treaty.

The First Lady's most memorable moment occurred at the Bolshoi Theater, when the Nixons entered the presidential box to attend a gala performance of *Swan Lake*, and she was delighted "to see the two flags, the Russian flag and the American flag on either side of the box and to hear the two national anthems played [which] made chills run up my spine." The Nixons invited the Soviet leaders to a banquet and a performance by the American classical pianist Van Cliburn, who was in Moscow to perform with the Moscow Orchestra. When Kosygin, sitting next to her, harangued her about arrogant American female politicians and reporters and complained about Americans' focus on consumerism, she politely but firmly defended American women and reporters. Later the Nixons toured Leningrad, visiting the cemetery where the victims of the Nazi siege were buried, and then flew back to Moscow to attend services at the city's only Baptist church.

As she had been in China, Pat was dogged by reporters who wanted information about the activities of the president, cordoned off from public view in meeting after meeting. "I haven't seen that guy," she laughingly told reporters. On her own the First Lady attended a rehearsal of the Bolshoi Ballet School, the circus, and classes at Moscow State University; she visited a Moscow watch factory, a fashion show, and the famous GUM department store. As one U.S. editorial saw it, "Any first lady who can execute a dance step for pleasure at the Bolshoi Ballet School, who can confront a Russian bear with equanimity, who can survive three wild subway rides and still put out a protective hand to Mrs. Brezhnev . . . is a first lady in quality as well as in position."

Pat wore bright colors and bold patterns, contrasting with the solid grays and browns of the Kremlin wives. Spouses of Soviet leaders traditionally stayed out of the spotlight, but they showed up for Mrs. Nixon.

When Pat accompanied Victoria Brezhnev and other Soviet leaders' wives on the Moscow subway, they were surrounded by KGB security guards to protect them from zealous reporters and cameramen. The guards thwarted Pat's efforts to speak to other passengers on the train and she was frustrated. She did tell the Metro administrator that the famously sleek Moscow subway system was the loveliest system she had ever seen. Mrs. Nixon and Mrs. Brezhnev linked arms in a gesture that symbolized détente.

As Nixon and Brezhnev concluded their meetings by professing the start of a new era of increased cooperation, Colson reported from Washington that the Strategic Arms Limitation Talks, negotiations that had begun Finland in 1969 and had culminated with the signing of the ABM Treaty and the Interim Offensive Agreement in Moscow, had had an enormous impact on public opinion and were "especially effective with the swing category" voters, as was Pat Nixon's performance. On their way back to the United States, the Nixons stopped in Warsaw. After attending a Chopin recital, Pat evaded her minders and plunged into an excited crowd outside the concert hall. Returning to Washington, the president and First Lady went directly from Andrews Air Force Base to Capitol Hill, where he addressed a joint session of Congress. Pat received a standing ovation when she entered the House chamber, and she acknowledged her admirers with outstretched hands.

The Nixons barely noticed the first indications of the coming Watergate crisis. On Sunday, June 18, 1972, while visiting Key Biscayne, Richard Nixon glanced at the *Miami Herald*'s front page and noticed a small story: "Miamians Held in D.C. Try to Bug Demo Headquarters." A former CIA employee, later identified as James McCord, and four Cuban Americans had been arrested for breaking into the offices of the Democratic National Committee at the Watergate Hotel and Office Building and apartment complex in Washington. Nixon claimed in his memoir he did not pay much attention to the article because he thought the burglary sounded like a silly prank. According to his account in *RN*, the next evening, as he was on his way back to Washington from Key Biscayne, Bob Haldeman gave him jolting news: James McCord, who was on the payroll of the Committee to Re-elect the President (CRP—commonly mocked afterward as CREEP), had been one of the men arrested for breaking into the Democratic headquarters to tap the phone of party chairman Lawrence O'Brien.

The Nixon team was, as usual, highly sensitive to anything that might generate negative public relations. Nixon could have fired anyone involved in the matter and he could have suggested an independent investigator to recommend whom to fire, but he decided to contain any political damage through monitoring his own administration's actions. The FBI told him that E. Howard Hunt, a former CIA employee, and G. Gordon Liddy, the legal counsel for CRP, had supervised the burglars. The president knew that Hunt had participated in the break-in at the office of Daniel Ellsberg's psychiatrist, the surveillance of Senator Edward M. Kennedy, and plans to break into the offices of the Brookings Institution, where Ellsberg's colleagues and Democratic foreign policy strategists were employed. Nixon also quickly realized that the Watergate break-in had occurred under the auspices of his campaign manager, John Mitchell. By June 23 Nixon and Haldeman were worried that the Watergate operation could be linked to the White House, and eventually to the president. In what came to be known as the "smoking gun" conversation that revealed Nixon's complicity in a cover-up, the two men talked about calling in CIA director Richard Helms and directing him to ask the interim head of the FBI, L. Patrick Gray, to stop his investigation. Pat remained unaware of her husband's actions, which would enmesh them all in a nightmarish crisis.

During the summer and fall of 1972, *Washington Post* reporters Carl Bernstein and Bob Woodward, along with a few other investigative reporters from the *Los Angeles Times* and the *New York Times*, confirmed an astounding list of possible tight links between CRP and the Watergate break-in. Among the most damning were: Watergate burglars had received cash that had been raised for the president's re-election campaign; Nixon's campaign manager, John Mitchell, controlled a secret fund that was used to pay for a wide variety of intelligence-gathering activities directed against the Democratic Party; and, according to the FBI, the Watergate incident was part of a massive political spying and sabotage operation associated with the effort to re-elect the president. The Republican dirty tricks had helped eliminate Senator Edmund Muskie, a candidate Nixon saw as a genuine threat, from the race for the Democratic presidential nomination.

During the fall presidential campaign, Nixon remained essentially unscathed by these revelations. Pat Nixon read about them in the papers. As far as is known, Dick did not reveal to her the truth he was hiding: that he had talked about authorizing payment to the Watergate burglars, that he had set the administrative tone that led to illegal activities, or that he was suppressing and thwarting the Watergate investigation. Nor did Pat, it appears, probe him for the facts. For her to believe her husband was a great man and at the same time engaged in criminal activities would have created a cognitive dissonance that she would not willingly endure. Pat tended to blame any wrongdoing in her husband's office on Bob Haldeman and his minions.

As she started an independent campaign tour in Chicago, Pat encountered her first hint that reporters were going after a bigger story than she was prepared to give. At a press reception younger reporters didn't merely agree to shake her hand in front of the television cameras but demanded a chance to ask questions and then pressed her with the type of inquiries she detested. Was she concerned that the investigation of the Watergate burglary would hurt her husband's re-election chances? "I really don't think so," Pat said. "All I know is what I read in the papers." When she discussed the campaign with her husband, did the Watergate situation concern him? "We don't discuss it," Pat answered. "I think it has been blown out of proportion." The reporters asked about an incident in which a Republican security operative reportedly threw John Mitchell's wife, Martha, down on the floor in her room and ripped the phone out of her wall. Martha Mitchell, who had been hospitalized in the past for alcoholism and depression, made many attention-seeking late-night calls to the media, giving them her anti-Nixon perspective on Watergate. She claimed that she had been held against her will in a California hotel room to keep her from contacting reporters. Pat, who could not stand the flamboyant wife of the Nixon campaign manager, deflected the question. "I don't know what happened in that room."

In July, South Dakota senator George McGovern accepted the Democratic nomination for president at his party's convention in Miami Beach. The McGovern campaign got off to a problematic start when it became known that his vice-presidential running mate, Missouri senator Thomas Eagleton, had received electroshock treatment for depression. Eagleton withdrew. After being turned down by a number of other prominent politicians, McGovern eventually replaced Eagleton with Kennedy in-law R. Sargent Shriver. Nixon had already prompted Charles Colson and Bob Haldeman to maximize public awareness that controversial leftist activists Abbie Hoffman, Jerry Rubin, and Angela Davis supported McGovern's presidential bid. Remembering the success Lyndon Johnson had had tying Barry Goldwater to ultra-right-wing supporters in 1964, Nixon knew that "nailing" McGovern to his left-wing supporters was "essential," as he put it, no matter what hardball methods he had to use.

On August 8, Pat surprised a group of reporters by spending an entire hour discussing a wide range of topics with them, including directly addressing political subjects. Her counterpart in the presidential campaign, Eleanor McGovern, was known for talking bluntly about the issues, and the First Lady was not going to lose a contest about substance with McGovern's wife. In October a hyperbolic *Time* magazine cover story would assert, "Never before in the history of U.S. politics have the wives of two presidential candidates squared off so directly." In her August interview Pat showed a surprising command of facts and figures about Vietnam and the economy and deftly handled questions about day care and abortion rights, articulating traditional Republican stands on those issues.

When a reporter brought up the charge by actress and activist Jane Fonda that the United States had deliberately bombed dikes in North Vietnam to flood the country—a false accusation arising from North Vietnamese propaganda—Pat vehemently denied the accusation and retorted that Jane Fonda "should have been in Hanoi asking them to stop their aggression. Then there wouldn't be any conflict." Declaring how important it was to elect a Congress controlled by the GOP, Pat tossed off a few zingers at the Democrats. Dick, who set Pat's campaign agenda, approved of her performance but noted in his diary, "The only problem is that she goes through such agony in preparing it that I hate to have to have her take on the assignment."

In mid-August Pat essayed another preconvention interview, with Marya McLaughlin of CBS. According to Haldeman, McLaughlin "made a big thing of Mrs. Nixon being separated from the president all the time." Nixon would have to stay in a hotel in Miami Beach, instead of being in his house in Key Biscayne, so as to avoid more nettling press speculation about the physical and emotional distance between him and his wife. As Nixon set up a tightly controlled convention that would project compelling images of his all-American family, he did not want any further commentary regarding the vitality of his marriage. Part of the convention's sales pitch included a laudatory documentary about Pat, a "Tribute to the First Lady." When Pat screened the documentary at the White House, Nixon told Tricia and Rose Mary Woods to rave about it so that Pat would not dare ask to have it remade. There was no time to repackage it to suit a perfectionist. Pat approved it.

Pat, Julie, and Tricia arrived in Miami Beach the day before the convention started and attended an afternoon reception for a thousand volunteers at the Hotel Fontainebleau. Listening to the band, the First Lady "threw up her hands, dipped her knees, and executed a dignified, but unmistakable little frug" while blurting out, "Oh, that music!"

Actor James Stewart narrated the nine-and-a-half-minute documentary tribute to Mrs. Nixon. "She has always been the kind who waits in the wings," he began, and then went on to declare, "Out of her desire to serve . . . she emerged as a force in her own right." The video highlighted the partnership between Pat and Dick, with Stewart intoning, "She believes in him, she's always there. Companion, helpmate, campaigner." Pat was a diplomat who "best represents the president's policy of reconciliation, the desire for a people-to-people bond that reinforces the universal desire for peace." A typically effusive campaign film geared to the Silent Majority viewers Nixon needed for his re-election, it lauded the Nixons as "this new force in diplomacy for goodwill." Mrs. Nixon was "elegant, but never aloof, unreachable." The video closed with a shot of the Nixons walking together along a beach.

When the film ended, Pat took the podium while a band played "Lovely to Look At," and received an ovation that lasted nearly as long as the film. Pat stood with her arms stretched out in a wide embrace. "It was a gesture uniquely hers," Nixon wrote, "graceful and gracious." Smiling and waving, she thanked the foot-stomping delegates for "the most wonderful welcome I've ever had." The delegates yelled in reply, "We want Pat" and "Four More Years." Pat playfully lifted an oversize gavel and acted as if she were pounding it to silence her admirers, then began her brief talk: "To those who say that we don't have the young people . . ." Stomping and cheering erupted again.

Pat was the first Republican First Lady to address a nominating convention. (Eleanor Roosevelt had spoken to the 1944 Democratic convention.) Her speech would set the model for future convention speeches by the wives of the nominees. Dick, watching the convention lovefest and seeing his daughters in action, was pleased. "No First Family ever looked better than they did," he wrote. "No family looked more the all-American type than they did." But afterward there were a few concerns about the worshipful film. It covered too many subjects, Dick told Haldeman; it needed a stronger architect. Feminists were not pleased that Stewart described Pat as someone who waits in the wings, and decried the focus on her role as patient wife whose husband carried out the important missions, but the documentary succeeded with men and with more traditional women.

For the first three days of the convention, television viewers and delegates might have been forgiven for mistaking the event as a coronation of Pat Nixon. The First Lady was everywhere, appearing at major events and state caucuses and celebrating the roles of women. At a "women of achievement" luncheon for 2,100 women at the Fontainebleau, Pat declared, "This year there are more women in high-level positions [in government] than ever before." Outside the cordoned-off convention area, three hundred demonstrators countered her, declaring that the "real women of achievement are welfare mothers and Vietnamese women."

In convention interviews, Pat denied that campaigning had ever been a burden to her, acknowledging that "sometimes the days are too long—but I like people very much." Representative Margaret Heckler from Massachusetts called Mrs. Nixon "the No. 1 liberated woman. She started with nothing. Look at her now." Pat told *Newsweek*'s Nancy Ball that the changing perceptions of her (there had been much talk of the "new" Pat) made sense because, as the president's wife, "People see me more, see more what I'm like and what I do."

Dick arrived in Miami on Tuesday afternoon and made an impromptu appearance at an evening open-air youth rally. Thousands of roaring young people, their hands above their heads, took up a cry that reverberated throughout the convention: "Four more years! Four more years!" Nixon would write that he was happy to be celebrated by a "new kind of Republican youth: they weren't square, but they weren't ashamed of being positive and proud."

On Thursday, as Nixon began his acceptance speech, he expressed his gratitude to the convention for honoring "the best campaigner in the Nixon family—my wife Pat." Smiling broadly, he beckoned her up to the podium and put his arm around her. "In honoring her," Nixon told the delegates, "you have honored the millions of women in America who have contributed in the past and will contribute in the future so very much to better government in this country."

Nixon had endeavored to create a strong first-term record to run on. He championed policies that removed power from the federal government and handed it over to the states. Yet while he dismantled some of the most inefficient programs of Lyndon Johnson's Great Society, he spent excessively on certain domestic programs, more in the tradition of LBJ than most people remember. Working with an overwhelming Democratic majority in Congress, Nixon pursued a remarkably progressive domestic agenda because he believed in some of the programs, because he needed congressional support for his foreign policy initiatives, and because social reforms could help expand support for his presidency among working-class voters. He launched wars on illegal drugs and on cancer, and accelerated desegregation of southern schools. He created wage and price controls, and dramatically increased funding for the National Endowment for the Arts and the National Endowment for the Humanities. One of his significant domestic accomplishments was the establishment of the Environmental Protection Agency (EPA), and the strengthening of the Clean Air Act.

Some of the social changes Nixon advocated were ahead of their time. Bob Dole said that we should have done welfare reform when Nixon proposed it and Senator Ted Kennedy said we should have listened to Nixon about health care reform. "That was the best deal we were going to get," Kennedy told *Boston Globe* columnist Farah Stockman shortly before he died. "Nothing since has ever come close."

Nixon distanced himself from McGovern, who was promising unconditional amnesty for draft resisters and prompt withdrawal of U.S. troops from Vietnam, while relying on the good faith of the North Vietnamese to release U.S. prisoners of war. "In negotiation between great powers," Nixon declared, "you can only get something if you have something to give . . . when the president goes to the conference table, he never has to negotiate out of weakness. . . . There is no such thing as a retreat to peace." Nixon refused to debate McGovern, and the Democratic nominee never really had a chance of victory. On August 30, polls showed Nixon with a lead of 69 to 30 percent.

Pat set another precedent for Republican First Ladies by making a solo campaign trip. In Chicago the First Lady kicked off her six-day, seven-state campaign swing that would "bring the White House to the people." She was greeted by the black R&B band the Spidells, singing, "Shake it to the left, shake it to the right. Nixon's got his thing on tight—right on." They then "twanged into soul-funk versions" of "Hail to the Chief." On the tour Pat endured sleety forty-five-mile-an-hour winds that blew her hair straight up in Montana, snow and sleet that froze her hands at the hundredth anniversary of the founding of Yellowstone National Park in Wyoming, thundershowers in Illinois, and 102-degree temperatures in Riverside, California. But it was not harsh weather but tough questions that tested her endurance.

When asked what she thought of her daughter Julie's comment that she would willingly die for the South Vietnamese government, Pat stated that she, too, would be "willing to die" to ensure the freedom of seventeen million South Vietnamese people. Ken Ringle of the *Washington Post* observed that there "was a look of panic in her eyes." When Pat gave Connie Stuart a signal to rescue her, Stuart inexplicably announced, instead, that the First Lady would continue to answer questions for five more minutes, which allowed for queries about abortion. Pat opposed "on-demand" abortion, she said, but believed that abortion was "the personal decision of the woman." The First Lady, defensive about Watergate and furious about not being adequately shielded from these questions, rushed off to her hotel room.

Two days later, Nixon sent orders through Haldeman to Dwight Chapin, who in turn wrote ex–television executive William Codus, the scheduler for the Nixon family, giving strict instructions about management of the media. From now on, Chapin declared, when Mrs. Nixon was confronted with reporters' questions, Stuart needed to move quickly to cut them off. No one in the Nixon family was to give speeches or do any partisan activities. Because Mrs. Nixon was "more ill at ease in speeches and Q and A," but "superb" at dealing with people, she should be put in front of the television cameras and appear at events that showed her off to best effect. She was never to respond directly in a political way to comments made by Eleanor McGovern.

Even if Pat did not generally offer her opinion on specific political issues beyond the need for more women in government and her feelings about abortion, it was a more political First Lady who entered her final campaign. Responding to press criticism that her campaign swing did not make much sense (the reporters thought she did not appear to be mentioning her husband's campaign often enough), on the return trip to Washington Pat went to the back of the plane to talk with reporters. "I hate people to be pessimistic and groaning around, and now they're [the American people] not," she told them. "They're saying we've had improvements, and now we are going to go right on up." A reporter asked whether people could be truly happy until the country was out of Vietnam. "Listen, you're never going to get a state of complete happiness," Pat responded. What about having the good feeling that we are not killing people, the reporters asked? "Well, they didn't kill anybody last week," the First Lady replied. "Oh yes, they [American forces] did kill South Vietnamese," a reporter countered. At that point Stuart came forward to remove Pat with the excuse that they would be landing soon.

From the end of August until Election Day, Pat, Julie, and Tricia did most of the campaigning while Dick worked in the White House. With a cabinet officer or a good speaker at the lectern, the presence of Julie, Tricia, and Pat "will simply hypo the publicity in an enormous degree," Nixon wrote. Nixon and Haldeman prepared the Nixon daughters carefully so that they would avoid any attacks on the Democratic nominee. Their job was to point out that most young voters were primarily interested in which of the two candidates was, in Nixon's words, "best qualified to lead the United States in international affairs and to build on the great peace initiatives we have begun in China and the Soviet Union."

In mid-October, Pat called Helene Drown to express her concern about how the campaign was being run. For Pat, too much power had been invested in just a few men, and her husband was not fully involved in many aspects of the re-election effort. Dick was increasingly insulated from his cabinet as well as the rest of his staff. When Julie later asked her mother about the reservations she had during the 1972 campaign and the Watergate scandal, she told Julie, "I think I made a mistake protecting Daddy too much and in giving in too much." Pat regretted not insisting that her husband act on her recommendations to fire staff members who were not acting in his best interest, nor did she press him hard enough to tell her the full story of the Watergate crisis. As she often did, Pat rationalized her action by focusing on her husband's preoccupation with running a war. She did not want to bother him with well-meaning advice.

Compounding Pat's stress during the campaign were the incidents when she faced the rage of antiwar demonstrators, as she did at a Republican fund-raising dinner in Boston. Several thousand protesters blocked traffic, smashed in storefront and car windows, burned a press car, and fought with police in riot gear outside the armory where the event was held. Pat slipped in the side door to avoid them. But as she started speaking about giving her husband four more years to "make this great country what it can be," antiwar activists inside the armory began shouting, "Stop international genocide." The police quickly removed and arrested them. Dick noted in his diary that Pat "was serene and natural" during the outburst, which "infuriated [the shouters] even more." But Pat's calm was only surface: Her husband wrote that the protesters had "no idea how much they had hurt her."

On Election Day the Nixons voted in San Clemente and then flew back to Washington. After the family dined at the White House, one of the caps on Dick's front teeth came off. His dentist rushed to the White House and created a temporary cap. While awaiting the results, Dick sat alone in the Lincoln Sitting Room soothing himself by listening to his favorite recording of the sound track of the television series *Victory at Sea*. He had few realistic worries about the likelihood of his re-election. By the end of the campaign the newspaper publishers he so reviled for being unfair to him had endorsed Nixon by a margin of 753 to 56. He ultimately won forty-nine of the fifty states and received 61 percent of the popular vote, the second-largest percentage of the popular vote to that point in history. Only Lyndon Johnson had bested him.

By fueling resentment against liberals and young people, Nixon had masterfully dismantled the New Deal coalition put together by Franklin D. Roosevelt, stripping off Catholics, evangelicals, working-class Democrats, and members of labor union families, the majority of whom voted with the Republicans for the first time. They joined southerners in building a new conservative majority that did not hold during the 1976 election. Nixon did, however, solidify the Republican hold on the South for years to come. Dick had a lot of help from George McGovern, who ran a terrible campaign, but, nonetheless, Nixon had changed American politics for future generations.

An astonishing 35 percent of Democratic voters cast ballots for the president. While Pat was thrilled with the extent of the victory and relieved to have completed her last campaign, Dick underwent a stronger version of his typical postvictory melancholy. He would never again be able to prove himself with an election victory. Moreover, the Republicans had lost seats in the Senate and lacked a majority in either house, and the war was not over.

At the end of a president's first term, cabinet secretaries were usually expected to submit pro forma letters of resignation. Nixon went far beyond the tradition of other twentieth-century presidents. The day after the election, agency directors, federal department heads, and presidential appointees were stunned when Haldeman, at the direction of the president, requested standby resignation letters from all of them; while he reorganized the executive branch, Nixon would take a month to decide whom he wanted to stay on for the second term. This was an act of bad judgment—not the generous deed of a triumphant visionary.

As Nixon reflected on the long journey toward a second term, he "knew that the road had been hardest of all for Pat." After twenty years of service as a campaigner she was, he wrote in his memoir, "loved by millions, and no woman ever deserved more. My deepest hope was that she felt that it had all been worth it." Based on this passage, he did not ask her if his deepest hope was true. Was it not in his nature to ask such a question, or was he afraid of her answer?

Throughout the fall campaign the Nixon administration had been negotiating with the North Vietnamese delegates at peace talks in Paris. He and Kissinger had hoped to reach a settlement of the war before Election Day. By October, after the North Vietnamese concluded that Senator McGovern was not going to win the White House and offer them a better deal, they agreed to the U.S. terms, but South Vietnam's President Thieu refused to assent to an agreement unless it included a commitment to withdraw North Vietnamese troops from the South. By mid-December, the negotiations were stalemated. To increase pressure on the North Vietnamese, Nixon ordered heavy bombing of airfields, rail yards, communication centers, and power plants in Hanoi and Haiphong, and the mining of Haiphong Harbor. The fierce attack, which began on December 18, continued for eleven days—with the exception of a thirty-six-hour bombing pause for Christmas—until the twenty-ninth of December, when Hanoi agreed to return to negotiations in Paris.

Thanks to the outrage over what was called the "Christmas bombing," and due to postelection letdown, Pat and Dick did not enjoy their holiday in Key Biscayne. It was their first Christmas alone, while their daughters vacationed in Europe with their husbands. Dick was not thrilled that Kissinger shared the cover of *Time* magazine with him as "Men of the Year." Pat and Dick felt so lonely and besieged that they did not even open their Christmas presents. They brought the wrapped gifts back to Washington and put them away.

The Nixons were separated on New Year's Eve. Dick remained at Camp David while Pat went to Pasadena to preside over the Rose Bowl revels. Dick ate a supper of bacon and eggs by himself. He was about to turn sixty and he had much to ponder; namely, how to end a war and integrate that triumph into a psyche accustomed to crisis.

Pat had celebrated her sixtieth birthday the previous March. Over the past twenty years she had visited 75 countries and had traveled more than half a million miles internationally and more than a quarter of a million miles at home. During her first four years as First Lady, she had been to 23 countries and 107 American cities. Apart from the nagging worries about Watergate, she had much to celebrate. She and Dick had successfully raised their daughters, who had entered into happy marriages. She was beloved in America and across the globe. Even the tetchiest reporters were beginning to show her new respect. Reporter Diana McLellan in the *Washington Star-News* asserted that even the foreign press had begun to relax its habit of critiquing American First Ladies. The *London Daily Mail* called Pat Nixon "this utterly stylish butterfly" emerging at age sixty from "the moth like woman" with the "mirthless smile set in concrete."

For the first time, in a Gallup poll in which half of the top-ten women made the list because of their independent accomplishments,

Pat Nixon was voted the "Most Admired Woman" in the world. She outpaced Prime Minister Indira Gandhi of India, Golda Meir, prime minister of Israel, Maine senator Margaret Chase Smith, and Shirley Chisholm, a female congressional representative who was the first major African-American candidate for the presidency. With all that she and Dick had accomplished in 1972, Pat felt she had a right to relax more often during her husband's second term in the White House. She did not think he needed as much help from her to thrive.

During a campaign interview, a reporter asked Pat, referring to her husband, "What trait of character does he prize most?" Pat answered quickly: "Honesty. I can remember him lecturing the girls about that a long time ago." When his daughters told him that some of their class-mates cheated on exams, he was "so shocked that he told them it was important to be honest . . . honest in every way . . . and to speak their minds and be straightforward." Pat's judgment would prove ironic in the months to come.

Falling Apart

*T*he Nixons' last nineteen months in the White House felt like a slow crucifixion punctuated by moments of hope, even triumph, and final gasps of glory. This tortured period ushered in yet another phase in the Nixon marriage. Despite presenting a staunch solidarity to the outside world, Pat and Dick became more emotionally distant than they had been in any other phase of their tumultuous partnership. They spent less time with each other. Their daughters often acted as emissaries across the widening gulf between their parents.

The Nixons' partial estrangement raises the question: How many secrets can a marriage withstand before the union loses its vitality and becomes unsustainable? The trauma of a quarter century of political and press attacks—whether merited or unmerited—had infused itself into their characters, so much so that, under siege, Dick felt his only option was to lie about his behavior, and Pat found herself partially withdrawing from the political world she had re-embraced in 1972. She shrank from asking her husband probing questions. It is surprising that their bond was not fatally splintered by the multitude of shocks they endured as everything fell apart during the fifth and most extensive crisis in their marriage. In the end, their only viable option was to choose the purgatory of political exile.

On a cold and sodden January 20, 1973, Pat held the Milhous family Bible as Richard Nixon took the presidential oath of office for the second time. Behind the podium, Pat and Dick held hands, but no one in the crowd in front of them could see this intimate gesture. In his inaugural address, Nixon pronounced a revival of the nation's spirit and the healing of deep divisions during his first four years in office. Believing a cease-fire in Vietnam was at hand, he said, "We stand at the threshold of a new era of peace in the world." Dick spoke about the need for all Americans, implicitly including himself, to answer "to God, to history, and to our conscience for the way in which we use these years." But there would be no real peace in Vietnam—a cease-fire would eventually unravel—and no respite from tumult in the nation's capital or in America itself.

According to Robert Bork, the incoming solicitor general, Pat's face looked like a "death mask" that inaugural morning. Certainly she and her husband did not demonstrate to the crowd a sustaining bond between them. Dick noted in his diary that he was relieved Pat did not kiss him after the swearing-in ceremony. On certain occasions "these displays of affection are very much in place," he wrote, "as was the case on election night," but at this time, "I didn't really think it quite fit." He, too, might have been feeling more stress than he revealed as he celebrated his accomplishments and heralded a new epoch. At the very same time he was overwhelmed by arduous negotiations to convince North and South Vietnam to agree to a cease-fire.

Riding to the viewing stand to watch their inaugural parade, Dick and Pat stood up in their limousine to wave to their supporters.

Demonstrators threw eggs and refuse at them, but the Nixons ignored Secret Service agents' orders to sit down. When a demonstrator lunged at the car, the agents promptly knocked him down. That evening, Dick danced at all five inaugural balls, bringing Pat to the dance floor as the band played "People Will Say We're in Love." Before leaving the final ball, Dick also danced for a few minutes with a gushing fan from Massachusetts. For his second term, he was determined to improve his uncongenial public image, but he wanted to make sure not to "overplay it," as he wrote in his memoir *RN*.

Pat and Dick maintained their visibility in the first months of Nixon's second term, attending funeral services for former presidents Harry Truman, who died in December 1972, and Lyndon Johnson, who died right after Nixon's inauguration in January 1973. When Alice Roosevelt Longworth, who was ill, did not attend Nixon's swearing-in ceremony—the first inauguration she had missed since 1900—Pat and Dick paid an unexpected visit to her Washington home on February 7. They spent ninety minutes with her, drinking tea, snacking on cookies, and talking about her upcoming eighty-ninth birthday. As the three of them posed at the front door while press photographers snapped pictures, Pat placed her stole around Alice's shoulders to protect her from the cold.

Julie and David did their bit to help make the Nixons appear more affable by convincing them to eat in a restaurant, and on February 13, the two couples, with Bebe Rebozo in tow, ambled through Lafayette Park, chatting with people they passed on the way to Trader Vic's in the Statler Hilton Hotel. The news that the Nixons were walking outside the White House zipped throughout Washington's press corps. Helen Thomas and CBS reporter Lesley Stahl raced to the restaurant and scrambled to find a table near the presidential party. They watched Pat indulge in an after-dinner cigarette, belying her rigorously wholesome public image. When the Nixons exited amid a crush of reporters, Thomas ended up beside Mrs. Nixon. When she asked the First Lady how she was faring, Pat said, "Helen, can you believe that with all the troubles Dick has had, all the pressures he's been under, he would do this for *me*?" But Nixon had also left the Executive

Mansion to please Julie and to confound his enemies, who were claiming that he had gone into hiding.

Nixon continued to look for opportunities to sell the brighter side of his presidency. Despite the press's appreciation of the "new" First Lady in 1972, the president was not satisfied with coverage of the East Wing's events. Nixon wrote Ron Ziegler, asking him to whip up fresh attention to the fact "that we have probably done the best job of any Administration in history in terms of making the White House open to all people of all races . . . in a very gracious and in many cases unprecedented way." The president charged that journalists who covered the East Wing seemed to report social events "only if they find some hot news" or "somebody . . . present [who] makes some jackass comment on national events." The East Wing press failed to realize, he thought, that "ten times as many women, as well as perhaps a few men, read the society pages more than they read the news pages."

Following Dick's landslide re-election victory, Pat decided to focus on herself again, as she had during her private years in New York City. "I'm going to relax in these last four years," she told her correspondence secretary Gwendolyn King. "I want to enjoy my family, spend more time with Julie and Tricia. I want to enjoy my grandchildren as they come along. I'm going to spend time with my friends, go out to lunch . . . I'm going to shop." When Connie Stuart resigned shortly after the inauguration, Pat decided to streamline her East Wing organization. She became her own de facto chief of staff, but relied on Julie to assume many of her responsibilities. Mrs. Nixon promoted Connie's popular assistant, Helen McCain Smith, to be press secretary, but reduced her staff from nine to three. Lucy Winchester stayed on as social secretary. Helen McCain Smith was close to Mrs. Nixon during the second term. Helen told Susan Porter Rose that "Mrs. Nixon has more sense in her little finger than the entire West Wing put together."

Stress persisted between the president's men and the First Lady's women. Smith fought with Ziegler, who regularly antagonized the East Wing. On occasion, Mrs. Nixon did not receive advance notice that she needed to attend important presidential announcements or watch them on television. Nor was she notified ahead of time about a news release concerning her appointment to an advisory council.

Nixon did not change his guard. Haldeman and Ehrlichman still manned the fortress even though Pat, Tricia, and Julie strongly disliked and distrusted them. Pat was increasingly disturbed by Dick's heavy dependence on Haldeman, whose purview over so many aspects of the president's life overextended him. Pat noticed that Haldeman had delegated many tasks to younger staffers who were not secure enough to elevate their own good judgment over blind loyalty to Haldeman. According to Julie, the Nixon family became convinced Dick's men "squeezed out" a large part of their father's "sensitivity and thoughtfulness." Pat, Julie, and Tricia did not yet realize how cynical and hard-bitten Nixon could be in his private conversations with his staff. Nor was Pat aware how often her husband ordered petty and vindictive actions against his press and political enemies, banishing them from events or ordering IRS audits of their taxes.

At the end of January 1973, Gordon Liddy, Howard Hunt, James McCord, and four Cuban burglars were convicted of conspiracy, burglary, and wiretapping. The presiding judge, John Sirica, delayed sentencing until March to induce the conspirators to reveal the higher-ups in their schemes. A week later the Senate voted unanimously to establish a committee to investigate Watergate and Nixon's campaign finances. Sam Ervin of North Carolina, a conservative and independent-minded Democratic senator, was chosen as the chairman of what became unofficially known as the Senate Watergate Committee.

Nixon continued to withhold the process of his political decision-making from his wife and daughters. "He liked to tackle problems by turning them over and over again in his mind until they became digested and resolved," Julie wrote. "Because my parents were very private people, their relationship was a delicate, polite one that did not allow for much second guessing." Concealing some work activities from a spouse is a somewhat common phenomenon, but withholding information about possibly illegal activities is toxic for a marriage. Pat could sense how troubled Dick was, but she could offer him only generic support—reminding him that his family stood behind him all the way. He shut her out.

In February 1973, a transfixed nation had watched on television as 591 Vietnam prisoners of war, some of them feeble and gaunt, arrived back in the United States under the terms of the January 23 cease-fire agreement with North Vietnam. Many of the men bore the marks of repeated torture. Their homecoming was a sign that the war was at last beginning to wind down and a cruel reminder of its costs. Pat held a formal White House dinner for the POWs and their families, a May 24 gala that proved to be the last great social event of the Nixon presidency and the largest the White House had ever hosted up to that point. Relieved to have a constructive challenge, Pat prepared for weeks. Under an enormous red and gold tent on the South Lawn, bigger than the White House itself, thirteen hundred people were seated at 126 tables. Chandeliers glowed within the tent. The official goal of the lustrous evening was to express the nation's gratitude for the courage of the POWs, but Nixon also hoped the publicity about the event would focus attention on what he saw as his success in resolving the war, and would be a way to recharge his presidency amid investigations by media, Congress, and the courts.

A rainy day, sopping muck on the South Lawn, and dresses spattered with mud did not dampen the Nixons' spirits or those of their guests. Beyond the tent, plenty of Americans thought Nixon could have brought the POWs home much sooner, had he not been so stubborn in negotiating the terms of their release. But inside the tent, celebration overshadowed those controversies. Pat and Dick visited with the POWs and their families and signed autographs for them. At dinner Dick offered a toast to Pat, to the POW wives and mothers, and to their sacrifices. The POWs themselves presented Nixon with a plaque reading, "Our leader—our comrade, Richard the Lion-Hearted." Bob Hope, Jimmy Stewart, Sammy Davis, Jr., country and pop singers, and movie stars entertained them. John Wayne struck a deep chord of appreciation when he told the men, "I'll ride into the sunset with you anytime." Men wept as the elderly Irving Berlin sang "God Bless America."

*　　　*　　　*

The Watergate cover-up unraveled with dizzying speed. A series of press revelations in March and April undermined the president's claim that the White House was not connected to Watergate. On March 21, White House counsel John Dean had told Nixon that there was "a cancer—within—close to the presidency, that's growing . . . daily. It's compounding." Dean explained that he did not believe it was possible to continue the cover-up because even with continued perjury and financial support for the burglars, the real story was sure to come out.

On March 23, Judge Sirica read aloud in court a letter from James McCord claiming that some of the defendants had succumbed to political pressure and had committed perjury to protect as yet unnamed conspirators in the burglary. In early April the *New York Times* reported that the cash payoffs to the Watergate burglars came directly from the Committee to Re-elect the President. On April 19, John Mitchell admitted in public that he had known about Gordon Liddy's intelligence activities, which included directing the Watergate burglaries of the Democratic National Committee offices. Additionally, White House staff members had begun to point the finger at each other to protect themselves. White House counsel John Dean started cooperating with the grand jury's prosecutors.

The Nixon family's Easter holiday in Key Biscayne was suffused with a deep underlying tension. Nixon withdrew into a shell, staying in his office and not calling to the main house to check in with his family as he normally would. Pat stopped trying to connect with her husband. She ensconced herself in a chaise longue, set comfortably between two shady palm trees, and distracted herself by reading. At this point it is likely that Pat, responding to a lifetime of feeling beset by enemies, still believed that staff members like Haldeman, unbeknownst to her husband, had betrayed him.

Julie judged her father's frost unfair to her mother, and she confronted him. In one of the rare breaks he took in Key Biscayne when he watched a movie with Julie, she spoke up in Pat's defense:

"Mother's trying so hard to make things right and you just don't realize it. It's hard for her too." "I guess so," Nixon said simply. Julie consequently felt guilty for further burdening a heavily encumbered president.

But when the movie ended, her father told her, "You're right, it's hard for her too. I'll try." Pat, Julie, and Tricia sensed his predicament, but had no way of knowing he was facing one of the most excruciating decisions of his life: whether to fire his loyal lieutenants in order to save himself.

Inexorably, that spring and summer, the Watergate story would become daily front-page news across the country. Returning to Washington after Easter, Nixon's family grasped just how much jeopardy Dick's top aides faced. Press reports picked up on leaks from John Dean that Nixon's top lieutenants were involved in both the Watergate break-in and the White House cover-up of the whole affair. Dick traveled solo to Camp David on Friday night, April 27, while his wife and daughters remained at the White House and fumed over the behavior of Dick's right-hand men. Tricia stayed up late that night discussing the situation with Julie and David. The next morning the trio consulted Pat, resulting in a decision to confront the president directly. They had to convince him of a view they had long held: He had to break with Haldeman and Ehrlichman.

Early on Saturday morning, April 28, the Secret Service drove Tricia to Camp David. Dick was stunned when he walked into the living room at Camp David's Aspen Lodge to discover Tricia sitting on a couch in front of the fireplace. She tearfully told her father that the family had concluded that the way his trusted advisors had handled people made it impossible for the advisors to continue serving him. "I want you to know that I would never allow any personal feeling about either of them to interfere with my judgment," she told him. She expressed the family's confidence in him and then returned to Washington. Dick was despondent. He summoned Haldeman and Ehrlichman to Camp David the next afternoon. Firing them was "like cutting off my arms," he told them. According to Ehrlichman, Nixon's eyes were "red-rimmed," and he "looked small and drawn." When Nixon started "crying uncontrollably," Ehrlichman put his arm around his boss to comfort him. Nixon went out on the terrace to compose himself, then said to Ziegler, "It's all over."

On Monday evening, April 30, Nixon addressed the nation on television to announce that he had fired Dean and accepted the resignations of Haldeman, Ehrlichman, and Attorney General Richard Kleindienst, who had been implicated in covering up the scandal. He did not tell the public that he had fired them. Without accounting for his role in the affair, he claimed he was taking over the investigation, planning to replace people who were engaged in wrongdoing, and that he was accepting general responsibility, as the "the man at the top," for the behavior of his associates. The president hoped firing his aides and speaking to the nation would cauterize the wounds of Watergate. However, his claims that he had known about the cover-up only since a March meeting with John Dean and his vague description "that he accepted full responsibility for the actions of his aides" did not make intuitive sense to the public; his comments only roiled the nation further. Nixon later wrote that he had "done what I thought was necessary, but not what I believed was right." He usually "prided" himself on standing by "people who were down." Plagued with guilt about abandoning his men when they were under attack and before all the facts were known, Dick was too drained to respond to most of the telephone calls that poured in after his speech from supporters. Nixon did speak to California governor Ronald Reagan, who told him "[M]y heart was with you. I know what this must have been in all these days and what you have been through. This too shall pass." Nixon agreed that "everything passes." He said, "Each of us has a different religion, but God damn it, Ron, we've got to build peace in the world and that's what I am working on here."

Pat, David, Tricia, and Rose Mary Woods answered many calls. Julie heard Dick mutter under his breath, "I hope I don't wake up in the morning," but Pat did not hear him say that. Nixon had good reason to feel like disappearing. By mid-May his approval ratings had dipped to 44 percent; more than half of Americans surveyed believed that he had participated in a cover-up. The day after the firings Pat soldiered on, holding a luncheon for the wives of senators and cabinet members.

On May 17, the day the Senate began the televised hearings on Watergate that would rivet the nation over the next months, Pat talked with the press after a White House reception. When one reporter asked if the president felt duped by his staff, she said, "I'm not going to say that they let him down until we find out whether they did or not." The First Lady proclaimed what would become her mantra for the next fifteen months: "I'm full of faith and confidence. . . . I'll have faith until I am proven wrong."

A week later, after hosting the formal White House dinner for the POWs on the South Lawn, the Nixons went back into the Executive Mansion. Dick kissed Pat good night and settled in the Lincoln Sitting Room to savor what he later wrote was "one of the greatest nights in my life." He read a note a former POW had handed to him, which said, in part, "Don't let the bastards get you down, Mr. President." His words appealed to Nixon's fighting spirit. But recognizing the sharp contrast between the evening's heartfelt resplendence and the "dreary daily drain of Watergate" sucked the vitality out of him. When Julie and Tricia joined him in the sitting room, they saw how agitated he was. "Do you think I should resign?" he asked. Realizing that their father was seeking reassurance, not advice, they told him he had to stay in office for the good of the nation. But it was a question he would begin asking himself and others with greater frequency. He did not query Pat because he knew she would urge him to fight on. There was no longer any triumph, nor any glorious moment that could assuage for long the agitated depression he often felt. In the midst of a long downward spiral, he was not fully aware of how and why he had created such forceful threats to himself and his administration.

Twenty-one years earlier, in 1952, Pat had been humiliated during the fund scandal that culminated in the Checkers speech. Now, in the last year and a half of her husband's presidency, the charges of wrongdoing again devastated her, including new accusations that questioned her own integrity. In May 1973 a House subcommittee leaked the information that the government had spent up to $10 million on improvements at the Nixons' vacation houses. Further revelations emerged. The Nixons had paid little or no state and federal taxes since 1969 because the president had taken a $500,000 writeoff for donating some of his vice-presidential papers to the National Archives in March 1969. His lawyers had not turned the paperwork in to the Internal Revenue Service before the deadline of July 25, 1969, after which time Congress had repealed deductions made for such papers.

On the advice of her husband's lawyer, Pat had signed the tax return without carefully studying it. In the later part of 1973 when Pat and Dick signed a statement preparing for an audit of their taxes, Dick "could sense her tightly controlled anger." She understood the politics of Watergate, but she was outraged the press attacks had spilled over into their private and financial lives. She could not acknowledge that it was legitimate to review large deductions, because she felt that it would give the press more ammunition against them.

In mid-June, Pat and Dick had a brief respite from the investigations; the Senate Watergate Committee postponed its hearings for a week while Nixon and Brezhnev conducted their second summit in Washington and at San Clemente. Brezhnev stayed in Tricia's frilly bedroom at La Casa Pacifica. Pat did not miss that Brezhnev brought his girlfriend into the house during the night right under the Nixons' noses. Brezhnev attended a dinner and a reception with an array of Hollywood stars milling around the Nixons' swimming pool. Brezhnev and Nixon signed a general agreement on the Prevention of Nuclear War at the White House and worked out modest agreements on atomic energy, trade, agriculture, and transportation. They could not agree on the structure for peace in the Middle East because Brezhnev was adamant that Israelis return the territories they had seized from the Arabs in the 1967 war.

Later in the month, at televised hearings before the Senate Watergate Committee, John Dean testified that the president was implicated in the cover-up of Watergate. During the hearings, Republican senator Howard Baker posed the question that would haunt the nation and both Nixons for the next thirteen months: "What did the president know and when did he know it?" By July, Nixon was so emotionally stressed that he developed chest pains. Hospitalized at the National Naval Center in Bethesda, Maryland, he was diagnosed with viral pneumonia.

Then, in mid-July, came a fateful pivot point in the investigation: Alexander Butterfield, Haldeman's former aide, gave sensational testimony that he had installed a secret audio taping system in the White House. Now it appeared that Nixon's conversations about the Watergate burglaries and cover-ups might be on tapes that investigators could hear. The Senate committee demanded Nixon appoint a special prosecutor to lead an independent investigation of Watergate. Attorney general Elliot Richardson chose Harvard law professor Archibald Cox, who joined the committee, the grand jury, and Judge Sirica in insisting that Nixon should release the tapes. The president refused, claiming executive privilege—the power of the president to resist subpoenas from the legislative and judicial branches of government because he is entitled to frank and confidential advice from his aides.

Pat believed taping private conversations was "something you just don't do." She was "appalled," Helene Drown said later. "She couldn't believe the stupidity involved." Mrs. Nixon did not hold her husband accountable for this questionable decision; she blamed her favorite scapegoat, the now-departed Bob Haldeman, for installing the recording system. In her view, her husband's guardians were not protecting him.

In August and September 1973 when the Watergate special prosecutor's office subpoenaed the White House for access to the Nixon audio tapes, Nixon decided to make transcriptions of some of the tapes for investigators to see. Pat believed publishing the transcripts was "foolish" and "silly" because they could be so easily misinterpreted, rife with swear words that appeared in brackets as "expletive deleted" and full of inaudible or ambiguous exchanges. She spent twelve hours reading 1,254 pages of transcripts that covered Nixon's conversations with staff members about Watergate and told Helene the tapes should be treated like "personal, sensitive diaries . . . never to be released to anyone." For Pat, "The tapes are like private love letters—for one person only." But she was engaging in wishful thinking, because they were official government documents and part of the president's archive.

She covered her dismay by joking with Helene about how the president's predecessors might have sounded cursing in tapes of their conversations, imagining LBJ erupting in "deleted expletives" in his Texas drawl or JFK cursing in his "broad Boston a's." When *Pageant* magazine, which mixed glamour photo features with informative text on a wide range of subjects, declared the Nixons were planning to divorce, Pat bantered with Helene about who could be listed as a corespondent. Dick had been tied up with affairs of state, but Pat said, "I've had more time, so let's think up someone I could name. Sam Dash [co–chief counsel for the Senate Watergate Committee]? Peter Rodino [chairman of the House judiciary committee]?" Pat's deepest regret about Watergate was that back in 1971 Dick had not asked her opinion about his plan to tape his conversations.

By October 1973, both the Nixon administration and the Nixon marriage faced increasingly challenging problems. The president was directing Henry Kissinger—newly appointed as his secretary of state—in managing the U.S. response to the Yom Kippur War. With the crucial assistance of airlifted arms provided by the United States, the Israelis humiliated the Arab states that had invaded them on the most holy day in the Jewish calendar. In the midst of this international turmoil, Vice President Spiro Agnew resigned after being charged with accepting bribes for public works contracts during his tenure as governor of Maryland. His departure escalated the atmosphere of constant scandal besetting the administration. Soon thereafter, on October 12, Nixon chose the House minority leader, Gerald Ford of Michigan, as the new vice president. Ford went on to win confirmation from the Senate in what was the first exercise of the Twenty-fifth Amendment to the Constitution.

Adding to Nixon's personal distress, that same month Kissinger and North Vietnamese diplomat Le Duc Tho—but not Nixon—were awarded the Nobel Peace Prize for constructing an accord intended to end the Vietnam War. Le Duc Tho, who had originally organized the rebellion against the government of South Vietnam, was honored for becoming the North Vietnamese negotiator at the Paris peace talks in January 1969.

One of October's few bright moments occurred during the state dinner for Prime Minister Norman Kirk of New Zealand. After dinner, the Nixons astonished their guests and perhaps even themselves. As the Marine Band played "The Sound of Music," Pat grabbed Dick's hand and they danced a foxtrot through the Grand Foyer to the stairs leading to their private quarters.

Also in October, the battle over the president's Watergate tapes sparked a monumental collision of judicial and presidential power. In what he called a compromise that he said would preserve the principle of executive privilege, Nixon offered to submit authenticated summaries of his conversations to the Senate Watergate Committee and to Special Watergate Prosecutor Archibald Cox instead of the actual tapes. Cox refused to accept Nixon's proposal. Nixon maintained that any material pertinent to national security information would have to be redacted from the tapes, that being involved in a battle over the tapes would impede his ability to take decisive action in foreign affairs, and that a president who accepted the dictates of a person who technically worked under him in the Justice Department would lose worldwide presidential authority and the respect of the Soviets, whose cooperation would be critical in resolving the conflicts in the Middle East.

Nixon's basic motive was to stop Cox from expanding the scope of his requests for White House material that would directly implicate the president in the Watergate cover-up. Nixon asked Richardson to fire Cox. But the attorney general and his deputy both quit rather than obey their boss. Solicitor General Robert Bork then dismissed Cox. What became known as the "Saturday Night Massacre" caused a hurricane of controversy, and Nixon's action was seen by many as the most egregious example yet of what historian Arthur M. Schlesinger, Jr., and others called "the imperial presidency," an aggrandizement of executive power, beyond prescribed constitutional limits, that had been expanding unchecked since at least the Kennedy and Johnson years. Within ten days of Cox's firing, Congress and the White House received 450,000 telegrams protesting Nixon's actions. The editor of *Time* wrote an editorial, an act unprecedented in the magazine's history, telling the president to resign. His approval rating sank to 17 percent in a Gallup poll. The president, digging in and buying time, appealed the matter of the tapes and the extent of executive privilege to the Supreme Court.

The Watergate crisis was compounded in November, when White House counsel Fred Buzhardt testified that two of the nine subpoenaed tapes did not actually exist. Even more shocking, he revealed a week later that an eighteen-and-a-half-minute segment of one tape had been erased. Rose Mary Woods later claimed to have erased it by accident. In response to the public outcry, Robert Bork appointed a new special prosecutor, Leon Jaworski.

Nixon, speaking before four hundred Associated Press managing editors in Orlando, Florida, defended himself in response to a question about an emerging new issue involving his tax returns—he was being questioned about paying minimal taxes in 1970 and 1971—saying, "People have got to know whether or not their president is a crook. Well, I am not a crook." His words would become one of his most memorable and perhaps most self-indicting utterances, the question and its answer an indication of how profoundly his presidency had been wounded by dishonor.

As the maelstrom of Watergate expanded, Dick and Pat rarely discussed it, at least according to his memoir. She believed, he said, that "we must not allow the attacks to depress us to the point where we would be unable to carry out our duties effectively." Avoidance was one of their few refuges from despair. Pat complained to Helene Drown, "It's right out of the *Merchant of Venice*. They're after the last pound of flesh." After nearly thirty years of a public life in which she had felt her husband had been unjustly attacked, she was choosing to stand by her husband and deliberately deafen herself to the possibility he had done anything wrong.

The family suffered public humiliation. At Yankee Stadium one day when the scoreboard flashed "Welcome Tricia Nixon," Ed and Tricia were vigorously booed. When Julie and David held a press conference in the East Garden of the White House to defend her father, she felt wounded when CBS reporter Robert Pierpoint reasonably inquired why she and not her father was answering questions about his mental state and his thoughts on resigning. While Julie, David, and, to a lesser extent, Tricia launched a campaign of interviews, speeches, and articles staunchly defending Dick, Pat avoided the subject of Watergate. Her staff arranged her schedule to minimize the potential for awkward and painful confrontations with White House visitors and reporters. Yet the more Pat and Dick retreated, the more the press, along with Americans in general, grew fascinated by analyzing the Nixons' psyches and the president's style of governing from a bunker.

Nixon wrote later that during the summer of 1973 the Washington press corps decided that "I was starting to go off my rocker." His public behavior intensified their concern. That August, emotionally run-down after days of news reports on the Senate Watergate hearings, Nixon went to New Orleans, counting on the emotional boost of seeing large crowds lining the route as his motorcade made its way into the city. When Secret Service agents, reacting to an assassination threat, shifted the motorcade to a quiet back road, Nixon grew angry. Shortly after arriving at the convention center for a speech to the Veterans of Foreign Wars, he lost his temper and mistreated Ron Ziegler in front of the television cameras. After retreating to a private area to gather his thoughts before he went on the stage, he saw Ron Ziegler and a posse of press following him, grabbed Ron's shoulders, turned him around, and shoved him hard toward the reporters and photographers. He later apologized to Ziegler off camera, but the footage led the press to portray his actions, Nixon said in his memoir *RN,* "as the desperate flailing of a man at the end of his tether." There was some truth to their depiction.

Such questions about Dick's and Pat's state of mind persisted until the end of his presidency. In January 1974, covering the First Lady's reception for the members of the Religious Broadcasters of America, reporters wanted to know only if the president was sleeping well. Pat's "eyes flashed" and she said, according to a UPI article, "He doesn't sleep long, but he sleeps well." Defiantly, she told them that sometimes his sleep was interrupted by important phone calls. Reporters asked if he got up in the middle of the night to play the piano. "He plays before he goes to bed," she parried. She had had enough. "Thrusting up an arm with her fist clenched," she reiterated her position. "He is in great health, and I love him dearly and I have great faith." Pat understood, her daughter Julie wrote, that the press was "just looking for cracks" in the family's state of mind. In her first four years in the White House, she had created an expansive and independent role for herself; now her world was narrowing. It was a painful step backward. Pat was fulfilling her desire to have less to do with the public and the press, but not in the manner she had imagined.

On her increasingly rare encounters with reporters, Mrs. Nixon asserted, "The truth sustains me because I have great faith in my husband." "He's an honorable, dedicated person and when you know the truth you have nothing to fear." But Pat did not possess the facts, facts she did not seek out, facts she probably would not have learned about even if she had asked about them. Her husband cordoned her off from the knowledge of his questionable activities and his campaign against the investigations into Watergate. Perhaps she sensed that the truth of her husband's complicity in Watergate would be too painful for her to bear. She had reason to believe, however, that once again he would triumph over adversaries who, as in the past, used every available strategy to deny Dick Nixon what he deserved. With the exception of the 1960 race for the presidency and the run for the California governorship two years later, Pat had witnessed Dick emerge miraculously intact from his crises. She could believe he would triumph over this predicament as well.

At the beginning of 1974, the Nixons secluded themselves at La Casa Pacifica for a gloomy two-week break from the unyielding torture of the Watergate revelations in Washington. Rain drenched Southern

California, and the deluge was compounded by a small earthquake and historically high tides. Dick had trouble sleeping and calmed himself by playing the piano in the middle of the night. Ed, Tricia, and Bebe Rebozo joined Pat and Dick on driving expeditions along the Southern California freeways.

In spite of beginning the year with a holiday together, the Nixons would spend far fewer hours in each other's company in 1974 as the crisis of the Nixon presidency estranged them from each other. Each spouse retreated to a private zone. The toll that year took on their relationship can be seen in the presidential diaries listing their events day by day. In the fall of 1973 Pat and Dick dined together at the White House an average of sixteen or seventeen nights per month. In the winter, spring, and early summer of 1974 they ate together an average of just three and a half times per month at the White House. They did, however, make a twice-weekly drive to visit Julie and David, who lived in Bethesda, Maryland, where they could talk about everything except Watergate, and where Dick could reminisce about the youthful trips he and Pat took by car and train in their first years together. These conversations sustained the president, Julie wrote, who was "steadfastly" working to "sustain a lifelong philosophy of never giving into defeat."

During the winter of 1974 Pat made "herself a virtual recluse in the White House," *People* magazine noted. She was becoming increasingly tense and angry because she believed that congressional Democrats and the press were determined to find ways to drive the Nixons out. She felt helpless to do anything to improve the situation. She stopped reading the newspapers and their glaring headlines about Watergate, relying instead on the news summaries that were prepared for the president. When she went to lunch with friends at Washington's trendy Sans Souci restaurant, an unsettling hush enveloped the room when she entered. Reporters turned her outing into a headline and wondered if she had specifically chosen the prominent restaurant to counter accusations that she was reclusive. "What in the world do they expect me to do," she asked Helene Drown, "go streaking along the Tidal Basin?"

*   *   *

In March, when Pat attended the inaugurations of the presidents of Venezuela and Brazil, the trip provided relief from what *People* magazine called the "drumfire of Watergate." Critical press reports—partially accurate—suggested that the major motivation for the trip was to divert attention from Watergate, which had by now moved beyond investigations of the Watergate cover-up and was looking into the profound constitutional question of whether the president's alleged illegal activities warranted impeachment by the House and trial by the Senate. NBC's Tom Brokaw claimed that the trip was all part of the "White House plan to demonstrate that the President is concerned with other matters than the impeachment investigations."

On the return flight from the six-day trip to South America, Pat, who had the flu, made an effort to be gracious to reporters and her staff members who surprised her with a cake and champagne to celebrate her sixty-second birthday. Noticing how wan she looked, they pressed her to talk about the personal strain of living through the Watergate investigations. She turned paler and her smile became "a blank stare." As she edged her way out of the reporters' section of the plane, she cut the questions short. "No," she replied, "I really don't want to speak of it. It's a personal thing. . . . Why bring that into the trip?" Attempting to end the encounter on a cordial basis, she urged them, "You all drink some champagne." Her goal was to be a model of tranquillity under pressure; she had only briefly failed to do so.

Pat flew directly to Nashville, where she joined Dick at the dedication of the new $15 million Grand Ole Opry House. Differing versions of that evening have played a key role in an enduringly negative public view of the Nixon marriage. Roy Acuff, known as the "King of Country Music," the master of ceremonies, and a local woman, Dorothy Ritter, presented the First Lady with what they declared was a "treasured heirloom," a Tennessee dulcimer, and saluted Mrs. Nixon as "a traveler from her husband's heart to the hearts and homes of all her countrymen." Dick was in an expansive mood that evening. When Acuff asked him to play the piano, Dick begged off, saying, "In this professional company I am a little embarrassed to play this thing." He pulled out of his pocket a yellow yo-yo, which Acuff had given him, and said, "I haven't even learned how to play this."

But then Dick sat down at the keyboard and offered piano renditions of "My Wild Irish Rose," "God Bless America," and "Happy Birthday" in honor of his wife's birthday. As he finished, Pat approached him with her arms open in an expression of appreciation. Dick had already turned back toward the master of ceremonies to indicate that he was finished with the program, and he and Pat never connected onstage. Reporters cited this incident as an example of Dick's insensitivity toward his wife. Her press aide, Helen Smith, inflamed the perception of the incident in a 1976 article in *Good Housekeeping* in which Smith wrote that she "winced" when Nixon "ignored her [Pat's] outstretched arms." Author Kati Marton, in her harsh portrait of the Nixon marriage, declared, "Those present never forgot the shocked expression on her face." Pat was momentarily stunned by the crossed signals, but she explained later that the misinterpretations of the incident hurt her far more than missing a public embrace with her husband.

The solution to travail on the home front was, once again, to go abroad. In June the Nixons embarked on their last two foreign trips together as president and First Lady. During these missions they shared bittersweet moments of exultation. At times during the travels, Dick found it difficult to walk; he was coping with a painful flare-up of phlebitis, an inflammation of his leg that had first occurred on a visit to Asia in the 1960s. During a seven-day trip in the Middle East in 1974, the Nixons became the first president and First Lady to visit Israel, Egypt, Syria, Saudi Arabia, and Jordan. "From the moment he set foot on Egyptian soil," *Time* magazine wrote, "the huzzas and hosannas fell like sweet rain." That portion of their visit was carefully staged by Egyptian president Anwar Sadat as what *Time* magazine called "a triumphal pageant, an exercise in diplomatic theater." Three hundred thousand Egyptians welcomed the Nixons in Cairo and one million thronged their public appearances in Alexandria. These jubilant events were beamed back to the United States for television viewers. Nixon was exploring multilateral approaches to strengthen Sadat's influence in the Middle East peace negotiations, while expressing understanding of Israel's military needs, reiterating the U.S. commitment to the long-term security of Israel, and encouraging the Israelis to focus on negotiated settlements. He also hoped these alliances would help reduce Soviet influence in the region.

After a brief return to Washington, the Nixons set out in late June 1974 on their very last presidential trip—to the Soviet Union for a third summit conference with Leonid Brezhnev. Pat and Dick stayed at Brezhnev's luxurious home on the Black Sea and the Soviet leader left them alone to have a dinner, just the two of them, in the moonlight, overlooking the sea, on a balcony outside their room. As they gazed at a three-quarter moon, Pat showed Dick how to spot an American flag in it. This was one of their last tranquil moments before the unthinkable happened. Observing the president in the Soviet Union, reporter Helen Thomas wrote, "All the life seems to have drained out of him. He appears to be only going through the motions." A crisis was arising that would test the consciences of Washington and the resilience of the Constitution itself.

That spring, Nixon had asked his family during a Camp David weekend whether he should resign the presidency. In May when reporters questioned whether her husband would leave the Oval Office before the end of his term, Pat retorted, "Why should he? There's no reason to." His wife and daughters told him to fight. On the issue of whether he was obligated to turn over his private taped conversations with aides to the Senate Watergate Committee and to the special prosecutor, Dick decided to "take this constitutionally down to the wire," as Julie told reporters in her White House East Garden press conference. But he clearly needed relief from the crushing pressure.

Pat found it an ordeal to fend off reporters who intended, in her opinion, to damage her husband. But defending her actions was a humiliation on top of a tribulation. The Constitution bans government officeholders from accepting presents from foreign governments; all foreign gifts must be recorded with the gifts unit to guarantee that they are being treated as public property even if they are going to be worn by the First Lady or the president.

Correspondence secretary Gwen King noted that on many occasions Mrs. Nixon had spoken about foreign gifts, saying "how careful she wanted to be about seeing that things got over to the gifts unit . . . I just don't feel comfortable having them around here, and I'm certainly not going to wear them." She asked King to register them and to put a gift of Saudi Arabian jewels in another safe. Yet before Gwen had a chance to do that, Maxine Cheshire in the *Washington Post* accused Pat of keeping a $52,400 matched set of emeralds and diamonds presented to the Nixons by King Fahd of Saudi Arabia on a state visit in May 1971. Cheshire reported that other state gifts had not been registered with the gifts unit in the White House in a timely fashion, even as she also brought up old charges that Pat and Dick did not return gifts when Nixon was vice president.

Publicly, Pat laughed at the allegations and said, "It's for the birds." Privately she was furious. "What more can they possibly want us to do?" she asked Dick. Emotionally exhausted that summer by these charges, Pat significantly curtailed her White House schedule. In June, the only White House events she held were a tea for Victoria Tolbert, the wife of the president of Liberia, a reception for the National Spelling Bee finalists, and a reception for the wives of the chiefs of missions. In July, she presided over two events: a tea for Irina Dobrynin, the wife of the Soviet ambassador to the United States, and a reception for the National Council of Negro Women.

On July 23, the Supreme Court ruled unanimously that Nixon must turn over sixty-four tapes to the Watergate special prosecutor and the Senate committee. He did so. The House Judiciary Committee voted four days later by a total of twenty-seven to eleven in favor of an article of impeachment charging that Nixon had tried to obstruct the investigation of the Watergate case. Six Republicans voted with the majority. The committee voted for two additional articles of impeachment: one for abandoning his constitutional duty to uphold the laws—including violating the constitutional rights of citizens by obtaining confidential information from tax returns for political purposes—and another for failing "without lawful cause" to produce the items subpoenaed by Congress.

Dick was standing barefoot in a beach trailer getting ready to swim near San Clemente when he learned that he was the first president recommended for impeachment in 106 years. He was disturbed about his own prospects, but later that evening he wrote, "But, God," he couldn't fathom how Pat "could have gone through" all that he had put her through in twenty-five years of politics. David Eisenhower worried about his mother-in-law, and he told a reporter she "is a shoulder to everyone, but whose shoulder does she lean on?"

Helene Drown tried to bolster Pat's morale by spending a week in late July with the Nixons in Washington. By this point, when reporters lobbed questions about Watergate in her direction, Pat pretended she did not hear them. She told Helene, "The next thing I know there will be a report that I am getting deaf." If she gave reporters "tidbits about people and issues," they would accuse her of being loose-lipped, but if she refused to talk to them, she told Helene, they would accuse her of "having no opinions or being capable only of small talk." She preferred the latter.

As the pressures of the Watergate investigations mounted, it would be understandable if Pat and Dick coped by drinking more than usual. Pat had often sworn to reporters that she did not drink or smoke, but in her last year as First Lady, she became more open about enjoying a Jack Daniel's whiskey and a cigarette. During their last year in the White House, there were many rumors in and outside the capital that the Nixons drank so heavily that their performance in the White House was impaired. These rumors passed into legend in 1976 when Bob Woodward and Carl Bernstein's best-selling book, *The Final Days*, covering the Nixons' last one hundred days in the presidency, claimed that, after drinking, Nixon spoke to the portraits on the White House walls and made decisions that put the country in danger. Pat's drinking, they asserted, caused her to withdraw from her role as First Lady. *The Final Days* was vigorously attacked by Nixon family members and White House staff.

Bob Haldeman, who did not shrink from criticizing the president, asserted that his boss did not drink excessively. However, according to his biographer Walter Isaacson, Henry Kissinger sometimes referred to Nixon as "our drunken friend." After the White House years Kissinger denied the statement—a decision that was politically wise. Through his press officer, Dr. Kissinger sent the following message to this author: "I have the highest regard for President Nixon to whom I had the opportunity to serve. I consider him the best prepared foreign policy president of the time I have known. These are my views. Any other quotations are an innaccurate description of my views."

Dwight Chapin explained that "Even after one or two beers, he [Nixon] might slur some words. I have always felt his system did not tolerate alcohol." Rose Mary Woods told Chapin that Nelson Rockefeller, who did not drink, "suggested to RN that he just sip a Dubonnet cocktail when he went to political events. . . . He could make one last all evening. I saw it many times." Steve Bull, Nixon's special assistant, had an office right outside the Oval Office and saw the president more often than anyone but Haldeman. He agreed that Nixon was a "lousy drinker" but says that he "never saw him incapacitated." On a couple of occasions he perceived him to "be mellow, but it was very, very rare." Bull, who had free access to the private residence, cannot remember seeing the president and First Lady drinking together. Pat's former press secretary Helen Smith wrote an article in *Good Housekeeping* declaring that as the pressure mounted, "she [Pat] kept to a very busy schedule right up to the resignation." Her social secretary Lucy Winchester, who "[s]aw her every day from early morning to late at night," declared that her social drinking had never become a problem.

On August 2, Dick asked Pat, Tricia, Julie, David, Ed, and Bebe to meet with him in the Lincoln Sitting Room. Dick described the contents of the June 23, 1972, tape in which he supported obstructing the FBI's investigation of the Watergate break-in. Nixon approved a plan for Deputy CIA Director Vernon Walters to call FBI head Pat Gray and say, "Stay the hell out of this . . . this is ah, business here we don't want you to go any further on." He told the family that this tape, which had been subpoenaed and was about to be released to the

Senate Watergate Committee and the special prosecutor, would make it impossible for him to continue his fight to stay in office. Tricia, Ed, David, and Julie took copies of the transcripts to their rooms and read them. Pat did not want to see them—not then anyway. She was quiet at the family meeting and for the next week did not answer phone calls from friends or respond to memos from her East Wing staff—a responsibility she usually handled with alacrity.

She distracted herself by working with curator Clement Conger on redecorating the Queen's Room and the Garden Room, substituting antiques for 1950s furniture, and matching draperies to a new rug in the State Dining Room. She played gin rummy with Helene, took long walks on Theodore Roosevelt Island, and listened to music. Only Helene saw her despair. "Dick has done so much for this country. Why is this happening?" As angry as she was about some of Dick's decisions, she retained her deep underlying respect for his abilities and his accomplishments, and her decision not to read the transcripts of the June 23 tape allowed her to maintain that respect and her support for her husband at a time of ultimate crisis.

Pat did her best to exude confidence and calm in front of her family and her staff. However, Helene said she was "more worn and fragile than I had ever seen her. . . . She looked forlorn. She had always been a doer and now there was nothing she could do." Pat told Conger, "They're out to get us. . . . They want us out of here. But it's all politics and will go away." Until late July, Pat believed that her husband would find a last-minute maneuver (like the Checkers speech) that would allow them to shed the active shadow of Watergate once and for all. She busied herself planning events for the fall, the holiday season, and the spring of 1975.

On the morning of August 2, the day Nixon would later ask his family to listen to the "smoking gun" tape, shortly before Helene left to return to California, Nixon told Julie that he had made a tentative decision to resign. Even without the release of the June 23 tape, he had little support left in Congress. Because of the "smoking gun" tape, the House was certain to vote to impeach him and a Senate trial would likely result in conviction and his removal from office. Dick could not endure telling his wife of his decision. Julie went to Pat's bedroom and found her mother standing expectantly in the doorway. When Julie told Pat the news, Pat's "mouth began to tremble." She asked, "But why?" Julie explained, and they hugged briefly. Mother and daughter were afraid a long hug would unhinge them both. When they came apart, Julie saw tears in her mother's eyes. For Julie, it was "perhaps the saddest moment" of their final weeks in the White House.

Nixon and his family spent that weekend at Camp David, walking in the woods, swimming, and watching movies. They did not discuss the president's dilemma until they finished dinner on Saturday night. The conversation was painful. His daughters and sons-in-law pressured him to stay on, as did Pat. Nixon told them he would wait until Monday, when the June 23 tape would be released and he could assess its impact. "It's fight or flight by Monday night," he told them. In her diary Tricia articulated the family's intentions during their final week in the White House: "Now we must all be as stoical as humanly possible and show him [our love] more than ever. We must not collapse in the face of this ordeal. We must not let him down."

After Nixon released the June 23 tape, acknowledging that he had misled his lawyers and the public, and had participated in the cover-up, his political support in Congress collapsed. Political commentators and allies called him everything from a madman to a dictator. Dick asked that his family join him for a final outing on the presidential yacht *Sequoia*. He did not want any of them to watch the evening television news. Word about the Nixons' dinner cruise spread quickly. Photographers lined the bridges over the Potomac and gathered at the pier where the boat was launched. The president was furious at the intrusion. When he disappeared below deck, Pat explained to Julie that her father had to elevate his leg, which was painfully swollen from phlebitis. A soft breeze vitalized the stifling hot night. Dick tried to buck up Pat and his children by telling them that the awful experiences they endured had brought the family closer. Pat told Dick she was "emphatically against resigning," Nixon remembered. As always, "She was a fighter to the last." He later realized that she, sensing what he had decided to do, had already begun packing their belongings and preparing to leave. For the Nixons, "the unspoken things go deeper than the spoken," aide Frank Gannon said about them. Pat had already asked Conger to cancel an order for a Nixon White House china pattern.

Several nights later, on August 7, the Nixons gathered in the third-floor White House solarium for dinner served on trays. Perched on the edge of the couch, Pat held her chin high. Dick recognized this as a sign she was tense. Pat got up and embraced him, saying, "We're all very proud of you, Daddy." Dick told his family, "Well, I screwed it up good, real good, didn't I?" Nixon had summoned White House photographer Ollie Atkins to take a portrait of the family, but Pat was disturbed when he arrived. "Ollie, we're always glad to see you," she told him, "but I don't think we need pictures now." For Dick, the imperative of history trumped his family's private feelings; he told Ollie to take the shots. Atkins used a flash camera that minimized the traces of tears on the women's faces. Pat would hate those photographs as much as she detested the pictures showing her fighting back tears while Dick conceded the 1960 election. "Our hearts were breaking and there we were smiling," she later said.

Nixon gave his televised resignation speech from the Oval Office at 9:00 p.m. on Thursday, August 8. Earlier that evening, in a crowded meeting with a group of fifty-five senior aides and members of Congress in the Cabinet Room, Republican House minority whip Leslie Arends, Nixon's friend for twenty-five years, put "his head on his arms and sobbed." Nixon "broke into tears," and left the room. Many wondered whether he would cry during his speech. Nixon barred his family from watching him in person lest they all become audibly distraught.

The president began by telling the nation that he had kept his inaugural promise to make the world a safer place. But using as his cover the statement that he no longer had political support in Congress to fight the charges against him, he told Americans, "Therefore I shall resign the presidency effective at noon tomorrow." He hoped his departure would help heal the national trauma, he declared, and went on to say he regretted the injuries he had inflicted on his fellow citizens and his bad judgments, which he claimed "were made in what I believed at the time to be the best interest of the nation." For years to come he would grapple with the extent to which he had kept the welfare of the nation in mind as he handled the Watergate crisis.

After his speech Dick hastened to the White House family quarters on the second floor. Pat enveloped him in an embrace. Tricia, Julie, David, and Ed huddled with them. His family was alarmed when Nixon began to shake violently. He had perspired heavily during his broadcast and had felt chilled walking back from the Oval Office, but he was reacting most violently to the anguish he had suppressed during his address to the nation. The muted sound of the crowds outside the White House filtered into the room. Pat summoned Dick to the windows to absorb what she assumed to be encouragement from Nixon supporters assembled to bid their president farewell. Instead, she heard the chant "Jail to the Chief."

The next morning, Nixon aide Steve Bull prepared the family to enter the East Room to say good-bye to the cabinet and approximately three hundred members of the White House staff. When Bull told the Nixons that there would be three television cameras in the East Room, Pat and Tricia became visibly upset. Julie heard torment in her mother's voice as Pat told her husband, "Oh, Dick, you can't have it televised." Nixon disagreed. "That's the way it has to be," he said. "We owe it to our supporters. We owe it to the people." While the president spoke, the three Nixon women took deep breaths to manage their grief.

With tears flickering in her eyes, Pat listened to Dick address the gathering. After giving a mawkish tribute to his mother ("a saint") and his father (a "great man because he did his job") and declaring them to be representatives of the kind of hardworking people who built America, Nixon read a passage from an account Theodore Roosevelt had written about the death of his young wife, Alice. Roosevelt believed then that "when my heart's dearest died, the light went from my life forever." Many of the guests in the East Room sobbed deeply at this point in his talk. Nixon used Roosevelt's words to emphasize that when "things happen that don't go the right way . . . that when we suffer a defeat," and think "that all is ended," it is "[n]ot true. It is only a beginning always."

Demonstrating the tenacity in the face of crisis and defeat that is part of his legacy, he told the nation, his family, and his staff that this moment was not a good-bye, but "au revoir," meaning that we "will see you again." Drawing on his personal credo that character resides more in rising to challenges than in winning, he asserted that "greatness comes and you are really tested when you take some knocks, some disappointments, when sadness comes, because only if you have been in the deepest valley can you ever know how magnificent it is to be on the highest mountain." He finished by offering advice he had failed to heed until the end: "Always remember, others may hate you, but those who hate you don't win unless you hate them, and then you destroy yourself." In his intense suffering, he had finally wrested some wisdom and a bit of grace out of anguish. Dick's speech, as disjointed and self-serving as it was, was also heartfelt and, in the end, strangely moving—even for some of his enemies. As Dick and Pat left the East Room, the crowd rose to their feet and applauded vigorously.

In the aftermath, Nixon faced widespread criticism for not mentioning Pat in his final address. Some people still wonder why in his last large public moment of retrospection, reflection, and renewed resolve, Richard Nixon could not have celebrated the woman who had made his best moments possible and stood by him in his most difficult times. Nixon justified the omission by saying, "I wasn't about to mention [Pat], or Julie or Tricia and have them break down in front of all the people in the country. That would have destroyed her. She had too much dignity, and she was always proud of that." He asserted that "she knew that I was mentioning her in my heart—that's what mattered."

The incoming president and First Lady, Gerald and Betty Ford, escorted the Nixons from the White House onto the South Lawn, where a helicopter would spirit them out of Washington on the first leg of the trip that would take them back to San Clemente. Pat and Betty linked arms. She told Betty, "My heavens, they've even rolled out the red carpet for us, isn't that something." In an intriguing final comment that suggested a private truth about her public life, she added, "You'll see so many of those . . . you'll get so you hate them." As Richard Nixon climbed the steps of *Marine One,* he turned back to offer the cameras and the assembled crowd an awkward wave, flashing a defiantly proud smile and stretching his arms wide into his trademark double V for victory. He had fought off defeat throughout his life, but now he surrendered to it with a surprising glint of dignity.

He would be haunted by how deeply he had harmed his wife. "Now she would not receive any of the praise she deserved," he wrote in his memoir. "There would be no round of farewell parties by congressional wives, no testimonials, no tributes." Reflecting on her resilience during these last wretched months in the White House, and throughout his career, Dick praised Pat as possessing "a strength of character unmatched in the history of American politics." For Dick, the year 1974 had been, he told Haldeman, "Eight months of pure hell and agony—for nothing." The corruption of power and the corrosive effects of the president's compartmentalization of his life had brought the Nixon marriage to the brink of emotional bankruptcy.

Now, as the helicopter rose from the White House lawn, Dick overheard Pat murmur, "It's so sad. It's so sad."

Part Four

Affliction and Recovery

If you are going through hell, keep going.
—*Winston Churchill*

The dogs bark but the caravan moves on.
—*An old Arab proverb*

There is a tonic strength, in the hour of sorrow and affliction, in escaping from the world and society and getting back to the simple duties and interests we have slighted and forgotten. Our world grows smaller, but it grows dearer and greater. Simple things have a new charm for us, and we suddenly realize that we have been renouncing all that is greatest and best, in our pursuit of some phantom.
—*William George Jordan*

20

Renewal in Exile

At noon Eastern Daylight Time that August 9, as *Air Force One* flew over Missouri with the Nixons inside, Gerald Ford took the oath of office as the thirty-eighth president of the United States. On board the plane, Pat, numb and dazed, sat alone in her small, private compartment, with occasional visits from Tricia and Ed, while Dick remained in his office, swiveling in his padded chair, planning his future. The thirty-four passengers, including Secret Service agents and Nixon staffers, spoke little on the long, somber flight across the country. Neither Pat nor Dick saw Ford tell the nation, "Our long national nightmare is over. . . . May our former president, who brought peace to millions, find it for himself."

But there would be no immediate peace for the Nixons. As the former presidential couple began their exile, they were plagued with freshly humiliating ordeals, and battered with legal, financial, and emotional challenges that would equal and even surpass at times the travails of their last months in the White House. The Nixons even skirted death. They would need years to recover from the disgrace of Dick's abrupt departure from the presidency, rebuild their battered and disaffected marriage, and find the peace at the center that his Quaker tradition promised.

When the plane landed at El Toro Marine Air Station near Irvine, California, Nixon swung open the door to the compartment where he had holed up and found Pat, Tricia, and Ed standing in the passageway. Pat reached out to hold his hand. Out the window they saw a huge crowd of supporters had gathered to welcome them home on this sunny California day. When Nixon appeared in the open doorway of the plane, the crowd cheered, some of them weeping and waving flags. When he gave the V-for-victory salute, they clapped even louder and followed the lead of one supporter who began singing "God Bless America." With Pat at his side, Dick briefly addressed the crowd, telling them that "having completed one task does not mean that we will just sit back and enjoy this marvelous California climate and do nothing." The family flew in the *Marine One* helicopter to the Coast Guard station next to La Casa Pacifica. Their friend Gavin Herbert, who had landscaped the San Clemente property, met them at the house. Nixon told Herbert, "It is good to be back in a house of peace." Sympathetic supporters sent four hundred floral arrangements.

That afternoon, while Dick walked down the slanted back lawn of their home and stood on a cliff watching waves crash across the beach, Pat gave herself a measure of peace by unpacking her husband's possessions and placing them in his bedroom. At least the next morning he could start his first full day as a former president surrounded by the photos and books he loved. Organizing their belongings allowed her to manage the pain she felt beneath her numbness.

Nixon had spent his life compensating for his feelings of being an outsider; now his resignation to avoid possible conviction for impeachable offenses had caused him and his wife to become, for many Americans, national pariahs. He had brought about the realization of his worst fears. But although they were outsiders to many in the nation they had led, they were not ignored. Two dozen reporters kept watch outside the compound's heavily guarded gates. Over the next months, the Nixons seldom ventured out. Julie asked author Lester David, "What do you expect her [Pat] to do, stand at the check-out line at the Alpha Beta supermarket? She'd be mobbed." Early in the former president's first term surfers had petitioned the state and won the right to use the beach in front of La Casa Pacifica, so Nixon had to travel thirteen miles to swim out of sight of curious bystanders.

During their first week, Pat and Dick's shock began to recede, replaced by what Nixon aide Jack Brennan called a deep "sadness brought by the sense of all that had been lost." Pat was "hurt beyond words," author Earl Mazo said. As for Dick himself, he later acknowledged that during this period he felt "that he was being forsaken by God."

While Pat and Dick maintained a bitter and defensive interpretation of Watergate (including the assertion that other presidents had acted similarly or worse), they were subjected to myriad humiliations. Within ten days of the president's resignation, a Gallup poll found how deep the public's fury with him reached: 56 percent of Americans wanted to put him on trial. Newspaper columnists, Nixon thought, remained determined to prove that he "represented the epitome of evil itself." *Saturday Night Live* and other television programs made Dick and Pat the object of jokes. Pat bitterly resented the Ford White House's confiscation of her personal letters, address books, souvenirs, and Julie's wedding dress as part of the Watergate investigation.

Reporter Maxine Cheshire impugned Mrs. Nixon's integrity when she revealed that, before its mandate ran out at the end of June 1974, the Watergate committee had subpoenaed Pat's cousin Edward Sullivan, Jr., to testify about the provenance of $580,000 of jewels he had appraised for the Nixons for insurance purposes between 1970 and 1974. Cheshire reported it was unclear whether some of these jewels were official gifts that belonged to the government and whether some of the jewelry might have been bought for Pat with misappropriated campaign funds. The matter was never fully resolved, but any mention of the issue distressed Pat.

Approximately twenty lawsuits, some of which were frivolous and attention-seeking maneuvers, were filed against Nixon for civil damages related to Watergate. He was subpoenaed to testify at the trial of his former aides and at other congressional investigations. The House of Representatives and later the Supreme Court decreed that he could not have possession of his papers and tapes because the materials were evidence in the judicial process. The Nixons' attorneys' fees and back taxes left them at the brink of bankruptcy. It would eventually cost him $1 million for legal fees to defend himself. He owed $225,000 in back taxes. Congress angrily allowed them only $60,000, much less than he had requested, for Nixon's expenses during the official six-month period of transition. All these problems swiftly took their toll on Nixon. After Benton Becker, President Ford's lawyer, visited Nixon to talk about the possibility of a pardon, he reported to Ford that the ex-president had aged significantly in the month since he left office. He was "shrunken in the mouth . . . his jowls were loose and flabby" and his "handshake was very weak." Benton worried that Nixon might commit suicide.

Dick coped by putting on a suit each morning, crossing the home's courtyard, and climbing the outdoor stairs to his blue-carpeted and blue-walled den-office, which had a view of the ocean. He made calls and conducted business as if he were still in power. He arranged with the flashy talent agent Irving "Swifty" Lazar, who represented everyone from Truman Capote to Cary Grant, to sell the rights to his memoirs to Warner Books for $2.5 million and began work on the book, assembling a team of researchers that included staffers Frank Gannon and Diane Sawyer. Writing his autobiography gave Dick the sense of purpose he needed and the assurance his voice would be heard once more.

When Pat was not looking after her husband, she retreated into reading biographies (Antonia Fraser's *Mary Queen of Scots* and Robert K. Massie's *Nicholas and Alexandra*) and current and classic fiction (Morris West's *The Ambassadors* and the works of Jane Austen, Pearl S. Buck, and Ernest Hemingway). As a gift, Gannon bought her fiction by the romance novelist Belva Plain and a box of soap that looked like candy. "After reading that novel," she told Gannon, "I needed the soap to wash my mouth out." She loved listening to music on the radio and show tunes on the stereo and still answered her mail, with the help of a volunteer staff. Gardening on their acre-and-a-half property—an activity to which she devoted up to seven hours a day—was her main therapy. She tore up a rose garden on the north side of the house and planted a colorful mass of pink and white geraniums along with purple gazanias. She planted roses that Dick loved so they were visible from his office and from the dining room.

Pat continued to regret deeply that she had failed to help her husband avert the tragedy of Watergate. Ten months after they returned to San Clemente, Pat told Julie that "there were two broken people here." Pat would have been justified in being furious at her husband for withholding key information from her while she defended him publicly, and for botching his second term, but there is no evidence that she had any ill feeling toward him. None of her friends revealed confidences to the press about her feelings of hostility and disappointment. Certainly any anger she felt at her husband was mitigated by her indignation at the press, the investigations, and the Republican representatives who deserted him in the last weeks of his presidency. According to Julie, Pat believed that Nixon had been cast out partly as a result of an international conspiracy. Perhaps, she thought, "double agents were involved" in the circumstances surrounding the break-in at the Democratic Party headquarters at the Watergate. Even amid her resentment and indignation, she focused on recognizing how well Dick had risen to the task of the presidency, and how he had opened doors in China and the Soviet Union and de-escalated the Vietnam War. Compared to shortsighted political cover-ups and even abuse of power, his accomplishments had enduring value for her.

On Sunday morning, September 8, Pat and Dick drove through the Southern California fog on their way to the secluded and lush 220-acre Palm Springs estate of their friends Walter and Lee Annenberg. While they were en route, President Ford addressed the nation on television, announcing he was granting Nixon a full pardon for all offenses he had committed or might have committed during his term in office. Ron Ziegler, who was now serving as Nixon's main assistant, released a statement Nixon had negotiated with Ford's representatives: "I was wrong in not acting more decisively and forthrightly in dealing with Watergate. . . . No words can express the depths of my regret and pain at the anguish my mistakes over Watergate have caused the nation and the presidency." Significantly, the admission of "mistakes and misjudgments" did not extend to any illegal acts. The acceptance of the pardon was an admission of guilt for his role in mishandling the Watergate crisis. Dick reluctantly accepted the pardon because, after discussing his situation with his lawyer, Nixon believed that there was little likelihood that he would be able to receive a fair trial in the foreseeable future. Dick told Pat that it was the "most humiliating day" of his life. It was "the saddest day" of hers, she told Julie.

That same night Dick began experiencing piercing abdominal pain. During the last few months of his presidency his left leg had become swollen, and now his thigh was enlarged, in a flare-up of phlebitis, an inflammation of the veins. For the next two weeks Pat and Dick denied the severity of the problem, daunted by the prospect of a physical ordeal at a time when they were contending with so much else. By September 23, Dick was so uncomfortable he accepted the recommendation of his physician John Lungren to check himself into Long Beach Hospital, where his medical team found a blood clot in his lung. He could not sleep at night; nurses awakened him every hour to refill his intravenous anticoagulants. Miserable, he told Pat that once he went home, he would never return to the hospital. Pat sympathized with his suffering, shared McDonald's hamburgers with him, and watched reruns of the TV show *Bonanza* in the room with him each night.

After twelve days of treatment Dick returned home. Soon thereafter, when she saw that the swelling in his leg was intensifying, Pat asked Walter Tkach, the White House physician, to fly to California to examine her husband. Tkach ordered him back to the hospital, but Dick resisted, telling him that he would "never get out of there alive." Dick was not yet ready to accept his political defeats and his deep emotional reactions to those losses, nor was he willing to admit that he had a serious physical problem. When former White House communications director Kenneth Clawson visited Nixon, the ex-president told him, "You can't break, my boy, even when there is nothing left. You can't admit, even to yourself, that it is gone. . . . But a man doesn't cry." Yet by October 23, he was readmitted to Long Beach Hospital, where doctors discovered an alarming clot higher up his left leg. They ordered emergency surgery.

Pat fed Dick ice chips in the recovery room. Alarmed by his pallor, she called Julie and Tricia and told them to fly to California at once. Pat grew even more frightened when she heard the hospital call the emergency staff to her husband's unit. For three hours doctors fought to stabilize Dick's blood pressure, which plummeted in response to extensive internal bleeding. His heart was failing. Dr. Lungren stepped out into the waiting area, to tell Pat that "we're just doing all we can." She felt helpless, she later told Helene, and prayed.

Pat and her daughters spent the night watching over him. Dick would write later that he and Pat had "seldom revealed our physical disabilities to each other." Enduring was their credo, not sharing. But now Dick, at the edge of his endurance, told Pat that he did not think that he "was going to make it." She grabbed his hand and spoke fiercely: "Don't talk that way. You have got to make it. You must not give up." Her grit reminded him of how firmly she had fortified him when he had faltered twenty-two years before, moments before giving his Checkers speech. Lying in his hospital bed and fearing he might not survive, Dick dictated his reminiscences about his life in politics to Pat. After two hours, she was exhausted; Ziegler and Gannon, terrified that they were recording Nixon's last words, took down four more hours of reflections that ranged from the bitter to the philosophical.

The former president remained on the critical list for several days. In the brief moments the doctors allowed Pat to be at his side, she reassured him that he would survive. Dick's right lung collapsed and he contracted a mild case of pneumonia before he finally emerged from danger. When he awoke each morning, Pat was holding his hand. His life-threatening illness put in perspective whatever disappointment she had with her husband and strengthened her feelings of tenderness toward him. Dick later told journalist Trude Feldman that when he was in pain, Pat appeared to feel his suffering "twice as much." A visit from President Ford, who was in California on a campaign trip, cheered Dick, but also brought up fresh memories of the ordeal they had been through.

In mid-November, after a twenty-three-day hospital stay, Dick was released. He had lost twenty-three pounds. Judge Sirica sent three doctors from Washington to examine him to determine whether he was physically able to testify at the trials of his aides. The physicians observed how difficult it was for him to walk across a room, or speak more than a couple of sentences without catching his breath. Dick was excused from testifying because, as he later said, "I was a physical wreck; I was emotionally drained; I was mentally burned out."

Starting that winter, Pat and Dick slowly rebounded as a couple. They often started their evenings with a short swim, an exercise recommended by Dick's physicians. They ate dinner on trays in front of a blazing fire in the living room. The Nixons liked to watch USC football games together. Sometimes Ed and Tricia would join them and they would all root for USC, where Pat's brothers Tom and Bill received scholarships to play football. Pat watched Dick's other favorite ballgames on television. She was becoming "quite an authority," with her own "favorite players and teams," she told Feldman. They doted on their dog. Pat made a huge concession to the convalescing Dick, allowing their dog to flop down on the living room furniture— an indulgence she had denied him in the White House. While Jack Drown was visiting to watch a televised ballgame with Dick, he noticed how carefully she monitored his diet: Pat placed Dick's lunch on a tray with a note saying, "This meets your doctor's standards for good health."

Dick knew that Pat herself needed the same kind of encouragement she was giving him. He gently prevailed upon her to eat more dinner, to try the "delicious squash from the garden." One morning Pat, in a moment of despair, asked her husband how he managed to "keep going." He told her firmly, "I just get up in the morning to confound my enemies." According to Julie, her parents had a remarkable ability to rally each other. One of the secrets of a successful long-term marriage is an emotional synergy that allows couples to balance each other's moods so that they do not both sink into despondency at the same time; the welfare of the couple becomes more important than the mood of either spouse. That Dick and Pat could sustain each other during the severe tribulations of late 1974—and later—indicated the resilience of their marriage.

Pat rarely left the compound in those first months. "It's as if she went underground or vanished into the sea," said one of her friends. On one occasion she donned a black wig and slipped out of La Casa Pacifica to go Christmas shopping with Helene Drown. Tricia, Julie, David, and Ed flew to San Clemente for the holidays, but it was not a festive occasion. Julie wrote that that Christmas and New Year's were "the lowest point in my father's life." Confined to bed, he could walk only a few yards at a time. His blood pressure was monitored three times a day. Pat herself was not as beset and beleaguered as her husband. While she might have felt like a failure, the American public did not hold Watergate against her; she was *Good Housekeeping's* most admired woman in the country for 1974 and 1975. She was puzzled why Americans continued to like her so much yet "say the things they do about Dick."

The year 1975 started off on a painful note. As Dick sat watching the Rose Bowl on television on New Year's Day, a news bulletin interrupted the game to announce that the Watergate jury had delivered guilty verdicts for H. R. Haldeman, John Ehrlichman, and John Mitchell. Each of them was sentenced to three years in prison. In the early months of 1975 two of Dick's closest associates were mired in the inquiry. Bebe Rebozo had to testify several times before the special prosecutor's staff and the Senate Watergate Committee; Maurice Stans, the Nixon campaign's political fund-raiser, faced multiple investigations about the use of money under his control. Pat and Dick felt guilty and dispirited about the suffering of their friends, former staff members, and their families. Once again Dick sank into a deep depression; he had difficulty sleeping and he did not want to eat. Pat became even more solicitous. Nixon recalled, "I'm told I was more dead than alive. . . . Pat's devotion kept me alive—I doubt if I would have made it without her."

As Dick's sixty-second birthday approached on January 9, Pat knew she needed to create a positive occasion for him. He relished celebrating her birthday but took little pleasure in observing his own. Pat summoned his friends Bebe Rebozo, Robert Abplanalp, Miami restaurateur Cy Mandel, and conservative columnist and author Victor Lasky. When the four arrived at La Casa Pacifica Pat was gardening, and she motioned for them to tiptoe up the outside stairs to Dick's office. Stunned when the men entered his room, he roared: "Well, goddamn!" As they gathered in the living room for drinks, Pat brought out crackers and a two-pound jar of caviar, which the shah of Iran had sent for Dick's birthday. His mood brightened. The group bantered and he opened gag gifts. Nixon told them how buoyed he was by receiving greetings from Chou En-lai, Ronald Reagan, and President Ford, and went on to give a toast that reiterated what he and his wife were endeavoring to do: "Never dwell on the past. Always look to the future." After drinking brandy and smoking cigars in the library, Nixon grew tired. As he and Pat bid their guests good-bye, Lasky hugged Nixon and was shocked to feel the bones under Dick's suit.

Another dinner party for several old friends was not so successful. During the group's conversation, one former high-ranking administration official began pushing Nixon to explain the full story of how the Watergate scandal unfolded. Pat was enraged. She did not, a friend said, think that "in his physical condition, he should be exposed to that sort of thing." Future dinner guests were more carefully vetted.

By the spring of 1975 Nixon's health had significantly improved, and he and Pat began venturing out occasionally. In early March they went to dinner at the home of their friends Jack and Helene, who rolled out a red carpet. Dick wrote them on March 3 that "above all the chance to relive 30 years of friendship made it an evening we will always cherish." He requested that when the Drowns visit them, they "bring the red carpet." That May, at Dick's behest, Pat made her first public appearance since she left Washington, attending the dedication of the Patricia Nixon Elementary School in Cerritos (formerly the town of Artesia, where Pat had lived as a child). She told the assembled crowd, "I am happy to tell you that I'm not gone—I mean really gone." Then in June Pat and Dick made a rare joint outing, to celebrate their thirty-fifth wedding anniversary, driving to Dana Point, where Dick had proposed to her. Helene and Jack Drown visited La Casa Pacifica often. While the men watched ballgames, the women played gin rummy. On one occasion Pat and Helene stole off for an incognito shopping excursion in Tijuana.

By 1977, as Dick regained his physical strength, he began planning to re-emerge into public life. Short on cash, he sold the rights to a series of four interviews to television host David Frost for $600,000 plus 20 percent of any profits (which would eventually add approximately $400,000 to Nixon's income from the project). Nixon and Frost taped nearly twenty-nine hours of interviews, which were distilled into a series of four riveting and popular ninety-minute television programs in which the former president answered questions about Watergate, foreign and domestic affairs, and his personality. The sessions were taped in March 1977 at a seaside home in Laguna Beach, California, and were aired weekly for four weeks starting on May 4, 1977. The first episode on Watergate drew a television audience of forty-five million viewers, unprecedented for a political interview. Frost, who was hoping to rejuvenate his television career, gave the ex-president plenty of room to energize his own political comeback. Nixon spoke assertively about his domestic and foreign policy accomplishments. In response to Frost's first questions on Watergate, Nixon, however, was evasive, protecting himself with lawyerly circumlocutions. He displayed a self-deprecating humor and, in his facial expressions, a palpable emotional vulnerability that may have astonished some viewers.

In the final interview Frost surprised Nixon. The ex-president had maintained that the first time he understood the "full import" of the Watergate cover-up was during a March 21, 1973, conversation with John Dean, but Frost's researchers had found a February 14, 1973, memo from Nixon to Charles Colson in which the president had written "the cover-up is the main ingredient." Nixon was shaken. After taking a break, Nixon refused, as he said, to "get down and grovel on the floor" or to state he had participated in an illegal cover-up, but he acknowledged, "I let down my country" and "I gave them a sword." His mistakes, he said, "were mistakes of the heart rather than of the head." At the end of the interview, "through moist half-closed eyes," Nixon granted, "I let down my friends." He poignantly finished by conceding: "I let down the country. I let down our system of government, and the dreams of all those young people that ought to get into government but now think it too corrupt. . . . I let the American people down, and I have to carry that burden with me the rest of my life."

The public and press reactions to the interviews were predictably mixed. A Gallup poll revealed that 44 percent of the viewers felt more sympathetic toward Nixon, although 72 percent still thought he was guilty of obstruction of justice. Pat and Dick did not watch the televised programs. Despite Dick's inability to take full responsibility, the interviews did cauterize Nixon's wounds and facilitated his relaunch into a role as an elder statesman.

Back in November of 1975, President Ford made a cordial but unproductive state visit to China that was followed by his promulgation of the Pacific Doctrine, which called for normalization of relations with China. Julie and David Eisenhower traveled to China the following month and were granted the unusual honor of a private meeting with an ailing Mao Tse-tung, who told the couple he wanted Julie's parents to visit him. In February 1976—on the fourth anniversary of the historic 1972 trip—Pat and Dick traveled to China for nine days. The Ford administration, including Secretary of State Kissinger, was alarmed at the prospect of the ex-president and his wife stealing headlines at a time when Ford was contending with Ronald Reagan for the Republican presidential nomination. Politicians and columnists condemned Nixon for upstaging the president and for what seemed at least the appearance of conducting diplomacy as a private citizen. James Brody's jeremiad in the *Washington Post* typified the outrage.

"The utter shamelessness of the man . . ." Brody wrote. "There is . . . absolutely nothing he will not do in order to salvage for himself whatever scrap of significance he can find in the shambles of his life." But no amount of invective could stop Richard Nixon from this essential first step in the recovery of his reputation. For Pat, the trip offered a sign that the worst period of their lives had come to an end.

When they arrived in China on February 21, the Nixons were not greeted with the bands and banners of 1972, but their hosts did literally roll out a red carpet for them. Dick was hampered by the lingering effects of phlebitis, but he plowed through the pain. He met privately with Mao, who had suffered a stroke and had a hard time speaking. Mao asked Nixon, "What after peace?" Nixon answered, "Justice." This exchange was the basis for Nixon's later book *Beyond Peace*. Nixon conferred several times with acting Chinese premier Hua Guofeng, but he spent the bulk of his time sightseeing with Pat—attending cultural programs and visiting agricultural centers, bomb shelters, and a university. The Nixons were treated to an evening that replicated the famous 1972 banquet (with the same ten courses of food and music). Pat and Dick experienced a reprise of their original public welcome from tens of thousands of citizens calling out their name on the streets of Canton in southern China.

At a lavish final banquet in the Great Hall of the People, Nixon, speaking as if he were still president, spoke about the process of reestablishing diplomatic relations, "We have not finished the bridge . . . there is more work to be done. But we are determined to complete it." Back in the United States his comments were taken as a criticism of Ford and Kissinger's progress on diplomatic normalization with China. The respect the Chinese leaders accorded the Nixons suggested to the press that the Chinese government was unhappy with the pace of Ford's progress in fostering relations between the two countries. Pat and Dick's pictures were back on the front pages of American newspapers for the first time since the resignation, but, after nearly thirty years, it was to be their last joint appearance in the international spotlight.

*   *   *

That summer Pat and Dick suffered a shock that permanently altered their relationship and led him to express a deeper level of tenderness and mutuality with his wife. On Wednesday morning, July 7, while reading Carl Bernstein and Bob Woodward's *The Final Days* on the patio at La Casa Pacifica, Pat felt weak. Against Dick's wishes, she had obtained from one of their secretaries a copy of the sensational book about the last months of the Nixon White House. Julie, who was spending the Fourth of July weekend at La Casa Pacifica with her husband, David, prepared dinner that evening, but Pat ate only a small portion and then stumbled back to her bedroom. Julie later found her mother lying fully clothed, sound asleep on her bed. She did not wake her to watch television.

The following morning, when Dick went into the kitchen to get a cup of coffee, he noticed Pat was struggling to open a bottle of juice. She slurred her words slightly. He saw that the left side of her mouth was drooping, recognized she had probably had a stroke, and raced to his office, and called Dr. John Lungren and then a doctor from Camp Pendleton. The marine base physician examined her, found her blood pressure was elevated, and concluded that she had suffered a small stroke. Dick called an ambulance and insisted that Pat go immediately to the hospital. Thirty-five percent of people who suffer a stroke die within the first forty-eight hours, and, as would be medically established in the following years, those who are immediately treated for strokes tend to recover more completely. Pat, who prided herself on her physical resilience, was stunned. "I can't believe this is happening to me," she told Julie. She insisted on walking to the ambulance by herself. On the ride to the hospital her left side became paralyzed. Doctors at Long Beach Hospital diagnosed a hemorrhage of the right cerebral cortex.

Dick stayed close by her during her initial assessment and treatment, and as he left the hospital that day, he told the gathered reporters, "She is a fighter. She is not giving up." But Helene Drown overheard Pat tell the head nurse, "I'm beat. I'm through." Pat later told Julie, "I'm so angry with myself" for getting ill. As doctors worked to stabilize her condition, Dick numbed his fear by fussing over the flowers, deliveries, and telegrams that flooded the hospital. Over a million letters of sympathy and support poured in. Each morning he entered her hospital room, kissed her, and asked to feel her grip. Then he read telegrams and newspaper editorials to her.

After six days he arranged an All-Star baseball game picnic, consisting of fried chicken and watermelon, in front of the television in the hospital's therapy room. She leaned unsteadily on Dick as he guided her into the room to join their daughters, sons-in-law, and Jack Drown. She was exhausted by the excursion, but her family was relieved to see she was making progress.

After two weeks of medication and inpatient physical therapy treatment, she was allowed to return home. The slurring in her speech had improved, but her left arm hung feebly at her side. As Dick somberly wheeled Pat through the hospital lobby, she covered up her vulnerability by motioning toward her husband and joking with photographers, "I feel fine, but I am a little frightened about the driver."

Pat had an exercise wheel installed on a wall in the outside patio at La Casa Pacifica so that she could rehabilitate her arm. As Dick walked between his outside office and their Spanish-style villa, he could see how relentlessly she turned that wheel. During periods in her therapy she saw little or no progress, but she persevered until she regained use of her left arm and hand. In 1990 Dick told *Time* magazine that critics who called her "Plastic Pat" had missed the point. Her "plastic was tougher than the finest steel."

The outside world continued to inflict humiliation on the Nixons. In June 1976, the New York Bar Association initiated disbarment proceedings against the former president. Pat was distressed to read rehashed views of her private life, based on Woodward and Bernstein's account of Watergate. On the basis of uncredited interviews, the two authors claimed that the Nixon marriage was loveless, that the Nixons had not slept together in sixteen years, and that Pat and Dick were heavy drinkers. They depicted President Nixon as mentally unbalanced and on the verge of suicide. Staff who worked closely with them, including Helen McCain Smith, Lucy Winchester, and curator Clement Conger, admitted that both Pat and Dick did drink more in their last year in the White House, but never to the point that it "caused her [Pat] to be out of sorts." Julie and David Eisenhower both rallied to defend her parents. She stood up for her mother by writing an article in *Newsweek*, and he issued a public statement reiterating that "the Nixon family is a close family." The country was divided. A large swath of the public was primed to believe the worst about the Nixons, but many others were furious about the treatment that such a moral couple endured.

Dick and his family blamed the book—which they believed was a despicable misrepresentation of them—for causing Pat's stroke. More than any incidental stress brought on by reading *The Final Days*, however, her stroke was more likely brought on by years of stressful living, suppressed emotions, and smoking. When Dick read excerpts of the book, which depicted her as a recluse sneaking drinks from the pantry, in *Newsweek*, he was apoplectic about its treatment of Pat. "The bastards have got no reason to talk about her," he told Ford's White House military office chief, William Gulley. "[She] never did anything to anybody."

A Peaceful Twilight

*I*n 1978 the Nixons cautiously emerged from exile. Dick was determined to engineer one of the most unlikely professional comebacks in American history, but he had yet to figure out how. Dick fought to restore his reputation as an international statesman while Pat maintained the quiet, private life that after more than thirty years of public service she felt she deserved. As a result of her stroke, Pat tired easily and felt stressed around strangers. According to Bebe Rebozo, her conviction that her husband "got a bum rap" during Watergate also caused her to decline an active public life for herself. As a woman who remained one of the most admired in American life, she had nothing more to campaign for. Only Dick could restore his own honor.

On January 9, 1978, Pat set aside her discomfort about going out in public in order to mark Dick's sixty-fifth birthday. Julie and David, who now lived twenty minutes away from Pat and Dick in Capistrano Beach, joined their parents along with an unexpected guest, the Nixons' friend Robert Abplanalp, for an early dinner at Dick's favorite local restaurant, El Adobe, in San Juan Capistrano. While Pat and Dick drank margaritas, Julie and David gave Richard Nixon a memorable birthday present: the news that they were expecting a baby that summer. Pat, after working for eighteen dreary months to recover from her stroke, savored a moment of joy. As the former president blew out the sixty-five candles on his fruit-flavored cake, patrons at other tables across the restaurant raised their glasses to toast him. "The greatest test is not when you are standing," Dick told journalist Nick Thimmesch, "but when you are down on the floor. You've got to get up and start banging again."

His memoir *RN* would be his third foray (after the second China trip and the Frost interview) in his campaign to restore himself to a place in American public life. Nixon claimed that "Watergate mattered so much less than the things I did well" in foreign policy. Watergate, as he saw it, was brought about by three major factors: a partisan, publicity-seeking, and politically opportunistic Senate Watergate Committee; an unscrupulous media and an irresponsible Congress; and an uninformed American public who were unduly influenced by his enemies. Repositioning himself as a sagacious commentator on American life, Nixon warned that the national character had become dangerously alienated from its core values of optimism, self-reliance, dedication to work, love of country, and commitment to a national mission to bring freedom to the world. His well-written book, which critics deemed self-protective, would be a sustained bestseller that summer of 1978.

He and Pat scheduled a publication party at La Casa Pacifica, but when Pat developed acute bronchitis, Tricia took her mother's place as host. Nixon allowed television cameras on the property for the first time since his presidency. Dick apparently did not share the contents of his book with his family as he was writing it, but he gave the first three printed copies he received to Pat and his daughters, asking them to read the book from the beginning. Pat cheated and went right to the section on Watergate. She told Julie that she "felt sick" when she realized that Dick's treatment of the scandal consumed one-quarter of the book.

Dick would exhibit different attitudes toward the scandal and his responsibility for it. In his memoir *RN*, Nixon said, "My actions and omissions, while regrettable and possibly indefensible, were not impeachable." By 1990, Nixon called Watergate "one part wrongdoing, one part blundering, and one part political vendetta by my enemies." He acknowledged that he "should have set a higher standard for the conduct" of his staffers and should have "established a moral tone" that would have made illegal actions "unthinkable" and avowed that his key mistake was a failure to take "a higher road than my predecessors and my adversaries."

Nixon conceded wrongdoing but not illegalities and did not fully acknowledge that the unlawful activities he inspired outdid those of his adversaries and previous administrations. He claimed the charge that he ordered hush money paid to Howard Hunt and other conspirators was a myth, but the March 21, 1973, tape of his conversation with John Dean shows Nixon seriously considering obtaining money for that purpose—whether he eventually gave such an order is not clear from the tapes.

Dick traveled extensively to polish his image while Pat chose carefully where to appear beside him. Over the course of 1978, Nixon further edged into political life and policy issues by speaking at the Oxford Union in Britain, being interviewed on French television, and making his first U.S. political appearance in Kentucky in the latter half of 1978. Pat made a rare public appearance when she accompanied Dick to the National Presbyterian Church in Washington on Friday, November 2, 1979, for a memorial service for Mamie Eisenhower. The former First Lady had died in her sleep shortly before her eighty-third birthday.

Throughout their retirement years, Pat and Dick's private lives revolved around their four grandchildren. Jennie Elizabeth Eisenhower was born in August 1978. The former First Lady and president were now known as "Ma" and "Ba." Sometimes, when Julie and David went away for a night alone, Ma and Ba skirmished over whose bedroom baby Jennie would sleep in—a domestic disagreement so minor that it could not even echo the fervor of their old conflicts. Tricia gave birth to Christopher Nixon Cox in March 1979 and Julie had a son, Alex, in 1980 and another daughter, Melanie, in 1984. After Julie and David moved to Berwyn, Pennsylvania, in 1979, it made sense for the Nixons to leave La Casa Pacifica to move closer to their daughters' families.

Discussing a transfer to the East Coast, Pat told Julie, "We're just dying here slowly." Life on the Pacific coast was pleasant, but it lacked the vibrancy the Nixons desired. Moreover, after an exile of nearly five years, Dick sought to be closer to the nation's political media center.

The Nixons approached the New York City real estate market assertively, but they were treated, at first, like ex-cons fresh from jail. In late July 1979, they put down a deposit on a nine-room, $750,000 penthouse apartment at 19 East Seventy-second Street, near Madison Avenue. The building's board approved the sale, but shareholders rose up in opposition, fearing the Nixons' presence would bring notoriety and that Secret Service agents would disrupt their lives. The co-op board reversed itself. When the Nixons agreed to buy a twelve-room condominium for $925,000 from parking garage magnate Abraham Hirschfeld at 817 Fifth Avenue at Sixty-third Street, the sale was put in limbo when residents of the building threatened to file lawsuits against the Nixons.

Lester Tanner, a Democratic trial lawyer, was appalled at the treatment New Yorkers gave the former president and his wife and wrote Nixon offering him the opportunity to buy his four-story, twelve-room town house at 142 East Sixty-fifth Street. The house, built in 1871, had six wood-burning fireplaces, four bedrooms, an elevator, and a sizable wood-paneled library that opened onto a terrace above the back garden. Neighbors included banker David Rockefeller, next door, and the distinguished historian and former Kennedy aide Arthur Schlesinger, Jr., on the other side of the Tanners' garden wall. In August 1979, Tricia, Pat, and Dick arrived to look at the Tanners' house, with the former president carrying his five-month-old grandson Christopher on his shoulders. According to Lester Tanner's wife, Marcella, Tricia loved the house, but Mrs. Nixon appeared wary. Stung by recent rejections, she chain-smoked.

In order to purchase the town house, the Nixons backed out of their Fifth Avenue contract and lost their $92,500 down payment. In October 1979 they paid $750,000 for the town house. Shortly beforehand, Mr. Tanner was awakened at midnight by a phone call from Nixon. "Pat can't sleep," Nixon told him. "She's sure we'll be rejected." "I don't need anybody's approval," Tanner said. "I told her that," Mr. Nixon explained. "She doesn't believe me." Tanner spoke to Pat, reassuring her that there would be no problems.

Pat and Dick moved into the town house in February 1980. Pat was excited to leave behind the long trips to Los Angeles for any shopping or cultural life. In New York she expected to find anonymity while her husband sought access to power. Beyond those considerations, they were faced with the challenge of building a sustaining life of culture, friendships, and socializing, to be achieved as much as possible on their own terms. Having family close by helped. Several times a week, Pat and Dick took a short walk to Tricia and Ed's home on East Seventieth Street. In the 1980s the Nixons ate frequently at Le Cirque restaurant in the Mayfair Hotel, which used to be between Park and Madison on Sixty-fifth Street, only five blocks south of the elegant Cox apartment at 10 East Seventieth Street. The Nixons often walked there from the Coxes' home to dine with Ronald and Nancy Reagan or other political figures. The owner, Sirio Maccioni, was close to Pat and Dick and proud whenever they came in. Sometimes Maccioni would dine with the Nixons, whose other favorite restaurant was Lutece.

Nixon made a point of telling gossip columnist Aileen Mehle (who wrote her column under the name Suzy), "What she [Pat] doesn't like are vacuous dinner parties with a lot of idle chatter." Pat and Dick had experienced their fill of fancy mansions, glitzy cocktail parties, and elaborate dinners. Pat met her needs for intellectual stimulation by reading; Dick needed more contact with people. They compromised. Dick held events at home without her, twice-a-month gatherings for politicians, intellectuals, economists, and former aides in their town house's golden-yellow first-floor drawing room, where Pat had placed her favorite porcelain figures and historical mementos. After a gourmet Chinese dinner and fine wines in the formal dining room that overlooked the garden, Nixon led discussions of topical issues, often on foreign policy. Guests saw a relaxed, jovial, and gracious man who loved to regale them with stories.

Ed Cox remembered that during this period "one of the highlights for the Nixons were the family christenings." In 1979 before the Nixons moved East, Norman Vincent Peale christened Christopher at the Cox apartment on East Seventieth Street. After Alex Eisenhower was born in 1980, Peale christened both Alex and his older sister Jenny at the same time at the Cox apartment.

Yet by the summer of 1981, only eighteen months after moving in, Pat and Dick had already grown disenchanted with aspects of their city life. Pat was often noticed and followed when she went for walks, and she was bothered by the sounds of the traffic on their heavily trafficked street. They wanted a spacious backyard like the one they enjoyed at La Casa Pacifica. Dick worried about Pat's ability to navigate the four flights of stairs on the central staircase in their town house. Their master bedroom and master bath were on the third floor and the kitchen was on the lower level. When Pat climbed the stairs, a friend told journalist Nick Thimmesch, "She has to watch it . . . there is always the possibility her leg could crumble. . . . Pat drags her left foot behind just a little. When her foot comes down, you can hear a little clump."

The Nixons sold their town house in September 1981 for $2.6 million to the Syrian government, to be used as a residence for its chief delegate to the United Nations. That fall they moved to a $1 million, two-story contemporary home, built in the Frank Lloyd Wright style, with a shingle mansard roof, on four acres in Saddle River, New Jersey. It was located on a quiet cul-de-sac near a peach orchard in a heavily Republican professional community in rural northern Bergen County. It was a fifty-minute ride to Nixon's office in lower Manhattan. The fifteen-room house had seven bedrooms, five upstairs and two in a separate guest wing. On the first floor there was an outside porch, a formal parlor, a living room with a big stone fireplace, a dining room, and a small library where Nixon worked. There was a den/playroom downstairs. It was a perfect place to enjoy their grandchildren and entertain prominent overnight guests. The properties adjacent to the Nixon home were not yet developed, and the grandchildren enjoyed running up and down the mounds of dirt on the cul-de-sac. They played hide-and-seek on the lots that were still forested.

Pat had the living room painted a favorite shade of pale yellow and hung Chinese landscapes on the wall. Expansive windows allowed the Nixons to feel immersed in the wooded landscape of hickory, white pine, birch, and red maple trees that enveloped them. Christopher Cox, even as a young child, enjoyed helping his grandmother garden. There was an elegant black marble swimming pool, "landscaped like a country pond," in the backyard, and a tennis court nearby. Guests drove up a circular drive graced with mountain laurel.

To maintain her energy, Pat rested every day after lunch and dinner and limited her appointments. When her husband held one of his seminar-dinners, she remained in her room, eating dinner from a tray, unless there were important guests she knew or other wives were in attendance. Dick found it relaxing to amble through the dozen shops of the village and chat affably with the owners and patrons. The former president walked into Oluf Hansen's candy store and bought a box of soft-center creams and a pound of handmade chocolate-walnut fudge for Pat. Thinking that Nixon looked a little disheartened, Hansen told him, "Mr. President, for all it's worth, I voted for you and I'd vote for you again." Dick responded by leaning over the counter and giving Hansen a bear hug.

Neither Pat nor Dick had to worry about food shopping—they hired a married couple to do that for them and to prepare meals. At times when they didn't prepare family dinners at home, Mr. Nixon would go out to McDonald's or to a Chinese restaurant and bring home meals for the grandchildren. The Nixon family (with the grandchildren) loved watching movies like *The Sound of Music* on RCA's electronic discs.

One day a large stray mutt, the size of a German shepherd, who was dying of hunger limped into the Nixons' Saddle River house. He was brown and had no hair on him. Chris Cox named him Brownie. The dog's hair soon grew back. He became Richard Nixon's best friend. Brownie tugged on the ex-president's shoe when he wanted to go out. It became a family joke to speculate about who was feeding Brownie under the table. Dick was the main culprit, but Pat would sometimes slip him food, too.

The Nixon family often enjoyed taking walks around their neighborhood with Brownie, who would run around. At night they used a flashlight. Dick took energetic walks to stay fit, but Pat did not have the strength for long walks. When Pat did leave the house with her grandchildren, she greeted neighbors she met along the country road.

Pat traveled into New York City twice a week to visit with Tricia and Christopher at the Cox apartment and to have her hair done at Elizabeth Arden. Richard Nixon used the library in the Coxes' apartment to meet with important guests such as Helmut Schmidt, the chancellor of West Germany, and James Baker, who served as secretary of the Treasury under President Reagan and secretary of state under President George H. W. Bush. On January 10, 1987, the day after his sixty-fourth birthday celebration at the Coxes' apartment, Nixon sent the Coxes a letter, saying: "Your beautiful apartment has been a haven."

Every second weekend the Nixons traveled two hours to see Julie and her family at their home, a less luxurious converted carriage house in the suburbs of Philadelphia. When Pat felt particularly energetic, Dick drove her around New Jersey villages or ventured into the Hudson Valley. During the holidays they took the grandchildren to Radio City Music Hall to see the Christmas show and then backstage, as Jennie Eisenhower remembered, "to pet the reindeer and meet the little people who played the elves."

The state of Pat's health, as well as her emotional well-being, remained a mystery to all but her closest friends, because she did not talk about it publicly. In October 1985 a *Washington Post* reporter spotted her shopping for a silk dress in Bonwit Teller. "I haven't been well," she told the reporter, "and I still get a little tired, but otherwise am fine." Pat declined a request for an interview. "I'm retired," she said. The reporter noticed that her speech bore only "slight traces of slurring."

When Nixon resigned the presidency in 1974, Ed Cox had been prescient about his father-in-law's future. Aboard the *Marine One* helicopter on the way to Andrews Air Force Base the Nixons flew past the Washington Monument. At this historic moment, Ed Cox had tried to encourage his father-in-law by saying that in ten years' time Nixon would be back (recognized on the world stage). He was, indeed, on the cover of *Newsweek* ten years later. In the late 1970s and then throughout the 1980s, Dick expanded his role as a senior statesman, consulting with President Carter about normalizing relations with China in 1978 and advising Reagan on the 1980 campaign against Carter and how to construct and staff his presidency. During the 1980s Nixon offered frequent advice to Presidents Reagan and Bush about arms negotiations and relations with the Soviet Union and China.

While Dick was counseling U.S. presidents, advising foreign leaders in Third World countries, and making frequent speeches and television appearances, Pat suffered a succession of illnesses that led her to contract her interactions with the outside world. In 1979 she had bronchial pneumonia and a few years later she had to be hospitalized for asthmatic bronchitis. In August 1983 she suffered a second, smaller stroke, which did not affect her speech but left her with a slight weakness in her left arm and diminished her resilience. Dick visited her for the five days she was in New York Hospital. "She doesn't quite have the stamina she used to have," he told the press, "and she doesn't like to go on faraway trips." He noted that she was still very beautiful: "She has the kind of classic beauty that lasts." In 1983, a month after accompanying her grandchildren to Disney World, she spent three days in Valley Hospital in Ridgewood, New Jersey, recovering from a pulmonary infection. In 1984, Dick accompanied her twice to New York Hospital to be treated for lung infections. Pat suffered from diminished lung capacity related to emphysema and asthma—the result of long years of smoking—and degenerative arthritis in her neck. In 1987 Dick took her to Manhattan's Lenox Hill Hospital for surgery to remove a small malignant tumor from her mouth.

Despite her declining health, Pat Nixon decided to hold a luncheon reunion for her female White House staff in the spring of 1985. Because of the pressures of the Watergate crisis, they had not had a chance to have a proper farewell party at the time of Nixon's resignation. Connie Stuart, Gwen King, and Lucy Winchester Breathitt joined seven other staffers at the Nixons' Saddle River home. Julie, Tricia, and their children attended; the women brought gifts for the grandchildren. Susan Porter Rose remembers that Richard Nixon joined the women in the living room and "he did not stop being the center of attention. He dominated—he didn't know how not to do it." Dick played Santa as the "kids" were "just tearing into paper." Nixon had a cocktail with the group and left so they could have a private lunch. The women "laughed and joked" about the fun times they had in the White House before that dismal last year in Washington. Connie remembered that Pat "seemed the same, although of course older and not quite as energetic . . . but all that old fired spirit was still there." A few years later Pat invited Susan Porter Rose, who worked in Barbara Bush's staff office, back to Saddle River to dine with the Nixons. Pat, who spoke with a "little bit of a speech slur," and the ex-president were very interested in hearing Susan's stories about working in the Reagan-Bush White House.

Remarkably, a 1979 Gallup poll listed Nixon as one of the ten most admired men in the world. Even as he looked after his wife's health, Dick traveled as often as he could, advancing his authority and presence as a senior expert in foreign policy. In July 1980, without the sanction of the State Department, he attended the funeral of his friend the former shah of Iran, in Egypt. Dick's campaign for renewed respect as an elder statesman received a huge boost in October 1981 when he was invited to accompany former presidents Carter and Ford as official U.S. representatives at the funeral of the assassinated Egyptian president Anwar Sadat. Five years later, as the Soviet Union seemed to be stirring into reforms of its ossified economic and governmental systems, its new leader, Mikhail Gorbachev, presented Nixon's foreign policy recommendations in a memo to President Reagan. Between 1983 and 1994 Nixon published eight best-selling books, seven of which focused on foreign policy and augmented his reputation as a pragmatic internationalist.

After returning to the East Coast, Richard Nixon did not feel it would be appropriate to accept invitations to be honored by Republican groups, but on October 17, 1985, he made an exception. Robert J. Brown, former special assistant to the president and the highest-ranking African-American official in the Nixon administration, wanted "to lift the old man up for all the things he had done to create progress for African-Americans." Under Nixon, in a Black Capitalism program, Brown had increased federal purchases from minority firms by 100 percent, set up a system for minorities to participate in government contracts, loans, and grants, and increased hiring of African Americans in governmental agencies. Brown arranged for 750 African-American entrepreneurs, civil rights leaders, ministers, and government officials from all over the country to fete Nixon and his former secretary of commerce, Maurice H. Stans. Nixon was initially reluctant to attend the $300-a-seat black-tie dinner in the Grand Ballroom of the New York Hilton Hotel, but decided to accept after he talked it over with Pat. Ed Lewis, the founder of *Essence*, a monthly magazine for African-American women, reportedly told Nixon that the president made it possible for him to start the magazine.

Despite Dick's vigorous travel schedule, the Nixons' longtime friend the author Victor Lasky, whose book *It Didn't Start with Watergate* was a defense of the president, wrote that by 1986 Pat and Dick were "closer than ever before. They have found their niche in life." The Nixons adored their young grandchildren. "We were their close friends, not their distant grandparents," Dick said. Taking after his famous grandfather, Christopher Cox was elected president of his grade school class each year and president of his school in ninth grade. While following Chris's successful grade school political career, Nixon would often pen him a congratulatory letter.

Like Richard Nixon, Tricia's son Christopher was an avid sports fan. During the late 1980s and early 1990s Dick enjoyed taking him to Yankees and Mets games and comparing notes about their favorite players and their batting averages. "I don't have to tell him," Dick wrote in his memoir *In the Arena*, "that when a man is on third with less than two out, a batter who doesn't drive him in deserves a reprimand from his manager."

On Saturday, February 29, 1992, Nixon took twelve-year-old Christopher and eleven-year-old Alex to a New York Knicks basketball game at Madison Square Garden. At halftime the cheerleaders noticed the ex-president in the audience. They sang and danced for him. In the midst of their "dance routine one of them landed in my lap!" Nixon told his assistant Monica Crowley. "I felt like Gary Hart on the *Monkey Business!*" he said, referring to the Colorado senator whose presidential bid collapsed in 1987 in the aftermath of a published photo of him on a yacht with a woman sitting on his lap. "I told Mrs. Nixon about it," he told Crowley, "and she thought the whole thing was very funny. She's such a good sport."

Pat played made-up games like "shoe store" with Julie's daughters Jennie and Melanie, as they lined up their grandmother's shoes to be sold in her bedroom. Playing circus, Alex helped his sisters perform the roles of ringmasters and performers in their three-ring spectacle. At age eleven, Jennie Eisenhower wrote a children's opera and put on special performances for her grandparents on their birthdays and on Christmas.

The day before the Nixons' fiftieth wedding anniversary, Tricia, Ed, and Chris's twelve-year-old poodle, Poo, died. Chris and Poo had grown up together. They were sad about the loss when they went to Saddle River for a family gathering.

In consideration of Pat's deteriorating health, the Nixons celebrated their fiftieth wedding anniversary on June 21, 1990, at home in the company of only their children and grandchildren. They allowed a photographer and reporter to be present, on the condition that no one would be quoted. As soon as the anniversary photograph was taken, Jennie, Melanie, Chris, and Alex dashed off to change into swimming suits for a dip in the backyard pool.

*　　*　　*

Fueled by guilt and disappointment that Pat had not received suitable recognition for her stellar career as his longtime partner, Dick insisted that Pat be commemorated in a separate section in his presidential library, which he started planning in the early 1970s. When the building opened, she was celebrated with a Pat Nixon room that displayed photographs and mementos from her life, a rose garden planted with the red-black Pat Nixon Rose developed by a French company in 1972, and a Pat Nixon amphitheater, a simple bowl-shaped area carpeted in fresh grass and terraced in concrete in an area south of the library's main building. Donated by Bob and Delores Hope, the amphitheater serves as a setting for dinners, weddings, and outside social activities. In 2012, on the hundredth anniversary of her birth, the Nixon Library and Museum organized an extensive and highly regarded Pat Nixon Centennial Exhibition, subtitled "People Were Her Project."

Nixon fought for decades with the National Archives for control over the papers and tapes documenting his presidency. Supporters raised $25 million for Nixon's library by 1990, but with possession of his presidential materials still a matter of contention, it began essentially as a museum. When the institution officially opened, its publicity materials emphasized that it was the only presidential library to be built without public funding. Without informing the public or calling much press attention to their activity, Pat and Julie quietly broke ground for the building in December 1988. It did not officially become a government library until after a 2004 act of Congress amended the Presidential Recordings and Materials Act of 1974, which had consigned Nixon's papers to the National Archives in College Park, Maryland. The Nixon Library was incorporated into the Federal Presidential Library system in July 2007.

Shortly before the opening of the Nixon Library, Dick published his third memoir, *In the Arena,* the style of which he assumed that he had totally rehabilitated himself and that he had earned, through his self-reflection in exile and his diligent comeback into political life, the role of a wise elder statesman—a stature that the library would be dedicated to enhancing.

Pat and Dick attended the library's dedication ceremonies, which lasted for two days in Southern California. Speaking at an opening event in the auditorium of a hotel in Anaheim, California, on July 18, 1990, Nixon repeated a remark by Kansas senator Frank Carlson when Dick was running for vice president: "Dick, you're controversial, but *everybody* loves Pat." The audience broke into a standing ovation to honor Pat, who was seated near her husband on the dais. It was obvious that she was frail. She leaned on the arm of her husband and walked gingerly to the microphone. Embarrassed by the attention, she raised both arms to quiet the crowd. "I just want to thank you for your years of loyalty and support," she said. Nixon put his arm around Pat and carefully guided her off the stage.

Pat eventually took an active interest in the development of the museum and library and her place in history. She was particularly concerned with the creation of quality exhibits in the library and committed to making the library accessible to visitors. Pat and Tricia met with the team members who were developing videos and other advanced techniques for the library exhibitions. Pat Nixon also attended fundraising meetings, in the library of the Coxes' New York apartment, with Maurice Stans, an accountant and the Nixon administration's secretary of commerce.

Fifty thousand people attended the opening of the Nixon Library and Birthplace on July 19, 1990, in Yorba Linda, California. Three brass bands played in the broiling heat. Adding a dash of grandeur, trumpeters in red suits heralded the entrance of four presidents: Republicans George Bush, Ronald Reagan, and Gerald R. Ford accompanied Nixon. It was the first time that four living presidents had attended a public event. Secretaries of State George P. Schultz, Alexander Haig, Henry Kissinger, and William P. Rogers also participated, as did many former Nixon staffers, including Dwight Chapin and H. R. Haldeman. The event was televised live; one thousand journalists were present. The museum celebrated Nixon's role as a peacemaker and mounted a controversial Watergate exhibition that minimized Nixon's role in the scandal by suggesting his resignation was the result of a partisan witch hunt.

The library dedication was Pat's first official public appearance in eleven years since her attendance at Mamie Eisenhower's funeral in 1979. Furors that had once centered on the Nixons had abated, to be replaced by controversies involving other issues and leaders. That hot July day there were few protesters carrying signs decrying Richard Nixon's role in the Alger Hiss case, the Vietnam War, or Watergate. Although one man carried a sign saying "Don't honor a crook," demonstrators focused on other issues, elsewhere, such as AIDS research and treatment, abortion rights, the plight of the homeless, the condition of the environment, and America's potential actions against Iraq over its designs on Kuwait.

Only President Bush mentioned Watergate in his remarks, referring to it simply as one of many crises in the Nixons' lives. Bush reminded the crowd that Nixon "came from the heart of America, not geographically perhaps, but culturally," and that he "loved good, quiet, decent people. And he spoke for them; he felt deeply, on their behalf." He saluted him as a leader who "knew that true peace means the triumph of freedom, not merely the absence of war."

President Reagan declared Pat to be "a true unsung hero of the Nixon administration." As for Richard Nixon, speaking on behalf of himself and his wife, he told the crowd, "Nothing we have seen matches this moment, to be welcomed home again so warmly on this day by our friends in California." He told them, "You will suffer disappointments and sometimes you will be very discouraged. It is sad to lose, but the greater sadness [is] to travel through life without knowing either victory or defeat."

Acknowledging Pat, as well as the other past and present presidential wives in attendance, Barbara Bush, Nancy Reagan, and Betty Ford, Nixon told the crowd that "there is no more important a position or career a woman could have than to be a First Lady, the wife of the president of the United States." The grand ceremony, twenty years in the making, lasted for two and a half hours. At its conclusion, the crowd sang "God Bless America" and red, white, and blue balloons were released into the sky. That evening at a banquet of fifteen hundred supporters at the Century Plaza Hotel in Los Angeles, Pat radiated joy, expressing her quiet satisfaction that her husband's reputation was being restored.

Monica Crowley, Nixon's last foreign policy assistant who worked with him on his last two books on foreign policy, observed the Nixon marriage closely in the early 1990s. She was impressed by the mellow, thoughtful, and playful bond the couple had forged: "They treated each other kindly and often surprised each other with small gestures of affection that meant far more to them than ostentatious displays. He fluffed her pillow when he knew she was preparing to rest; she chilled his favorite drink, white grape juice. He brought her cold water when she was sick and chocolate when she was well. . . . Like many couples a silent language seemed to pass between them; they exchanged glances of recognition when words were burdensome, and they understood." Crowley was also struck by her boss's willingness to listen to Pat's advice: "His reliance on her was absolute . . . he grew stronger and more patient, just by being around her. When she cautioned him against a certain course of action, he almost always heeded her suggestion."

Crowley enjoyed Nixon's "wonderful sense of humor," which, she thought, "didn't necessarily come across" in public. On Mrs. Nixon's birthday in 1992, Dick told Monica, "You know what I got her for a gift? I'm leaving for two weeks." Raising her thumbs, Pat looked at Monica, smiled, and said, "That's right."

Couples who share similar upbringings and values are more likely to maintain long-term marriages. Dick, speaking again to columnist Aileen Mehle, elaborated on this point and explained that their success over a half century was related to having a similar point of view based on coming from a common background. Nixon told Mehle that Pat "can discuss anything with anyone as an equal—from a head of state on down."

When Nixon introduced Crowley to Pat in July 1990, Pat, smiling, told her, "Don't let Dick give you a hard time now. If he does—well, just report to me." Dick asked Crowley if she was going to "squeal on me." "Only if you give her a reason to," Pat said. Mrs. Nixon winked at Crowley. Dick gave his wife an "affectionate squeeze" on the arm. Pat could tease him about his exacting behavior without eliciting defensiveness from him.

Pat told Crowley that Halloween was Dick's favorite holiday. "He just *loves* it. . . . He's like a child. It's as if he is the one trick-or-treating." Pat laughed as she told Crowley, "It's good for him, though. He needs a pick-me-up like this once in a while." On October 31, 1990, Dick invited his new assistant to watch as the Nixons opened up their yard at 4:00 p.m. for local children and their parents to come in to trick-or-treat. When Nixon appeared on the porch, cameras flashed and the children rushed toward him. A man in a Nixon mask approached the former president. Dick extended his hand, saying, "Well, Mr. President, it's a pleasure to meet you!" Laughing, the neighbor took off his mask and introduced his young son. Pat watched the antics from inside the house.

Approaching the age of eighty, the Nixons drew the circle of their lives tighter by 1991. It no longer made sense to try to maintain a house on four acres. Pat and Dick had lived in their Saddle River house longer than any other home, but they downsized by giving up their seven-bedroom house with its own pool for a three-bedroom, four-story town house condominium in the Bear's Nest luxury gated community four miles away in Park Ridge, New Jersey. The condominium had an elevator for her and suitable space to entertain the grandchildren. Pat created an appealing fourth-floor study for Dick, with views in three directions and plenty of room for his massive collection of books and historical mementos. Dick was delighted by the study, which he called the "Eagle's Nest." He worked there in the afternoons; Pat joined him there after dinner to watch the evening news and their favorite television programs.

Pat looked fragile and needed support to walk when she made her last public appearance at the opening of the Reagan Library on November 4, 1991. She was not immediately told the diagnosis when doctors found lung cancer in early 1993. But Dick knew, and his assistant, Monica Crowley, saw his despair and helplessness: "Sadness crept into everything he did and every word he spoke. . . . He often left sentences unfinished and walked aimlessly down the hallways of his office and home." As Pat's pain became unbearable, she refused to use a wheel-chair. "I don't want to be a burden," she insisted. "I have to try to walk again. I must try to get well."

On Monday, June 21, 1993, Pat and Dick celebrated their fifty-third wedding anniversary at home. Julie and Tricia presented her anniversary cards and flowers. Her thin frame wasted away, Pat sat in a chair with her eyes closed. Dick told her, "Your family loves you, the country loves you, and people all over the world love you." She smiled. "I kissed her on the forehead and that was it," Dick would say later. Shortly thereafter she lapsed into a coma and died at five-forty-five the next morning with Dick, Tricia, and Julie at her side.

On June 26, funeral guests were seated in the inner courtyard of the Nixon Library facing the library's reflecting pool. The library's back doors opened and the Reverend Billy Graham led Dick Nixon—his face distorted in grief—and his somber family outside. As soon as Dick saw the hushed crowd of 372 friends, colleagues, and former staff members who had come to mourn his wife, he was overcome with wrenching sobs. While Graham guided Nixon and his family to their chairs—adjacent to the rose garden Pat loved and facing the reflecting pool—Dick tried to regain control. He covered his mouth with a handkerchief. But this man, who had been so careful not to show vulnerability in nearly fifty years of public service, could not contain himself. With his "shoulders hunched forward" and his body quivering, he continued to weep. Later when he greeted the Reagans, he "broke down a bit on Nancy's shoulder" and Reagan put his arm around him.

Nixon listened to California governor Pete Wilson eulogize Pat as a woman who was "almost visibly protective of a man whose courage and commitment she so admired." Wilson reminded everyone that in "that fragile body beat a great Irish fighting heart." Senator Bob Dole of Kansas mentioned one of her greatest accomplishments, the consistent expression of her caring for others: "Washington, D.C., is a town where the monuments are tall, and the egos are even taller," but "Pat treated everyone like a head of state."

Pat was her husband's strength and his solace and he was lost without her. For Dick Nixon, theirs had been a true love story. The Rodgers and Hammerstein song "You'll Never Walk Alone" was played during the service. During the war he wrote Pat, "You are the only one for me. It's been that way from the start." A man whose mind was brilliant but rife with weaknesses and shadows, he had followed his heart to its brightest possible place when he married Pat Nixon. "If he had not been the best picker of men," Julie Nixon Eisenhower declared in 1973, he had courted and won a woman who represented his most positive aspirations. Dick himself agreed with that assessment. He was confident that "the best decision I ever made was choosing Pat to be my wife, my partner in life."

After the public memorial service, Dick delivered his own eulogy of his wife to a private group of friends and family: "Let me tell you about the real Pat—the Pat I knew and loved for more than half a century. She was beautiful and intelligent and wise. . . . She loved people. . . . She loved a good time. . . . She always knew how to bring sunshine into a room. Above all, she was strong. . . . She always thought of others, not herself . . . when you think of Pat, I hope you will always remember—the sunshine of her smile."

Two days later Monica Crowley showed up for work at the former president's New Jersey town house. "There is no one here," he told her. "Can you hear how quiet it is? . . . Listen to that silence. My God!" A fierce protector of his wife's reputation, he was furious that President Bill Clinton did not send his wife, Hillary, or a high-ranking official to the funeral service. "What the hell was he thinking?" Dick asked Crowley. Nixon carefully monitored the press coverage of Pat's life. He was enraged when he read *U.S. News & World Report*'s conclusion that Pat Nixon was a woman without a "professional identity" or an "adoring public."

On the day of Pat's funeral, a mourner told Nixon aide Leonard Garment that "Dick would be dead within the year." He was. While Nixon prepared for dinner at home on the evening of April 18, 1994, ten months after Pat had died and the day the galleys of his last book, *Beyond Peace,* arrived, he suffered a severe stroke. He died four days later, with his daughters at his side.

On Tuesday, April 26, eight military pallbearers carried Richard Nixon's coffin into the lobby of the Nixon Library. Over the next twenty-four hours, fifty thousand largely middle-class mourners shivered and huddled under umbrellas—fending off pouring rain and hailstones— and waited for up to eighteen hours to walk past the casket to pay their respects to the man who had been their champion.

President Clinton declared the next day's funeral a full state occasion; all U.S. flags on ships and federal buildings were lowered for the first time since the death of President Johnson in 1973. Four past presidents, Gerald Ford, Jimmy Carter, Ronald Reagan, and George Bush, and their wives joined President and Mrs. Clinton and four thousand mourners at the service. Former vice president Spiro Agnew attended, as did more than two hundred members of the diplomatic corps and more than one hundred members of Congress. A military band played "Hail to the Chief," and the Reverend Billy Graham, who gave the funeral sermon, led the joint military services pallbearers, carrying Nixon's coffin, into the courtyard. Highlighting Nixon's life's arc from simple origins to historic accomplishments, his flag-draped coffin was set on a bier in front of the modest home his father had built and where Nixon was born.

In a service of healing and forgiveness, Senator Robert Dole famously predicted that "the second half of the 20th century will be known as the age of Nixon . . . because he always embodied the deepest feelings of the people he led." Dole acknowledged that "to tens of millions of his countrymen, Richard Nixon was an American hero" who "shared and honored their belief in working hard, worshiping God, loving their families and saluting the flag." With a sob in his voice, Dole eulogized him as a man who lived "every day of his life to the hilt" and as "the largest figure of our time whose influence will be timeless."

Kissinger said an eloquent good-bye to "our gallant friend," who "stood on pinnacles that dissolved into precipices" and "never gave up." Kissinger saluted Nixon for moving the United States from "rule by domination to leadership by example" and for envisioning "a new international order that would reduce lingering enmities, strengthen historic friendships, and give new hope to mankind—a vision where dreams and possibilities conjoined."

In the most indelible moment of the day, President Clinton, who had protested against the Vietnam War as a college student and whose wife, Hillary, had worked on the House Judiciary impeachment process, initiated a healing between the two Americas that had warred over Nixon's politics and his vision for the country, declaring: "May the day of judging President Nixon on anything less than his entire life and career come to a close." Some Nixon detractors were moved, while many others adamantly opposed this historical rehabilitation. Amid loud criticism from some columnists and commentators, America's thirty-seventh president was honored as a great statesman and mourned with full military honors, including a twenty-one-gun salute and an air force flyover.

Following the service, Dick was laid to rest beside Pat. After lives at the center of the nation's story, no conflict or controversy can separate them now.

On Patricia Ryan Nixon's simple gravestone is engraved "Even when people can't speak your language, they can tell if you have love in your heart."

Richard Milhous Nixon's gravestone bears the phrase: "The greatest honor history can bestow is the title of peacemaker."

Epilogue

All lives have triumphs and tragedies, laughter and tears,
and mine has been no different. What really matters
is whether, after all of that, you remain strong
and a comfort to your loved ones.
—*Pat Nixon in her final interview, June 1992*

Pat was always stronger. Without her,
I could not have done what I did.
—*Richard Nixon,* In the Arena, *1990*

*I*n a culture that celebrates extroverts, encourages public displays
of emotion, and fosters the idea that relationships can be discarded when troubles arise, much of the American public and press
still does not understand the private, spacious, and committed nature
of the Nixon marriage. The Nixons' friends saw a tender side to Dick,
and a man who depended heavily on his wife. In Pat they witnessed
resolve and authentic engagement. Her surprising, deft, and enduring partnership with her husband over nine political campaigns was
central to his rise to power and to his enduring impact on the nation.
Their union, complex and mysterious, intrigued Americans for half
a century. The Nixons' swift ascent into prominence and power was
followed by repeated plunges into public humiliation, and then, each
time, a tenacious recovery. Their marriage represented both the fulfillment and the failure of the American dream of self-invention and
worldly success.

Pat Nixon was the loyal and at times angry and resentful wife of a brilliant, sentimental, and sometimes distant man she admired. She proved herself a humane and shrewd team player to a politician who considered her an essential helpmate. A modern, wise, and playful woman with a wicked sense of humor, she was also sometimes catty, small-minded, and fiercely partisan. Publicly silent but powerful in private, she influenced and tempered her husband, his actions, and his policies.

Twenty years after her death, Pat Nixon has not been fully appreciated for her role in helping her husband make the second half of the twentieth century into what Bob Dole called "the age of Nixon." Pat Nixon and her husband promulgated the belief that self-made Americans could, by dint of perseverance, industry, and determination, surmount early hardships to achieve their life goals.

Pat was astute in her assessments of people and situations in ways that facilitated her husband's political career and diplomacy. She had "a good sixth sense about people," according to her son-in-law Ed Cox. To powerful effect, she studied the subtleties of international politics, combining her fascination with foreign cultures with an ability to open her heart to people she met on her travels. Dwight Eisenhower rated her an excellent political spouse, able to converse intelligently with any world leader. Her husband agreed. She believed, along with her husband, in the American myth of mission, divinely ordained—that America should serve as an example of justice and freedom, and encourage the people of other nations to believe in their right to liberty and democracy. With her exemplary character she directly confronted negative communist propaganda and fostered a more generous, welcoming and successful image of her homeland. As a goodwill ambassador—representing the best of the American spirit—from the 1950s to the 1970s, she significantly advanced her husband's career at home and elevated the status of the United States abroad, often in countries tottering between democratic and authoritarian forms of government. It is a shame that she did not have a greater opportunity to use her diplomatic gifts; like Jean Kennedy Smith, she might have made an excellent ambassador to Ireland.

In the 1950s and later in her husband's presidency, Pat became an international advocate for women's rights—more by what she did (inviting foreign women to events they had never been allowed to participate in, representing the president in disaster relief efforts in Peru and at the inauguration of the president of Liberia, and addressing the Ghanaian National Assembly)—than by giving lectures.

When he is viewed through the lens of his marriage and the humanizing portrait of his wife, Richard Nixon, always a conundrum, takes on new dimensions. At those times in his life when he was not obsessed with obtaining and wielding power, he could be surprisingly relaxed and engaging, as he revealed in his early married years, his middle age in New York City, and his retirement in New Jersey. His mind worked so quickly that he could often be impatient and awkward in public, but he was far more sensitive and thoughtful in private with his wife, his daughters, and his friends. His wife understood the vulnerability that underlay the polarizing and vindictive aspects of his public character. She was not able to prevent the harm he did.

Dick knew that her positive persona was important to his bid to make his presidency successful, but he genuinely wanted her to feel valued by the American public and the press for her stellar qualities. Even when he was preoccupied with his own career and public agenda, he cared deeply about how his wife was perceived. He valued her as an asset to his administration and sought to safeguard her place in history. While his controlling behavior caused contention between his West Wing and her East Wing, he fought diligently to assist his wife in her first years in the White House and, later, to counter her negative image as a passive First Lady, a "Plastic Pat." The president and First Lady worked together to rectify harsh portrayals of their marriage: When the Nixon union was attacked as lifeless, the couple cooperated on television documentaries and in print interviews to correct portrayals of them that they felt were hurtful and inaccurate.

No one marital style predicts whether a couple will be successful over the long term. Both couples who fight frequently and those who bury their differences can survive the rigors of married life and live contentedly into old age. Pat and Dick often handled problems by avoiding them. They fought by moving apart for brief periods or communicating through others when tensions peaked. Nonetheless, they always found a way to reconnect before their injuries led to a permanent estrangement. The last year of Watergate, for example, understandably corrupted the bond between the Nixons, but during their subsequent exile in California they painstakingly renewed their connection to each other, amid life-threatening illnesses, disgrace, and defeat. Many onlookers wondered whether Pat should have stayed with Dick, but her apparent contentment during their last years together suggests it was the right decision for her.

Presidential speechwriter William Safire recognized that Pat shared her husband's "prejudices and scar tissue." "Pat and I come from similar backgrounds," Dick said in a 1982 interview with *Good Housekeeping* magazine. "We have compatibility and the same general beliefs. I married her because I loved her and admired her intelligence and her great sense of humor." Their common underlying values allowed them to surmount a vast difference in their enthusiasm for politics, but prevented them from fully acknowledging how their view of themselves as outsiders impeded their public performance. They had become so embattled that they saw slights where there were none, and they divided the public by withdrawing when honest engagement would have built greater consensus.

The Nixons' well-documented traumas and conflicts led them to discover their strength, courage, and resilience as a couple. Over fifty-three years of marriage each remained a solid comfort to the other. Within the marriage, Pat treaded close to the troublesome line between self-abnegation and healthy love, but in the end she felt that she had received and given enough love to make her life meaningful. Dick had trouble balancing ambition, intimacy, and relaxation in his home life, but he learned from his close brush with death in 1974 to live more fully in the moment, savoring quiet and relaxed times with his wife, and, thus, recalibrating his marriage.

The Nixons haunt and inspire our national psyche. They strove to portray the best of America's moral character and they succeeded, but they also represented the worst aspects of our culture—the pursuit of achievement and a preoccupation with public image at the expense of self-awareness, personal contentment, and integrity. Their marriage— rich with flaws and virtues, constantly reinvented in crisis after crisis, enduring for half a century in the public arena—makes them figures crucial to, and emblematic of, the American story.

Acknowledgments

I am a lucky man. Four years ago I cofounded a small biographers' support group in Manhattan. My fellow writers, with good humor and kind hearts, have shepherded me through the process of changing agents, writing a proposal, and awaiting publishers' responses to it. My group celebrated my book contract and encouraged me through a patch of bad health early in the writing process. When I presented pages, they offered me invaluable editing suggestions. I am grateful to Anne Heller and to Betty Boyd Caroli, Gayle Feldman, Kate Buford, Stacy Schiff, Carl Rollyson, Justin Martin, and Ina Caro for their contributions to this book and to my life. This is the first biography to emerge from this group since it was formed in 2010. I don't know how to thank Kate Buford, Anne Heller, and Carl Rollyson. Despite their remarkably busy schedules, they read my manuscript on short notice and offered crucial feedback. I was inspired by one of our first members, the late Hazel Rowley, who wrote so beautifully about another presidential couple, Franklin and Eleanor Roosevelt. Jamie McGrath Morris, the founder of the Biographers International Organization, has been a strong supporter and an inspiration. Nancy Milford, Sally Bedell Smith, Amanda Foreman, and Debby Applegate have provided moral and practical support.

The community of Nixon scholars (Irv Gellman, Mel Small, Gil Troy, Conrad Black, Frank Gannon, Jonathan Aitken, Iwan Morgan, Jeffrey Frank, Luke Nichter, John Farrell, and Evan Thomas) and First Lady experts (Betty Boyd Caroli, Mary Brennan, Carl Sferrazza Anthony, research director Martha Regula, and the staff of the National First Ladies Library) have provided crucial assistance. Irwin (Irv) Gellman is the most generous and thoughtful scholar I have ever worked with. With a prodigious memory, a depth of research knowledge, and uncanny wisdom about how to approach people, he has been an invaluable supporter and fact-checker for this project. Betty Boyd Caroli has also been my mainstay, reading the entire manuscript and making terrific suggestions. Melvin Small, Mary Brennan, John Farrell, Jim Byron, and Gil Troy carefully read the book for factual and contextual errors. I am particularly grateful to Frank Gannon for his superb and meticulous last-minute editing of the manuscript and for more than seven hours of phone and Skype conversations about *Pat and Dick*. I am indebted to Mary Brennan's meticulous research in the Patricia Ryan Nixon Collection at the Nixon Presidential Library and for sharing research from archives in Texas. Carl Sferrazza Anthony gave me encouragement, thoughtful advice, and help with photographs.

Over the course of many trips to the Nixon Presidential Library in Yorba Linda, California, I sustained myself by meditating in the Pat Ryan Nixon rose gardens during breaks from intense hours of research in the voluminous Richard and Patricia Ryan Nixon files. I am grateful to the library staff for their patience and expertise. Gregory Cumming, the supervisory archivist, and Meghan Lee-Parker gave me thorough introductions to the Patricia Ryan Nixon collection. Paul Wormser, the acting director of the library, and Timothy Naftali, the former director, gave me feedback. Easygoing and thorough, Jon Fletcher and Ryan Pettigrew provided superb, timely help with photographs and audiovisual materials. Olivia Anastasiadis aided me with the library exhibition materials, and archivists Carla Braswell, Dorissa Martinez, Craig Ellefson, and Pamla Eisenberg were friendly, efficient, and resourceful.

The Nixon Foundation initially approached me with wariness, but ultimately embraced this project. Sandy Quinn, the president of the Nixon Foundation, arranged for me to interview a wide variety of Nixon staff members and friends, opened the Jonathan Aitken files for me, and met with me whenever I was in Yorba Linda. Foundation staffers Jonathan Movroydis and Cheryl Saremi were particularly effective and enthusiastic supporters of this project. Cheryl arranged many important interviews. As my deadline for submitting the book approached, Jonathan found a number of important photographs for me. I am grateful to Ed Nixon, and Ed and Tricia Nixon Cox, for their support and the memories they shared. Special thanks to Ed Cox's wonderful assistant Cathy Scandariato. Julie Nixon Eisenhower also assisted. The Nixons' secretaries Loie Gaunt and Marje Acker were generous with their time and their recollections. Lucy Winchester Breathitt granted me several particularly valuable interviews. Maureen Drown Nunn was particularly generous with her time and her observations about her mother and Pat Nixon. Frank Gannon, General Don Hughes, Dwight Chapin, Steve Bull, Susan Porter Rose, Gavin Herbert, Robert Nedelkoff, Cynthia Hardin Milligan, Hubert Perry, Bruce Herschenshon, Ken Khachigian, Ray Price, Robert J. Brown, and Ruth Wiley Buchanan offered insights about the Nixons. Reporters Alvin Spivak, Bonnie Angelo, Helen Thomas, and Bernard Kalb spoke with me. Gavin Herbert, who now owns La Casa Pacifica, arranged for me to tour the property and talked with me. Generous Paul Carter, who created the wonderful map "Native Son: Richard Nixon's Southern California," provided me with a last-minute Facebook miracle. When he saw my posting saying that my deadline for submitting photographs to the publisher had passed, he offered to send me two early photographs of Pat that I had not been able to find. Late that night my editor granted me a twenty-four-hour extension, and the next morning I woke up to Paul's email with jpegs of the missing photos.

This book is based on previously unavailable oral histories at Whittier College, oral histories at California State University, Nixon biographer Fawn Brodie's papers in the special collections at the Marriott Library at the University of Utah, the interviews in the Bela Kornitzer collection at Drew University, and Jonathan Aitken's personal interviews with Richard Nixon and his staff members. Highly knowledgeable, Joe Dmolhowski at Whittier College was a terrific support, and librarian Joanna Perez provided me with oral histories from the college. Joe interrupted his vacation to go to his office at Whittier College to locate some superb early photographs for this book. Stephanie George at Cal State Fullerton also provided me with research materials. I am grateful to William (Bill) David in the legislative archives and David Langbart, the archivist at the National Archives, Resources Administration, Reference Services, and administrative aide Marie Carpenti. Myra Hillard was a delightful and resourceful tour guide for the Nixon collection at the Whittier historical society and for the town of Whittier.

Timothy Rives, the deputy director of the Eisenhower Presidential Library, and archivists Chris Abraham and particularly Mary Burtzloff helped me with research questions about the Eisenhowers, the 1952 presidential campaign, and the letters between Mamie Eisenhower and Pat Nixon. At the UVA Miller Center, Mike Greco, the director of information, archivist Sheila Blackford, and David Colman, the chair of the Presidential Recordings program, gave me guidance. Dexter Guerrier, the president of Vandenberg: The Townhouse Experts helped me understand the layout of the Nixons' town house on East Sixty-fifth Street in Manhattan.

For this complex project, I relied on research assistants more than I am accustomed to: I could not have written as thorough a book without John Dalzell's dogged, brilliant, and resourceful Internet and New York library research. Alicia Fernandez, an extremely gifted and delightfully obsessive Nixon Presidential Library freelance researcher, saved me many headaches and a great deal of time with her meticulous research, her painstaking review of my footnotes, and her speed in photographing materials in the Nixon Library files. Dianne Swift studied the Presidential Daily Diaries, worked with the Eisenhower Presidential Library, and offered helpful insights. Elizabeth Powhida and her staff at the Valatie library and Julie Johnson at the Kinderhook library answered innumerable calls for last-minute books.

My agent Michael Carlisle at Inkwell Management believed in *Pat and Dick* from the day we met. He helped me develop and find the right home for it. His assistant Lauren Smythe brought her terrific attitude and superb editing skills to the project. She made sure that my proposal was in the best possible shape before it went out to publishers. My creative editor Mitchell Ivers, at Threshold, was enthusiastic and made impressive revisions in the manuscript. His assistant Natasha Simons was a terrific source of support and made superb suggestions about improving the book. I am grateful to Jean Anne Rose for her friendly availability and her extraordinary proactive public relations work on this book.

I am fortunate to have a wonderful group of friends who take an active interest in my writing life. I would like to thank Anne Schomaker, Russ and Tini Pomeranz, and especially Jacqueline Pomeranz, Sue Chiafullo, Rod and DeGuerre Blackburn, Ralph Blair, Ed Parran and Jim Guidera, Samuel Kirchner and Gayle Labelle, Michael Laudati and Despina Leandrou, Melinda Moreno, David Black and Barbara Weisman, John Cooley and Jack Millard, Doug Cohen and Jody Dalton, Lyrysa Smith and Larry Steele, Chuck Olbrecht and Chuck Hewitt, Jeffrey Young, Martin Sloane and Karen Koop, John Levin, Steve Plimpton, Ciaran and Elizabeth Grant, Michael First and Leslee Snyder, Dan Bauman, Ruth Randall and Alyne Model, Helen Whitney and Kent Carroll, and Marion Roach and Rex Smith. My friends Dr. Robert Abramson, his wife, Shari, and Dr. Linda Lancaster kept me healthy and happy amid the stress of writing and research. I am grateful to my novelist cousin Jim Wilcox, my literary cousins Leslie, Zachary, Sophie, and Luke Maher, my sister Sara, my brother Jed, nieces Anna and Naomi, son Dylan, and daughter-in-law Brittany for their unconditional support.

My partner, Kevin Lee Jacobs, a gifted lifestyle writer and an extremely busy gardening, decorating, and cooking expert, has sustained me in more ways than I can mention—not the least of which was reading and editing many first and twentieth drafts of my manuscript. He tolerated and sometimes enjoyed listening to my endless conversations about the Nixons at home and at dinner parties. Literary spouses of biographers deserve a special medal. I nominate Kevin for the first award.

Notes

*D*espite my conviction that it is time for all the Nixon papers to be opened to the public (What more do they have to lose?), the Nixon Foundation is not yet willing to release Nixon's White House diaries or the audiotapes of conversations between President and Mrs. Nixon.

Abbreviations Used in Notes

BOOKS

AS   Anthony Summers, *The Arrogance of Power: The Secret World of Richard Nixon*. Paperback, London: Phoenix, 2001.

BK   Bela Kornitzer, *The Real Nixon: An Intimate Biography*. Paperback, New York: Literary Licensing, LLC, 2011.

CA   Carl Sferrazza Anthony, *First Ladies Volume II: The Saga of the Presidents' Wives and Their Power, 1961–1990*. Paperback, New York: William Morrow, 1991.

CB   Conrad Black, *The Invincible Quest: The Life of Richard Milhous Nixon*. Hardcover, Toronto, Ontario: McClelland & Stewart, 2007.

CM   Christopher Matthews, *Kennedy and Nixon: The Rivalry That Shaped Post-War America*. Paperback, New York: Touchstone, 1997.

DF   Daniel Frick, *Reinventing Richard Nixon: A Cultural History of an American Obsession*. Hardcover, Lawrence: University Press of Kansas, 2008.

DG	David Greenberg, *Nixon's Shadow: The History of an Image.* Paperback, New York: W.W. Norton, 2004.
DH	David Halberstam, *The Fifties.* Hardcover, New York: A Fawcett Book, 1993.
DP	David Pietrusa, *1960: LBJ vs. JFK vs. Nixon: The Epic Campaign That Forged Three Presidencies.* Hardcover, New York: Union Square Press, 2008.
EC	Madeleine Edmondson and Alden Cohen, *The Women of Watergate.* Hardcover, New York: Stein and Day, 1975.
EK	Edmund F. Kalina, Jr., *Kennedy vs. Nixon: The Presidential Election of 1960.* Paperback, Gainesville: The University Press of Florida, 2010.
EM	Earl Mazo, *Richard Nixon: A Personal and Political Portrait.* Paperback, New York: Harper & Row, 1986.
EN	Ed Nixon and Karen Olson, *The Nixons: A Family Portrait.* Hardcover, Bothell, Washington: Book Publishers Network, 2009.
FB	Fawn Brodie, *Richard Nixon: The Shaping of His Character.* Paperback, New York: W.W. Norton, 1981.
GT	Gil Troy, *Mr. and Mrs. President.* Paperback, Lawrence: University Press of Kansas, 2000.
HHD	H. R. Haldeman, *The Haldeman Diaries.* Paperback, New York: Berkley Books, 1995.
HTD	Helen Thomas, *Dateline: The White House.* Hardcover, New York: MacMillan Publishing, 1995.
HTDF	Helen Thomas, *Front Row at the White House.* Paperback, New York: Touchstone Book, 2000.
IG	Irwin Gellman, *The Contender: Richard Nixon: The Congressional Years 1946–1952.* Paperback, New York: The Free Press, 1999.
IM	Iwan Morgan, *Nixon.* Paperback, London: Arnold, 2002.
ITA	Richard Nixon, *In the Arena: A Memoir of Victory, Defeat and Renewal.* Paperback, New York: Pocket Books, 1991.
JA	Jonathan Aitken, *Nixon: A Life.* Paperback, Washington, D.C.: Regnery Publishing, 1993.
JBW	J. B. West, *Upstairs at the White House: My Life with the First Ladies.* Hardcover, New York: Coward, McCann & Geoghegan, 1973.
JE	John Ehrlichman, *Witness to Power: The Nixon Years.* Paperback, New York: Pocket Books, 1982.
JNE	Julie Nixon Eisenhower, *Pat Nixon: The Untold Story.* Paperback, New York: Simon and Schuster, 1986.

JW   Jules Witcover, *The Resurrection of Richard Nixon*. Hardcover, New York: G. P. Putnam's Sons, 1970.

KEM   Keith Melder, *Hail to the Candidate: Presidential Campaigns from Banners to Broadcast*. Paperback, Washington, D.C.: Smithsonian Institution Press, 1992.

KM   Kati Marton, *Hidden Power*. Paperback, New York: Anchor Books, 2002.

LD   Lester David, *The Lonely Lady of San Clemente*. Hardcover, New York: Thomas Y. Crowell, 1978.

LM   Lance Morrow, *The Best Year of Their Lives: Kennedy, Johnson, and Nixon in 1948: The Secrets of Power*. Hardcover, New York: Basic Books, 2005.

MB   Mary Brennan, *Pat Nixon: Embattled First Lady*. Hardcover, Lawrence: University Press of Kansas, 2011.

MC   Monica Crowley, *Nixon in Winter: His Final Revelations About Diplomacy, Watergate, and Life Outside of the Arena*. Hardcover, New York: Crowley & Baron, 1998.

MM   Margaret MacMillan, *Nixon in China: The Week That Changed the World*. Paperback, Toronto: Penguin Group, 2006.

MS   Melvin Small, *The Presidency of Richard Nixon*. Paperback, Lawrence: University Press of Kansas, 1999.

ND   Nancy Dickerson, *Among Those Present: A Reporter's View of 25 Years in Washington*. Hardcover, New York: Random House, 1976.

PNMT   Patricia Ryan Nixon, *Memorial Tributes in the Congress of the United States*. Hardcover, Washington, D.C.: U.S. Government Printing Office, 1993.

RA   Robert Sam Anson, *Exile: The Unquiet Oblivion of Richard M. Nixon*. Paperback, New York: Simon and Schuster, 1984.

RIR   Richard Reeves, *President Nixon: Alone in the White House*. Paperback, New York: Simon and Schuster, 2007.

RM   Richard Morris, *Richard Milhous Nixon: The Rise of an American Politician*. Paperback, New York: Henry Holt, 1990.

RN   Richard Nixon, *The Memoirs of Richard Nixon*. Hardcover, New York: Grosset & Dunlap, 1978.

RNSC   Richard Nixon, *Six Crises*. Paperback, New York: Touchstone, 1990.

RR   Robert V. Remini, *The House: The History of the House of Representatives*. Hardcover, New York: Smithsonian, 2006.

SA   Stephen Ambrose, *Richard Nixon, Volume One: The Education of a Politician 1913–1962*. Paperback, New York: Touchstone, 1988.

SK   Stanley Kutler, *Abuse of Power*. Paperback, New York: Touchstone, 1998.

SS   Deborah Hart Strober and Gerald S. Strober, *The Nixon Presidency: An Oral History of the Era*. Paperback, New York: Harper Perennial, 1996.

TW   Theodore White, *The Making of the President, 1960*. Paperback, New York, Harper Perennial, 1961.

WJR   W. J. Rorabaugh, *The Real Making of the President: Kennedy, Nixon, and the 1960 Election*. Hardcover, Lawrence: University Press of Kansas, 2012.

WTP   John Ehrlichman, *Witness to Power: The Nixon Years*. Paperback, New York: Pocket Books, 1982.

WW   John Whitcomb and Claire Whitcomb, *Real Life at the White House: 200 Years of Daily Life at America's Most Famous Residence*. Hardcover, New York: Routledge, 2000.

RESEARCH COLLECTIONS

AMR   Alice Martin Rosenberger, *Collection of Sixty Interviews for Pat Ryan Nixon* in Whittier Public Library.

CSO   Constance Stuart Oral History, August 19, 1988, Nixon Presidential Library (NPL).

DC   Drown Collection, NPL.

FLPO   White House Central Files (WHCF), Staff Member Office Files (SMOF), First Lady's Press Office, Nixon Presidential Library (NPL).

HRH   Haldeman Personal Files, NPL.

JDWC   Jack Drown Whittier College Oral History, Whittier College.

JHD   Jack and Helene Drown interview, March 11, 1959. Bela Kornitzer interview, Nela Kornitzer Collection, Drew University Library, Madison, New Jersey.

MFF   Main Motion Film File, Audiovisual Department, NPL.

NFC   Nixon Family Collection, NPL.

NPL   Richard Nixon Presidential Library and Museum, Yorba Linda, California.

PCE   Pat Nixon Centennial Exhibition, NPL, 2012.

POF   President's Office Files, NPL.

PPF   President's Personal Files, NPL.

PPS	Pre-Presidential Series, NPL.
PRNC	Patricia Ryan Nixon Collection, NPL.
RMN	Richard Milhous Nixon papers, Nixon Family Collection (NFC), NPL.
RNCE	Richard Nixon Centenary Exhibition, NPL, 2013.
RNOH	Richard Nixon Oral History, Whittier College.
WHCF, SMOF	White House Central Files, Staff Member's Office Files, NPL.
WHSF, SMOF	White House Special Files, Staff Member Office Files, NPL.
YN	*Young Nixon* Collection of Oral Histories (OH).

NEWSPAPERS AND MAGAZINES

BG	*The Boston Globe*
CT	*Chicago Times*
GH	*Good Housekeeping*
LAT	*Los Angeles Times*
LHJ	*Ladies' Home Journal*
MC	*McCall's*
NYJA	*New York Journal American*
NYT	*New York Times*
UNWR	*U.S. News & World Report*
WN	*Whittier Daily News*
WP	*Washington Post*

Prologue

1 The most helpful resources for the prologue were RM, pp. 758–849; SA, pp. 276–95; JA, pp. 208–20; CB, pp. 216–61; RN, pp. 92–108; JNE, pp. 117–26; RNSC, pp. 73–129; LeeHubner, "TheCheckers Speech After 60 Years," http://www.theatlantic.com/politics /archive/2012/09/the-checkers-speech-after-60-years/262172/.

2 "Secret Rich Men's Trust Fund Keeps Nixon in Style Far Beyond His Salary." JA, p. 210; JNE, p. 118; SA, p. 276.

2 "Senator Nixon knows it is morally wrong." RM, p. 765.

2 "Donate Here to Help Poor Richard Nixon." CB, p. 227.

2 "Maybe I ought to resign." CB, p. 229; RNSC, p. 87.

3 "Your life will be marred." RM, p. 781; CB, p. 229.

3 "What Are You Going to Do with the Bribe Money?" RM, p. 785; EM, pp. 106–7; RNSC, p. 88.

3 "Nickels for Poor Nixon." CB, p. 233.

3   "like a bruised little kitten." RM, p. 791; JNE, p. 119.

4   "Why do we have to parade." JA, p. 215; RM, p. 813.

4   "I don't think I can do it." RM, p. 827; RN, p. 103; SA, p. 288; JNE, p. 122.

4   "GI bedroom den." CB, p. 247; Hubner, "The Checkers Speech."

4   Cameraman Ted Rodgers had told her that he might zoom in on her. Interview with Irwin Gellman.

4   "The *best* I was able to do." Patricia Nixon, "Crises of a Candidate's Wife," *LHJ*, November 1962, p. 57.

4   "And you know, the kids." RM, p. 832; RNSC, pp. 114–15.

5   "You're my boy." RN, p.106; SA, p. 292; RM, p. 847.

Chapter 1: "Will You Think of Me Sometimes?"

9   Julie Nixon Eisenhower's biography of her mother, *Pat Nixon: The Untold Story*, serves as the main narrative account about her parents' courtship and early marriage. Her book is the source for many of the Nixons' love letters. Three of the letters in this chapter (Pat's letters inviting Dick for a hamburger, and thanking him for a gift, and Dick's letter from a "struggling barrister") were released in 2012 as part of the Pat Nixon Centennial exhibition. Richard Morris and Stephen Ambrose, drawing heavily on Julie's book, also provide accounts of their relationship before marriage. Jonathan Aitken supplements his account of that period with personal interviews Nixon, friends, and family granted him. Lester David's slightly less reliable account, portraying Pat as a victim, is based on interviews with friends. Ed Nixon provides his perspective in *The Nixons: A Family Portrait*.

9   bitterly disappointed. RM, pp. 182–83; CB, p. 38.

9   ignored Tom Bewley's phone calls. Parsons OH, YN; RM, p. 183; CB, pp. 38–39.

10   "lacking in aggressiveness." RM, p. 184; CB, p. 39.

10   representing the Garrett party. RMN, Box 17, "Richard Milhous Nixon: Lawyer, [Appointment Book—1938]," NFC, NPL.

10   Boston Café. Tom Bewley OH, second interview, August 13, 1971, p. 18.

11   still wore gloves and hats. Hortense Behrens OH, YN, p. 32.

12   "an eddy on the stream of life." Merton Wray OH, YN, p. 14.

12   "You could kid." Virginia Endicott OH, AMR.

12   "Miss Ryan was quite a dish." Robert Blake OH, AMR.

12   "She expected." Jean Lippiatt OH, AMR.

13   knock on her door. MB, p. 12.

13   staked out her apartment. Mildred Eason Stouffer OH, AMR; JNE, pp. 69–70.

14 "dark, sullen beauty." Script of *The Dark Tower*, pp. 17–18; JNE, p. 70.

15 "a faintly collegiate, eager, blushing youth." Script of *The Dark Tower*, p. 23; JNE, p. 71.

15 Dick fell in love. RN, p. 23.

15 "slight recollection." Grant Garment OH, AMR.

15 "was most attentive all evening." Elizabeth Cloes OH, YN, p. 2; RM, p. 205.

15 "with titian hair." RN, p. 23.

15 "always kind of serious." Hubert Perry interview, April 19, 2011.

16 "did not have social." Hubert Perry interview, April 19, 2011.

16 She found him to be. Hortense Behrens OH, YN, p. 226; RM, p. 220.

16 "was nuts or something." EM, p. 27.

16 "I'd like to have a date." Elizabeth Cloes Whittier College OH, January 20, 1972, pp. 7–8; LD, pp. 47–48.

17 "No, I'm not going to do it." Hortense Behrens OH, YN, p. 226.

17 "a role which called for temperament." JNE, p. 75.

17 "it rather a pity." DH, p. 216.

17 "sons of bitches." LD, p. 59.

17 "she did her part nicely." LD, p. 59.

18 For Pat's twenty-sixth birthday. RN to PRN, Navy, [March 17, 1944], PPS 265, Box 2, "No Title," PRNC. First opened for RNCE, NPL.

18 although his peers had esteemed him. SA, pp. 85–86; RM, pp. 140–41.

18 maneuvered cleverly and judiciously behind the scenes. RM, pp. 150–56, 178.

19 "the worst ice-skater in the world." JA, p. 91.

19 Filibuster Club. Virginia Stouffer Endicott OH, AMR.

20 "*you* were the most important." Sherril Neece OH, AMR.

20 asking her to go for a drive or to join him on walks. RM, p. 219.

20 "He's a bit unusual," LD, p. 60; RM, p. 219.

20 "My Irish Gypsy" or "Miss Vagabond." JNE, p. 76.

20 "that vagabond." JNE, p. 78.

20 "I like it [the clock]." JNE, p. 79.

20 "like a rat." LD, p. 59; RM, p. 219.

20 "a star fell right in front of me." JNE, pp. 77–78.

21 "Yes—I know I am crazy." JNE, p. 77.

21 Faculty consultant to the high school Pep Committee. LD, pp. 40–41; JNE, p. 81.

21 "I never spent a weekend." JNE, p. 54.

21 Dick paced around the city. DL, p. 60; RM, p. 220.

21 "Don't know whether I like." NFC: Box 17, Subseries F. Folder: Richard Milhous Nixon: Lawyer, [Appointment Book—1938], 17:12, NPL.

22 "I'd like so very much." JNE, p. 80.

22 He led a public discussion. *WN*, November 5, 1938.

22 "Awful Life Saver." RMN, Box 17, "Richard Milhous Nixon: Lawyer, [Appointment Book—1938]," NFC, NPL.

Chapter 2: Going Places

24 helped him win her over. Frank Gannon interviews, Day One, Tape Four, http://www.libs.uga.edu/media/collections/nixon/transcriptintro.html.

25 "four billion dollars." PPS 265, Box 2, "Early Marriage—WWII," PRNC, NPL.

25 "bore her with his thoughts." RN to PRN, "Love Letters," [undated], PPS 265, Box 2, "No Title," PRNC. First opened for PCE (2012), NPL.

25 "[W]hy don't you come." PRN to RN, "Love Letters," [undated], PPS 265, Box 2, "No Title," PRNC. First opened for PCE (2012), NPL.

25 "Gee, Dick." PRN to RN, "Love Letters," [undated], PPS 265, Box 2, "No Title," PRNC. First opened for PCE (2012), NPL.

25 He delighted his brother. EN, pp. 103–6.

26 "unusual for a busy girl." RM, p. 223; Pat and Hannah in BK, p. 136.

26 gold-rimmed cap. JA, p. 90; RA, p. 580; CB, p. 45.

27 Nixon had started out. Paul Carter, "Before He Was President, He Was a Local Attorney," *Orange County Lawyer*, March 2011, vol. 53, no. 3, pp. 34–36.

27 He spent midday in the La Habra. SA, pp. 89–90; RM, pp. 197–99.

28 Citri-Frost. RMN, Box 18, "Citri-Frost," NFC, NPL; SA, p. 89; RM, pp. 195–97; CB, p. 44; RA, pp. 83–84.

28 "Dick worked his heart out." Tom Bewley interview with Fawn Brodie, FB, p. 154; RM, p. 196.

28 sold less than two-thirds. RMN, Box 18, "Citri-Frost," NFC, NPL.

28 home-cooked spaghetti dinner. RM, p. 30.

28 went to an ice-cream parlor. LD, p. 51.

29 "so sorta' lonesome." JNE, p. 85.

29 "Some people felt." RM, p. 224; YN; Loubet interview, p. 21.

29 "Seriously, little one." JNE, p. 88.

29 "You have the finest ideals." JNE, p. 461; RM, p. 225.

29 "Now for the first time." RN, p. 22.

30 "my dearest heart." JNE, p. 86.

30 "lovely smile." JNE, p. 84.

30 "he was going places." JNE, p. 75.

31 "From the first days." JNE, p. 92.

31 "going to be president someday." JNE, p. 76.

31 a navigational landmark for ships. Doris Walker, *Images of America: Dana Point.* Paperback, Mount Pleasant, S.C.: Arcadia Publishing, 2007.

Chapter 3: Married, Happily

33 "broke the romantic spell of the evening." JNE, p. 89.

33 Pat's family had. JNE, pp. 89–90.

33 "too quiet." JNE, p. 89.

33 obsessed with deciding what ring. LD, p. 53; RM, p. 226.

33 "A man only buys a ring." RM, p. 226; LD, p. 53.

34 the $315 cost. It was $324.25 including taxes. PPS 265, Box 2, "No Title (9)," PRNC, NPL.

34 "it wasn't like he rushed." Helen Noll interview, April 2011.

34 the ring hidden. In early May, after the ring had been sized, Dick went to Los Angeles to pick it up. He arranged to meet Pat at his parents' home at noon that day to present it to her. Pat arrived on her lunch break and waited for an hour at the Nixons' house—but her husband-to-be did not show up. Disgruntled, she returned to school. Richard Nixon does not mention this puzzling incident in his memoirs, and daughter Julie, who explained and justified many of her parents' motivations and actions in her biography of her mother, was conspicuously silent about why Dick did not present the ring to his fiancée in person. If there had been an acceptable reason, Julie would most likely have mentioned it. She would not comment on it further for this book. Either Pat would not tell her daughter the truth about what happened or Julie knew but did not want to highlight her father's inconsiderate behavior. Given his boldness throughout the courtship, it does not make sense that his behavior was motivated solely by shyness. Why didn't Dick, the ardent pursuer, phone his parents' home or the school to explain what held him up? Was Dick preoccupied with a work project and forgot, taking his hard-won fiancée for granted, or was he unable to extricate himself from a client meeting? There is another, less plausible explanation: Friends say that Tricia believes that Richard Nixon thought about how to give Pat the ring in a special manner that would allow her to digest the experience in a private way, and that it was a romantic way to do it. In any case, Pat was not happy.

34 Pat was grading papers. JNE, p. 91 and interview with Ed Cox.

35 "You have always had that extra something." JNE, p. 92.

35 "one of the unjustly unsung." CB, p. 79.

35 aborted plans for a campaign. RN, p. 23; SA, p. 91; RM, pp. 201–2.

35 "I someday shall return." JNE, p. 92.

36 often had dinner dates there. EN, p. 118.

36 tea and shower for Pat. PPS 265, Box 2, "No Title (9)," PRNC, NPL.

37 "not just another wedding." Helen Noll interview, April 2011.

37 "with a veiled bride." JNE, p. 94.

37 "really splurgy." EM, p. 34.

38 "That's what we still like." EM, p. 34.

38 Mrs. Bell, the mother. RM, p. 228.

38 "We probably got more." JA, p. 93.

38 July as firecrackers burst in the evening air. LD, p. 56.

38 "Our life was happy and full of promise." RN, p. 25.

38 reception at their Worsham Drive estate. EN, p. 119.

39 students' school spirit. She had the school's shortest boys don the uniforms of its biggest rival, and staged a fight with the football players on the school lawn, which—to the delight of their classmates—the home team theatrically won. For a football pep rally, she devised a skit about how the smudge pots (oil burning devices used to raise air temperatures and prevent frost on fruit trees) were used to save Whittier's orange crop. "It must have been terribly corny," Pat's fellow teacher and roommate (later Mrs. Carl Brown) remembered, "but it was certainly fun." RM, p. 217.

39 "bobby sox and a school sweater." RM, p. 217.

39 "an aloof friendliness." RM, p. 218. Name of friend from Morris, WP, October 12, 1960.

40 "the highlight of the party." EM, p. 34.

40 "Remember the time." JNE, p. 110.

40 "I will never forget one night." EM, p. 34.

40 "think he has never had a good laugh." BK, pp. 138–39.

40 "you always make people have a good time." JNE, p. 110.

40 "a really outstandingly beautiful." JHD, pp. 2–4.

41 "pooled our resources." JHD, p. 15.

41 On their first double date. JDWC, pp. 8–9; EM, p. 35.

41 "jovial" that night. JDWC, pp. 8–9.

41 "He liked to exchange." JDWC, p. 10.

42 rowdy adventures together. JDWC, pp. 10–11; JNE p. 71.

42 "wide double revolving turntable." http://en.wikipedia.org/wiki/Earl _Carroll_Theatre.

42 "then they'd call some [of] us." JDWC, p. 10.

42 Cocoanut Grove nightclub. http://www.hollywood.co.uk/ambassador-hotel.htm.

43 visited British Columbia and Yosemite Park. JA, p. 94.

43 at the world-renowned Restaurant Antoine. PPS 265, Box 2, "1940 Vacation Souvenirs," PRNC, NPL.

43 Hitler had invaded Russia. RN, p. 25.

43 "often called the most immoral spot in the world." JNE, p. 98.

44 "vice-versa" evening. JNE, p. 98.

44 "just a gypsy at heart." JNE, p. 99.

Chapter 4: Love After Pearl Harbor

45 "We're at war, mister." RN, p. 26.

46 chief of interpretations. JA, p. 96.

47 serving in the theater of war. CB, p. 56.

47 the navy was seeking lawyers for administrative work. CB, p. 57.

47 "was the longest I've ever known." JNE, p. 104.

48 ("I am certainly not the Romeo type"). JNE, p. 105.

48 "It's two o'clock." JNE, p. 105.

48 "Its uncompleted runway." RN, p. 27.

49 position as an administrative aide to the executive officer. RM, p. 245.

49 "coffee socials with navy wives." Jerry Szumski, "When the Nixons lived in Iowa," *Des Moines Register*, February 8, 1970; RM, p. 246; CB, p. 58.

49 showed off the bounty. RMN, Box 17, "Correspondence 1942–1944," NFC, NPL.

50 "wasn't a move I made because." JA, p. 100.

50 "painful meal full of sad silences." RN, p. 27; RM, p. 246.

50 "Eddie, you take care of your mother." JA, p. 100.

50 "I would have felt mighty uncomfortable." BK, pp. 139–40; CB, p. 57.

50 "simple and inexpensive a funeral as possible." Nixon's Will, PPS 265, Box 2, "Early Marriage—World War II," PRNC, NPL.

51 "Your letters are my only happiness now." RN to PN, August 24, 1943, quoted in IG, p. 22.

51 "wishing that you and I." RN to PRN, Navy, [June 21, 1943], PPS 265, Box 2, "No Title," PRNC. First opened for RNCE, NPL.

51 "Remember how you treated me then?" RN to PRN, Navy, [June 21, 1943], PPS 265, Box 2, "No Title," PRNC. First opened for RNCE, NPL.

51 Dick claimed that her job with the OPA. RN to PRN, Navy, [April 15, 1944], PPS 265, Box 2, "No Title," PRNC. First opened for RNCE, NPL.

51 "When I feel blue." IG, p. 22.

51 number and date their missives. JNE, p. 107.

51 "Everybody raved." RN to PRN, Navy, [undated], PPS 265, Box 2, "No Title," PRNC. First opened for RNCE, NPL.

52 "You rode." And samples of flora in letters. JNE, p. 111; RM, p. 248.

52   "I love you just the same up here as down below." RN to PRN, Navy, [September 8, 1943], PPS 265, Box 2, "No Title," PRNC. First opened for RNCE, NPL.

52   "We will see sunrises from the air together." RN to PRN, Navy, [September 9, 1943], PPS 265, Box 2, "No Title," PRNC. First opened for RNCE, NPL.

52   "get good dinners." JNE, p. 114.

53   "It isn't really as bad." IG, p. 23.

53   "won over a thousand to date." RN to PRN, Navy, [July 4, 1944], PPS, 265, Box 2, "No Title," PRNC. First opened for NCE, NPL.

53   "I'm anti-social." JNE, p. 108.

53   No one "below him was a threat." SA, p. 110.

53   He formed a close friendship. JA, p. 104.

54   "It meant so much." RM, p. 252.

54   "Snack Shop, etc." RN to PRN, Navy, [May 14, 1944], PPS 265, Box 2, "No Title," PRNC. First opened for RNCE, NPL.

54   "What fun we could have" RN to PRN, Navy, [February 11, 1944], PPS 265, Box 2, "No Title," PRNC. First opened for RNCE, NPL.

54   "For all the years to come." RN to PRN, Navy, [March 17, 1944], PPS 265, Box 2, "No Title," PRNC. First opened for RNCE, NPL.

54   She turned down several invitations from married friends. JNE, p. 113.

55   "I always look first for that." JNE, p. 111.

55   "she [Pat] felt she should not be participating." Gretchen King OH, RNOH, p. 3.

55   She was pictured in the San Francisco News. PPS 265, Box 2, "Early Marriage—World War II," PRNC, NPL.

55   "She seemed a well-disciplined person." Gretchen King OH, RNOH, p. 6.

55   "the most beautiful eyes." Gretchen King OH, RNOH, p. 4.

55   "seemed so alone." Gretchen King OH, RNOH, p. 3.

56   "I'm going to walk right up to you and kiss you." JNE, p. 115.

56   "her eyes lighted up." RN, p. 33.

56   "I will have to admit that I am pretty self-reliant." JNE, pp. 114–15.

57   "I was the chief janitor." JNE, p. 119.

57   "seemed so right for each other." Gretchen King OH, RNOH, p. 7.

57   "idealistic dreamer." BK, p. 150; RM, p. 263.

Chapter 5: Giant Slayers

58   "very conservative." James Cobey interview in Fawn M. Brodie Research Collection, University of Utah, quoted in RM, p. 263.

59   Pat and Dick debated the pros and cons. RM, p. 271.

59   "we're not starting off." JA, p. 114.

59   "I could see that it was." *Time,* February 29, 1960, p. 26.

60   "Why, this girl doesn't." RM, p. 290.

60   "aggressive and vigorous campaign." RN, p. 35; JA, p. 116.

60   "electrifying personality." Jorgensen OH in *Richard M. Nixon in the Warren Era,* as quoted in DG, p. 3; *Alhambra Post-Advocate,* November 13, 1968, quoted in RM, p. 281.

60   "Dick, Dick, the nomination is yours!" Herbert Parmet, *Richard Nixon and His America,* hardcover, Boston: Little Brown, 1989, p. 141; JA, p. 116.

61   Bewley, Knoop, and Nixon. RM, p. 285.

62   set up their campaign headquarters. LD, pp. 64–65.

62   "jungles of the Solomons." LD, p. 65.

62   "stayed safely behind the front in Washington." LD, p. 65.

62   Pat would angrily wonder. JNE, p. 128.

62   Historians are divided about whether. Roger Morris supports vandalism: RM, p. 291; as does Conrad Black: CB, p. 76. Irwin Gellman debunks it as a myth: IG, p. 86. Mary Brennan and Stephen Ambrose mention only that volunteers took pamphlets from Pat and threw them away: MB, p. 23; SA, p. 125.

63   "I've known an indescribable . . . periods of despondency" and help of a nearly blind woman. "I Say He's A Wonderful Guy," *Saturday Evening Post,* September 6, 1952, pp. 17–22.

63   "One morning Pat." Charles Cooper interview in JA, p. 123.

64   Pat's labor was complicated. JNE, p. 87; RM, p. 289; LD, p. 67.

64   "the perfect young lady" and her "lovely mother." DG, p. 19.

64   The *Monrovia News Post* reported. *Monrovia News Post,* March 11, 1946, quoted in IG, p. 44.

65   She served as the campaign office manager. JA, p. 121; RM, pp. 290–91; JNE, pp. 125–28; SA, pp. 120–26; LD, pp. 64–65.

65   "it was a very exciting life." Evlyn Dorn interview, Fawn Brodie Collection, quoted in RM, p. 290.

65   Pat could talk about little. Georgia Sherwood interview, quoted in FB, p. 178; Tom Dixon, quoted, SA, p. 125.

65   small Spanish-style stucco house. Jorgensen OH in *Richard M. Nixon in the Warren Era,* quoted in RM, p. 290; JA, p.121; JNE, pp. 124–25.

65   she burst into sobs. SA, p. 125; LD, p. 65.

66   "Nixon flared at her." Interviews with Sherwood and Dixon, Fawn Brodie Collection, Ms 360, Box 43, Folder 16, University of Utah, J. Willard Marriott Library; also SA, p. 125. Dixon, who broke with Nixon

over his 1950 senatorial campaign, related the incident to biographer Fawn Brodie, who was hostile to Nixon.

66 "thoughtful and sometimes quite persistent critiques." RN, p. 36.

66 "God, she made it rough." Adela Rogers St. John interview notes, Fawn M. Brodie Research Collection, University of Utah, Ms 360, Box 43, Folder 17.

67 traveling throughout the district. PPS 266, Box 1, "1946," PRNC, NPL.

67 Dick paced and fretted. LD, p. 68; RM, p. 306.

68 "Elect Nixon and needle the P.A.C." JA, p. 124.

68 Republican congressional strategy. SA, pp. 128–29.

68 GOP national chairman had set. RM, p. 312.

69 "the better man." "I Say He's A Wonderful Guy," p. 20.

69 "I can't say I was exactly." Jerry Voorhis, *Confessions of a Congressman*, hardcover, Westport, Conn.: Greenwood Press, 1970, p. 333.

70 "Huh Boy!" Donald Fantz OH, quoted in IG, p. 81.

70 listened to the vague early election returns. RM, p. 333.

70 "I think today." *Los Angeles Examiner*, November 6, 1946; RM, p. 334.

70 Kyle Palmer. RM, p. 334.

71 "Let's save it." JA, p. 129.

71 "were happier on November 6, 1946." RN, p. 40.

71 "VICTORY!" PPS 266, Box 1, "1946," PRNC, NPL.

71 Black calls the campaign "mischievous." CB, p. 82.

72 "husky ex-footballer." IG, p. 43.

72 "dark, lank Quaker." "New Faces In the House," *Time*, November 18, 1946.

72 "giant-killer." Clippings in the *Whittier News*, RMN, Box 18, "1946 Campaign clippings," NFC, NPL.

72 "someday he would be president." YN, Black, p. 8; RM, p. 339.

72 "start getting acquainted." *Temple City Times*, November 14, 1946; RM, pp. 338–39.

Chapter 6: The Faces of America's Future

75 "time . . . growing desperately short." WP, December 17, 1946.

75 "Virginia countryside." LM, p. 55.

76 "perform something worthy." www.en.wikipedia.org/wiki/United _States_Capitol.

76 "In the late forties." LM, p. 55.

76 with a housekeeper and a valet. CM, p. 56.

77 "the graceless, vacant." Robert S. Allen and William V. Shannon, "Rumblossoms on the Potomac" in *Katherine Graham's Washington*, paperback, New York: Vintage, 2003, p. 156.

77 "like a fish out of water." IG, p. 91.

77 Congressman Nixon was also uncomfortable. John Ehrlichman, quoted in LM, p. 162.

77 Donald Thompson contacted Catherine Rippard. IG, p. 91.

77 "Washington society is like lemon meringue." Robert S. Allen and William V. Shannon, "Rumblossoms on the Potomac" in *Katherine Graham's Washington*, p. 155.

78 was listed as "informal." JNE, p. 135.

78 "scarcely a moment to themselves." Nixon letter to friend, quoted in IG, p. 91.

78 "He can keep right on thinking." KM, p. 178.

78 "They would always solve." *WP*, December 20, 1972; RM, p. 367.

78 Her letters to her close friend. DC, NPL.

79 "We were like a family." JNE, pp. 136–37.

79 "the greenest congressman in town." *WP*, January 1947; LD, p. 70.

79 "He is as typically American." *Washington Times Herald*, January 21, 1947.

79 "Serious and energetic." *Washington Times Herald*, January 21, 1947.

80 perfect subjects for a photograph. RM, p. 358.

80 feared that he would fall off. JNE, p. 136.

81 saw the Broadway sensation *Oklahoma!* EN, p. 135; RN, p. 7; RM, p. 363.

81 The elder Nixons had moved. EN, pp. 128–32.

81 "nurses in attendance." PPS 266, Box 1, "1947–Corresp," PRNC, NPL.

81 Greek woman whose breast. RN, pp. 49–51.

82 "Europe would be plunged." RN, p. 49.

82 "This place is another." PPS 266, Box 1, "1947–Corresp," PRNC, NPL.

82 four or five pairs of long black Italian gloves. IG, p. 138; JNE, p. 138.

82 lightning-fast tour. SA, pp. 156–57.

83 fostering world peace through American leadership abroad. JA, p. 147.

Chapter 7: Crises on the Home Front

85 As a woman who never allowed. JNE, p. 97.

85 Dick had an accident. IG, p. 156.

86 "how deep her discontent was." JNE, p. 140.

87 "Eight years into their marriage." KM, p. 177.

88 "his abiding love." JNE, p. 140.

88 the birth of their second child. JNE, pp. 140–41.

88 "What's that thing?" JNE, pp. 140–41.

89 "the camaraderie and carefree time." JNE, p. 97; RM, p. 368.

89 "unseen malignant forces." LM, p. 173.

90 "Terrible Republican Eighty." Lou Gannon tapes, Day 1, Tape 6 (35:46), www.libs.uga.edu/media/collections/nixon/nixonday1.html#Tap6.

90 Historians disagree whether Nixon had inside information about Hiss. That debate is beyond the scope of this book. Take a look at Melvin Small, ed., *A Companion to Richard M. Nixon,* chapter five: "The Alger Hiss Case," pp. 84–101.

90 "a devastation of empty sockets." CB, p. 107.

91 "immersed himself in the case." JNE, p. 144.

91 "period of doubt." SC, p. 19.

91 "Crisis can indeed be agony." SC, p. xx.

92 "back in 1948 before the scope." SC, p. 18.

92 "quick-tempered." SC, p. 41.

92 A Herblock cartoon. *WP,* August 5, 1948; LM, p. 240; RM, p. 398.

92 "the entry of our society." *WP,* August 6, 1948; RM, p. 405.

93 "it is the Committee." *WP,* August 7, 1948.

93 Pat read "voraciously." ITA, p. 271.

93 "She knew we were on the right side." ITA, p. 271.

93 "the press's fair-haired boy." JNE, p. 144.

93 "the terrible attacks." EM, p. 54; SA, p. 174.

94 "more un-American than the activities." *NYT,* September 23, 1948.

94 "there was a great statesman." JDWC, pp. 12–13.

95 "This time," he told Pat. SC, p. 46.

95 "have the heart to tell Pat the bad news." SC, p. 49.

95 "I'm going out to sea." William Miller, *Fishbait: The Memoirs of the Congressional Doorkeeper,* hardcover, New York: Warner Books, 1978, pp. 41–42; RM, p. 465.

95 to avoid being interrupted by telephone calls. SA, p. 191.

95 SECOND BOMBSHELL. RN, p. 65.

96 "Here we go again." JA, p. 171.

96 "Oh my God." JA, p. 171.

96 "hardly able to believe." JNE, p. 146; RM, pp. 471–72.

96 "conclusive proof of the greatest." *NYT,* December 7, 1948; RM, p. 473.

97 Pat was enraged. JNE, p. 147.

97 "He did what he felt." JNE, p. 101.

97 GOP as "we." MB, pp. 67–68, and her examples of such comments in letters to Drown, in MB, footnote 116, p. 194.

Chapter 8: Safeguarding the American Home

99 "Julie just bit Tricia." Ruth Haroldson OH, AMR.

101 either freedom or "state socialism." EM, p. 65.

101 "I like to do." JNE, p. 108.

101 "fighting, rocking, socking campaign." *LAT*, November 4, 1949; JA, p. 181.

101 "return to normal living." KM, pp. 152–57.

102 "seriously interested in national affairs." JNE, p. 158.

102 "displayed photographs." DG, p. 30.

102 "Dick Nixon fought communism." GT, p. 173.

102 "The Douglas-Marcantonio Record." JA, pp. 187–88; RM, pp. 581–82.

102 "pip-squeak" and a fascist. RN, p. 77.

103 "could be waspy." Richard St. Johns interview, quoted in RM, p. 594.

103 secondhand wood-paneled station wagon. JNE, p. 152.

103 "Safeguard the American Home." IG, p. 300.

103 sixty-five thousand thimbles. IG, p. 300.

103 "They were all over the map." Interview with close Nixon staffer, May 12, 2012.

103 "You know I don't want." Tom Dixon and Richard St. Johns interview, quoted in RM, pp. 593–94.

103 "a curious thing happened." "I Say He's a Wonderful Guy," *Saturday Evening Post*, September 6, 1952.

104 "the girls missed their parents." Helen Daniels OH, AMR.

104 "Politics was a harsh." JNE, p. 132.

104 "pink right down to her underwear." Frank Gannon, in "The Pink Lady Revisited," TheNewNixon, www.thenewnixon.org/2008/10/02 /helen-gahagan-douglas-redux.

105 "You Pick the Congressman the Kremlin Loves." JNE, p. 155.

105 "If I Knew You Were Coming." JNE, p. 156.

105 Dick's insistence on talking about the dangers. JA, p. 191.

105 They decamped to a Los Angeles beach. "I Say He's a Wonderful Guy."

105 "Dick was so exuberant." SA, p. 223; FB, p. 244.

105 "there was the United States." Quoted by Frank Gannon, in "The Pink Lady Revisited."

106 "dirtiest" campaign. RM, p. 615.

106 "brazen demagoguery . . . astonishing capacity for petty malice." RM, p. 615.

106 Dick was sworn in. RM, p. 614.

106 "thought that was the height of viciousness." LD, p. 81.

106 "they had the nerve to invite us." PN to HD, [undated], "Correspondence 1942–1951," Box 1, DC, NPL.

106 "I had a wonderful opportunity." PN to HD, [November 3, 1951], "Correspondence 1942–1951," Box 1, DC, NPL.

106 Herbert Block's (Herblock's) cartoons. Interview with Alvin Spivak, October 14, 2011.

107 "bright California look." JNE, p. 161.

107 Pat went to sewing classes. RM, p. 244.

107 sold their Whittier home. RM, p. 653.

107 "I have moved." PN to HD, [May, 20, 1951], "Correspondence 1942–1951," Box 1, DC, NPL.

107 "electric kitchen with *dishwasher* and disposal." PN to HD, [undated], "Correspondence 1942–1951," Box 1, DC, NPL.

107 "What a luxury to have." PN to HD, [February 1951], "Correspondence 1942–1951," Box 1, DC, NPL.

107 The entire family "fell." PN to HD, quoted in IG, p. 349.

108 "the vessel for hopes." DG, p. 30.

108 was on the road more than he was in the Senate. SA, p. 225.

108 "Dick is more tired." letter PN to HD, [September 4, 1951], "Correspondence 1942–1951," Box 1, DC, NPL.

108 "Yes, Saturday night." PN to HD, [sometime in 1951], "Correspondence 1942–1951," Box 1, DC, NPL.

108 WELCOME HOME DADDY sign. PPS 266, Box 1, "1946–1952," PRNC, NPL.

109 "sensible non-medical advice." Hutschnecker, JA, pp. 196–97.

109 "emotional conditions" including "misery." RM, p. 655.

109 about Hutschnecker's role. Nixon biographer Irv Gellman has examined Hutschnecker's medical records on Nixon. Gellman claims that there were fewer than a dozen recorded appointments and that there is no mention of mental problems or therapy in the doctor's notes. Might the doctor have purposely not recorded sessions or might he have been telling tales to gain attention? Perhaps both. It is mystifying. Gellman has Hutshnecker medical records. Interview with Irv Gellman, May 5, 2011.

109 "a glorious ten days." PN to HD, [November 3, 1951], "Correspondence 1942–1951," Box 1, DC, NPL.

110 "a secluded beach." PN to HD, [Winter 1952], "Correspondence, 1952," Box 1, DC, NPL.

110 "he doesn't drink whiskey." Charles Smathers interview and Charles Rebozo interview with Jonathan Aitken, quoted in JA, pp. 197–99.

110 Bebe and Dick developed. AS, pp. 100–115; JNE, pp. 217–19; CB, pp. 496–97; William Safire, *Before the Fall,* paperback, New York: Belmont Tower Book, 1975, pp. 613–16.

111 "Bebe's favorites are RN." AS, p. 105.

111 "Bebe's like a sponge." *GH*, July 1976; quoted in AS, p. 105.

111 Julie fondly called him "Beebes." Interview with Susan Porter Rose, May 2, 2013.

111 "failed Asian policies." IG, p. 366.

111 Pat decided to attend. PN to HD, [May 20, 1952], "Correspondence 1952," Box 1, DC, NPL.

112 "some combination!" PN to HD, [May 20, 1952], "Correspondence 1952," Box 1, DC, NPL.

112 "which was a riot." PN to HD, [undated], "Correspondence 1942–1951," Box 1, DC, NPL; IG, p. 349; MB, pp. 32–33.

112 "the last carefree vacation I ever had." JNE, p. 162.

Chapter 9: "Heroes" and "Housewives": Dick, Ike, Pat, and Mamie

115 "I was speechless." *Chicago Daily Tribune,* July 12, 1952.

115 "amazed, flabbergasted, weak." *NYT,* July 12, 1952; IG, p. 444.

116 "surface glamour of the idea." JNE, p. 114.

116 Chotiner, sensing that Pat. RM, pp. 727–28.

116 "The junior senator." EM, p. 88; RM, pp. 727–28.

116 "I guess I can make it through another campaign." RN, p. 86.

117 "statesman-like." *Chicago Sun-Times,* July 12, 1952; IG, p. 446.

117 taking $52,000 from the oil industry. SA, p. 296.

118 "I want my mommy." LD, p. 83.

118 "tired of photographers and reporters." *WP,* July 14, 1952.

118 "What do you think of Senator Nixon." "Miss Bouvier's Telling Questions," *WP,* May 28, 1994.

118 "When are you going away?" Isabella Taves, "Pat Nixon: Problems of a 'Perfect Wife,'" *Redbook,* May 1956.

118 "always work as a team." *NYT,* July 11, 1952.

118 "terrifically thrilled." AS, p. 139.

118 "who still believe." *Chicago Daily Tribune,* September 28, 1952.

119 "Mr. and Mrs. Horatio Alger, Jr." *Colliers,* July 9, 1954, p. 33.

119 "there was a great deal of hue." Sherman Adams OH, April 12, 1967, Columbia University Oral History Project, OH-162, pp. 95–97.

119 "as clean as a hound's tooth." http://millercenter/presidenteisenhower/essays/biography/3.

119 explain the fund in a televised appeal. Lee Huebner, "The Checkers Speech After 60 Years," *The Atlantic,* September, 22, 2012.

120 "There comes a time." SA, p. 282; CB, p. 241; JA, p. 212.

120 "It seemed like the last mile." RNSC, p. 112.

120 "GI bedroom den." RM, p. 826; RN, p. 103.

120 "financial striptease." Lee Huebner, "The Checkers Speech After 60 Years."

120 "Well, that's about it." http://www.americanrhetoric.com/speeches/richardnixoncheckers.html.

121 he tossed down his notes. CB, p. 251.

121 "had not stayed on the defensive." RNSC, p. 118.

122 three million letters, telegrams, and phone calls. www.wikipedia.org/wiki/Checkers_speech.

122 "fund crisis made me feel suddenly tired and old." RN, p. 108.

122 "hardest" and "sharpest." RNSC, p. 128.

122 "It kills me." JNE, p. 126.

122 "zest" for "political life." RNSC, p. 128.

123 took her a while. CB, p. 260.

123 214 cities. RN, pp. 111–13.

123 "more veneer than substance." SA, p. 297; CB, p. 263.

123 "Fighting Quaker." *Time*, August 25, 1952.

123 "We Like Nixon" banners. *Chicago Daily Tribune*, September 30, 1952.

123 Drew Pearson wrote a column. JNE, p. 127.

123 women were 5 percent more likely. Jo Freeman, "Gender Gaps in Presidential Elections," www.uis.edu/orgs/cwluherstory/jofreeman/polhistory/gendergap.htm.

124 Nixon became the chief spokesman. Irwin Gellman's chapter on civil rights in his forthcoming *The President and the Apprentice: Dwight Eisenhower and Richard Nixon, 1952–1961*.

124 to hide his underlying goal. Interview with Irv Gellman.

124 "one and a half times around the world!" PPS 267, Box 4, "1953 Diary Oct 5–17, 1953," PRNC, NPL.

124 "We suddenly discovered." Isabella Taves, "Pat Nixon: Problems of a 'Perfect Wife,'" *Redbook*, May 1956.

125 "dominated and saddened." PPS 267, Box 4, "1953 Diary Oct 5–17, 1953," PRNC, NPL.

125 "But a job had to be done." JNE, p. 199.

125 "rather than all the useless gadding." PN to HD, [February, 8, 1956], "1956," Box 2, DC, NPL.

125 This expanded role allowed Pat. Isabella Taves, "Pat Nixon: Problems of a 'Perfect Wife,'" *Redbook*, May 1956; SA, p. 326.

125 Pat in Australia and New Zealand: First draft of chapter 11, page 13,

in Irwin Gellman's forthcoming *The President and the Apprentice: Dwight Eisenhower and Richard Nixon, 1952–1961.*

126 "Wives had never been invited." *WP*, November 20, 1953, Box 2, "Far East Trip," Series 375, RNL.

126 "with the energetic enthusiasm." *UNWR*, December 4, 1953.

126 visit to a slum area in Hong Kong. *UNWR*, December 4, 1953.

126 the Nixons called "inspiring." PN to HD, [undated], "Correspondence 1953," Box 1, DC, NPL.

126 "Everywhere I went it helped women." JNE, p. 210.

126 "Imagine me—a farm girl." Isabella Taves, "Pat Nixon: Problems of a 'Perfect Wife,'" *Redbook*, May 1956.

126 "gave great impetus." RN, p. 120.

127 When the Nixons returned. SA, p. 326.

127 "But the reports on you, Pat." JNE, p. 211.

127 Tricia had been sick while her parents were abroad. PPS 271, folder: *Redbook* article, May 1956, Taves.

127 visit to the Pale Seco Leprosarium. *LAT*, February 25, 1955; Irwin Gellman's forthcoming *The President and the Apprentice: Dwight Eisenhower and Richard Nixon, 1952–1961.*

127 "The Patients are still talking." Aida Hurwitz letter to Pat Nixon, [April 21, 1955], PPS 207.205, NPL.

128 "made a greater impression." "Are Goodwill Trips Worthwhile?: I've Got a Question," *LAT*, July 31, 1955.

128 "shooting wildly." Quoted in CB, p. 290.

128 "magnificent" speech. SA, pp. 337–38.

128 she intuitively mistrusted. Pat Nixon biography in http://www.firstladies .org/biographies/firstladies.

129 "for socializing American institutions." SA, p. 355.

129 *Washington Post* cartoonist Herblock depicted. DG, p. 58.

129 "the most charming of the lot." JNE, p. 222.

129 "You are probably laughing." PN to HD, [August 16, 1954], "Correspondence 1953," Box 1, DC, NPL.

129 "How I do enjoy your letters!" PN to HD, [undated 1959], Box 2, "1959 HD's Talk on PN-1960," DC, NPL.

130 "She was most friendly." PN to HD, [February 3, 1953], "Correspondence 1953," Box 1, DC, NPL.

130 "as two of their best friends." Ellis D. Slater, *The Ike I Knew* (privately printed, 1980); MH, p. 139.

130 increasingly valued Nixon's intelligence. Conversation with Irwin Gellman.

130 "we should meet regularly for breakfast or lunch." They did so throughout 1954. Memo, November 12, 1965, PPS 324.38, NPL.

130 "It has been much too long since." Memo, January 12, 1955, PPS 325(1955), 1, NPL. Nixon and Eisenhower's monthly meetings in Eisenhower daily diary in Louis Galambos and Daun Van Ee, eds., *The Presidential Papers of Dwight David Eisenhower* (2005 electronic edition) and in *The Papers of Dwight David Eisenhower: The Presidency,* hardcover, Baltimore: The Johns Hopkins University Press, 2001, vol. 14–17 and 18–21, see pp. 259, 2612, 2624, 2635, 2643, 2657, 2661, 2675, 2676, 2697.

131 interested in international affairs and did her homework. Isabella Taves, "Pat Nixon: Problems of a 'Perfect Wife,'" *Redbook,* May 1956.

131 "My crystal ball." DDE to PN, [March 17, 1961], PPS 268, Box 1, "Eisenhower Correspondence 1961–1966," PRNC, NPL.

131 were not as physically robust. MH, p. 65.

131 "wonderful fun being with you." MDE to PN, [June 1, 1956], PPS 268, Box 1, "Eisenhower Correspondence 1953–1960," PRNC, NPL.

131 "single perfect universe." DH, p. 591.

132 as many as four nights a week. JNE, p. 195.

132 "Oh, joy, I can hardly wait." PN to HD, [October 25, 1954], "Correspondence 1954," Box 1, DC, NPL.

132 "two, three and sometimes four." *Collier's,* July 9, 1954, p. 35.

132 Despite her hectic schedule. *Collier's,* July 9, 1954, p. 34.

132 an orderly assemblage of outfits. *Collier's,* July 9, 1954, p. 33.

132 Pat Nixon was named. *Hartford Courant,* December 11, 1957; *Chicago Tribune,* March 16, 1958; GT, p. 175.

132 She allowed photographers. LD, p. 96.

133 "That's my steam iron!" Isabella Taves, "Pat Nixon: Problems of a 'Perfect Wife,'" *Redbook,* May 1956.

133 "hero of the lighting performance." PN to HD, [undated], "Correspondence 1954," Box 1, DC, NPL.

133 "again enjoying (?)." PN to HD, [August 16, 1954?], "Correspondence 1954," Box 1, DC, NPL.

133 "We've never quarreled." *Collier's,* July 9, 1954, p. 33.

133 Anthony Summers cites. AS, pp. 158–59.

133 Jessamyn West asserted. SA, p. 350; AS, p. 159.

133 avoided confrontations with each other. JNE, pp. 213–14.

134 Pat felt increasingly trapped. JA, p. 234.

134 agreement with her that he would serve for only one term. EM, p. 139; LD, p. 75.

134 "were not in control." JNE, p. 223.

134 Dick was worn out. RN, pp. 384–99; CB, pp. 321–31; JA, pp. 238–42.

135 the president had suffered a heart attack. RN, pp. 164–66; SC, pp. 131–45.

135 'The president isn't going to die, is he Daddy?" RNSC, pp. 133–34.

135 Dick and Pat attended. RNSC, p. 144.

135 "I just wish." PN to ME, October 1955, Box 32, Nixon file, MDE papers, White House Series, Eisenhower Library.

135 "They visit and prowl." PN to HD, [October 1, 1955], "Correspondence 1955," Box 1, DC, NPL.

135 "great stream of history." EM, p. 157.

136 officially hosting the visits. Marilyn Irvin Holt, *Mamie Doud Eisenhower,* hardcover, Lawrence: University Press of Kansas, 2007, p. 114.

136 Eisenhower thought deeply about. SA, pp. 384–99; RN, pp. 167–68; JA, pp. 238–42.

136 "I have asked." SA, p. 390; RN, p. 170.

136 "dreadfully wounded and hurt." JA, p. 239.

136 Nixon was depressed and had difficulty. Interview with Irwin Gellman, November 5, 2011.

137 "did not want her to be upset." Eisenhower diary, quoted in interview with Irwin Gellman, November 5, 2011.

137 "No one is going to push." JA, p. 240; JNE, p. 232.

137 "delighted by the news." CB, p. 350.

137 "In politics you can never count on anything." *NYT,* August 21, 1956.

Chapter 10: A Turbulent Ascent

138 "Pat knitting." DH, p. 322.

139 held her own press conference. "Straws in the Wind," *San Diego Union,* August 21, 1956.

139 "with mixed pleasure and confusion." *San Diego Union,* "Coffee Hour" The Mark Hopkins Pat Stories, August 25, 1956.

139 "I have been cussed." *Time,* August 3, 1956.

139 "Dick, you keep fighting." AS, p. 160.

139 "Ike and Dick." http://people.cohums.ohio-state-edu/childs1/Mamie %20Eisenhower%20and%20Pat%20Nixon.htm.

139 Pat set aside her belief. *NYT,* September 26, 1956.

139 target of opposition attacks. DG, p. 58.

139 ("Nixonland"). JA, p. 244; FB, p. 357.

140 "a guardian of the hydrogen bomb." DA, p. 62.

140 "who takes the low road." RN, p. 178.

140 Liberian female political leaders. JNE, p. 245.

140 "took it like a pill." Interview with General Don Hughes, February 4, 2012.

141 "a phenomenon of our times." Ruth Montgomery, "Mrs. Pat Nixon's Winning Ways," February 15, 1957, Vertical File, "Nixon, Patricia," NPL.

141 "peasants by the thousands." Earl Mazo, *New York Herald Tribune,* April 12, 1957.

141 "I think all of us will agree." George Smathers, PPS 272, Box 2, "1957 Clippings," PRNC, NPL.

141 "a warm, engaging, sincere personality." *Pittsburgh Courier,* May 25, 1957.

141 Louise Johnson led a group of friends. *Hartford Courant,* June 4, 1957.

142 "We didn't realize." RN to HD and JD, [April 3, 1957], "1957," Box 2, DC, NPL.

142 Nixon met with over one hundred. CB, p. 355.

142 a state dinner for King Mohamed V. PPS 273, Box 3, "PN-Newspaper Clippings Nov. 1957," PRNC, NPL.

142 "Ike apparently prefers." Nixon platter, December 3, 1957, quoted by Irwin Gellman. Interview with Gellman.

142 She badly sprained her back. JNE, p. 252.

142 "It did hurt me to know." HD to PN, [undated], "1958," Box 2, DC, NPL.

143 diplomatic trip to South America. SC, pp. 183–234; JNE, pp. 254–64; CB, pp. 356–63; SA, pp. 462–82; RN, pp. 185–92.

143 "At first the spit looked like giant snowflakes." JNE, p. 174.

144 "she was as brave as any man." Paul Harvey, May 22, 1958, transcript of "Mrs. Nixon," PPS 273, Box 3, "1958," PRNC, NPL.

145 Pat and Dick returned. JA, p. 254; JNE, pp. 263–64.

145 "You should get purple hearts." HD to PN, [undated], "1958," Box 2, DC, NPL.

145 "stayed in the front lines." Paul Harvey, May 22, 1958, transcript of "Mrs. Nixon." And Hoover letter, PPS 273, Box 3, "1958," PRNC, NPL. Also MB, p. 65.

145 *Los Angeles Times'* Washington bureau chief. Reprinted in the *LAT,* May 18, 1958.

146 she joined him on a brief stopover in Indianapolis. Polly Cochran, "Second Lady of the Land Smiles for Everyone in Indiana," *Indianapolis Star,* September 30, 1958, and Betty Preston, "Vice President's Wife Shares Husband's Views," *Glendale News-Press,* October 1, 1958, PPS 273, Box 3, "1958," PRNC, NPL.

146 "I feel sorry for." Interview with Ruth Buchanan, November 5, 2011.

147 "We should adopt as our primary." JA, p. 257.

147 "uncouth adventurer." *NYT*, July 30, 1958; CB, p. 375.

147 Pat met the women of the Fleet Street. *Hartford Courant,* November 27, 1958.

147 "doll that would be smiling." "Mrs. Pat—A British View," *Spectator,* reprinted in *New Republic,* December 22, 1958, p. 5.

147 on December 19. *WP,* December 20, 1958.

148 "with over a hundred at each." PN to HD, [December 3, 1958], "1958," Box 2, DC, NPL.

148 "Tricia had a gala." PN to HD [undated], "1958," Box 2, DC, NPL.

148 "correct treatment." RNSC, p. 246.

148 The Nixons took a brief stroll. *NYJA,* July 24, 1959.

149 NIXON AND KHRUSHCHEV ARGUE. *NYT,* July 25, 1959.

149 "I felt like a fighter." RNSC, p. 258.

149 "like a fight between." Interview with Don Hughes, February 4, 2012.

149 "to carry good will." *New York Herald Tribune,* July 21, 1959.

149 "We must be friends." *NYJA,* July 26, 1959; and *Seattle Post Intelligencer,* July 27, 1959.

149 She prodded Khrushchev. SA, pp. 529–30; MB, p. 66.

150 his lavish stone dacha. RNSC, p. 263.

150 "On matters of substance." RNSC, p. 274.

150 "Now look here." RNSC, pp. 263–64.

150 "I'm surprised that there is." RN, p. 211; JNE, p. 273.

150 a radio and television address. RNSC, p. 278.

150 "masterpiece—a tough, but sympathetic statement." *Life,* August 10, 1959.

150 applauded them at the Kirov Opera House. *LAT,* July 28, 1959.

150 Pat danced the polka. *LAT,* August 1, 1959.

151 "friendship, friendship." *New York Herald Tribune,* August 6, 1959.

151 "Your grandchildren will be raised." Interview with Ruth Buchanan, November 2011.

151 "catching them like a baseball player." *New York Herald Tribune,* August 3, 1959, p. 1.

151 "one of the most moving experiences." SA, p. 532.

151 "hugging and kissing spree." *Pittsburgh Sun,* August 5, 1959.

151 "A Barnstorming Masterpiece." *Life,* August, 10, 1959.

151 "perfect way to launch a campaign." *NYT,* July 27, 1959.

151 "might of changed the course of history." CB, p. 386; SA, p. 529.

151 "Diplomat in High Heels." *NYT,* July 28, 1959.

152 "probably did more to convince." Russia Trip, Dorothy Roe article, "Women World Over Know How to Size Each Other Up," PPS 274, Box 2, "July 1959-PN and RN," PRNC, NPL.

152 But the Nixon daughters. *WP,* August 6, 1959.

152 a special homecoming premiere. PN to HD, [July 1959], PPS 274, Box 2, DC, NPL.

152 Christmas Day celebrations. *WP,* July 26, 1958.

Chapter 11: Enduring Defeat

153 This chapter draws on accounts of the 1960 and 1962 elections in: SC, pp. 293–426; RN, pp. 214–47; SA, vol. I, pp. 544–608; JNE, pp. 276–319; LD, pp. 115–24; JA, pp. 265–306; AS, pp. 200–238; CM, pp. 133-219; MB, pp. 70–87. And the four books on the 1960 election: DP; EK; TW; CM.

155 "I would be willing to debate." *NYT,* September, 29, 1960; SA, pp. 576–77.

155 "unless I wore sable underwear." Originally quoted from *Women's Wear Daily* in CB, p. 409; SA, vol. 1, p. 576; JNE, p. 190.

156 "too serene, too tightly controlled." *Time,* February 29, 1960, p. 25.

156 "I've . . . been called the super-efficient wife." Pat Nixon to Christine Hotchkiss, "What Keeps Me Going," *LAT,* June 5, 1960.

156 "I may be dying." *Time,* February 29, 1960, p. 25.

156 "invoke the name of Abraham Lincoln." www.americanrhetoric.com /speeches/jfk1960dnc.htm.

157 was enjoying a ten-point lead. RN, p. 215.

157 "America will not be pushed around." CM, p. 136.

157 "When Mr. Khrushchev says." *NYT,* July 29, 1960.

157 "promised everything to everybody." SA, p. 554.

157 Nixon had regained the lead by. Gallup results, quoted in WJR, p. 128.

157 where Democrats outnumbered Republicans. RN, p. 214.

157 "time America started moving again." Quoted in WJR, p. 133.

158 "I have sat with." TW, p. 303.

158 "If you give me a week." EK, pp. 114–15.

158 he was hospitalized. RN, p. 218; JA, p. 276; SC, p. 327.

158 "Pat, who seems to feel." James Bassett to Wilma Bassett, September 4, 1960, Bassett papers, quoted in AS, p. 221.

159 goal of garnering as much. WJR, p. 132.

159 During the day they drove. MB, p. 77.

159 "flung them into such." TW, quoted in JNE, pp. 285–86.

159 "nothing was as draining." Interview with Don Hughes, February 2012.

159 In a famous incident. WJR, p. 131.

160 "where she took an aggressive approach." Interview with Don Hughes, February 2012.

160 she was often furious. Interview with Dwight Chapin, August 2012.

160 "flickering, often snow-speckled." DP, p. 355.

160 Kennedy prepared carefully. SA, p. 571.

160 "erase the assassin image." TW, p. 324.

161 Stressed, gaunt with a one-hundred-degree temperature. JA, p. 277.

161 He banged his knee. JA, p. 277.

161 On television Nixon looked. IM, p. 61.

161 "almost frightened, at turns." TW, p. 289.

161 "sucker punch." RP, p. 53.

161 "get the country moving again." WJR, p. 152.

161 what bothered Pat most. JNE, p. 192.

162 radio listeners thought Nixon. DP, p. 345.

162 "Image had replaced." Quoted in AS, p. 208.

162 "None of us disillusioned him." Klein interview with AS, p. 208.

162 "couldn't imagine why he looked that way." AS, p. 208.

162 "had no comment." AS, p. 208.

162 thought he had won on substance. JNE, p. 285.

162 October 3 "Pat Week." PPS 275, Box 3, "Republican National Convention, Chicago—July 25, 1960 (4)," PRNC, NPL.

163 "the stronger one." *Newsweek,* October 10, 1960; William Costello, "Nixon on the Eve," *New Republic,* November 7, 1960; FB, p. 419.

163 "Dick didn't give me a thing." *LAT,* June 22, 1960; FB, p. 420.

163 330,000 Americans had lost their jobs. CM, p. 176.

163 "little of the near-hysteria." *NYT,* November 3, 1960.

164 "fluffing of a phrase." TW, p. 302.

164 Even when covered with rotten eggs. SC, p. 374.

164 Pat's weight dropped from 115 to 103 pounds. *NYT,* October 10, 1960.

164 "I value the sense of connection." Pat Nixon to Christine Hotchkiss, "What Keeps Me Going," *LAT,* June 5, 1960.

165 final campaign rally. RNSC, p. 376.

165 Dick had traveled sixty-five thousand miles. RN, p. 223; JNE, p. 290.

165 Ambassador Hotel in Los Angeles. DP, p. 396; SC, p. 377.

165 "I knew Kennedy too well." JNE, p. 290.

165 "no talk of elections or politics." Interview with Don Hughes, February 2012; DP, p. 398; SC, p. 378; TW, pp. 7–8.

165 They agreed not to turn on the television. TW, p. 217; DP, p. 400.

166 "I simply cannot bring myself." RNSC, p. 386.

166 "How can we let the American people." JNE, p. 288.

166 Kennedy's campaign shenanigans. AS, pp. 209–16.

166 "especially frustrated by what seemed." CM, p. 177.

167 "I think we should go down." RN, p. 223.

167 Pat began to cry. RNSC, pp. 389–90.

167 As they left the ballroom. LD, p. 119.

167 "the saddest day of my life." RNSC, p. 386.

167 "a long bony arm." WB to FB, March 27, 1975, FB, p. 433.

167 "Kennedy's organization approached campaign dirty tricks." RN, p. 225.

167 Nixon declined to demand a recount. IM, p. 62.

167 "in the end, the cost." JA, p. 291.

168 "because I spent too much time." RNSC, p. 422.

168 "Nineteen sixty disillusioned her beyond redemption." JNE, p. 303.

168 "Mrs. Nixon still says we should order a recount." Monica Crowley, *Nixon Off the Record*, paperback, New York: Random House, 1998, p. 30; EK, p. 208.

168 "state of numbness." PN to HD, November or December 1960, "1960," Box 2, DC, quoted in MB, pp. 78–79.

168 Pat vented her rage. AS, pp. 220–21.

168 "completely depressed." Herb Klein, quoted in AS, p. 218.

168 At Christmas the family sought. RNSC, pp. 414–15.

169 Joann Lynott noticed. *LAT*, January 21, 1961.

169 "would never hold hands." *Jacqueline Kennedy: Historic Conversations on Life with John F. Kennedy*, hardcover, New York: Hyperion, 2011, p. 326.

169 that Pat had snubbed Jackie that day. LD, p. 120.

169 Pat shares her pleasure in snubbing enemies. PN to HD, [February 1951] and [November 3, 1951], "Correspondence: 1942–1951," Box 1, DC, NPL; MB, pp. 34–35.

169 "You could see." *Jacqueline Kennedy: Historic Conversations on Life with John F. Kennedy*, hardcover, New York: Hyperion, 2011, pp. 149 and 326.

169 "one of the most trying days of my life." Quoting what Nixon told his friend Elmer Bobst, AS, p. 219.

170 "I vowed that I would never." RN, p. 226.

170 "after a few days of shallow talk." RNSC, p. 423; JNE, p. 302.

170 "I am not fit company." HD to PN, [undated], 1960, Box 2, DC, NPL.

Chapter 12: Darkness

171 She made several trips to Los Angeles. FB, p. 443.

171 "difficult to concentrate." RN, p. 232.

172 Harpo and Groucho Marx were their neighbors. LD, p. 122; JNE, p. 303.

172 "a miracle of peace, friendliness, and good will." "Crises of a Candidate's Wife," *LHJ*, November 1962, p. 57.

172 "We were enjoying a breathing space." "Crises of a Candidate's Wife," *LHJ*, November 1962, p. 57.

172 "The people who lose." *Time*, February 29, 1960, p. 25.

173 "probably in our hearts we always knew better." "Crises of a Candidate's Wife," *LHJ*, November 1962, p. 57.

173 "Virtually everything I did." RN, p. 232.

173 see them less often. RN, p. 236.

173 working intently on the book. See interesting discussion in DF, pp. 21–45.

173 fears of failing, of being indecisive. FB, p. 445.

173 "I was almost ten pounds." RN, p. 237.

173 "I Also Ran." *CT*, March 20, 1960.

174 "a major new crisis for me and my family." RN, p. 237.

174 "has always been one of those." RN, p. 240.

175 "the most vicious people in the world." FB, p. 451.

175 "Why you?" *GH*, March 1962, p. 71.

175 "As nearly as I can define my attitude." "Crises of a Candidate's Wife," *LHJ*, November 1962; LD, p. 123.

175 "would not be going out campaigning." RN, p. 240.

175 "All I want is." *GH*, March 1962, p. 71; FB, p. 455.

175 "I am not sure." RN, p. 240.

176 "Well . . . that is life." JNE, p. 306.

176 "I am more convinced than ever." JNE, pp. 306–7; RN, p. 240.

176 According to Nixon's account. RN, p. 240.

176 "I'm trapped." JNE, p. 308.

176 "He can't help it." "Crises of a Candidate's Wife," *LHJ*, November 1962, p. 118.

177 Hoffa's Teamsters' Fund lot. FB, pp. 448–49; JNE, p. 211; SA, p. 629.

177 "her lips quivering." *WP, Times Herald*, October 18, 1962.

177 "We never have fights." *LAT*, February 21, 1969.

178 willing to debate Mrs. Nixon on television. *WP, Times Herald*, June 18, 1962.

178 "by gushing ladies." Tom Wicker, quoted in FB, p. 456.

178 "People paid to get in." PPS 279, Box 1, "PN-Misc. Press Clippings," PRNC, NPL.

179 "didn't want to ask for pity." *Hartford Courant*, December 2, 1962.

179 "We had to play the dreary drama." RN, p. 244.

179 removed herself to a separate room to grieve. JW, p. 13.

179 "The boss won't be down." JW, p. 15.

179 "the next twelve years." RNSC, p. 70.

179 When a CBS reporter asked Klein. JW, p. 17.

180 "Good morning, gentlemen." JW, pp. 16–22.

180 a night of too much drinking. WTP, pp. 21–22; MB, p. 86.

180 Pat yelled "Bravo." JNE, p. 318. Note: there were unsubstantiated rumors, cited by Anthony Summers, that Dick beat Pat after the 1962 election loss. But when tapping new sources unavailable to Summers, and weighing denials of the Nixon intimates I interviewed, I find no further evidence to support the charge. The reader should keep in mind that Nixon was the most polarizing of all American politicians, and was the target of many malicious myths and falsehoods during his life and afterward. AS, pp. 234–36.

181 "You just go on." JNE, p. 319.

181 "There was a sadness." AS, p. 236.

Chapter 13: Your Turn, My Turn

182 This chapter is based on material in: RN, pp. 247–351; JA, pp. 307–72; JNE, pp. 320–73; SA, pp. 11–222; MB, pp. 87–131.

182 one of the happiest seasons. RN, p. 250.

183 itinerary for the trip. RN, pp. 248–49; JNE, p. 323–24; JA, pp. 318–19.

183 "pulled out all the stops." Interview with Maureen Nunn, April 13, 2012.

183 "I realize that you have." RN, p. 248; JA, pp. 318–19.

184 "in French provincial." JW, p. 52.

184 the outdoor barbecue. Peter Kihss interview, *NYT*, December 29, 1963.

184 none of them were as close. MB, p. 93.

184 "I hope we never." RN, p. 250.

185 the Nixons dove. SA, p. 26 and p. 62.

185 often took Julie and Tricia. Peter Kihss interview, *NYT*, December 29, 1963.

185 they liked to dine and dance. Interview with Ed Cox, January 7, 2013.

185 small dinner parties. Robert Donovan, "Over-Nominated Under-elected, Still a Promising Candidate," *NYT*, April 25, 1965.

185 neighbor Kathleen Stans. JNE, p. 325.

186 joined two posh. LD, p. 125.

186 famous invitees including. PPS 283, Box 1, "1966 (1)," PRNC, NPL.

186 he told local journalists. SA, p. 262.

186 "It's just terrible." RN, p. 252.

186 watching the events unfolding on television. SA, p. 262.

187 "While the hand of fate." RN, p. 253.

187 "We never value life." RN, pp. 254–55.

187 to arrange for an official invitation. JA, p. 317.

188 he often put on a record. JNE, p. 327.

188 "He tries hard." JNE, p. 328.

188 testimony Marina Oswald gave. Marina Oswald's testimony suggests this incident did not occur in November when Nixon was in Dallas, but in April of that year, when he was elsewhere. In his memoir Nixon implied that he was a target in November 1963. He either misinterpreted Marina Oswald's testimony or lied to gain sympathy for himself. Story about Oswald and Nixon, JA, p. 316; RN, p. 252.

188 Pat at first refused. JNE, p. 329.

188 "Extremism in the defense." Wikipedia.org/wiki/1964_Republican_National_Convention.

189 Nixon made 150 appearances. RN, p. 263.

189 "I would be mentally dead." RN, p. 265.

189 Pat and the girls hightailed it. JNE, p, 329.

189 "slaving 14 hours a day." PN to HD, [November 1964], Box 2A, DC, NPL.

189 "Miss Ryan." JNE, p. 331.

189 "panic-stricken campaigners." PD to HD, [undated], 1964, Box 2A, DC, NPL.

190 "The years fly so fast." PN to HD, [May 1965], 1964–1974, Box 3, DC, NPL.

190 "After you have been." SA, p. 63; JNE, p. 334.

190 "If Dick is going." HD to PN, [February 21, 1965], 1964–1974, Box 3, DC, NPL.

190 an affair between Nixon and Marianna Liu. Marianna Liu inadvertently fueled rumors of a liaison with Nixon when she moved briefly to Whittier, California, to take a job as a housekeeper upon her 1969 emigration to the United States. Rumors about Marianna Liu and Nixon and J. Edgar Hoover's role: AS, pp. 269–70; *NYT*, June 22, 1976; *National Enquirer*, August 10 and 24, 1976; *People*, October 4, 1976. J. Edgar Hoover's use of pressure on Nixon, Anthony Summers, *Official & Confidential: The Secret Life of J. Edgar Hoover*, hardcover, New York: Putnam, 1993, pp. 371–76.

191 a twenty-fifth-anniversary trip. JNE, pp. 334–35.

191 four hundred appearances in forty states. RN, p. 272.

191 "We all have to contribute." JNE, p. 338.

192 "Dick keeps scheduled." PN to HD, [undated], "1967," Box 3, DC, NPL.

192 was not failing her husband. JNE, p. 338.

193 "goodwill ambassador for Pepsi Cola." RN, p. 280; CB, p. 493.

193 "flatly, almost tonelessly." JNE, p. 343.

193 Helene served as a sounding board. JNE, p. 344.

193 more important for her husband. Jo Ann Levine, "A Private Person Faces Great Public Challenge," *Christian Science Monitor*, March 15, 1968.

193 "I was not sure." RN, p. 291.

193 On Christmas Day, Nixon. RN, p. 292.

193 Julie thought he was depressed. JNE, p. 347.

194 "Whatever you do." RN, p. 292.

194 "It's like living under." Flora Rheta Schreiber, "Pat Nixon Reveals for the First Time: 'I Didn't Want Him to Run Again,'" *GH*, July 1968.

194 Graham encouraged Dick to run. RN, pp. 292–93.

194 "I have decided to go." RN, p. 294; SA, p. 132.

194 "should go through it." Flora Rheta Schreiber, "Pat Nixon Reveals for the First Time: 'I Didn't Want Him to Run Again,'" *GH*, July 1968.

195 and dropping over the course. Vera Glaser, "The Pat Nixon Story III: Sincere, understated, she draws women's vote," *BG*, December 31, 1968.

195 "with an only slightly glazed." MB, p. 97.

195 up to fifty letters a day. SA, p. 152.

195 "What is your greatest contribution." JNE, p. 355; SA, p. 153.

195 "If people work." Charlotte Curtis, "Pat Nixon: 'Creature Comforts Don't Matter,'" *NYT*, July 3, 1968.

196 "I never had time to think." Gloria Steinem, "In Your Heart You Know He's Nixon," *New York* magazine, October 28, 1968. Email comments from Gloria Steinem, May 2011.

196 "think the world owes them a living." Mary Wiegers, "The Same Pat Nixon—She's Polished," *WP*, May 27, 1968.

197 "Mr. Nixon, Excuse me." RN, p. 305.

197 "Dick, that poor boy." RN, p. 306.

197 "saddened and appalled." RN, p. 306.

197 "the safety factor." Lynn Lilliston, "1968: Year of the New Nixons," *LAT*, July 23, 1968,

197 CBS program *60 Minutes* filmed. CB, pp. 535–36.

197 "just screeched and clapped." *LAT*, August 12, 1968; RN, pp. 309–13.

197 greeted with "deafening" roar. RN, p. 314.

198 "courageous wife and loyal children." JA, p. 358.

198 "enveloped in smoke and flame." JA, p. 357.

198 "A child . . . hears a train." RN, p. 315.

198 "And every time . . . all the time." William Scranton interview with Jeffrey Frank, May 13, 2010.

198 "help me make that dream." SA, p. 176.

198 motorcade through the Loop. SA, p. 182.

199 "New Nixon." In "The Impact of Vietnam on Domestic Politics: The Election of 1968," www.faculty.smu.edu/dsimon/change-viet3b .html.

199 "new" Pat Nixon. "1968 Campaign Sees new Pat Nixon," UPI story printed in the *Montreal Gazette*, August 20, 1968.

199 Pat styled herself as a campaign volunteer. Mary Wiegers, "'Volunteer': I Don't Think They Like to Listen to Women," *WP*, October 8, 1968; "For Pat It's Win or Lose . . . Just Don't Drop Out," *WP*, April 24, 1968. Also see MB, p. 98.

199 "I'd rather be his right-hand man." Marilyn Goldstein, "Long Road to First Lady," *Newsday*, November 7, 1968.

199 "the eyes and ears of women voters." "For Pat It's Win or Lose . . . Just Don't Drop Out," *WP*, April 24, 1968.

199 "I fill him in on what women think." "For Pat It's Win or Lose . . . Just Don't Drop Out," *WP*, April 24, 1968.

199 were faced with protesters. RN, p. 319.

200 Haldeman failed to instruct. JNE, pp. 358–59.

200 Pat Nixon and Bob Haldeman did see eye to eye. Lynn Lilliston, "The Year of the New Nixons," *LAT*, July 23, 1968.

200 "gets very tense when he is on a heavy schedule." Vera Glaser, "The Pat Nixon Story III: Sincere, understated, she draw's women's vote," *BG*, December 31, 1968; Mary Wiegers, "Pat Soft-Sells Lighter Side of the Nixons," *WP*, August 9, 1968.

200 controlled appearances in the media. "The Election of 1968," Melvin Small in Melvin Small, ed. *A Companion to Richard M. Nixon*, hardcover, Chichester: Wiley-Blackwell, 2011, p. 154.

200 "win the peace in the Pacific." RN, p. 298.

201 "Even though it will be." RN, pp. 330–31.

202 "want them to keep up." RN, p. 332.

202 "He would come out into our suite." Interview with Ed Cox, January 7, 2013.

202 She vomited in the bathroom. RN, p. 334; JNE, p. 368.

202 "You got it. You won." RN, p. 333.

202 "there wasn't the elation." RN, p. 234.

202 "But Dick, are we sure of Illinois." RN, p. 334.

203 "Bring Us Together." RN, p. 335.

203 Back at home at 810 Fifth Avenue. RN, p. 335; JNE, p. 371.

203 "This comeback for Dick." Trude Feldman, "Pat Nixon 'Jumped for Joy' at Her Husband's Election Success," *Hartford Courant*, November 10, 1968.

Chapter 14: Adjusting to the White House Fortress

207 The most helpful sources for this chapter were: RN, pp. 355–454; JNE, pp. 377–422; CA, pp. 166–89; WW, pp. 383–90; MB, pp. 103–20; HRH, pp. 23–159; GT, pp. 179–88; LD, pp. 127–40.

207 Julie married Dwight David Eisenhower. Marie Smith, *WP,* December 23, 1968.

207 Nixon walked his daughter. RN, pp. 360–61; JNE, pp. 388–90; SA, pp. 240–41.

208 regretted that he had not spent. RN, p. 360.

208 twirled her around. RR, pp. 601–2; CB, p. 566.

209 "Expression on his face." HRH, p. 24.

209 bowed low to her. JNE, p. 379.

209 "We cannot learn." www.bartleby.com/124/pres58.html.

210 they watched in horror. CB, p. 568.

210 ordered the bubble top removed. CB, p. 568.

210 "byzantine scrolls of gold and silver bullion." WHCF, SMOF, Gwendolyn King, Box 7, "68 [i.e., '69] Inaugural Gown and Costume," NPL.

210 Dick sat down at the piano. RN, pp. 366–67; JNE, pp. 382–83.

211 felt genuine hostility toward them. RR, p. 579.

212 "a bit of sunlight into the hall." Tricia Nixon comment during Tricia Nixon's Tour of the White House on *60 Minutes,* MFF-549, May 26, 1970. "Main Motion Film File," NPL.

212 formal memo to his wife. RN to PN, [February 5, 1969], WHSF, SMOF, PPF, Box 1, "Memos–February 1969," RMN, NPL.

212 Pat chose Sarah Jackson Doyle. JNE, p. 394.

213 "*Nobody* could sleep with Dick." JBW, p. 357.

213 "Politics had literally bred strange bedfellows." RN, p. 367.

213 Nixons removed from the bedroom. RN, p. 167; JBW, pp. 356–58.

213 On the Truman Balcony. MFF-549, May 26, 1970, "Main Motion Film File"; Tricia Nixon's Tour of the White House on *60 Minutes,* NPL.

213 Ehrlichman invited Tricia. WTP, pp. 42–43.

214 "First Lady's Garden." LD, p. 132.

214 mantelpiece bore two plaques. JNE, p. 397; LD, pp. 132–33.

214 "It really upset Mrs. Nixon." Gwendolyn B. King, OH, May 24, 1988, pp. 40–41.

215 "The Berlin Wall." "H. R. Haldeman Dies," *WP,* November 13, 1993.

215 The president gave Haldeman orders. HRH, pp. 58–59; CB, p. 578.

215 "a sense of and a desire for accomplishment." Raymond Price, *With Nixon,* hardcover, New York: Viking Press, 1977, p. 132.

215 "schedule deviations, people allowed to get too close . . . fair and considerate . . . had a lot of fun with him." Haldeman Interview, Jonathan Aitken Collection, Series II: Interviews, Box 9, "Haldeman, H.R.," p. 4, NPL; Chapin Interview, Jonathan Aitken Collection, Box 8, "Chapin, Dwight," p. 2, NPL.

216 "by imposing a rigid self-discipline." HRH, pp. 69–70.

217 "a great equalizer." Alice E. Anderson and Hadley V. Boxendale, *Behind Every Successful President: The Hidden Power and Influence of America's First Ladies,* hardcover, New York: S.P.I. Books, 1992, p. 122.

217 "was the warmest First Lady." HTD, p. 165.

217 "never forgets her days." LD, p. 140.

217 Pat had long been irritated. CA, p. 188.

217 "We're going to invite our *friends.*" CA, p. 165.

217 raised platform for a choir. LD, p. 134.

217 "feels that we have too many non-VIPs." HRH to Rose Mary Woods, WHSF, SMOF, PPF, Box 4, "Memos-September 1969," RMN, NPL.

218 adored "pomp and ceremony." RR, p. 35.

218 "trying not to look as tickled." HRH, p. 32.

218 new "Student Prince" outfits. CA, p. 188.

218 "white tunic, gold braid, and pillbox hats" on guard uniforms. WW, p. 386; SA, p. 325.

218 Recalling how excited she was. JNE, p. 46.

218 "When I get into my own room." *Life,* August 25, 1972; CA, p. 166.

218 "We are shut up in this house." HTD, p. 173.

219 "it was like living." Charles Colson, quoted in WW, p. 383.

219 Pat's correspondence served. MB, p. 117.

219 "When a letter from the White House." LD, p. 136.

219 Pat Nixon took action. CA, p. 169.

219 emergency heart surgery. Gwendolyn B. King, *OH,* May 24, 1988, pp. 18–19.

219 "the paradoxical combination." RN, p. 434.

220 The president's 1969 daily diary. www.nixonlibrary.gov/virtuallibrary /documents/dailydiary. php.

220 surprise fifty-seventh-birthday party. Author interview with Lucy Winchester.

221 where the Nixons awoke. HRH, p. 51; Molly Meyer Wertheimer, ed., *Inventing a Voice: The Rhetoric of American First Ladies of the Twentieth Century,* paperback, New York: Rowman & Littlefield, 2004, p. 298.

221 had trouble falling asleep. WW, p. 383.

221 "delightful as a couple." CSO, August 15, 1988, p. 46.

221 Once at the Western White House. William Safire, *Before the Fall*, paperback, New York: Belmont Tower Books, 1975, p. 611.

221 rarely spent more than half an hour eating. *Presidential Daily Diaries*, www.nixon.library.gov/virtuallibrary/documents/dailydiary.php; RR, p. 578.

221 "maintain a certain figure." WW, p. 390.

222 "I want to go. God take me." Michael Korda, *Ike: An American Hero*, hardcover, New York: Harper, 2007, p. 723.

222 "I knew that he had been sinking fast." RN, p. 375; RR, p. 63; HRH, p. 55.

222 Nixon eulogized the president. The American Presidency Project, www.presidency.ucsb.edu/ws/?pid=1987#axzz2gqybutw2.

222 "Oh, he could be aroused." "1969 Year in Review: Eisenhower, Judy Garland die," UPI, October 25, 2005, http://www.upi.com/Archives/Audio/Events-of-1969/Eisenhower-Judy-Garland-Die/. Retrieved May 3, 2010.

223 "I shall pick a name—gentle." RN, p. 540.

223 "Evenings at the White House." SA, p. 332.

224 dinner for Andrew Wyeth. Christopher Andreae, *Christian Science Monitor*, February 24, 1970.

224 "two historical firsts." www.presidency.ucsb.edu/ws/?pid=2876#axzz2gqybutw2.

224 "a non-political, non-prejudiced person." Judy Klemesrud, "Peggy Lee Is Back on Top—Is That All There Is?" *NYT*, April 26, 1970.

224 entertained more than forty-five thousand people. JNE, p. 428.

225 "the social scene." "Washington Society Isn't Exactly Swinging," *NYT Magazine*, March 8, 1970.

Chapter 15: "We Had Held Our Own"

226 The most helpful sources for this chapter were: RN, pp. 355–454; JNE, pp. 377–422; CA, pp. 166–89; WW, pp. 383–90; MB, pp. 103–20; HRH, pp. 23–159; GT, pp. 179–88; LD, pp. 127–40.

226 "This is a time the program." Nixon to John Ehrlichman, [February 5, 1969], WHSF, SMOF, PPF, Box 1, "Memos-February 1969," RMN, NPL.

227 "Mrs. Nixon is off to an excellent start." Nixon to John Ehrlichman, [February 4, 1969], WHSF, SMOF, PPF, Box 1, "Memos-February 1969," RMN, NPL.

227 hired Gerry van der Heuvel. Herbert Klein, *Making It Perfectly Clear*, hardcover, New York: Doubleday, 1980, pp. 385–86.

227 she chose Lucy Winchester. CSO, p. 30.

227 "age-old tug-of-war." CSO, p. 16.

228 "absolutely hated the large." HRH, p. 73; GT, p. 185.

228 Service was "way too slow." H. R. Haldeman to Lucy Winchester, [July 17, 1969], WHSF, SMOF, H. R. Haldeman, Box 51, "Memos/Lucy Winchester (July 1969)," NPL.

228 "to make sure that none." H. R. Haldeman to Lucy Winchester, [September 19, 1969], WHSF, SMOF, H. R. Haldeman, Box 52, "Memos/Lucy Winchester (September 1969)," NPL.

228 "as far from our table" WHSF, SMOF, PPF, Box 2, "Memos April 1970," RMN, NPL.

228 "I know it is none of my business." H. R. Haldeman to Lucy Winchester, [September 30, 1969], WHSF, SMOF, H. R. Haldeman, Box 52, "Memos/Lucy Winchester (September 1969)," NPL.

228 "PN thing is a real problem." Haldeman Notes, [August 8, 1969], WHSF, SMOF, H. R. Haldeman, Box 40, "H Notes July-Dec '69 [July–Sept. 1969] Part 1," NPL; GT, p. 186.

228 East Wing reporters were complaining. "Reporter Gerry var den Heuvel Donovan dies; ambassador's aide," *WP*, November 3, 2009.

229 "badly organized." *Newsweek*, May 27, 1969, p. 85; "Pat Nixon: The Image," *WP*, June 3, 1969; GT, p. 186.

229 "determined to run." HRH, p. 107.

229 "Mrs. Nixon would initiate." CSO, p. 12.

229 Pat "bristled." JE, pp. 57–58.

230 plan for reorganizing the East Wing. CSO, pp. 3–4.

230 East Wing staff was enlarged. GT, p. 187.

230 coordinated with Dwight Chapin. Connie Stuart exit interview, March 15, 1973, pp. 5–8.

230 "rolled her eyes." Interview with Lucy Winchester.

231 "If you ignore." CSO, p. 32.

231 "What have I done wrong?" CSO, pp. 46–47.

231 To address complaints. CSO, p. 9.

231 "before it became a husband and wife issue." CSO, p. 12.

231 "volumes of memos." "Social Entertaining" from Constance Stuart to Bob Haldeman, [November 3, 1969], WHSF, SMOF, H. R. Haldeman, Box 54. "Memos/Connie Stuart (November 1969)," NPL.

232 On February 18, 1969. Eugenia Sheppard, "Nixon Talk a Surprise Item on Pat's Luncheon Menu," *LAT*, February 21, 1969.

232 "to reach beyond government." www.bartleby.com/124/pres58.html.

232 "The Government has taken over." *UNWR*, August 2, 1971, p. 54.

232 "national recruitment program." National First Ladies Library online at www.firstladies.org/biographies/firstladies.aspx?biography=38.

233 allowed her to complement. MB, p. 109.

233 "Vest Pockets of Volunteerism." JNE, p. 402; "Boosting Volunteerism,"

Time, June 22, 1969; "Traveling with Pat Nixon—A Different Type of Tour," *UNWR*, June 30, 1969.

233 "violence and destruction." Marie Smith, "Applause for Pat," *WP*, July 11, 1969.

233 "warm as always." Nan Robertson, "Pat: The Lady Unbends a Little," *NYT*, June 22, 1969.

233 sent letters of "commendation." National First Ladies Library online at www.firstladies.org/biographies/firstladies.aspx?biography=38

234 "the so-called women's pages." Herb Klein, *Making It Perfectly Clear*, hardcover, New York: Doubleday, 1980, p. 386.

234 "Mrs. Nixon's Journey." ND, pp. 161–62.

234 made a last-minute appeal. "A Press for Pat," *WP*, July 22, 1969.

234 Four days later, when the Nixons embarked. MFF-552, August 1969, "Main Motion Film File"; NBC special, "Mrs. Nixon's Journey," with Nancy Dickerson, NPL.

234 Pat and her daughters had watched. Tricia Nixon's Tour of the White House on *60 Minutes*, May 26, 1970.

235 "Because of what you have done." RN, p. 429.

235 official state dinner, at the Century Plaza Hotel. blog.nixonfoundation .org/2012/08/8-13-1969-honoring-the-astronauts/.

235 highlight of the Nixons' first White House year. MFF-552, August 1969, "Main Motion Film File"; NBC special, "Mrs. Nixon's Journey," with Nancy Dickerson, NPL.

235 first time a president and his wife traveled in a war zone. JNE, pp. 408–10.

236 "a moment of fear going into the battle zone." CA, p. 171.

236 "I came to see the boys." MFF-552, August 1969, "Main Motion Film File"; NBC special, "Mrs. Nixon's Journey," with Nancy Dickerson, NPL.

236 took down the wounded soldiers' names. MFF-552, August 1969, "Main Motion Film File"; NBC special, "Mrs. Nixon's Journey," with Nancy Dickerson, NPL.

236 "droned on." ND, p. 168.

237 "often portrayed as a disciplined." MFF-552, August 1969, "Main Motion Film File"; NBC special, "Mrs. Nixon's Journey," with Nancy Dickerson, NPL.

237 "kept pounding the table." ND, pp. 168–69.

238 "contemporary woman." "The Power of a Woman," September 1969, p. 93; Lisa Burns, *First Ladies and the Fourth Estate: Press Framing of Presidential Wives*, hardcover, DeKalb: Northern Illinois University Press, 2008, pp. 108–12.

238 "a dutiful wife in the old-time sense." Lisa Burns, *First Ladies and the Fourth Estate: Press Framing of Presidential Wives*, p. 111.

239 "She speaks in platitudes." Marie Smith, *WP*, September 5, 1969; SA, p. 318.

239 "that almost tragic epitome." Leonore Hershey, "Compassion Power," *LHJ*, September 1969, p. 88; GT, p. 182.

239 Gallup polling found. Harry S. Dent to RN, [July 9, 1969], WHSF, SMOF, POF, Box 2, "July 1969," RMN, NPL.

239 Richard Nixon enjoyed a 56 percent. Charles Stuart to John Ehrlichman, [September 2, 1969, p. 2], WHSF, SMOF, John D. Ehrlichman, Box 17, "East Wing, 1969," NPL.

240 Charles Stuart wrote a twenty-four-page memo. Charles Stuart to John Ehrlichman, [September 3], WHSF, SMOF, John D. Ehrlichman, Box 17, "East Wing, 1969," NPL.

240 "ostensible lack of impact." Nan Robertson, "A Starring Role is Not for Mrs. Nixon," *NYT*, January 26, 1970.

241 "I know it is hard to get the press." WHSF SMOF, PPF, Box 2, "Memos—Jan 1970," RMN, NPL.

241 "a tenseness in the air." JNE, p. 416.

241 "It will be necessary for me." Nixon to H. R. Haldeman, [November 24, 1969], WHSF, SMOF, PPF, Box 1, "Memos—November 1969," RMN, NPL.

242 "great silent majority." RN, p. 409; CB, pp. 637–38.

242 "to mobilize the silent majority." WHSF, SMOF, PPF, Box 1, "Memos—December 1969," RMN, NPL.

242 "We had held our own." RN, p. 434.

Chapter 16: A Private Marriage in the Public Spotlight

243 "a long, dark night of the American spirit." www.presidency.ucsb.edu/ws/?pid=3110#axzz2gqybutw2.

244 visited college volunteer programs. Louise Hutchinson, "Pat Nixon Trip Found to Be Fascinating," *CT*, March 8, 1970; Isabelle Shelton, "Most Students Are Idealists, Mrs. Nixon Found on 5-State Tour," *WP*, [March 8, 1970], WHCF, SMOF, FLPO, Series II: Events, Sub-Series A: Trip Files, Box 77, "Tour 3/2/70-3/6/70," NPL. See also Linda Reiniger, "Mrs. Nixon Warms to College Student," *St. Louis Dispatch*, [March 8, 1970], WHCF, SMOF, FLPO, Series II: Events, Sub-Series A: Trip Files, Box 77, "College Trip: Point Lookout & Springfield, Missouri," NPL.

244 "kill for peace." Barbara Browne, "Mrs. Nixon Ignores Chanting Pro-
testers," *Rocky Mountain News*, March 5, 1970.

244 "She wanted to listen." Quoted in CA, p. 182.

244 "all idealists." "Pat Nixon Trip Found to Be Fascinating," *CT*, March 8,
1970.

245 "smoothly oiled professionalism." Kandy Stroud, "The Hard Sell and
Mrs. Nixon," *Women's Wear Daily*, March 14, 1970.

245 "her ability to face." Marie Smith, "Mrs. Nixon's Trip," *WP*, March 7,
1970; MB, p. 111; quoted in JNE, pp. 424–25.

245 "Whatever happened." "Signs of Life," *Time*, March 16, 1970.

245 *Mary Tyler Moore Show.* MS, p. 177.

246 "bums blowing up campuses." RN, p. 454.

247 "turn into bitter hatred." Nixon to H. R. Haldeman, [May 13,
1970], WHSF, SMOF, PPF, Box 2, "Memos—May 1970," RMN, NPL;
RL, pp. 392–94; RN, pp. 458–66.

247 "the great question." en.wikisource.org/wiki/Richard_Nixon%27s
_First_State_of_the-Union_Address.

247 "That S.O.B. will go." Tom Wicker, *One of Us: Richard Nixon and the
American Dream*, hardcover, New York: Random House, 1991, pp. 634–
35.

248 "the weirdest day so far." HRH, p. 163.

248 "play removed from reality." JNE, pp. 437–39: RL, pp. 392–94.

249 "urban underground of political terrorists." RN, pp. 469–71.

249 "Why do you keep." *Newsweek*, May 25, 1970.

249 "he was wrong." Unpublished Diaries of Harry R. Haldeman, March
3, 1970, p. 1, NPL.

249 "Fuck Julie and David Eisenhower." JNE, p. 290.

250 version of graduation. JNE, pp. 439–40.

250 "There are many who would." Judith Viorst, "Pat Nixon Is the Ulti-
mate Good Sport," *NYT Magazine*, September 13, 1970.

251 "Mort" Allin. MS, p. 233.

251 "hints of strain." Vera Glasser and Malvina Stephenson, "Much Ado
About Nothing," from Knight Newspapers, Inc., WHCF, SMOF, FLPO
Series VII: Miscellaneous Files, Sub-Series B: Press Coverage, Box 128,
"Newspaper Articles—Nixon Family [2 of 2]," NPL.

251 "definitely on the undemonstrated side." Helen Thomas, "Pat Nixon
Says It's Lot of Fun," *Hartford Courant*, September 27, 1970.

251 "from time to time." Susan Porter Rose in SS, p. 37.

251 Secret Service agents wondered. Ronald Kessler, *Inside the White House*,
paperback, New York: Pocket Books, 1996, pp. 38–39.

252 "an emotional, chemical." President's Interview with 9 Press Ladies, [March 11, 1971], WHCF, SMOF, FLPO, Series I: Chronological Files, Box 9, "President's Interview with 9 Press Ladies 3/11/71," NPL.

252 "the President should show." Roger Ailes to H. R. Haldeman, "White House Television," Item Four, May 4, 1970, quoted in CSO, August 15, 1988, pp. 43–44.

252 "he was [being] a rather typical male." Constance Stuart OH, RNPL, August 15, 1988, pp. 44–45.

252 "Frankly, I saw them." Constance Stuart OH, RNPL, August 15, 1988, pp. 44–45.

252 Dwight Chapin watched. Dwight Chapin interview, August 20, 2012.

253 "had that sort of dingy." SS, p. 36.

253 "the president didn't speak to her much," and Bobby Baker, "she gave eighty and he gave twenty percent." SS, p. 36.

253 "this dance of unhappiness." Diane Sawyer, quoted in KM, p. 171.

253 "who compliments." Helen Thomas, "Pat Nixon Says It's Lot of Fun," *Hartford Courant*, September 27, 1970.

253 "He wrote her perfectly darling." EC, p. 224.

253 "I never picked up." Interview with Cynthia Milligan, January 2011.

254 with his family at Camp David. H.R. Haldeman in SS, p. 34.

254 Marje Acker, a secretary. Interview with Marje Acker.

254 "he worshiped Pat." Alexander Haig in SS, p. 37.

254 "geek who couldn't believe." Interview with Frank Gannon, May 19, 1972.

254 "She looked like a young model." JNE, p. 505.

254 "in a few years?" *NYT*, February 4, 1972.

254 "He's very dear personally." Frances Lewine, *Courier-Journal & Times*, Louisville, Kentucky, [January 24, 1971], WHCF, SMOF, FLPO, Series I: Chronological Files, Box 7, "Mrs. Nixon: Miscellaneous [1 of 4]," NPL.

254 "Yes. Completely." "Mrs. Nixon's Own Style," *Washington Star*, [September 25, 1972], WHCF, SMOF, FLPO, Series VII: Miscellaneous Files, Sub-Series B: Press Coverage, Box 128, "Newspaper Articles, Nixon's Family [1 of 2]," NPL.

254 "very vulnerable." CA, p. 173.

254 "Let Frank play." Frank Gannon interview, May 19, 1972.

255 "I know how close." Susan Porter Rose in SS, p. 37.

255 did not have grand arguments. Eugenia Sheppard, "Nixon Talk a Surprise Item on Pat's Luncheon Menu," *LAT*, February 21, 1969.

255 "a respected, but limited partner." WTP, p. 39.

255 "was never hesitant." Quoted in CA, p. 179.

255 "Big League." "Mrs. Nixon's Own Style," *Washington Star*, [September 25, 1972], WHCF, SMOF, FLPO, Series VII: Miscellaneous Files, Sub-Series B: Press Coverage, Box 128, "Newspaper Articles, Nixon's Family [1 of 2]," NPL.

255 "her criticisms." Quoted in CA, p. 179.

256 "troop withdrawals." President's Interview with 9 Press Ladies, [March 11, 1971], WHCF, SMOF, FLPO, Series I: Chronological Files, Box 9, "President's Interview with 9 Press Ladies 3/11/71," NPL.

256 "I don't think anything." Winzola McLendon at MC: WHCF, SMOF, FLPO, Series III: Subject Files, Box 109, MC: "The Nixons Nobody Knows, Public Marriage"; "Winzola McLendon [1 of 2]," MC, May 1971; RR, p. 313.

258 "He is so thoughtful." Allen Drury, *Courage and Hesitation: Notes and Photographs of the Nixon Administration,* hardcover, New York: Doubleday, 1971, pp. 226–35; RR, pp. 311–12; CB, pp. 719–20.

258 thirtieth wedding anniversary. *WP,* June 21, 1970; *LAT,* June 2, 1970.

258 Pat was surprised when Dick mentioned. "Pat Is Surprised but It's Ole! with Her," *LAT,* July 22, 1970.

259 "I just wish." CA, p. 185.

259 A tour by Pat. JNE, pp. 440–43; MB, pp. 120–21; LD, p. 156; CA, pp. 185–86.

259 "no possibility of unfavorable reaction." Pat Buchanan talking points so she wouldn't have to "wing it." Haldeman Notes, [June 23, p. 4], WHSF, SMOF, H. R. Haldeman, Box 41, "H Notes—April–June '70 [May 6–June 30, 1970] Part II," NPL.

260 "Sometimes Mrs. Nixon grabbed." UPI reports quoted in press summary, "The First Lady's Trip to Peru, July 7, 1970," WHCF, SMOF, FLPO Series II: Events, Subseries A: Trip Files, Box 80, "Peru: Connie's Files on Peru Trip [1 of 3]," NPL.

260 "The greatest need." Pat Nixon to Mrs. Charles Taft, [July 9, 1970], Constance Stuart to First Lady, [July 13, 1970], WHCF, SMOF, FPLO Series II: Events, Subseries A: Trip Files, Box 80, "Peru-Connie's Files on Peru Trip [1 of 3]," NPL.

260 "leadership, imagination, and energy." Press reports quoted in "The First Lady's Trip to Peru, July 7, 1970," WHCF, SMOF, Constance Stuart, memo from Constance Stuart to First Lady, Box 80, FLPO, July 13, 1970.

261 "spirit of détente and cooperation." Constance Stuart to H. R. Haldeman, August 11, 1970, quoted in HD, pp. 167–70.

262 "unfailingly courteous to each other." WTP, p. 64.

262 created a floor plan. J. F. Ter Horst and Ralph Albertazzie, *Flying White House: The Story of Air Force One,* hardcover, New York: Coward, McCann & Geoghegan, 1979, p. 250; Ronald Kessler, *Inside the White House: The Hidden Lives of the Modern Presidents and the Secrets of the World's Most Powerful Institution,* pp. 56–57; HDTF, p. 173; MB, p. 140.

262 She canceled Haldeman's orders. CA, pp. 184–85.

263 "That is just plain hokey." Interviews with Lucy Winchester Breathitt.

263 When Haldeman eliminated Herb Klein's job. CA, p. 185.

263 "Pat's conduit for complaints." WTP, pp. 46–48.

264 "leave at once." H. R. Haldeman to John Ehrlichman, [January 21, 1982], "1980–1985," DC, NPL.

264 "blasted me and P." HHD, pp. 247–48.

265 to light the White House at night. JNE, pp. 304–5.

265 Pat called Haldeman at home. HHD, pp. 263–64.

Chapter 17: Love in the White House

266 In February 1971. CA, pp. 189–90; LD, pp. 151–52; JNE, pp. 309–10; RN, pp. 502–3.

268 "Every family should put." LD, p. 152.

268 John spilled his milk on the table. Caroline Kennedy video comments at the PCE.

268 "live in a dream world." RN, p. 503.

268 "You were so kind." Letter found in Opinion Center, JFK, Jr., His Legacy, Handsome Lost: Manners Live. www.opinioncenter.com/JFK/JFKjr.ntm.

268 working clandestinely to undermine. MS, p. 251.

269 "an opera singer's nightmare." WHCF, SMOF, FLPO, Series II: Events, Sub-Series E: Evenings at the White House, Box 97, "2/2/71 Beverly Sills, Evening at the White House," NPL.

269 "make the Johnson years almost barbaric." Bruce Oudes, *From the President: Richard Nixon's Secret Files,* hardcover, New York: HarperCollins, 1989, p. 266.

269 "kind of like dealing with politicians." Constance Stuart to H. R. Haldeman, Haldeman Notes, [November 15, 1971], WHSF, SMOF, H. R. Haldeman, Box 44, "H Notes October–December 1971 Part II," NPL.

269 visits from British royalty. WHCF, SMOF, FLPO, Series II: Events, Sub-Series D: Dinner Files, Box 91, "Prince Philip, Duke of Edinburgh Dinner 11/4/69"; WHCF, SMOF, FLPO, Series II: Events, Sub-Series D: Dinner Files, Box 91, "4/14/70 Dinner for the Duke and Duchess

of Windsor [2 of 2]"; WHCF, SMOF, FLPO, Series V: Press Releases, "Press Releases-1970-from July [3 of 4]"; WHCF, SMOF, FLPO, Series I: Chronological Files, Box 6, "11/5/70 Lord Mountbatten Stag dinner," NPL.

270 "a new sparkle added." Marie Smith, *WP,* January 18, 1970.

270 "Do you think there will." Transcript of Barbara Walters interview with Nixon, WHCF, SMOF, FLPO, Series I: Chronological Files, Box 9, "President's Interview with Barbara Walters 3/15/71," NPL.

270 Dennis Day performed. HTD, p. 162.

270 "I understand I am supposed." Charlotte Curtis, "Nixon Announces Patricia's Engagement," *NYT,* March 17, 1971.

270 Edward Ridley Finch Cox. en.wikipedia.org/wiki/Edward_F._Cox.

270 He and his fiancée. JNE, pp. 472–73; MB, p. 118; LD, pp. 14–143.

271 "That 'Terrible-tempered Tricia.'" Kandy Stroud, *Detroit News,* April 1, 1971, reprinted from *Women's Wear Daily.*

271 Grace Slick of the rock group. MS, p. 225.

271 "largest, costliest public relations staff." Harriet Van Horne, "Pat Nixon's Image," *San Francisco Chronicle & Examiner,* [March 28, 1971], WHCF, SMOF, FLPO, Series I: Chronological Files, Box 7, "Mrs. Nixon: Miscellaneous [1 of 4]," NPL.

272 "ride herd." HH, p. 312.

272 "All of us were beautifully." RN, p. 508.

272 "a little sad." MFF-552, June 12, 1971, "Main Motion Film File"; "The Honor of Your Presence: A White House Wedding," ABC, June 12, 1971.

272 "It's a little difficult." *LAT,* June 22, 1971.

272 "Absolutely venomous." "Woman's World," *Evening Star,* Washington, [July 31, 1970], WHCF, SMOF, FLPO, Series VII: Miscellaneous Files, Sub-Series B: Press Coverage, Box 127, "Newspaper Articles— Washington Star," NPL.

272 "No," she answered. LD, p. 143.

272 "I was married twenty years." HTD, p. 181.

273 "She's determined to have a Rose Garden wedding." MFF-552; June 12, 1971; "Main Motion Film File"; "The Honor of Your Presence: A White House Wedding," ABC, June 12, 1971; RN, p. 504.

273 "limp Viet Cong flags." *NYT,* June 22, 1971.

274 "most precious." WHCF, SMOF, FLPO, Series III: Subject Files, Box 116, "Tricia's Wedding, 6/12/71," NPL.

274 "happier than I have ever seen them before." HTD, p. 182.

274 "standing pretty straight." HH, p. 363.

274 "akin to American royalty." *Life,* June 18, 1971.

274 "It may be the closest thing." GT, p. 193.

275 an infuriated Nixon ordered. Nixon to H. R. Haldeman, [June 15, 1971], WHSF, SMOF, PPF, Box 3, "Memo re: New York Times-6/15/71," RMN, NPL.

275 "good sport." Nixon to H. R. Haldeman, [June 2, 1971], WHSF, SMOF, PPF, Box 3, "Memos—June 1970," RMN, NPL.

276 "where the people are." http://hnn.us/node/115611.

276 "Nixon Speaks with a Forked Tongue." Marion Christy, *BG*, August 18, 1971.

276 "we're such good friends." CA, pp. 179–80; MMF-529: "Main Motion Film File"; "A Visit With the First Lady at San Clemente," includes Virginia Sherwood interview and parts of ABC "Legacy of the Parks" Special, NPL.

277 "a paper doll." Judith Viorst, "Pat Nixon Is the Ultimate Good Sport," *NYT Magazine*, September 13, 1970, p. SM13.

277 "Pat a Political Bonus for Nixon." *CT*, September 13, 1972.

277 "I think it will be great." "Pat Wants Woman on High Court," *BG*, October 20, 1971.

278 "Boy is she mad." HHD, p. 447.

278 "We tried to do the best we could, Pat." JNE, p. 487.

278 "I'm liberated." "Pat Nixon Says She's Liberated," *LAT*, October 28, 1971.

279 To prepare for the trip. WHCF, SMOF, FLPO, Series VII: Miscellaneous Files, Sub-Series B: Press Coverage, Box 127, "Newspaper Articles-Christian Science Monitor," NPL.

279 During her eight-day trip. CA, pp. 195–98; JNE, pp. 499–502; MB, pp. 122–24, 156–58; "Time for Celebration," video of Mrs. Nixon's trip to Liberia, Ghana, and the Ivory Coast.

279 "courage, strength of character, and fortitude of spirit." MB, p. 123.

279 presented her with Liberia's top honor. CA, p. 196.

279 "Being First Lady." FLPO, Series VII: Miscellaneous Files, Sub-Series B: Press Coverage, Box 127, "Newspaper Articles-LA Herald Examiner."

279 "I'm taking orders." "A Medal for Mme Nixon," *NYT*, January 9, 1972; *Time.* January 17, 1970.

279 "don't have so much fun." "A Medal for Mrs. Nixon," *NYT*, January 9, 1972.

280 "I want to cash in on my diary." "The First Lady of the Land at 60," *NYT*, March 16, 1972.

280 "Pat a Hit as Liberian Pres. Sworn In." Mort Allin to Charles Colson, [January 2, 1972–January 9, 1972], WHSF, SMOF, PPF, Box 5, "Africa—Mrs. Nixon," RMN, NPL.

432 / Notes to pages 280–286

280 "The TV coverage." RN to PN, WHSF, SMOF, PPF, Box 5, "Africa—Mrs. Nixon," RMN, NPL. Also JNE, p. 500; GT, p. 195.

280 "Pat had press conferences." Nixon's diary, quoted in JNE, p. 501.

280 "They loved her in Monrovia." "A Medal for Mrs. Nixon," *NYT*, January 9, 1972, p. E3; MB, p. 124.

280 "Mrs. Nixon has broken through." Charles Colson to RN, [January 19, 1972, pp. 1–2],WHSF, SMOF, H. R. Haldeman, Box 91, "Charles Colson, January 1972," NPL.

281 "Thought you would be amused." JNE, p. 505.

281 Pat was "very put out." CA, p. 197, and his reference.

281 interview with Barbara Walters. Transcript of January 13, 1972, interview, WHCF, SMOF, FLPO, Series I: Chronological Files, Box 7, "Mrs. Nixon—*Today* Show Interview," NPL.

282 they were "vicious." White House tapes 018-0709 071/072, January 11, 1972; JNE, pp. 503–4.

282 set up a White House Television Office. MS, p. 229.

282 She wasted no time. Constance Stuart to the Staff Secretary, [March 8, 1971], WHSF, SMOF, H. R. Haldeman, Box 76, "Constance Stuart-March, 1971," NPL.

Chapter 18: The Zenith

283 historic trips to China. RN, pp. 554–80, 609–21; JNE, pp. 506–11; MB, pp. 124–28, 515–21; LD, pp. 158–60; CA, pp. 198–201; MM, pp. 1–329.

283 "bombing human beings." Dorothy McCardle, "Singer's War Protest Startles Nixon Dinner," *WP*, January 29, 1972, p. A1; blog.wmfu.org /free-form/2010/02/the-richard-nixon-ray-coniff-incident.html.

284 "Throw her out." Dorothy McCardle, "Singer's War Protest Startles Nixon Dinner," *WP*, January 29, 1972.

284 Pat was angry. HHD, p. 490.

284 "angry isolation." Richard Nixon, "Asia after Vietnam," *Foreign Affairs* vol. 46, no.1, October 1967.

285 "I'm putting my name on the sign-up list." *CT*, August 14, 1971.

285 would go to Ireland. "Pat Nixon: Not Going to China," *WP*, August 5, 1971.

285 "The P's [president's] now concluded." unpublished entry in Diaries of Harry R. Haldeman, October 26, 1971, p.1, RNL.

285 "people contact is more important." HHD, p. 443.

285 "a journey for peace." CB, p. 777.

286 "sick to her stomach." JNE, p. 506.

286 "Of course I wouldn't." GT, p. 196.

286 Speechwriter Pat Buchanan. MM, p. 269.

286 Nixon spent over forty hours. CB, p. 778.

286 "unprecedented opportunity." Briefing paper, "Notes for Mrs. Nixon," 1972. WHCF, SMOF, Susan Porter, Box 43, "Visit of Richard Nixon President of the United States to the People's Republic of China February 1972 [1 of 2]," NPL. Quoted in MB, p. 125.

286 "That handshake." RN, p. 560.

287 "came in vast silence." Hugh Sidey, "A President Wrapped In an Enigma," *Life*, March 3, 1972.

287 Pat Nixon made her own bold statement. See www.blog.nixonfoundation .org/2012/02/pat-nixons-part-in-the-week-that-changed-the-world.

287 brought Mao a friendship gift. In David Whitney's *The Week That Changed The World*. WHCF, SMOF, FLPO, Series VII: Miscellaneous Files, Sub-Series C: Publications, Box 130, "Misc. Files-Publications *The Week That Changed The World*," NPL.

288 Echoing Lincoln's Gettysburg speech. CB, pp. 784–85.

288 Chinese were wary of authority. Colonel John Brennan's comments at the "First Lady Pat Nixon: Ambassador of Goodwill" Legacy Forum, held at the National Archives, April 5, 2012.

288 "Yes, I am acquainted with the philosophy." HTD, p. 190; CA, p. 198.

288 "I think it's sort of rude to watch." *Time*, March 6, 1972, p. 15.

289 "Male chauvinist[s]." HTD, p. 142; MM, p. 271.

289 "Ah, the elephant." *Time*, March 6, 1972, pp. 14–15; MB, p. 126.

289 thought they would fit "Ricardo." Colonel John Brennan's comments at the "First Lady Pat Nixon: Ambassador of Goodwill" Legacy Forum, held at the National Archives, April 5, 2012.

289 Barbara Walters, who tried. Colonel John Brennan's comments at the "First Lady Pat Nixon: Ambassador of Goodwill" Legacy Forum, held at the National Archives, April 5, 2012.

289 CBS's Walter Cronkite and ABC's Harry Reasoner. *Life*, March 3, 1972.

289 "Pat Nixon was the only show in town." *Guardian*, March 7, 1972.

289 "prompting from their mothers." *NYT*, February 26, 1972.

289 "took revolutionary patience." Interview with Bernard Kalb.

290 "so graceful winding." Pat's comments, [October 1972], WHCF, SMOF, Gwendolyn King, Box 7, "Comments: On Being First Lady," NPL.

290 "on the enduring symbol." GT, p. 196.

290 "We do not want walls." *WP*, February 24, 1972.

290 "a charmer." HTD, p. 190.

290 "Aren't they cute?" JNE, p. 510.

291 Shanghai Communiqué. RN, pp. 576–77.

291 "the week that changed the world." RN, p. 580.

291 "A smiling dragon." *NYT*, February 25, 1972.

291 "seems to have taken a second look." Kandy Stroud, "Pat Nixon," *Women's Wear Daily*, [March 1, 1972], WHCF, SMOF, FLPO, Series VII: Miscellaneous Files, Sub-Series B: Press Coverage, Box 127, "Newspaper Articles—Women's Wear Daily," NPL.

292 "the important work." JNE, pp. 508–9.

292 "a vital role." CA, p. 201.

292 "enormous price the Chinese people have paid." Pat Buchanan to Mrs. Nixon, WHSF, SMOF, John Scali, Box 2, "China follow-up," NPL.

292 prime-time television special. John Scali to H. R. Haldeman, [March 28, 1972]; John Scali to Steve Bull, [March 28 and March 29, 1972], WHSF, SMOF, John Scali, Box 2, "China follow-up," NPL. The Nixons' trips to China and Russia, RN, pp. 554–80, 609–21; JNE, pp. 506–11; MB, pp. 124–28, 515–21; LD, pp. 158–60; CA, pp. 198–201.

292 Dick escalated efforts to plant. Nixon to H. R. Haldeman, [March 13, 1972], WHSF, SMOF, PPF, Box 3, "Memos March 1972," RMN, NPL.

293 ability to act properly and to make acute observations. "The Nixon /Gannon Interviews," May 27, 1983, day 6, tape 2, 00:58; 27 and 00:20:39, accessed July 28, 2012, www.libs.edu/media/collections /nixon/nixonday6.html; also quoted in MB, p. 121.

293 to meet with Irina Dobrynin. CA, p. 200; JNE, pp. 512–13; RN, p. 589.

293 Pat showed "great skill and subtlety." RN, p. 589.

294 Pat asked to sit in. RN, p. 616.

294 "to see the two flags." Pat's comments, [October 1972], WHCF, SMOF, Gwendolyn King, Box 7, "Comments: On Being First Lady," NPL.

294 "I haven't seen that guy." "First Lady Tours While Nixon Works," *WP*, May 25, 1972.

294 "Any first lady who can execute." WHCF, SMOF, FLPO, Series VII: Miscellaneous Files, Sub-Series B: Press Coverage, Box 127, "Newspaper Articles—LA Herald Examiner," NPL.

295 When Pat accompanied. Robert Sample, Jr., "Mrs. Nixon Tours with Soviet Wives," *NYT*, May 24, 1972.

295 Mrs. Nixon and Mrs. Brezhnev linked arms. CA, p. 200.

295 "especially effective with the swing category" voters. HHD, p. 568.

295 Pat evaded her minders. MB, p. 127.

295 Nixon glanced at. RN, pp. 525–643.

297 "I really don't think so." *BG*, September 29, 1972.

297 "We don't discuss it." "The Other Campaigners," *Time*, October 9, 1972.

298 knew that "nailing" McGovern. Nixon to H. R. Haldeman and Colson, WHSF, SMOF, PPF, Box 3, "Memos—June 1972," RMN, NPL.

298 On August 8, Pat surprised. Vera Glaser, "In a Tough Job, She's Grown Accustomed to the Pace," *Herald Washington Bureau*, WHCF, SMOF, FLPO, Series VII: Miscellaneous Files, Sub-Series B: Press Coverage, Box 27, "Mrs. Nixon Press Coffee 8/8/72 [1 of 2]," NPL.

298 "Never before in the history." "The Other Campaigners," *Time*, October 9, 1972.

299 "should have been in Hanoi." JNE, pp. 527–28.

299 "made a big thing." HRH, p. 601.

299 Nixon told Tricia and Rose Mary. HHD, August 2, 1972, p. 595.

299 "threw up her hands." "Pat Gets a Tribute; Nixon Heads for Show," *Times-Union*, [August 22, 1972], WHCF, SMOF, FLPO, Series VII: Miscellaneous Files, Sub-Series B: Press Coverage, Box 128, "Misc. Files Newspaper Articles: Mrs. Nixon-Republican National Convention [1 of 2]," NPL.

299 "Out of her desire to serve." MFF-391, "Main Motion Film File," NPL; GT, p. 197.

300 and received an ovation. CA, p. 20; JNE, pp. 516–21.

300 "It was a gesture uniquely hers." RN, p. 678.

300 "the most wonderful welcome." "Pat Gets a Tribute; Nixon Heads for Show," *Times-Union*, [August 22, 1972], WHCF, SMOF, FLPO, Series VII: Miscellaneous Files, Sub-Series B: Press Coverage, Box 128, "Misc. Files Newspaper Articles: Mrs. Nixon-Republican National Convention [1 of 2]," NPL.

300 "To those who say." "Pat Nixon Wins Vote of Approval," *Richard New Leader*, August 25, 1972.

300 "No First Family." RN, p. 678.

300 Feminists were not pleased. Marianne Means from King Features Syndicate, "'Liberated' Women Admired," [January 7, 1973], WHCF, SMOF, FLPO, Series VII: Miscellaneous Files, Sub-Series B: Press Coverage, Box 127, "Newspaper Articles—Mrs. Nixon Most Admired Woman," NPL.

301 "This year there are more women." "Mrs. Nixon Lauds Her Husband for Appointing Women to Office," *NYT*, August 23, 1972.

301 "sometimes the day." *Newsweek*, September 4, 1972.

301 "Four more years!" RN, p. 678.

301 "the best campaigner." Nixon's 1972 acceptance speech, www.4president .org/speeches/nixon1972acceptance.htm.

302 Bob Dole and Edward Kennedy's comments: Interview with Ed Cox, January 7, 2013.

302 "In negotiation." http://www.4president.org/speeches/nixon1972-acceptance.htm.

302 "bring the White House." *Newsweek*, October 2, 1972.

303 "willing to die." "But where is the real Pat Nixon?" *BG*, September 29, 1972.

303 Dwight Chapin, who in turn. Dwight Chapin to William Codus and David Parker, [September 20, 1972], WHSF, SMOF, Dwight L. Chapin, Box 18, "Chronological-Dwight Chapin-Chron-Sept. '72 I [2 of 2]," NPL.

303 "I hate people to be pessimistic." Helen Thomas, "Mrs. Nixon Backs Viet Regime," *WP*, September 19, 1972; "Pat Nixon Backs Julie on Dying for S. Vietnam," *LAT*, September 19, 1972.

304 "will simply hypo." Nixon to H. R. Haldeman, [January 28, 1972], WHSF, SMOF, PPF, Box 3, "Memos—January 1972," RMN, NPL.

304 "best qualified to lead." Nixon to H. R. Haldeman, [June 6, 1972], WHSF, SMOF, PPF, Box 4, "Memos—June 1972," RMN, NPL.

304 "I think I made a mistake." JNE, pp. 530–32.

305 "make this great country what it can be." *Berkshire Eagle*, November 1, 1972. The event also covered in JNE, p. 533.

305 "was serene and natural." RN, p. 686.

305 had endorsed Nixon by a margin of 753 to 56. MS, p. 260.

305 He ultimately won. RN, pp. 715–17.

306 "knew that the road." RN, p. 687.

306 had been negotiating with. RN, pp. 717–58; JNE, pp. 537–39.

307 "Men of the Year." RR, p. 555.

307 "this utterly stylish butterfly." Diana McLellan, "Most Admired Woman," *Washington Star-News*. WHCF, SMOF, FLPO, Series VII: Miscellaneous Files, Sub-Series B: Press Coverage, Box 127, "Newspaper Articles—Mrs. Nixon Most Admired Woman."

307 in a Gallup poll in which half. WHCF, SMOF, FLPO, Series VII: Miscellaneous Files; Sub-Series B: Press Coverage, Box 126, "Magazine Articles, Ladies' Home Journal," NPL.

308 Pat Nixon was voted. Marianne Means from King Features Syndicate, "'Liberated' Women Admired," [January 7, 1973], WHCF, SMOF, FLPO, Series VII: Miscellaneous Files, Sub-Series B: Press Coverage, Box 127, "Newspaper Articles—Mrs. Nixon Most Admired Woman," NPL.

308 "What trait of character." Pat's comments, [October, 1972], WHCF, SMOF, Gwendolyn King, Box 7, "Comments: On Being First Lady," NPL.

Chapter 19: Falling Apart

309 Most helpful for this period are: JA, pp. 467–528; CA, pp. 206–20; GT, pp. 198–206; RN, pp. 741–1090; JNE, pp. 547–659; SA, pp. 52–445; MA, pp. 157–65; RR, pp. 556–609; WW, pp. 395–97; MS, pp. 269–96; SK, pp. 1–619.

310 Pat and Dick held hands. CA, p. 206.

310 "We stand at the threshold." http://www.bartleby.com/124/pres59.html.

310 "death mask." AS, p. 443.

310 "these displays of affection." RN, p. 753.

311 "People Will Say We're in Love." AS, p. 443.

311 "overplay it." RN, p. 751.

311 paid an unexpected visit. WP, February 8, 1973; SA, p. 71.

311 "Helen, can you believe. HT, p. 263; SA, pp. 71–72.

312 "that we have probably done." Nixon to Ron Ziegler, [March 15, 1973], WHSF, SMOF, PPF, Box 4, "Memos—March 1973," RMN, NPL.

312 "I'm going to relax." Connie Stuart OH, pp. 18–19; Gwen King interview with Kati Marton, KM, p. 193; GT, pp. 198–99.

312 "Mrs. Nixon has more sense." Helen McCain Smith interview with Susan Porter Rose, May 2, 2013.

312 Smith fought with Ziegler. Helen Smith memo to Ron Ziegler, January 18, 1974, quoted in CA, p. 211.

313 "squeezed out." JNE, p. 550.

313 "He liked to tackle." JNE, p. 560.

314 White House dinner for the POWs. SA, pp. 149–52; RN, pp. 864–69; JNE, pp. 564–68.

315 press revelations in March and April. Keith W. Olson, "Watergate" chapter in *A Companion to Richard Nixon*, Melvin Small, ed., hardcover, Chichester: Wiley-Blackwell, 2011, pp. 481–84; RN p. 791.

316 "Mother's trying so hard." JNE, pp. 558–60.

316 "I want you to know." RN, pp. 845–46; JNE, p. 561; SA, pp. 132–33.

316 "like cutting off my arms." WTP, p. 357; http://www.bartleby.com/124 /pres59.html; CB, p. 893; H. R. Haldeman and Joseph DiMona, *The Ends of Power*, paperback, New York: Dell, 1978, p. 296.

317 "red-rimmed." WTP, p. 357.

317 "It's all over." RN, p. 848.

317 "done what I thought was necessary." SA, pp. 135–36; RN, pp. 849–51; JNE, pp. 562–63; JA, p. 490; CB, pp. 893–94.

317 Conversation with Reagan. www.abcnews.go.com/blogs/politics/2013 /08/bush-41-reagan-consoled-nixon-during-watergate-scandal/.

317 "I hope I don't wake up in the morning." JNE, p. 563.

318 "I'm not going to say." *NYT*, May 18, 1973.

318 "one of the greatest nights." SA, pp. 149–52; RN, pp. 864–69; JNE, pp. 564–68.

319 Further revelations emerged. In April 1974, the Internal Revenue Service would order him to pay $400,000 in back taxes for improper deductions. RN, p. 993; CB, p. 953; JNE, p. 406.

319 "could sense her tightly controlled anger." RN, p. 963.

319 Nixon and Brezhnev conducted. RN, pp. 875–87; JNE, pp. 569–71; SA, p. 452; CB, pp. 904–7; SA, pp. 173–77.

320 diagnosed with viral pneumonia. R. W. Apple, *NYT*, July 14, 1973.

320 "something you just don't do." EC, p. 217.

321 "deleted expletives" in his Texas drawl. "Watergate Wife," *People*, May 27, 1964, vol. 1, no. 13.

322 state dinner for Prime Minister Norman Kirk. RN, p. 963.

323 approval rating sank to 17 percent. Quoted in SA, p. 459.

323 "People have got to know." SA, p. 462; CB, p. 942.

323 "we must not allow." EC, p. 217; "Watergate Wife," *People*, May 27, 1964, vol. 1, no. 13; LD, p. 168.

324 Ed and Tricia were vigorously booed. AS, p. 463.

324 Julie and David held a press conference. WHCF, SMOF, FLPO, Series V: Press Releases, Box 122, "Press Release: 5/11/74. The White House Interview with Julie and David Eisenhower," NPL.

324 "I was starting to go." RN, pp. 961–62.

324 mistreated Ron Ziegler. JNE, pp. 599–600; SA, p. 455.

325 "eyes flashed." JNE, pp. 613–15; SA, p. 312.

325 "The truth sustains me." Baltimore, Maryland, *News American*, [April 16, 1974], WHCF, SMOF, FLPO, Series I: Chronological Files, Box 40, "Pat Nixon Showing Strain," NPL.

326 they ate together an average of. *Presidential Daily Diaries, 1969–1974*, www.nixon.library.gov/virtuallibrary/documents/dailydiary.php, NPL.

326 Dick could reminisce. SA, p. 312; JNE, pp. 610–11.

326 "herself a virtual recluse." "Watergate Wife," *People*, May 27, 1974, vol. 1, no. 13.

326 "What in the world." LD, p. 170.

327 "drumfire of Watergate." "Watergate Wife," *People*, May 27, 1974, vol. 1, no. 13.

327 "White House plan to demonstrate." GT, p. 202.

327 "a blank stare." Sara Fritz, "Mrs. Nixon Showing the Strains of Watergate," UPI, [April 21, 1974], WHCF, SMOF, FLPO, Series I: Chronological Files, Box 40, "4/21/74, Mrs. Nixon, Showing Strain

of Watergate," NPL; "Watergate Wife," *People*, May 27, 1974, vol. 1, no. 13; CA, p. 211, birthday cake; RN, p. 1023.

327 "a traveler from her husband's heart." Viewed videotapes of the event, index No 1211-180-74 (Roll 4/5), March 16, 1974, NPL.

328 "winced" when Nixon "ignored," Helen McCain Smith, "Pat Nixon's Final Days in the White House," *GH*, July 1976.

328 "Those present never forgot." KM, p. 195.

328 the misinterpretations of the incident. SA, p. 314.

328 "From the moment." *Time*, June 24, 1974, p. 12.

328 "a triumphal pageant." *Time*, June 24, 1974, p. 14.

329 how to spot an American flag. RN, p. 1034.

329 "All the life seems." Interview with Helen Thomas.

329 "Why should he?" CA, p. 214.

329 "take this constitutionally down to the wire." Julie and David's press conference, WHCF, SMOF, FLPO, Series V: Press Releases, Box 122, "Press Release: 5/11/74. The White House Interview with Julie and David Eisenhower," NPL.

330 "how careful she wanted to be." Gwendolyn King OH, p. 21, May 24, 1988, NPL.

330 Maxine Cheshire. Maxine Cheshire, "Kings, Princes, Foreign States, Jewels, and the 'Gifts Unit,'" *WP*, May 14, 1974, p. C1; Donnie Radcliffe, "A Story 'For the Birds,'" *WP*, May 16, 1974; CA, p. 213; MB, p. 161.

330 "It's for the birds." RN, p. 963.

330 Pat significantly curtailed. Mrs. Nixon's Activities, 1974, Lucy Winchester, WHCF, SMOF, FLPO, Series VII: Miscellaneous Files, Sub-Series A: Background Information, Box 123, "Misc. Files-Background Information-Activities for Mrs. Nixon and Girls [1969–1974] (1 of 4)," NPL.

331 "But, God." RN, p. 1053.

331 "is a shoulder to everyone." CA, p. 215.

331 "The next thing I know." JNE, pp. 636–39; SA, pp. 400–401.

331 Nixon's drinking. See a discussion of the evidence in MB, pp. 172–73; see also SA, p. 313 and pp. 494–95.

332 "our drunken friend." In Walter Isaacson, *Kissinger: A Biography*. Paperback, New York: Simon and Schuster, 2005.

332 "I have the highest regard." Email communication from Dr. Kissinger through press officer Jessica Le Porin, September 20, 2013.

332 "Even after one." Communications with Dwight Chapin, August 23, 2013.

332 "lousy drinker." Conversation with Steve Bull, September 15, 2013.

332 "she [Pat] kept to a very busy schedule." Helen McCain Smith and Elizabeth Pope Frank, "Ordeal! Pat's Final Days in the White House," GH, July 1976, pp. 127–33.

332 "[s]aw her every day." Interview with Lucy Winchester.

332 "Stay the hell out of this." SK, p. 67.

333 "Dick has done so much." CA, p. 215.

333 "more worn and fragile." JNE, pp. 636–39; SA, pp. 400–401.

333 "They're out to get us." LD, p. 178; CA, p. 215.

333 She busied herself planning. LD, p. 178.

333 "But why?" JNE, pp. 639–40.

334 "It's fight or flight by Monday night." RN, p. 1062.

334 "Now we must all be as stoical." Quoted in KM, p. 196.

334 outing on the presidential yacht. RN, pp. 1063–64; SA, pp. 415–16; JNE, pp. 644–45; CB, p. 975.

334 "emphatically against resigning." RN, pp. 1059–61; SA, pp. 410–11; JNE, pp. 641–44.

334 "the unspoken things." Interview with Frank Gannon.

335 "We're all very proud of you." JNE, p. 424.

335 "Well, I screwed it up." Quoted in GT, p. 205.

335 "Ollie, we're always glad." KM, p. 196.

335 "his head on his arms." JA, pp. 517–25.

335 "Therefore I shall resign." www.pbs.org/newshour/character/links/nixon_speech.html.

336 "Jail to the Chief." RN, pp. 1084–85.

336 "Oh, Dick, you can't have it televised." JNE, pp. 653–56; RN, pp. 1087–89; CA, p. 217.

336 After giving a mawkish tribute. www.cnn.com/ALLPOLITICS/1997/gen/resources/watergate/nixon.farewell.html; RN, p. 1089; SA, pp. 440–46; CB, pp. 984–86; JA, pp. 522–25.

337 "I wasn't about to mention." "The Nixon/Gannon Interviews," June 10, 1983, tape 3, 00:57:42; accessed October 5, 2013. www.libs.edu/media/collections/nixon/nixonday7/html.

337 "My heavens." CA, p. 218.

338 "Now she would not receive." RN, p. 1086.

338 "a strength of character." RN, p. 1023.

338 "Eight months of pure hell and agony." H. R. Haldeman and Joseph DiMona, *The Ends of Power*, paperback, New York: Dell Publishing, 1978, p. 310.

338 "It's so sad." RN, p. 1090.

Chapter 20: Renewal in Exile

341 Helpful resources for this chapter were: RA, pp. 1–215; JNE, pp. 431–57; SA, vol. III, pp. 446–530; MB, pp. 166–79; LC, pp. 198–209.

341 On board the plane. RA, pp. 19–22; SA, pp. 446–47.

341 "Our long national nightmare." http://www.historyplace.com/speeches/ford-sworn.htm.

342 "God Bless America." RA, p. 22.

342 "having completed one task." SA, p. 446; RA, p. 23.

342 "It is good to be back." ITA, p. 13.

342 four hundred floral arrangements. LD, p. 199.

342 Pat gave herself a measure. RA, pp. 24–25.

343 "What do you expect." Julie Nixon Eisenhower to Lester David, LD, p. 200.

343 "sadness brought by." Jack Brennan, *NYT*, October 15, 1974; SA, p. 452.

343 "hurt beyond words." Author Earl Mazo interview with Lester David, LD, p. 200.

343 "that he was being forsaken by God." Nixon to Conrad Black, 1992, CB, p. 992.

343 Gallup poll found how deep. SA, p. 453.

343 "represented the epitome of evil itself." ITA, p. 15.

343 Pat bitterly resented. Helen McCain Smith, "Pat Nixon's final days in the White House—the truth behind those stories," *GH*, July, 1976, p. 131.

343 provenance of $580,000 of jewels. Maxine Cheshire, "Kin insured Pat Nixon gems," *CT*, September 23, 1974.

344 Watergate cover-up trial: Geoffrey Shepard has uncovered new information suggesting prosecutorial and judicial misconduct that suggests the defendants did not receive a fair trial. www.theatlantic.com/politics/archive/2013/08/the-watergate-cover-up-trial-justice-denied/278522/.

344 "shrunken in the mouth." SA, p. 459.

344 He made calls and conducted. RA, pp. 29–30.

344 she retreated into reading. LD, p. 3; JNE, p. 680.

345 "After reading that novel." Interview with Frank Gannon, May 17, 2012.

345 Gardening on their acre-and-a-half. JNE, p. 673.

345 "there were two broken people here." JNE, p. 681.

345 Certainly any anger. MB, p. 167.

345 "double agents were involved." JNE, p. 680.

346 "I was wrong." RA, p. 54.

346 "most humiliating day." JNE, p. 666.

346 "never get out of there alive." SA, p. 465.

347 "You can't break." RA, p. 68.

347 "we're just doing all we can." JNE, p. 669.

347 "seldom revealed our physical disabilities." ITA, p. 17.

347 "was going to make it." ITA, p. 17.

347 "Don't talk that way." ITA, p. 17.

347 Zeigler and Gannon. ITA, p. 17.

347 she reassured him. LD, p. 204.

348 "twice as much." Trude B. Feldman, "The Quiet Courage of Pat Nixon," *MC*, May 1975, p. 115.

348 "I was a physical wreck." ITA, p. 19.

348 The Nixons liked to watch USC football games. Interview with Ed Cox, January 7, 2013.

348 "quite an authority." Trude B. Feldman, "The Quiet Courage of Pat Nixon," *MC*, p. 115.

348 "This meets your doctor's standards." Trude B. Feldman, "The Quiet Courage of Pat Nixon," *MC*, May 1975, p. 115.

348 "delicious squash from the garden." JNE, p. 676.

349 "keep going." JNE, p. 676.

349 According to Julie. JNE, p. 676.

349 "It's as if she went." Kandy Stroud, "Pat Nixon Today," *LHJ*, March 1975, p. 132.

349 "the lowest point in my father's life." JNE, p. 673.

349 Confined to bed. RA, pp. 83–84.

349 "say the things they do about Dick." Helen McCain Smith, "Pat Nixon's final days in the White House—the truth behind those stories," *GH*, July 1976, p. 130.

350 "I'm told I was more dead." Winzola McLendon, "Pat Nixon Today," *GH*, February 1980, pp. 128–29.

350 "Well, goddamn." RA, pp. 88–89; SA, pp. 476–77; LD, pp. 200–201.

350 "in his physical condition." Kandy Stroud, "Pat Nixon Today," *LHJ*, March 1975, p. 133.

350 "above all the chance." RN to Helene and Jack Drown, [March 3, 1975], "1974-Aug. 197," Box 4, DC, NPL.

351 "I am happy." JNE, pp. 678–79.

351 a series of four interviews. RA, pp. 151–70; JA, pp. 540–42; en.wikipedia .org/wiki/The_Nixon_Interviews; www.dailymail.co.uk/tvshowbiz/article -1127039/Nixon-v-Frost-The-true-story-really-happened-British -journalist-bullied-TV-confession-disgraced-ex-President.html; www .huffingtonpost.com/elizabeth-drew/ifrostnixoni-a-dishonorab_b_150948

.html;www.smithsonianmag.com/history-archaeology/Presence
-Frost-Nixon.html.

352 "the cover-up is the main ingredient." JA, p. 541; RA, pp. 166–67.

352 Pat and Dick traveled to China. RA, pp. 122–33; SA, pp. 488–93; JA, pp. 542–44.

353 "The utter shamelessness." *WP*, February 25, 1975; SA, p. 490; RA, pp. 124–27.

353 "What after peace?" Interview with Ed Cox, January 7, 2013.

353 "We have not finished." RA, p. 131.

354 Pat felt weak. *Time*, April 2, 1990; JNE, pp. 687–96; RA, pp. 141–42; *Time*, July 19, 1976; SA, p. 498.

354 "I can't believe this is happening to me." Winzola McLendon, "Pat Nixon Today," *GH*, February 1980.

354 "She is a fighter." *WP*, July 10, 1976; RA, pp. 141–42.

354 "I'm beat. I'm through." JNE, p. 691.

354 "I'm so angry with myself." JNE, p. 695.

355 "I feel fine." LD, p. 209.

355 "plastic was tougher." *Time*, April 2, 1990, p. 44.

356 "caused her [Pat] to be out of sorts." "Pat Nixon: Those Drinking and Sex Allegations: They are all fiction, angry friends and former aides protest," *Washington Star*, Vertical File, "Nixon, Patricia," NPL.

356 "the Nixon family is a close family." JNE, p. 686.

356 "The bastards have got no reason." Bill Gulley, quoted in RA, p. 135.

Chapter 21: A Peaceful Twilight

357 Helpful sources for this period: ITA, pp. 268–76 and 421–33; MC, pp. 361–402; JNE, pp. 455–61; DG, pp. 284–303 and 338–47; JA, pp. 560–77; SA, pp. 526–97; CB, pp. 1016–59.

357 "got a bum rap." Nick Thimmesch, "The Unsinkable Pat Nixon," MC, April 1979, p. 89.

358 Dick's sixty-fifth birthday. Joann Barrett, "Pat Nixon's Happiest Night," GH, May 1978, p. 153.

358 "The greatest test." Nick Thimmesch, "The Unsinkable Pat Nixon," MC, April 1979, p. 146.

358 "Watergate mattered so much less." RN, p. 973.

358 Watergate, as he saw it. See discussion in DF, pp. 46–69.

359 "felt sick." JNE, p. 702.

359 "My actions and omissions." Quoted in Carl Bernstein and Bob Woodward, "Woodward and Bernstein: 40 years after Watergate, Nixon was far worse than we thought," WP, June 8, 2012.

359 "one part wrongdoing." Time, April 2, 1990, p. 38.

360 "Ma" and "Ba." JNE, pp. 456–57.

360 The Nixons approached the New York City real estate market. WP, October 3, 1979; RA, p. 212.

361 "Pat can't sleep." "Richard Nixon's Search for a New York Home," NYT, July 30, 2008; RA, p. 212.

361 Pat and Dick moved. JNE, pp. 457–59.

361 ate frequently at Le Cirque. Interview with Ed Cox, January 7, 2013.

361 "What she [Pat] doesn't like." Aileen Mehle, "Nixon Talks About His Life With Pat," WP, July 21, 1982.

361 Pat and Dick had experienced their fill. RA, p. 219; Julie Baumgold, "Nixon's New Life in New York," New York, June 9, 1980.

362 Guests saw a relaxed. RA, pp. 219–21.

362 "one of the highlights." Interview with Ed Cox, January 7, 2013.

362 Dick worried about Pat's ability. Lester David, "Pat Nixon's Golden Years," MC, October 1986, p. 137.

362 "She has to watch it." Nick Thimmesch, "The Unsinkable Pat Nixon," MC, April 1979, p. 143.

362 sold their town house. NYT, September 6, 1981.

362 The fifteen-room house had. Interview with Ed Cox, January 7, 2013.

363 "landscaped like a country pond." Lester David, "Pat Nixon's Golden Years," MC, October 1986, p. 137.

363 eating dinner from a tray (and description of their life at home in

Saddle River). Lester David, "Pat Nixon's Golden Years," *MC*, October 1986.

363 "Mr. President, for all." Michael Reese, John Lindsay, and Madlyn Resener, "Nixon: 'Never Look Back," *Newsweek*, June 14, 1982.

363 would go out to McDonald's. Interview with Ed Cox, January 7, 2013.

364 "Your beautiful apartment has been a haven." Interview with Ed Cox, January 7, 2013.

364 "to pet the reindeer." *Pat Nixon: Life After the White House*, www .youtube.com/watch?v=A_EG1-5nECY.

364 "I haven't been well." "Pat Nixon, Look Shipshape," *WP*, October 29, 1985.

365 Ed Cox had been prescient. Interview with Ed Cox, January 7, 2013.

365 "She doesn't quite have." Carl Sferrazza Anthony, "Pat Nixon: The Golden Years," *GH*, pp. 105–6.

366 reunion for her female White House staff. CSO, pp. 33–34.

366 "he did not stop being the center." And the later visit for dinner with Pat, who spoke with "little bit of a speech slur," Interview with Susan Porter Rose, May 2, 2013.

366 Pat "seemed the same." Connie Stuart, *Pat Nixon: Life After the White House*, www.youtube.com/watch?v=A_EG1-5nECY.

366 1979 Gallup poll listed Nixon. MS, p. 306.

367 $300-a-seat black-tie dinner. Interview with Robert J. Brown, March 19, 2013, and press materials he sent, including *Jet*, November 4, 1985; article from *Washington Times*, October 22, 1985; and booklet *Nixon and Black America: An Insider's View of the Nixon Presidency*.

367 "We were their close friends." MT, p. 57.

367 While following Chris's successful. Interview with Ed Cox, January 7, 2013.

368 "I don't have to tell him." ITA, p. 431.

368 "dance routine." MC, p. 368.

368 games like "shoe store." JNE, p. 459.

368 put on special performances. ITA, p. 431.

368 They were sad about the loss. Interview with Ed Cox, January 7, 2013.

368 celebrated their fiftieth wedding anniversary. "Nixons Mark Fiftieth Wedding Anniversary." *LAT*, June 21, 1990.

370 "Dick, you're controversial." Carl Sferrazza Anthony, "Pat Nixon: The Golden Years," *GH*, pp. 105–6.

370 Pat's involvement with Nixon Library planning: Interview with Ed Cox, January 7, 2013.

371 "came from the heart of America." Remarks at the Dedication of the

Richard M. Nixon Presidential Library in Yorba Linda, California, Public Papers, 1990. Accessed through Lexis-Nexus.

371 "a true unsung hero." Carl Sferrazza Anthony, "Pat Nixon: The Golden Years," *GH*, p. 106.

371 "Nothing we have seen." SA, pp. 576–80; "Nixon Library Opens With Pomp, Tributes: Dedication: Three Former Presidents at Yorba Linda Ceremony. Bush Makes the Only Mention of Watergate," July 20, 1990; CB, pp. 1044–45. See also Anette Haddad, "Nixon library dedicated by four presidents," UPI, July 19, 1990.

372 Pat radiated joy. JA, p. 569.

372 "They treated each other kindly." MC, p. 363.

372 "His reliance on her." MC, p. 367.

372 "didn't necessarily come across . . . That's right." Monica Crowley video, http://on.aol.com/video/monica-crowley—nixons-sense-of-humor -517770845.

372 "can discuss anything as an equal." "Nixon on His Life with Pat," *WP*, July 20, 1982.

372 "Don't let Dick give you a hard time." MC, p. 365.

373 "Eagles Nest." JA, pp. 570–71; Nixon Library exhibition on Richard Nixon: Text and replica of the "Eagles Nest."

373 "Sadness crept into everything." MC, p. 382.

374 "I don't want to be a burden." PNMT, p. 56

374 anniversary cards and flowers. PNMT, p. 77.

374 "Your family loves you." MC, p. 393.

374 "shoulders hunched forward." MC, p. 393.

374 Nixon listened to California governor. PNMT, pp. 48–49.

375 "You are the only one." JNE, p. 81.

375 "Let me tell you." PNMT, pp. 56–57.

375 "There is no one here." MC, pp. 394–95.

375 "Dick would be dead within the year." Leonard Garment, *Crazy Rhythm: From Brooklyn and Jazz to Nixon's White House, Watergate, and Beyond*, paperback, New York: Da Capo Press, 2001, p. 384.

376 waited for up to eighteen hours. *LAT*, April 27, 1994.

376 funeral a full state occasion. *Services for Richard Nixon, 37th President of the United States, Wednesday, April 27, 1994*, souvenir program produced by the Richard Nixon Library and Birthplace Foundation; DF, pp. 1–6.

376 "the second half of the 20th century." www.cnn.com/ALLPOLITICS /1997/gen/resources/watergate/dole.speech.html.

376 "our gallant friend." CB, p. 1053.

377 "May the day of judging." *Services for Richard Nixon, 37th President of the United States, Wednesday, April 27, 1994*, souvenir program produced by

the Richard Nixon Library and Birthplace Foundation, p. 14; DF, p.4. See also pp. 2–8 for interesting commentary on diverse reactions to his funeral.

Epilogue

378 "All lives have triumphs." Trude B. Feldman, "Pat Nixon Recounts 'Triumphs and Tragedies.'" *NYT,* March 15, 1992; PNMT, p. 77.

379 "a good sixth sense about people." Interview with Ed Cox, January 7, 2013.

381 "Pat and I come from." "Nixon on His Life with Pat," *WP,* July 20, 1982.

Index

ABC News, 202, 289
    filming of Tricia's wedding by,
        273–74
    Pat as First Lady documentary on,
        276–77
    See also specific reporter
ABM Treaty, 293–94, 295, 371
abortion rights, 298, 303
Abplanalp, Robert, 350, 358
Abzug, Bella, 278
Acheson, Dean, 123
Acheson, Lila, 283
Acker, Marje, 111, 254
Acuff, Roy, 327–28
Adams, Penny, 217
Adams, Sherman, 119, 134
Africa
    Pat and Dick's trips to, 140–41, 193,
        279–80, 281
    See also specific nation
"age of Nixon," 376, 379
Agnew, Spiro T., 197, 201, 235, 249,
    259, 321, 376
Ailes, Roger, 252
Aitken, Jonathan, 50, 59, 71, 109, 136,
    188, 215
Alameda Air Station (California):
    Nixon's naval assignment at, 57
Aldrich, Winthrop, 112

Aldrin, Edwin F. Jr. "Buzz," 234, 235
Alexandria, Virginia: Nixon home in,
    46, 328
Allen, George, 147
Allen, Robert S., 77
Allin, Lyndon K. "Mort," 251
Ambrose, Stephen, 53
American Bar Association, 277
American Dream: and Pat and Dick's
    relationship, 378, 379
American Heart Association, 219
Amherst College, 192, 249
Anderson, Jack, 225
Andreae, Christopher, 224
Anne (princess of Great Britain), 269,
    271
Annenberg, Lee, 345
Annenberg, Walter, 345
anniversaries, Pat and Dick's wedding,
    43, 51, 163, 191, 258, 351, 368, 374
Anthony, Carl Sferrazza, 217
Apollo 11 moon landing, 234–35
Arbuthnot, Ray, 141–42
Arends, Leslie, 335
Argentina: Nixon's vice presidential
    trip to, 143
Armstrong, Neil, 234, 235
Arnold, William "Bill," 86, 104
Artesia, California

Artesia, California (*cont.*)
 Patricia Nixon Elementary School
 in, 351
 Pat's childhood and youth in, 13,
 351
Asia
 Nixon's mid-1960s trips to, 190,
 193
 See also specific nation
Associated Press (AP), 79, 152, 167,
 323
Atkins, Ollie, 335
Atlanta Constitution, 261
Atlantic Alliance, 183
Attlee, Clement: Nixon's meeting with,
 80–81

Bahamas: Pat and Dick's vacation in,
 170
Baker, Bobby, 253
Baker, Howard, 319–20
Baker, James, 364
Baker, Russell, 162
Ball, Kenny, 19
Ball, Nancy, 301
Baltimore Sun: HUAC stories in, 93
Bassett, Jim, 158, 167
Bassett, Wilma, 158, 167
Becker, Benton, 344
Behrens, Hortense, 16, 17
Berlin, Germany, 89, 150
Berlin, Irving, 314
Bernstein, Carl, 296, 331, 354, 355
Bewley, Tom, 9–10, 28, 29
Bird's (Laguna restaurant), 18, 54
Black, Conrad, 35, 71
Black, Hugo, 277
Black Panthers, 249
Black, Wallace, 72
Blake, Robert, 12
Block, Herbert (Herblock), 92, 106,
 129
Bobst, Elmer, 169
Boddy, Manchester, 101, 102
Boehm, Edward, 287
Bohlen, Charles E., 183
Bolshoi Ballet: and Pat and Dick's

presidential trip to Soviet Union,
 294
Bork, Robert, 310, 322, 323
Borman, Frank, 234
Boston Café (Whittier, California), 10
Boston Globe: Kennedy (Edward) com-
 ments about Nixon's health care
 proposal in, 302
Boston Herald: HUAC stories in, 93
Botton, Alain de, 113
Boy Scouts, 210
Bradlee, Ben, 253
Brazil: Pat's trip to, 327
Brennan, Jack, 288, 289, 343
Brezhnev, Leonid, 293–94, 295, 319,
 329
Brezhnev, Victoria, 294–95
British Columbia, Pat and Dick's trips
 to, 29, 43
Brodie, Fawn, 66
Brody, James, 352–53
Brokaw, Tom, 327
Brookings Institution, 296
Brown, Bernice, 178
Brown, Edmund "Pat," 174, 178, 179,
 180
Brown, Robert J., 367
Buchanan, Patrick "Pat," 199, 250, 251,
 259, 286, 292
Buchanan, Ruth, 146, 151
Buchanan, Wiley, 146
Buckley, William F., 289
Bull, Steve, 332, 336
Burdlong, Marion, 39, 62
Burger, Warren, 273
Bush, Barbara, 366, 371, 376
Bush, George H.W., 364, 365, 370, 371,
 376
Butterfield, Alexander, 253, 264, 272, 320
Buzhardt, Fred, 323

cabinet, Eisenhower: Nixon proposed
 for post in, 136–37
cabinet, Nixon, 306, 336
California, 171–72, 174–81, 193
California State Assembly: Nixon con-
 siders running for, 27, 35

Cambodia: U.S. invasion of, 242, 246, 249
Camp David
  and firing of Ehrlichman and Haldeman, 316–17
  Julie's graduation party at, 250
  and Nixon family relationships, 254, 255
  Pat and Dick at, 220, 246, 248, 307, 316–17, 329, 334
  as safe haven for Nixon family members, 246, 248
  and Washington visits of British royalty, 269
Canadian Rockies: Pat and Dick's vacation in, 67–68
Captive Nations resolution, 148
Caribbean cruise: Pat and Dick's 1948, 95–96
Carlson, Frank, 370
Carruthers, Bill, 282
Carter, Jimmy, 365, 366, 376
Cash, Johnny, 262–63
Central Intelligence Agency (CIA), 186, 296, 332
Chamberlain, Neville, 247
Chambers, Whittaker, 89, 90–91, 92, 93, 95, 96
Chancellor, John, 165–66
Chapin, Dwight, 160, 199, 202, 215, 230, 252, 264, 303, 332, 370
Chapin School (New York City), 185
Charles (prince of Great Britain), 269, 271
"Checkers speech," Nixon's, 3–5, 119–22, 318, 333, 347
Cheshire, Maxine, 330, 343
Chiang Ching, 289
Chicago Seven, 249, 271
Chicago Times, 173, 195
Chicago Today, 292
Chicago Tribune, 119, 244, 277
China, 111, 125, 190, 279, 283, 284–92, 352–53
  Carter and, 365
  de Gaulle–Nixon discussions about, 183
  and Douglas-Nixon campaign of 1950, 105

Eisenhower administration and, 284
Eisenhowers (Julie and David) trip to, 352
elections of 1972 and, 304
Ford and, 352, 353
Korean war and, 105
in late 1940s, 99, 124
musk oxen as U.S. gift to, 290
and Nixon as elder statesman, 365
Nixon presidency and, 211, 215, 279, 283, 284–92, 345
Chisholm, Shirley, 308
Chotiner, Murray, 104, 116, 165, 174, 177–78
Chotiner, Phyllis, 115
Chou En-Lai (Zhou Enlai), 285, 286, 287–88, 290, 291, 350
Christian Science Monitor, 224
Churchill, Winston, 339
CIO (Congress of Industrial Organizations), 68
Cioran, Emil, 205
Citri-Frost project, 27–28, 34
civil rights/liberties, 92–93, 124, 188, 209–10, 302
Clawson, Kenneth, 347
Clean Air Act, 302
Cliburn, Van, 294
Clinton, Bill, 375, 376, 377
Clinton, Hillary, 375, 376, 377
Cloes, Elizabeth, 14–15, 16
Cobey, James, 58
Cocoanut Grove nightclub (Los Angeles), 42–43, 94, 172
Codus, William, 303
Coelho, Paulo, 113
Cole, Sterling, 95
Collier's magazine, 132, 133
Colson, Charles, 219, 262, 269, 280, 281, 295, 298, 351–52
Columbia University: demonstrations and protests at, 196
Committee of 100 (California Republicans), 60, 63, 71
Committee for Congested Production Area: Pat's job with, 55
Committee for the Preservation of the White House, 214

Committee to Re-elect the President
(CRP), 296–97, 315
communism
and Douglas-Nixon campaign of
1950, 100, 102, 105–6
elections and, 68, 82, 117, 119, 129,
136, 157
GOP reputation and, 96
Khrushchev-Nixon "kitchen debate"
about, 149, 173
McCarthy speech about, 99
in 1950s, 89–94
Nixon Doctrine and, 235
and Nixon as vice-president, 124,
128
Nixon's comments about, 68, 92,
128, 147
and Nixon's decision to run in elec-
tions of 1968, 194
Nixon's early concerns about, 57,
82–83, 84
Nixon's reputation and, 99, 117
Pat's reactions to, 379
See also House Committee on Un-
American Activities; specific person
or organization
Conger, Clement, 267, 333, 334,
355–56
Congress, U.S.
Captive Nations resolution in, 148
Democratic control of, 98, 128–29,
306
elections of 1954 and, 128–29
elections of 1970 and, 264
elections of 1972 and, 306
and Kennedy-Nixon relationship,
154
and Nixon as vice-president, 124
Nixon's finances and, 344
Nixon's lack of support in, 333, 334,
335
Nixon's relations with, 257
and Nixon's return from Venezuela
trip, 145
Nixon's views about, 358
and Pat and Dick's return from
presidential trip to Soviet Union,
295

Republican control of, 90
See also House of Representatives,
U.S.; House Un-American Activi-
ties Committee (HUAC); Senate,
U.S.; Senate Watergate Commit-
tee; specific person
Congressional Wives Club, 77
Conniff, Ray, 283–84
conservatives
elections of 1972 and, 305
Nixon's relationship with, 97
Cooper, Charles, 63
Copland, Aaron, 38
Courage and Hesitation: Notes and Photo-
graphs of the Nixon Administration
(Drury), 257
Cox, Archibald, 320, 322–23
Cox, Christopher Nixon, 360, 361,
362, 363, 364, 367, 368
Cox, Dorothy, 79, 136
Cox, Edward F. "Ed," 197, 202, 210,
248, 307, 341, 355, 361, 362, 368
and Dick's resignation, 334, 335–36
and Pat and Dick's New York City
move, 361, 362
and Pat and Dick's post-Watergate
activities, 342, 348, 349, 365
and Pat and Dick's reactions to
Watergate, 326
personal and professional back-
ground of, 270
Tricia's engagement to, 270–71
views about Pat, 379
Watergate and, 324, 332
wedding of, 271–74, 275
and Yankee Stadium incident, 324
crisis: Pat and Dick's views about, 91
Cronkite, Walter, 202, 289
Crowley, Monica, 168, 368, 372–74,
375
Cuban Missile Crisis, 179
Cultural Revolution, 289

Daley, Richard J., 198, 202
Dallas, Texas
Kennedy assassination in, 186–87
Nixon visit to, 186

Daniels, Helen, 104
The Dark Tower (Kaufman-Woollcott
    play): Pat and Dick as actors in,
    14, 15, 16
Dash, Samuel, 321
Daughters of the American Revolution
    (DAR), 130
David, Lester, 169, 343
Davis, Angela, 298
Davis, Rennie, 249
Davis, Jr., Sammy, 314
Day, Dennis, 270
Day, Roy O., 60
de Gaulle, Charles, 183, 256, 284
de Gaulle, Yvonne, 183, 256
Dean, John, 315, 316, 317, 319–20,
    351–52, 359
defeat: Nixon's views about, 181
Democratic National Committee. *See*
    Watergate
Democratic National Conventions,
    143–45, 186, 196, 198, 199,
    200, 210, 233, 241–42, 244–45,
    246–50, 273, 283–84, 298, 305,
    311, 371
  Pat's views about, 284
    Tricia-Cox wedding and, 273
    in Venezuela, 143–45, 186, 210
    in Washington, D.C., 246–50
Deng Yingchao, 290
Dewey, Thomas E., 94, 120, 186
Dickerson, Nancy, 234, 235–37, 276
divorce
    Nixon's views about, 10, 41
    rumors about Pat and Dick's, 321
Dixon, Tom, 65, 66
Dobrynin, Anatoly, 293
Dobrynin, Irina, 293, 330
dogs, Pat and Dick's, 26, 185, 221, 257,
    348, 364
Dole, Bob, 302, 374–75, 376, 379
domestic issues
    Frost-Nixon interviews about, 351
    and Nixon's 1972 re-election cam-
        paign, 301–2
    See also specific issue
Donahue, Giggs, 106
Dorn, Evlyn, 27, 39–40, 50, 65

Douglas, Helen Gahagan: elections of
    1950 and, 99–106
Douglas, Melvyn, 101
Downey, Sheridan, 101, 106
Doyle, Sarah Jackson, 212
drinking: Pat and Dick's, 331–32,
    355–56
Drown, Helene, 40, 64, 71, 112, 113,
    115, 120, 129, 141–42, 143, 145,
    166, 170, 181, 182, 183, 193, 202,
    333, 354
  Dick's relationship with, 263–64
  and Pat and Dick's early married
      life, 40–41
  and Pat and Dick's post-Watergate
      activities, 349, 350, 351
  and Pat and Dick's relationship, 263
  Pat's relationship with, 40–41, 263,
      264, 331, 351
  Pat's stroke and, 354
Drown, Helene—Pat's letters/conver-
    sations with
    about Dick's activities around the
        house, 107, 108
    about Dick's health, 108, 110, 347
    about Dick's vice-presidential candi-
        dacy in 1956, 137
    about Dick's work obsession, 192
    about Drew Pearson, 106
    about Eisenhower's health, 135
    elections of 1948 and, 94
    elections of 1950 and, 105
    elections of 1952 and, 3
    elections of 1968 and, 193
    elections of 1972 and, 304
    about Mamie Eisenhower, 130
    about Nixon family move to New
        York City, 184
    about Pat and Dick's relationship in
        vice presidential years, 134
    about Pat and Dick's social life, 112
    about Pat and Dick's vacations, 109,
        129
    about Pat and Dick's vice-
        presidential travels, 125
    about Pat's defense of Dick, 323
    about Pat's early days as a congres-
        sional wife, 78

Drown, Helene (*cont.*)
   about Pat's health, 142
   about Pat's loneliness, 108
   about Pat's mid-1960s activities,
      189
   about Pat's midlife crisis, 190
   about Pat's reactions to elections of
      1960, 168
   about Pat's views about Kennedy
      family, 169
   about Pat's views about Republican
      Party, 97
   about public admiration for Pat,
      281
   about rumors of Pat and Dick's
      divorce, 321
   about vacations in mid-1950s, 133
   about Washington social life, 112,
      132, 148
   about Watergate, 320–21, 326, 333
Drown, Jack, 71, 94, 105, 109, 112, 120,
      129, 141–42, 181, 182, 183, 193,
      202
   Dick's relationship with, 41–42
   and Nixon-Drown (Helene) rela-
      tionship, 264
   and Pat and Dick's early married
      life, 40, 41–42
   and Pat and Dick's post-Watergate
      activities, 348, 350, 351
   Pat's relationship with, 40
Drown, Maureen. *See* Nunn, Maureen
   Drown
Drury, Allen, 257–58
Duke University Law School: Dick as
   graduate of, 9, 24

Eagleton, Thomas, 298
earthquake, Peruvian, 258–61
East Whittier Friends Church: Nixon
   as member of, 29
Egypt
   and Nixon as elder statesman, 366
   Pat and Dick's presidential trip to,
      328–29
Ehrlichman, John, 177, 180, 199, 218,
      249

Drown (Helene)-Nixon relationship
   and, 263, 264
   firing of, 316–17
   and Haldeman-Pat relationship, 262
   Nixon's relationship with, 313
   and Pat and Dick's relationship, 255
   Pat, Julie and Tricia's distrust of, 313
   and Pat's activities as First Lady, 226,
      227, 229–30, 232–33, 240, 281
   "plumbers" and, 275
   and reorganization of White House
      office, 215, 230
   trial and sentencing of, 349–50
   Tricia's discussion with, 213–14
   Watergate and, 316–17, 349–50
Eisenhower, Alex (grandson), 360,
      362, 368
Eisenhower, Barbara, 147
Eisenhower, Dwight D. "Ike"
   China relations and, 284
   death/funeral of, 222–23
   elections of 1952 and, 1, 2, 3, 4, 5,
      115–17, 119–20, 121, 122, 123
   elections of 1954 and, 128, 129, 134
   elections of 1956 and, 134–35,
      136–37, 139, 140
   elections of 1960 and, 147, 157–58,
      160, 161, 163, 164
   elections of 1968 and, 197, 222
   health of, 131, 135–36, 142, 173, 222
   and Julie-David's wedding, 208
   Kennedy inauguration and, 169
   and Khrushchev invitation to visit
      U.S., 151
   legacy of, 223
   Nixon's eulogy for, 222–23
   Nixon's relationship with, 5, 116–17,
      119–20, 121, 122–23, 124, 127,
      129, 130–31, 134–35, 136, 137,
      142, 145, 147, 158
   and Nixon's vice-presidential travels,
      128, 145, 146, 151
   Pat's relationship with, 130–31, 147,
      379
   Pat's views about, 136, 137
   as supporter for Nixon's 1962 guber-
      natorial race, 174
   White House life of, 213, 221

Eisenhower, Dwight David III "David"
(son-in-law). 210, 213, 249, 307,
326, 352, 358, 360
  demonstrations and protests and,
  249
  and Dick's resignation, 334, 335–36
  and drinking allegations about Pat
  and Dick, 356
  and elections of 1968, 198, 199, 201,
  202
  and impeachment charges against
  Dick, 331
  Julie's reacquaintance with, 192
  and Kennedy (Robert) assassination,
  197
  and Nixon tapes, 332
  and Pat and Dick as grandparents,
  360
  and Pat and Dick's image, 311
  and Pat and Dick's post-Watergate
  activities, 349
  and Pat and Dick's relationship, 253
  and Pat's stroke, 354, 355
  Watergate and, 316, 317, 324, 332
  wedding of Julie and, 207–8
Eisenhower, Jennie Elizabeth (grand-
  daughter), 359–60, 362, 364, 368
Eisenhower, John, 147
Eisenhower, Julie Nixon. *See* Nixon,
  Julie
Eisenhower, Mamie, 145, 169
  death/funeral of, 359, 371
  Dick and Pat's relationship with, 147
  and Dick's Checkers speech, 121
  elections of 1952 and, 118, 121
  elections of 1956 and, 139
  health of, 131, 142
  and Ike's health issues, 135
  and Julie-David's wedding, 208
  Pat compared with, 212, 240–41
  Pat and Dick's relationship with,
  122–23, 131
  Pat's relationship with, 130, 131, 142
  Tricia-Cox wedding and, 274
Eisenhower, Melanie (granddaughter),
  360, 368
elder statesman: Nixon as, 351, 352,
  357, 365, 366–67

elections of 1932, presidential, 94
elections of 1936, presidential, 94
elections of 1940, presidential, 39, 59
elections of 1946, congressional
  break-in at Nixon campaign head-
  quarters during, 62
  charges of dirty campaign tactics
  for, 71
  funding for, 61, 62, 63, 65, 67, 68,
  69, 70
  Nixon campaign during, 60–70, 73,
  74, 85, 103
  Nixon family image and, 79
  Nixon's decision to run in, 59
  Nixon's nomination for candidacy
  in, 59–60
  and Nixon's post-election activities,
  71–73
  Nixon's primary win in, 67
  Nixon's victory in, 70–71
  Pat's role in, 60–61, 64–65, 66–67,
  70, 72
  Republican victory in, 71–72
  Tricia's birth during, 63–64
  Voorhis-Nixon debates during, 67,
  68–69
elections of 1948, congressional:
  Nixon's campaign during, 82,
  93–94, 98–99
elections of 1950, congressional
  Douglas-Nixon campaign during,
  99–106, 186
  Nixon victory in, 105–6
  Pat's reactions to, 116, 186
elections of 1952, presidential
  calls for Nixon resignation during,
  2–5, 119, 120, 121
  "Checkers speech" during, 3–5,
  119–22, 318, 333, 347
  Eisenhower-Nixon relationship dur-
  ing, 116–17, 119–20, 122–23
  Eisenhower-Nixon victory in,
  123–24
  fund crisis story and, 1–5, 117,
  119–22, 130, 170, 173, 318
  impact on Pat and Dick's relation-
  ship of, 122
  media and, 117–19

elections of 1952, presidential (*cont.*)
  Nixon's campaign during, 1–5,
    117–23
  Nixon's ethics/integrity as issue dur-
    ing, 117, 119–22, 123
  and Nixon's selection as vice-presi-
    dential candidate, 115–17
  Nixon's views about, 122
  Pat and Dick's relationship during,
    118–19, 122
  Pat's image during, 117
  Pat's reactions to, 116, 123
  Pat's role in, 118–19, 123
  and Pat's views about politics, 117
  women's role in, 118, 123–24
elections of 1954, congressional,
  128–29, 134
elections of 1956, presidential, 134–35,
  136–37, 139–40, 154
elections of 1958, congressional, 146,
  174
elections of 1960, presidential
  communism and, 157
  Eisenhower-Nixon relationship and,
    147
  election day activities during,
    165–66
  Kennedy-Nixon campaign in,
    154–65
  Kennedy-Nixon debates during,
    121–22, 159, 160–62
  and Kennedy-Nixon relationship,
    154
  Kennedy's Democratic nomination
    speech for, 156–57
  media and, 155, 162, 166, 168, 177
  Nixon campaign during, 106, 200
  and Nixon family's post-election
    activities, 168–70
  Nixon's decision about running in,
    142–43
  Nixon's health problems during,
    158, 159–60
  Nixon's mistakes during, 160
  Nixon's nomination for, 138, 154,
    157
  Nixon's reactions to, 167–68, 169,
    170, 325

  Nixon's writings about, 173
  and Pat and Dick's different views
    about public life, 154
  "Pat Week" during, 162–63
  Pat's role in, 156, 158–59, 162, 164
  Pat's views about, 142–43, 154,
    166–68, 169, 170, 180, 193, 202,
    325, 335
  results of, 165–68, 202
  role of First Lady candidates in,
    154–55
  television and, 159, 163
  voting irregularities in, 166, 167–68
elections of 1962, California guber-
  natorial: Nixon as candidate in,
  174–81, 325
elections of 1964, presidential, 174,
  187, 188–90, 191, 193, 298
elections of 1966, congressional, 191,
  192
elections of 1968, presidential
  demonstrations and protests during,
    196, 198, 199, 200
  Johnson and, 196, 200–201
  "New Nixons" in, 199
  Nixon's campaign during, 192,
    195–96, 198–201
  Nixon's decision to run in, 191–92,
    193–95
  Nixon's election night activities dur-
    ing, 201–2
  Nixon's nomination for, 197–98,
    203
  Nixon's victory in, 170, 201–3
  Pat's role in, 195–96, 199–200
  Pat's views about, 193, 194–95, 203
  Vietnam War and, 199, 200–201
elections of 1970, congressional, 264
elections of 1972, presidential
  Democratic National Convention
    for, 298
  demonstrations and protests during,
    305
  Kennedy (Edward) as contender in,
    268–69
  McGovern campaign for, 298, 302,
    305
  media and, 303, 305

Nixon family image and, 255–56,
281, 300
Nixon's campaign during, 298–306
and Nixon's image as world leader,
292–93
Nixon's victory in, 305–6
Pat and Dick's reputation and, 266
Pat as First Lady image and, 282
Pat's announcement about Dick's
run for re-election in, 280
Pat's campaign tours for, 297, 302–3
Pat's comments about her relation-
ship with Dick during, 254
Pat's concerns about, 304
Pat's role in, 298–305
Republic National Convention for,
299–301
television and, 266
Tricia's wedding and, 271–72
Vietnam War and, 266, 298–99, 302,
303, 304, 305
Watergate and, 297, 303
women's issues and, 300–301
elections of 1976, presidential, 305,
352–53
elections of 1980, presidential, 365
Elizabeth (queen of England), 146
Ellington, Duke, 223
Ellsberg, Daniel, 274–75, 284, 296
Endicott, Virginia, 12, 28–29
English Speaking Union: Nixon
speech to, 146
environmental issues, 247, 261–62,
276, 302
Environmental Protection Agency
(EPA), 302
Erskine, Helen Worden, 132, 133
Ervin, Sam, 313
Essence magazine, 367
"Evenings at the White House,"
223–24, 269, 271
executive privilege issue: Watergate
and, 322–23

Fahd (king of Saudi Arabia): gift of
jewelry from, 330
Federal Bureau of Investigation (FBI),
10, 55, 186–87, 190, 191, 201, 296,
297, 332
Federal Trade Commission, 270
Feldman, Trude, 348
Feraci, Carole, 283–84
The Final Days (Woodward and Bern-
stein), 331, 354, 355–56
finances, Nixon
"Checkers speech" and, 3–5
and Citri-Frost project, 27–28
and Dick as member of Congress, 75
and Dick with OPA, 44, 47
and Dick's autobiography, 344
and Dick's early law career, 27
in early 1950s, 107
and elections of 1940, 59
and elections of 1946, 61, 62, 63, 65,
67, 68, 69, 70
Frost interviews and, 351
and fund crisis of 1952, 2–5, 120–21
House investigation of, 318–19
and media criticisms of Pat, 106
and Nixon family move to New York
City, 184
and Pat and Dick's honeymoon, 37, 38
Pat's engagement ring and, 33–34
and sales of *Six Crises*, 174
tax audit of, 319, 323, 331
Watergate aftermath and, 344
during World War II, 55
Finch, Carol, 176, 190
Finch, Robert, 176, 177
Finch College, 189, 192, 213, 271
First Lady, Pat as
access to, 217
activities of, 212–13, 219, 226–27,
231–32, 233–34, 239, 244–45,
265–66
awards and honors for, 260, 307–8
and comments about Pat and Dick's
marital relations, 250–57
contradictions confronting, 212, 245
death threat against, 244
demonstrations and protests and,
244, 246, 248, 305
depression of, 237
Dickerson interview of, 234, 235–38,
276

First Lady, Pat as (cont.)
Dick's comments about, 256
Dick's honesty comments of, 308
and Dick's state of mind, 324–25
Drury interview of, 257–58
and expansion of role as First Lady, 233
fears/insecurity of, 214, 236–37
"firsts" of, 241
and gifts from foreign governments, 330
health of, 327
image of, 225, 252, 277, 280–81, 311
Mamie Eisenhower compared with, 212, 240–41
McLaughlin (Marya) interview of, 299
overarching national project of, 212
and Pat as perfect, 244
Pat's views about being, 205, 279, 312
popularity/approval ratings of, 239, 276, 281, 291–92, 306, 307–8
preparation of, 216
public relations program for, 240
as recluse, 326
reputation of, 266
role of, 291–92
Secret Service agents for, 248
and "Tribute to the First Lady" documentary, 299–300
Walters interview of, 281–82
See also specific person or topic
Fonda, Jane, 298–99
football: Pat and Dick as fans of, 24, 28, 41–42, 254, 307, 348, 349
Ford, Betty, 337, 371, 376
Ford, Gerald
as Agnew replacement as vice president, 321
China and, 352, 353
elections of 1976 and, 352–53
and Nixon family departure from White House, 337
at Nixon's funeral, 376
Nixon's pardon by, 344, 345–46
Nixon's post-presidential visits with, 348
Sadat funeral and, 366
takes presidential oath of office, 341
foreign affairs
Frost-Nixon interviews about, 351
and Nixon's 1946 campaign, 68
and Nixon's support of Marshall Plan, 82
Nixon's views about accomplishments in, 358
See also travels, Nixon's official; specific person or nation
Foreign Affairs magazine, 284
Franco, Francisco, 250
Frank, Jeffrey, 198
Friedan, Betty, 238
Frondizi, Arturo, 143
Frost, David, 351–52, 358
Fuchs, Klaus, 99

Gandhi, Indira, 269, 308
Gannon, Frank, 24, 104, 254, 293, 335, 344–45, 347
Garment, Grant, 15
Garment, Leonard, 375
Gaunt, Loie, 111
Gellman, Irwin, 71, 136
Ghana: Pat and Dick's trips to, 140, 279–80, 380
gifts from foreign governments: for U.S. presidents, 329–30
Glasser, Vera, 251
Goldstein, Marilyn, 199
Goldwater, Barry, 188–89, 193, 298
Goldwyn, Samuel, Jr., 175
Gonzales de Velasco, Consuelo, 259–60
Good Housekeeping magazine, 174, 194, 328, 332, 349, 381
Goode, Mark, 282
Gorbachev, Mikhail, 367
Gose, Barbara, 34
government, role of
Nixon presidency and, 232
Nixon's views about, 46–47
Graham, Billy, 194, 235, 273, 374, 376

Graham, Katharine, 228
Grand Ole Opry: Pat and Dick at, 327–28
Gray, L. Patrick, 296, 332
Great Britain
honoring of World War II U.S. servicemen by, 146
Nixon's travels to, 80–81, 146, 250
and Washington visits of British royalty, 269–70
Great Depression, 39, 101
Great Society program, 188, 192, 232, 301
Great Wall of China: Nixon at, 290
Greenberg, David, 102, 108
Grim, Peter, 112
Gromyko, Andrei, 293
Gulley, William, 356

Hagerty, James "Jim," 135, 137
Haig, Alexander, 254, 370
Halberstam, David, 131
Haldeman, H.R. "Bob," 160, 177, 199, 200, 209, 222, 234, 242, 248, 249, 259, 262–63, 265, 272, 275, 281, 298, 299, 300, 303, 304, 338, 370
and Dick's public treatment of Pat, 252
and East Wing–West Wing staff relations, 264–65, 269, 272
functions/responsibilities of, 215, 228–29, 257, 313
Klein firing and, 263
media relations and, 215, 262, 275, 303
and Mitchell's (Martha) comment about Feraci, 284
and Nixon as family man, 254
Nixon's dependence on, 313
Nixon's drinking, 332
Nixon's firing of, 316–17
and Nixon's Supreme Court appointments, 278
and Pat and Dick's relationship, 200, 229, 230, 231, 259, 263
and Pat and Dick's trip to China, 285
Pat's blame for Watergate on, 297
Pat's relationship with, 200, 228–29, 230, 259, 262–63, 264–65, 298, 313, 315, 320
and reorganization of White House office, 215, 230
and resignations of cabinet secretaries, 306
Stuart's (Connie) relationship with, 231, 261–62, 269
trial and sentencing of, 349–50
views about Nixon of, 215, 216, 218
Watergate and, 295–98, 316–17, 321, 349–50
and White House church services, 217
and White House staff hierarchy, 227
Hall, Leonard, 174, 177
Hallett, Doug, 281
Halloween: as Dick's favorite holiday, 373
Hansen, Oluf, 363
Harlan, John, 277
Harlow, Bryce, 166
Haroldson, Ruth, 99
Harris, Eleanor, 106
Harris, Lou, 124
Hartford Courant, 179, 253
Hartmann, Robert, 145
Harvey, Paul, 145
Hawaii: Pat and Dick's vacation in, 112
health care
Kennedy (Edward) comments about, 302
Nixon presidency and, 276, 302
Hearst, William Randolph Jr., 184
Heath, Edward, 250
Heckler, Margaret, 301
Helms, Richard, 296
Herbert, Gavin, 342
Herblock cartoons, 92, 106
Hersh, Seymour, 246
Hershey, Lenore, 239
Herter, Christian, 77–78, 81, 137
Herter Commission, 81
Hilberg, Eloise, 39

Hildegard (singer), 94
Hillings, Pat, 187
Hirschfeld, Abraham, 360
Hiss (Alger) case, 371
    and criticisms of HUAC and Nixon,
        92–93, 97, 177
    and Dick's return from Caribbean
        cruise, 95, 96
    elections of 1948 and, 98
    and Hiss's personal and professional
        background, 90
    HUAC testimonies of, 90
    importance of, 96–97
    indictment and conviction of, 96
    and Nixon-media relationship, 179,
        180
    Nixon reputation and, 89, 97
    and Nixon's bitterness, 170
    Nixon's role in, 89, 91, 92, 93, 94
    Nixon's writings about, 173
    Pat and, 91, 92, 93, 97
Hitler, Adolf, 36, 43, 102, 247
Hoffa Teamsters Fund, 177
Hoffman, Abbie, 271, 298
Home and Garden magazine, 240
honesty: Pat and Dick's views about,
    308
Hoover, J. Edgar, 145, 187, 190, 191,
    273
Hoover, Lou, 219
Hope, Bob, 42, 223, 314, 369
Hope, Delores, 369
Hotchkiss, Christine, 156, 164
House Beautiful magazine, 240
House of Representatives, U.S.
    impeachment charges against Nixon
        by, 327, 330–31, 333
    investigation of Nixon finances by,
        318–19
    Nixon as member of, 74–83, 84–89
    Republican control of, 71–72
House Un-American Activities Com-
    mittee (HUAC), 84, 86, 89, 90–91,
    92–93, 94, 96–97, 100
Houston Chronicle, 227
Hua Guofeng, 353
Hughes, Donald "Don," 140, 143, 144–
    45, 149, 159–60, 163, 165, 166

Hughes, Howard, 163, 166, 177
human rights, 126, 279
Humphrey, Hubert H., 198, 200, 201,
    202
Humphrey, Muriel, 198
Hunt, E. Howard, 269, 296, 313, 359
Hurwitz, Aida, 127
Hutchinson, Louise, 195, 277
Hutschnecker, Arnold A., 109

"I am not a crook" statement, Nixon's,
    323
impeachment, Nixon's, 327, 330–31,
    333
Interim Offensive Agreement, Soviet-
    U.S., 293–94, 295
Internal Revenue Service (IRS), 313,
    319
Iran, shah of, 366
Ireland
    Pat and Dick's presidential trip to, 250
    Pat's proposed trip to, 285
isolationism: Nixon's views about, 68
Israel, 319, 329
Ivory Coast, Pat's trip to, 279–80

Jami, Criss, 7
Jaworski, Leon, 323
Johnson, Lady Bird, 208, 212, 213, 214,
    224, 231, 233, 239, 266–67
Johnson, Louise, 133, 141, 170
Johnson, Lyndon B., 157, 188, 191,
    196, 200–201, 213, 214, 224, 231,
    269, 298, 305
    assumes presidency, 188
    civil rights and, 188
    "credibility gap" of, 243
    death/funeral of, 311, 376
    Great Society program of, 188, 192,
        301, 302
    and Kennedy (Jackie) White House
        visit, 266–67
    as member of congress, 76
    and Nixon transition, 208
    Vietnam War and, 192, 200–201,
        274–75

War on Poverty and, 188
Johnson Nugent, Luci, 213, 272
Johnson Robb, Lynda, 272, 274
Johnson, Roger, 170
Jordan, William George, 339
Junior Chamber of Commerce, 94
Justice Department, U.S., 322

Kalb, Bernard, 289
Kennedy & Nixon (Matthews), 166
Kennedy, Caroline, 267, 268
Kennedy, Edward M. "Ted," 197,
    268–69, 296, 302
Kennedy, Jacqueline, 118, 154–55, 185,
    212, 218, 221, 225, 231, 267
  approval ratings for, 239
  comments about Pat by, 169
  and inauguration of JFK, 169
  JFK's relationship with, 169
  legacy of, 223
  Nixon letters to and from, 187
  Pat compared with, 155–56, 212
  Pat's relationship with, 169
  Tricia interviewed by, 118
  and White House flower garden, 214
  White House portrait of, 267
  White House visit of, 266–68
Kennedy, John F., 214, 225, 231, 249
  ambitions of, 155
  assassination of, 186–87, 188
  Cuban Missile Crisis and, 179
  elections of 1960 and, 154–68
  funeral/mass of, 187
  health problems of, 154, 159
  inauguration of, 169
  Jackie's relationship with, 169
  legacy of, 223
  as member of congress, 76
  Nixon compared with, 14
  Nixon's relationship with, 154, 174,
    187
  Pat's views about, 156, 165, 166
  Vietnam War and, 274–75
  White House portrait of, 267
  womanizing of, 156, 166
Kennedy, John F. Jr., 267, 268
Kennedy, Robert F., 196, 197

Kennedy family
  Dick's comments about, 170
  Nixon family compared with, 76
  Pat's views about, 169
Kent State University, 246
Kepple, Gerald, 35
Khrushchev, Nikita, 148–49, 150, 151,
    157, 173
Khrushchev, Nina, 149, 150
King, Coretta Scott, 163
King, Gretchen, 55–56, 57
King, Gwen, 214, 312, 330, 366
King, Martin Luther Jr., 163, 196
King, Robert, 55–56, 57
Kirk, Norman, 322
Kirwin, Mike, 95
Kissinger, Henry, 279, 370
  China relations and, 284, 285, 286,
    287, 291, 292, 352, 353
  and Nixon's drinking, 332
  at Nixon's funeral, 376–77
  and Nixon's image as world leader,
    292–93
  Nobel Peace Prize for, 321–22
  and Pat and Dick's trip to China,
    284, 285, 286, 287, 291, 292
  Pentagon Papers and, 275
  as *Time* Man of the Year, 307
  Vietnam War and, 306, 321–22
  Yom Kippur War and, 321
Kitchell, Alma, 87
Kitchen Debate, Khrushchev-Nixon,
    149, 173
Kiwanis Young Professionals Club
    (Whittier, California), 17
Klein, Herbert, 162, 168, 179–80, 227,
    234, 255, 263
Kleindienst, Richard, 317
Knowland, William F., 174, 179
Koch, Alice, 34
Korean War, 99, 105, 124
Kornitzer, Bela, 40, 50
Kosygin, Aleksei, 293, 294
Kunstler, William, 244

La Casa Pacifica (Nixon home). *See*
    San Clemente, California

labor unions, 68, 71, 72, 100, 305
Ladies' Home Journal, 132, 172–73,
    174, 175, 176–77, 238, 239, 254,
    278
Laird, Melvin, 222
Laos: U.S. invasion of, 242
Lasky, Victor, 186, 350, 367
Latch, Edward Gardiner, 274
Latrobe, Benjamin, 214
lawyer, Nixon as
  at Adams, Duque & Hazeltine, 171
  at Bewley, Knoop and Nixon, 61
  early law career of, 9–12, 20, 22, 27,
    29, 39, 41
  New York disbarment proceedings
    against, 355
  at Nixon, Mudge, Rose, Guthrie and
    Alexander, 184
  at Wingert and Bewley, 9, 10, 14,
    27, 29
Lazar, Irving "Swifty," 344
Le Cirque (New York City restaurant),
    361
Le Duc Tho, 321–22
Lee, Peggy, 224
"Legacy of the Parks" program, 276,
    278
leprosy, 127
Lewine, Frances, 197, 254
Lewis, Ed, 367
liberals
  elections of 1968 and, 200
  elections of 1972 and, 305
  Nixon's relationship with, 97, 129
Liberia
  Nixon's vice presidential trip to, 140,
    279
  and Pat as First Lady trip to, 279,
    280, 380
Liddy, G. Gordon, 296, 313, 315
Life magazine, 127, 150, 151, 218, 274,
    287
Lillie, Mildred, 277
Lincoln, Abraham, 156, 213, 214
Lincoln Memorial: Nixon's visit with
    students at, 247–48
Linkletter, Art, 273
Lippiatt, Jean, 12–13

Liu, Marianna, 190–91
Lodge, Henry Cabot Jr., 157, 160,
    163
London Daily Mail, 307
Long Beach, California, Nixon home
    in, 38
Longworth, Alice Roosevelt, 80, 119,
    268, 272, 273, 311
Longworth, Nicholas, 272
Los Angeles, California
  Pat and Dick's home in, 171, 172
  and Pat's youthful social life, 21
Los Angeles Daily News, 101, 106
Los Angeles Herald Examiner, 291
Los Angeles Times
  and Douglas-Nixon campaign of
    1950, 101
  Nixon's 1946 endorsement by, 67,
    71
  and Nixon's 1946 victory statement,
    70–71
  and Nixon's 1962 gubernatorial
    campaign, 178
  and Nixon's 1968 presidential nomi-
    nation, 197
  and Nixon's return from Venezuela,
    145
  and Nixon's vice-presidential travels,
    128
  and Pat's comments about 1960
    campaign, 164
  Pat's comments about elections of
    1962 in, 177
  and Pat's comments about her crit-
    ics, 156
  and Pat's comments about women's
    issues, 278
  and Pat's trip to Africa, 280
  and Sheppard comments about Pat
    and Dick's relationship, 255
  Watergate and, 296
Los Angeles Times-Mirror: Nixon as col-
    umnist for, 173
Luce, Clare Boothe, 112
Lucke, Jane, 111
Lungren, John, 159, 346, 347, 354
Lutece (New York City restaurant),
    361

Lynch, John (Irish prime minister), 250, 270

MacArthur, Douglas, 52, 111
Maccioni, Sirio, 361
MacMurray, Fred, 172, 270
Madison, James, 268
Mafia: Rebozo and, 110
Maine: Dick and Pat's vacations in, 47, 133
Manchester Union Leader, 260
Mandel, Cy, 350
Mao Tse-tung, 105, 286, 287, 288, 289, 291, 352, 353
Marcantonio, Vito, 102
Marlborough School (Beverly Hills, California), 172
marriage: Dick's views about, 252
Marshall, George, 81
Marshall Plan, 81, 82
Marshburn, Olive, 36
Martin, Joseph Jr., 60
Marton, Kati, 87, 328
Mary Tyler Moore Show (TV show), 245
Massing, Hede, 112
Matthews, Chris, 166
May Day Tribe, 273
Mayflower Hotel (Washington, D.C.): as Pat and Dick's home, 75
Mazo, Earl, 16, 40, 93, 141, 175, 343
McCall's magazine, 132, 256, 257
McCardle, Dorothy, 238
McCarran-Wood bill, 100
McCarthy, Eugene, 196
McCarthy, Joseph, 97, 99, 128, 130, 136
McCord, James, 295, 296, 313, 315
McGovern, Eleanor, 298, 303
McGovern, George, 298, 302, 305, 306
McLaughlin, Marya, 299
McLellan, Diana, 307
McLendon, Winzola, 256, 257
Medal of Freedom, Presidential, 223, 228, 235, 283–84
media
  criticisms of Pat in, 106

Dick's comments about Pat to, 255–57
Dick's relationship with, 97, 106, 179–80, 257, 262, 275, 303, 313, 324
Dick's views about, 93, 257, 282, 358
and Nixon family's farewell to White House staff, 336
and Pat and Dick's relationship, 147, 250–57, 328
Pat's final interview with, 378
Pat's relationship with, 133, 139, 147, 151–52, 196, 200
Pat's views about, 97, 262, 345
Republican Party bias against, 211
and women as journalists, 238
and "you won't have Nixon to kick around anymore" statement, 180
See also specific reporter, news organization, or topic
Meehan, Thomas, 225
Mehle, Aileen, 361, 372
Meir, Golda, 308
Mendenhall, William, 37
Mesta, Perle, 80, 111
Metropolitan Club (New York City), 185
Mexico
  Pat and Dick's trips to, 37–38, 72–73, 165, 191, 258
  and Pat's barbed-wire fence incident, 276
Miami Herald, 295
Middle East
  Brezhnev-Nixon meetings about, 319
  Nixon presidency and, 211, 319, 321, 328–29
  Nixon's mid-1960s trips to, 193
  Pat and Dick's presidential trip to, 328–29
  Soviet influence in, 329
  Watergate impact on discussions about, 322
Mikoyan, Anastas, 150
Milan, Italy: Nixon's congressional trip to, 82
Milhous, Alvira (Nixon's maternal grandmother), 49

Miller, Jeffrey, 246
Miller, William "Fishbait," 95
Milligan, Bob, 253
Milligan, Cynthia, 253
Mission Inn (Riverdale, California):
    Pat and Dick's wedding at, 36–37
Mitchell, John, 199, 273, 296–97, 315,
    349–50
Mitchell, Martha, 273, 284, 297–98
Mitchell, Stephen, 2
Mohamed V (Sultan of Morocco), 140,
    142
Mondo Cane, 191
Montgomery, Ruth, 140–41
moon landing, Apollo, 234–35
Moore, Mrs. Clifford, 78
Morrow, Lance, 75, 76
Mountbatten, Lord, 146, 270
movies: Pat and Dick as fans of, 28,
    42
Mundt-Nixon bill, 84
musk oxen: as U.S. gift to China, 290
Muskie, Edmund, 297

Nader, Ralph, 270, 273
National Archives, 319, 369
National Council of Negro Women,
    330
National Day of Protest (1970), 246
National Endowment for the Humani-
    ties, 302
National Enquirer
    Kennedy (Edward) picture in, 269
    Liu-Nixon story in, 190
National First Ladies Library, 128
National Institutes of Health, 219
National Park Service, 265
National Republican Committee: elec-
    tions of 1952 and, 121
National Security Council, 135, 157
National Spelling Bee, 330
National Women's Political Caucus,
    278
Naval Reserve, U.S., 48
Nave, Doyle, 24
Navy, U.S.
    Dick in, 47–50, 51–57

Dick's discharge from, 61
NBC
    and Dickerson-Pat interview, 234,
        235–38, 276
    Nixon's "Checkers speech" on, 3–5
    See also specific reporter
Neece, Sherril, 20
Nelson, Drusilla, 135
Nelson, Harriet, 129
New American Revolution programs,
    275–76
New Deal, 35, 60, 305
New Federalism program, 232
New Frontier, 156, 157
New Orleans, Louisiana
    Nixon VFW speech in, 324
    Pat and Dick's early travels to, 43
New Republic: and Douglas-Nixon sen-
    ate campaign of 1950, 106
New York Bar Association, 355
New York City
    Dick and Pat's meetings/socializing
        in, 46, 81, 112
    Nixon family visits to, 168–69
    Nixon's presidential visits to, 229
    Pat and Dick's mid-life home in,
        184–86, 212
    Pat and Dick's retirement home in,
        360–62
    Pat's hospital job in, 18, 218
    Pat's visits from Saddle River to, 364
    social life in, 185–86, 361–62
New York Daily News, 227
New York Herald Tribune
    1952 fund crisis story in, 2
    Pat story in, 141
New York Post: elections of 1952 stories
    in, 2, 119
New York State: disbarment proceed-
    ings against Nixon in, 355
New York Times, 129, 149, 151, 163
    and demonstrations at Tricia-Cox
        wedding, 273
    and Khrushchev-Nixon "kitchen
        debate," 149
    Liu-Nixon story in, 190
    and Lynott's Pat–Jackie Kennedy
        story, 169

Nixon's views about, 275
Pat as First Lady story in, 240
and Pat as First Lady trip to Africa, 280
Pat's volunteerism tour and, 233
Pentagon Papers story in, 274–75
Tricia-Cox wedding story in, 274
Viorst story about Pat and Dick's martial relations in, 250–51
Watergate stories in, 296, 315
New York Times Magazine, 225
Newsday, 199
Newsweek, 72, 151, 229, 301, 356, 365
Nietzsche, Friedrich, 7
Nixon, Arthur (brother), 30
Nixon daughters (Julie and Tricia), 99, 172, 210, 234, 267, 268, 280
and antiwar protests, 246, 248
care of, 72, 81, 88, 104, 112
"Checkers speech" and, 4
and Dick as family man, 72, 108, 188, 253
and Dick's death, 376
and Dick's health issues, 158, 347
Dick's relationship with, 78, 81, 109, 133, 158, 191–92, 208, 315–16, 380
elections, pre-presidency, 3, 102, 104, 105, 116, 118, 161, 164, 165, 166, 175, 176, 180–81, 186
elections of 1968 and, 193–94, 197, 198, 199, 201, 202
elections of 1972 and, 299, 300, 304
Haldeman's relationship with, 313
Herblock cartoons and, 129
impact of politics on, 106
and New York City social life, 185
and Nixon family celebrations, 368, 374
and Nixon family image, 64, 80
and Nixon family move to New York City, 184, 185
Nixon family vacations and, 168–69, 171–72, 182, 183, 191, 193
Nixon Library and, 369, 370
and Nixon tapes, 332
and Pat and Dick as grandparents, 360

and Pat and Dick's post-Watergate activities, 349
and Pat and Dick's post-Watergate return to San Clemente, 342, 343, 348, 349
and Pat and Dick's retirement years, 364
Pat's health and, 142, 354, 355
Pat's relationship with, 312
and Pat's White House staff reunion, 366
Rebozo's relationship with, 111
and resignation of presidency, 318, 329, 334, 335–36
RN book and, 358–59
and vice presidential years, 125, 127, 131, 133, 135, 145, 148, 152
as volunteer workers for Republican Party, 172
Washington social life and, 148
and Washington visits of British royalty, 269, 271
and White House farewell, 336–37
White House life of, 212, 213–14, 221, 222, 233
and Woodward and Bernstein book, 331
See also Nixon, Julie; Nixon, Patricia "Tricia"
Nixon, Donald (brother), 16, 25, 33, 36, 62, 163, 165, 166, 177
Nixon, Edward (brother), 25–26, 39, 50, 81, 165
Nixon, Frank (father), 49, 50, 61, 70, 72–73, 81, 85
and care of Julie and Trisha, 72, 75
death of, 139
and Dick and Pat as actors, 17
and Dick and Pat's courtship and wedding, 17, 26–27, 33, 38–39
Dick's relationship with, 261
health of, 85
jobs of, 11
Milhous family relations with, 17
and Nixon family's farewell to White House staff, 336
as Nixon Market owner, 11–12
and Nixon's early law career, 10

Nixon, Frank (*cont.*)
  and Nixons in Iowa, 49
  and Nixon's swearing-in as member
    of congress, 75
  Pat's relationship with, 26–27, 85
Nixon, Hannah Milhous (mother), 17,
    49, 50, 61, 62, 64–65, 70, 75, 81,
    85, 92, 117–18
  and care of Julie and Trisha, 64–65,
    72, 75, 88, 92, 104
  death/funeral of, 194
  and Dick's early law career, 9, 10
  and Dick's farewell to White House
    staff, 336
  Dick's relationship with, 17, 336
  elections of 1960 and, 165
  family background of, 17
  health of, 85, 88
  and Pat and Dick in Iowa, 49
  and Pat and Dick's courtship and
    wedding, 17, 18, 26, 29, 33, 37,
    38–39
  and Pat and Dick's relationship,
    133
  Pat's relationship with, 17, 18, 26,
    33, 85
  Pat's similarity to, 30
  as role model for Dick, 261, 336
Nixon, Harold (brother), 30
Nixon, Julie (daughter), 265, 307,
    360
  biography of Pat by, 86, 108, 174,
    175
  birth of, 88
  childhood/youth of, 4, 88, 99, 102,
    104, 105, 107, 108, 109, 112
  China trip of, 352
  confiscation of wedding dress of,
    343
  David's relationship with, 192
  Dick defended by, 324
  and Dick's birthday, 358
  and Dick's views about politics,
    104
  and Dick's World War II activities,
    57
  and drinking allegations about Pat
    and Dick, 356
  education of, 171, 172, 185
  and Haldeman-Pat relationship,
    200
  image of, 281
  media and, 152, 325, 329
  and Nixon family's state of mind,
    325
  and pardon for Dick, 346
  and Pat and Dick's image, 311, 312
  and Pat and Dick's relationship,
    133–34, 175, 191–92, 253, 254,
    258, 309, 313, 315–16, 333
  Pat and Dick's visits with, 326
  pregnancy of, 358
  at Smith College, 192, 241–42,
    249–50
  Tricia's wedding and, 272, 273, 274
  Vietnam War and, 303
  Watergate and, 304, 313, 316, 317,
    324, 326, 329, 332, 333, 334, 343,
    345, 359
  wedding of, 207–8
  See also Nixon daughters (Julie and
    Tricia); Nixon (Richard) family
Nixon, Pat Ryan "Thelma"
  as actress, 14–17, 19, 40
  admiration/popularity of, 6, 123,
    156, 162–63, 349, 357
  ambitions of, 74
  awards and honors for, 132
  birth of, 19
  birthdays of, 18, 25, 54, 220–21,
    255–56, 270, 307, 327, 328, 350,
    368, 369, 372
  childhood/youth of, 13, 16, 19, 78,
    195, 216, 217, 289
  critics of, 156
  death and funeral of, 374–75
  as Democrat, 94
  distaste for public life of, 87
  final interview of, 378
  grandchildren and Pat and Dick's
    retirement years, 359–60, 362,
    363, 364, 365, 366, 367–68
  and Pat as First Lady, 312
  and Pat's White House staff reunion,
    366
  gravestone of, 377

health of, 142–43, 179, 327, 354–55, 356, 357, 358, 362, 364, 365–66, 368, 373–74
image of, 97, 117, 132–33, 138
independence of, 108
isolation/loneliness of, 86, 108
Jackie Kennedy compared with, 155–56
jewelry of, 343
midlife crisis of, 189–90
as pioneer activist political spouse, 60–61
"Plastic Pat" caricature of, 5, 195, 239, 245, 355, 380
pregnancies of, 58, 62, 63–64, 82, 85
Republican cloth coat of, 3, 4, 121, 245
retirement years of, 359–73
"saddest day" for, 346
self-identification of, 189
teaching career of, 12–13, 20, 21, 34, 39
unforgiving nature of, 106
youthful jobs of, 19
See also First Lady, Pat as; Nixon (Richard) family; Pat and Dick; *specific person or topic*
Nixon, Patricia "Tricia" (daughter) 189, 192, 222, 307, 341, 361
birth of, 63–64, 65, 88
at Chapin School, 185
childhood/youth of, 3, 4, 65, 85, 86, 99, 102, 104, 105, 107, 108, 112
Cox's engagement to, 270–71
Dick's accident with, 86
Dick's first public comment about, 64
and Dick's swearing-in as member of congress, 75
education of, 171, 172
Ehrlichman's discussion with, 213–14
and Finch College alumnae tea, 271
media and, 152, 271
and Pat and Dick's New York City move, 360–61

and Pat and Dick's reactions to Watergate, 326
and Pat and Dick's relationship, 192, 253, 258, 309
and Pat as stay-at-home mom, 79, 85
and "Tribute to the First Lady" documentary, 299
Watergate and, 313, 316, 317, 318, 324, 329, 332, 334
wedding of, 271–74, 275
and Yankee Stadium incident, 324
See also Nixon daughters (Julie and Tricia); Nixon (Richard) family
Nixon, Richard "Dick"
accident and injuries of, 86
as actor, 14, 15, 17, 22, 40
admiration/popularity of, 366
ambitions of, 9–12, 18–19, 28, 30, 35, 53, 57, 59, 72, 74, 116, 154, 155, 189, 193
awards and honors for, 56, 94, 132–33
birthdays of, 221, 350, 358, 364, 368
as campaign strategist, 104
childhood/youth of, 18, 261
complex character of, 6
death of, 375–76
depression of, 318
gravestone of, 377
health issues of, 86, 108, 109–10, 139, 158, 159–60, 208, 320, 334, 346–48, 349, 350, 353, 381
image/reputation of, 14, 40, 97, 107, 135–36, 138, 145, 181, 183, 186, 194, 252, 266, 275, 282, 311–12, 353, 357, 359, 367, 372
isolation and self-absorption of, 53, 219, 229
as loner/outsider, 40, 53, 215, 257, 342–43
lying by, 310
"most humiliating day" for, 346
Quaker background of, 49–50
resilience of, 19
secretiveness of, 248–49
self-confidence of, 22

Nixon, Richard "Dick" (cont.)
  self-image/self-analysis of, 20, 25,
    173, 215, 216, 257
  "Tricky Dick" caricature of, 5, 102
  vindictive instincts of, 4, 215, 223,
    248–49, 313, 380
  vision of America of, 57
  will of, 50
  work obsession of, 66, 78, 85, 87, 95,
    96, 107, 170, 173, 192, 344
  See also Nixon (Richard) family; Pat
    and Dick; specific person or topic
Nixon, Richard "Dick"—writings by
  Beyond Peace, 353, 376
  In the Arena (Nixon), 93, 368,
    369–70, 378
  RN, 126, 167, 172, 174, 175, 193,
    293, 295, 311, 324, 358–59
  Six Crises, 91, 92, 95, 149, 162, 164,
    170, 173–74, 287
Nixon (Richard) family
  Atkins photograph of, 335
  Christmas celebrations of, 82, 152,
    168, 185, 186, 193, 258, 307, 349,
    368
  Dick's relationships within, 250–57,
    258
  and Douglas-Nixon campaign of
    1950, 102
  Eisenhower (David) public state-
    ment about, 356
  elections of 1972 and, 300
  image of, 64, 72, 102, 152, 261,
    280–81
  Irish heritage of, 250
  Kennedy family compared with, 76
  media coverage of, 152
  and 1968 election night activities,
    201–3
  and Pat and Dick's retirement years,
    363
  and Pat as First Lady, 312
  resignation, 333–36
  state of mind, and Watergate,
    325–26
  White House departure of, 336–38
Nixon Doctrine, 235
Nixon Library and Museum (Yorba

Linda, California), 369–72, 374,
    376
Nixon Market (Whittier, California),
    11–12, 15, 29, 34
Nixon tapes/papers, 320–21, 322–23,
    329, 330, 334, 344, 369
Nobel Peace Prize, 321–22
Noll, Helen, 34, 37
nuclear weapons test ban, 150
Nunn, Maureen Drown, 182, 183

O'Brien, Lawrence, 296
Office of Civilian Defense: Pat's job
    with, 49, 55
Office of Price Administration (OPA)
  Nixon's appointment in, 44, 45–47
  Pat's job with, 46, 48, 49, 51, 55
O'Grady, Margaret, 20, 29
Oldfield, Elizabeth, 79
Onassis, Aristotle, 267
Onassis, Jacqueline Kennedy. See Ken-
    nedy, Jacqueline
Order of the Hounds Tooth, 122
Oswald, Lee Harvey, 188
Oswald, Marina, 188
Ottumwa, Iowa: Nixon's naval assign-
    ment in, 48–49
Oxford Student Union: Nixon at, 147,
    359

Pacific Doctrine, Ford's, 352
pacifism: Nixon's views about, 49–50
Pageant magazine, 321
Palmer, Kyle, 70–71
Panama
  Nixon's vice-presidential travels to,
    127–28
  Pat and Dick's cruise to, 43–44
pandas: and Pat and Dick's presiden-
    tial trip to China, 290
pardon, presidential: for Nixon, 344,
    345–46
Park Ridge, New Jersey: Nixon home
    in, 373
Pat and Dick
  American Dream and, 378

avoidance and, 323
common values of, 382
complexity of relationship between, 5–6, 378–82
courtship and wedding/honeymoon of, 5–6, 15–21, 22–23, 24–27, 28, 29–31, 32–35, 36–38, 51, 211, 375
and Dick's ambitions, 31
and Dick's eulogy for Pat, 375
and Dick's image as ideal husband, 107
Dick's media comments about, 255–57
and Dick's praise for Pat, 338, 378
and Dick's public treatment of Pat, 251–52, 328
and Dick's resignation, 333, 334, 335–36
and Dick's will, 50
early married life of, 38–44
estrangement of, 309–10, 326
first crisis for, 97
handling of difficult issues by, 153–54
happiness of, 71
jokes between, 237
Julie as buffer between, 175, 191–92, 309, 313, 315–16
loyalty and, 176–77
marital ambivalence of, 86–87
and marriage as equal partnership, 87–88
media questions about, 147, 250–57
as national heroes, 97
overview of, 378–82
and Pat as stay-at-home mom, 85–89
and Pat's belief about wife's first duty, 112
and Pat's *Collier* comments about Dick, 133
and Pat's comments about Dick's honesty, 308
and Pat's comments about Dick's state of mind, 324–25
and Pat's influence on Dick, 104
and Pat's mistakes, 176

and Pat's pet name ("Plum") for Dick, 48
and Pat's support of Dick, 97
as prototypical young family, 74–83
resilience of marriage of, 349
retirement years of, 359–73
and romance outside marriage, 190
sadness in relationship of, 181
separations of, 47–48, 51–57, 81, 171–72, 307
and *Six Crises* dedication, 173–74
"three marriages" of, 216
Tricia as buffer between, 309
and vice presidential years, 131, 133–34
See also specific topic
Pat Nixon Rose, 369
Patricia Nixon Elementary School (Cerritos, California), 351
Paul VI (pope), 250
Peale, Norman Vincent, 185, 208, 362
Pearson, Drew, 106, 123, 163, 166, 211
Pentagon Papers, 274–75
People magazine, 264, 326, 327
Pepsi-Cola Company, 186, 193
Perdue, Dick, 42
Perlstein, Rick, 161
Perry, Herman, 27, 35, 58–60, 65, 71
Perry, Hubert, 15–16
Peru: Pat and Dick's trips to, 143, 258–61, 379
Peru Earthquake Voluntary Assistance Group, 260
Pew, Joseph, 111–12
Pew, Mrs. Joseph, 111–12
Philip (duke of Edinburgh), 270
piano-playing, Nixon's, 71, 105, 152, 186, 211, 223, 247, 254, 258, 325, 326, 327–28
Pierpoint, Robert, 324
Pietrusa, David, 160
"Pink Sheet," 102
Piping Rock Club (Long Island): Pat and Dick at, 112
Pittsburgh Courier, 141

"Plastic Pat" caricature, 5, 195, 239, 245, 355, 380

"plumbers," 275, 296

Podgorny, Nikolai, 293

Political Action Committee (PAC), 68

politics
and Dick's campaign against communism, 57
Dick's early interests in, 22, 27, 31, 35, 39
Dick's impact on American, 305
Dick's personality and, 53
Dick's views about, 62–63, 104, 154, 173, 189, 194, 382
impact on Pat and Dick's relationship of, 57
and Pat and Dick's courtship, 31
Pat's concern about Dick's interest in, 87
and Pat's influence on Dick, 104
and Pat's support of Dick in early years, 35
Pat's views about, 62, 87, 97, 106, 117, 122, 128, 137, 154, 168, 172, 175, 177, 189, 193, 195, 256, 278, 310, 382
women in, 278
and World War II impact on Dick, 57

Pompidou, Georges (president of France), 224

Pompidou, Mrs., 224

POW dinner, White House, 314, 318

Powell, Lewis F. Jr., 278

presidency, Nixon
access to Nixon during, 215, 217, 304
accomplishments of, 345
and Agnew's resignation, 321
approval ratings for, 239, 317–18, 323
assassination threats against, 324
and comments about Pat and Dick's marital relations, 250–57
"credibility gap" of, 243–44
demonstrations and protests during, 210, 233, 241–42, 244–45, 246, 283–84, 311
and Dick's preparation for presidency, 216, 257
executive privilege issue in, 322–23
and expansion of presidential power, 323
and first night in White House, 210–11
Ford named vice president during, 321
and gifts from foreign governments, 329–30
goals for, 222
image/reputation of, 225, 275, 280, 282, 292–93, 311–12
impeachment and, 327, 330–31, 333
inauguration of, 208, 209–11, 212, 232
and isolation of Nixon, 229
1946 victory as first step toward, 72
and Nixon's resignation, 318, 323, 324, 329, 333, 371
second inauguration of, 310–11
State of Union Addresses during, 243, 275–76
and Walters-Nixon interview, 270
See also staff, White House; White House; specific person, nation, or issue

Prevention of Nuclear War agreement, Brezhnev-Nixon, 319

Price, Raymond, 199, 215

Pumpkin Papers, 96

Quinn, Sally, 269

race relations, 124, 209–10, 211, 302, 367

Radio Free Europe, 151

Rather, Dan, 274

Ray Conniff Singers, 283–84

Reader's Digest, 186, 283

Reagan, Nancy, 251, 361, 371, 374, 376

Reagan, Ronald, 151, 196, 350, 352, 365, 367, 370, 371

comments about Nixon of, 371
New York City visit of Nixon and, 361
Nixon as advisor to, 365, 367
Nixon compared with, 251
Nixon's comments about Watergate to, 317
at Nixon's funeral, 376
Nixon's relationship with, 374
and Pat as "unsung hero," 371
at Pat's funeral, 374
Reagan Library: opening of, 373
Reasoner, Harry, 289
Rebozo, Charles "Bebe," 110, 165, 194, 250, 274, 350
comments/views about Dick of, 110–11
Dick first meets, 110
Dick's relationship with, 110, 192
Dick's vacations with, 129, 137, 170, 194, 220
Drown (Helene)-Nixon relationship and, 264
Mafia and, 110
and Nixon tapes, 332
Pat and Dick socializing with, 311
Pat and Dick's Mexican vacation with, 191
and Pat and Dick's reactions to Watergate, 326
and Pat and Dick's relationship, 192
Pat's views about, 111
and Pat's views about Watergate, 357
Tricia and Julie's relationship with, 111
Watergate and, 332, 349
Red Cross: Pat as volunteer for, 46, 111
Red Scare, 89, 99
Redbook magazine, 126, 127, 132
Reed, Donna, 156
Rehnquist, William, 278
Religious Broadcasters of America, 324–25
Republican cloth coat, Pat's, 3, 4, 121, 245
Republican National Committee, 3, 122, 162–63

Republican National Convention, 117, 139, 157, 188, 197–98, 208, 222, 299–301
Republican Party, 97, 99, 108, 117, 128, 172, 174, 175, 191, 192, 211
resignation, Nixon's, 333–38
Reston, James, 151
Revell, Nellie, 87
Reynolds, Frank, 273
Rice, Una, 94
Richardson, Elliot, 320, 322
Ringle, Ken, 303
Rippard, Catherine, 77
Ritter, Dorothy, 327
Rivera, Alex, 141
Robertson, Nan, 233, 240, 241
Rockefeller, David, 360
Rockefeller, Nelson A., 163, 184, 332
Rockwell, Norman, 152
Rodgers, Ted, 4
Rodino, Peter, 321
Roe, Dorothy, 152
Rogers, Adele, 251
Rogers, Ted, 120
Rogers, William, 135, 285, 286, 370
Roosevelt, Alice, 336
Roosevelt, Eleanor, 7, 19, 61, 101, 126, 218, 219, 232, 235, 236, 300
Roosevelt, Franklin D. "FDR," 35, 39, 43, 90, 94, 218, 305
Roosevelt, Mrs. Theodore Jr., 112
Roosevelt, Theodore, 205, 268, 336
Rose, Susan Porter, 251, 255, 312, 366
Rubin, Jerry, 249, 298
Russia. *See* Soviet Union
Ryan, Katherine Halberstadt (Pat's mother), 19
Ryan, Neva (Pat's half-sister), 19, 33
Ryan, Pat. *See* Nixon, Pat Ryan "Thelma"
Ryan, Thomas "Tom" (Pat's brother), 19, 33, 36, 62, 348
Ryan, William "Bill" (Pat's brother), 19, 33, 36, 348
Ryan, William M. (Pat's father), 13, 16, 19, 30

Sadat, Anwar, 328–29, 366
Saddle River, New Jersey
  Nixon family gatherings in, 368
  as Pat and Dick's retirement home,
    362–73
  Pat's White House staff reunion in,
    366
Safire, William, 186, 240, 381
Sahl, Mort, 138
San Clemente, California
  Brezhnev-Nixon summit in, 319
  media in, 343
  Nixon family's departure from
    White House to, 337
  Nixon family's vacations in, 220
  Nixon home in, 220, 240, 305
  Pat and Dick in seclusion in,
    325–26
  and Pat and Dick's move to New
    York City, 360
  Pat and Dick's post-Watergate life in,
    341–56
  and Pat and Dick's relationship, 255
San Diego Union, 139
San Francisco Examiner & Chronicle, 271
San Francisco News, 55
Sanchez, Fina, 184, 194
Sanchez, Manolo, 184, 194, 246–47,
  248
Sans Souci restaurant (Washington,
  D.C.): Pat at, 326
Saturday Evening Post
  Pat's comments about 1946 cam-
    paign in, 63
  Pat's comments about Dick in, 107,
    108
Saturday Night Live (TV show), 343
"Saturday Night Massacre," 322–23
Sawyer, Diane, 253, 344
Schlesinger, Arthur Jr., 169, 322, 360
Schmidt, Helmut, 364
Schultz, George, 250, 370
Scranton, William, 198
Screen Actors Guild, 151
Sea Island, Georgia: Pat and Dick's
  vacation at, 109
Secret Service, 221, 247, 248, 251, 286,
  311, 324, 341, 360

Senate Ladies group: Pat as member
  of, 111
Senate, U.S.
  and Nixon swearing-in as senator,
    106
  and Nixon as vice-presidential candi-
    date, 116
  Nixon's early years in, 108
  Nixon's maiden speech before the,
    111
  Pat's role in Dick's office in, 111
  Republican control of, 71–72
Senate Watergate Committee, 313,
    318, 319–20, 321, 322, 324, 329,
    330, 333, 349, 358
separations, Pat and Dick's
  in early 1960s, 171–72
  on New Year's in 1973, 307
  and Nixon's congressional trips, 81
  and Pat's independence, 56
  during World War II, 47–48, 51–57
Sequoia (yacht): Nixon family outing
  on, 334
Serkin, Rudolf, 224
Sevareid, Eric, 165–66
Shanghai Communiqué, 291
Shannon, William V., 77
Sheppard, Eugenia, 255
Sherwood, Georgia, 65, 66
Sherwood, Jack, 143, 165
Sherwood, Virginia, 273, 276–77
Shikler, Aaron, 267
Shoreham Hotel (Washington, D.C.):
    Pat and Dick's social life at, 89
Shriver, R. Sargent, 298
Sidey, Hugh, 287
Sills, Beverly, 269
Sirica, John, 313, 315, 320, 348
60 Minutes (TV show), 197
Skelton, Red, 223, 273
Slick, Grace, 271
Smathers, George, 109–10, 141
Smith College, 192, 241–42, 249–50
Smith, Helen McCain, 230, 253, 312,
    328, 332, 355–56
Smith, Jean Kennedy, 379
Smith, Margaret Chase, 100, 308
Smith, Marie, 195, 233, 239, 245, 270

socialism, 68–69, 71, 101, 129

Sorensen, Ted, 157

Soviet Union, 43, 89, 99, 329, 367
China relations with, 284–85, 291
de Gaulle–Nixon discussions about, 183
elections of 1972 and, 304
Fuchs case and, 99
and Nixon as elder statesman, 365, 366–67
Nixon presidency and, 211, 215, 275, 283, 345
and Nixon's 1946 campaign, 68
Nixon's mid-1960s trips to, 193
and Pat and Dick's presidential trip to China, 286, 291
Pat and Dick's presidential trips to, 283, 293–95, 329
Pat and Dick's vice presidential trip to, 148–52, 173, 186
Pat's role in U.S. relations with, 293–95
Vietnam War and, 286, 293
Watergate impact on U.S. relations with, 322

Spivak, Al, 106

SS Panama (ship): Pat and Dick's Caribbean cruise on, 95–96

St. Johns, Adela Rogers, 66

St. Johns, Richard, 103

St. Mathias Episcopal Church (Whittier, California), 14, 15

St. Matthew's Cathedral (Washington, D.C.), Kennedy funeral mass at, 187

staff, White House
and East-West Wing staff relationships, 216, 227–28, 230–31, 261–63, 264–65, 272, 281, 282, 292, 312–13, 380
firing of, 316–17
hierarchy among, 227, 230
Julie's role with, 312
and media reports of Pat's trip to Peru, 260–61
and Nixon family relationships, 254
Nixon family's farewell to, 336
and Nixon's birthday party, 221

Nixon's relationship with, 313
Nixon's reorganization of, 214–15, 230–31
and Pat and Dick's presidential trip to China, 292
and Pat and Dick's relationship, 221, 227–29, 230
Pat's confrontation with Dick about, 264–65
Pat's East Wing, 216, 227–31, 312, 366
and Pat's trip to Africa, 280, 281
and privacy for Nixon family, 219
reactions to Woodward and Bernstein book by, 331
reunion of Pat's, 366
Tricia's wedding and, 271, 272
Watergate and, 324
See also specific person

Stahl, Lesley, 311

Stalin, Joseph, 90, 102, 124

Stans, Kathleen, 185–86

Stans, Maurice, 349, 367, 370

Stassen, Harold, 137

State Department, U.S.
Chambers-Hiss case and, 96
Hiss at, 90
and Nixon as elder statesman, 366
and Nixon's vice-presidential travels, 124, 125, 127, 143
and Nixon's views about communism, 128
and Pat and Dick's presidential trip to China, 286, 287

stay-at-home mom, Pat as
and Dick's absences from home, 108–9
in early 1950s, 107–8
and Pat and Dick's relationship, 85–89
and Pat as First Lady, 238–39
in post–World War II years, 74–83
vacations and, 95

Steinem, Gloria, 196, 278

Stephenson, Malvina, 251

Stevenson, Adlai, 121, 123, 139–40

Stewart, James B. "Jimmy," 53–54, 186, 299, 300, 314

Stockman, Farah, 302
Strategic Arms Limitation Talks, 293, 295
Strober, Deborah Hart, 255
Strober, Gerald S., 255
Stroud, Kandy, 245, 271, 291
Stuart, Charles, 230, 231, 240
Stuart, Connie
  and East–West Wing staff relationships, 231, 261–62, 269
  elections of 1972 and, 303, 304
  functions of, 230–31, 241
  Haldeman's relationship with, 231, 261–62, 269
  and Haldeman's role in Pat and Dick's relationship, 229
  and Pat and Dick's relationship, 231, 252, 253, 255
  as Pat's East Wing staff director, 221
  Pat's hiring of, 230
  and Quinn story about entertaining at White House, 269
  "rescuing" of Pat by, 303, 304
  resignation of, 312
  Tricia's wedding and, 272
  and Walters-Pat interview, 282
  and White House staff hierarchy, 227
  and White House staff reunion, 366
students
  demonstrations and protests by, 244–50
  Nixon's Lincoln Memorial talk with, 247–48
Sulgrave Club (Washington, D.C.), 106, 111–12
Sullivan, Edward, Jr., 343
Summers, Anthony, 110, 133
Sunday church services, White House, 217–18, 228
Supreme Court, U.S., 35, 77, 275, 277–78, 323, 330, 344

Taft, Eleanor, 260
Taft-Hartley Act, 100
Taiwan, 286, 288, 291

Tanner, Lester, 360–61
Tanner, Marcella, 361
Task Force on Women's Rights and Responsibilities, 278
Taves, Isabella, 127
tax returns, audit of Nixon, 319, 323, 331
Teamsters Retirement Fund, 177
television
  Checkers speech and, 3, 122, 305
  and Dick-daughters relationship, 158
  and Douglas-Nixon campaign of 1950, 105
  elections of 1960 and, 159, 163
  elections of 1972 and, 266
  HUAC hearing on, 93
  and Nixon family's farewell to White House staff, 336
  Nixon family's interests in, 107
  and Nixon's address to Russian people, 150
  Nixon's resignation on, 335
  Nixon's views about, 122
  and Nixon's Watergate address, 317
  and Pat and Dick's presidential trip to China, 288, 292
  and Pat's First Lady trip to Africa, 280
  Pat's use of, 122
  and Watergate hearings, 318, 319–20
Thieu, Nguyen Van, 201, 235, 306–7
thimbles, Nixon, 68, 103
Thimmesch, Nick, 358, 362
Thomas, Helen, 217, 218–19, 251, 274, 288, 289, 311, 329
Thompson, Donald, 77
Thompson, Robert, 292
Timberlake, Edith, 36
Time magazine, 90, 123, 298, 328
  call for Nixon resignation by, 323
  and criticisms of Pat, 156
  Dick's comment about "Plastic Pat" in, 355
  Kissinger and Nixon as "Men of the Year" for, 307

and Nixon's 1946 victory, 72
and Pat as First Lady, 245
Pat's comments about Dick's ambitions in, 59
Pat's comments about impact of politics on children in, 172
Tito, Josip, 250
Tkach, Walter, 222, 247, 346
Tolbert, Victoria, 330
Tolbert, William, 279, 280
Toledano, Ralph de, 112, 151
Trader Vic's restaurant: Pat and Dick dining at, 311–12
travels, Pat and Dick's official
as congressman, 80–82
demonstrations and protests during, 143–45, 186, 210
Nixon's image and, 146
Pat's role during, 125, 140–41, 147, 149, 150, 151–52, 284–92
as president, 220, 232, 233, 234, 235–36, 250, 258–61, 279–82, 283, 284–92, 293–95, 307, 327–29
round-the-world, 234
as vice-president, 124–27, 130, 140–41, 143–45, 146–47, 148–52, 173, 186, 281
See also specific nation
travels/vacations, Pat and Dick's
in congressional years, 89, 92, 95–96, 109–10
and Dick as elder statesman, 359
Dick's early return from, 95–96
in early and mid-1960s, 168–69, 170, 171–72, 182–83, 189, 190, 192–93
on honeymoon, 37–38
and Pat and Dick's early married life, 43–44
and Pat and Dick's post-Watergate trip to China, 352–53
of Pat in mid-1950s, 129, 133
of Pat, Tricia and Julie, 189
Pat's youthful, 18, 19, 22, 28–29
during presidential years, 220, 295, 307, 315–16
reminiscing about, 326
during vice presidential years, 133, 137

and Washington–California drive of Nixon family, 99
See also specific location
Trilling, Lionel, 90
Troy, Gil, 102, 290
Truman, Bess, 111
Truman, Harry S.
and Douglas-Nixon campaign of 1950, 100
elections of 1948 and, 94, 98
elections of 1952 and, 2, 119
funeral of, 311
and HUAC hearings, 90, 94, 96
and MacArthur firing, 111
Nixon's attacks on, 111
White House living of, 208, 213, 214

Ulua (cruise ship): Pat and Dick's trip to Panama on, 43–44
United Nations: Nixon speech to, 229
United Press International (UPI), 167, 260, 269, 325
University of Southern California (USC), 13, 24, 28, 40, 348
U.S. News & World Report, 126, 224, 225, 232, 375

vacations. *See* travels/vacations
van der Heuvel, Gerry, 227, 228–29
Van Horne, Harriet, 271
Vanocur, Sander, 161
Vecchio, Mary Ann, 246
Velasco Alvarado, Juan Francisco, 258, 260
Venezuela
Pat and Dick's vice presidential trip to, 143–45, 173, 186, 210
Pat as First Lady trip to, 327
Veterans of Foreign Wars: Nixon's New Orleans speech for, 324
vice president, Nixon as
and Eisenhower-Nixon relationship, 122–23, 124, 127, 130, 134–35, 136, 137, 142, 145
and Eisenhower's health issues, 135–36, 142

vice president, Nixon as (*cont.*)
  and family privacy, 219
  functions of, 124, 138, 142
  global popularity of, 138
  and Nixon's image, 135–36
  papers of, 319
  Pat and Dick's relationship and,
    133–34
  and Pat's image, 138
  and Pat's role, 127–28, 140–41, 149
  Pat's views about, 134
  press conference of, 142
  reputation of, 147
  and selection of Nixon, 115–17
  social life of, 131–32
  travels of, 124–27, 130, 140–41,
    143–45
  See also elections of 1952; elections
    of 1956
Vietnam War
  cease-fire in, 310, 314
  "Christmas bombing" during,
    306–7
  Clinton protest against, 377
  elections of 1968 and, 199, 200–201
  elections of 1972 and, 266, 298–99,
    302, 303, 304, 305
  Johnson and, 192, 200–201, 274–75
  Kennedy and, 274–75
  My Lai massacre during, 246
  Nixon Library opening and, 371
  Nixon presidency and, 209, 211,
    215, 221, 224, 229, 235–36,
    241, 242, 243, 244, 246–50, 266,
    283–84, 286, 288, 291, 293, 304,
    306–7, 310, 314, 321–22, 345
  Nobel Peace Prize and, 321–22
  Paris peace talks and, 306–7, 322
  and Pat and Dick's presidential trip
    to China, 288, 291
  and Pat and Dick's trip to Vietnam,
    235–36
  Pat's views about, 284, 298–99, 303,
    304
  prisoners of war from, 302, 314,
    318
  Soviet Union and, 286, 293
Viorst, Judith, 250–51

Voice of America, 151
volunteerism
  and Pat as First Lady, 226, 231,
    232–34, 239, 244
  and Pat's volunteer work, 189–90
Voorhis, Jerry, 59, 61, 62, 63, 67, 68–69,
  70, 71, 72, 73, 79

Wallace, DeWitt, 283–84
Wallace, George C., 202
Wallace, Lila Acheson, 283–84
Walters, Barbara, 270, 281–82, 289
Walters, Vernon, 332
War on Poverty, 188
Warner Books, 344
Warren Commission, 188
Warren, Earl, 209
Washington, D.C., 58, 75, 106–7,
  141–42
  Brezhnev-Nixon summit in, 319
  demonstrations and protests in,
    246–50
  Pat and Dick move to, 72–73
  in post-World War II years, 75
  social life in, 77–78, 79, 89, 111–12,
    147–48, 213, 218, 220, 223–25
Washington, D.C, *See also* Congress,
  U.S.; staff, White House; White
  House;
Washington Post
  attacks on Nixon by, 92–93, 106,
    228
  Brody story about Pat and Dick's
    China trip in, 352–53
  Cheshire story about gifts to Pat as
    First Lady in, 330
  election stories, 2, 106, 118, 129,
    195, 280, 364–65
  Herblock cartoons in, 92, 106, 129
  HUAC stories in, 92–93
  Moore's comments about Pat and
    Dick's relationship in, 78
  and Nixon family celebrations, 152
  and Nixon's image, 79
  Nixon's relationship with, 275
  Pat and Dick as young congressional
    couple story in, 75

Pat and role of women stories in, 238, 245
and Pat's Vietnam comments, 303
Pat's volunteerism tour and, 233
"Profile of Pat" in, 239
Watergate and, 296
and White House social activities, 228, 269, 270
See also specific reporter
Washington Star-News, 307
Washington Times Herald, 79, 118
Watergate
beginnings of, 295–98
convictions related to, 313
elections of 1972 and, 297, 303
firing of top aides during, 316–17
Frost-Nixon interviews about, 351–52
impeachment discussions and, 327, 330–31, 333
and inquiry about confiscation of Pat's personal belongings, 343
and Julie as buffer between Pat and Dick, 192
lawsuits filed against Nixon related to, 344
media and, 315, 318, 324, 331, 345
Nixon approval ratings and, 317–18
and Nixon family's state of mind, 325–26
Nixon Library and, 370–71
Nixon tapes and, 320–21, 322–23, 329, 330, 334, 344, 359
and Nixon's diplomatic influence, 291
Nixon's mistakes concerning, 352, 359
and Nixon's resignation, 318, 323, 324, 329, 333–36
Nixon's televised address about, 317
Nixon's views about, 122, 170, 343, 346, 351–52, 358, 359
and pardon for Nixon, 346
Pat and Dick's relationship during, 255, 313–14, 325, 326, 381
Pat's deepest regret about, 321

Pat's knowledge about, 296, 297–98, 304, 313–14, 325
Pat's views about, 297–98, 303, 304, 307, 316, 317, 318–19, 320–21, 324–25, 326, 327, 331, 332–33, 343, 345, 350, 357, 359
pivot point in, 320
and public views about Nixon, 316–17, 343
"Saturday Night Massacre" and, 322–23
"smoking gun" conversation and, 296, 332, 333, 334
televised hearings about, 318, 319–20
trial and sentencing of former aides of, 344, 348, 349–50
unraveling of cover-up for, 315–21
See also Senate Watergate Committee; *specific person*
Waters, Ethel, 273
Wayne, John, 314
welfare reform, 211, 276, 302
West, J.B., 213
West, Jessamyn, 17, 133
White House, 212, 213, 214, 215, 221–22, 223, 225, 231, 267–68, 269, 326, 334–35
candle-light tours of, 265
flower garden at, 214
and Johnson-Nixon transition, 208
Kennedy (Jackie) and children visit to, 266–68
Kennedy portraits in, 267
night lighting of, 265
Nixon family's departure from, 336–38
Nixon family's early days in, 210–25, 226–42
Nixon family's first night in, 210–11
Nixon family's privacy in, 219
Pat and Dick's dinners/entertaining at, 213, 218, 220, 223–25, 228, 231, 263, 269–70, 312, 314, 322, 330
Pat and Dick's "three marriages" during years in, 216

White House (*cont.*)
  Pat at Senate wives' luncheon at Truman, 111
  Pat's birthday party in, 220–21
  Pat's redecoration of, 212–13, 267–68, 333
  Pat's views about, 208
  Pat's youthful tour of, 218
  police uniforms for, 218
  POW dinner at, 314, 318
  Slick-LSD incident at, 271
  Sunday church services at, 217–18, 228
  Tricia-Cox wedding at, 271–74
  Truman family at, 208, 213, 214
  visitors to, 218
  See also staff, White House
White House Correspondents' Dinner, 275
White, Theodore H., 159, 161, 164
White, William L., 112
Whitney, John Hay, 147
Whittier, California
  and Dick's decision to run in 1946 election, 59
  Dick's early law career in, 9–12
  Pat and Dick 1960 voting in, 165
  Pat and Dick return to, 60
  Pat and Dick's homes in/near, 39, 65, 99, 107, 133, 184
  social life in, 11
Whittier College, 10, 18, 28, 37, 38, 41, 65
Whittier Community Players: Pat and Dick's first meetings at, 14–18
Whittier Daily News, 17, 64, 70
Whittier Union High School: Pat as teacher at, 12–13, 20, 21, 34, 39
Wicker, Tom, 178, 195
Willkie, Wendell, 39
Wilson, Pete, 374
Winchester, Lucy, 217, 220, 227, 228, 230–31, 263, 264, 312, 332, 355–56, 366
Windsor, Duchess of, 270
Windsor, Duke of, 270
Wingert, Jefferson, 29
Wingert, Judith, 29

Witcover, Jules, 179
Woman's Day magazine, 87
women's issues
  in Africa, 140
  in China, 286
  and Dick's public treatment of Pat, 252
  and Douglas-Nixon campaign of 1950, 101–2
  in early 1950s, 101
  elections of 1952 and, 118, 123–24
  elections of 1968 and, 199
  elections of 1972 and, 300–301
  and empty nest syndrome, 189
  feminist movement and, 238, 245
  Kosygin-Pat discussion about, 294
  Nixon presidency and, 232, 277, 278
  and Nixon as vice president, 132, 141
  Nixon's views about, 104, 278, 281, 285
  and Pat and Dick's trips to Soviet Union, 149, 294
  and Pat as First Lady, 245, 277, 278, 294, 300–301
  Pat as international advocate concerning, 125–27, 140 and Pat's awards and honors, 132–33
  and Pat's self-identification, 189
  and Pat's volunteerism program, 233
  in post-World War II years, 59, 78–79, 87
  in pre-World War II years, 32
  and Supreme Court appointments, 277
Women's Wear Daily magazine, 245, 271, 291
Woods, Rose Mary, 111, 162, 189, 194, 217
  and Drown-Nixon relationship, 264
  and Nixon's drinking, 332
  Pat and Dick's socializing with, 188
  Pat's relationship with, 160
  and "Tribute to the First Lady" documentary, 299
  Watergate and, 317, 323
Woodstock Music Festival (1969), 224

Woodward, Bob, 296, 331, 354, 355
World War II
  and bombing of Pearl Harbor, 45
  British honoring of U.S. servicemen
    from, 146
  Dick's commendations during, 56
  Dick's letters to Pat during, 375
  Dick's naval activities during, 47–50,
    51–57
  Dick's OPA appointment during,
    45–47
  and Hitler's invasion of Russia, 43
  impact on Dick of, 57
  influence on Pat and Dick's wedding
    of, 36
  Pat's activities during, 46, 49, 51,
    55–57

  Roosevelt (Eleanor) visit with troops
    during, 235, 236
Worley, Chandler, 54
Wray, Merton, 12
Wright, Frank Lloyd, 362
Wyeth, Andrew, 224

Yom Kippur War, 321
"you won't have Nixon to kick around
    anymore" statement, 180
Young Republicans Club, 35
Youth for Nixon, 199

Ziegler, Ron, 177, 208, 230, 282, 312,
    317, 324, 346, 347